AF342143

Errant Bronzes

ERRANT BRONZES

George Grey Barnard's Statues
of Abraham Lincoln

FREDERICK C. MOFFATT

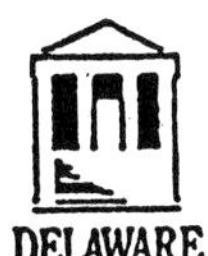

Newark: University of Delaware Press
London: Associated University Presses

Associated University Presses
440 Forsgate Drive
Cranbury, NJ 08512

Associated University Presses
16 Barter Street
London WC1A 2AH, England

Associated University Presses
P.O. Box 338, Port Credit
Mississauga, Ontario
Canada L5G 4L8

The paper used in this publication meets the requirements
of the American National Standard for Permanence of Paper
for Printed Library Materials Z39.48–1984.

Library of Congress Cataloging-in-Publication Data

Moffatt, Frederick C.
    Errant bronzes : George Grey Barnard's statues of Abraham Lincoln
/ Frederick C. Moffatt.
        p.   cm.
    Includes bibliographical references and index.
    ISBN 0-87413-628-8 (alk paper)
    1. Barnard, George Grey, 1863–1938—Criticism and interpretation.
    2. Lincoln, Abraham, 1809–1865—Statues. I. Title.
    NB237.B33M63   1998
    730′.92—dc21
                                                    97-33147
                                                    CIP

PRINTED IN THE UNITED STATES OF AMERICA

Contents

Acknowledgments

THIS STUDY WAS MADE POSSIBLE BY THE GENEROUS financial support of the Smithsonian Institution and the University of Tennessee, Knoxville. This assistance included a senior postdoctoral fellowship which was administered by the Smithsonian's National Museum of American Art in Washington, D.C. for the year 1989–1990, as well as salary supplements which originated from a University of Tennessee professional development award, and from the College of Liberal Arts and the Department of Art. The Faculty Research Council helped me in the purchase of photographs and the Southern Regional Educational Board of Atlanta, Georgia, kindly underwrote incidental travel expenses in the early stages of my research. I have Albert Boime, Philipp P. Fehl, and Allen S. Weller to thank for having graciously recommending my project to the NMAA's fellowship committee, and I have NMAA Curators Lois M. Fink, George Guerney, and William H. Truettner to warmly thank for their ever wise and friendly counsel before, during, and after my fellowship year. I am especially indebted to David W. Tandy of the UT Department of Classics for being my editorial taskmaster and Michael H. Logan of the UT Department of Anthropology for his many thoughtful suggestions. I can only single out a few of the many technicians, archivists, and librarians who patiently and expertly aided me and this project: Louise F. Rossmassler and Gina Kaiser of the Philadelphia Museum of Art Library; Cynthia B. Altman, of the Pocantico Conference Center of the Rockefeller Brothers Fund, Judy Throm, Liza Kirwin, and Eva Crider, of the Archives of American Art; Joan Stahl, of NMAA; Cecilia A. Chinn and Patricia M. Lynagh, of the NMAA/National Portrait Gallery Library; Lee Stout, of the Pennsylvania State University Archives; Anne L. Chandler, of the Kankakee County (Illinois) Historical Society Museum and Archives; Gilbert T. Vincent, of the New York State Historical Society at Cooperstown; David Brook, of The Sterling and Francine Clark Institute, Williamstown, Massachusetts; Gladys Murray, of the Centre County (Pennsylvania) Library and Historical Museum. I sincerely thank Tony Barnard and Wendy Barnard Gessner for valuable information on the Barnard family. Gregory Giacona and Erin Moore provided photographs and information from London and Manchester. Throughout the ten years I have spent in the research, writing and production of this book, Betsy Fahlman has kept me on track with her insights, good humor, and encouragement James F. Moffatt has been a good brother and Anne G. Moffatt, a truly good wife.

Introduction

NO PUBLIC IMAGE IS MORE FAMILIAR THAN THAT OF Abraham Lincoln. We need not bother to read pedestal legends or search out trencher beards and stovepipes to know who is being portrayed; the gaunt face, spindling proportions, disheveled hair, and period dress give him away at once. The fair-sized army of plaster, stone, and metal Lincolns that populate this country reinvent his protean identity: the young frontiersman, the soldier, rail splitter, lawyer, the President, the Commander-in-Chief, the Great Emancipator, and the slain martyr. He greets us as an orator at the Douglas debates, at Cooper Union, Gettysburg, and at the Capitol during the Second Inaugural. A wooden Lincoln surmounts a totem pole; others stand before public schools, libraries, outside and inside state halls and corporate headquarters, and in parks and cemeteries. As the custom of erecting statues went into its decline in the 1920s, sculptors and patrons continued to commemorate him. Even today, when Richard Serra's steel abstractions have come to symbolize both the promise and limitations of public sculpture in an urban setting, commissions for Lincolns are not unknown.[1]

Three bronze Lincoln statues, a prototype and two replications, stand apart from the others. Created by New York artist George Grey Barnard between 1912 and 1922, they are by all accounts gloriously ugly and at the same time touchingly pathetic; they assume awkward stances, they are noticeably ill-proportioned and disfigured, they are attired in unkempt costumes several sizes too small, and their grimacing faces express a mixture of pain, anger, and

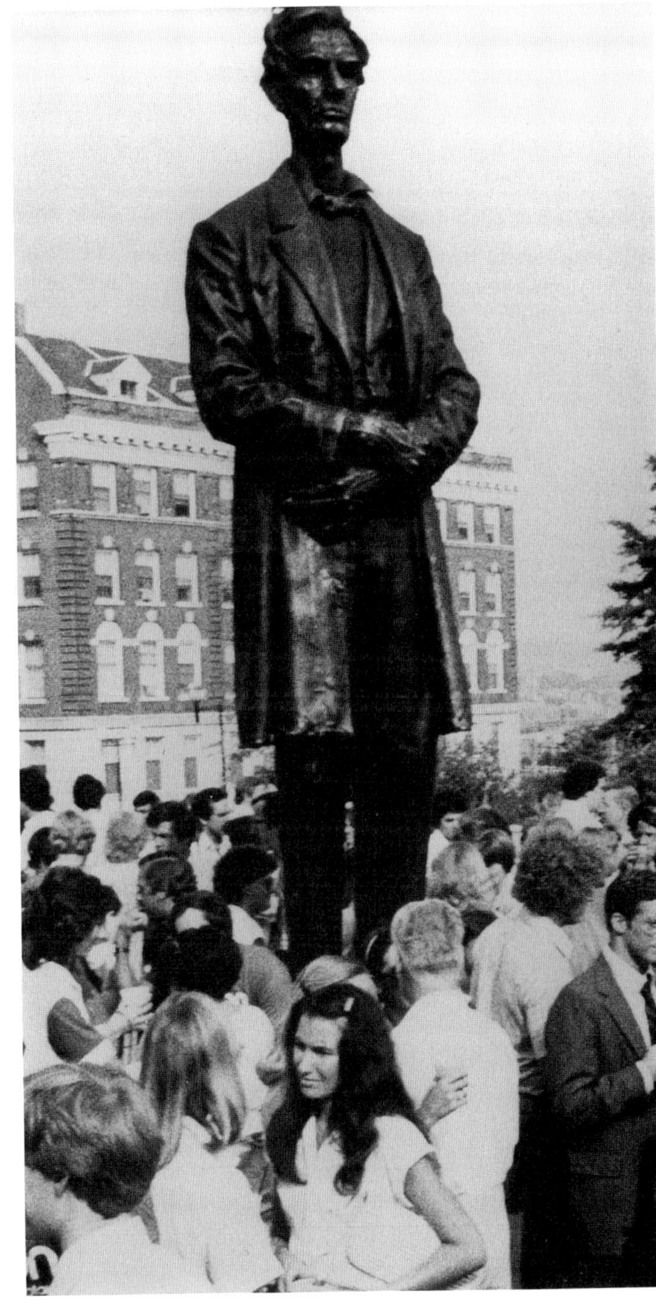

George Grey Barnard, Abraham Lincoln. *1916. Bronze, 13'4". Cincinnati Ohio. [Photo ca. 1980]. Courtesy of the Cincinnati Historical Society.*

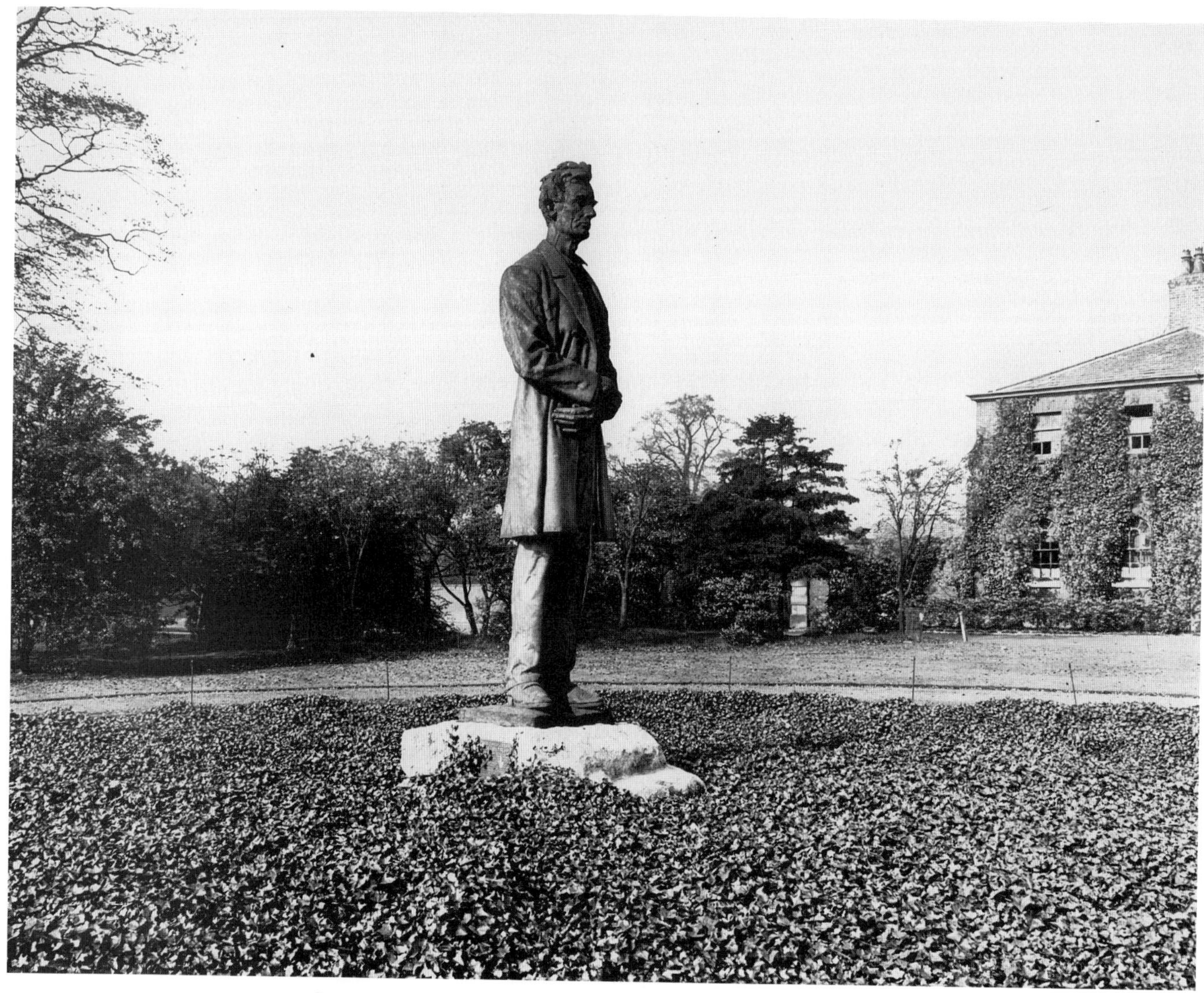

George Grey Barnard, Abraham Lincoln. *1919.*
Bronze, 13'4". Manchester, England. [Photo, 1923].
Manchester Central Library, Local Studies Unit.

frustration. When surrounded by happy crowds, their expressions of "silent desperation" seem at times ludicrous; when contemplated in isolation, their abjection is more deeply felt. Although no one engaged in sculpting Abraham Lincoln's likeness before or shortly after the turn of the century could ignore his physical appearance, Barnard's characterizations went far beyond acceptable boundaries. To the degree the public ideal of the man had assumed iconic finality, these works are better categorized as anti-Lincolns, negations not only of what the popular will demanded of the "public" Lincoln, but also of what it demanded of all heroic public statues.

Like the "counter monuments" designed by contemporary German artists like Hans Hoheisel, Jochen Gerz, and Esther Shalev-Gerz, which mock the general practice of building memorials and specifically renounce their country's Nazi past, Barnard's bronzes are visible forms of cultural dissent for which he was fully responsible. Because they did not disown the statues, Barnard's patrons also were morally obliged to accept limited responsibility for his conception and had full authority over the siting of the works. But no one could be held responsible for what was to occur at the moment of the unveilings or for the ways the public chose to "read" the works in accordance with the ongoing rush of events thereafter. The first bronze cast appeared at a time of extreme social and political unrest. Completed in 1916, the prototype was briefly exhibited in New York City before being permanently mounted in Cincinnati, Ohio, on the eve of President Woodrow Wilson's declaration of war. The second was privately ordered for immediate shipment to London, England, to serve as a "public" token of American sympathy for her future ally. If, as Walter Lippmann wrote of his generation, "we live in a revolutionary period and nothing is so important than to be aware of it," then March 1917 was the month of revolution and no one viewing Barnard's first bronze needed reminding.[2] What course could one expect the revolution to take if this degraded portrayal of America's greatest hero were to be raised in a foreign city on behalf of the American people? The daunting uncertainty of this question had much to do with the fact that the second cast was kept in storage for the duration of the war.

Even after its release following the Armistice, the statue was not forwarded to London, but at the last minute diverted to Manchester, England, where its dedication occurred in the fall of 1919. A far less tendentious social atmosphere surrounded the unveiling of the final bronze in Louisville, Kentucky, in 1922. Even so, the public regard for Lincoln in this, his native state, was still not undivided. Furthermore, this replica was a farewell gift from a prominent Jewish citizen whose religion had prevented his full integration into Louisville's social order.

In this book I position the statues at the center of a broad examination of patronage and politics, preferring to study them as cultural markers that relate to human conflict and historical accident. While pursuing an overlapping chronological history, I focus upon the adversarial roles that existed between the artist, his peers, his model, and his patrons; between the patrons, their allies, and their political and social detractors; between rival promoters, critics, journalists, bureaucrats; and between differing patterns of urbanization that affected the three host cities. A final chapter assesses recent history, showing how the postindustrialized policies adopted by the respective city governments allocated new uses for these once-endangered bronzes. To a degree, this book is also a partial history of Abraham Lincoln, in that it reviews how this national hero's memory was not unselfishly appropriated by social and political contenders in their campaigns for dominance or survival.

Despite their accessibility and eminence, public statues remain at the fringes of high scholarly interest. Like Jasper John's flag, we know them only too well, but rarely do we look at them or study them. Practitioners of American Studies and devotees of Lincolniana have demonstrated considerable interest in the iconic portrayal of Lincoln; since midcentury, three illustrated texts have appeared that deal singly with Lincoln statues: F. Luristan Bullard, *Lincoln in Marble and Bronze* (1952), Donald C. Durman, *He*

Belongs to the Ages (1951) and Lincoln National Life Foundation, *Heroic Lincoln Statues in Bronze* (1957). However, it is not surprising that the bulk of ongoing historical research in the area of American public sculpture is bound up with Modern and Post-Modern criticism. Harriet F. Senie's *Contemporary Public Sculpture*, and Erika Doss's *Spirit Poles and Flying Pigs; Public Art and Cultural Democracy in American Communities*, evaluate the inevitable connection between public sculpture and public controversy and suggest what should be done about it. Even so, as the authors of these studies attest, the entire field of American sculpture, even that in the Modern area, has been unjustly overlooked.[3]

It is not simply a lingering puritanical fear of idolatry that takes the blame for this disinterest and for the consequent crisis facing public sculptors and their patrons, but also the old statue-making tradition itself. Modern and contemporary abstraction is usually regarded as the evolutionary successor to the ubiquitous Victorian-Edwardian monument, and to its continental counterpart, the École-des-Beaux-Art-inspired statue and pedestal. Rosalind Kraus locates the mutant gene that separates the old from the new in Auguste Rodin's *Gates of Hell* (1880) and in his *Balzac* (1891), two works that conclusively demonstrated the "failure" of the monument and the aspiring ascendancy of abstract form. The "statue" had to be discredited before Modernism could be born. While the old "logic of representation" well served the statue's didactic purpose—it reminded a populace of exemplary leaders and actions and thus served, as Marvin Trachtenberg phrased it, "as crystallizations of social energy"—its modern offspring advanced "significant form" as a prescription for cultural amnesia.[4]

Efforts to salvage the reputation of American sculpture have not entirely centered upon the modern tradition. Important work on eighteenth- and nineteenth-century American artists has in recent years inspired a number of articles, exhibition catalogues, and monographic studies that in conventional fashion organize a body of work around the life and times of individuals. Although they hardly fill the large gaps that remain, these studies build upon a slender publishing tradition inaugurated at the turn of the century by Truman Bartlett, Henry James, and Lorado Taft. It was notably a 1903 publication by the last author that remained the first and (until the appearance of Wayne Craven's ambitious compendium, *Sculpture in America* in 1968) only attempt at a comprehensive survey of American sculpture. The necessary task of expanding the monograph into an examination of the social, economic, political, and institutional horizons of American statuary has only recently begun. Books, essays, and catalogues by Daniel Robbins, Timothy Garvey, and George Gurney lead the way, while Michele Bogart's *Public Sculpture and the Civic Ideal in New York City, 1890–1930* (1989) evidences the most serious attempt so far to plumb the depths of this topic. With the recent appearance of Vivien Fryd's *Art and Empire,* another highly focused study that concentrates in part on the social and political content of sculpture made for the United States Capitol, one is encouraged to believe a movement is at last underway.[5]

While Bogart's subject—the so-called American "Beaux-Arts" style—and the manner in which she addresses it—a scrupulous documentation of contracts, political events, correspondence, and iconography—has been an important model for this study, the sheer quantity of material the period-location topic forces upon the author somewhat belabors the project. Could not a single work, or a related series of works, if wisely chosen, also be sufficient for an extended cultural study? Given the success of his *Michelangelo's David, A Search for Identity* (1967), it is surprising more authors, Americanists as well as others, have not followed Charles Seymour's lead, even for lesser-known monuments. Most noteworthy among recent single-work monographs that deal with statuary are Marvin Trachtenberg's classic contextual analysis, *The Statue of Liberty* (1976), Albert Elsen's *Rodin's Thinker and the Dilemmas of Modern Public Sculpture* (1986), and the same author's *The Gates of Hell by Auguste Rodin* (1985).[6] Like Seymour's, however, these books feature relatively famous icons made by foreign sculptors—one of them whose reputation is equal to that of Michelangelo—which underlines the fact that one-statue books continue to be a highly restrictive form of study. It is for this reason that the subject of *Errant Bronzes,* which has so far been relegated to one article, Harold E. Dickson, "George Grey Barnard's Controversial Lincoln," *Art Journal* (1967), and a few fleeting chapters in surveys, most notably in Craven, Durman, and Bullard, is not better known. Indeed, Barnard himself is one of the many important American sculptors whose life and career remains largely unexamined.

This book touches upon many issues that will strike familiar resonances today: the often opposed interests that divide Federal and privately initiated projects in the public sphere; the ongoing argument whether public sculpture should stand as an aspiring monument to lasting human values or as a freely expressive work of art; the claim that public sculpture should represent one or another special interest group instead of the common lot; the question whether the architect or the artist is the best judge in making site decisions and, most importantly, the consideration whether any kind of statuary is ultimately an appropriate medium for expressing secular and religious beliefs. The enormous increase in memorial projects earmarked for the National Mall in Washington over the past decade has helped make these issues more timely than ever.[7]

Public statue controversies feed upon a convergence of disassociative factors that are both internal and external to the activities of the artist, patrons, promotional agents, and administrative committees.[8] Thus, during the Barnard Lincoln affair, no single party seemed capable of controlling events. The first commission was prompted more by blind reaction than premeditation. Similarly, the second statue offering to England was instigated by a remarkably clumsy attempt at influence peddling. Thereafter, "the historical tissue of circumstance," combined with the irrational logic of political posturing, social recrimination, vanity, and the haughty claims of artistic genius, assumed full command over the fate of Barnard's wayward statues.

This book is divided into six parts. The first, "Unveilings," brings biographical and regional material into line with the commissioning of Barnard's Lincolns. The chapters "The Tafts and Their Lincolns" and "The Charles Tafts in Art" set the stage for later chapters by discussing the way art patronage, in particular the commissioning of Lincoln statues, related to the conservative ideology of the Taft brothers and to their failing political careers. The second chapter concludes with the contestation that surrounded the signing of the Taft-Barnard contract. Part 2, "Creations," reviews the artist's early life and works, and details his labors on the Lincoln prototype. His embrace of the myth of genius and his estrangement from the American Beaux-Arts coterie presage the difficulties that threatened to derail his work on the Taft commission. The early history of the first two castings, the temporary exhibit in Manhattan, and the promotional scheme concocted by John Stewart for sending the second cast to London's Parliament Square, are the subjects of Part 3. "Profiles of Controversy" examines the dramatic consequences of Stewart's promotion as they personally affected former president Taft and fueled the public debate in newspapers and journals, most notably in Frederick Ruckstull's *Art World* and Adolph Och's *New York Times.* Part 5 picks up the chronicle in 1918 and 1919 when antagonists instituted a campaign to divert Barnard's work from London. Eventually successful, this counterpromotion placed a replication of Saint-Gaudens's standing bronze statue of Lincoln (Chicago, 1887) at the same location Stewart formerly secured for the Barnard. The Barnard, meanwhile, was accepted by the city of Manchester, England, for temporary placement in a park in 1919. The commission and placement of the final Barnard Lincoln cast is examined in Chapter 10, "Louisville and The Bernheim Lincoln." Part 6 and its single chapter update the histories of the three Lincolns by discussing recent urban renewal projects that included the refurbishing, and in the example of the Manchester Lincoln, the relocation of the statues.

Errant Bronzes

Part One
Unveilings

1

The Tafts and Their Lincolns

O N THE COOL, CLEAR AFTERNOON OF 31 MARCH 1917, a statue of Abraham Lincoln was unveiled in a small public park in Cincinnati, Ohio.[1] Former president William Howard Taft, his voluminous figure in striking contrast to the tall, skeletal image close by, delivered the dedicatory address. Weary from weeks of speech-making in Southern states on behalf of the League to Enforce Peace, he chose Cincinnati for his final appearance before returning to his teaching du-

ties at Yale University Law School. Taft's participation in the ceremony offered him an opportunity to acknowledge old personal debts; here in Cincinnati he had finished his education, had married, and had launched a career in the Federal judiciary that eventually led to the White House. Here, as well, his older half brother Charles Taft, and wife Anna Sinton Taft, presided as the community's wealthiest and most influential citizens, its chief benefactors, and most en-

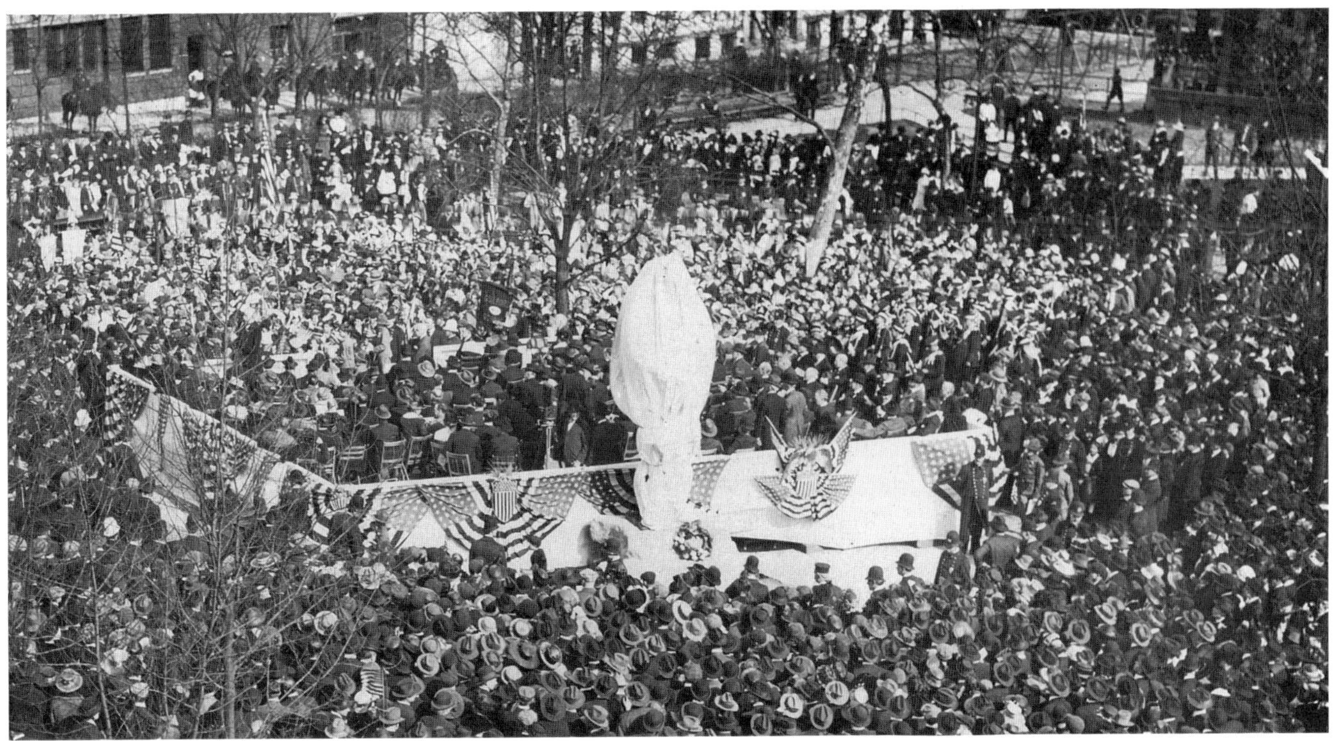

Dedication of George Grey Barnard's Abraham Lincoln, *Cincinnati, March 31, 1917. Courtesy of the Cincinnati Historical Society.*

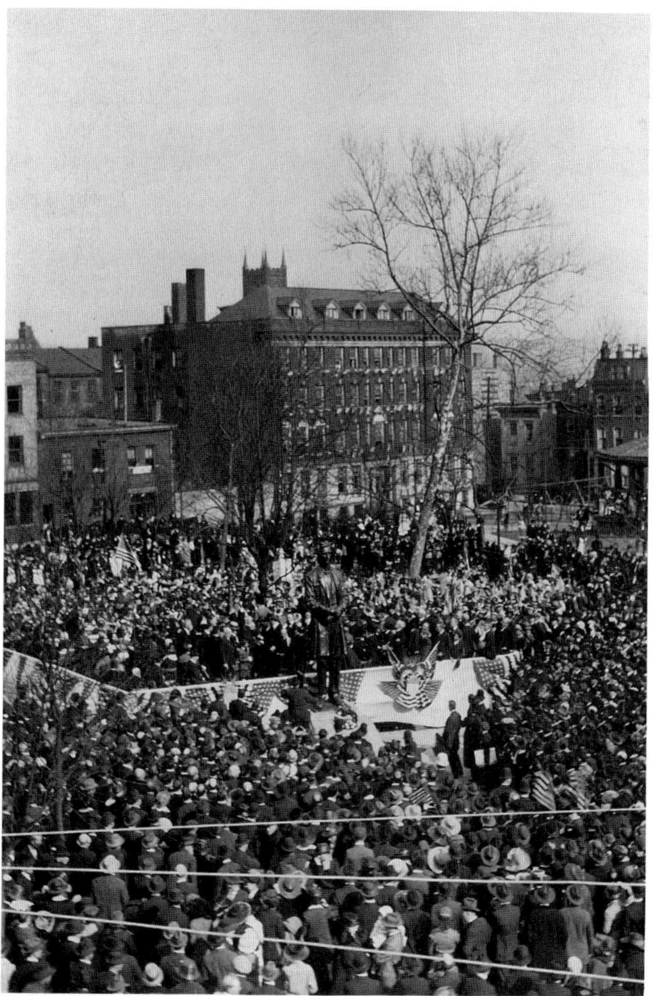

Dedication of George G. Barnard's Abraham Lincoln, *Cincinnati. Courtesy of the Cincinnati Historical Society.*

the practice of unveiling, as one congressman described it, enabled deceased heroes to once again walk "out upon us through the parting veil of the changeless past [and consequently] the multitude carries away the indefinable something that makes men true and good and brave." While young Charles and William were contemplating careers in law and jurisprudence, their father, jurist-statesman Alphonso Taft, often lectured them on the history of art and architecture, underlining his conviction that politically liberal governments unfailingly erected noble monuments to their leaders and outstanding citizens. Nobility could not be equated with mere representation, he insisted, but reflected what Emerson held to be a moral beauty which "belongs to the soul and illuminates with expression features not otherwise deemed beautiful and makes them active."[3] As guardians of what they perceived to be the inviolable principles of good government, the brothers stood ready to reaffirm their father's convictions.

Yet, for influential citizens who had a stake in the promotion of statues like the Lincoln, unveilings presented untold risks. No matter how generally re-

lightened patrons of art. The Lincoln statue was their latest, most significant, donation.

For a half century William Taft had profited from Charles's political counsel and financial support and thanks to him had gained an abiding respect for the civilizing influence of art. Wealthy Cincinnatians had been generous patrons. This magnanimity was seen in a large memorial fountain in the central square and in heroic statues of Ohio-born presidents James Garfield and William Henry Harrison that had been financed through public subscription and fashioned by local sculptors.[2] No less indicative was the community's distinguished contribution to the Arts and Crafts movement, its art academy and museum, its extensive collections of painting, statuary, and objets d'art, especially that of the Charles Tafts which adorned the family homestead near the new statue.

The Tafts lived in an era when the practice of unveiling portrait statues was a cogent device for educating the public about great national and moral issues. The origins of the custom were obscure, but

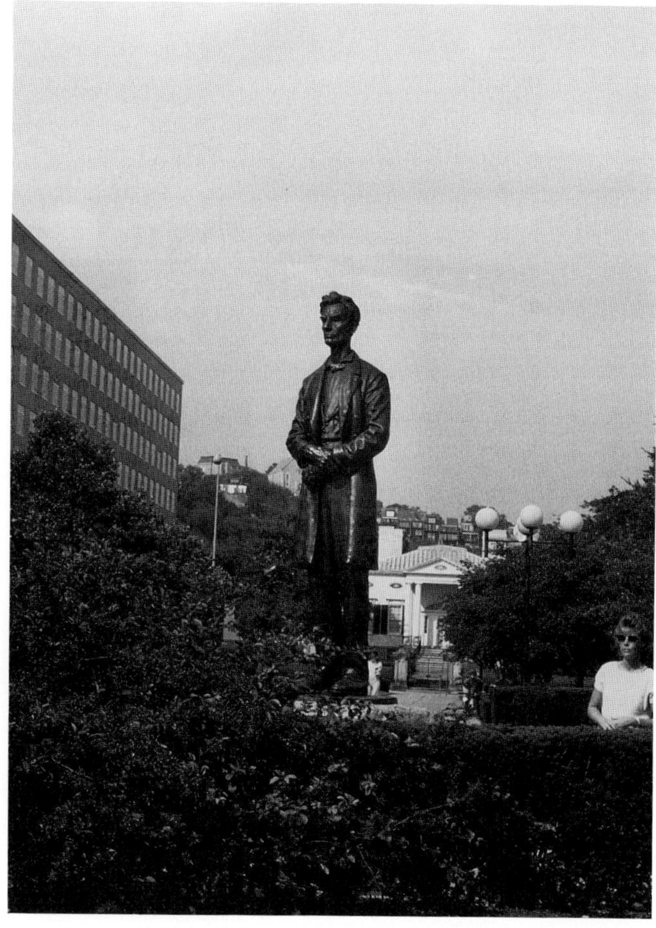

George G. Barnard, Abraham Lincoln. *Cincinnati. [Contemporary photo].*

spected the subject of a statue might be, nor how successfully an artist may have captured the moral essence of an honored patriot, there was no way to predict what effect, in the short or long term, a monument might have upon the living who were fated to share its space. History presented too many instances of statue presentations that for various reasons had ignited controversy and caused their sponsors untold anguish. For a close-at-hand example, the fraudulent handling of the Harrison statue competition in the early 1890s cast a dark shadow over this presumably generous donation.[4] Thus, the Tafts and

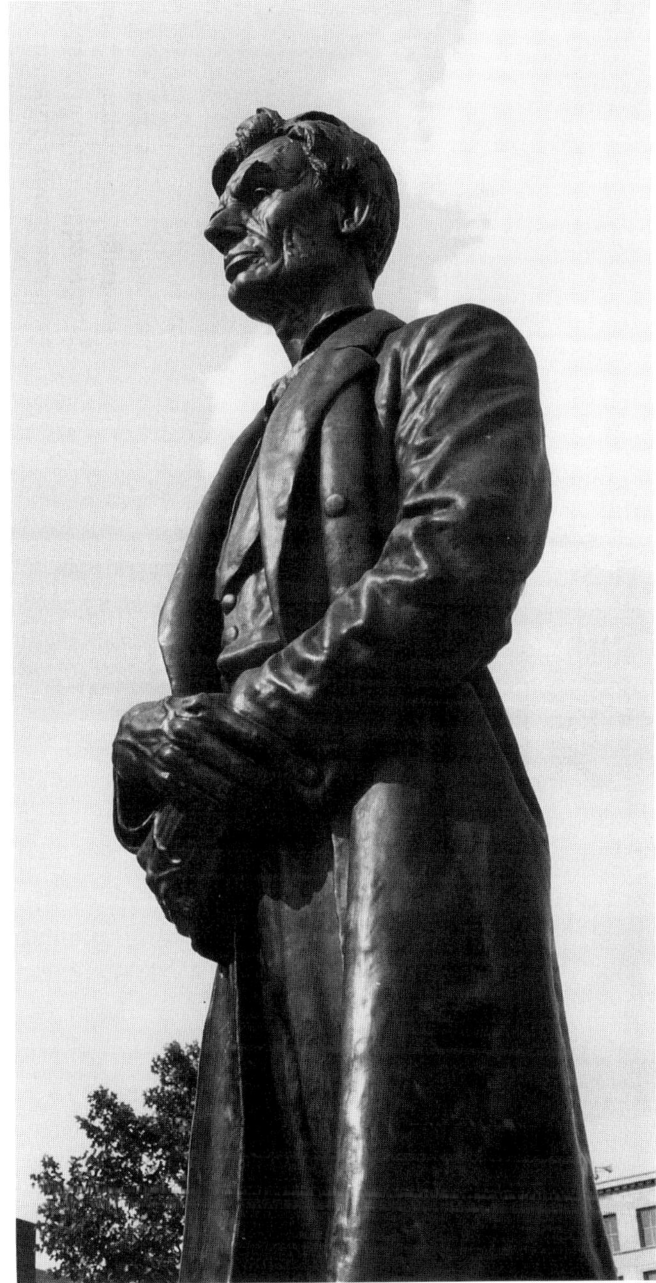

George G. Barnard, Abraham Lincoln. *Cincinnati. [Contemporary photo].*

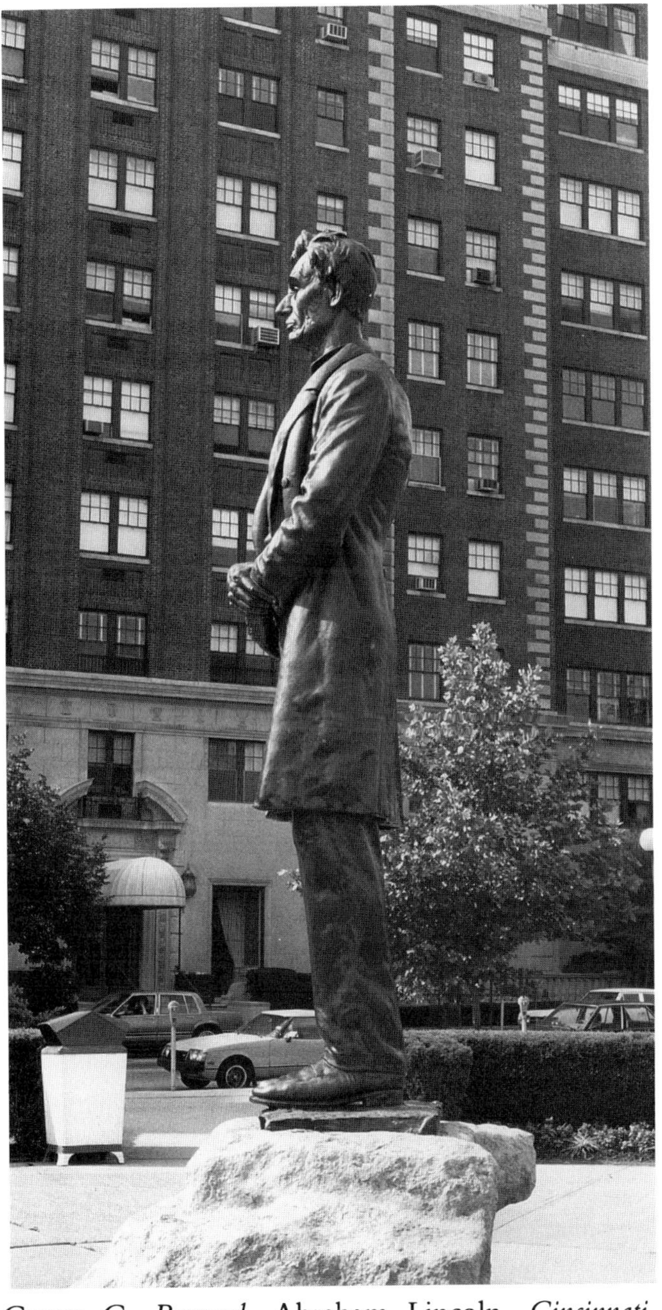

George G. Barnard, Abraham Lincoln. *Cincinnati. [Contemporary photo].*

their friends turned anxious eyes to the proceedings on that spring afternoon.

The subject of the statue was bound to arouse mixed impressions in the minds of the city's oldest residents. In life, Lincoln visited Cincinnati on four occasions, the first two as an unknown attorney, then as a presidential candidate, and finally as the president-elect en route to his inauguration. Local historians best remembered him as a lonely figure wandering city streets or as the innocent who was bullied by unprincipled adversaries. In 1855, following a public humiliation at the hands of cocounsel

Edwin M. Stanton, Lincoln regretfully assured his hosts he had "nothing against the city, but things have so happened here as to make it undesirable for me ever to return here." His reappearance as a candidate came on the heels of the Douglas debates, when he certified his aversion to the uncontrolled expansion of slavery. Mindful that it was a mixed audience that greeted him, however, Lincoln hastened to reassure all pro-slavers within hearing that he intended to honor the Constitutional Ordinance of 1787, which permitted the ownership of slaves as property in certain states. During his final appearance this olive branch was rudely rejected by the militant abolitionists of the German Free Workingmen.[5]

Lincoln's unusual physical presence was as much at issue as was his stand on slavery. Moncure Conway and Rutherford B. Hayes, both associates of Alphonso Taft, recorded their impressions in 1859. Conway wrote:

> His face had a battered and bronzed look, without being hard. His nose was prominent and buttressed a strong and high forehead. His eyes were high-vaulted and had an expression of sadness; his mouth and chin were too close together, the cheeks hollow. On the whole, Lincoln's appearance was not attractive until one heard his voice, which possessed a variety of expression, ernestness, and shrewdness in every tone. The charm of his manner was that he had no manner; he was simple, direct, humorous.

Riding with the Lincoln entourage as the American Party's vice-presidential candidate, Hayes was similarly struck by the contradictions existing between the man's character and appearance.

> Mr. Lincoln has an ungainly figure, but one loses sight of that, or rather the first impression disappears in the absorbed attention which the manner of his speech commands. He is an orator of an unusual kind, so calm, so undemonstrative, but nevertheless an orator of great merit. It is easy to contrast him after the manner of Plutarch, but his like has not been heard in these parts.

Three years later such approving reminiscences were overbalanced by Lincoln's handling of the war. A disciple of Emerson who for several years ministered to Cincinnati's Unitarians, Conway became a raging critic; after exile to England he proclaimed Lincoln to be the most detested president in American history.[6]

Determined to export New England values to the wilderness, Alphonso Taft moved to Cincinnati in 1838, following graduation from Yale College and admittance to the bar. He had little reason to regret his departure from hallowed ground, since next to Boston, Cincinnati was home to the most concentrated gathering of freethinkers in the country; here Hegelians, evolutionists, and transcendentalists tirelessly labored to expose the fallacies of parochialism and supernaturalism in social and religious practice. Keeping pace with the liberal revolt against Calvinism in the East, he severed old family ties with the Baptist Church and in the 1840s joined Cincinnati's Unitarians. Equally bound to worldly concerns, he opened a thriving law practice, served on the state superior court, and assisted in founding the Republican party. Alphonso admired Lincoln's performance in the Douglas debates, supported his candidacy, and personally greeted the future president in Washington at the end of 1860. But the following year Alphonso and his second wife, Louise, were expressing outrage at Lincoln's equivocations on a clear moral issue. The president's countermanding of Gen. Freemont and advancement of generals McClellan, Buell, and Halleck at the beginning of 1862 symbolized to them and other New Englanders in their circle Lincoln's total capitulation to Southern conservatives and monarchists.[7] His refusal to allow the enlistment of Blacks because of the prejudice that existed in border states and within regular army ranks seemed nothing more than a pretext that augmented that prejudice. Above all other abuses and omissions, they could not forgive Lincoln's tragic misreading of the Constitution regarding the human ownership of other human beings.

Family correspondence makes clear Alphonso's bitter indictment was not simply the isolated protest of a private citizen, a judge, a lawyer, or a politician; however much condensed or simplified, it was a blow struck in defense of sectional values. New England liberalism was on trial, and a crude Western sophist was temporarily obstructing its destined expansion across the continent. The elder Tafts gained hope when Grant took command and old generals were replaced. But neither the Emancipation Proclamation nor the assassination could entirely redeem Lincoln's reputation in the Taft household.[8]

By the time Alphonso Taft entered President Grant's cabinet in 1876, he had gained a more moderate perspective on the Civil War president. Among the few gala events he was expected to attend during his brief tenure as secretary of war was the unveiling east of the Capitol of Thomas Ball's *Emancipation Group,* a heroic monument that had been partly financed by former slaves. He was quite possibly offended by Ball's portrayal, for it presented a dapper

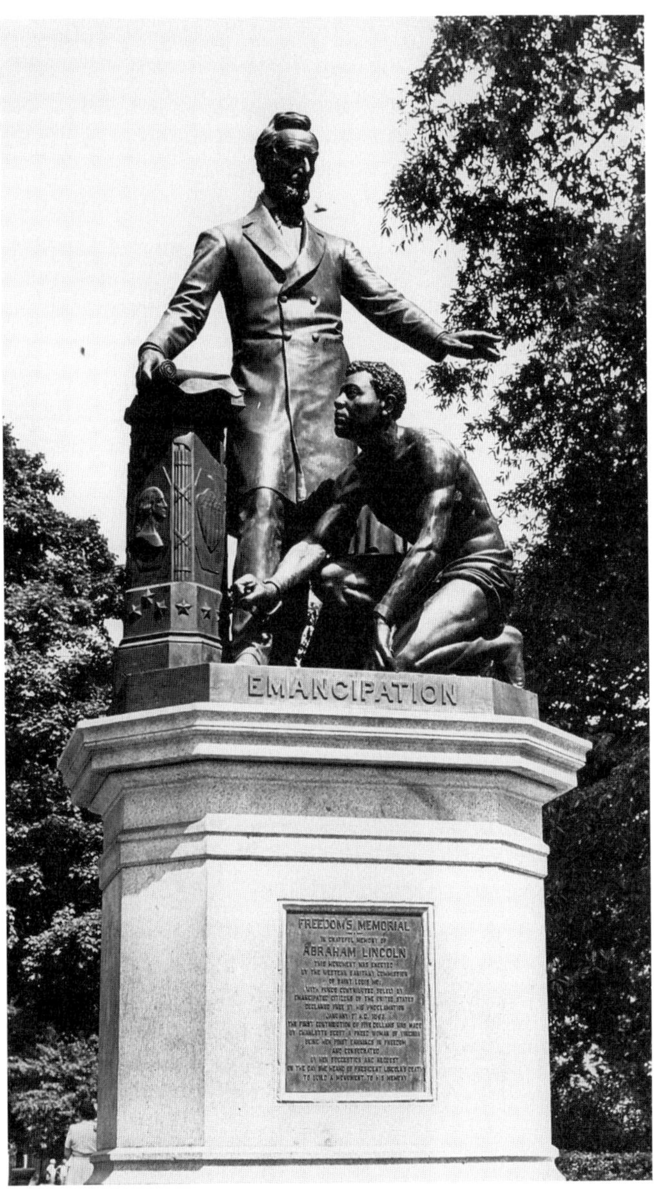

Thomas Ball, The Emancipation Monument. *1875. Bronze, Lincoln figure, 7'. Washington, D.C.*

emancipator standing in slave-master fashion above a crouching black man. However, Alphonso would have been moved by Frederick Jackson Douglass's oration, which after paying rhetorical homage, harshly scorned Lincoln for his equivocations.[9] From his new perspective inside Grant's troubled administration, the elder Taft had less cause than before to condemn a monument that deified a mere mortal.

During the Taft Lincoln dedication forty years later, similar reflections on Lincoln's role in history were overwhelmed by the startling events of the hour. On that day, banner headlines heralded President Woodrow Wilson's declaration of war on Germany; two weeks earlier, first reports out of Petrograd gave notice the Russian Revolution had begun its long and bloody course. Once more soldiers

patrolled Cincinnati streets and bivouacked on public grounds. There were random acts of violence and rumors of dark plots. Some local seamen were feared lost in the German sinking of a merchant vessel.

It is no wonder the assembled sensed the relevance of Lincoln's memory to present circumstances, but they did so from opposing views: neutralists and radical pacifists decried America's foreign adventure, just as they regretted Lincoln's decision to resort to military force half a century earlier. Others equated Prussian aggression with the same slave-master mentality Lincoln sacrificed his own and thousands of other lives to eradicate from American soil. America seemed poised to enter the second and final stage of the Civil War. In his address, William Taft observed the statue "could not have been dedicated at a more fitting time," and Mayor George Puchta, himself of German descent, did not hesitate to proclaim Lincoln a true American "whose personality and quality of statesmanship is attracting the love of all humanity during these trying times."[10]

Still others present differed with the speakers on what Lincoln's role would be were he to miraculously return from the grave. One of these dissenters sat beside the Tafts and special guests before the podium. He was George Grey Barnard, the New York sculptor Charles Taft commissioned to produce the statue six years earlier. Barnard believed his figure presented more a victim of international class repression than a righteous crusader who was preparing to lead the forces of good against those of evil. By extension, he perceived the European conflict to be a class war of extinction being waged by the rich against the poor—not an argument between neighboring countries—and he condemned President Wilson for waiting two years before committing American military forces to the conflict. In other respects, however, Barnard believed the war was having a salubrious moral and cultural effect: it was leading the allies to a new understanding of democracy and social justice, while it was also giving rise to a new art style. Founded upon the spirit of universal brotherhood, this style promised to "help crush the baleful influence of the German school, always stiff and constrained, and strongly tinged with the German militaristic idea."[11] Furthermore, he noted with satisfaction that the war was helping the cause of American art, since it was forcing wealthy collectors of European masterworks like the Charles Tafts to acquire, and hence better appreciate, the work of native artists like himself. A group of Eastern liberals who had been closely following Barnard's career agreed with the artist's prognostications about a resurgent style and regarded the *Lincoln* as its leading example. While the statue was on temporary exhibit in Manhattan during the previous winter, citizen committees ordered replicas for London, Paris, and Petrograd to serve as tokens of American sympathy and good will. Charles Taft heartily endorsed each project and pledged to finance the casting and transportation of the London statue.

As a guest of his patrons, Barnard was to spend several days in Cincinnati, appearing before civic groups, giving newspaper interviews, and posing for photographers. The evening following the unveiling, he was honored at a patriotic celebration at the Businessmen's Club. A tour of the city convinced him Cincinnati's passion for all forms of creative art, music, dance, as well as painting and sculpture, not Taft money alone, had predestined it to receive his great work.[12] Given to extreme emotional shifts, Barnard was momentarily ebullient and boastful; he had devoted the best years of his life to the statue, while suffering financial insecurity, emotional turmoil, and physical trauma, and he was now prepared to bask in the glory due him.

Unlike the German press, which rapidly passed over the unveiling ceremonies, Cincinnati's English language newspapers gave them full coverage and found Barnard's statue above reproach. A journalist approvingly remarked that the "veins stand out clearly visible in the haggard face and lean hands, the hair is matted on the head, the trousers bag at the knees, the shoes run over at the side. From the forehead the bronze hair stands up in what is known in Lincoln's country as a cowlick. A large nose, enormous hands and feet, distinguish the statue." The writer confirmed that individuals who had known the living Lincoln considered the statue a convincing portrait. The *Cincinnati Post,* a Democratic newspaper which on principle opposed the Tafts, admiringly quoted a child's reaction to the statue: "'Why, it's just a plain man.'" The reporter confirmed "the knarled hands [were like those of] any who works in the shoe factory that stands close by the statue," and that "the clothes are wrinkled and hang loosely as on one who cares nothing at all about looks that do not count." There was an especially warm response from poets whose sentimental verse preached the social gospel. Lyman Whitney Allen's dedicatory ode sublimated each disfigurement—the "unshapely" feet, the "ungainly" hands—before assessing the entire statue as "commonality glorified." Among the creases traversing the statue's back, the poet discerned a double cross, a configuration that suggested "the emblem of a statesman's Calvary!" Some months later Edwin

Markham was moved to rewrite his standard tribute, "Lincoln, the Man of the People." Other Lincoln statues, he found, present an idealized figure, but only the Barnard "gives us Lincoln the man, Lincoln the plain man of the people, Lincoln the man who had swung the ax among the woods at Sangamon, the man who had followed the plow on the prairies, the man who had passed through all the grim experiences of the common life." Lincoln had earned those "big, sturdy hands" in honest labor. "Those hands," Markham contended, "might well be made the symbol of our Americanism, the emblem of our hopes and aspirations. For do we not claim to base democracy upon labor, upon honest toil?"[13]

Barnard also chose the medium of free verse to address the social significance of his figure. In forcefully scribbled notations, he confirmed his intention had been to depict in combination a radical prophet, a Westerner, "a Christ-like man of the American soil," a democrat, and a bone-weary farmer. The enormous vein-swollen hands were likewise those of a pioneer that "opened the doors of Heaven to the Paths of Labor." Nor did William Taft dispute these effusions in his remarks. There was no denying the image before him reflected a man of the soil, whose exterior was "rough and apparently unrefined."[14] He commended Barnard for having presented Lincoln in the "habit and garb of his origin and his life among the plain people—a profound lesson in democracy and its highest possibility." The clear signs of impoverishment were apt reproofs to a contemporary society besotted by material comfort and extravagance. Now facing Armageddon, American citizens would have to exchange false goals of national wealth for the material sacrifices Lincoln asked of himself and the country in his day.

But Taft was incapable of explaining just how it was possible, short of a miracle, that Barnard's rustic should acquire the intellect, the innate genius, the uncommon wit, and the unrelenting propensity for self-examination which distinguished his Promethean struggle with slavery. Certainly, the uneven fall of the cloak, the tilted collar and tie, and the overlarge hands and feet did not in themselves evidence the "pure soul and commanding intellect" to which Taft directed his attention. Indeed, in ordinary circumstances, the professional class to which Taft belonged regarded such roughness and physical deformity as unalterable signs of social depravity and ineptitude.

William Taft's days as a political front-runner were now well behind him, but he continued to speak for wealthy conservatives and the capitalist system. By no means was his intellectual outlook entirely doctrinaire: since his Yale days he had embraced both laissez-faire and protectionist theories. Furthermore, of the six Taft children who survived into adulthood, William alone accepted Unitarianism, the precepts of that buttressed his vision of American neutrality and of a postwar international peace tribunal. Still, he never questioned the premise that civilization, the ultimate repository "of [the] higher instincts of the human mind and soul," rested upon a citizen's constitutional right to own property and accumulate capital."[15] It followed, therefore, that the courts of the land had no higher purpose than to protect property rights to the fullest extent of the law. Bound up with these principles was the absolute requirement that a professional elite should occupy the highest offices of government. Thus, even if Lincoln's exceptional rise out of poverty provided an instructive lesson, it did not justify Labor's attempt to overthrow Capitalism. The fact remained that the subject of the statue in no manner resembled the informed citizen who normally qualified for high political or judicial office or who could be expected to honor property rights.

The Cincinnati unveiling was not the first time William Taft was obliged to portray Lincoln as a strict constitutionalist. Similar pronouncements were routine during his presidency when his political future lay in the balance. No sooner had he entered the White House than he was attacked by progressive Republican legislators of Western states, the so-called Insurgents, for whom Taft had become a symbol of an intransigent Eastern banking establishment, and of a judiciary controlled by special interests.[16] The Insurgents espoused a popular ballot for primary elections, the rights of initiative, referendum, and recall of judges and judicial decisions, pressed for an extension of the franchise to women, and strenuously fought to keep Federal lands out of the hands of private developers. Following a brief retirement, former president Theodore Roosevelt took up the cause, singling out the man he once groomed to replace him for harsh rebuke. Taft defensively styled himself a moderate, but provided the Progressive opposition with a clear target when he signed the protectionist Payne-Aldrich tariff and refused to censure a powerful obstructionist, Illinois Representative Joseph Cannon. When Roosevelt and his rebellious coalition charged into the presidential campaign of 1912 as members of the Progressive, "Bull Moose," party, they insured Woodrow Wilson's triumph. Even so, Roosevelt claimed a moral victory for Progressivism by soundly defeating Taft.

A marked increase in the production of Lincoln statues attended these critical moments of the progressive-conservative engagement. While between 1866 and 1900 Lewiston Bullard estimates fourteen full-length Lincolns were raised in this country, over twenty were sculpted between 1909 and 1919.[17] The upsurge was prompted in part by the centenary anniversary of Lincoln's birth (12 February 1909) and by the rapidly increasing mortality of surviving Grand Army of the Republic veterans that conveniently coincided with this anniversary; before it was too late, old soldiers wished to bid their former commander an appropriate farewell. It also helped that children of abolitionists like the Tafts, and of pro-slave Copperheads who once resided in the border states, were now willing to forgive and forget. It was inevitable that as they mapped out their campaign plans, Taft and Roosevelt would put the new crop of statues and monuments to political use.

The contenders freely compared themselves to two distinct Lincolns. Taft's obeyed the law and for this was slandered by his own party and members of his cabinet. While not disputing Lincoln's capacity for coolheaded sanity, Roosevelt sketched for his audiences a man of rugged strength and valiant courage, a righteous individual who followed the dictates of his conscience rather than law. He reminded his Western listeners of a Lincoln remark affirming that labor was in advance of, and independent of, capital in the American economic hierarchy.[18] He pointed to Lincoln's embittered reaction to the Supreme Court ruling on Dred Scott—a reaction Taft considered warranted by the exceptionally unjust nature of the decision—in an attempt to prove Lincoln continually questioned that which William Taft held sacrosanct: the Court's constitutional authority.

For his rebuttal, Taft enlisted the aid of Abraham Lincoln's lawyer son Robert, an individual whose limited political talents, tightfisted management of the George M. Pullman Company, and blatantly aristocratic views had not blunted his authority to speak for his father. Accusing Roosevelt of having usurped the "Gettysburg Address," Robert proclaimed in a public letter solicited by Taft that above all else, his father honored a balanced representational government; that he favored deliberation over "shortsighted impulse"; that unlike the Bull Moose candidate, Abraham Lincoln opposed unchecked democracy and revolution. Also coming to Taft's aid was Judd Stewart, a collector of Lincolniana and a champion of conservative principles, who published a pamphlet detailing how Roosevelt had deceitfully altered the meaning of Lincoln's speeches by quoting them out of context.[19]

As the speeches also make clear, Taft's Lincoln differed quite as much from the Lincoln his father and the New England abolitionists thought they knew as it did from the Lincoln pictured by the Progressives. When in early November 1911 Taft addressed a crowd at Lincoln's Kentucky birthplace, he attributed the president's ineffective handling of McClellan, the conspiring generals, and cabinet officers not to moral cowardice, but simply to a lack of managerial experience. Once gained, this experience enabled him to disarm his enemies with "strategic suggestion," which in the long run proved more effective a weapon than righteous anger. Even more injurious to the Union cause than were the conspirators, Taft had to admit, were the moral reformers "who pounced on Mr. Lincoln with emphatic denunciation and bitter attack, but he knew better than they what was necessary before he took the step of emancipation they were pressing."[20]

Notwithstanding the outcome of the presidential election of 1912, President Taft won something of a moral victory of his own in February of 1911 when Congress named him chairman of the Lincoln Memorial Commission, an appointment successive presidents reconfirmed until the project's completion in 1922. His appointment as Chief Justice of the Supreme Court overshadows his directorship of this multimillion dollar project. Indeed, some biographers assert that Taft did not especially like art. But it could be more accurately stated that during the construction of Henry Bacon's Greek temple, and during the sculpting of Daniel Chester French's colossal seated statue, Taft assumed a position that for lack of a better term could be designated the national art czar. When at the memorial's dedication he declared it to be a national shrine "in which those who love country and love God can find inspiration and repose," Taft fully recognized that but for his own tireless defense of the troubled project, the Lincoln Memorial would have been anything but an inspiration.[21]

Taft's history of the project encapsulates a chronicle of American art in which he saw the architect as the dominant force.[22] Not the painter or sculptor but the architect was in a position to bring all branches of the fine arts into a unified balance. At the large expositions of the late nineteenth century, Taft recalled, American artists first learned the value of community effort. The spectacular Chicago Columbian Exposition of 1893, which assembled the architects Daniel Burnham, Charles McKim, and Charles Atwood, the landscape planner Frederick Olmsted Sr., as well as painter Frank Millet, and, at least in spirit, Augustus Saint-Gaudens, the "dean" of American sculptors, demonstrated the cultural and spiritual advantages of civic planning. The exposition's influence led to the founding of the American Academy in Rome, a city that remained a "reservoir of Greek art." In Washington, the creators of Chicago's "White City" and "Court of Honor" undertook a loftier mission as designers of a master plan for their nation's capital, a plan that gave major focus to a Lincoln memorial. Designed in the Greek Doric style, the resulting monument embodied "the highest art of which America is capable." It was the architects, especially Charles McKim, Taft contended, who "did the most among us to bring the art of Greece to appreciative and noble use."

The critical master plan to which the present form of the Lincoln Memorial owes its existence is the United States Senate Park Commission Plan, also known as the McMillan Commission Park Plan, a document faintly resembling Major L'Enfant's original design for the capital city. Conceived by Burnham, McKim, and Frederick Olmsted Jr., and approved by the Senate in opposition to House action

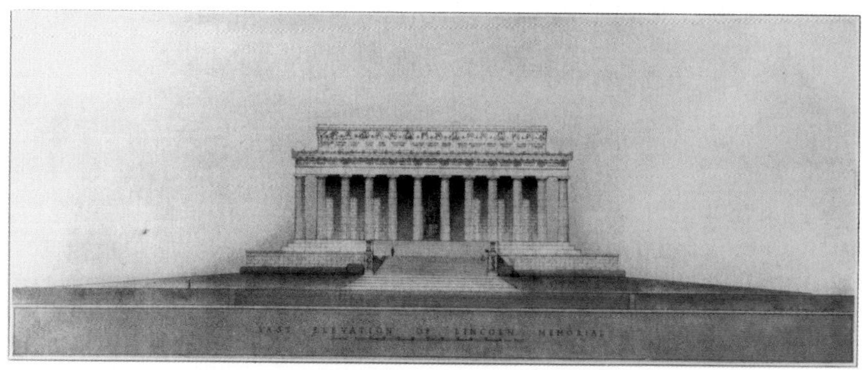

Proposed East Elevation of the Lincoln Memorial, *from
U. S. Congress, 62d., 3d Sess.,* Senate Documents
(Washington, D.C.: G.P.O., 1913) 7, pl. 3.

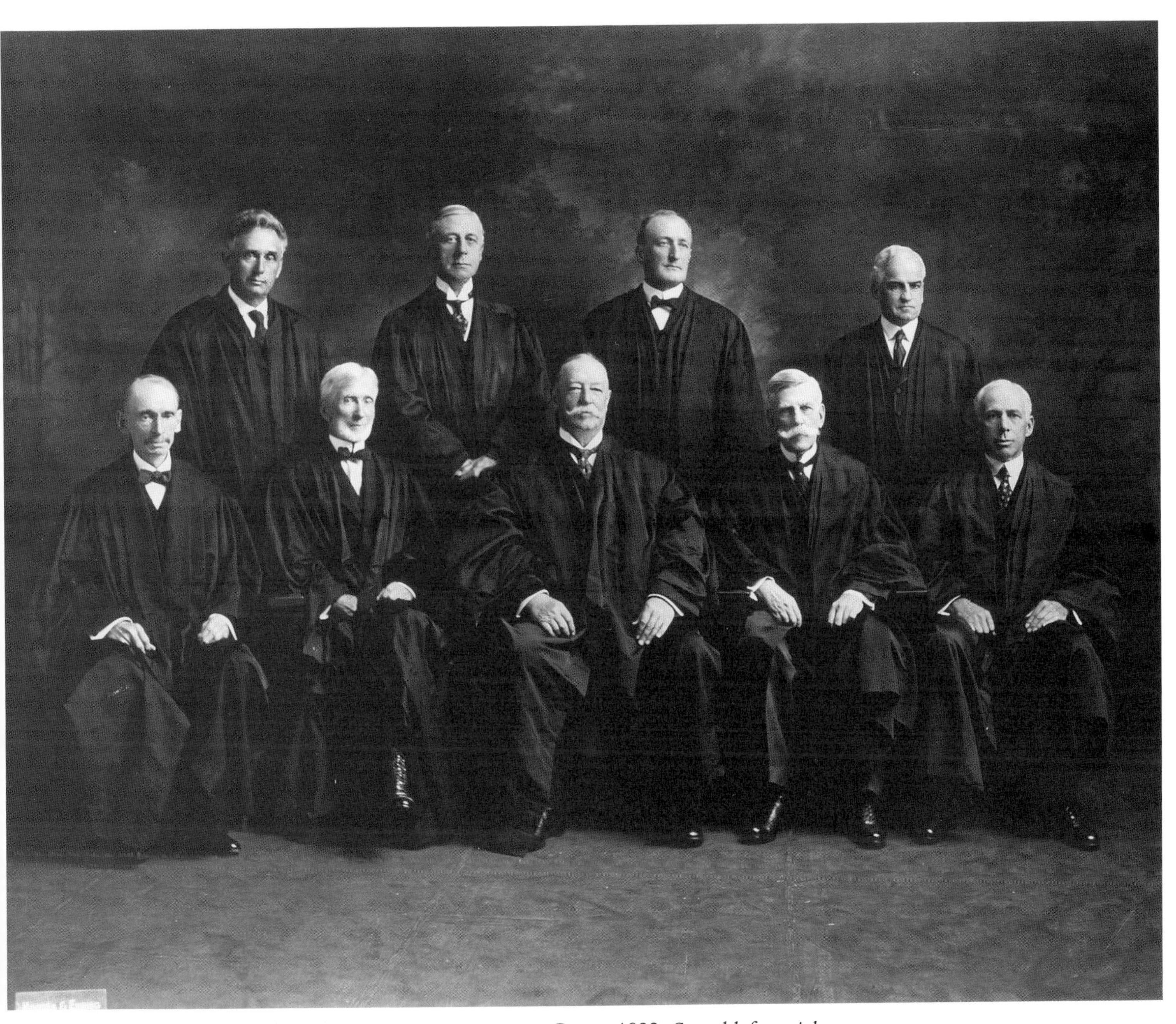

United States Surpreme Court, 1922. Seated left to right, William R. Day, Joseph McKenna, Taft, Oliver Wendell Holmes, Jr., and Willis Van Devanter. Standing, from left, Louis D. Brandeis, Mahlon Pitney, James C. McReynolds and John H. Clark. Courtesy of the Library of Congress.

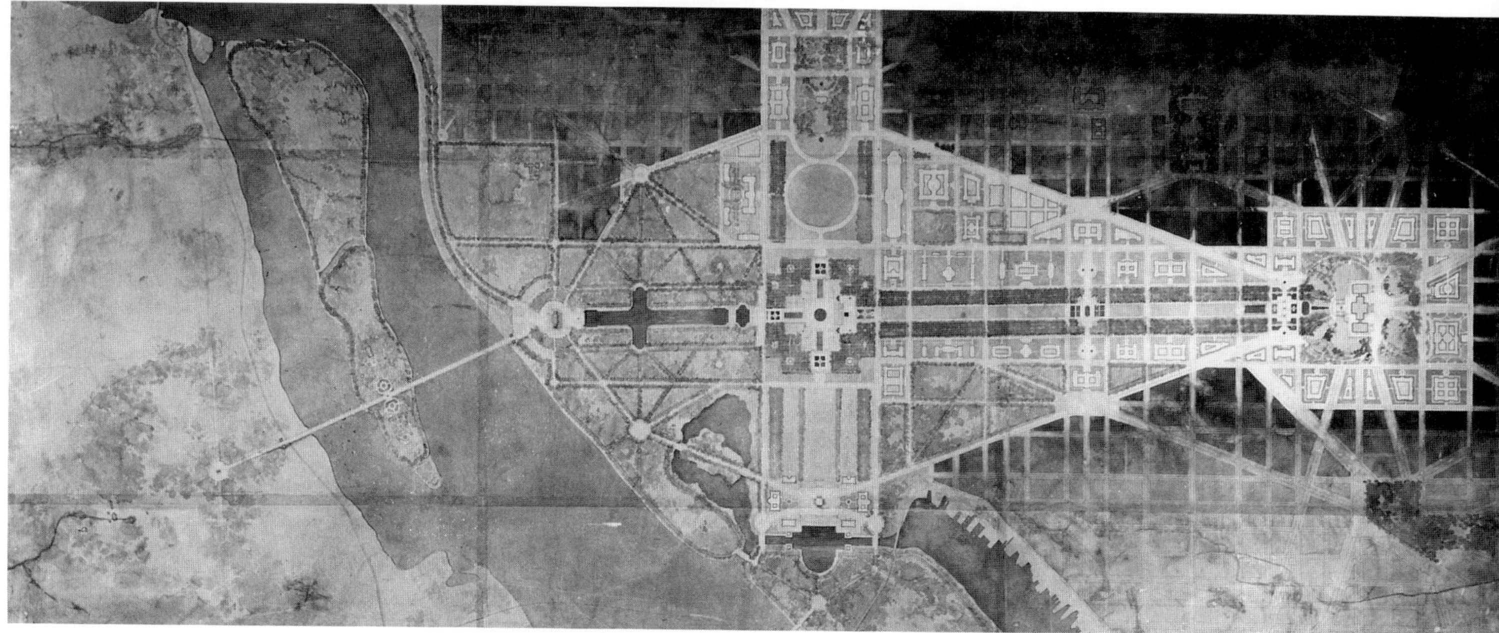

United States Senate Park Plan *[McMillan Commission Park Plan]*, *Washington, D.C. 1901. Courtesy of
the United States Commission of Fine Arts.*

in 1901, the document seemed defiantly aristocratic
to powerful House members such as Joseph Cannon.
In it, the proposed Lincoln Memorial takes its place
in an ellipse at the western terminus of the projected
mall, directly on line with the Capitol dome and
Washington Monument. In accord with Burnham's
design for Chicago's "White City," the McMillan design emphasized wide boulevards, adjusted proportions of buildings to space, regulated plantings, and
"healthy spaciousness and ordered amenities." Not
objects or details, but proper scale, "the finding of
the relationship between a composition and its surroundings," guided Burnham to an aesthetic as well
as spiritual solution. Such a plan, Taft could well appreciate, functioned as a constitutional document did,
in confirming man's innate desire for geometric order
and balance. Said Burnham, "a logical diagram once
recorded will never die."[23] It left no room for innovation, originality, and vibrant expression, aesthetic
factors Taft might easily have equated with political
insurgency. It was manifestly an outline of authority
and power.

The park commissioners considered a Lincoln
statue essential to the proposed memorial and requested the ailing Saint-Gaudens to join their deliberations. The sculptor had created two bronze
Lincoln statues for Chicago, both in close collaboration with architects, and he was McKim's choice to
receive a handsome commission for sculpting the memorial statue. After his death in 1907, Saint-Gaudens

was by no means forgotten, and it was in commemoration of his old friend that Burnham insisted the
appointed sculptor "be one who has the severest
taste, not the richest fancy."[24]

The history of the Senate park plan's survival in a
decade of intense warfare between members of both
Houses and the efforts of the American Institute of
Architects, President Roosevelt, and his secretaries of
war, Elihu Root and William Taft, to preserve the
integrity of the fragile document, is an involved one.
Here it need only be mentioned that repeated attempts to change the recommended form and location of the Lincoln Memorial, whether to render it
more publicly accessible, thus more "democratic," or
modify it in order to appease one sectional interest or
another, were in principle opposed by the Roosevelt
administration. Like Root before him, Secretary Taft
steadfastly upheld provisions of the park plan and
was wholly sympathetic to the long range goals of
Burnham's commission.[25]

During the Taft administration, the park commission was at long last given solid administrative footing. In 1910, six months prior to his selection by
Congress to head the Lincoln Memorial Commission
(LMC), President Taft, with Congressional approval,
created the (Federal) Commission of Fine Arts
(CFA), appointing Burnham its first chairman.
Sculptor Daniel French assumed the chairmanship
following Burnham's demise in 1912. As it claimed
advisory jurisdiction over all Federal art and architec-

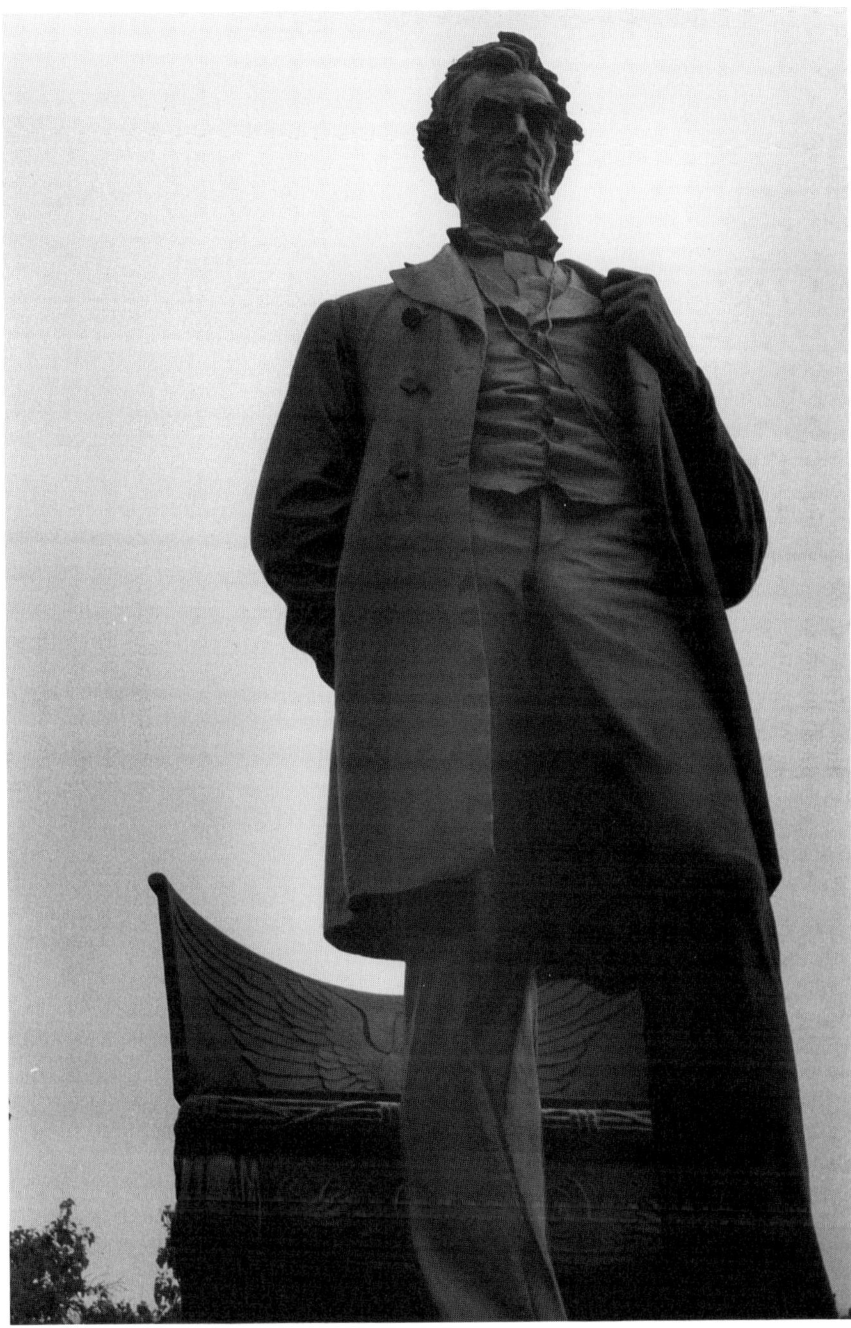

Augustus Saint-Gaudens, Abraham Lincoln. *1885–87.*
Bronze, 12'. Chicago, Illinois.

ture projects planned for the District of Columbia, the CFA accepted an American Institute of Architects (AIA) mandate regarding the appointment of architects, collaborating sculptors, and decorators. This dictated that because high classical standards were essential, the directing architect was to be directly chosen by a commission of enlightened professionals. Once appointed, he then recommended the sculptors, painters, muralists, and artisans he deemed suitable for the tasks at hand. While open competitions gave a semblance of democratic process, this unwieldy procedure handicapped those of proven ability and too often led to political abuse. This Taft could confirm from his own experience as Secretary of War when in his normal course of duties, he routinely administered Federal monument commissions and arbitrated disputes between sculptors and their respective lobbyists.[26]

The first major responsibility facing the CFA was to judge plans for the Lincoln Memorial. After reviewing the proposals of two invited architects—the other being John Russell Pope—the CFA recommended Henry Bacon's appointment. An École-des-Beaux-Arts graduate, a former partner with McKim, Mead, and White, and a prominent New York member of AIA with offices on Park Avenue, Bacon was a highly connected, if otherwise unexceptional, exponent of the classical school. Even though he was appointed in April 1912, almost three years passed before the LMC, after having requested French to submit a model for the central figure, officially appointed the latter to be the sculptor of the Lincoln statue. French then reluctantly resigned from the CFA. It was not Bacon's disinterest in the statue that forced the delay; immediately after his own appointment, the architect ventured the opinion that "the most important object [in the Memorial] is the statue of Lincoln, which is placed in the center of the Memorial, and by virtue of its imposing position in the place of honor, the gentleness, power, and intelligence of the man, expressed as far as possible by the sculptor's art, will predominate." An unusually detailed illustration in the LMC's first official publication in 1913 represented a figure seated in a chair of state (see p. 77). Nor did Bacon doubt what sculptor would best qualify: from the beginning of his involvement, he wanted Taft to directly select French. The two were longtime collaborators; appropriately, their last commission, which was still receiving finishing touches, was for a Lincoln statue in Lincoln, Nebraska. Bacon was convinced they made a successful team because "we each have given in to the other when points arose, but were finally satisfied in combined efforts."[27] Other Daniel French proponents agreed that next to Saint-Gaudens, he was that rare individual who could create an "ideally perfect," rather than a merely striking, statue.

Before French's appointment, Taft, Bacon, and the LMC were naturally beset with inquiries and unsolicited suggestions. Charles Taft informally recommended Barnard, a proposal William received with a decided lack of enthusiasm. William himself advanced the name of Cartaino S. Pietro, who was sculpting his bust for the Hague Peace Palace in Holland. Pietro's efforts to articulate the "nobility" of Taft's features in the bust failed to impress Bacon, who reproved Taft for daring to think the portrait passable. Pressure came from an unexpected source when Saint-Gaudens's widow, Augusta, implored Bacon to make the memorial's centerpiece a bronze replica of her husband's highly regarded standing Lincoln in Chicago's Lincoln Park. Like her husband's vociferous Washington supporters, Augusta's opinion was that Saint-Gaudens the sculptor, like Lincoln the political leader, had attained a unique position in American history; thus, even a replica of the Chicago bronze would be far more appropriate for the memorial than an original work by a lesser living artist. Meanwhile, Myron T. Herrick, United States Ambassador to France, urged Taft and the LMC to consider Auguste Rodin, since in Herrick's view, a world-renowned leader deserved to be sculpted by the "Michel Angelo of this century."[28]

Taft also received by way of Herrick a lesson in French democracy. An unsigned letter written to him by American sculptors denounced direct selection or limited invitational competitions since these could only yield "some steriotyped [sic] form of poor modern ideas, or still worse, that of a huge uninteresting mythological God."[29] The latter was in obvious reference to Horatio Greenough's much maligned colossus, *George Washington* (1841). The democratic model was to be found in France, where open competition had brought forward such once-unknown artists as Jean François Millet and Rodin. Taft was also reminded that the practice of issuing guidelines for scale and design improperly limited the aesthetic possibilities a Lincoln statue might inspire. Why not allow sculptors the same freedom in conceiving their work as architects enjoy when designing buildings and leave to the Commission, rather than to the architects, the decision as to which was better?

It was hardly the first time sculptors had assaulted the classical ramparts already built around the proposed Lincoln statue. Utilizing the tactics of political insurgency, the scrappy self-advocate John Gutzon Borglum began attacking the memorial's Beaux-Arts styling in 1912. Borglum's progressivism, his Western origins, and journalistic acumen made him a model Bull Mooser. For a time he was on intimate terms with Roosevelt; the latter heartily praised Borglum's tender portrayal of Lincoln in a marble bust of 1907—it was temporarily displayed in the White House—and in the seated bronze figure in Newark that Roosevelt dedicated in 1911. In league with architect William G. Purcell, Borglum authored numerous newspaper and magazine articles that unfavorably compared the cold classicism of French and Bacon's collaboration to the passionate spontaneity of Rodin's bronzes. While these wrathful denunciations did not openly indict the memorial project's chief officer, the sculptor obviously considered William Taft directly responsible for the disastrous turn of events at the building site.

In an open letter to the LMC addressed to one of its members, Sen. George P. Wetmore, Borglum ridiculed both the LMC and its advisory council, the CFA, for their joint decision to slavishly copy classi-

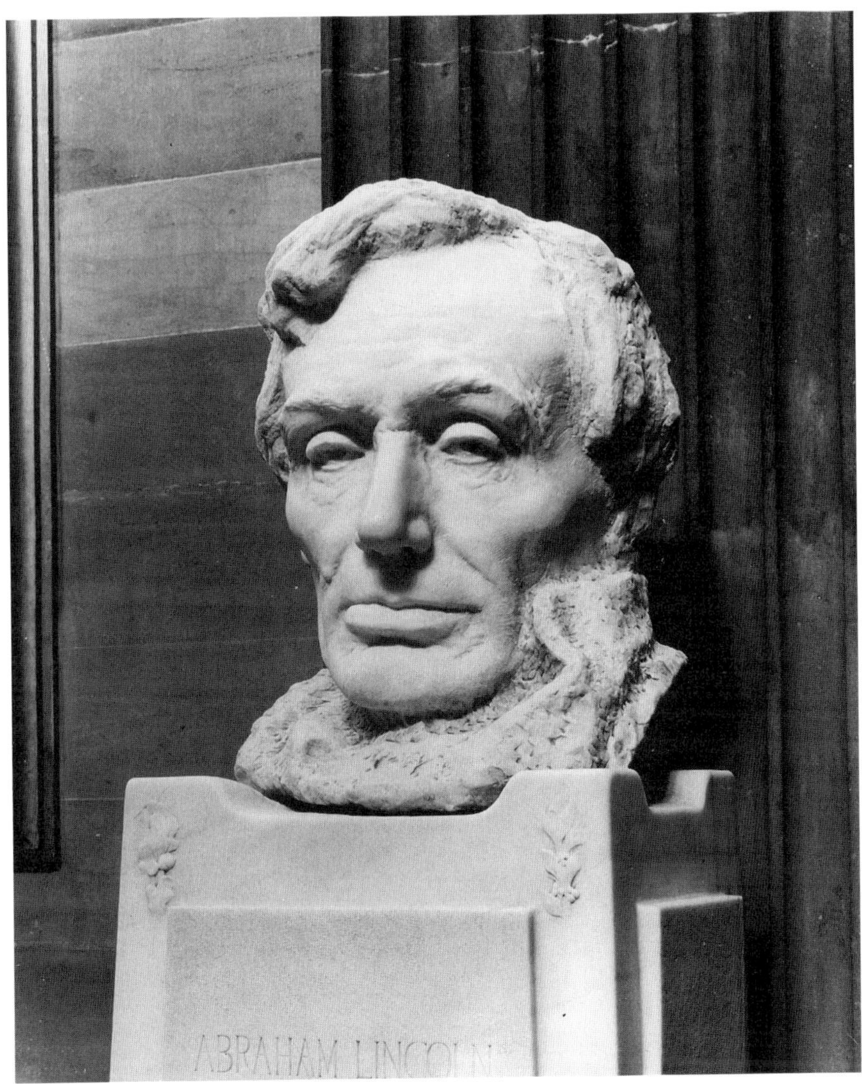

John Gutzon Borglum, Abraham Lincoln. *1908. Stone,
3'4". United States Capitol, Washington D.C. Gift of
Eugene Myer. Photo courtesy of the Library of Congress.*

cal Greek architecture and for daring to incorporate into the design the printed text of Lincoln's speeches. Still smarting from his own brush with the AIA and its bevy of collaborative sculptors, Saint-Gaudens and French chief among them, Borglum pointed out that the CFA was conspicuously overstocked with classical architects and urged that the membership be distributed equally among painters, sculptors, architects, and landscape architects.[30] He branded a classicist's contention that there was no possibility of surpassing the Greeks as "slanderous to the times." What was required were prominently displayed friezes and sculptural groups that would convey to the masses the forgotten sagas of America's ongoing struggle for freedom. Neither Taft nor the Lincoln Memorial commissioners responded to Borglum's challenge.

Like the Tafts, French was the son of a New England-born lawyer and like them had also come under the influence of New England transcendentalism.[31] Emerson himself presided at the unveiling of French's early triumph, *The Minute Man,* the famous bronze that stands near Concord bridge. Following study in Rome and later in Paris, he fully participated in the 1893 Columbian Exposition, creating the fair's principal symbol, the colossal *The Republic,* a gilded-staff figure that greeted visitors from the head of the lagoon. Thereafter, French was often identified with Burnham's City Beautiful Movement, and he acquired an ingratiating disposition that stood him well in the ongoing work of the urban renaissance at the turn of the century.

Like Burnham and McKim, French preferred homogeneous styling and mathematical stasis to indi-

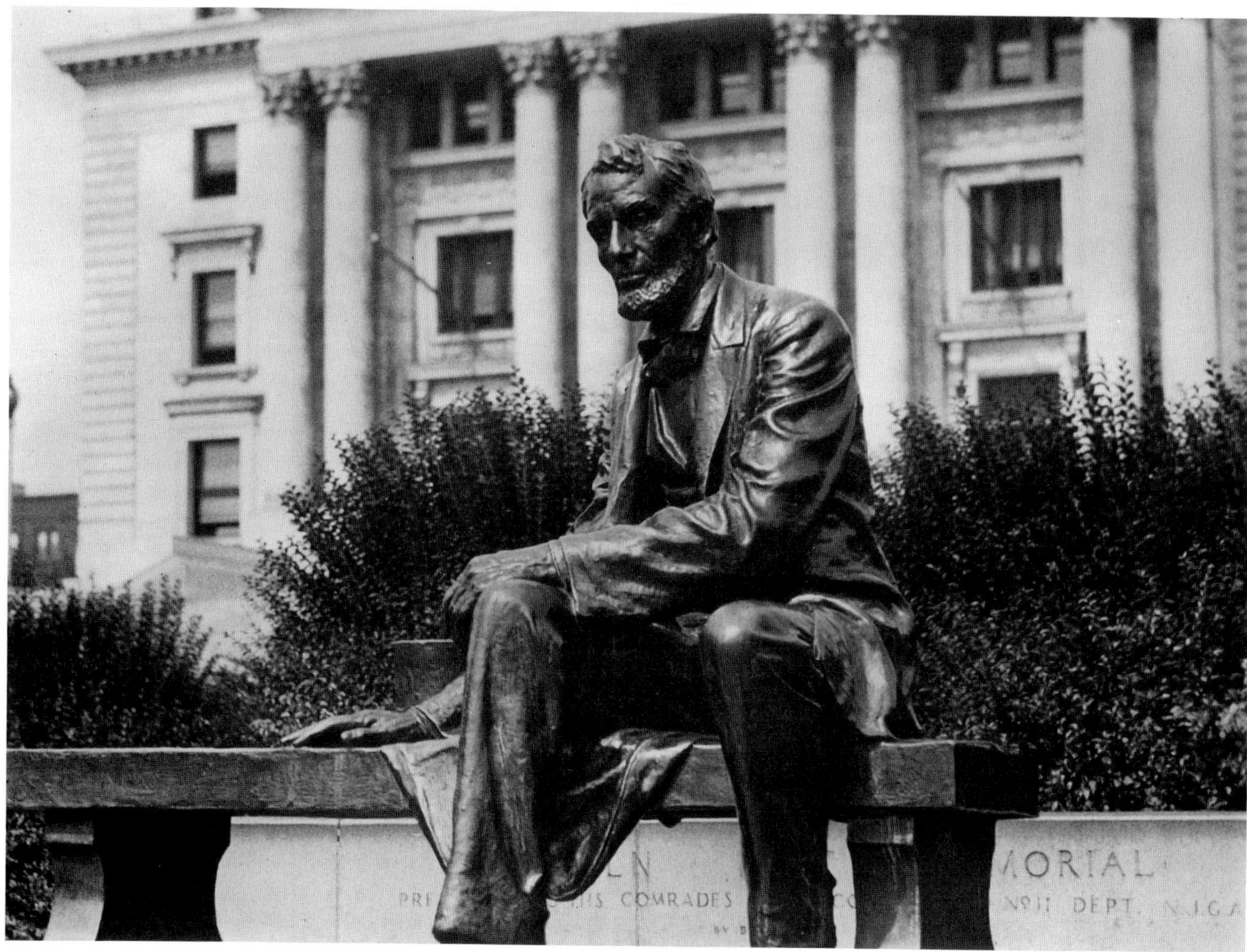

John Gutzon Borglum, Abraham Lincoln. *1911.*
Bronze, figure 6'. Newark, New Jersey. Courtesy of the
Library of Congress.

vidual expression. Acknowledging the architect's dominant role in sculptural projects, he accepted without complaint contract stipulations allowing the architect, rather than the sculptor or painter, an added fee equal to 6 percent of the construction cost of an entire project, even if that figure included cost overruns for sculptural or decorative work. For his part, French concerned himself with subtle adjustments and transient effect. One had to bring a literary idea "out over the footlights"; consequently, such matters as publicity and proper lighting were ultimately more important than the material existence of a work. The sensitive matter of how a statue's completion and dedication was announced, and when, where, and what photographs were published, these considerations together decided for all time a statue's public reputation. Even a masterwork could be destroyed by something no more momentous than a "leaked" photograph.[32]

Daniel French's Lincoln models portrayed a figure in deep thought seated in a curule chair, a conception that distantly resembled Phidias's legendary statue of Zeus and Greenough's overblown rendition of America's founding president. Recalling the sentiments of John Hay, Lincoln's secretary and biographer, who said in regard to the projected memorial that one "must not approach too close to the immortals," French's figure was to be elevated on a tall base far above the grasping hands of the crowd. A loose-fitting jacket emphasizes the width of shoulder and the full roundness of the thighs. The inclined head reflects equanimity; the left hand closes gently, and the right leg advances in easy stride, suggesting purpose and resolve without tenseness. Taft recognized in it something more admirable than an enshrined god or philosopher king; here Lincoln was nothing less than a supreme judge perpetually engaged in the act of judging. Taft once characterized his regard for

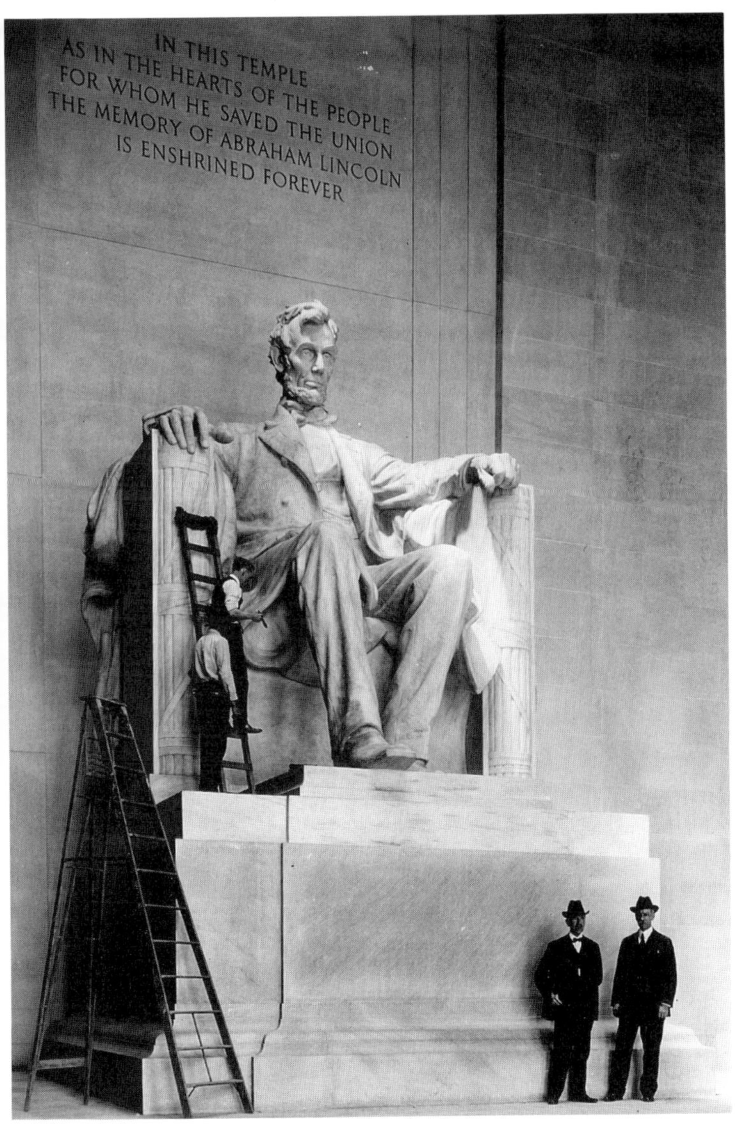

*Daniel C. French, Abraham Lincoln. 1916. Plaster, 7'.
Courtesy of the Library of Congress.*

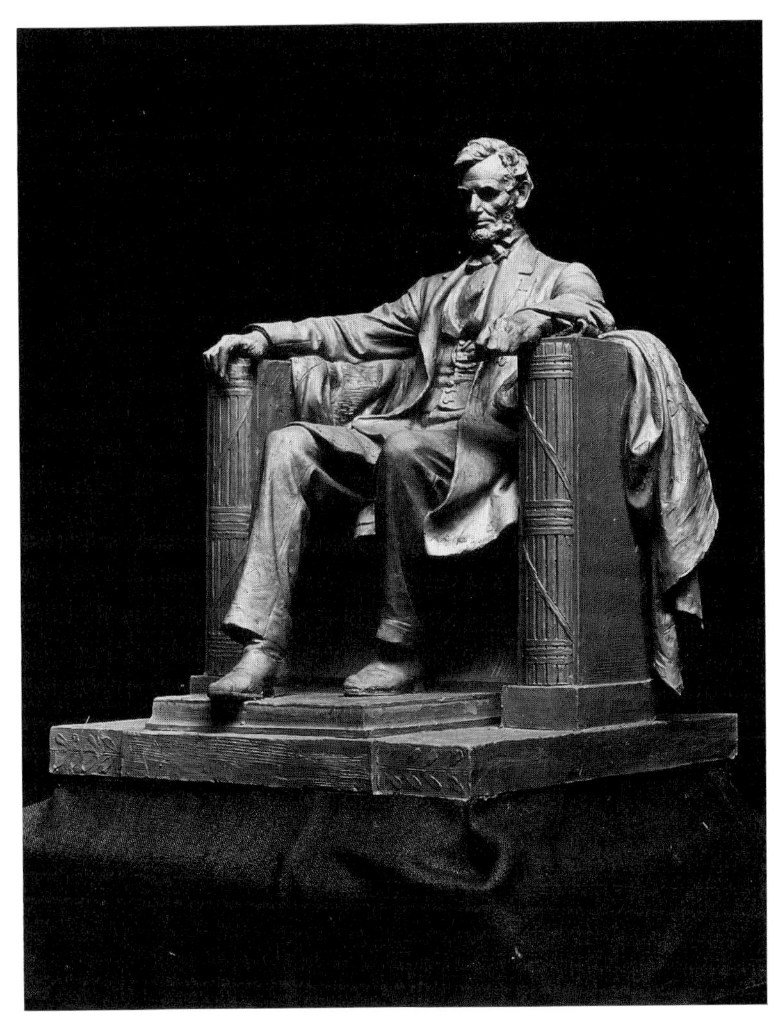

*Daniel C. French, Abraham Lincoln. 1919–20. Stone,
19'. Lincoln Memorial, Washington, D.C. Photo courtesy
of the Library of Congress.*

the logical mind at work in a generalization that could be applied to this colossus: "but the greatest argument for a God is law—law that works more accurately than any which can be devised by man, in fact we only mar law and the logic of law. It is too unerring to be chance . . ."[33]

French's modeling of clay maquettes and scheduled commission approvals of models proceeded apace until late 1916. His objective was to produce a marble figure, although bronze remained an option, measuring twelve feet high. Working at his Eighth Street studio in Manhattan and at his Massachusetts summer home at Stockbridge, he studied an edition of Leonard Volk's life cast of Lincoln's hands and face, relics that had become required references for any Lincoln portraitist.[34] Over the mask's smoothly

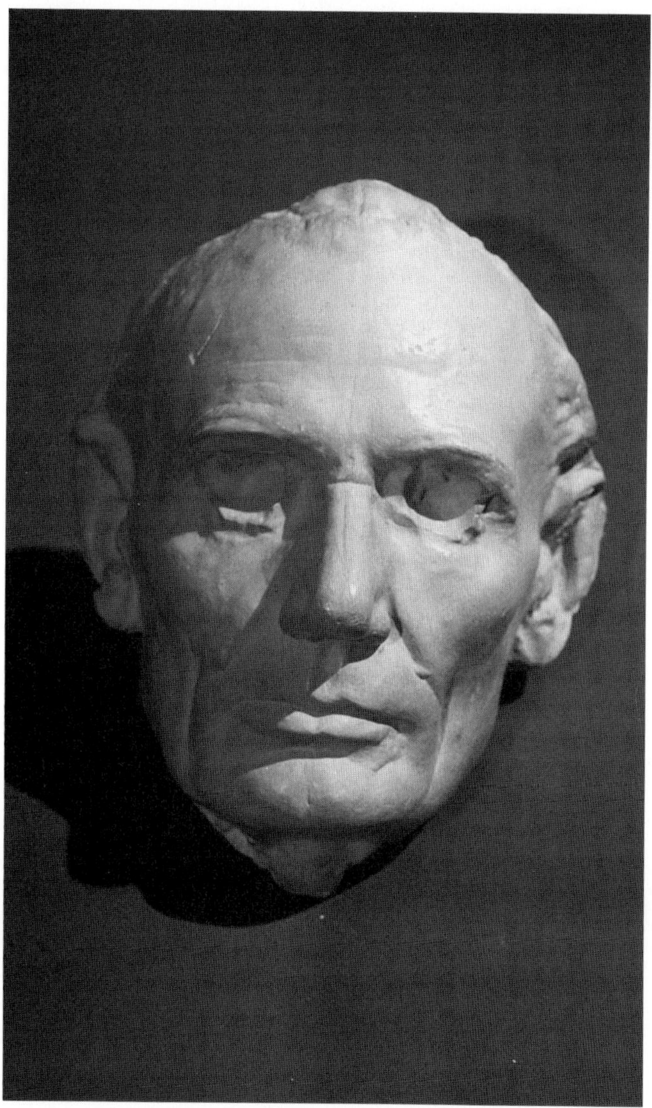

Leonard Volk, Face cast of Abraham Lincoln. 1860. Plaster, 8¾". National Portrait Gallery, Smithsonian Institution.

shaven chin, he superimposed a version of the beard familiarly seen in presidential photographs. The jacket was modeled from one the artist retrieved from a New England antique shop. There is no evidence he studied a live model, as had Saint-Gaudens for his standing Lincoln, although the hands ultimately derived from sketches the artist made of his own hands.

Publicity and budgetary problems aside, the most troubling concern for Daniel French and company was determining the proper scale of the figure. In October of 1916, just as Barnard was readying the Taft Lincoln for its temporary exhibit at the Union Theological Seminary in upper Manhattan, French and Bacon discovered that they had made an error in calculating the size of the statue, an oversight that would cost the LMC an additional fifty-seven thousand dollars, as well as other incidental expenditures, and would delay the project's completion by a full year. In order to "give [the Lincoln] dignity and dominating influence which it must have to fulfill properly its office in the Memorial," a ten-foot figure was to be increased to nineteen feet, and its pedestal adjusted accordingly. The ultimate responsibility for the miscalculation would seem to have rested squarely on Bacon's shoulders. Nevertheless, the architect benefited from an additional fee proportionate to the increased costs for marble, while French was left to ponder the damage the incident might inflict upon his professional reputation. He feared the error and resulting delay in the delivery of the statue— twenty-eight sectioned blocks of Georgia marble were finally assembled in 1919—would be attributed to his own dilatoriness.[35]

Throughout the travails of the memorial commission, William Taft stood ready to address Congress or enter litigation whenever the majority of the LMC deemed it necessary to sacrifice economy for aesthetic reasons. For example, in a controversy involving the choice of marble for the exterior walls of the memorial, Taft, with the approval of Robert Lincoln, forcefully overruled Wilson's secretary of war by insisting that a higher grade of white Colorado Yule should be selected over a more pinkish Georgia stone, the material from which the statue itself was produced. During later stages of construction, Taft and the conservatives were heartened when Joseph Cannon, who originally joined the LMC with intentions of holding the line on costly "artistic" refinements, became a primary spokesman for aesthetic considerations. In 1916, Cannon allowed that artistic beauty was preferable to economy so long as the laws permitted it.[36] This review of the construction history of a famous monument makes clear that William Taft was not simply a figurehead or a processor of documents. Not just his close involvement with every phase of its construction, but also his creation and governance of an administrative system that safeguarded the project, as well as his determination to "read" the monument and statue in terms of his personal sociopolitical and religious views, make clear Taft's proprietary regard for the project. But his embrace of the memorial and all it stood for as a cultural symbol, also pointed to the predicament he faced in regard to the Charles Taft's Cincinnati Lincoln. How was he now to respond to queries about the contradictions that existed between the works? The differences embodied more than stylistic questions, such as might be tested in a classroom comparison, but in fact grew out of fundamentally differing formal propositions. The one attached the recollection of Lincoln to a unified formal presentation that commands authority and admiration; the other associated Lincoln with material dissolution, social degradation, and despair. If he were to accept both on an equal footing, Taft would be compromising his reputation as a cogent judge and advocate; if he were to renounce the one for the other he would be betraying family honor for the sake of ideology, on the one hand, or, on the other, would be retreating from ideological consistency in favor of family sentiment.

But we have not quite examined the full depths of William Taft's quandary, and to do so will require yet another return to the events surrounding the Cincinnati dedication. When, a week before the scheduled unveiling, his tour train approached Atlanta, Taft had begun rereading a popular biography of Lincoln authored by the Englishman, Lord Charnwood, a book and author that will occupy an important place in a future chapter. Otherwise, he knew relatively little about the statue he was to dedicate. Furthermore, despite timely updates on preparations from Charles, William had not been informed that his brother was sponsoring a replica of Barnard's statue for England and endorsing yet another for Paris. William was therefore stunned by a communication from his old political ally Robert Lincoln that awaited his arrival in Nashville on 26 March. Addressed to "My dear Mr. President," it read as follows:

> When I first learned through the newspapers that your brother, Mr. Charles P. Taft, had caused to be made a large statue of my father for presentation to the city of Cincinnati, I very naturally most appreciated the sentiment which moved him to do this; when, however, the statue was exhibited early this winter, I was deeply grieved by the result of the commission which Mr. Taft had given to Mr. Barnard. I could not understand and still do not understand any rational basis for such a work as he has produced. I have seen some of the newspaper publications inspired by him, one of which printed in the North American of Philadelphia in November and another in the Literary Digest for January 6th last, attempt to make explanations which are anything but satisfactory, to me at least. He indicates, if I understand him, that he scorned the use of the many existing photographs of President Lincoln and took as a model for his figure a man chosen by him for the curious artistic reasons that he was six feet four and one-half inches in height; was born on a farm fifteen miles from where Lincoln was born; was about forty years of age and had been splitting rails all his life.
>
> The result is a monstrous figure which is grotesque as a likeness of President Lincoln and defamatory as an effigy. I understand that the completed statue has gone to Cincinnati to be placed; as to that I have nothing more to say, but I am horrified to learn just now that arrangements are being made for a statue of President Lincoln by the same artist, and I assume of a similar character, to be presented for location, one in London and one in Paris; I understand also that these statues are to be gifts by Mr. Taft. I do not think I have ever had the pleasure of meeting him and I am therefore venturing to beg you on my account to intercede with him and if possible to induce him to abandon this purpose if it is true that he has it in mind. I should of course have filial pride in having a good statue of my father in London and in Paris, of a character like the two great statues of him made by Augustus Saint-Gaudens, and that which I have good reason to expect in the Lincoln Memorial, now being modelled by Daniel Chester French. That my father should be represented in those two great cities by such a work as that of which I am writing you, would be a cause of sorrow to me personally, the greatness of which I will not attempt to describe.

Seldom had William Taft confronted so acute a conflict between personal loyalties, one made more severe by Charles Taft's curious lack of candor. William was quite possibly reminded of the instance when he, as Roosevelt's secretary of war, urged John Quincy Adams Ward to resign from a federally supported commission for the General Sheridan equestrian statue because the family of the intended subject objected to the artist's conception. But that was a federal matter, while this circumstance was entirely unofficial and personal. Several days later, while en route to Dallas, William explained the situation to Mrs. Taft.

I dont know what to do about it. It will make Charlie and Annie angry. Barnard will blow up about it and R L will continue his rage. R L says of course he can't prevent the Cincinnati statue but he is anxious to prevent the London and the Paris ones. I am confident that Charlie has no purpose to spend any such sums as a repetition of the statue would involve but Annie and Charlie are partisan if they are anything and this will be a big fly in the ointment. I am inclined to think I'll not say anything to them about it and only inquire as to the wisdom as to London and Paris and if it proves useless, write Lincoln accordingly.[37]

Upon his return to New Haven he broke the news to Lincoln. His brother, he wrote, "says that he has offered the statue [to London] and it has been accepted, and that he has paid $5,000 in performance of the contract, so that it seems to be impossible now to turn back. It is of course a great pain to him that you feel as you do about the statue." Despite his political indebtedness, Taft made it clear he would no sooner compromise deeply felt obligations to family honor than Robert Lincoln would his, when he concluded that "I confess that I don't share your feelings, though I don't bear the same relation, either as a witness or a son. But it seems to me that the work is a strong one, and that were you to study it yourself, you might become reconciled to it as its strength manifests itself in your study."[38]

If Taft sensed his chances to be the principal architect of the eventual pacification of Europe might be compromised by this "big fly in the ointment," he successfully concealed his concerns from Charles and Anna. One incident that occurred as the Cincinnati unveiling exercises were concluding, however, suggests the Tafts were under some strain as they exited from the park. A reporter observed that Charles, Anna, and William seemed reluctant to pose with Barnard before motion picture cameras. Pressing them to comply, Barnard was quoted as saying, "Come, you must get into this, this is the penalty you must pay."[39]

2

The Charles Tafts in Art

I N THE MUSIC ROOM OF CINCINNATI'S TAFT MUSEUM hang Raimundo de Madrazo's pendant portraits of Charles and Anna Phelps Taft. Charles appears as a thin-featured ascetic approaching sixty years; Anna resembles the grand dames that sat to Gainsborough and Reynolds around the time Cincinnati was emerging from the wilderness.[1] Adorned in a white dress with roses at the breast, she displays a pearl necklace and pendent she had newly acquired from Tiffany's of Paris. At the moment of posing—1902—the couple had reached a critical turning point in their thirty-year marriage. Anna's father, Irish-born industrialist David Sinton, had died in 1900; now his fortune and the cheerless old mansion he shared with the Tafts since their marriage was entirely at their disposal.

Charles was born in 1843, the oldest of the two surviving sons of Alphonso and his first wife, Fanny (Phelps) Taft. He was not the most brilliant or ambitious of the Taft sons, Peter and William held title to these distinctions; nor was he at first unusually attracted to aesthetics, which was Harry Taft's domain; but Charles was easily the most worldly and urbane of them all.[2] After earning bachelor's and master's degrees at Yale, he took graduate law degrees from Columbia University and the University of Heidelberg. He pursued further studies at the Sorbonne in Paris. Returning to Cincinnati in 1869, Charles dutifully practiced in his father's law firm. However, his proficiency in civil law, the humanities, and languages promised more distinguished attainments, by his estimate, a seat in the United States Senate. A rank-and-file Republican, he often served as a delegate to national conventions, he was elected to the Ohio State Legislature in 1871, and, eventually, in

1895, he won a seat in the United States House of Representatives. Yet, even after masterminding William Taft's defeat of William Jennings Bryan in the 1908 presidential race, Charles's ultimate personal goal continued to elude him.

His true destiny lay in the hands of David Sinton, who agreed to the Taft-Sinton marriage in part because he wanted a capable manager for the Sinton financial empire. Insofar as the elder Tafts were concerned, Anna's "foreign culture," her unobtrusiveness and poise, more than her wealth, made her a worthy mate for their eldest son.[3] Having earned his first million dollars in the manufacture of iron, Sinton knew that the secret to capital growth lay in diversification, and Charles found no reason to divest himself of the far-flung interests in transportation, utilities, amusements, and newspapers that his father-in-law had accumulated. Nowhere did their partnership operate more successfully than in the publishing field. Having already acquired interest in the *Cincinnati Volksblatt,* they assumed control of what through merger became the *Cincinnati Times-Star,* thereafter a lucrative and politically powerful property. Seldom did this newspaper stray from bedrock conservatism, but Taft successfully clothed its partisanship in a mantle of moderation, fairness, and antisensationalism.

He was equally successful with another Sinton venture: a large Texas ranch near Corpus Christi, the one-hundred-thousand-acre Coleman Fulton Pasture Company. Sinton acquired the property solely as an investment, but Taft, with the managerial assistance of Sinton's former partner, developed what was essentially barren acreage into a scientifically managed cotton and cattle ranch. Under his presidency, the

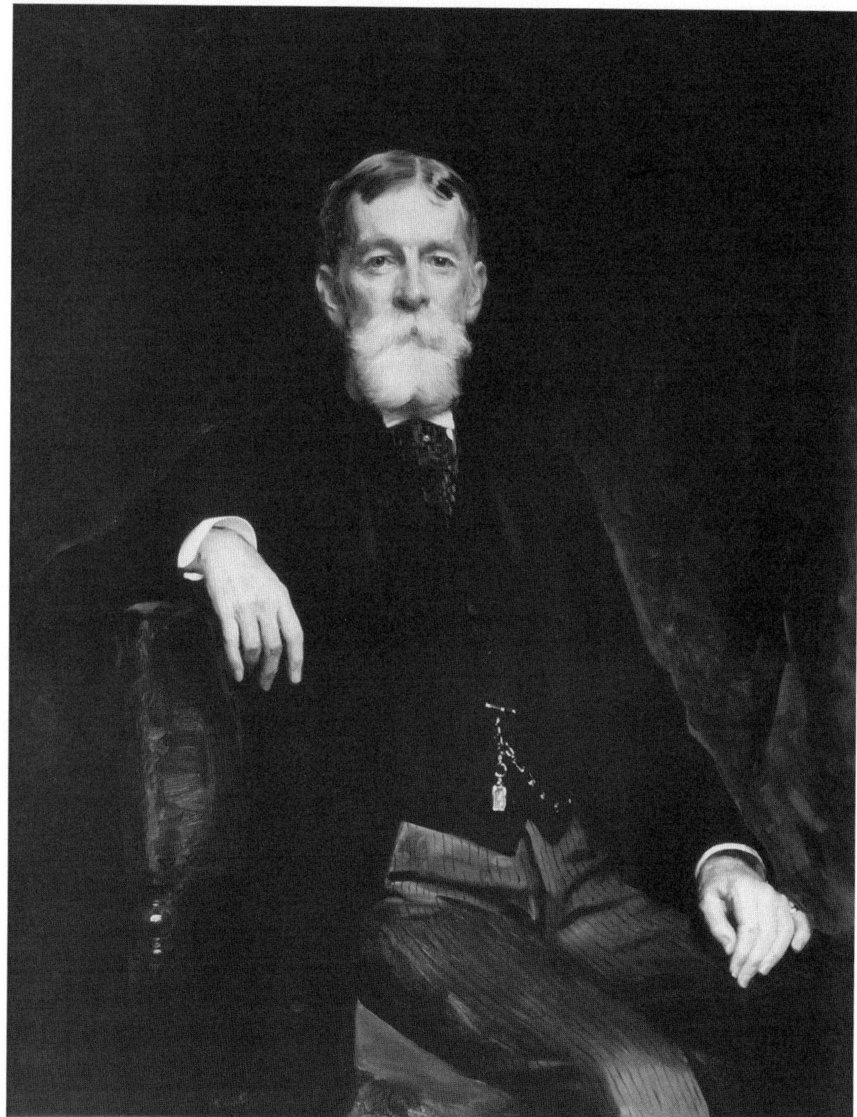

Raimundo de Madrazo Garreta, Charles Phelps Taft.
*1902. Oil on canvas. 49⅛" × 38¼". 3.1931. Bequest of
Mr. and Mrs. Charles Phelps Taft, The Taft Museum,
Cincinnati, Ohio.*

ranch assumed the characteristics of a utopian capitalist society in which labor, commerce, and small industry found their properly proportioned places.
Within its borders, the towns of Sinton, Taft, Gregory, and Portland sheltered some five thousand laborers, tenant farmers, and managers. Modern
housing, churches, banks, stores, schools, and a Presbyterian industrial college for Mexican women, provided model components of an integrated social
community. In an effort to eliminate the most pre-
dictable source of inefficiency and social discord, Taft
prohibited the use of alcohol on ranch property. But
an indispensible segment of the working population
was less easily governed. This was comprised of the
piscadores, the migratory cotton pickers who, on their
northward trek each spring, paused at the ranch long
enough to bring in the harvest. Even by 1940, little
had changed in the gypsylike existence of these wandering laborers as they passed through Sinton and
Taft: "whole families toil under the blazing sun, drag-
ging their elongated sacks down the rows." "Spontaneous corridos," one could observe, "furnish rhythm
for dances, as piscadores sing of work, of hands
gnarled from picking cotton, of romances born over
the lint."[4]

Charles had a far easier time controlling the destiny
of the ranch than the social matrix of Cincinnati. No
ingenious management technique or political tradeoff
could finally safeguard the priorities of property and
wealth or bring the German, Irish, Eastern Euro-

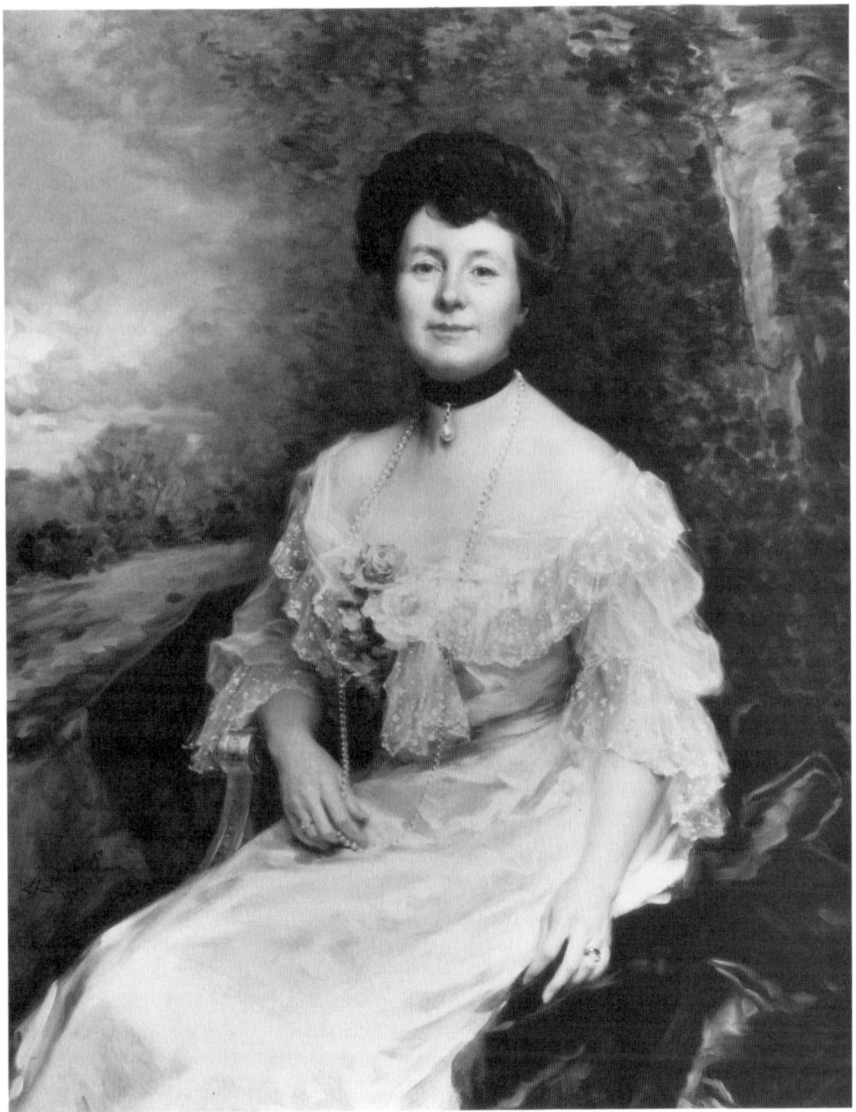

Raimundo de Madrazo Garreta, Mrs. Charles Phelps
Taft. *1902. Oil on canvas. 49¼″ × 38⅛″. 4.1931. Bequest
of Mr. and Mrs. Charles Phelps Taft, The Taft Museum,
Cincinnati, Ohio.*

pean, and Black laboring classes of the city to a common table.[5] In their efforts to "Americanize" the local
population Taft and his fellow patricians also confronted the disruptive maneuverings of the politically
dispossessed, the progressive Republicans, the inde-
pendents, and Democrats. It was precisely at the
point where politics failed in this mission to unify
social diversity that philanthropy became the civic
leader's weapon of choice. In a city often beset by
natural disasters, afflicted by social unrest and political corruption, charity and art paid special dividends.
None of Cincinnati's wealthy merchants or investors
could afford not to selectively support the opera, art
museum, the university, the symphony orchestra,
the various music festivals, and religious charities,

because this support, as it was faithfully indexed in
biographical summations of notable citizens, legiti-
mized wealth and power.

Since before the Civil War, art collecting in Cincinnati was a highly acceptable pastime for the male professional. A primary figure behind the art boom of
the 1840s was Nicholas Longworth, a lawyer who
arrived from New Jersey in 1803. Having made his
fortune in real estate, Longworth eased himself into
the life of gentleman farmer and *literatus.* His collecting commenced in about 1830, the year he acquired
"Belmont," the future Taft-Sinton residence, from
Martin Baum. Belmont's collection politely deferred
to the Old Masters; several Dutch canvases "of the
time of Rembrandt," and a copy of a Carlo Dolci

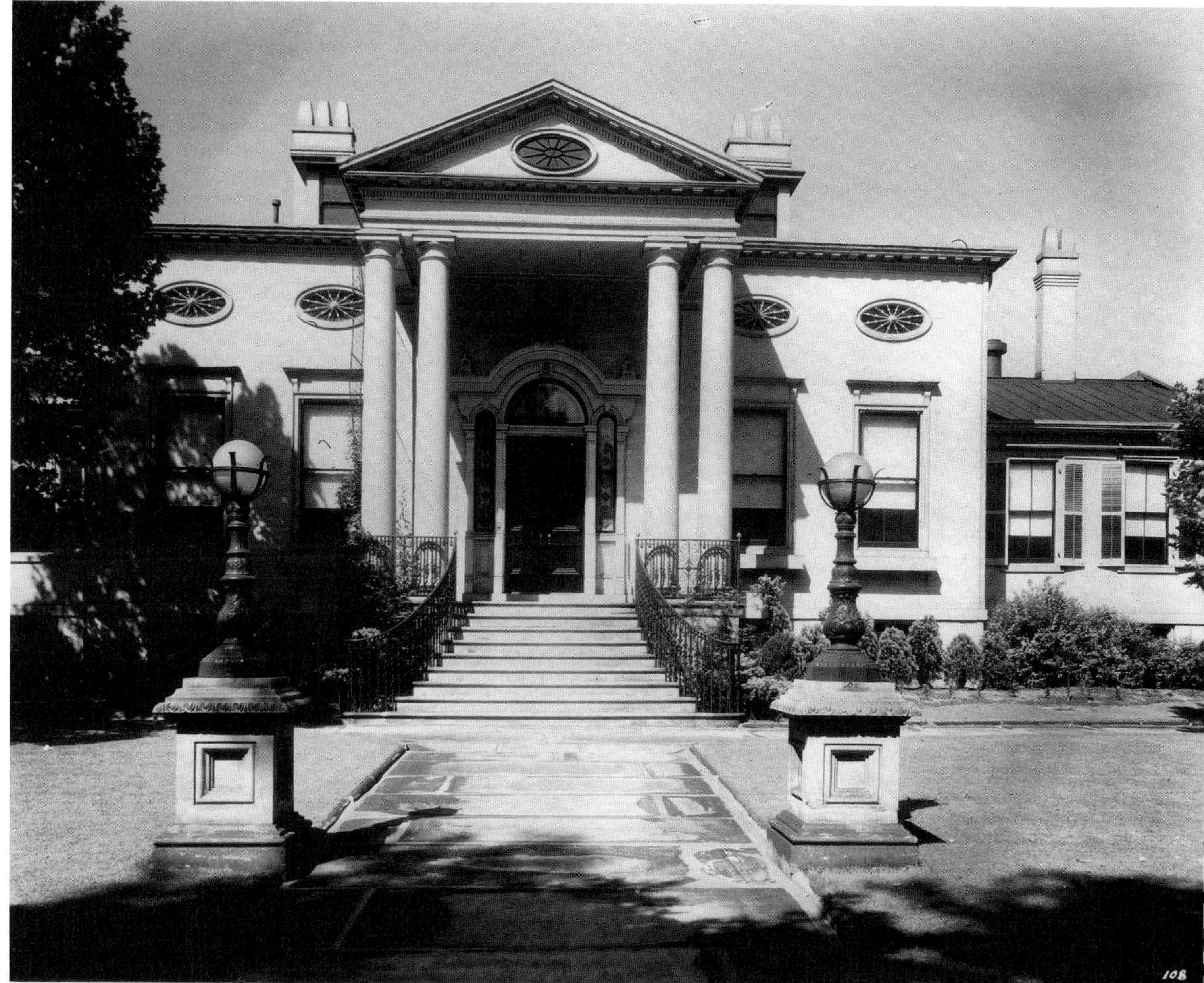

Martin Baum, The Baum-Taft House, *formerly "Bel-mont." [photo ca. 1900]. Cincinnati. Photo courtesy of The Cincinnati Historical Society.*

Madonna hung beside Benjamin West's *Ophelia and Laertes,* painted in 1792. But the collection was essentially an American one, stocked with works by artists who had contact with Cincinnati and who were personally known to Longworth.[6]

The city's postwar recovery witnessed a resumption of efforts to make it the "cradle of American art," but now patrons wanted European rather than homegrown art to lead the way. The most extraordinary symbol of the Queen City's rebirth was to be the aforementioned *Tyler Davidson Fountain,* which was given to the city by Henry Probasco and un-veiled in Fountain Square in 1871. This complex bronze monument was a thoroughly German work; it had been designed and modeled by Germans, it was the product of a German foundry, and even the syenite base was quarried from "the old pine woods of Bavaria."[7]

Cincinnati's large German population naturally took pride in this triumph of Bavarian art and craftmanship, but non-Germanic native-born sculptors, especially as they contemplated Germany's crushing defeat of France the very year it was dedicated, had less reason for enthusiasm. What most shielded Pro-

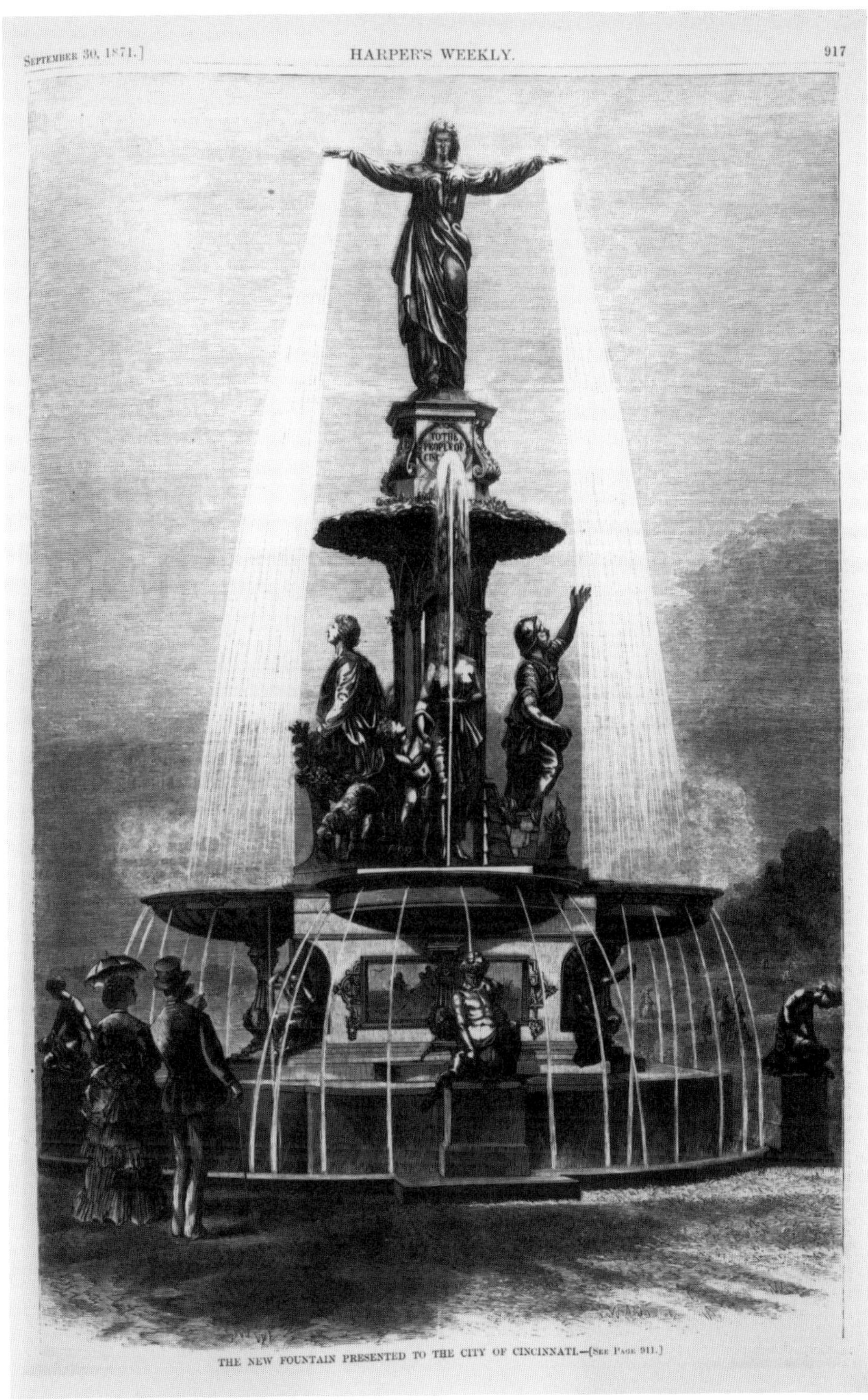

August von Kreling et al., Tyler Davidson Fountain.
From Harper's Weekly, September 30, 1871.

basco's gift from stern patriotic resentment was its thematic appeal to the city's working classes. Beneath "Genius's" outstretched arms were no helmeted soldiers and charging cavalry, but a farmer who leans on a plow while watching water replenish his field, a mother who leads her child to a bath, and a woman offering water to her aged father. Speeches presented at the unveiling by religious leaders and by Ohio Governor Rutherford B. Hayes admonished wealthy citizens for not doing more to help the poor. The Catholic archbishop predicted class warfare would result unless the disparity between social classes was not immediately eliminated. Trusting that Probasco's magnanimous gesture would instruct others, Hayes

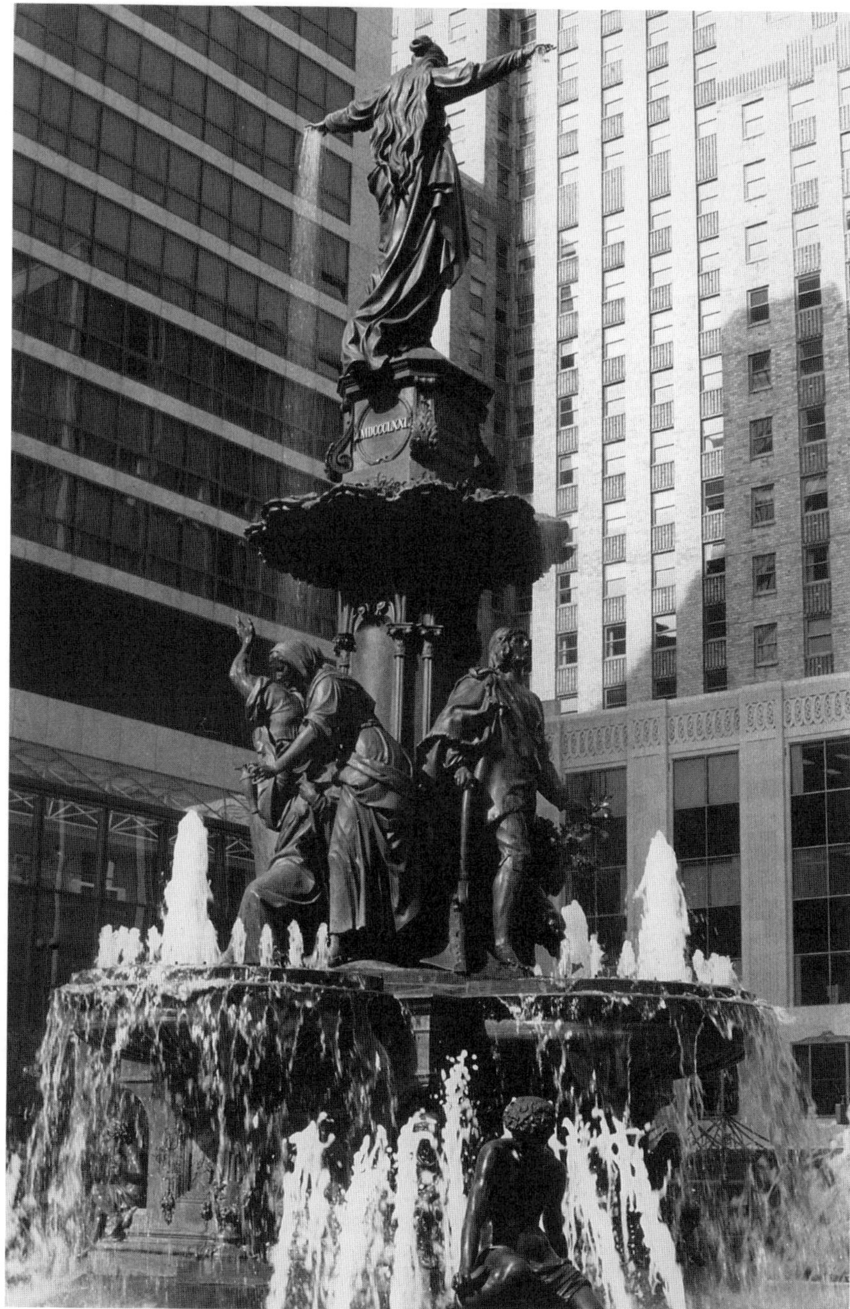

August von Kreling et al., Tyler Davidson Fountain. *1869–71. Bronze, 25'. Cincinnati. [Contemporary photo].*

warned the audience, that "no rich man who is wise will in the presence of this example, willingly go to his grave with his debt to the public unpaid and un-provided for."[8]

The fountain's social message failed to mitigate the hard evidence it presented of America's and Cincinnati's woeful lag behind Europe in the production of arts and crafts. National greatness and regional supremacy would arrive only when native artists could model, carve, and cast as well as, if not better than, the Germans, French, Italians, or English. The sense of cultural inferiority dovetailed with a growing appreciation of the arts-and-crafts precepts of John Ruskin and William Morris. In the 1870s and '80s, the wives and daughters of Cincinnati civic leaders began to believe that a beautiful living environment induced the inhabitant to become a better person, and that the time and effort spent in manual labor strengthened an individual's moral disposition while also strengthening creative skills. Machine work merely debased the product and depressed the human spirit. Even before the Philadelphia Centennial Exposition publicized the early results of the English craft revival, Cincinnati was already becoming a thriving center for the arts and crafts. Benjamin Pittman, Henry and William Fry, all English-born disciples of Ruskin and Morris, were instructing local women in woodworking and ceramics.[9]

The Philadelphia Exposition reviewed the innovative design principles taught in conjunction with exhibits housed in London's South Kensington Museum, now the Victoria and Albert Museum. In Cincinnati, the South Kensington legacy, later supplemented by the Aesthetic Movement and the Arts and Crafts Movement, shifted emphasis from an artist's ability to imitate material form to the individual's power to develop taste, to be responsive to just relationships among forms, spaces, and colors as these were exhibited in fine decoration or on tools of everyday use. An ever expanding state of consciousness, having little to do with national styles or periods, was sure to insulate the artist and his public from the tyranny of materialism. South Kensington's system required cooperative affiliations between teaching museums and craft schools; since the goal was to stimulate the creative faculties, rather than store precious masterworks, a teaching museum could do no better than exhibit facsimiles, plaster copies, photographs, and engraved illustrations of admired originals.

Like many of their friends, the Tafts enlisted in the cause of establishing Cincinnati's museum and art school. The funding campaign was in the hands of the Women's Art Museum Association—the director was Elizabeth Perry, wife of Alphonso's former law partner, Aaron—but its success naturally depended upon the financial resources of males. Charles West was the principal contributor to the museum fund, while David Sinton made a substantial donation to the future Cincinnati Art Academy, where the main building was to bear his name. Charles Taft broadly supported the idea of a teaching museum; in 1878 he presented the third in a series of lectures sponsored by the Women's Art Museum Association, a program to which former abolitionist Moncure Conway also contributed. Taft disparaged the relatively inferior position presently occupied by American artisans and predicted an industrial art museum, modeled upon that at South Kensington, could in a mere twenty-five years reverse the situation.

The designer of furniture should know the history of that branch of manufacture; he should be familiar with the church wood-work of the middle ages, the ornaments and inlaid work of the chests of the fifteenth century, and the chairs and cabinets of the renaissance, and the woodcarving of Queen Anne's time. The potter should know the struggles, the hardships and at times, the despair of a Palissy, and be familiar with the history and result of his work.[10]

Despite Taft's resolve, the new museum's governing policies shifted unsteadily between instruction and the conventional display and the storage of precious art objects. Here the remnants of Longworth's gallery was sandwiched between an enormous gathering of recent German work, antiques, armor, and pottery. The delicate line separating facsimiles and originals continued to vex administrators; patrons were dismayed to learn the most esteemed masterwork, a signed and dated Rembrandt, and a much-admired Sevres cup and saucer, were in fact copies.[11] Shortly after its opening next door to the Museum in 1887, the new art academy began deemphasizing craft production in favor of the traditional fine arts media of painting and sculpture.

Charles Taft's call for the native production of quality industrial design was already being answered in large measure by Cincinnati's art pottery movement; in 1880 Maria Longworth Nichols, the early patron's granddaughter, founded Rookwood Pottery, a company whose wares were soon to be internationally acclaimed. This hopeful development came with mixed blessings, for it occasioned continuous feuding among high-spirited female artists, and between them as a group and the begrudging male business community that eventually gained control of the movement. When in 1883 William Watts Taylor commenced managing Rookwood, its status changed from that of an experimental enterprise directed by female amateurs to a highly systematized industry. Fending off patent suits and advancing new marketing techniques, Taylor adroitly nurtured Rookwood's industrial promise. The Tafts assisted his reorganization on several fronts; while serving as judge of the Circuit Court of the Southeastern District of Ohio, William ruled for Taylor when former Rookwood designer Laura Fry lodged a patent infringement suit against the manager. Charles otherwise welcomed the expanded use of Rookwood designs in new architectural projects with which he was associated.[12]

However Charles and Anna Taft perceived the events affecting public patronage in their city, their personal venture into art collecting would not be encumbered by the vagaries of popular sentiment. For

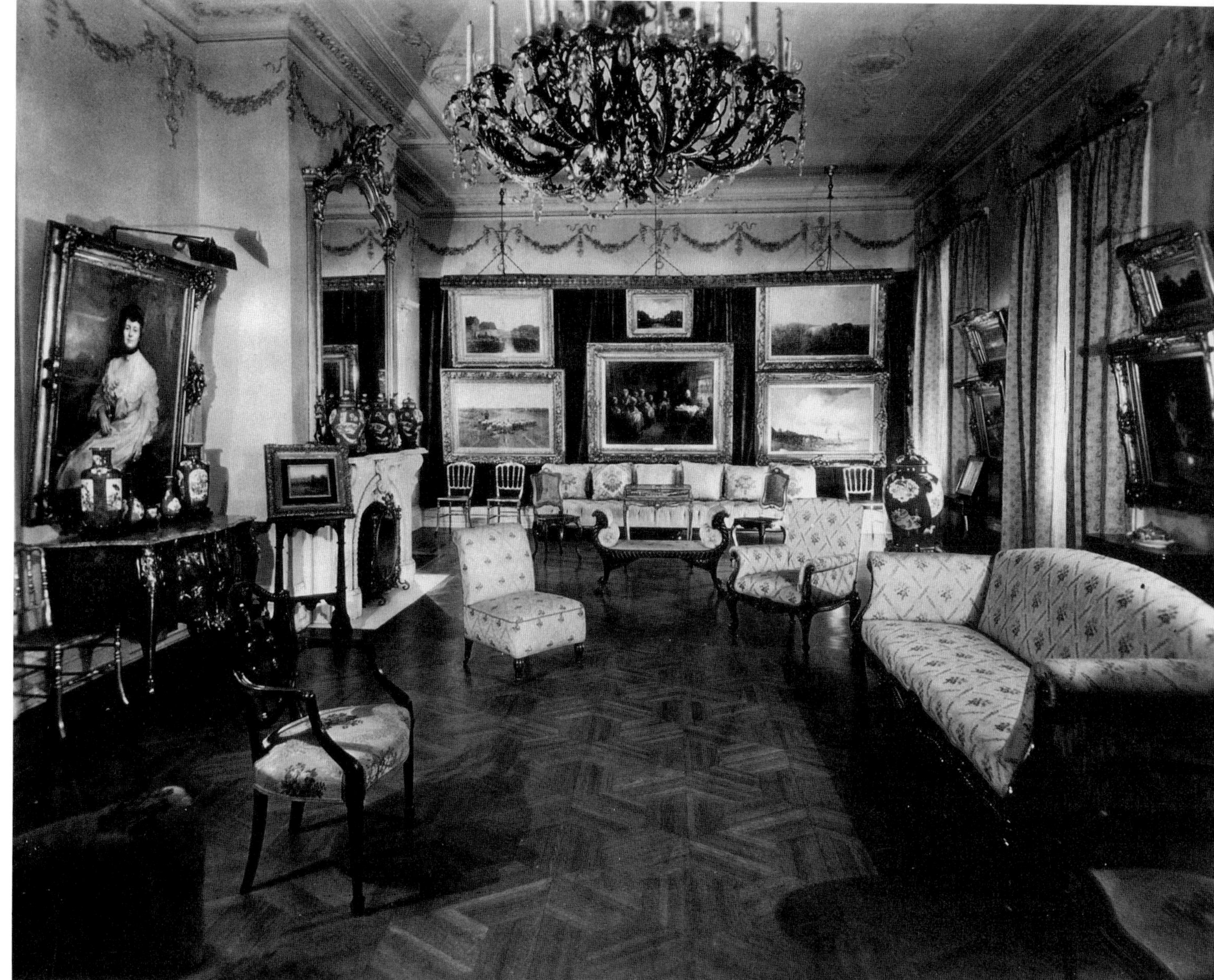

Drawing Room, The Baum-Taft House. *Ca. 1910. The
Taft Museum, Cincinnati, Ohio.*

them, the acquisition of art was an inherently selfish
and uncompromising occupation; if such an activity
was to have an effect upon public taste, it would do so
through personal example, not through cooperative
effort. As the Tafts entered the art market in 1902,
America's rage for the Old Masters was being paced
by J. Pierpont Morgan. Renaissance, baroque, and
rococo canvases bearing flawless pedigrees were purchased upon the advice of connoisseurs, historians,
and knowledgable dealers. The Philadelphian John
G. Johnson, the most sporting and wily of America's
leading collectors, attempted to blaze new trails into
unpopular categories, keeping scholars busy tracking
"problem paintings." Less particular buyers like Peter

A. B. Widener and Henry C. Frick responded more
readily to the salesmanship of such dealers as Joseph
Duveen. Since the turn of the century, money and
fashion had swung to works by Rembrandt and Hals,
and by 1909, when Benjamin Altman purchased his
twelfth Rembrandt, the popularity of the Dutch baroque in all classifications had peaked.[13] While Johnson pioneered in the field of the fifteenth-century
Flemish masters and primitives, only the most unorthodox collector would consent to American or contemporary European works.

The first sustained phase of Taft collecting, which
was marked by frequent trips to New York and Europe, occurred between 1902 and 1909. Itineraries

were routed around critical stops at the dealerships as Scott and Fowles, the Duveen Brothers, Jacques Seligmann, and Tooth and Sons. Works were usually purchased in single allotments, then hung en masse in the Pike Street home. The couple's experimentation with various modes of display was guided by the broad scope and casual arrangement of Baron Gustave Rothchild's Paris collection, where small bronzes, Limoge enamel paintings, easel paintings, and sculpture were freely integrated with living spaces. As the Tafts attempted to approximate this model of informality, they struggled with inherited problems of space, atmospheric conditions, and lighting. Protective glass that shielded paintings from coal dust also threw off distracting reflections.[14]

By 1909 the Taft collection divided between eighteenth- and nineteenth-century landscapes, Dutch and English portraits and a large quantity of objets d'art: Limoges enamels, faience, majolica, and marquetry. An early preference for French Barbizon and eighteenth-century English portraits remained the core around which new selections were added. Works by Millet, Corot, Theodore Rousseau, Reynolds, Gainsborough, Hoppner, and Romney survived later prunings and trades. In 1905, late nineteenth-century examples of the Hague school entered the collection, as did Van Dyke's *Paolina Adorno, Marchesa di Brignole Sale,* J. M. W. Turner's *Trout Stream,* and six Turner watercolors. Among 1906 acquisitions was a Hals and a Hobbema; in 1907, Turner's *Rape of Europa* and Gainsborough's *Edward and William Tomkinson* were purchased; and in 1908, the first Rembrandt arrived, *Portrait of an Elderly Woman,* of 1642, which was with the Sir Hugh P. Lane collection. But 1909 was the banner year as two Hals portraits and Rembrandt's *A Young Man Rising From a Chair,* of 1633, a valued momento of the Pourtales collection that had been consigned to Scott and Fowles's London office, were added to the Taft holdings.[15]

The Tafts did not hesitate to publicize their collection. They periodically issued catalogs, loaned works to exhibits, and opened their residence to connoisseurs and journalists. When in November 1909 Scott and Fowles hung a sampling of the collection in their New York gallery, a flurry of appreciative reviews appeared in art magazines and New York newspapers. Dealer Stevenson Scott estimated it to be one of the three greatest private collections in the country.[16] Excepting J. P. Morgan's European collection, this claim would rank it just below the Widener and the Frick. Certainly, nothing could approach it in Western America.

Typically, the collection was evaluated according to artists' names and validated provenances. Not only did lists of previous collectors help establish the legitimacy of an attribution, the social standing of such former owners as Comte Edmund de Pourtales of Paris, bequeathed social legitimacy to the paintings and, naturally, to their new owners who outbid competing collectors. Discernable resemblances between the Taft purchases and familiar works in other collections, especially those published in other catalogues, also contributed to their overall worth. The London-based *Burlington Magazine* reluctantly resigned itself to America's brash invasion of the European market, but allowed the Tafts due credit for their selections, which it stiffly observed "will be familiar to English connoisseurs."[17] The Tafts' dealers would not divulge the prices paid for the masterpieces, but published listings of comparative sales provided a fair idea of the amount of their investment. For example, Scott confided that Widener had recently paid five hundred thousand dollars for pendant portraits by Van Dyck that closely resembled the Tafts's *Portrait of Paolina Adorno.*

The catalogue that historian Maurice Brockwell produced in 1919 subjects the collection to somewhat contradictory discourses. Dividing works by subject category and room location—rooms often being designated by wall coloring—Brockwell devoted the most space to anecdotal descriptions of the sitters in the English portraits. Gainsborough's *Portrait of Maria Walpole, Duchess of Gloucester,* which hung in the entrance hall over concealed murals painted for Longworth by Robert S. Duncanson, was of special interest. Brockwell dealt with her inordinate beauty, quoting at length her uncle Horace Walpole, while also speculating on the persistent rumors concerning the young woman's illegitimacy and her mother's low birth. Obviously, her "fine eyes, brown hair, fine teeth, and infinite wit and vivacity" were inconsistent with such scandalous details, but the author could assure the Tafts and their guests that Maria was, after all, daughter to Sir Edward Walpole, K. B., and when baptized at St. James, Westminster, was granted the same preeminency "as the daughter of an Earl of Great Britain." The eminent connoisseur Sir Claude Phillips adequately settled the matter by indicating that whatever her defects, Maria had become the subject of an "important Gainsborough." No such justification was possible for the homely woman who posed for Millet's *Maternité: A Young Mother Cradling Her Baby,* which found its place in the Green Room. Here was pictured a Barbizon peasant "dressed in the coarse brown homespun of her kind and looking down upon the small bundle of human-

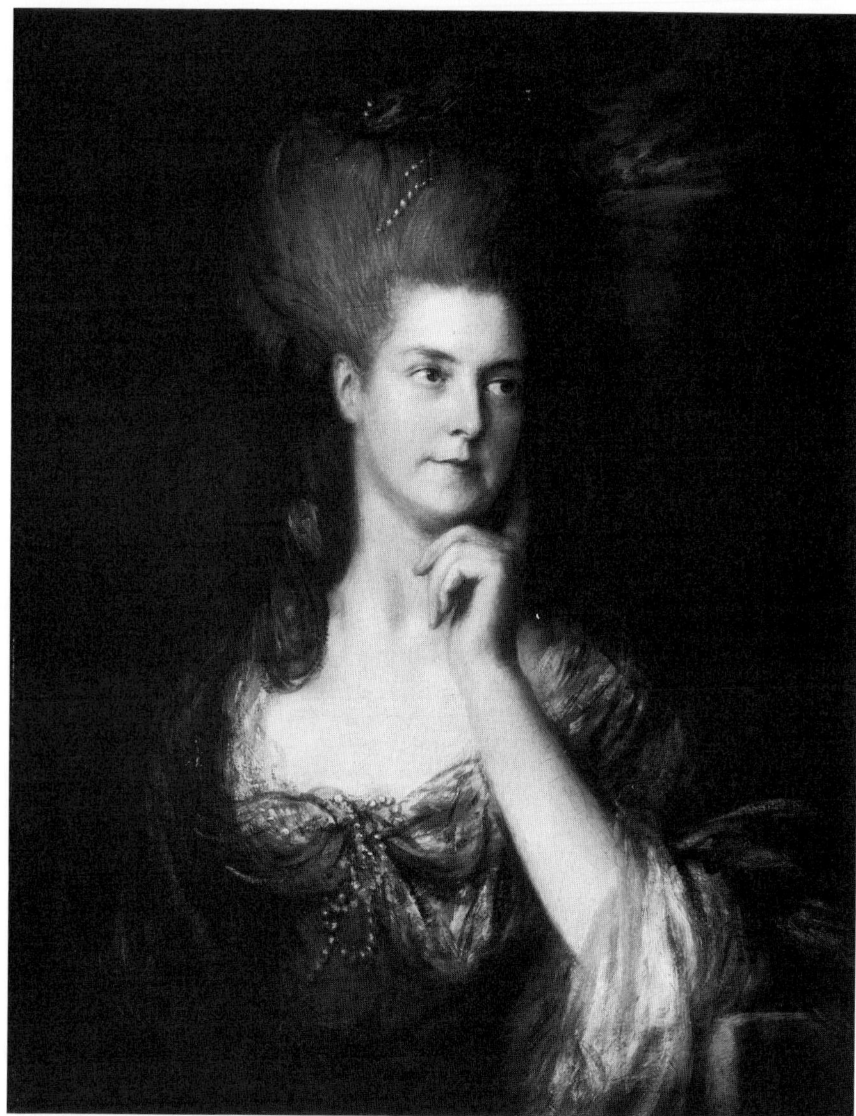

Thomas Gainsborough, Maria Walpole, Duchess of
Gloucester. *Ca. 1779. Oil on canvas. 36¼" × 28¼".
1931.406. Bequest of Mr. and Mrs. Charles Phelps Taft,
The Taft Museum, Cincinnati, Ohio.*

ity in her arms."[18] No less than the Van Dycks and the
Gainsborough, the Millet belonged with a coveted
classification of the collector's art. Yet while the former justified and confirmed the Tafts's social aspirations, the latter example called forth the simple,
pathetic, truths of humanity with which they remained deeply concerned.

Neither the social content nor the investment potential of the paintings warranted as much interest in
family discussions as did the pathetic and aesthetic
dimensions. Charles continuously reminded William
of the personal satisfaction he and Anna gained from
the pictures. As Charles described it, the pleasure derived from a gradual quickening of the appreciative
faculties; he wrote that it "was hard to get out of the

house when I get settled down at the pictures and the
porcelains." He associated this aesthetic pleasure with
a deepening interest in family history. At the conclusion of the Tafts's 1910 European tour in Britain,
Charles gave close study to tombs, old family pictures, to "the general mass of books, pictures, objets
d'art, and especially traditions likely to gather in such
a place when kept in the possession of one family
since before the discovery of America."[19]

Personal disappointments in his public life stimulated Charles's desire to make the collection an emblem of family identity and renewal. Shortly before
the Scott and Fowles exhibition introduced the Tafts
to the art world and Eastern society, Charles's political territory was being invaded by northern Ohio

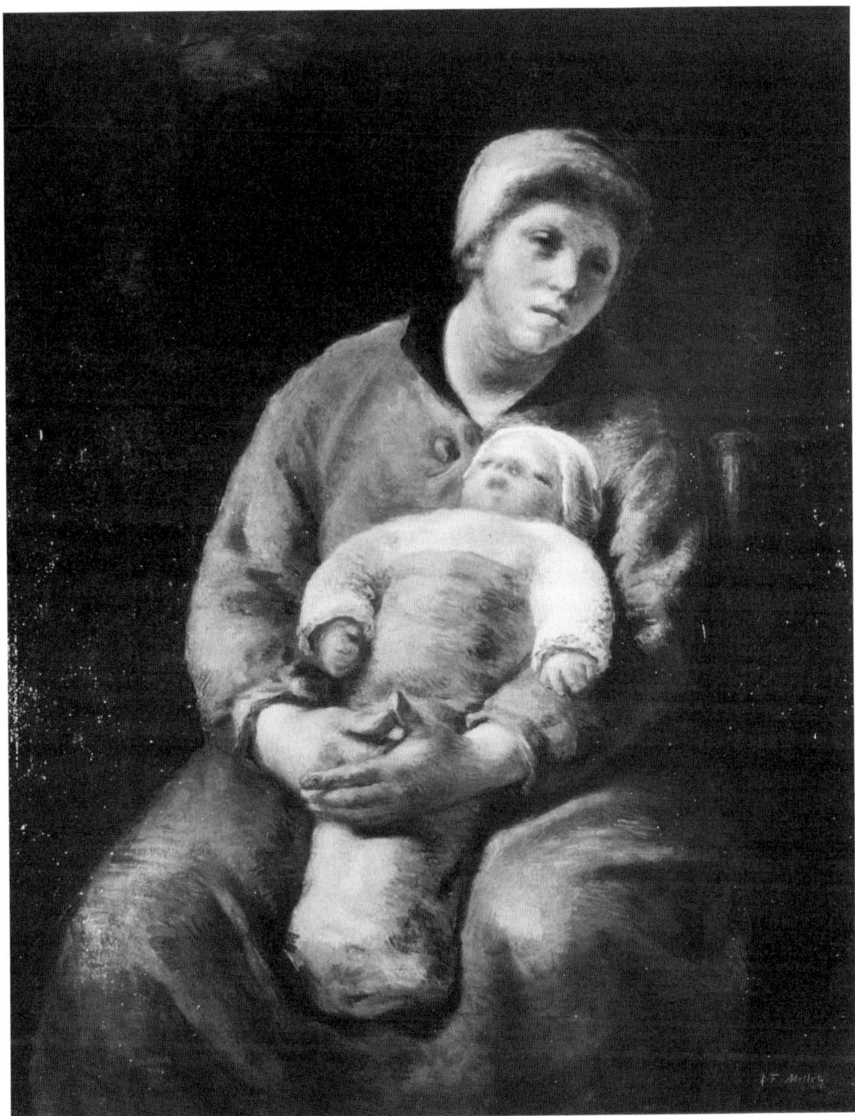

Jean François Millet, Maternite: A Young Mother Cradling Her Baby. *1870–73. Oil on canvas. 48⅛″ × 35¾″. 1931.448. Bequest of Mr. and Mrs. Charles Phelps Taft, The Taft Museum.*

Republican Theodore Burton. Certain that his best opportunity for winning a Senate seat would be during his brother's presidency, Charles was forced to resign his candidacy in the face of Burton's unexpected strength. It was a disastrous moment for all the Tafts: not only had the seasoned older brother failed miserably in his last attempt, he had also embarrassed William who was himself beginning to feel the displeasure of the progressives. The intensity of this distress was made apparent a week after his withdrawal when national headlines announced Charles had severed ties with Cincinnati's Presbyterian Church of the Covenant because during the presidential campaign its pastor had criticized William's affiliations with Unitarianism. In March 1909 Charles

abruptly notified William that he was "disgusted with politics" and was currently "ousting [from the state Republican organization] men who were vicious toward us in the state campaign."[20]

As a measure of reassurance, William frequently deferred to Charles's aesthetic tastes. At his brother's request, the president sat to Joaquin Sorolla y Bastida for a half-length portrait that soon hung with the collection, and he continually sought Charles's advice when having other portraits made. In September 1910, William directed a cabinet meeting at the Taft home "with its beautiful pictures [that were] sources of never ending pleasure." The paintings, he confirmed, "grow more beautiful as I see them oftener." William's sincerity in voicing these sentiments cannot be questioned, but his attestations were also intended to reaffirm the substance and hierarchical structure of the Taft family in its manorial setting. In another context, similar paintings may not have been able to work their magic so easily. For example, William held entirely different views of comparable works in the Frick collection which he inspected while attending a party at the magnate's Massachusetts home in 1909. Frick's boorish attempts to buy his way into society and acquire political influence reminded Taft of the way he also haggled over a Van Dyck.[21]

However he regarded Frick's motivations, William was destined to assist Charles's and Anna's passion for art, as well as that of other like-minded collectors, in a direct and practical way. The Payne-Aldrich Tariff, the legislation that had so incensed Roosevelt and the Insurgents, contained a clause that eliminated all import duties on nonutilitarian paintings and sculpture more than one hundred years old. The enactment of this provision served to increase the already sizeable importation of old master works by Americans. It can hardly have been a coincidence that the Taft purchase of their prize work, the Pourtales Rembrandt, was finalized in London immediately after the president signed the tariff.[22]

Unlike Nicholas Longworth, the Tafts had little interest in adding sculpture to their collection. The unidentified "marble" that Charles purchased from Duveen in 1904 was an exceptional addition.[23] Nor were they keen on acquiring works by living artists, especially Americans, nor in possessing objects that could not be advantageously displayed within the living spaces of their home. It was thus as much a surprise to the Tafts as to others that they would become the sponsors of a large public statue.

The Barnard Lincoln commission climaxed a chain of events that began in 1907. In that year the Cincinnati lawyer-politician Harry Probasco, unrelated to the patron of the *Tyler Davidson Fountain,* established the Committee on a Permanent Memorial of the Lincoln Centennial Memorial Association to which he named some thirty-five prominent citizens. His goal was to raise by public subscription a sum sufficient to attract a name artist for the memorial statue. Even though a figure as high as one hundred thousand dollars was being considered, the committee managed to clear only thirty dollars above expenses by June 1909. However, on 1 June 1909 Mrs. Frederick H. Alms announced her intention to donate one hundred thousand dollars for a Lincoln memorial that would be presented to the city under the condition it would be maintained, repaired, and cleaned in perpetuity. The former memorial association was reconstituted

under Probasco's directorship as The Frederick H. Alms Lincoln Memorial Fund. Probasco appointed a ways and means committee consisting of Louis Grossman, Rabbi of the Plum Street Synagogue, ex-officio; A. O. Elzner, a partner in the architectural firm of Elzner and Anderson, secretary; William W. Taylor, treasurer; and Charles Taft. From the beginning, Probasco made it clear he would "defer entirely to the judgement and taste of the majority of the board."[24]

Almost alone among Cincinnati's political contenders, Attorney Harry R. Probasco appreciated the significance of the Lincoln centennial. Born a lawyer's son in 1856, he followed the well-worn path into law and politics, becoming both corporate defender and progressive reformer. Having married the daughter of a jurist who was related to Gen. William T. Sherman, Probasco sought high Republican office and social prominence. But he was an Independent Republican whose colorful populist tactics severely limited his political options. William and Charles ridiculed Probasco, when, during the 1906 state elections, he attempted to unseat a Taft-Roosevelt Congressional Republican. More unforgiveable was his continuing alliance with Ohio Senator Joseph Foraker, a chief enemy of the regulars. Nonetheless, Probasco attempted from time to time to mend fences, especially after the 1908 presidential election.[25] Charles entertained no illusions about his appointment to the Alms Lincoln committee. Yet Probasco's conciliatory gesture gave him an opportunity to be identified with an unusually ambitious project, one that could not fail to further his national reputation as art collector and connoisseur and at the same time help to counterbalance his recent political failures.

Frederick H. Alms, another of Cincinnati's merchant-princes, died intestate in 1898, leaving his widow, Eleanora (Unzucker) Alms, full discretion in the dispersal of his estate.[26] The Alms fortune derived from the earnings of a family dry goods firm, Alms and Doepke, which Frederick joined at fourteen. The son of an immigrant from Hanover, Germany, he did not receive the educational advantages of the Tafts, nor was he driven by the political ambitions that afflicted much of Cincinnati's population. His deep regard for Lincoln, and for the Republican party grew out of a soldier's love for his commander in chief and for fellow warriors. Alms served with the Sixth Ohio Regiment at Bull Run, Shiloh, Stones River, and Chickamauga; while Charles Taft was studying at Yale, Alms was under fire, slept amid corpses, and often found himself without food or warm clothing. Such experiences did not oppress him, but reaffirmed a belief in the human capacity for compassion and for selfless devotion to duty. Through his membership in the Grand Army of the Republic, Alms kept in touch with other Cincinnati men who fought on the front lines, including future senator Joseph Foraker. He left no specific instructions for erecting a Lincoln statue, but Eleanora Alms was determined to initiate a project that would honor both her husband and the man he and his soldier comrades worshiped.

While contemplating their grand scheme, Mrs. Alms and Probasco no doubt gave considerable thought to a Lincoln moument that had been erected in the northern suburb of Avondale in 1902 at a cost of four thousand dollars. Charles Clinton, a former captain with the Missouri Regiment of Cavalry Volunteers, financed the erection of a bronze statuary group which survives at the corner of Rockdale and Main Avenues.[27] A replication of a design prepared by the English-born W. Granville Hastings, the monument consists of an eight-foot-high figure mounted on a granite pedestal. Before the pedestal, a bronze figure of Fame has begun inscribing the opening words of Lincoln's Second Inaugural address on a tablet. Financed by public subscription, the pedestal and surrounding stone benches were the design of the architectural firm of Elzner and Anderson. Probasco's selection of Elzner for his committee suggests he and Alms contemplated building a similar architectural ensemble around their statue, but in all other respects, the Alms Lincoln, an original creation of colossal dimensions, would eclipse the comparatively modest Avondale group.

John Gutzon Borglum, who as we have noted was to lead the progressive assault against the Lincoln Memorial, became a prime contender for the Alms Lincoln contract. In mid-1909, he was once again licking wounds he received while campaigning for a statue commission, a farcical struggle over the Lincoln, Nebraska, *Abraham Lincoln* that pitted him against his brother, Solon. The Borglums literally fought to a draw, then retired from the contest to watch the perplexed building committee award the contract to Daniel French and Henry Bacon. Amid an outpouring of invectives and soulful pronouncements, Gutzon then set his sites on the Alms Lincoln Memorial statue. Soon after the commission sent out its call for applications, the sculptor began sizing up the membership in order to press home his advantages. Borglum's initial contact is contained in a letter to Probasco on 29 July 1909 that advises the committee on possible designs and materials. He had in mind a colossal seated figure of Greek Pentelic marble, set roughly to twice the scale of his Lincoln bust of 1907,

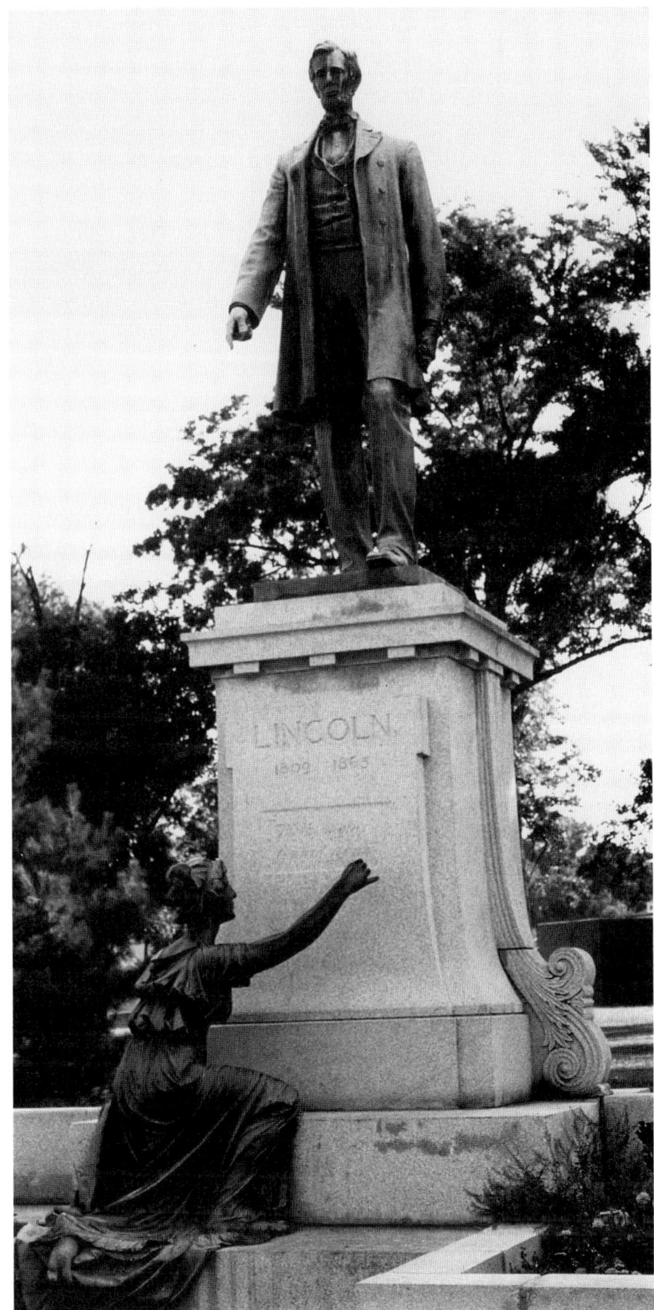

W. Granville Hastings, Abraham Lincoln. *1902. Bronze and stone, figure, 7'. Cincinnati, Ohio.*

a statue that would soar twenty-five feet high but would cost only thirty thousand dollars. There would be no architectural confinement and even though he could envision secondary figures or accessories, Borglum felt nothing should "interfere with the aloneness of the central motive," which, in this case, represents a simple man.

Psychologically, a statue has a certain personality, a sphere of influence. I mean a direct influence. That influence may extend twenty feet around it, it may go two hundred feet; that boundary is so to speak, sacred ground, as the ancient made it and thereby some token relative to the nature of the monument, something that minds you of it should mark the approach.[28]

Probasco confirmed that the committee wanted a colossal seated figure but insisted upon bronze, which, compared with marble, would be more acceptable "to the people and those of artistic culture," and presumably would be less expensive. Furthermore, since it was Probasco's personal preference to place the monument out of doors, possibly in Government Square, marble, because of its vulnerability to weather, would be inappropriate. Borglum's return estimate for bronze was in fact higher than that for marble, but he was still willing to undercut the total amount of the Alms bequest by a considerable margin: he would complete the statue in eighteen months at a total cost of forty thousand dollars.[29]

Borglum's proposal for a seated statue of Lincoln that would be positioned in its own "psychological" space resembled the over-life-sized bronze he was then preparing for Newark, New Jersey, a gift of the late GAR veteran, Amos H. Van Horn (see p. 30). Eventually dedicated by Theodore Roosevelt on 30 May 1911, Borglum's figure distantly resembled Rodin's *The Thinker,* a plaster version of which had its premier American showing at the St. Louis World's Exposition in 1904. Awaiting war news, the brooding President, his stovepipe close beside him, sits at the far edge of a bench, his head inclined and eyes lowered. Having finished a plaster of this work in October of 1909, Borglum was able to forward photographs of it along with reproductions of his large Lincoln bust to Probasco's committee.

But the sculptor's political instincts warned him that more would be required than a simple demonstration of his ability, efficiency, and experience if he were to capture the contract. He questioned Charles L. Pack, a political sage of Cleveland, Ohio, about the state's political climate. Pack briefed the sculptor on the Charles Taft/Theodore Burton feud, confirming that Probasco was "his own man," but emphasized Borglum would have to deal with the Tafts if he wished to garner success. Reminding Borglum that he was momentarily scheduled to sculpt William Taft's bust, Pack advised him to use the occasion to cement relations. There was a hint of disapproval in Pack's concluding remark: "of course, I know you do not want influence except to keep the wolves away so that you can have a fair straight-forward chance without being done up by politics."[30]

So long as he was assured victory, Borglum was willing to restrain himself. In quick order Probasco received recommendations from a well-appointed stable of referees: Elihu Root, Auguste Rodin, Robert Lincoln, the last paying Borglum the unwanted compliment of being second in ability only to Saint-Gaudens, and from William Taft's recalcitrant postmaster general, Frank H. Hitchcock. Another tribute originated from the office of Woodrow Wilson, president of Princeton University, who justified his institution's decision to confer an honorary degree upon Borglum in June of 1909. Not only was Borglum personally attractive, Wilson affirmed, but his work was permeated with a "very noble simplicity devoid of decadence and triviality, a classical character that was wholly American in thought." In November 1909, while the Taft paintings were on view at Scott and Fowles, Borglum gained what he considered a successful interview with the Charles Tafts, received Alms committee members at his Manhattan studio, visited Cincinnati at the committee's invitation, and won over Charles's nephew, Hulbert Taft, managing editor of the *Cincinnati Times-Star.*[31] Probasco was on the verge of declaring for Borglum in January 1910, but lacked a model, and was uncertain about contract procedures and obligations.

As negotiations dragged on into the new year, Borglum's prospects began to fade. Immediately after he pointedly reminded Probasco on 10 January he would under no circumstances enter a competition, a lapse occurred in the Borglum-Probasco correspondence. Quite possibly the hiatus had to do with a legal complaint filed against Borglum by another competitor, Charles Niehaus. Borglum's future was also made less certain by the fact that Solon Borglum was also in the running. It was not Niehaus or Solon, however, but George Grey Barnard, whom the embattled Borglum had now to face. In February, after twenty-five applications had been received, the Alms committee narrowed its search to Barnard and Borglum and, on 25 March 1910, imposed invitational competition rules: the two artists would submit models to scale by 1 November 1910 and be duly compensated. While Probasco and Mrs. Alms assured Borglum of their continuing favor, the chairman confided in May that the others wanted Barnard. This news elicited from Borglum the first of similar predictions concerning the fate of the Cincinnati Lincoln: "Your Lincoln monument," he chided Probasco, "begins to look to me like a hopeless, interminable, failure."[32]

While yet attempting to save the situation, Borglum reasoned Taft had engineered the rules change because he feared that Taylor, Elzner, and Grossman actually preferred him. He thus appealed directly to Taylor's presumed aesthetic sensitivity when arguing for the direct selection process, a procedure long preferred by his enemies in the National Sculpture Society and the AIA. In conformity to his insurgent political views, Borglum valued direct selection, not for its service in protecting the interests of a small conservative clique, or for insuring architects continued authority over sculptors, but for the possibility it offered of bringing forth genius. "What would your [William] Taylor say," Borglum inveighed Charles Taft, "if Wagner or Verdi should compete in writing an opera; who should say which is greater? Or Wagner and Beethoven; would a competition ever have produced the Ring of the Niebelungen, Michelangelo's David? Rodin, how has he fared?"[33] Competitive judging, he trusted Taylor would understand, had the unfortunate effect of aborting inspired creative effort. He professed to have no fear of competing with Barnard, but was certain that only inferior designs and added expense would result. Since the only basis of greatness "is all of a man's work," each committee member, it seemed, had to intuitively assess an artist's potential for greatness, man to man.

Borglum remained technically in the contest despite his renunciation of rules, since the deadline for submitting models had not passed. But now the sympathetic Probasco had to field complaints along with praise for Borglum. The architectural firm of Carrier and Hastings, for whose New York Public Library Barnard and Paul Bartlett were supplying statuary, endorsed Barnard and discredited Borglum. This, the latter assured Probasco, was an understandable response from a concern he had once attacked for being two hundred years behind the times, and which now insisted upon "putting sculpture on their library that belongs on a church." J. Scott Hartley, representing the NSS, questioned the ethics involved in Borglum's earlier capture of the Federal commission for the Gen. Philip H. Sheridan monument.[34]

If the decision for rules was a Charles Taft maneuver to disqualify Borglum, it was destined to backfire, for on 4 May 1910, Borglum learned Barnard had also refused to compete. Borglum thus resumed his courtship of the committee and Alms as if nothing had transpired. Now both sides embarked on a propaganda campaign designed to uphold or castigate Barnard's artistic ability and character. Borglum, Probasco, and their associates pressed home the fact that Barnard's Harrisburg work was unworthy of the praise it had received, that his inability to manage his own financial affairs should disqualify him from signing lucrative contracts, and that Charles Taft's

interest in Barnard rested on the fact that the patron was part of the financial cartel that had underwritten the cost of the artist's Harrisburg statuary. By emphasizing his own efficiency and productivity, Borglum hoped to disprove the widely held myth that insisted genius and a mind for business were mutually exclusive. The Taft-Barnard coalition attempted to turn the non compos mentis issue to advantage, asserting that Barnard's "total disregard of time and labor" proved him to be a passionate creative being who, in obvious contrast to Borglum, gave no thought to commercial interests. From Borglum's perspective, the contest was one in which a man of "prolific, poetic, character" faced the "bluster and bragg" of a bankrupt and failed artist. A popular journalistic summation of the case portrayed in Cincinnati's Democratic newspaper featured a satirical match between pugilists. The *New York Evening Journal* enticed its readers with a dramatic and entirely fictional account of two women, Eleanora Alms and Anna Taft, battling over three statues. Hulbert Taft, on the other hand, gave the affair a more dispassionate and balanced treatment, printing side-by-side interviews with Walter H. Page, editor of *Outlook Magazine,* who was a member of the Barnard cartel, and Probasco.[35]

Taft and another Alms committee member, most probably Taylor, separately viewed Barnard's Paris Salon exhibit. In June, before the Salon concluded, Barnard was unofficially told he would receive the contracts, which the artist described as an "assignment to a long expected duty."[36] He was not to visit Cincinnati until the Autumn of 1910, at which point he was considering making a complex figural group that would replace the *Tyler Davidson Fountain* in Fountain Square. For its part, the Alms committee had shifted the preferred locale from Eden Park to Inwood Park, where the statue, to be set close by a bandstand, would be in full view of passing trollies.

During the first week of December 1910, four members of the Alms committee awarded the contract to Barnard. Probasco declared the contract null and void because, in his opinion, the Alms committee was a joint and several agency that was legally bound to a unanimous vote. He could only guess Barnard had exerted some mesmeric hold over the committee, but maintained that "no matter what happens, Mrs. Alms cannot be deprived of the generous, high-minded and patriotic impulse born of her love for her husband and her adoration of Lincoln." Led by Taft, the dissenting trustees challenged Alms to ratify the contract, claiming Probasco was unfairly resorting to a technicality and that he had "poisoned"

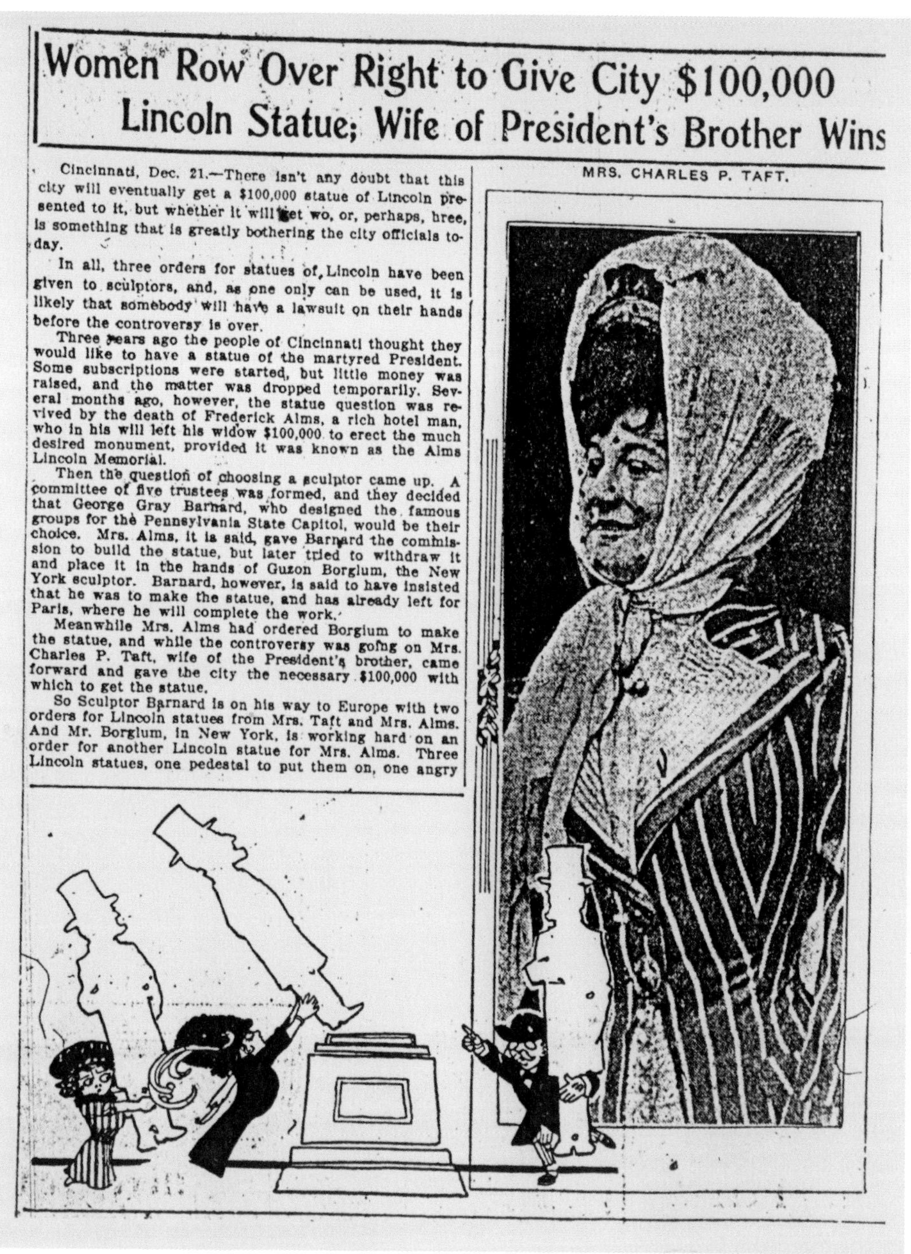

New York Evening Journal, 21 December 1910.

Mrs. Alms's mind against Barnard. They assured her that Barnard was fully capable of creating a monument that "will redound not only to the glory of Cincinnati, but will be a lasting and worthy memorial to your beneficence." Charles's seeming composure shrouded burning resentment. He wrote William: "I have been so mad today that I have not been able to do anything . . . if ever a confidence game has been practiced we certainly are in it."[37]

In the artist's presence, Charles and Anna signed a separate one hundred thousand dollar contract with Barnard on 15 December. The statue was to be executed in America, over the period of from two to three years, and would be positioned before their home in Lytle Park as their gift to the people of Cincinnati. Alerted by Probasco, Borglum also rushed to Cincinnati, arriving shortly after the signing. Both artists proceeded to give interviews that were printed under bold headlines in local and national newspapers on 17 December. Borglum spoke of trickery and deception, accusing the Tafts of having stolen the proposed Lincoln statue from a sick woman. He suggested that the Tafts sponsor a separate statue dedicated to Christopher Columbus. Headlined "Borglum Attacks the Tafts," the New York Times article aroused the president, who clearly wished to distance himself from the fracas. "It seems to me," William wrote his distraught brother, "[Borglum] is making an ass of himself."[38]

The standoff continued through 20 December. On that day Charles Taft, reacting to the news that Mrs. Alms had suspended immediate plans to erect a Lincoln monument, publicly indicated he would proceed with the Taft Lincoln only if Mrs. Alms withdrew. Borglum and Probasco urged her to stay the course, the former insisting that an Alms Lincoln already legally existed, since he knew of an Alms will that specifically mandated the building of such a monument. The sculptor then sent a joint communication to Charles and William Taft beseeching them to withdraw the competing contract or else the dispute "must grow into the very monuments we purpose [*sic*] building and be revived at the setting of every stone."[39]

Borglum later surmised the Tafts did not want a monument to be built, since an Alms Lincoln would cast a large shadow over their own family's standing with the community. To his way of thinking, Charles chose a notoriously untrustworthy sculptor precisely because he hoped Barnard would not complete the work, thus defeating the competing project without incurring the expense of building a statue himself. Following the debacle, the wrathful conspirator imagined, Charles went to Washington "head over heels" and William probably considered appointing Probasco to a national office in order to reconcile him to the defeat of the Alms Lincoln. These fanciful conjectures did much to sustain the Probasco-Borglum comradeship years after the stillbirth of the Alms memorial. One of Probasco's favorite contributions to the postmortem recounted his chance meeting with Charles Taft on a Cincinnati street. He remembered bowing while Charles smirked. "Think of it," he wrote Borglum, "the richest man in Hamilton County, and the brother of the President of the United States, taking that method to show contempt."[40] The fact remained that Barnard returned to New York on 16 December holding two separate contracts in equal amounts for Lincoln statues, only one of which, the Taft Lincoln, he intended to execute.

Thus, the Tafts' first decade as art collectors was about to end under a cloud of recrimination and despair. An elderly bedridden woman was being besieged by anonymous letters demanding she stop bluffing. A Cincinnati attorney who yet hoped for national office had further disgraced himself in the eyes of the nation's leading political family, and this without recompense from the widow Alms. A leading sculptor had lost his most cherished commission while his successful challenger, even though momentarily relieved of pressing debt, was soon to walk the gantlet of public opinion. A prominent Cincinnati citizen and his wife had in the heat of anger decided to gamble their reputations on an artist of uncertain ability and temperament—this after they had experienced a disastrous political reversal. They also stood accused of bullying a generous, public-spirited, woman whose only apparent fault was to love the memory of Lincoln a bit more intensely than did they. A first-term president, who watched his chances for reelection grow increasingly dim, was bound to defend a statue for which he would otherwise have had little sympathy. However, like the great patron princes of the past, the Tafts could for the moment contemplate the exalted promise of genius.

Part Two
Creations

3

The Genius of George Grey Barnard

I N HIS *FORERUNNERS OF LINCOLN IN THE OHIO VALLEY,* Rev. Lucien V. Rule compared Lincoln's creation of the "Middle Western Pioneer Democracy" with the Old Testament "Forerunners" and "Restorers" who founded Christianity. Among the great preachers of the Presbyterian Log College system none more tirelessly dissiminated the Lincoln prophecy to their far-flung parishioners than did Rev. Joseph H. Barnard. Having interviewed the minister and his artist son at their Madison, Indiana, home in 1925, Rule demonstrated how the example of Lincoln's early tribulations had sustained yet another Midwestern family. That the selfless Nancy Hanks prepared her son for a life of service and ultimate sacrifice by reading him the Scriptures reminded Rev. Barnard of his mother Elizabeth, "who gave her boy to God, to be a prophet of the Lord." The pungent recollection of having presided at Elizabeth's funeral overlay another mental image, that of young Lincoln constructing his mother's coffin. Again, with Lincoln in mind, the elder Barnard looked back to the day he and his wife Martha buried an infant son whose unclosed "great blue eyes" seemed to peer into the face of God. The heaviest burden was the illness and death of Martha herself, whose open piano in the parlor remained a sacred memorial.[1]

Rev. Joseph H. Barnard (1838–1926), a bearded man who in his maturity more resembled the Renaissance image of Moses than Lincoln, was of Anglo-

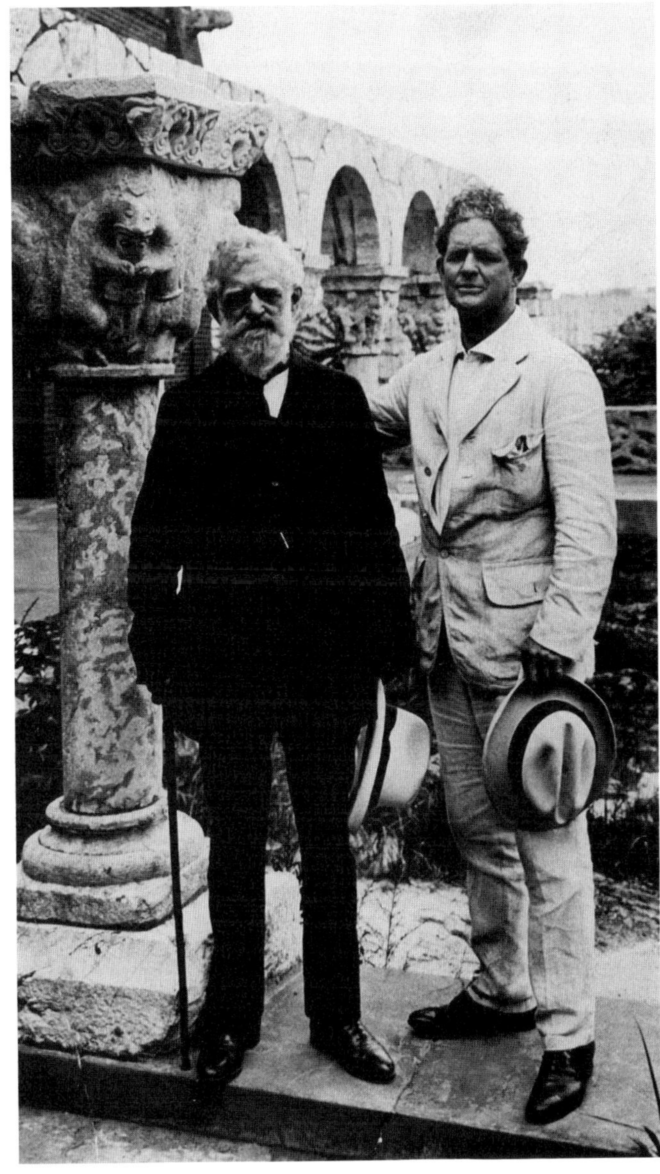

George Grey Barnard with Joseph H. Barnard at The Cloisters in New York City, 1922. George Grey Barnard Papers, Archives of American Art, Smithsonian Institution.

Irish and German extraction. Born in Tuscarora, Juniata County, Pennsylvania, he was initially drawn to ministerial studies at the Presbyterian log college of Tuscarora Academy, received further training at Lafayette College, and at Princeton Theological Seminary, where the conservative Charles Hodge was his principal mentor. Following his marriage to Martha Gray Grubbe in 1860, Joseph accepted short-term pastoral assignments at Huntington, Tyrone, and Bellefonte, Pennsylvania. George Grey, the eldest of four surviving children, was born in Bellefonte in 1863. In 1867 the family traveled west to Waukesha, Wisconsin; then to Chicago; to Kankakee, Illinois; and, in 1878, to Muscatine, Iowa. In 1883 Joseph was called to his final destination, the Second Presbyterian Church of Madison, where he presided for forty years.[2]

Martha Barnard spent her first years in a house near the Lincoln homestead in Springfield, Illinois. Her father, George Grubbe, savored memories of their famous neighbor; family legend identified Lincoln as the first man, other than her father, to have lifted Martha in his arms. Both sides of the family included musicians and artists; George believed he inherited his creative talent from the Grubbes, while his fondness for philosophical speculation came directly from Joseph. Joseph's familiarity with a wide range of theological, historical, literary, and social topics is reflected in the preserved texts of his sermons, which date from the Muscatine period through to the mid-1920s. Resisting Hodge's rigidity, he emphasized the theme of forgiveness, "the love side of Calvinism," and at times seemed ready to make peace with New England Transcendentalism. But there was no sparing of the rod when he preached the social gospel, especially during the McKinley and Taft presidencies. For in these years Joseph frequently found it necessary to warn special interest groups, monopolists, and the greedy sponsors of high protective tariffs, that the "imprisoned and enslaved God of Labor will yet rise up in its might" against "its bondage to Mammon."[3]

If like Lincoln, George Grey Barnard's moral being was strengthened by family loss—Martha's death in 1919 visited upon him a "vision of eternal things"— it was not a willful or vengeful strength. His study of Lincoln's personality made clear the death of Nancy Hanks awakened in the gaunt-featured giant a desire to "mother" the nation. Lincoln "held motherhood within him as great in its strength and gentle spirit, its forgiveness and yearning, as the wisdom and will of the manhood within him."[4] For the past dozen years Barnard had been testing this revelation in his

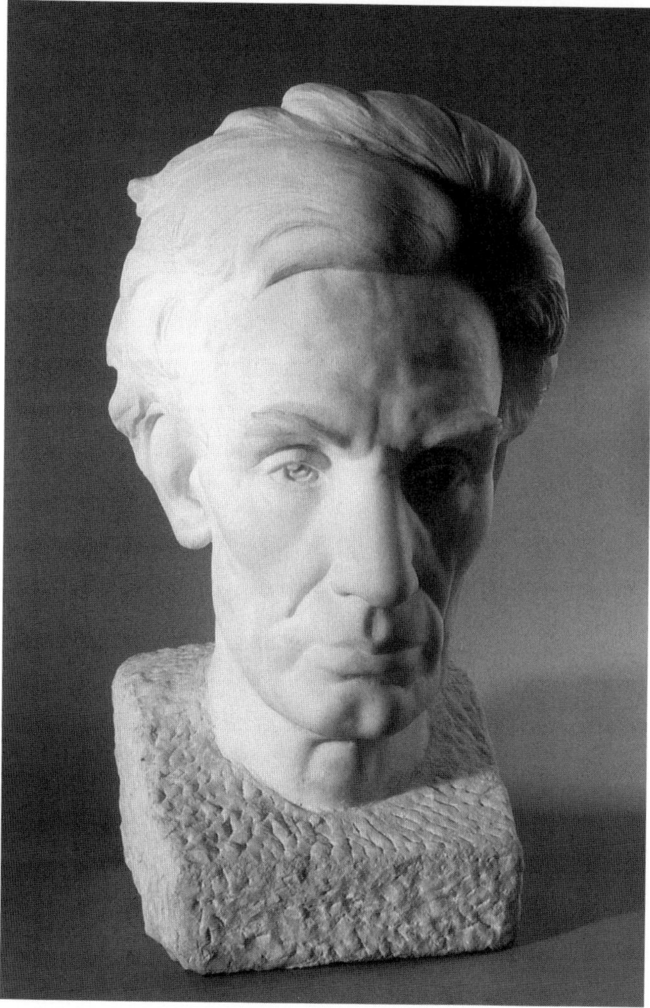

George G. Barnard, Abraham Lincoln. *Ca. 1918. Marble, 21". Memorial Art Gallery of the University of Rochester, Marion Stratton Fund.*

Manhattan studio. Here, among a storehouse of plaster and marble busts, were Lincoln images that manifested contrasting personae: one, a feline-faced youth, whose tender gaze fixes on the viewer *d'une maniere seduisante;* another, a faintly-smiling exquisite attired in a fulsome cape and scarf; another, a tearful materfamilias. In one experiment, a rough plaster mane and shaggy beard were reapplied to the youth's face, thus producing an individual that Barnard christened "The Christ Lincoln." As evidenced by a studio photograph, Barnard reached the limits of his intentions when simply by draping a bust with an actual shawl and adding cotton hair, he created a "grandmother" Lincoln. The will to visualize the bisexuality of this patriarch was a personally redemptive act, since Barnard would forever require the nurturing and shielding this model promised.

Martha Barnard was the first of a succession of companions who stood ready to console and protect him. For example, in 1896 she attempted to assuage his anger and frustration after he lost a statuary commission for the *Indiana Soldiers and Sailors Monument* at Indianapolis.[5] In a letter penned on delicate Japanese paper that opened with the salutation "My Precious Son," she discusses the apparent fact that head architect Bruno Schmitz had paid for the lucrative contract expressly to steer sculpture assignments to friends. Martha assured George no artist should have to "contend with the world in a business way," even though success demanded that he avail himself of the kind of manipulative practice that ruled the day. She beseeched him not to lose sight of priorities, since he was of a "finer artistic nature" than most sculptors and should concern himself only with the studio's domain. In regard to his recent marriage and the birth of a daughter, Martha firmly instructed that even domestic responsibilities should come second to his creative work.

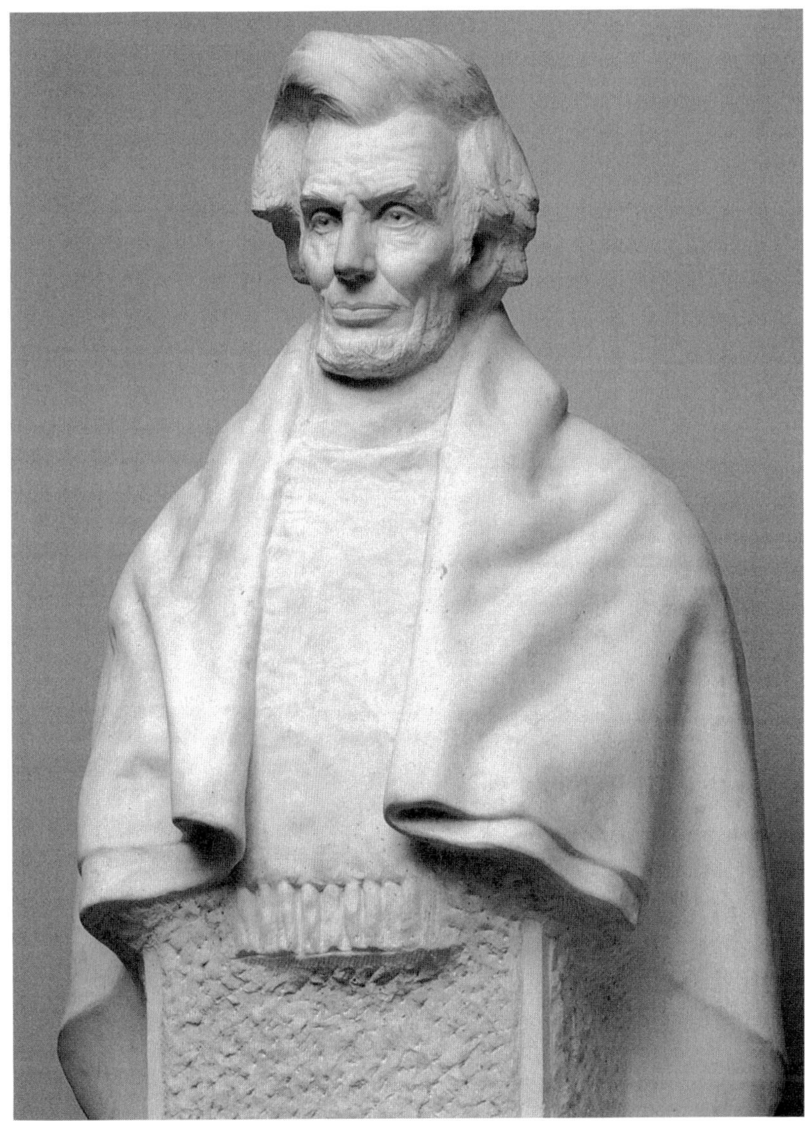

George G. Barnard, Bearded Lincoln With Cape. *Ca. 1920. Marble, 54". Courtesy of the Barnard family and the Kankakee County Historical Society Photo:* Kankakee Daily News.

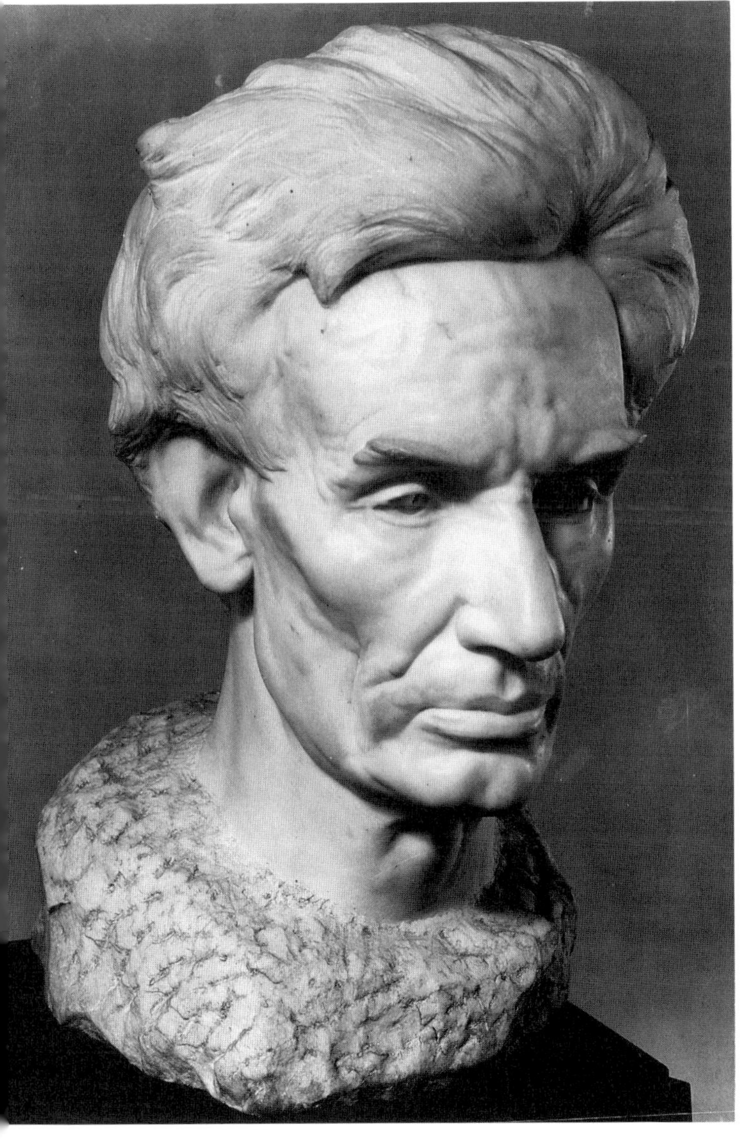

George G. Barnard, Abraham Lincoln. *N.d. Marble, 21 ½". The Metropolitan Museum of Art, New York. Morris K. Jesup Fund, 1929 (29.161).*

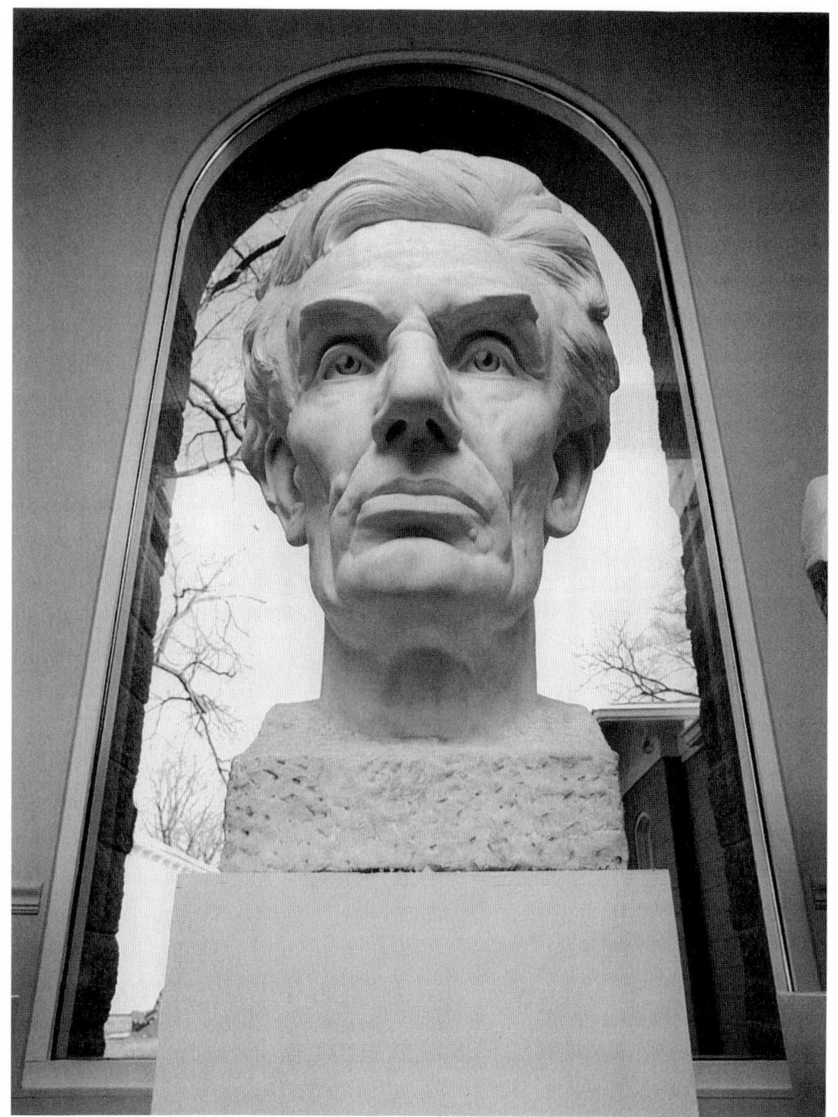

George Grey Barnard, Abraham Lincoln. *Plaster, 18".*
Courtesy of the Kankakee County Historical Society.

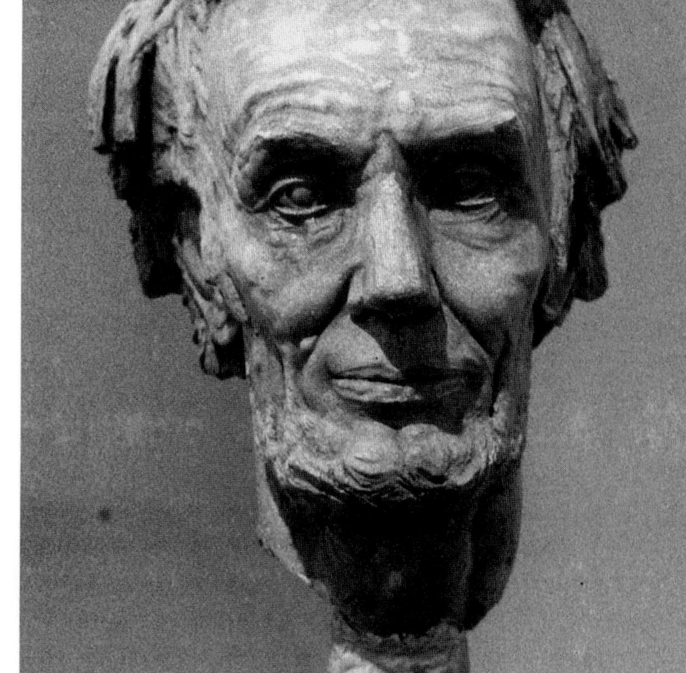

George Grey Barnard, Abraham Lincoln. Ca. 1920.
Marble, 40" inclusive. Courtesy of the Barnard family and
the Kankakee County Historical Society. Photo: Kankakee Daily News.

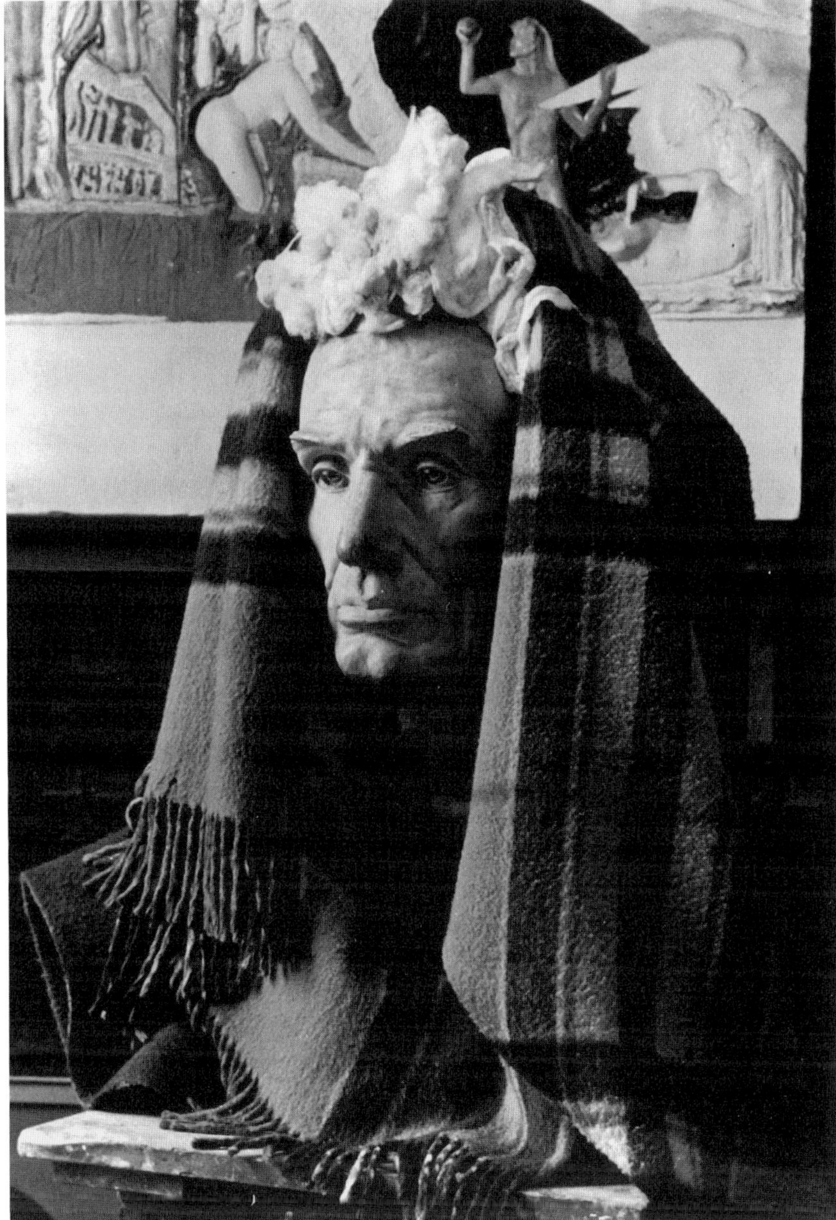

George Grey Barnard, The Christ Lincoln. *Ca. 1920. Plaster, 18″. Courtesy of the Kankakee County Historical Society.*

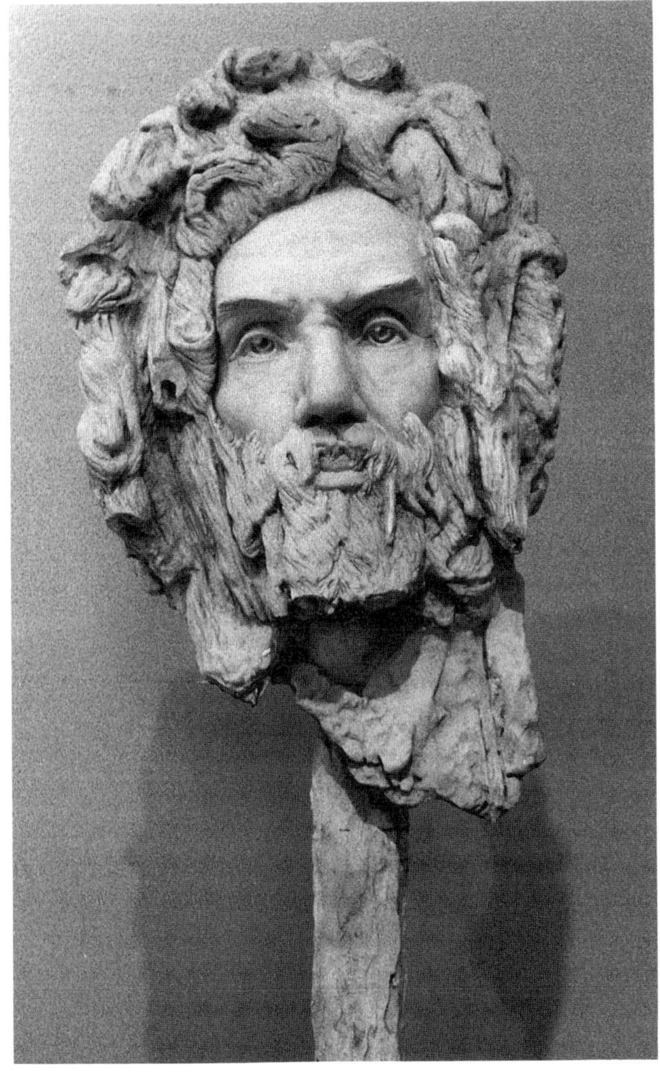

George Grey Barnard, Abraham Lincoln (draped with shawl). Ca. 1920. Photo courtesy of the National Museum of American Art, Smithsonian Institution.

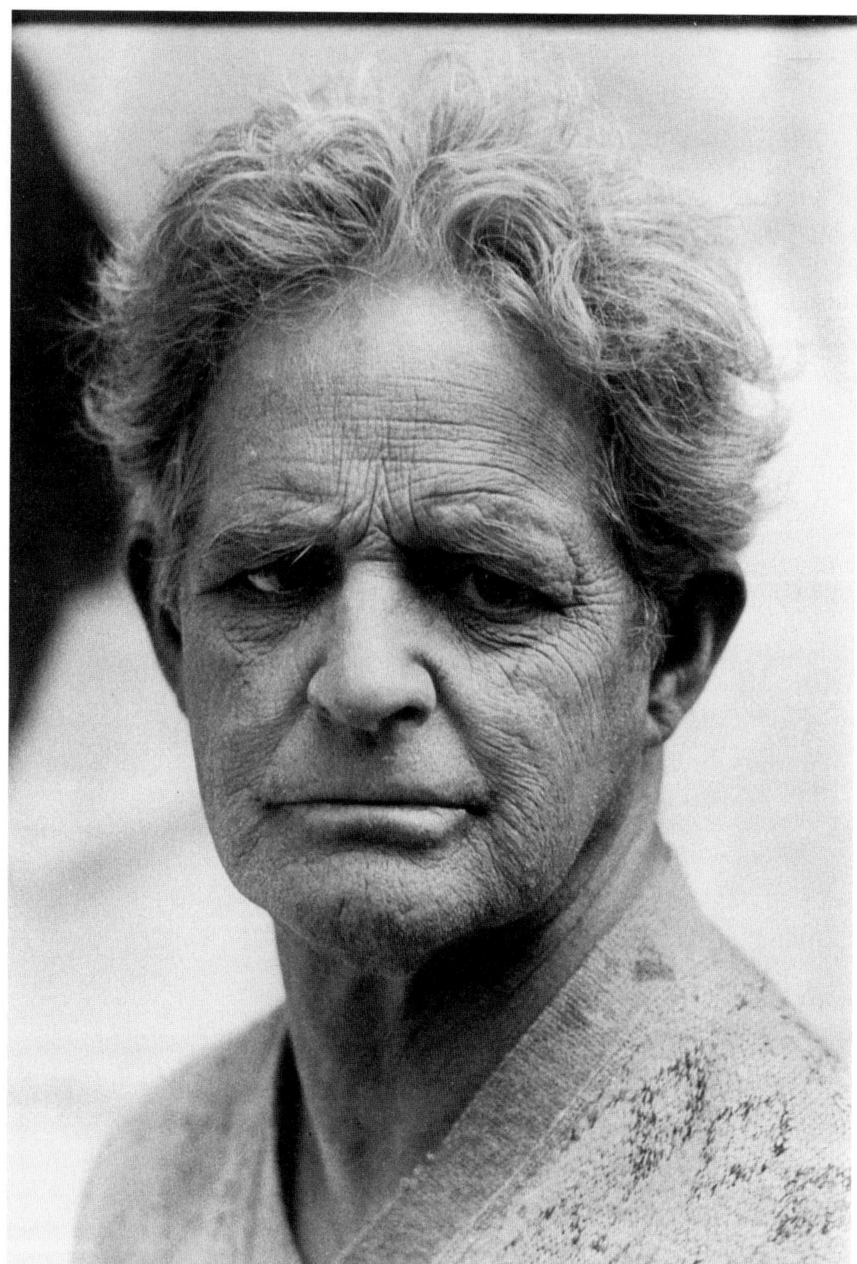

*George Grey Barnard. Photograph ca. 1925. George Grey
Barnard Papers, Archives of American Art, Smithsonian
Institution, Washington, D.C.*

George Barnard was small in stature, possessed
thick shoulders, and bore a cast in his left eye, a feature that lends satanic intensity to photographic portraits. On one hand he could exert a magnetic hold
over friends, but his obsessions and egotistical boast-
ing could just as easily repel associates, even family
members. The Kankakee years were his happiest; indeed, "KKK," as he later referred to the community
and the free-spirited gang with which he associated
there, bears a remarkable resemblance to Mark
Twain's portrait of Hucklebury Finn and life on the
Mississippi. A brother, Evan G. Barnard, published a
family history describing the impact popular Western
culture had upon the boys as they moved about the
midlands. They dressed as cowboys and kept abreast
of the latest adventures of "Dead Eye Dick" and
"Wild Bill." Inevitably, George's rebellion against
authority and polish brought him into conflict with
his father; when ordered to either write an essay or
leave home, the boy without hesitation struck out for
Chicago. His intolerance for grammar and mathe-
matics aside, young Barnard nurtured a propensity
for systematically collecting objects of varying gen-
era, an inclination that eventually served him when

he became an art collector and dealer. At age six, while living in Chicago, he assembled a collection of fossils, seashells, and geological specimens. Later, when assisting a Muscatine taxidermist, he amassed a managerie of stuffed animals. His first pictorial work was produced at a comparatively advanced age of twelve, when he commenced printing images of birds and modeling clay figures.[6]

Family impoverishment cut short George's high school term at Muscatine. He returned alone to Chicago in 1880, preparing to enlist in that city's burgeoning commercial graphics industry. He enrolled in preprofessional evening classes at the Chicago Academy of Design which, after reorganization in 1882, became the Chicago Academy of Fine Arts, or the Chicago Art Institute. The original academy was founded by Leonard Volk, the first of his profession to sculpt Lincoln's portrait and, thereafter, one of the Midwest's leading sculptors of memorials. Volk remained on the faculty, but only as an instructor of commercial printmaking; rather it was his son, the painter Douglas Volk, who encouraged Barnard's sculpting. Barnard remembered that while visiting Douglas's studio for the purpose of receiving a critique on his clay modeling, the instructor presented him with a set of the Lincoln casts made by the elder Volk in 1860. With no hint as to what may have motivated this generosity, Barnard mused, "there was enough in [the casts] to make a human religion."[7]

Barnard's graphic work at the Institute seems to have disappointed both Leonard Volk and himself and, in 1881, he transferred to the fine arts division for sculpture study under David Richards. Richards had charge of several plaster casts, including a reproduction of the Michelangelo *Moses*. Although assignments were restricted to drawing from this and other casts, the lessons provided Barnard with a sufficient introduction to the heroic figurative tradition and sparked his interest in the mythology of genius that surrounded Renaissance artists, most particularly Michelangelo. No doubt Barnard, Richards, and the Volks were familiar with William J. Clark Jr.'s *Great American Sculptures* (1878), the introduction to which devoted as much space to the "inspiration of prophecy" the author detected in the *Moses,* as it did to the chief American monuments of Horatio Greenough and Hiram Powers. Maintaining that this figure was the most "sublime memorial ever undertaken in honor of our own religion" as well as a "miracle of genius," Clark offered it as the supreme model for Protestant American artists to follow. Barnard was anxious to affirm this recommendation. Regarding his art institute days, Charles Caffin described an occasion when Barnard fell asleep in the lap of the plaster cast of the *Moses.* In connection with this event, he quoted Barnard as saying, "His work belongs to me. Michelangelo lived and worked for me as Jesus did."[8]

Within the expanding body of the Barnard mythology, accounts of his evangelical awakening before the *Moses* were joined in the following years with others that emphasized his proud acceptance of poverty and solitude for the sake of art. It was later discovered that during his Chicago tenure he rejected offers of financial assistance, elected to lodge in a rent-free cellar, and, as final proof of his dedication, survived a full year on one hundred dollars.[9] The full impact of his self-denial was brought home for Chicago readers when they learned the artist's maternal grandfather had been a wealthy real-estate speculator when the city was still in its rude infancy.

Barnard's Chicago studies were abruptly terminated when a chance commission for a bust made possible his transfer to Paris. Amid a rising tide of ambitious American art students, he arrived in the city in December 1883, preparing to enter the École des Beaux Arts. Classes at the École, the Académie Colorossi, Jardin des Plantes, Académie Julian, and a bevy of private studios were filled to capacity. A considerable number of unaffiliated artists and former art students also preferred to remain close to the city's exhilarating aesthetic and social ambiance. Ever since the early 1870s, when Saint-Gaudens enrolled there, the École remained the most respected school, but the "Beaux-Arts style" also designates the recognizable product of the many less prestigious Parisian ateliers through the first decade of the twentieth century. Barnard was to reside in France for two sustained periods, the first extending eleven years to 1894, the second lasting from 1902 to 1911.

Having gained entrance into the École for the first term of 1884, his principal concern would be modeling from the live figure. The sculpture division was then under the direction of an aging faculty: Augustin Dumont, François Jouffroy—who had been Saint-Gaudens's instructor—and Pierre-Jules Cavelier, all recipients of the Legion d'Honneur. His primary contact was with the classicist Cavelier, whose career had peaked twenty years previously. For the three and one-half years he was at the school, Barnard followed a grueling daily routine that typically began at five a.m. After a walk to the École to begin a full day's work, he proceeded to Colorossi's atelier for an additional evening session before the model, then retired to his apartment where home lessons in architectural design awaited him. Among his closest friends at the school were sculptors George Bissell (1839–1920),

Frederick MacMonnies (1863–1937), and Lorado Taft (1860–1936), and the painters William Dodge (1867–1935) and Frederick A. Bridgman (1847–28).[10]

New contacts induced Barnard to disengage himself from this fraternity and the educational structure that bound it. In the mid-1880s he befriended the half brothers Frank Holman and Charles Holman-Black, protégés of Alfred Corning Clark.[11] Son of a Boston physician, Frank Holman studied painting under Carolus-Duran and Cabanel at the École, but had few successes. A former resident of Philadelphia and Indianapolis, Holman-Black was a vocalist who received minor notice for appearances in Continental and American opera. Obviously, Clark's financial assistance, rather than professional notoriety, enabled the men to remain in Paris where they shared a garden apartment.

Clark was the son of Edward Clark, cofounder with Isaac Singer of the Singer Manufacturing Company. At the death of his father in 1882, Alfred inherited an estimated forty-million-dollar estate; but beyond real estate investment, he took no interest in commercial enterprise, turning instead to the pleasures of literature, language, drama, and the fine arts, to travel, philanthropy, and patronage—obsessions he carefully hid from public view. Although married to a Cooperstown, New York, debutante who bore him four children, Clark preferred the company of men, particularly that of vocalists like Holman-Black and the Norwegian tenor Lorentz Severin Skougaard. A participant in the fin-de-siècle glorification of the Nordic male hero, Clark distanced himself from conventional American values and popular culture.[12] For him, the Bible shown but dimly beside Teutonic legend in the galaxy of world mythology; neither could he tolerate restrictive Victorian mores or the frivolity and vulgarity that debased the American stage and concert hall.

Clark entertained a more distant view of the fine arts. Having translated into English the Swedish text of Viktor Rydberg's *Roman Days,* he had acquired a Northern perspective on ancient Roman sculpture. Yet, by the time he met Barnard through Holman-Black in May 1886, Clark had not advanced far as a patron of contemporary sculptors. Once the meeting occurred, he hastened to make up for this neglect; he engaged Barnard to complete his first major figurative piece, *Figure of a Boy,* promised him further commissions, and commenced dispensing a monthly stipend of one hundred dollars to his new friend. The sculptor's poverty and relative intellectual innocence were obviously as attractive to Clark as were any indications of creative potential; he gave Barnard

books, offered to underwrite the debt on his parents' Madison home, financed Joseph Barnard's visit to Paris in 1887, and helped the sculptor secure spacious new quarters in Paris. Shortly after meeting Clark, Barnard ceased attending École classes.[13]

Thus Clark's beneficence enabled Barnard to extricate himself from an academic system which appeared to honor proficiency and productivity above all else. Henceforth, his life in Paris more generally conformed to a literary definition of Parnassian aesthetics and the artist-poet. George Sand explained it was the latter mythical personage who "grows pale during ten years, in an attic, over a work which would have made his fortune, but which he will not release as long as it is not finished according to his conscience." The books Barnard received from Clark, a choice selection of holy texts, tracts on ancient religions, and mythology, were intended to impress upon him a consciousness of heroic action he could readily imitate. Clark insisted that this model not be drawn from standard Protestant iconology or America's less-than-stirring political history. Carlyle was favored among moderns. Barnard consumed *Heroes and Hero Worship* and *Sartor Resartus* with rapt attention; it was obviously the author's portrayal of the mad Teufelsdröckh that Barnard had in mind when he described his own dreamlike state of mind while at work in his studio. The extravagant syntax of his home letters became increasingly Carlylean in tone. Equally admiring of Victor Hugo, whose formulation of the "mage," the poet-priest who even while asleep "keeps open the eyes of his soul," Barnard found a firm model for developing his selfimage.[14]

Many commissions Clark gave Barnard connected in some way with Norway and a lifelong friend, Lorentz Severin Skougaard. Since 1866, when Edward Clark launched Skougaard's American career after inviting him to stay at the Clark's Cooperstown estate, Alfred and Severin were inseparable companions. A tour of Norway with Lorentz in 1870 inspired the younger Clark to establish a home on Langøen, "Long Island," near the coastal city of Langesund, Norway. In Langesund he frequently visited the Skougaards, whose house he partly owned, and in New York, Clark and Severin took neighboring apartments.[15] After Lorentz's death, which occurred in Clark's New York apartment in February 1885, the latter commissioned from Barnard a funerary monument entitled *Brotherly Love,* which sculptor and patron personally transported to Severin's grave at Langesund. With reference to Michelangelo's *Slaves* in the Louvre Museum, the relief depicts two

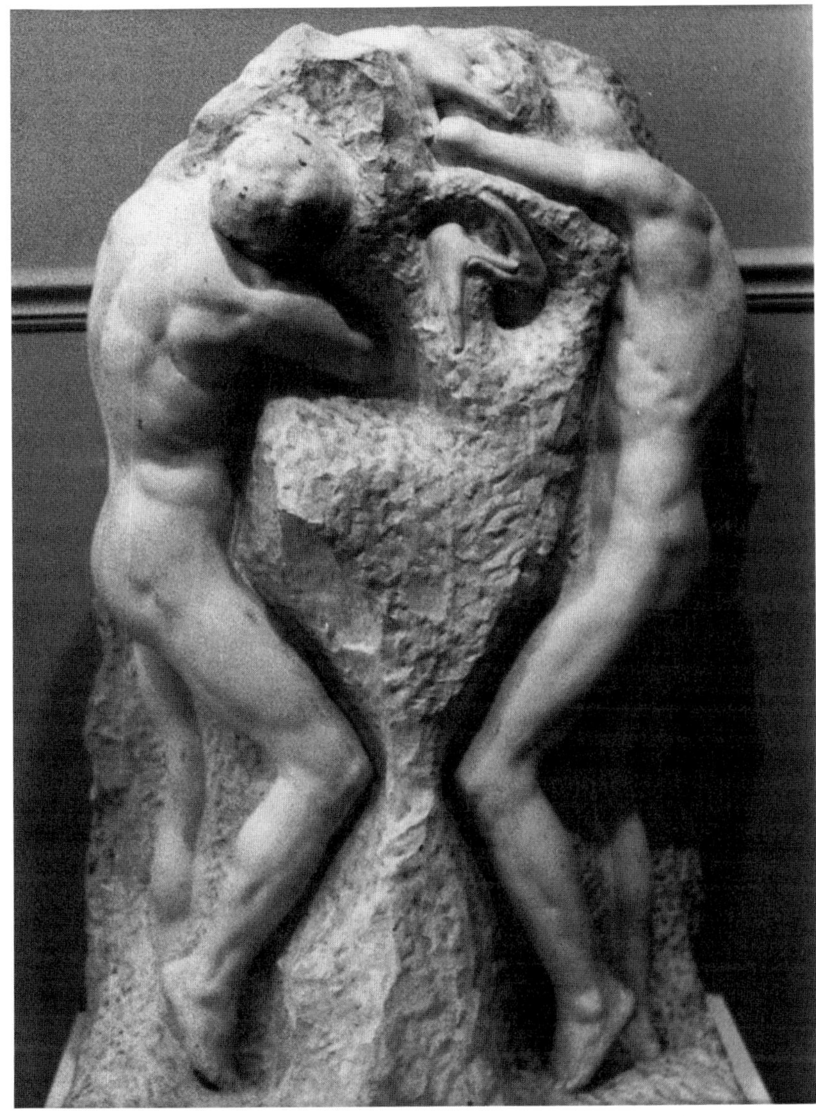

George Grey Barnard, Brotherly Love. *1886. Plaster, 43¾". Courtesy of the Kankakee County Historical Society.*

youthful nude males furtively groping for one another through a rubbly wall.

Several years later, Clark and some Norwegian associates ordered a porcelain stove, the swirling Rodinesque design of which illustrated scenes from the classic Norse chronicles, the *Eddas.* Barnard later transferred this ensemble to a large wooden clock case and, following Rodin's lead, proceeded to develop from its overall composition individual figurative fragments to which individual titles were assigned. *The Great God Pan,* which he began modeling in clay in January of 1894, was initially meant to decorate a fountain inside the Dakota Hotel in Manhattan, the showcase of Clark's real estate holdings.[16]

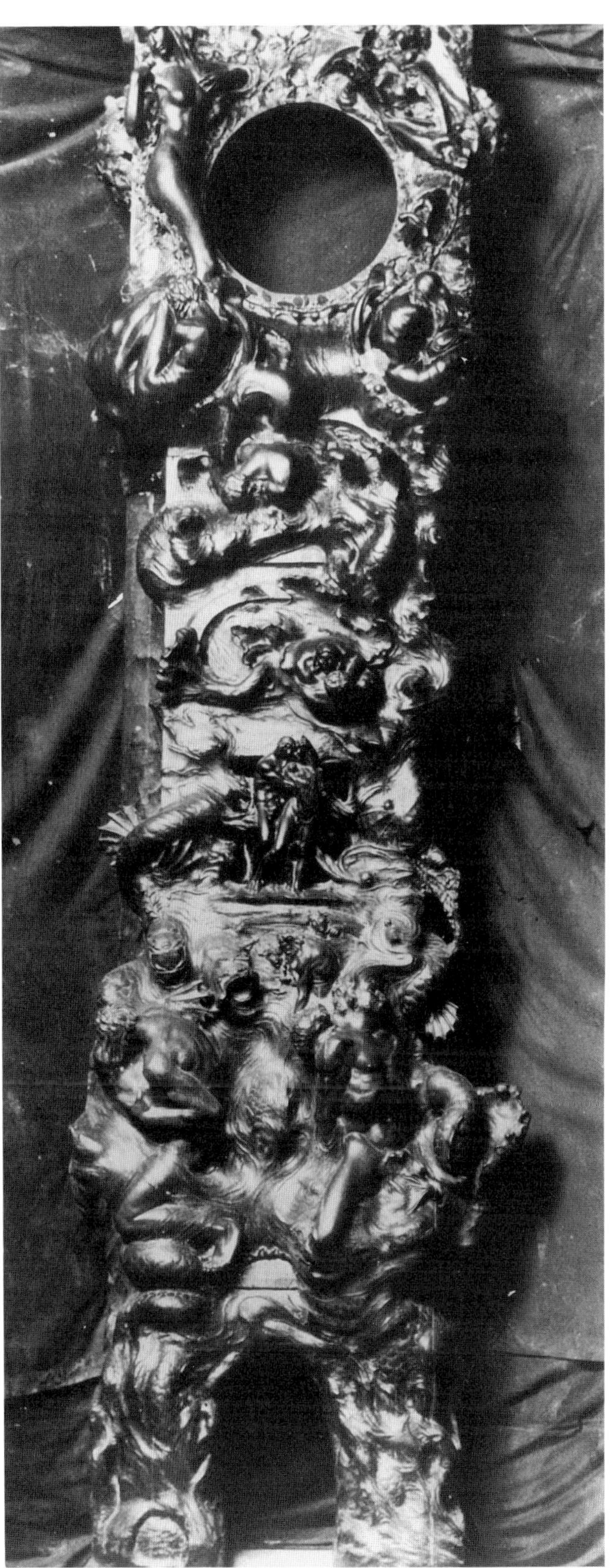

George Grey Barnard, Norwegian Clock. *Ca. 1898. Wood, 12'6". Courtesy of the Kankakee County Historical Society.*

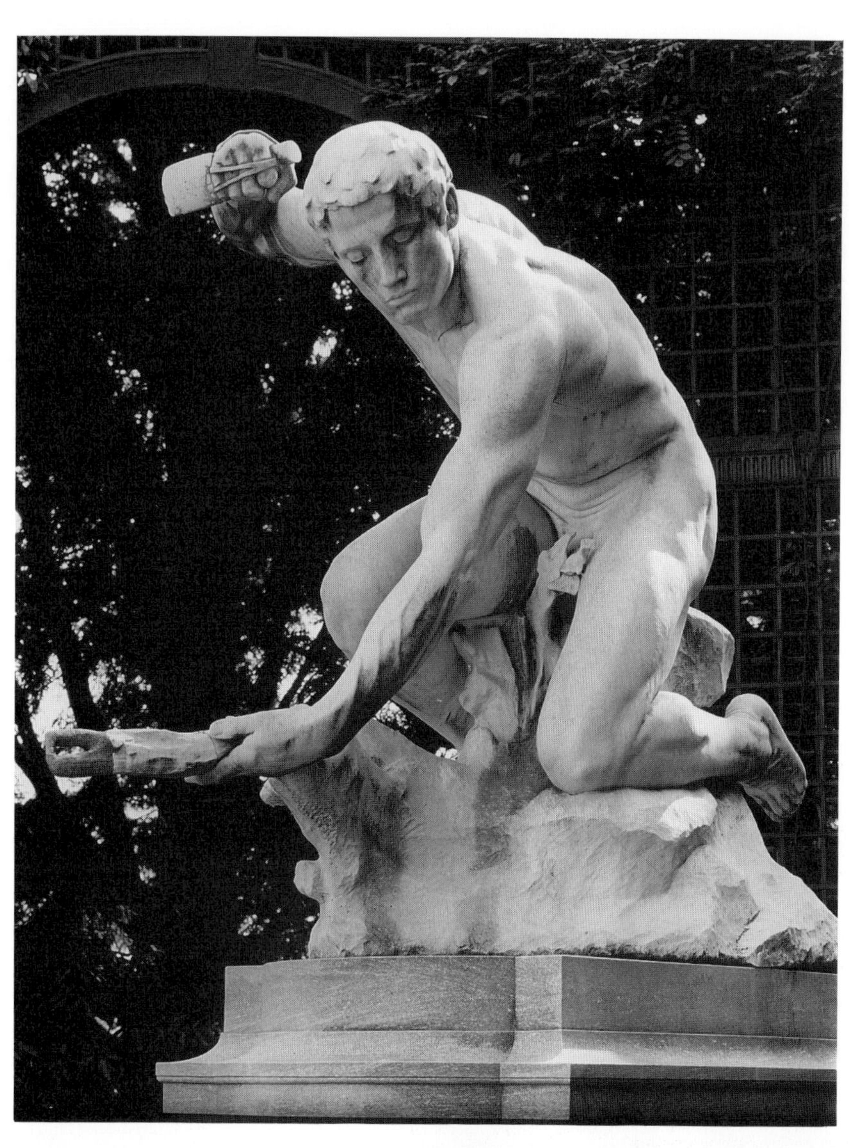

George Grey Barnard, The Hewer. *1902. Marble, 6'. Formerly in the collection of John D. Rockefeller Sr. Courtesy of the National Trust for Historic Preservation, Pocantico Hills Historic Area.*

George Grey Barnard, The Great God Pan. *Cast, 1898. Bronze on green granite plinth, 13'9" × 5'7". Courtesy of Columbia University in the City of New York. Gift of Edward Severin Clark, 1907.*

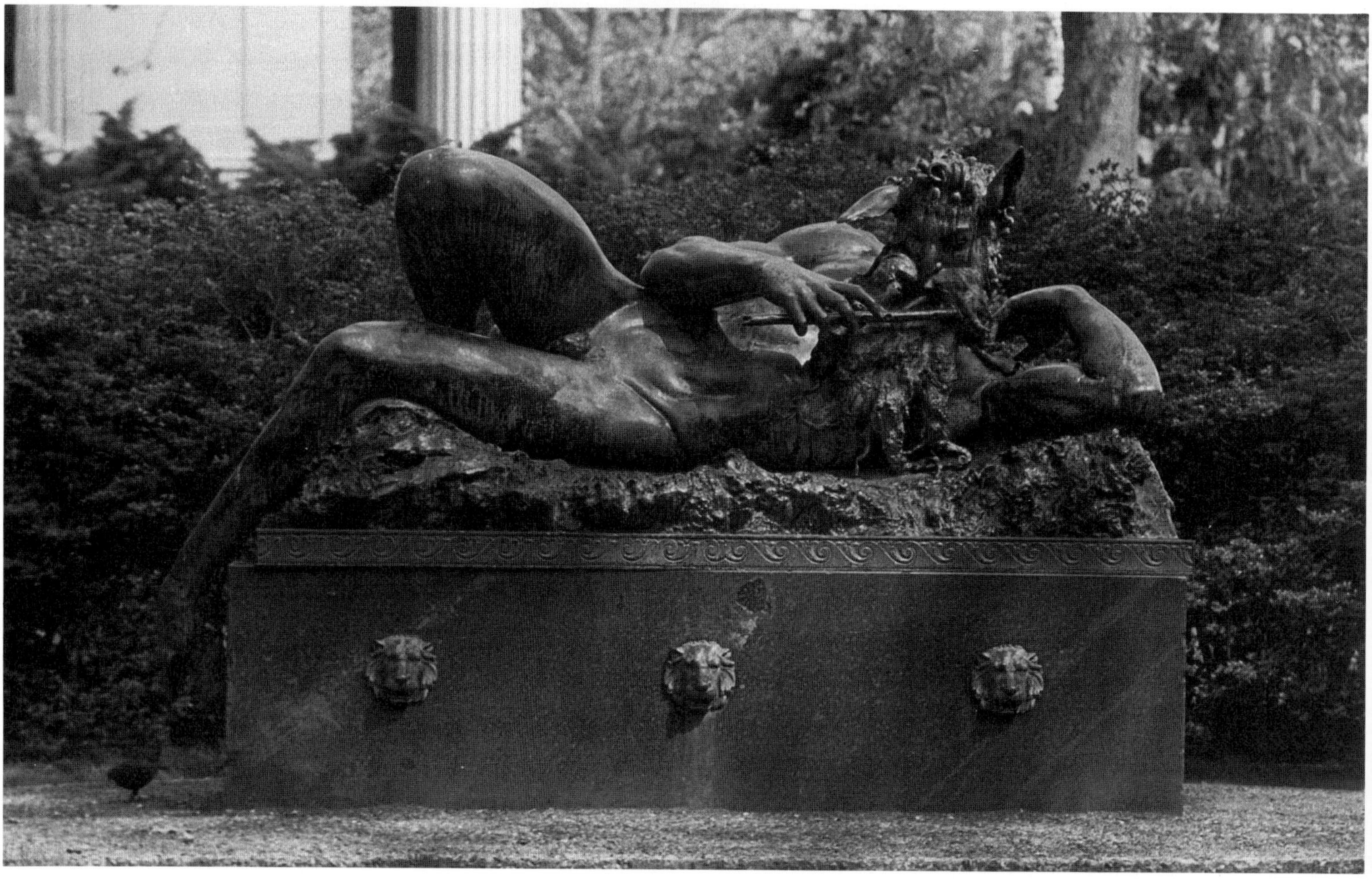

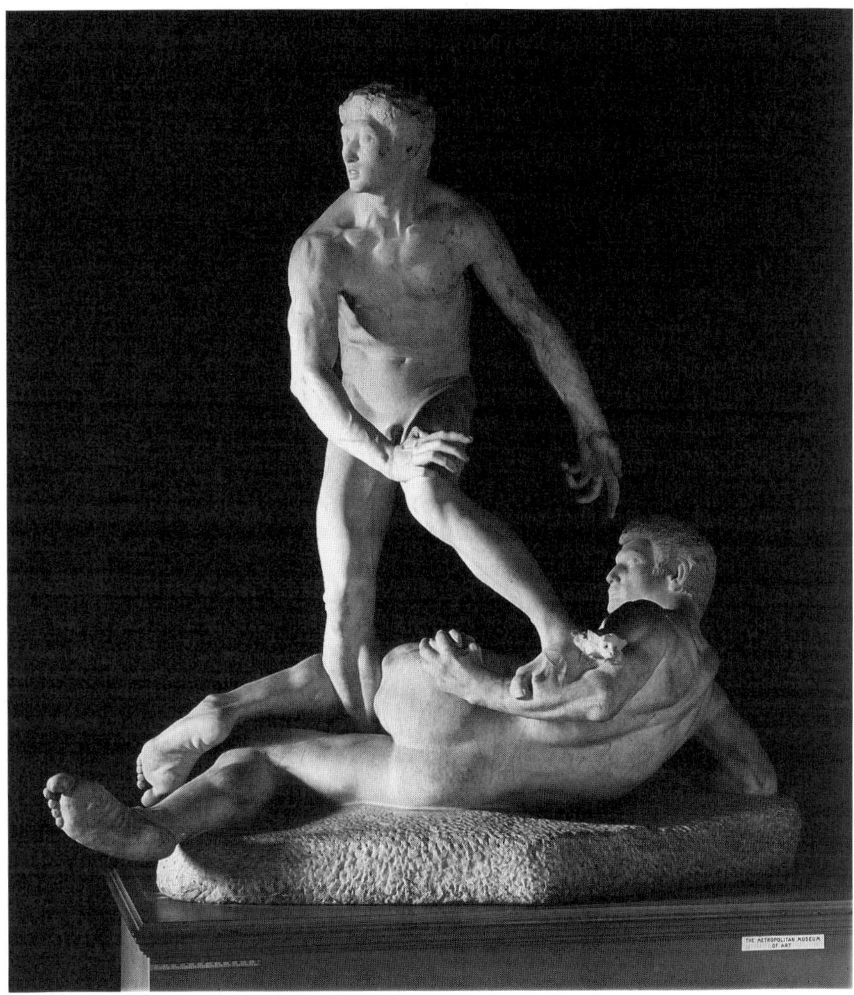

George Grey Barnard, Struggle of the Two Natures of
Man. *1894. Marble, 8′5″ Metropolitan Museum of Art.
Gift of Alfred Corning Clark, 1896 (96.11)*

In the winter of 1888, Barnard began modeling the heroic group, *Je sens deux hommes en moi,* or *The Struggle of the Two Natures in Man,* apparently on his own initiative. At first intended to be a conventional allegory of Liberty, it acquired a less certain psychological connotation when the artist settled on its permanent title, which derived from a Victor Hugo lyric.[17] At the time of its completion, Barnard affirmed that the group symbolized the ironic relationship that existed between the victor and the vanquished: both were ultimately condemned to suffer even if for different reasons.

A journalist later commented that Barnard's fanciful account of the statue's production resembled the plot of *Trilby,* but without the presence of the heroine or a Svengali. A typical workday began as one of the two models proceeded to guide Barnard, whose eyes remained closed, to a position before the statue. As he gradually opened his eyes, Barnard began to distinguish points of light, and "it was with these points of light that I modeled the group." He occasionally labored at night with candles attached to the brim of his hat, as was Goya's custom, this procedure helping him to more readily distinguish relationships between shadow and light. Barnard averred that his life's blood went into the clay model, since his fingers were often lacerated by the interconnecting wires of the armature. Bronchitis forced him to interrupt work for half a year. Nor was the health of the models incidental to the creative process and the ultimate sacrificial meaning Barnard attached to the work. One contracted tuberculosis, but fled the hospital because of his overwhelming desire to assist in completing the masterwork. When it became obvious the model was too ill to continue, Barnard placed him and his wife on a train bound for their native Pisa. The man expired before they reached their destination, but his widow was gratified to see through the train window a large marble block marked with Barnard's name, awaiting shipment to Paris.[18]

Once the plaster was finished in March of 1891, "the Governor," as Clark was known to his coterie, ordered the marble edition for a price of twenty-five thousand dollars. Given the close association between artist and patron at this time, Clark no doubt took a keen interest in Barnard's progress. A measure of the patron's involvement is quite possibly revealed in a portrait painted of Barnard in 1890 by the Polish artist Anna Bilinska (1858–93). It depicts the artist, roguishly attired in leather blouse, knee trousers, laced stockings, and sandals, proudly kneeling, clay in hand, before the large model. In this extravagently theatrical pose, the sculptor closely resembles young Prince Hamlet as first played by the famed tragedian Edwin Booth twenty years earlier. Clark would have admired this dual tribute to the genius of the stage, and of the studio, and since he also admired Bilinska's work, one might reasonably assume he had a hand in

inspiring the painting. Certainly the painting's bold affectation and coyly phrased title, *Portrait de M. Geo. B . . . ,* would have astonished Barnard's fellow Beaux-Arts students when it appeared at the Salon of 1890.[19] *The Two Natures* was completed in the Spring of 1894, in time to be included with other Clark-commissioned works in a much-heralded exhibit at the Salon Champ-de-Mars. As a consequence of this success, Barnard was elected Associate of the Société National des Beaux-Arts.

The homoerotic nature of the Clark commissions was not generally discussed by Barnard's new following, although critic William Coffin regretted that the caressing fingers featured in *Brotherly Love* were not made "a little more manly in character." It may be observed that the spontaneous posturings of the figures in *The Two Natures* are more suggestive of frolic than serious combat. Pan, whose initial act is

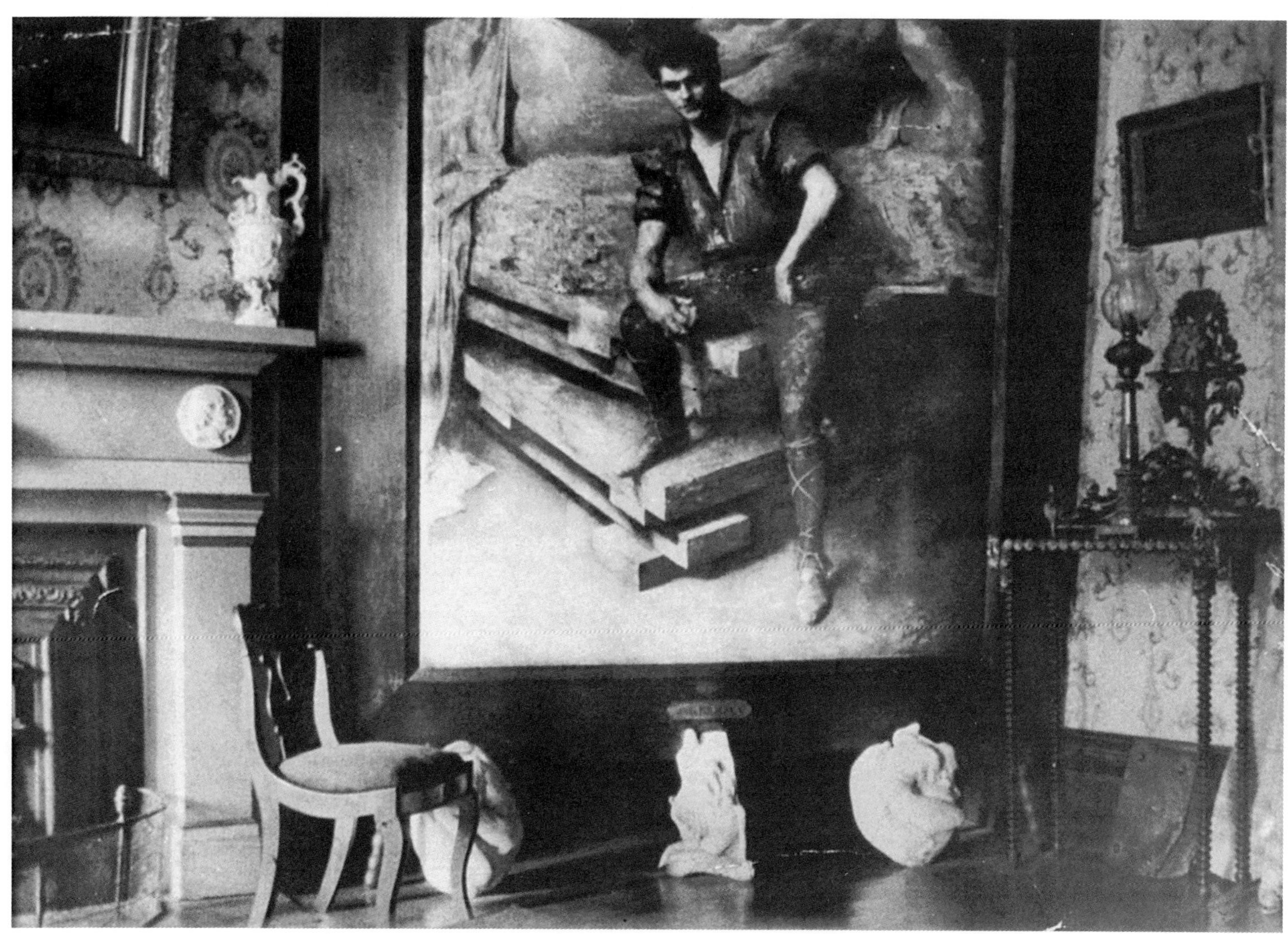

Anna Bilinska, Portrait de M. Geo. . . *1890. Oil on canvas. Location unknown. Photo courtesy of the Archives of American Art, Smithsonian Institution.*

to seduce the young mortal Olympos, has long been associated with the cult of homosexuality, and Barnard's interpretation does nothing to discourage this convention. Quite likely the Clark entourage was familiar with the recent publications of John Addington Symonds and Walter Pater that highlighted Michelangelo's and Cellini's homoerotic sensibilities. Rydberg's *Roman Days* deals at length with the Platonic relationship between Hadrian and Antinoüs, and with an ancient Roman statuary group, a composition comparable to *Brotherly Love,* which the author supposed allegorized this sexual love of one man for another. Clark and Barnard were thus encouraged to consider the historical precedent of their own association, so suggestive it was of the pairings between Donatello, Michelangelo, and Cellini, and powerful father figures, all of whose reputations remained intact.[20] It was also obvious, however, that Victorian society did not extend the same tolerance to the living.

Barnard's loudly acclaimed Salon success thus brought a forbidden historical aspect of the artist-patron paradigm into new focus. In terms of his career, however, the exhibition marked the ending rather than the beginning of an erotic revisiting of the past. Clark's death in New York on 8 April 1896 climaxed a ten-year period in which a substitute father had extended to him total financial, intellectual, and emotional support, this despite Barnard's self-righteous credo to stand alone. Nevertheless, an event that occurred before Clark's death already served to end the relationship. In 1893 the sculptor met Edna Monroe, daughter of a prominent Boston educator and herself an elocutionist, musician, and musical theorist. In mid-1894, before the adjournment of the Salon, Barnard and Edna left for the Monroe summer home in Dublin, New Hampshire. Here they were to be married the following year in a ceremony conducted by Rev. Barnard.[21] The couple settled near Fort Washington Heights, on the Manhattan's northern tip, to await the birth of their first child, Vivia.

The precipitous break from Paris was greeted by outcries from Barnard's friends, artists, and critics, most notably Rodin and Thiebault-Sisson of *Le Temps,* who reminded him that only in Paris "can your artistic garden be cultivated." The most critical was Clark, who firmly warned him "to give up America and give up home, or give up art." Clark backed this ultimatum with the offer of a fifty thousand dollar annual stipend and use of a garden studio if he would remain in Paris.[22]

In an early tribute to Rodin, Truman Bartlett des-

ignated France as the one place in the Western world where an artist could "make his representations of love's manifold expressions, the chastity of passion, and its amorous glow without fear, and in undisturbed confidence that he will find his due audience, without waiting for the 'sane serenities of futurity.'" Barnard fully agreed that Paris offered a far more congenial climate for art than did America, where "political methods," which he defined not only as political favoritism in the awarding of contracts but also as any contractual limitations that imposed deadlines and dictated subject matter, discouraged creativity. On the other hand, his sudden repatriation allowed him to avoid the repercussions of an Italian lawsuit claiming compensation for some unused Carrara marble, a complaint that threatened court seizure of his sculpture and his Paris studio. Publicly, Barnard avowed his return was entirely motivated by patriotism: he wished only to "identify himself with his own people and to aid in the upbuilding of American art."[23] Marriage and family life were the necessary conditions of patriotism, and would promise his full participation in the nation's greatest sculptural commissions.

In their early marriage, Edna Monroe energetically assumed the task of protecting her husband from life's tribulations. She was joined in this effort by a sympathetic community of poets, dramatists, academics, and performance artists who readily accepted the fact Barnard was a genius. The Monroe family had long been paired with the Mackayes, a dynasty of writers and actors dedicated to bringing about a synthesis of the arts. Lewis B. Monroe (1825–79) was the dean and founder of the School of Oratory of Boston University In the early 1870s he joined with the dramatist Steele MacKaye in an effort to establish a new American theater based on the precepts of François Delsarte's "cours d'esthétique applique," Wagner's *Gesamtkunstwerk,* and New England Transcendentalism.[24] Denied their value as independent media, sculpture and painting, along with pantomime, singing, oratory, poetry reading, costumes, lighting effects, and moving stage sets, would be incorporated into an enthralling spectacle of sight and sound. More than mere entertainment, this mighty synthesis would revive the necessary link between dramatic expression and "character, morality, aesthetics, and religion."

In the 1870s, the terms "genius" and "soul" carried considerable weight in any art discussion. But over the next twenty years, as architects took command of the nation's cultural destiny, as great art museums began their work of compartmentalizing old masterworks, and as religion went into its decline, the poet's concept of "genius" came under attack from other quarters. The financial collapse of MacKaye's "Spectatorium," a multimedia theater three times the size of Wagner's showcase at Bayreuth that had been planned for Chicago's Columbian Exposition, symbolized this national shift in cultural expectations. New institutions would arise that paid lip service to an American theater and to cultural synaesthesia—The New Theatre of New York and the National Academy and Institute of Arts and Letters—but in the eyes of MacKaye's followers these organizations were bereft of a unifying force and did not "attempt to fathom the religious incentives of art, without which dramatic art can only be an aberration."[25] But for the efforts of MacKaye's many talented descendants, their friends, and associates, his dream would have died altogether.

After the turn of the century, this progeny continued to meet in small New England towns like Dublin and Cornish, New Hampshire, to share their masques, music, poetry, and other creative endeavors. Foremost among Steele MacKaye's children was playwright-poet Percy MacKaye (1875–1956).[26] Along with brothers Will and Harold, Percy remained close friends with Lewis Monroe's widow and his daughters, Edna and May. After the Barnard wedding, the couple occasionally visited MacKaye and his wife, Marion, at the Monroe summer home in Dublin and at the MacKaye residence in Cornish. At the turn of the century, when Percy was writing his first major play, *The Canterbury Pilgrims,* the Barnards and MacKayes also shared the same New York apartment building. Barnard's effusively imaginative narrations and poetic extravagance fascinated his friends.

In 1907, while the MacKayes were entertaining Barnard at Cornish, Marion recounted Barnard's story about finding a wax imprint of Michelangelo's thumb on the Sistine Chapel ceiling, and candidly described his captivating mannerisms. In response to the same performance, Stephen Parrish observed: "You feel as if [Barnard] might indeed be a Michelangelo, that he could be anything, make anything; he is such a powerful, marvelous creator." However, none of Barnard's friends left a more vivid sketch of the sculptor's magnetic presence than did Marion herself.

And in truth he is marvelous—very beautiful, almost like a Greek statue, with a radiant, piercing sweetness, eyes which are like mirrored sparks and give the effect of light. As you are blinded by their radiance, you cannot see the thing which produces it behind. He has an extraordinary grace, an elusive cast in the eye, for one eye seems to wander. His big voice is of like quality, large—very large, with such resonance that, in a small room, it fills it to discomfort, but vibrant, sweet, penetrating, a marvelous musical instrument, whereon temperment plays in every key a never-changing drama. He is actually a small person, but every minute seeming as if the spirit leaping out of him shot up to heights where his stature followed; a neck of Hercules, with the straightness of the rectitude of his character; a thumb like Michelangelo's which seems made to create. One of his gestures is the modeling one of making curves with the thumb. He forgets to eat while talking, and the meals were hours long.[27]

A typical expression of Barnard's esteem for MacKaye is found in a congratulatory letter of 1906 in which the sculptor also alludes to his own current difficulties with the Pennsylvania Capitol sculpture commission.

Beloved Percy—I did wish strongly to be with you for the rehearsals and opening [of *Jeanne d'Arc*]. I hope by this time you have captured Philadelphia—therefore, the world! For who so waketh the Quakers by drama shaketh the world by the tail. . . . My creations are long since done (waiting on Quaker politics!).[28]

But neither the MacKaye circle nor a sympathetic press could rescue Barnard from the political maelstrom of American life. Despite such acclamatory notices as "Is a Great Genius," "Parentage of Genius," "Hard Climb to Fame," and "A Great American Sculptor," the seven-year period following repatriation proved generally disappointing. A retrospective of Paris work opened at Manhattan's Café Logerot in 1896, and *The Great God Pan,* temporarily earmarked for Central Park, was sand-cast in bronze by the Henry-Bonnard Bronze Company in August of 1898. But the complex engineering feat this casting required tended to overshadow Barnard's aesthetic achievement. The sculptor had no small role to play in the decoration of the Pan-American Exposition in Buffalo in 1901, to which he contributed a major group for the *Electric Tower.* Yet it was primarily student work produced in an earlier decade that kept Barnard's name before the public. *The Two Natures of Man* and *The Great God Pan* won medals at the Buffalo and St. Louis fairs, respectively, and through the efforts of Clark's widow, the former work became the first statue created by an American sculptor to enter the Metropolitan Museum of Art. His most ambitious project, also conceived before his first homecoming, was to be a monument to human labor that would be based upon early Norse legends, a tableau depicting some fifteen to twenty over-life-sized figures surrounding a vessel. By 1902, only one of the figures, *The Hewer,* had been developed past the sketch stage. Barnard might otherwise have found teaching an ideal profession, the perfect outlet for his spellbinding monologues. Jacob Epstein remembered them vividly when he attended Barnard's evening school classes at the Art Students League.[29] Nevertheless, after a two-term assignment as Saint-Gaudens's replacement at this institution ended, he made no further effort to join other faculties.

Perhaps the most indicative sign of the difficulties Barnard was having in adjusting to the American art world was his failure to land important public commissions. Despite his high hopes, a proposed monument to the Marquis de Lafayette for the Louvre went to Paul Bartlett. A widely publicized commission he accepted for a memorial to Pennsylvania Governor Andrew Curtin for Bellefonte, the artist's birthplace, was suddenly aborted. As we have seen, he was denied participation in the extravagant *Indiana Soldiers and Sailors Monument* at Indianapolis. Contract stipulations and deadlines that would have forced him to rush work that required time and consideration induced him to decline an invitation to sculpt figural groups for the Library of Congress. Thomas Hastings, his one friend among influential architects, did directly select Barnard to contribute pedimental sculpture to the New York Public Library, but this long-delayed and highly controversial project proved to be another unhappy experience.[30]

In a highly competitive profession, every sculptor could expect disputations and rejections. In the novel *The Genius* (1915), Theodore Dreiser characterized the combative spirit which dominated the actual sculpture studios he had visited as a journalist.[31] Barnard's perplexities seemed to reflect even more serious behavioral deviations. He was out of step with the practical world in which the contemporary studio artist had to survive. It was the sculptor, especially, who needed to keep his wits about him, for he was not only at war with other sculptors, but with architects and painters who from different directions attacked the integrity of his chosen medium. Like most other contemporary professionals of the day, American sculptors regarded prosperity as an index of worthiness, a sign that the individual had a legitimate claim to be a sculptor. Social Darwinism and Protestant values fed this belief, but so did the overarching issue of gender. Commercial success related directly to masculine prowess. Once returned to America,

Barnard thus found himself in a situation for which Clark's patronage, and the ongoing appreciation of the MacKaye circle, ill-prepared him. Nowhere is this better seen than in Barnard's first major confrontation with Frederick Wellington Ruckstull (1853–1942).

Shortly after Barnard met Clark, Ruckstull, then a student at the Académie Julian, casually discussed with MacMonnies, George Bissell, and others the idea of forming an association of American sculptors that would battle against the public's indifference to sculpture as an independent aesthetic medium. Although nothing immediately transpired, the plan resurfaced in New York in 1893 when Ruckstull and art critic Charles De Kay cofounded the Sculpture Society, later renamed the National Sculpture Society (NSS), and secured John Q. A. Ward as its first president. The NSS was never to have the lobbying power of the American Institute of Architects, since as we have observed in the single example of John Gutzon Borglum, its membership constantly quarreled. But it offered its affiliates their best opportunity for improving national aesthetic standards and for gaining significant commissions. Barnard was accepted as a member soon after the NSS was founded, and applied for commissions through Ruckstull, who acted as project coordinator.[32] From the beginning, their dealings became snared in conflicting aesthetic views.

After Barnard applied for an assignment to decorate the New York Appellate Court Building in 1898, an exasperated Ruckstull chided him for failing to follow directions for submitting models to the architect in charge, James Brown Lord. Ruckstull then proceeded to lecture his fellow sculptor on the ways of the world.

I am considerably older than you and have passed through the mental and spiritual phases you are now traversing 15 years ago. No artist ever started in art with a larger charge of lofty, noble, soul-full enthusiasm to live, and lead others to live, a grand life than I did. But the material facts of life forced me to come down to the level of earth. It was a question of root, hog, or die! and I rooted ! And buried my "soul" for safe keeping. Had I done so earlier it would have been to my advantage. The sooner you do so—the better, not only for you and your family but—for art—. Be logical—so long as you are forced to deal with the real world of business, deal with it in a business-like way—or do not have any relations with it. By this course alone will you save yourself much heart-burning—. Hamlet was not strong enough to set right a world out of joint—and even a Michelangelo could not revolutionize the art conditions under which we live—;

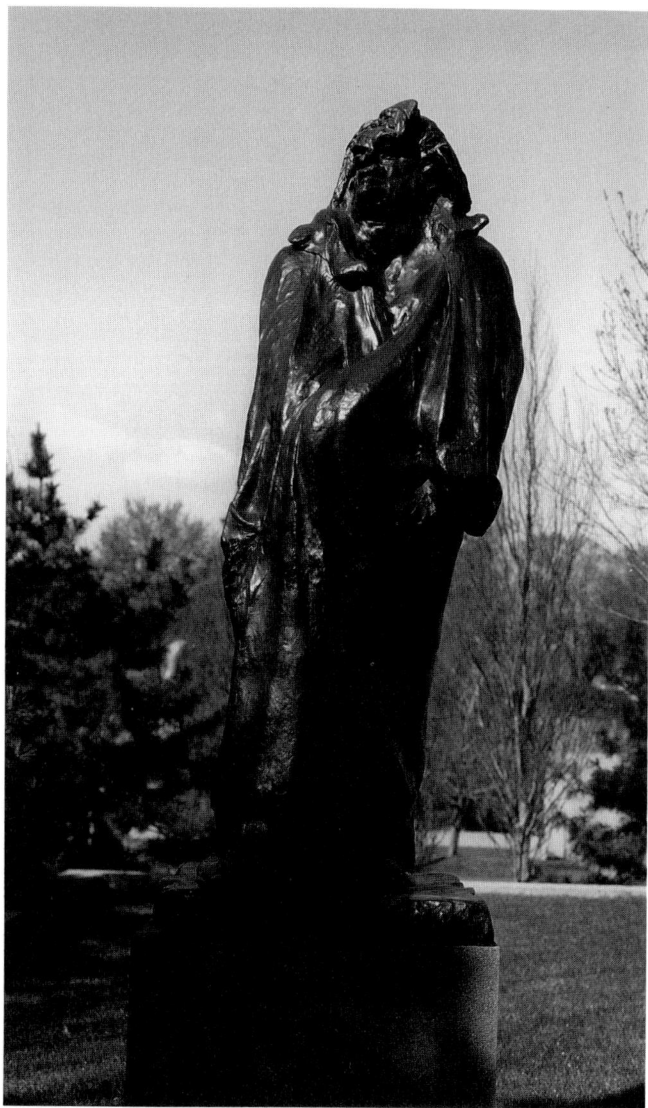

Auguste Rodin, Monument to Balzac. *1891–98, cast 1965–1966. Bronze, 8′10″. Hirshhorn Museum and Sculpture Garden, Smithsonian Institution. Gift of Joseph H. Hirshhorn, 1966. Photo: Lee Stalsworth.*

their improvement is a matter of development. You are not the only one who is strenuously working toward that end . . . In short—only one thing will excuse you ever from not following the specifications of Mr. Lord, in total, and that is physical inability.[33]

Ruckstull's reaction was a chilling reminder of how far leaders of the profession had strayed from the domain of creative genius. When in the summer of 1898 the controversy over Rodin's *The Monument to Balzac* broke in the American press—a contest that, thanks to Charles De Kay and the *New York Times,* produced some strong American support for Rodin—another aspect of Barnard's remote aesthetic position began to emerge. Convinced of Barnard's stylistic depend-

ency upon Rodin, critics were hard-pressed to explain why he ignored and occasionally denounced the French master. Not only did he appropriate themes and compositional devices from Rodin's oeuvre, Barnard was also obviously inspired by the French sculptor's miraculous rise from out of the ranks of the tradesman, by his reputation as the brooding artist-poet and as a soul-companion to Labor, and by Rodin's total devotion to work. It is true the Frenchman's often quoted observation concerning Barnard—that he was "too strong"—was not as complimentary as supposed, for it suggested the American had overstepped the boundaries that even Rodin considered proper for student work. Such strength often attracted too much praise at once, thus tempting a journeyman away from a "desire for thorough work."[34]

There were, after all, important technical differences between the works of Barnard and Rodin. Even though Barnard may not, as he claimed, have done all of his own stonecutting, he did in his early career cut a significant amount, and with considerable skill. When completing a clay model which he intended to reproduce in marble, Barnard routinely smoothed away most of the impromptu touches, dentings, and scratches the modeling process normally occasions. Clay work for such early bronze statuary as *The Great God Pan* was likewise defined by smooth surfaces and crisply defined details, not the spontaneous modeling preferred by Rodin for his bronzes.[35] Furthermore, Barnard insisted upon fixed, stationary, poses, not the transitory positionings of the moving body. Thus, even in its imbalance, *The Two Natures of Man* attains a semblance of permanence, even calculation, that is entirely foreign to the work of Rodin.

As had Rodin, John Gutzon Borglum, and other artists, Barnard took his turn with Isadora Duncan. The famous dancer's descriptions of how her performance fared before respective artists provides a new perspective from which one might view the diverse attitudes of those who would represent her dance. Rodin, as we learn, passionately caressed her body as if it were clay; "beneath his hands, the marble [*sic*] seemed to flow like molten lead"; only "absurd" Puritanical inhibitions averted Duncan's total surrender to Rodin's desire. Her dance before Barnard occurred in October 1908, after Duncan had returned to New York for appearances on Broadway. The sculptor frequently attended the performances, bringing with him people who might help restore the dancer's lagging American career. She remembered him as the central figure among such "young revolutionaries of

Greenwich village" as the editor Max Eastman, painters George Bellows and Robert Henri, the theatrical producer David Belasco, and Percy MacKaye. Together, dancer and artist envisioned a sculpted tableau vivant based on Walt Whitman's incantation "I Hear America Singing," to be entitled, "I See America Dancing." In order to insure the successful completion of this great national work, Duncan was even more disposed to give herself to Barnard than she had been to Rodin, so as "to become the mobile clay under his sculptor's hands." That she discerned that Barnard "was one of those men who carried virtue to fanaticism" only led her to intensify her efforts, but to no avail. Several other factors helped to doom the project; in the short term, the sudden illness of Edna Barnard, but more essentially, as Duncan recalled years later, the oppressive shadow of Barnard's Lincoln that fell across her and the artist.

Ah, George Grey Barnard, we will grow old, we will die, but not those magic moments we spent together, I the Dancer, you the Magician who could have seized this dance through its fluid reflection—you the Master Power to send the lightening stroke of the moment down to Eternity. Ah, where is my masterpiece—my chef d'oeuvre—"America Dancing"? I look up and encounter the gaze of Human Pity—of his colossal statue of Abraham Lincoln dedicated to America— the great brow, the furrowed cheeks, furrowed by tears of Human Pity and Great Martydom—and I the slight, futile figure dancing before this ideal of superhuman faith and virtue.[36]

As previously noted, Barnard's completion of the Pennsylvania State Capitol groups helped set the stage for the collapse of the Alms Memorial Lincoln Committee and the emergence of the new Taft initiative. We now turn to this project, as well as Barnard's collecting activities, before taking up with the early history of the Lincoln statue. Barnard received the Pennsylvania commission in 1902. Being a native son of the Commonwealth, he satisfied initial requirements. He was directly chosen by architect Joseph M. Huston to complete all sculptural motifs, and, because the architect's commission was proportionate to total construction costs, the sculptor, like the selected muralist Edwin Austin Abbey, seems to have been encouraged to enter an ambitious proposal. Barnard calculated the total cash amount of the original agreement for multi-figural groups at seven hundred thousand dollars, a sum that was considerably reduced by the time he signed a three-year contract in December 1902. Even so, *Harper's Weekly* estimated the resulting three-hundred-thousand-dollar contract to have been "the most important single commission yet given out in this country."[37] Artist and family traveled to France at the beginning of 1903, settling at Moret-sur-Loing, a farming community close by Fontainebleau, where a large stone barn was converted into a studio.

As originally conceived, the theme of the Harrisburg project was an apotheosis of Labor. Large bronze and marble groups, descriptive of Pennsylvania's debt to the immigrant worker, were to have embellished the entire front facade.[38] The reduced contract called for two flanking marble groups at each side of the central staircase. Barnard envisioned the banisters as proscenium stages upon which heroic nudes, in the attitudes of pantomimists, strode forward to silently engage their audiences. Each group was assigned either to good or bad societies; the former being the fruit of Man's Labor, the latter allegorizing a civilization that had ignored or suppressed Labor, and thus had violated the laws of God and Nature. "The Burden of Life," or "The Broken Law," eventually found its place on the south side of the stairs, opposite "Love and Labor," or "The Unbroken Law." Although certain figures correspond to such Biblical characters as Adam and Eve and the Prodigal Son, and obvious reference is made to the "saved" and "damned" of the Christian Last Judgement, Barnard's typology more directly illustrates universal brotherhood, facing Westward, into the "Sunset of Labor's long day."

Through 1904, Barnard worked from live models and engaged a professional molder to ready the plaster forms; yet by October 1906, the scheduled date of the Capitol's dedication, he had yet to order marble from which the finished pieces were to be carved. Barnard blamed this situation on the architect, who he publicly accused of having withheld payments. Begrudgingly, he agreed to supply duplicate plaster casts for the dedication, but failed to comply with this promise. Just as President Roosevelt was delivering the dedicatory oration before the capital's naked west facade, disclosures surfaced of funding irregularities. Further work on embellishments was immediately suspended.

As these events transpired, Barnard was already much absorbed in his alternate profession as art dealer and collector, a pursuit he claimed was made necessary to meet the expenditures he committed to the Harrisburg groups.[39] In 1905 he was gathering scattered remnants of Romanesque and Gothic monasteries, chapels, and related statuary with the intention of selling them to museums, dealers, or private individuals. Traveling from the environs of Paris to Dijon, the Vosges region, and the Pyrenees, he recovered statuary from farmyards and rescued whole sections of cloisters from vernacular use. Eventually, major portions of four cloisters, including that of Saint-Michel-de-Cuxa, originally located at Prades in Catalonia, and Saint-Guilhem le Desert, formerly near Montpellier in southern France, were assembled. Relying upon questionable financial arrangements, and often at the edge of bankruptcy, the artist borrowed large sums in anticipation of windfall profits. His limited success in placing objects with French galleries as well as with the Louvre Museum, yielded only temporary financial relief. A main objective, to which he ascribed a purely patriotic motive, was to place major works with American museums before the French government declared them *monuments historique,* thus preventing their exportation. This proved far more difficult than he had anticipated.

Romanesque and Gothic art and architecture were still unknown quantities in the museum world, thus Barnard had to "sell" curators on the aesthetic importance of medieval craftsmanship, the remarkable power of the "patient Gothic chisel," before hoping to affect a transaction. A great disappointment in this endeavor was the Metropolitan Museum of Art, whose director, Sir Purdon Clarke, remained unimpressed by pre-Renaissance art and disbelieved Barnard's claims and motivations. For example, Clarke suspected Barnard had retouched a photograph of a Burgos patio he offered the Museum.[40] Barnard's suggestion that a cloisters might provide an effective gallery setting for a display of medieval antiquities was also ignored. As we have since learned, this was only the beginning of long struggle between the future creator of The Cloisters Museum and its eventual sponsor, the Metropolitan Museum of Art.

In his negotiations with Clarke, Barnard won the support of British aesthetician Roger Fry, who was temporarily serving as curator of the Metropolitan Museum's department of painting. Fry's varied interests in old and new masters, in pre-Renaissance sculpture and painting, in the art of children and "primitive" artisans was predicated on the expressive nature of the creative act; in his mind, late Gothic painting held its own with that of the finest products of the Greeks, of the Renaissance, or of the Post-impressionists, because it shared with all art a formal construction, in Clive Bell's words, "a significant form," which could arouse the viewer's emotions. Being himself a painter, as well as a man of letters, Fry gave special authority to his tastes. Thus, he was most receptive when, in 1906 and 1907, Barnard asked him to advance new offers of medieval statuary and architecture to Museum officials. In his correspondence to Clarke, Fry attested to Barnard's sincerity and to the high quality of the architecture he offered. The curator admonished his director for having earlier refused objects offered at a fraction of what the Louvre eventually paid Barnard for them. Fry endorsed Barnard's plan for organizing an entire gallery around an architectural ensemble, concluding, "I certainly think we ought never in the future to neglect his offers as they have been neglected in the past." Fry relayed Barnard's final offer to Clarke, the Saint-Michel-de-Cuxa cloister, on 13 February 1907, but again, there was no response.[41]

Four months later Barnard returned to New York to find that his indebtedness in the Harrisburg affair would be underwritten by a committee of prominent New York educators, editors, and businessmen, which also rather curiously included Sir Purdon Clarke. Headed by Edwin R. A. Seligman, professor of political economy at Columbia University, the committee also consisted of Columbia professors William H. Carpenter, and wife Anna M. Carpenter, Robert E. Ogden, Frederick Bourne, Archer Huntington, Albert Shaw, Walter Hines Page, and possibly other unnamed individuals. The consortium first assisted Barnard in paying a twenty-thousand-dollar bond that came due because of Barnard's default on delivering the Harrisburg order within the specified deadline. But when it became apparent the artist would incur further debts, the committee became a self-perpetuating financial agency invested with the power to process all funds and make new contracts for the duration of the project.[42] Following a retrospective exhibition of his statuary at the Boston Museum of Fine Arts in October 1908, Barnard returned to France and Moret now prepared to begin cutting marble for the Harrisburg figures.

The Seligman committee included no artists, poets, dramatists, or ministers; they were all men—and a woman—of affairs who preferred to draw distinctions between themselves and the "artist type," an individual who was brooding, mediatative, intensely passionate, and hopelessly impractical. Bourne, an associate of Alfred Clark, was president of the Singer Manufacturing Company and, with Mrs. Clark, remained an influential member of the Metropolitan Museum of Art. Ogden lived two lives, one as the capable manager of John Wanamaker's department store in Philadelphia, the other as the director of a progressive educational system for Southern Blacks. The Carpenters, no doubt Clark acquaintances, were

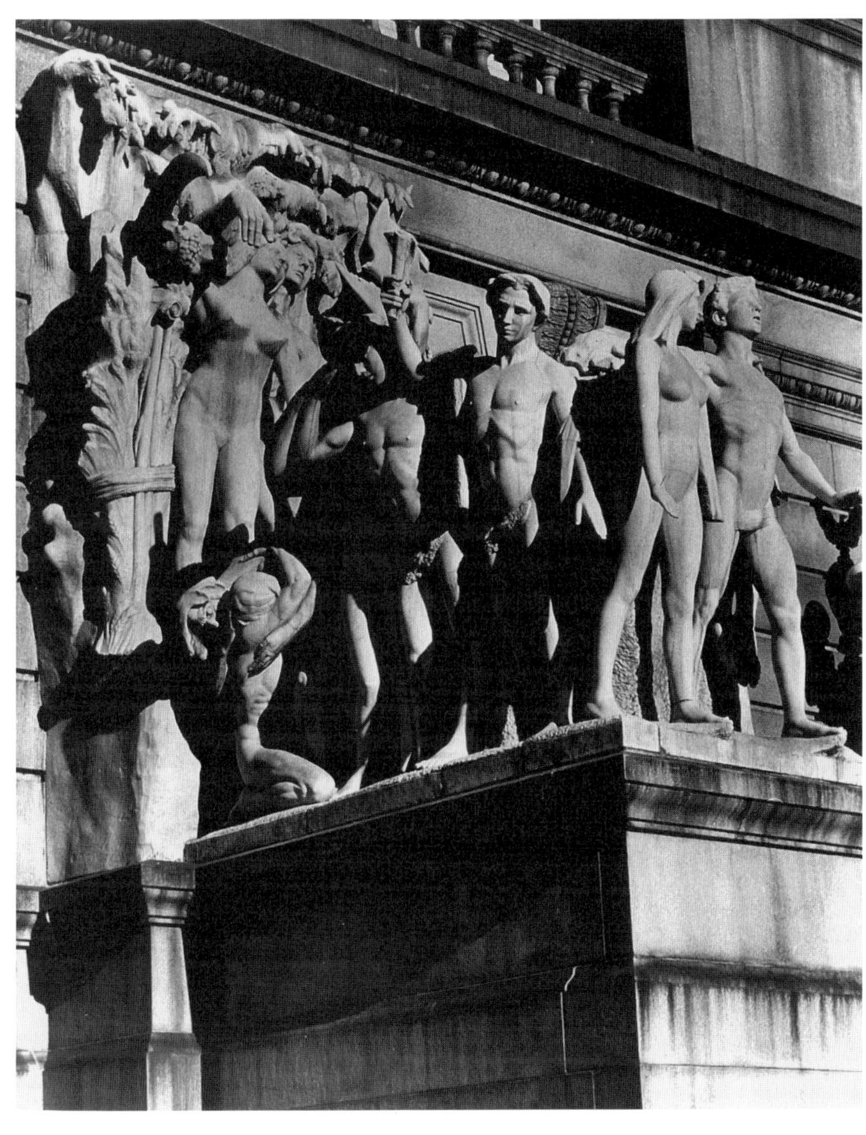

George Grey Barnard, Love and Labor: The Unbroken Law. *1910. Marble, full-standing figures ca. 9″. Pennsylvania State Capitol, Harrisburg.*

specialists in Germanic and Scandinavian languages. The culturalist Archer Huntington was the founder of New York's newly opened Hispanic Society. Page was editor of *World's Work,* a partner in the publishing house of Doubleday, Page and Company and an editorial advisor to the Houghton Mifflin Company. A proponent of urban reform, Shaw edited *Review of Reviews.* Both editors published articles on Barnard at the turn of the century. Perhaps the most crucial assistance the Seligman committee was to receive came from a nonmember: Adolph Ochs, publisher of the *New York Times.* At a meeting between Ochs, Ogden, and Barnard, the publisher promised to publicize the artist's plight, and it was indeed in the *Times* the public learned of the Seligman committee and of Barnard's version of how materialistic greed had forced a great American artist to the brink of bankruptcy.[43]

Despite a flood that inundated the Moret studio in January of 1910, Barnard was able to finish the groups in time for their exhibition in the Salon des Champs-de-Mars, where they were to be seen by Charles Taft and William Taylor. The statues were displayed under the dome of the Grand Palais in much the same kind of arrangement they would assume at Harrisburg. Preparing for his campaign to undermine William Taft's conservative constituency, former president Roosevelt took a press opportunity before the groups in order to offer a Progressive's interpretation of the statues.

I perceive two symbols in the general plan, and they oppose each other in supreme contrast. One represents humanity arrested and dominated by debasing error. The other is humanity advancing, inspired by the principle of work and brotherhood. These groups are my ideal of that which should decorate a capitol and they realize sculpturally what should constitute the ideal of the next genera-

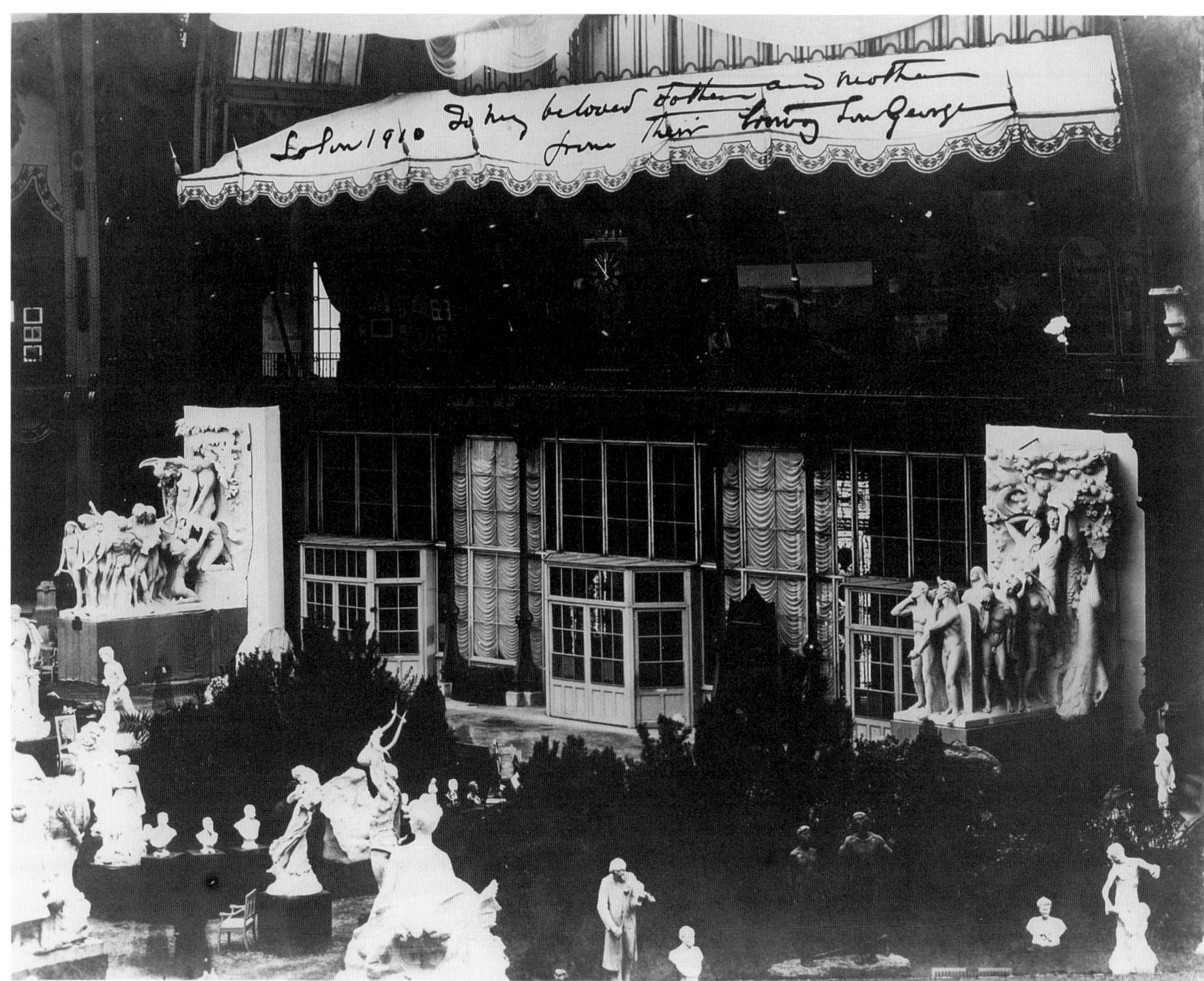

*Barnard's Pennsylvania State Capitol Groups at the Salon
de Champ de Mars, Grand Palais, Paris, 1910. Photo
signed by GGB. Photo courtesy of the National Museum
of American Art.*

tion. I am proud of this work, proud, three
times proud.[44]

American readers could not help but think Barnard's Harrisburg groups held all of Paris spellbound.
Among tributes was one Rodin personally delivered
to United States Ambassador Robert Baker. Re-
peating the late Cavelier's comments on *The Two Natures of Man,* M. Hippolyte LeFebvre unhesitatingly
named Barnard "the greatest artist in the world." The
press reassurred Americans as to why Barnard had
not been given a gold medal, this because a splinter
group of the Société des Artistes Français, known as

"The Free Society," opposed honoring a foreigner.
Barnard was reported to have removed his name
from consideration in a sharply worded note to the
Salon jury. Meanwhile, the troubled governor of
Pennsylvania made efforts to reverse the public perception that his state had abused a native-born genius. He urged the State Department to issue a
patriotic rebuff to "The Free Society." President Taft
refused to personally enter the case but authorized
the State Department to issue a position paper declaring such official sanctions inappropriate and potentially embarrassing to the American government.[45]

Yet, as John Gutzon Borglum and Henry Probasco

happily discovered, there was another side to the story of Barnard's Harrisburg groups. Adrian A. Buck, an employee of Paris art editor Friedrich Goldsheider, informed Borglum that the statues were "rotten" and that the French Salon committee did not think them worthy of even a third-class medal. Furthermore, it was Barnard's bad judgment to choose marble that would be vulnerable to Pennsylvania winters. In a summary of Buck's observations forwarded to Probasco, Borglum assumed the Seligman committee was raising money primarily to fund the shipment of the groups from Moret to Paris and for advertizing the Salon exhibition, this despite the fact the Salon committee "has not seen fit to give Barnard even a third class medal, or even vote on it . . ."[46]

Now assurred by Charles Taft he would receive the Alms Lincoln contract, Barnard returned to New York in November of 1910, arriving just in advance of his statues. He was again seeking money and appealed directly to the Pennsylvania House of Representatives. The Governor approved an added $80,000 reimbursement to cover additional expenses, including shipping costs, this bringing the total budget for production and delivery to $180,000. When the groups were finally dedicated on 4 October 1911 with the male genitalia now safely "blurred" by a team of marble workers, the state officially forgave all of Barnard's alleged contract violations. A half-day state holiday was declared so that Harrisburg might properly enjoy the pageantry planned for "Barnard Day." Had Percy MacKaye wanted to contribute to the occasion he could have done no better than recite part of a poem he later composed in praise of Barnard's *The Hewer*.

> Though from Carraran hills, by alien hands,
> Those forms of plastic vision are unfurled,
> Yet in their glowing, marble chastities
> America in naked splendor stands
> Inviolate, and looms across the world—
> Labor's impassioned apotheosis.[47]

The artist's parents hoisted a laurel wreath tied with white ribbon to the base of "The Unbroken Law" group and Rev. Joseph Barnard, that faithful sustainer of Middle Western Pioneer Democracy, offered the invocation.

4

The Modeling of Lincoln

As DIRECTED BY THE INITIAL CONTRACT, BARNARD was to begin work on the Taft Lincoln in 1910 almost a full year ahead of the unveiling of the Pennsylvania Capital groups. With the tangled circumstances of that project in mind, Charles Taft instructed his legal representatives, brother Henry and nephew Walbridge Taft, to keep tight reigns on fund disbursements.

At the close of 1911, Barnard's financial outlook was considerably improved. The initial ten-thousand-dollar installment of the Lincoln contract was paid him in May 1911. On 13 December, Commodore Frederick G. Bourne, Barnard's chief creditor for the Pennsylvania contract, received seventy thousand dollars on account from Harrisburg in settlement of contested payments. None too soon did this money arrive; even so, mortgage loans Ogden and Bourne disbursed to Barnard for his Fort Washington property were not covered by this windfall. As late as August 1917, Bourne was still owed eight thousand dollars, a sum that would have tripled if interest were added.[1] He pointedly reminded the sculptor of this when Barnard injudiciously asked for more money.

Before the reimbursement arrived, Bourne found it increasingly difficult to control his debtor. Independently, Barnard implored Taft and Edwin Seligman to safeguard his residence and studio from foreclosure or eminent domain proceedings until the statue was completed, while at the same time he contemplated selling this property in order to liquidate the mortgage and construct a new studio. Surmising that Barnard's trepidations may have "upset [his] head," Bourne firmly lectured him on simple economics, carefully explaining that the heavily encumbered land and buildings had no equity value, and thus he had no choice but to continue his lease. In any case, Bourne would not underwrite any new projects, and wished Barnard to remember:

> I entered into an agreement with the Commonwealth of Pennsylvania for your account and did all in my power to have the details carried out in every particular. If you did not succeed, it was not my fault nor the fault of the gentlemen who represented me both in Paris and New York, and if I am to be of any assistance whatever to you in the future it must be with full and complete understanding of all the conditions and the possibilities of your being able to live up to them.[2]

Five months before the Pennsylvania funds were made available, Barnard and the Tafts tentatively approved alternate funding procedures.[3] The Pennsylvania receipts would be applied to all property debts; Barnard would then sign a new mortgage with the Tafts to serve as contract security. If the money was not forthcoming and the mortgage remained in other hands, Barnard would then submit vouchers to Walbridge Taft certifying as to the work completed. Payments would be approved only after on-site verification by the attorney. As it happened, the Pennsylvania money was not applied to Barnard's mortgage. Thus, lacking this security, the parties entered a modified agreement on 27 October 1911 that specified the level of Taft's deposit would not exceed fifty percent of the total amount due until a completed plaster model was ready for casting. Payments would be contingent upon progress reports and inspections, with a final completion date set at two years. In theory, the "carrot-and-stick" principle would insure steady progress and prompt delivery of the bronze.

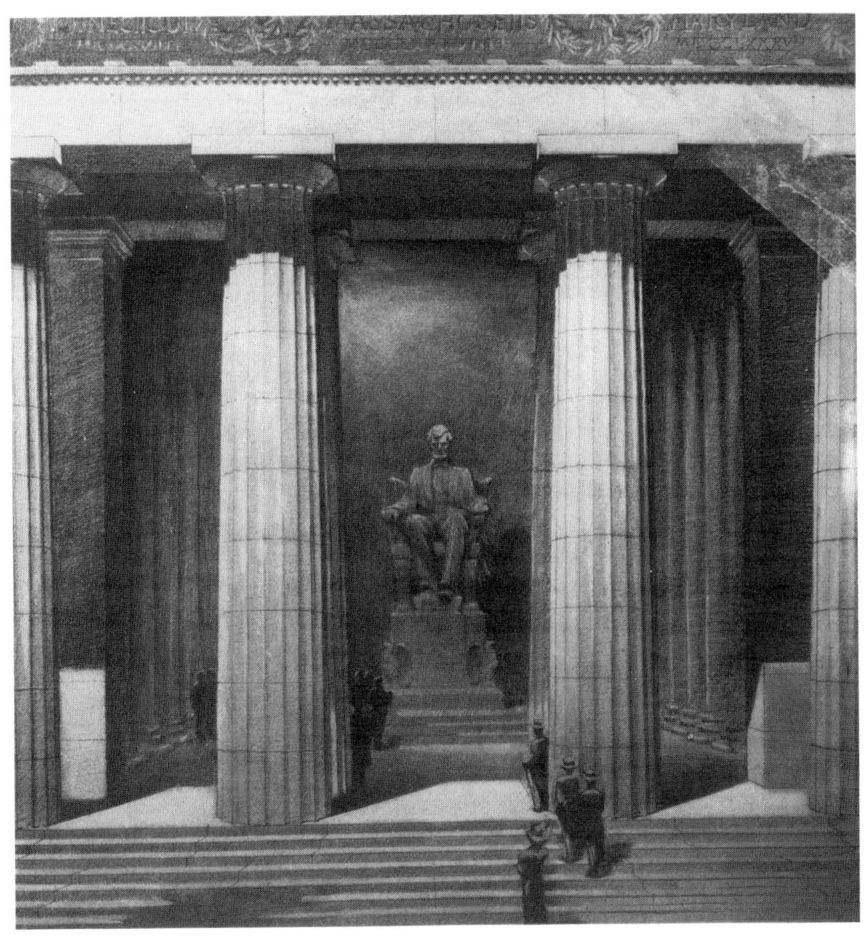

Proposed East Elevation of the Lincoln Memorial, from U. S. Congress, 62d., 3d Sess., Senate Documents *(Washington, D.C.: G.P.O., 1913) 7, pl. 6.*

As Barnard began gathering Lincoln photographs and biographical material, his research was assisted in a negative way by a suggestion emanating from the White House. Charles D. Hilles, President Taft's secretary, recommended Barnard study the illustrations accompanying a Richard W. Gilder article in *Century Magazine,* for he knew of "none better in Washington." Gilder's "Lincoln the Leader" was illuminated with wood engravings and halftone reproductions of familiar photographs that his production staff had cosmetically enhanced; the frontispiece was a candy-colored image derived from a 1860 campaign miniature owned by Robert Lincoln, while the concluding page included a glamorous cut of Saint-Gaudens's standing Lincoln statue. Since Barnard was among the many sculptors who retained hope they might be chosen for the Lincoln Memorial project, the Hilles communication, quite possibly a reflection of LMC chairman Taft's own thinking, was doubly discouraging. Barnard noted with suspicion Taft's claim that no artist had been approved, and that specifications had not been formulated. Indeed, as if prejudging the selection process, the LMC released a sketch of the proposed statue in 1913, which closely matched Saint-Gaudens's second Chicago statue, the somber *Seated Lincoln* of 1906 (see p. 78).

A faint ray of hope was visible, however, in Rep. Champ Clark's widely circulated proposal that "the people of the country [should decide] as to the character the memorial should take."[4]

Insofar as the Taft Lincoln was concerned, Barnard's most practical reference was Truman Bartlett's seminal study of Lincoln's physiognomy, which appeared in 1907. Building his case on detailed analyses of the Volk mask, and on photographs, as well as on verbal descriptions of the living man, Bartlett challenged conventional language that adversely compared the "awkward," "uncouth," Westerner to canonical examples of classical beauty; it was rather Lincoln's stature against which classical standards should be judged. Barnard was struck by the author's description of an isolated figure, one whose "suggestiveness multiplies until it becomes a text for a discourse upon the entire character of the man, its sadness, its pathos, its isolation. It seems like a solitary dolmen in a deserted, barren plain, that has withstood the ravaging decay of centuries."[5]

Beside copies of the Bartlett material in Barnard's study notes is a clipping which he obviously found equally provocative. An undated editorial contributed by E. W. Thompson to the *Boston Evening Transcript* urged some future sculptor "to save the living

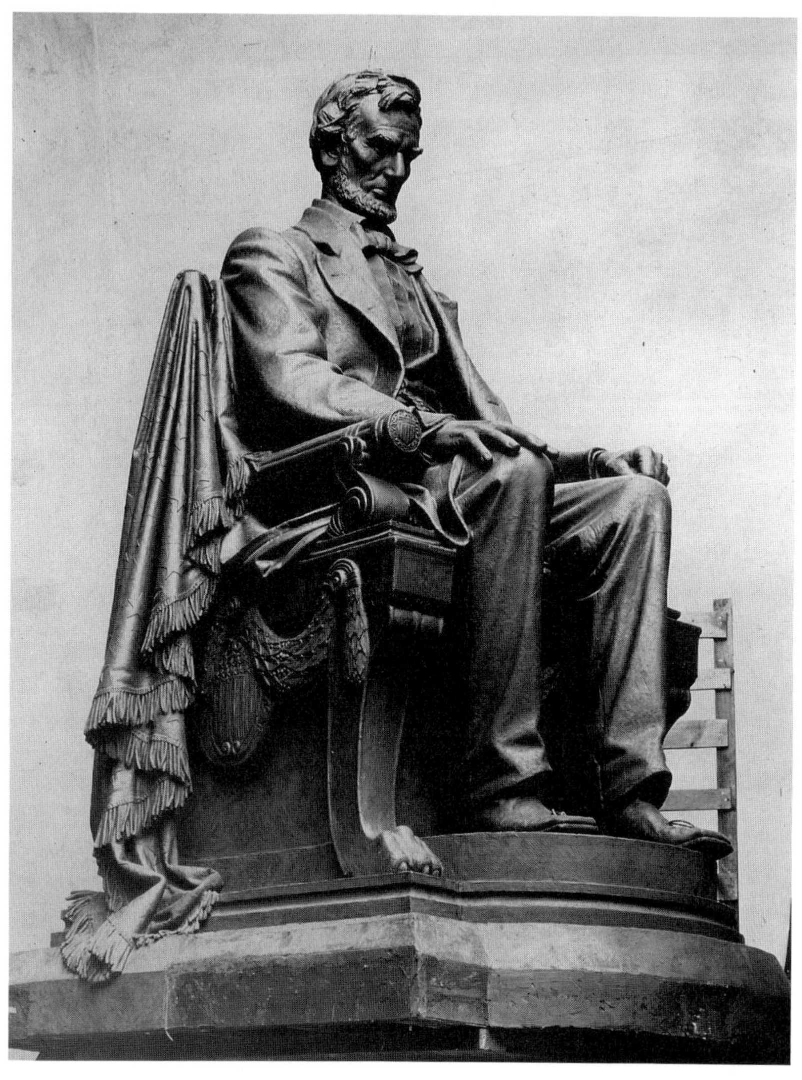

splitters were extremely rare, college president William G. Frost nevertheless forwarded to the sculptor photographs of mountain families and a copy of a college quarterly wherein Lincoln's education was explored in the context of mountain culture.[7]

Charles Taft was himself increasingly drawn to the subject of Lincoln's Kentucky origins. In November 1911 he accompanied William to the presidential dedication of Adolph Weinman's standing Lincoln statue in the Kentucky state capitol at Frankfort. Afterwards the brothers inspected Lincoln's Hodgenville farm memorial, where a "magnificent granite structure of fine architecture," as Charles characterized it, was being constructed around the cabin in which Lincoln was reputedly born. Favoring Barnard with his reflections, the experienced rancher took keen interest in the harsh economic conditions which surrounded the Thomas Lincoln family, marveling that such a bleak environment could have produced a man of such great stature. The cabin's cramped enclosure was oppressive and Taft noted at once the poor quality of the soil. But these factors disproved a popular body of opinion that celebrated Thomas's initiative in moving West, for Taft viewed the migration as simply an act of survival. Little had changed in the Hodgenville area in the intervening years until the founding of the Lincoln Farm Memorial, an enterprise Charles financially supported.[8] Thus, as a result of the generosity of wealthy philanthropists like himself, the "large, raw boned people" of the region had more reason for hope: new, comfortable, homes were beginning to appear amid the cabins. Taft discreetly withheld from Barnard any comments on Weinman's much-heralded statues at Frankfort and Hodgenville (see pg. 79). But did he not consider these stately portraits also to be worthy symbols of Lincoln's social emergence?

By 1912, Barnard decided his statue would present an prepresidential "Lincoln of the People." Work would proceed from small quickly-modeled clay sketches to a four-foot, ten-inch, plaster image and finally, to a full-scale thirteen-foot, four-inch, plaster figure, from which negative molds would be produced. He commenced modeling with two immediate objectives in mind: to complete a separate full-sized head and, in small clay sketches, to decide upon

Lincoln [for] all future ages—as he appeared to the people of his time—to retain that familiar air which the caricaturists of his day seized so truly that the man of their sketches seemed more like the man himself." With the authority of one who had personally known Lincoln, Thompson recognized a virulent and majestic beauty in the man's homeliness. With obvious feeling, the writer recounted the almost miraculous fact that a "tall, gaunt, hard-handed, long laborious, gigantic backwoodsman" had risen through the business classes and into the nation's highest office despite strong opposition. Noting that among contemporary sculptors only Rodin had demonstrated that ugliness was superior to "tailor standards," Thompson implored, "Oh sculptors, give us back our rail-splitter!"[6]

This radical entreaty stimulated Barnard's interest in the particular physical effects rail splitting normally had upon the body. A likely source for this kind of information was Kentucky's Berea College, an institution dedicated to the "recovery" of the long-isolated Appalachian farmer. Confiding that rail-

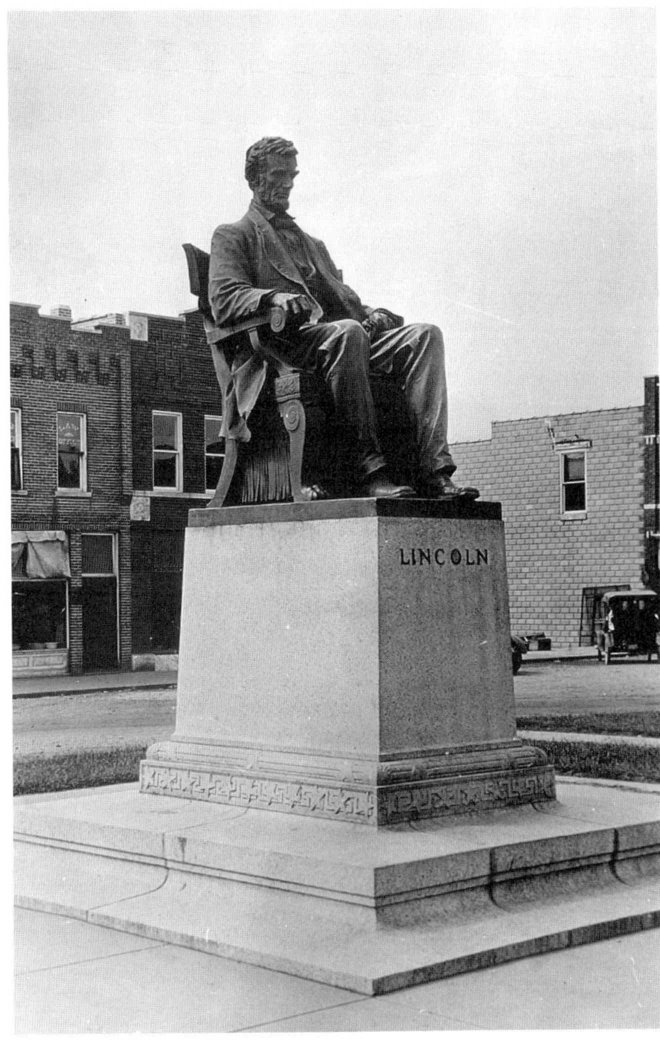

Adolph Weinman, Abraham Lincoln. 1909. Bronze, 8'. Hodgenville, Kentucky. Photographic Archives, the University of Louisville, Louisville, Kentucky.

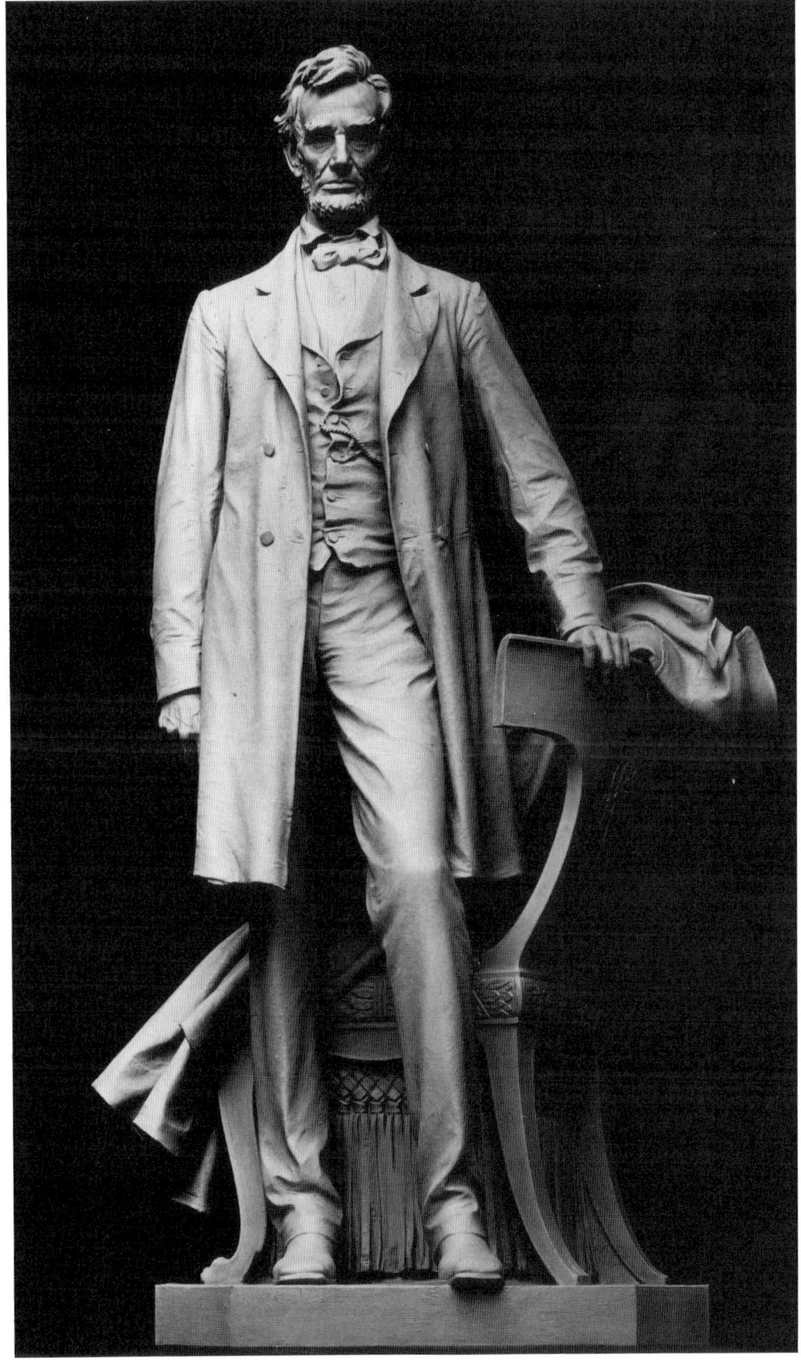

Adolph Weinman, Abraham Lincoln. 1911. Bronze, 12'. Kentucky State Capitol, Frankfort. Photo courtesy of the Library of Congress.

a satisfactory pose. Although he studied early photographs of the beardless Lincoln, such as Alexander Hesler's 1860 prints, he complained that too many photographic portraits had been spoiled by the "photographer's art." The Volk mask, on the other hand, far excelled all available visual models.

A large quantity of clay sketches were made, "several hundred" by Harold Dickson's account, to which Barnard selectively added sparing details. In a manner similar to that of Rodin, he inspected these small figures through squinted eyes in order to detect the light rhythms, or, "light vibrations," they emitted—a method he also followed while creating *The Two*

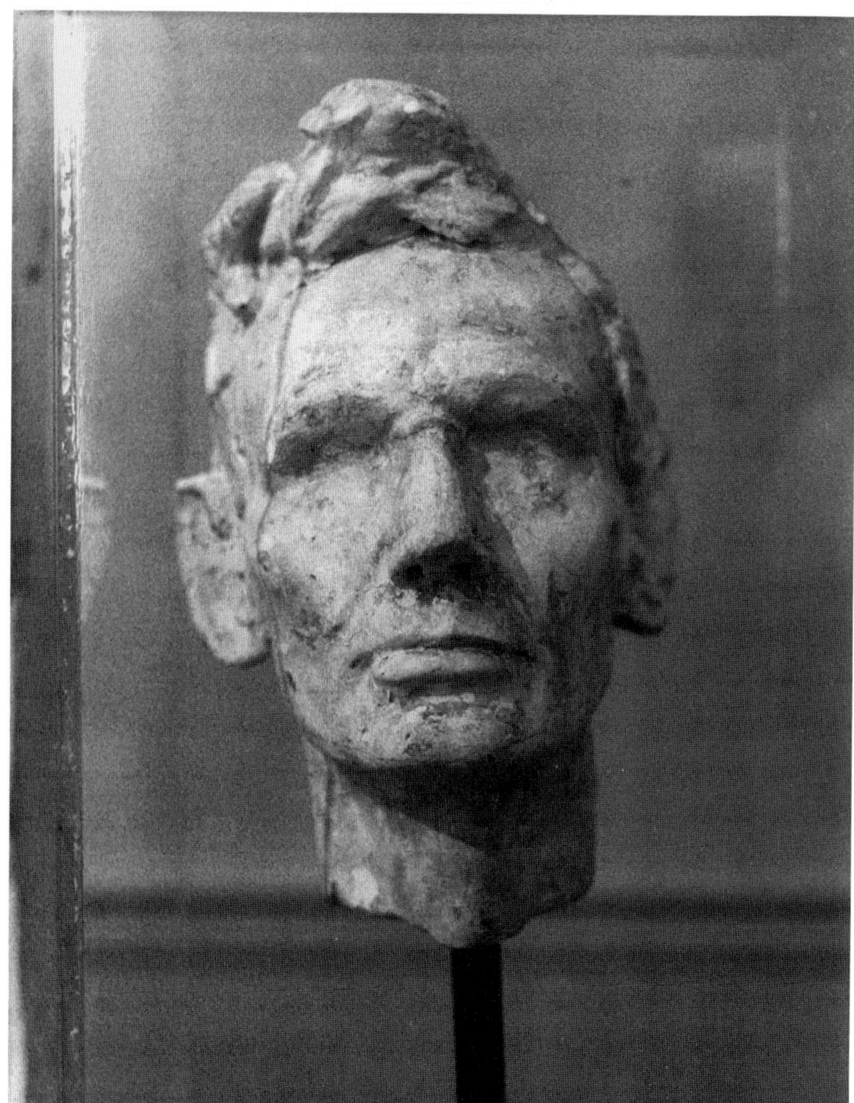

George G. Barnard, Abraham Lincoln *(preliminary head for standing statue). Ca. 1912. Plaster, 8½". Courtesy of the Kankakee County Historical Society.*

Natures of Man. While thus engaged, Barnard reverted to the ascetic habits of his Chicago and Paris days. Like an actor preparing for a leading role, he attempted to psychologically bond with the "real" Lincoln by mimicking his language and manner: Expansive commentary in family correspondence reflects moments of creative frenzy. Barnard wrote, "I can not wait to wash face, hands and especially shave in the mornings, I am so impatient to get to the studio. Each day it's the same passionate tempest of concentration from 9 A.M. to 6 P.M., only eight or 10 minutes for eating my sandwiches." He at one point observed that the head had "more great art in it than anything I have done." After four months of labor a full-sized head was entirely finished and by April 1912, the composition was "ready to go." These ti-

dings signaled the lawyers he was ready for another payment. Thus summoned, Walbridge released ten thousand dollars.[9]

At this point, Barnard estimated the bronze would be finished by October 1913, that it would reach a height of fourteen feet, and would be supported by a pedestal of four to five feet. Like Bartlett's ideal statue, it would stand alone in a park opposite the Taft homestead like a votive image in an open-air sanctuary. Barnard was thus disappointed to learn that a bandstand was to occupy the "same plot of ground which should be sacred to Lincoln's presence." A tawdry symbol of popular entertainment would not only infringe upon the sanctity of the statue and the man it depicted, it would also mock the artist's worshipful labor. He informed a Cincinnati Park commissioner that "[his] entire life and art (regardless of orders) is being given to call back to life this beloved man." It was enough to expect city officials to honor his sacrifice by saving the site. Respectful of their community's enthusiasm for music festivals, the Tafts stood firm, though they reassured Barnard the platform would be located at a respectful distance from the statue.[10]

The bouts of physical illness and emotional turmoil that were to continuously disrupt the project began in mid-1912. Between 25 April 1912, when Charles Taft's total commitment stood at twenty thousand dollars and 31 January 1914, no further payments were approved. In April 1912, Barnard reported he had taken ill and during the following winter was hospitalized after a fall in the studio. The latter incident occurred just prior to the opening of the International Exhibition of Modern Art, or "The Armory Show," which convened in New York in February 1913, an exhibition to which he sent *The Prodigal Son* (1904), a separate marble group he developed from the Harrisburg statues.[11]

His recovery was well underway by February 1913, but he did not immediately resume work. Instead he was busy challenging Daniel French for a Federal commission to sculpt the *National Indian Memorial* at Fort Wadsworth, in New York Harbor, and was preparing to escort Alfred Clark's sons, Stephen and Sterling, on a high-rolling shopping tour of European art and antique centers. This excursion would also permit him to further his dealings in medieval antiquities and ready a last section of St. Michel de Cuxa at Prades for shipment to New York. With this bit of unfinished business out of the way, the sculptor returned to New York on 30 May 1913, prepared to locate a suitable living model for his great statue.[12]

The canvass would entail considerable effort, since Barnard not only required an individual whose proportions accorded with Lincoln's, but also a man whose character and social background were closely similar. A national screening was announced in an advertisement that read: "Wanted—A man of the Abraham Lincoln type, facial resemblance not desired, giant in stature, six feet three inches or more, big-boned, sinewy, age 40 to 50 years, to pose for Lincoln statue at $10 per day. Several month's work."[13] Barnard began concentrating on applicants who lived in the western Kentucky farming district of Lincoln's youth. In this more concentrated search he was to be assisted by Rev. Barnard.

Solid French precedent existed for the concept that the living model used for an historic portrait should be drawn from the same social class, racial back-ground, and region that had originally produced the subject. Barnard would have known of the positivist teachings of Hippolyte Taine at the École that stressed the importance of the social and geographic environment in the formation of an individual's character. In accordance with this theory, Rodin searched for a living Balzac in that author's homeland of Tours, and while there, foraged for relics that related to his subject, even going to the extreme of ordering a suit from Balzac's personal tailor. But following Lincoln's assassination, no sculptor had ventured West to find a model or articles of clothing. Saint-Gaudens, who also had ample opportunity to sample Taine's thoughts, was determined to portray Lincoln as a classically-proportioned New England Puritan. Despite Bartlett's close study, he, too, preferred to believe the Northeast, rather than the rough Western frontier, was Lincoln's natural habitat. The insurgent John Gutzon Borglum perhaps came the closest to refuting the New England bias, but he found the mountainous terrain of Volk's plaster life mask to be a more than sufficient reference for his own work on Lincoln's physiognomy.[14]

It fell to a new generation of "living sketch" biographers to amend the popular view of Lincoln's pre-presidential existence. In 1895 Ida Tarbell, an old friend of the Monroes, MacKayes, and, thereafter, Barnard, registered at a Louisville, Kentucky, hotel as she prepared to reconstruct a history of Lincoln's early life, a study that was to be serialized in *McClure's* magazine and published in book form in 1896.[15] Availing herself of the newly perfected devices of photojournalism, Tarbell enlivened her biography with copious illustrations, both archival portraits and present-day views of structures where her subject resided or worked, of objects he or family members made or used—Thomas Lincoln's Holy Bible was a conspicuous inclusion—of pathways and streams along which young Lincoln once traveled. Her text ran beside facsimiles of Lincoln's school calculations and miscellaneous records, as if to prove his life began like that of many other youths. Ultimately Tarbell added little to the Hay-Nicolay compendium— she bitterly complained that Hay and Robert Lincoln withheld unpublished source material—but the most significant achievement of her biography was that it persuasively set forth a mental picture of the social and material environment that had molded the now legendary hero.

Following in Tarbell's as well as Lincoln's footsteps, Barnard traveled to Louisville in mid-June 1913. There he resided at the Seelbach Hotel, awaiting responses to an advertisement purchased in the *Louisville Courier-Journal*. Charles Abraham Thomas, a forty-four-year-old employee of the Illinois Central Railroad Company who was formerly from St. John, close by Hodgenville, answered the advertisement on 15 June and, directly following an interview with Barnard three days later, was selected to be the Lincoln model. Barnard's first choice, a man with fine tendons and hands, a flat chest, strong back muscles at the shoulders, thin legs and hips, an individual who "stands straight but at ease more like [a] Lincoln stoop," was for unexplained reasons passed over.[16]

Until shortly before the hiring, Thomas had been a farmer, an avocation that displeased him, and, according to Barnard, had once lived in a log cabin and had split rails. Even though it was now a moot point, since the head had been completed, Barnard approvingly noted that Thomas was clean-shaven. Years at the plow quite possibly had caused a pronounced curviture of Thomas's upper back, as well as a forward tilt of his neck. By Barnard's estimate these deformities were his greatest assets, placing him well above the typical European who posed for allegorical statuary. The sculptor commented, "I have seen the models of Europe—men of Greece and Italy—symmetrical and beautiful in a classical way but nothing ever appealed to me like the form of this Kentuckian."[17] A decided advantage was also Thomas's unusual ability to hold himself motionless for extended periods.

Thomas was to pose nude and then clothed for both the small model and full-sized statue. Other than to "personate a great American statesman," he was assigned to locate an old suit of clothes that would fit his six-foot-four-inch frame and, for reasons that are unclear, to find a log cabin similar to the Lincoln birthplace. So ardently did he devote himself to these additional chores, Thomas was compelled to resign his railroad position and consequently would remain unemployed for another eight years. He arrived at Barnard's studio for an initial two week session in July 1913. A four-foot nude plaster figure was completed in mid-November and, a month later, a clothed duplicate stood ready.[18]

Its weight evenly distributed on both feet, the statuette stands stiffly erect with hands crossing the abdomen, with steeply sloping shoulders and with a head, under disheveled hair, facing directly forward. The frontal view betrays no sense of motion, but from the angles one can see that the pantlegs tilt slightly outward as they rise from the base to the hips. An illusion that the knees are flexed, and that the figure is thus preparing to hop forward, arises

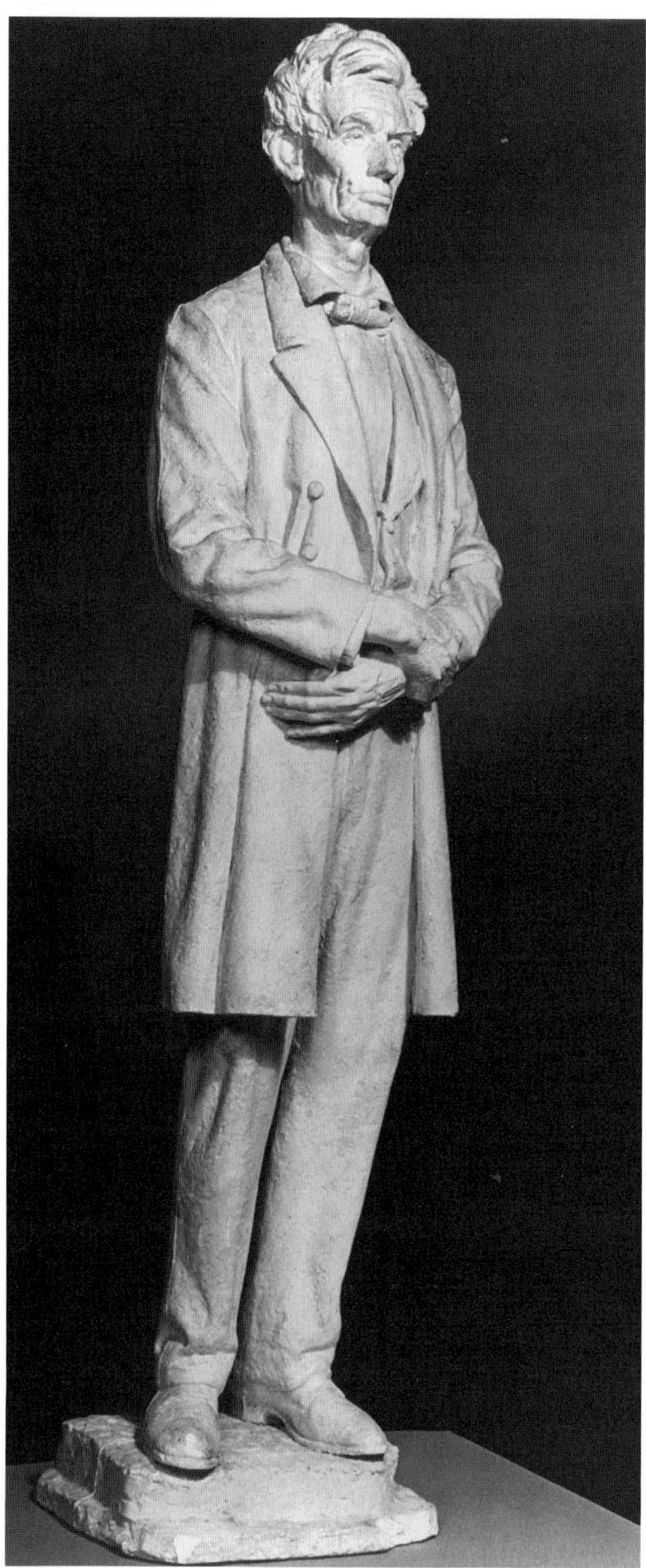

George G. Barnard, Abraham Lincoln. *1913. Plaster, 58". Courtesy of the Archives, Pennsylvania State University, University Park.*

from the fact that the coat hem flares outward at knee level and, from that point upward, partially obscures the position of the thighs. The immobility and nar-

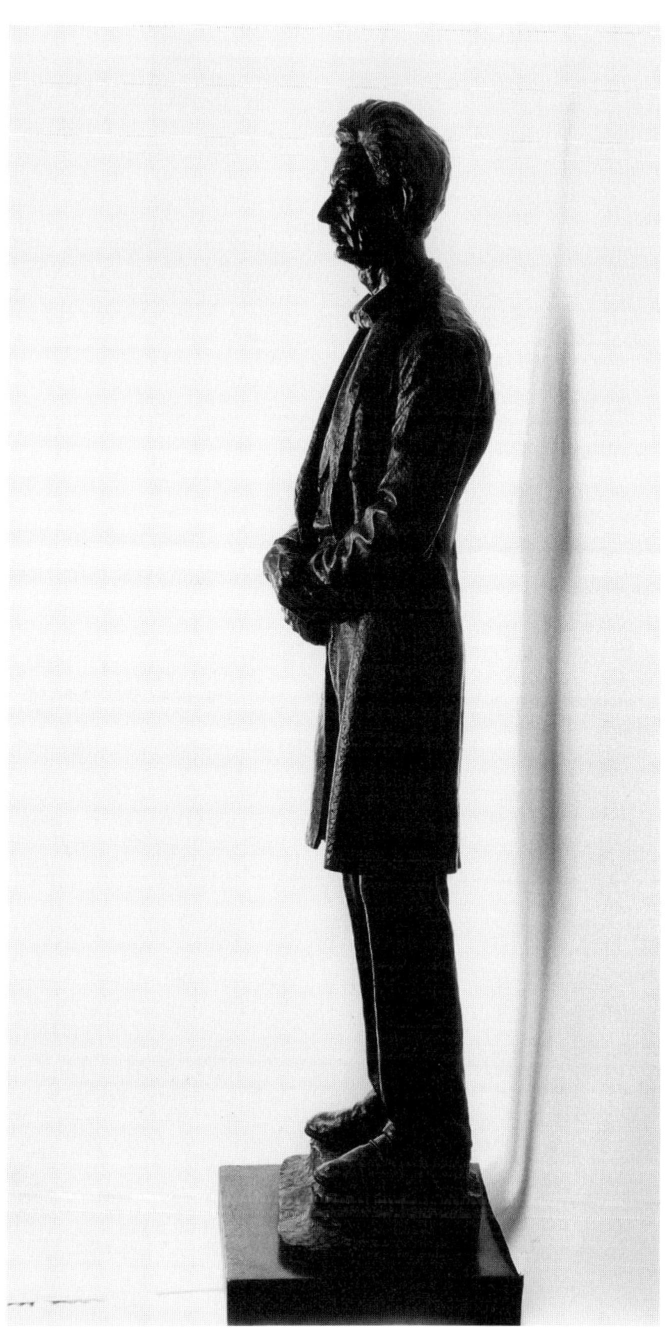

George G. Barnard, Abraham Lincoln (bronze version of fig. 51 cast ca. 1970) view of Barnard Lincoln.

Detail of Barnard Lincoln.

row shape recalls jamb figures on Gothic cathedrals. Only minor alterations—a lengthening of the coat, the marking of additional pleats, the downward tilting of the solidly-rooted boots—would have made the statue a fair match for the left-hand figures at the portal of Chartres Cathedral. The crossed arms more resemble the ubiquitous tomb figures Gothic artisans carved in relief on horizontal slabs, carvings with which Barnard was quite familiar. In this context, the stiffened and constrained body quite naturally suggests a corpse turned on end, specifically, the young Lincoln laid in an invisible coffin. A profile view exposes the swollen mound of the upper back, bringing to mind a far less exalted classification of

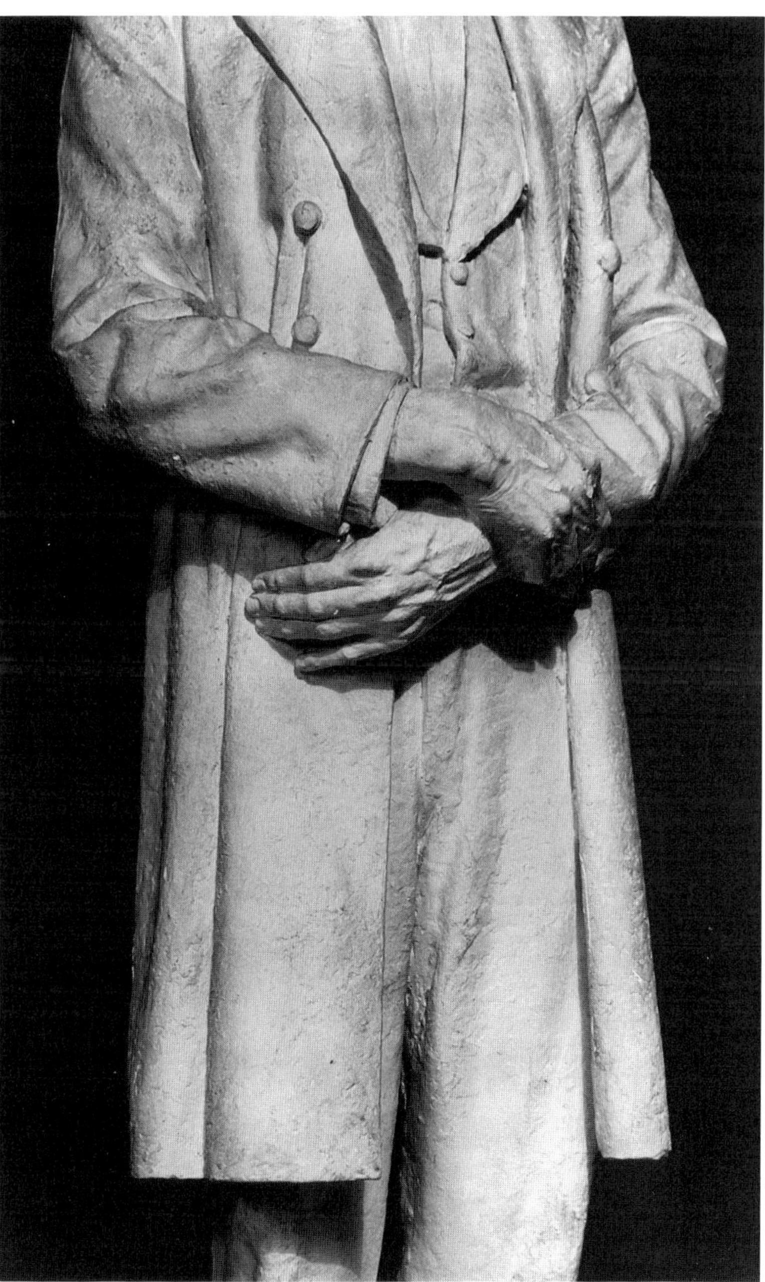

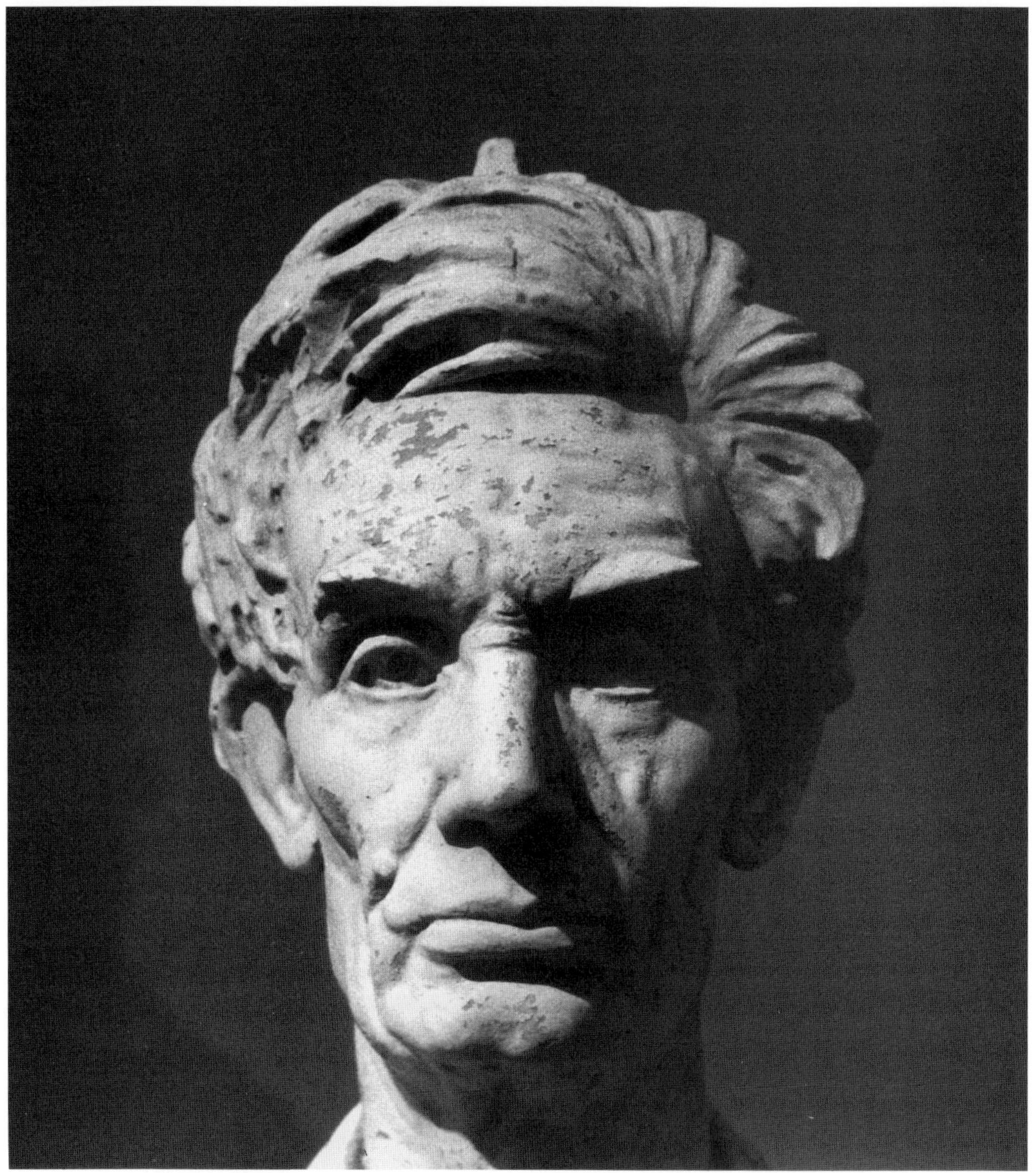

George G. Barnard, Abraham Lincoln, *(detail of model). 1913. Plaster, 10", (crown to Adam's apple). Courtesy of the Kankakee County Historical Society.*

cathedral sculpture: the hideously deformed stone creatures that populate the upper reaches. In a single change of perspective, Lincoln's saintliness is replaced by the savage specter of Quasimodo, Hugo's invented counterpart to the sculpted grotesqueries, the "misshapen ape" who "was savage because he was ugly."[19]

Volk's mask is confirmed in every aspect of the head. On the shaven contour of the face are met the familiar creases, moles, the dry leathery stretch of skin across bone, the uneven chin, the protruding lower lip, and massive ears that the cast makes evident. But only early life photographs could convey crucial information about the neck. With these im-

ages and perhaps reproductions of Donatello's late statues of emaciated saints at hand, Barnard emphasized the knotted thyroid cartilage, and the taut tendons that encircle it. As did Volk himself, when he made his first sculpted busts of Lincoln, Barnard departed from the mask when he designed the steep arching brows that under sunlight would cast their heavy shadows across the eye sockets. At the same time, by manipulating a modeling tool as he might a brush, Barnard virtually "painted in" the highlights of the eyes, by suspending small clay corbels just before the indented tunnels of the irises. Similar coloristic accents were applied to the tumultuous spray of hair and, in anticipation of a lively incandescence on

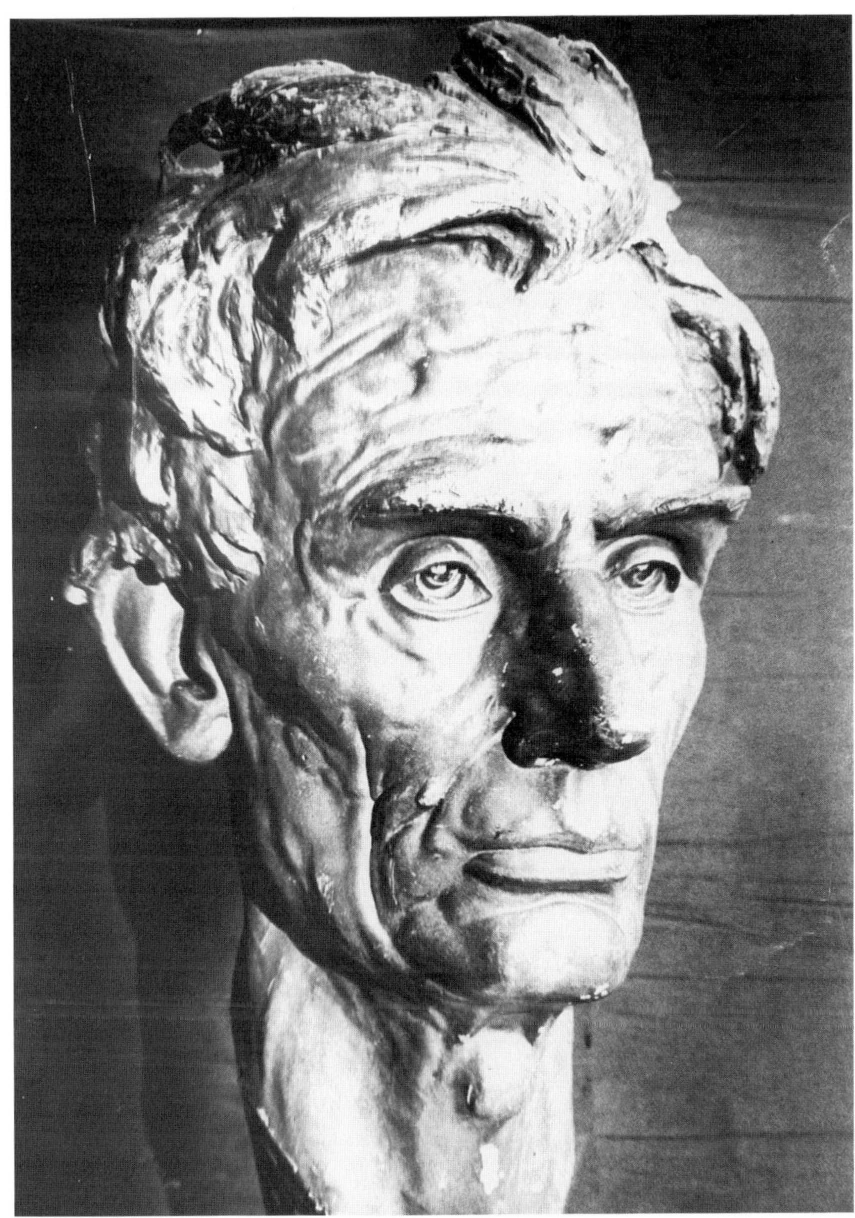

George G. Barnard, Abraham Lincoln. 1916. Bronzed plaster, 33" inclusive. Courtesy of the Kankakee County Historical Society.

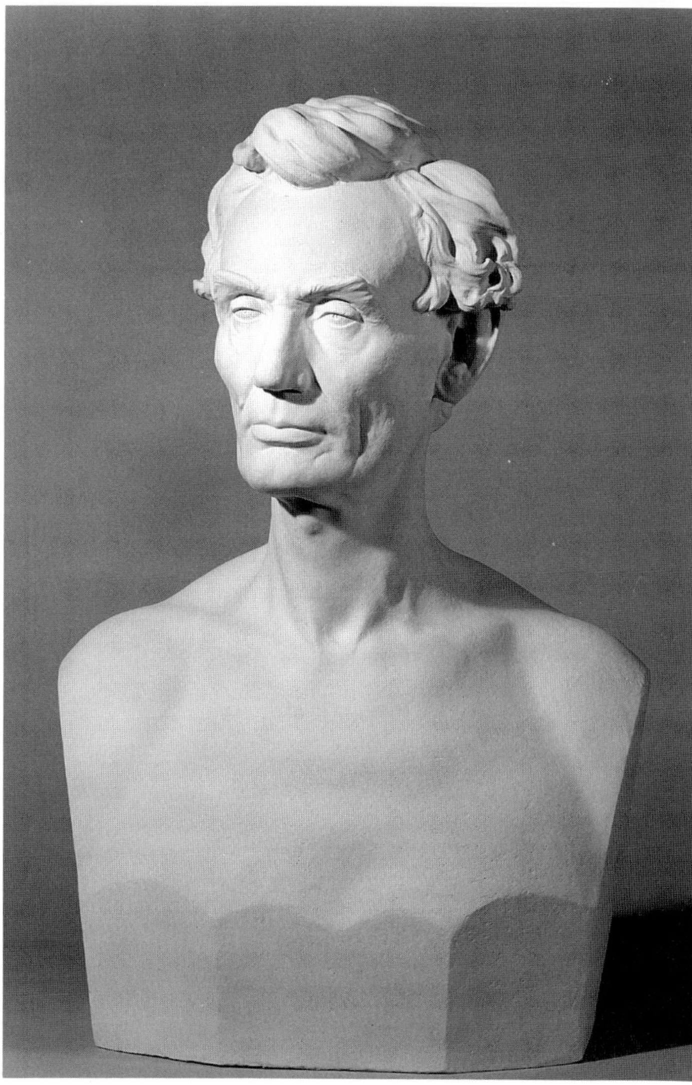

Leonard Volk, Abraham Lincoln. *1860. Plaster, 26".*
National Portrait Gallery, Smithsonian Institution.

the bronze surface, the sculptor added a rough texture, and irregularly waving currents to the surfaces of the clothing.

If like Borglum and most other Lincoln portraitists Barnard was generally respectful of the Volk mask when modeling the small Lincoln head, he also managed to instill in it the look of an unusually abject individual. Here is registered no brooding sadness or heroic resolve, not even impatience and frustration, but, we might be tempted to conclude, the bleak psychological response of one who has been deeply wounded. This could be confirmed in the way the muscles of the upper lip pull downward, and by the angry knit of the brow; there is no whisper of the smile Borglum discovered about the left corner of the lip, nor the stolid glower of the Weinmans, or any trace of the warming glance many post-Saint-Gaudensian Lincolns train on their viewers. As one

considers the staring eyes and the stiffly fixed position of the head, one perceives the subject of the statue is perhaps unconscious, that he dreams rather than thinks.

This interpretation leads us to the doorstep of Freudian-derived aesthetics, a topic widely supported in postmodernist theory. Barnard provided no evidence that he was a textbook follower of Freud, but given his fervent interest in spiritual and psychological speculation, it is reasonable to assume he had at least a superficial understanding of *The Interpretation of Dreams* (1900), and of the theory of the unconscious. When restudied within a Freudian context, the face, the hand gestures, the physical deformities, and the formal displacements that result from a contradictory relationship of parts—the large head juxtaposed with the small torso—remarkably confirm opposing positions in Freud's theory, the antiformalist energetics of "desire" in "Dream Work" and the formal unity and rules that reside with conscious thought.[20] The positioning of the out-of-scale hands, for example, suggest they belong to an altogether different statue. In another circumstance they might have satisfied a particular narrative and convincingly blended with a more massive organic structure, but in this instance they challenge the logic of Lincoln. As if reacting to a spasmodic attack, the powerful right hand seizes the left wrist in a vicelike grip. The opened left hand, by contrast, turns protectively inward, its long, finely wrought, fingers gently touching the contour of the abdomen beneath the coat. This particular action contributes significantly to the asymmetrical hang of the frock, for the pressure of the gripping hand pushes the left border of the garment against the hip, while the right hem hangs freely over the right knee. Saint-Gaudens's standing Lincoln controls the fall of its coat by thoughtfully clutching his lapel (see p. 27).

The hand gesture signals an urgent biological impulse, a reflex such as one might experience while falling asleep, or when suddenly striken, but it contributes nothing to the viewer's understanding of Lincoln's statesmanship or unique personality. Fin-de-siècle paintings occasionally employed similar gestures to connote impoverishment or social isolation, but rarely is it encountered as a sculptural motif. Rodin chose a comparable hand position, albeit reversed, for a nude study of the *Monument to Balzac*. When eventually seen as a protrusion beneath the author's gown in the completed work, this feature suggested to one observer the gesture of masturbation.[21]

Under the compulsion of desire, the neo-Freudian acknowledges, the artist substitutes references to his

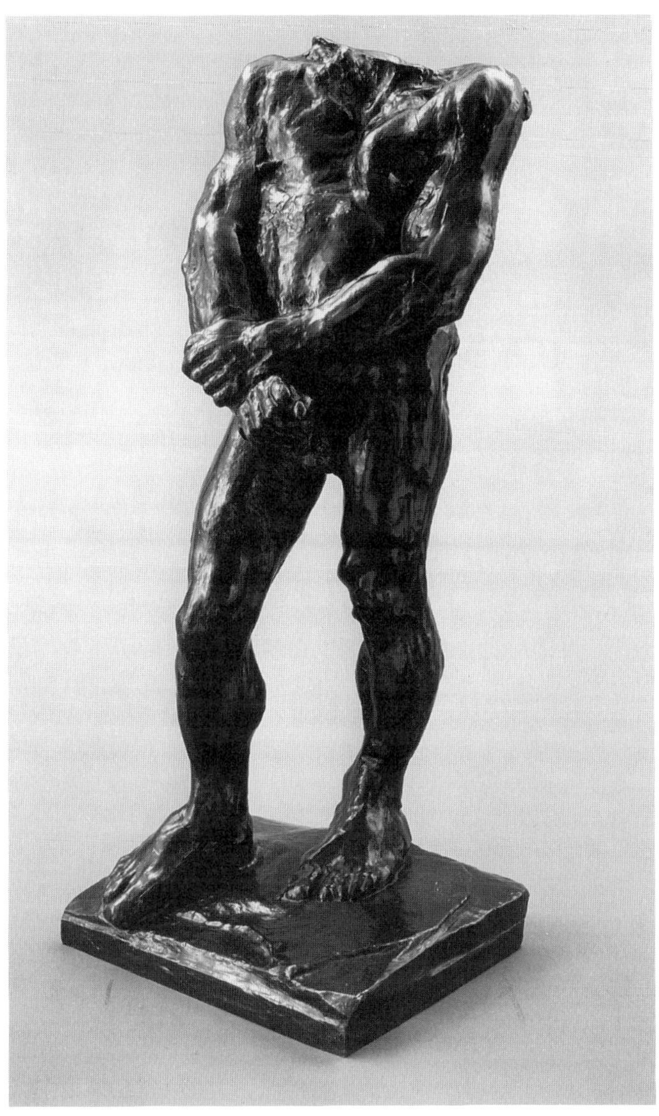

Auguste Rodin, Headless Naked Figure Study for Balzac. *1896–97. Bronze, 39″. The Museum of Modern Art, New York, gift of the Cantor, Fitzgerald Collection. Photo (c) 1998, The Museum of Modern Art.*

own body for those that in the conscious realm belong with the body of an objectively studied subject. As products of Barnard's dream work, the heavily-veined hands could not fail to remind him of his own hands, which after years of modeling and chiseling were afflicted with arthritis. The growthlike mound of the upper back invited additional comparisons with his own massively proportioned shoulders and bulging biceps. While in the process of forming these features in clay, Barnard both "labored" and created; the act of making became that specific activity through which his own body became the "corporate host" for the bodies of a common laborer and a mighty statesman.

The choice of clothing and the way it would fit the body may never have entirely satisfied him. The artist hinted at Carlyle's sartorial concepts when he observed "the whole statue must be face," that, in other words, the creases and lines of the outer garment, like those that line the face, should properly express the character and soul of the subject. When he finished the clothed one-third scale model at the end of 1913, Barnard contemplated making later alterations as he and Thomas continued to look for suitable clothing. However, for reasons to be addressed momentarily, no appreciable changes in either pose or clothing were made before the final casting. Thomas continually complained that the single-breasted "Lincoln" broadcloths he obtained in the Louisville area were excessively small or short when he tried them on. He obviously held the same opinion of the Kentucky colonel's wedding suit that local tradition insists Barnard finally chose for the small model.[22]

In company with William Taft, Charles and Anna viewed the the small plaster model shortly before Christmas of 1913 and gave Barnard clearance to proceed. In the following month an additional five thousand dollars went into the sculptor's account. Shortly thereafter, in February 1914, Barnard met once again with his patrons to review the modified contract, but no significant changes were made. The Tafts concluded Barnard's desire for money would hereafter overbalance his errant tendencies. Payments still remained fifteen thousand dollars short of the critical fifty-thousand-dollar barrier that signified unqualified approval of the fourteen-foot-high plaster model, and, as the patrons hoped, Barnard pressed ahead during the spring of 1914. Thomas was recalled from Kentucky in May for work on the full-size nude model, and Walbridge and Charles Taft were invited to inspect this plaster before Barnard applied its final dressing in August.[23] In anticipation, Barnard hired workmen to remove scaffolding and kept Thomas and the "wedding suit" at the ready.

But now it was Charles Taft's turn to delay. Without explanation, neither he nor Walbridge appeared at the studio. From Barnard's perspective this discourtesy was somehow linked to the lagging payment schedule; even though another five thousand dollars was immediately consigned to his account, the total paid him remained ten thousand dollars short of the fifty percent threshold. On 22 July, Barnard's attorney sent Charles an informal complaint that argued the artist's personal hardships took precedence over the terms of the contract.[24] Atty. Alex O. Jones assured Taft of Barnard's sense of mission; because of this dedication he had delayed other commissions from esteemed patrons like Alfred and Stephen Clark and, because of economic hardship, was on the verge of selling one-hundred-thousand-dollars worth of antiques he would have preferred to donate to the city of New York. These circumstances, then, had momentarily forced an otherwise solvent man into financial hardship and were entirely the fault of Charles Taft.

From the family compound at Murray Bay, Canada, Taft informed Jones an attack of gout had forced his immediate, unannounced, departure from New York.[25] But he reaffirmed that whatever claims might be made in defense of artistic temperment, he intended to stay with the "ready-for-casting" stipulations of the modified contract before releasing more funds. But having made his point, Taft agreed to bring the balance paid to within two thousand of the fifty-thousand-dollar level.

While this correspondence was being exchanged, Barnard had reached a final crossroads. For a sculptor whose goal was to produce an over-life-sized figure, the first small working model was an important indication but not the deciding factor in determining its final appearance. From the Renaissance onward, the sculptor of bronze statuary realized that when the scale of the first model was enlarged, the proportions, pose, even sometimes the configuration of clothing, had to be restudied for the final model, if the desired visual effect was to be retained. Barnard had indeed begun the full-scale nude in Thomas's presence, but the latest delays and financial withholdings prompted the sculptor to forego a restudy of the costumed figure. Instead, utilizing the pointing method, he indiscriminately transferred the configurations of the coat, pants, and shoes from the small plaster "onto the [large clay nude] figure as it stood."[26] While he admitting this maneuver violated the usual practice of a conscientious artist, he complained that the overly rigorous governance of the contract had left him no choice.

The next work stoppage occurred in November 1914, ostensibly as Barnard's reaction to the outbreak of war began to take hold. He was especially dismayed by Germany's attack on Belgium, the home of the renowned sculptor of social themes, Constantin Meunier. At the same time, he rushed to complete "The Cloisters," a brick structure resembling a monastery adjoining his home and studio in which his collection of medieval art was to be displayed in a period setting. He advanced its opening date to 14 December 1914 so that entrance fees might be immediately distributed to French artists who were afflicted by the war. Even so, there was no slackening in Barnard's work on sculpture projects other than

the Taft commission. In fact, the war seems to have stimulated his interest in a more unorthodox category of sculpture altogether.

At the beginning of the previous chapter I made reference to some of the Lincoln portraits the sculptor executed in his later career. In fact, since the very beginning of his work on the Taft Lincoln in 1912, the artist frequently took time out to produce Lincoln heads that significantly differed from the plaster head he intended for the bronze. Produced for speculative purposes, this grouping features life-sized marble studio busts of beardless Lincolns that bear smoothly chased surfaces, full, sensuous lips, macrocephalic heads, softly dressed coifs, and rubbly bases (see pp. 56–58). An early example of this series was eventually accepted by the French government for placement in the Versailles Museum.[27] Like the intended bronze head, the marbles also derived from preliminary plaster models, but in their production Barnard obviously intended to exploit the delicate refinement that high quality stone made available to him, in countradistinction to the rough expressiveness the lost-wax-to-bronze process so amply encouraged for his rustic statue. As we shall see, a plaster head that was the model for a large marble bust that is now in the Kankakee Illinois County Historical Society collection, was to have no small role to play in the upcoming controversy (see p. 58).

But there was to be an even more notable diversion than the marble series. In 1915 he commenced a fifteen-foot-high colossal plaster bust of a beardless Lincoln with closed eyes and cropped hair. Entitled *Lincoln in Thought,* or *Lincoln's Thought,* the colossus made boldly visible the "wonders of [Lincoln's] physiognomy" to the widest possible audience. More specifically, it expressed Barnard's stunned incredulity over America's passivity in the face of German aggression, a subject to be considered in a future chapter. For several years, *Lincoln in Thought* was the central feature of a continuous studio exhibition that adjoined the Cloisters. Barnard circulated photographs of himself triumphantly attending the head. In one remarkable example, a photograph of about 1916, he, like the biblical Jacob, mounts a ladder in order to administer finishing touches to the head's "Eventuality zone," while below, Ida Tarbell, arrayed in furs, looks up in wonderment.[28]

The manner in which this curious work advances hysterical and obsessive manifestations of megalomania could lead us far afield. However, several additional observations are in order. Charles Blanc once said of the artist who would attempt a colossus: "he is brought face to face with struggles which few art-

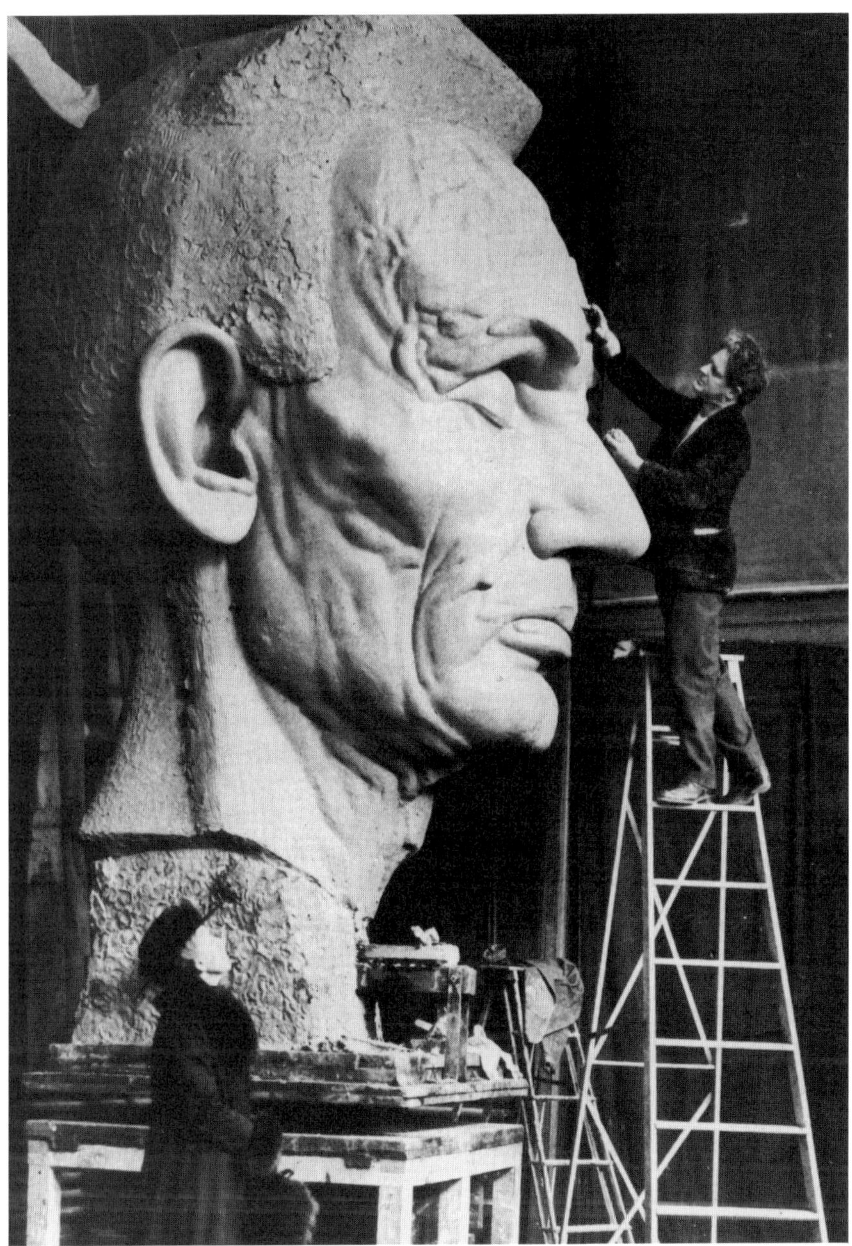

George G. Barnard and Ida Tarbell with Lincoln in
Thought, *ca., 1916. Photo courtesy of the Archives,
Pennsylvania State University.*

ists have experienced . . . that no one can advise him,
nothing can guide him except his instinct, faith and
courage. . ."[29] While over-large statues had been
common fare since the Renaissance and America was
to receive from France *The Statue of Liberty,* the
largest existing figurative statue in the world, Launt
Thompson, Thomas Ball, and John Gutzon Borglum
sustained a new American taste for oversized portrait
busts (see p. 29). Borglum pushed this trend as far
as it would go in his Mount Rushmore presidential
group of the 1930s. Yet, at approximately two- and
three-times life size, respectively, Borglum's first

Lincoln head and Barnard's later beardless Lincoln
marble bust, did not convey that special psychological thrill which monstrous scale otherwise lends to
familiar images. The swollen veins, astringent
creases, and trancelike immobility of Barnard's giant
head was clearly meant not just to impress, but aston-
ish, particularly when studied alongside smaller religious works in the Cloisters collection.

At least one visitor to the Cloisters and the studio
questioned whether the unsettling effect of the head
was appropriate to the theme of contemplation.
George Bissell, who had produced a Lincoln statue

for Edinburgh, Scotland, in 1892 and a related bronze bust that exists in a number of casts, cautioned his old Paris colleague not to stray from the physical evidence provided by the Volk mask.[30] Steeped in Truman Bartlett's physiognomical inquiries, Bissell expounded upon the similarities that existed between the Volk impression and the facial appearances of other American statesmen, most notably Washington. While in Bissell's view Barnard had correctly interpreted the facial mask, the bulging forehead and narrow jaw otherwise falsely conveyed qualities of "an erratic genius," not the exceedingly practical and level-headed man Bissell portrayed in his own sculpture.

In mid-1915, after a hiatus of eight months, Barnard regained his composure. Charles and Anna inspected the full-sized model in July while enroute to Murray Bay. What they saw was the plaster with clothes intact, and the colossal Lincoln head. That much of the Tafts' inspection was carried out in silence led Barnard to believe they were critical. Anna reassurred him they were "deeply impressed," reminding him that art patrons, like artists, sometimes tended to be hypercritical of objects they helped to inspire, just as Lincoln himself was critical of the Gettysburg Address.[31] The implication that they indeed did have reservations did not help to immediately clear the air. But, by early November, all had been forgiven.

In an effort to generate a file of congratulatory comments, Barnard privately exhibited the plaster model in mid-November 1915. Among those attending were Theodore Roosevelt, Roosevelt's then-close friend; the ornithologist Frank M. Chapman; Columbia University philologist William Carpenter, a chief organizer of the Barnard rescue team; and Denver attorney L. Ward Bannister. The most remarkable of the resulting approbations was Bannister's. Couched in language that was remarkably free of soulful sentiment, his statement was the first of many to associate the bronze with the ethos of progressive democracy. Bannister perceived the image represented Lincoln at the time of the Douglas debates, correctly presenting him,

> stooped as to shoulders, wearing clothes more or less ill fitting and shoes of the coarse, heavy type then worn in the country districts. The hands, large and rough, are crossed in front, and the expression of the face especially the eyes is that of sadness and isolation. The very homeliness of the garb and posture accentuates this expression and makes Lincoln to be all the more in Art what he was in nature—the embodiment of a great but as

yet in many ways uncultivated democracy. If the American people fail to appreciate this statue it will be because they do not know themselves.[32]

Charles Taft took pleasure in this vindication of his and Anna's faith in Barnard's genius, yet he required a more official endorsement before releasing further funds.[33] Thus, he called upon two senior faculty members of the Cincinnati Art Academy to visit Barnard's studio in November for the purpose of filing a report. The team consisted of Frank Duveneck, dean of faculty, and senior sculptor instructor Clement J. Barnhorn. Barnhorn, whose early promise earned him a Cincinnati Museum Association scholarship to Paris in the 1890s, had lately confined himself to decorative ornament and ecclesiastical statuary. Even though Taft was soon to take a singular interest in Duveneck's paintings, this once famous mainstay of the Munich Royal Academy had also succumbed to the leveling influences of the academy. The Tafts could not have expected these aging local artists to report objectively on a statue, already four years in production, which had so far cost them fifty thousand dollars; however, the Barnhorn-Duveneck assessment would serve as an important civic reference should the real recipients of the statue, the people of Cincinnati, decide to question its aesthetic qualities.

On the surface, the summary was fully reassuring: the statue was "original and individual." It predicted some among its viewers would consider it "the greatest Lincoln that has ever been produced in this country." The authors agreed with this judgment and wished the work to be prominently displayed so that "its beauties and importance may be adequately discovered." In a more discretionary tone, however, the testimony warned that other observers, at least at first, would not like the statue. In conclusion, the respondents stood with an effusive greeting Chapman sent the Tafts: "I congratulate Mr. Taft in having been priviledged to give to his country so impressive a statue of its first citizen that its resting place would always be a mecca for every lover of liberty and freedom."[34] Still smarting from the rancor that surrounded the genesis of the commission, Taft also requested his team to evaluate Borglum's Newark Lincoln, and his Lincoln bust in the Capitol, as well as his Sheridan equestrian. The nature of their response is unknown, but one suspects it was in Barnard's favor.

The payments to Barnard resumed on 4 December 1915, with the first of several small increments which would boost the total contribution well past the fifty percent plateau. Separate negative plaster molds for the head, torso, and legs were finished on 17 March 1916, and liquid wax had been run into the head and torso molds the following month. Barnard contemplated retouching the wax head in early May. Walbridge Taft assisted him in drawing up a supplemental contract with the Roman Bronze Works, a document that gave the artist full financial and aesthetic control and set minimum standards for the quality of the cast, its material, and for the joining of the several sections.[35] The head, the trunk to the lower edge of the coat, and the legs, with shoes set into a thin plate, were to be joined as separate pieces. With the date for the casting set for early June, the Tafts anticipated an October 1916 unveiling.

Throughout 1916 Anna and Charles Taft urged their sculptor forward. But while in the past Anna was the peacemaker, Charles now posed as Barnard's advocate. He regularly reported on his wife's impatience and of his own desire to satisfy her, but also confided his personal concern was for an aesthetic perfection that could not be measured by time. This perfection was one that only Barnard could evaluate and acclaim. The next funding plateau arrived on 3 August 1916, when the Taft contribution stood at just under three-quarters of the full amount. At this point, another work suspension occurred that was to delay the unveiling for an additional three months. Belatedly, Barnard blamed the foundry for being overly cautious during the casting procedure, but illness, this time Edna Barnard's, was also a contributing factor. Edna's recuperation obliged the Barnards to spend the summer at the Monroe's estate in Dublin. Here, in a barn close by the home of his painter friend Abbott H. Thayer, Barnard took advantage of this unplanned respite by completing the marble *Rising Woman,* which was to join his *The Hewer,* and the large relief *Adam and Eve,* before the garden entrance of "Kykuit," John D. Rockefeller Sr.'s Pocantico Hills mansion in North Tarrytown, New York.[36]

In September Barnard obtained from the Roman Bronze Works a tinted plaster cast of the Lincoln, which he placed on a variety of low pedestals in a lot adjoining the Fort Washington studio. This he carefully hid from public view. Now firm in his resolve to use a low uncut boulder rather than a tall architectural pedestal, he might have expected Charles Taft to have second thoughts. Charles had recently read with interest Homer Saint-Gaudens's biography of his father—a study Taft recommended to Barnard—and no doubt had formed strong opinions about the way in which the standing Lincoln related to Stanford White's expansive architectural

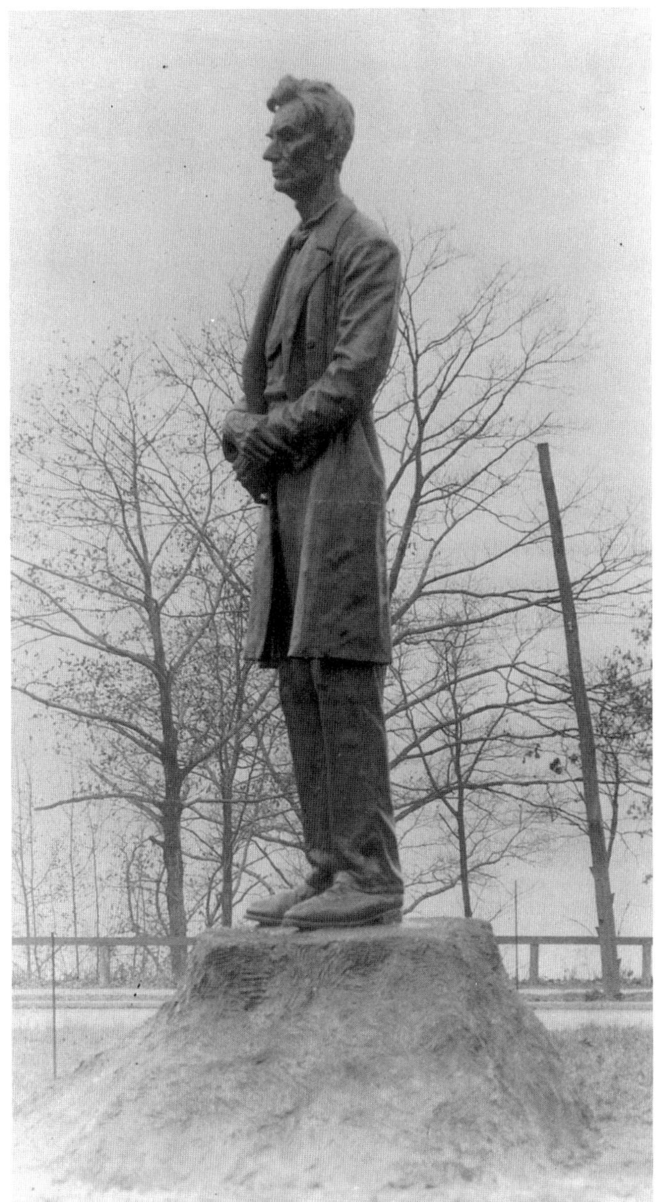

Plaster cast of Barnard's Abraham Lincoln *positioned near artist's studio, 1916. Photo courtesy the National Museum of American Art.*

ensemble. Barnard insisted that a low boulder naturally "goes with the great democrat and man of earth (and Heaven)" while "a polished base belittles (Lincoln's) personality . . . he is too great a Human to stand on a polished base."[37] The on-site inspections convinced him that light pink Vermont granite would most effectively set off the dark bronze. All but the three-foot summit of an eight-ton stone, which would be roughed into a step-like platform, was to be embedded in the earth. In late October, the bronze casts had been produced; all that remained to be accomplished was the assembly of parts, and last-minute adjustments to the patina.

At that moment, several of Barnard's New York friends began urging him to consider a temporary exhibit of the statue in the city, prior to its shipment to Ohio. Since the sculptor's property mortgage yet hung in the balance, he decided fringe expenses for the event should be drawn from the balance of the Lincoln account, and he thus beseeched his weary patrons to break yet another funding plateau for the sake of New York "artists and others who love Lincoln." But he quickly assured his sponsors he would instantly ship the figure if the exhibition did not materialize. While in principle Charles was not opposed to a one-week exhibit, he would under no circumstances consider advancing the requested four thousand dollars to finance it.[38]

After three weeks, an exhibition site had not been secured, and Barnard realized a highly favorable press notice remained his only chance for holding off the Tafts and saving the proposed exhibition. To this end, he invited Leigh M. Hodges, editor of the *Philadelphia North American,* to a private viewing at the Roman Bronze Works. Hodges's eulogistic appraisal, "A New Tradition in American Art," which appeared in his paper on 25 November, had its intended effect. Charles immediately released the requested funds, while also forwarding to Hodges his summary view of the commission's troubled history.

> We believed in Barnard and had a great fight to put this through. It resulted really through the effort of a lady in Cincinnati to award the making of a Lincoln statue to a personal friend of one of the commissioners and as there were four of us who believed in Barnard over this rival sculptor, Mrs. Taft and I thought we should carry out our wishes and give Mr. Barnard an opportunity of producing his Lincoln in bronze. It certainly is a masterpiece.[39]

The first, and most laudatory of published analyses, the editorial synthesized evangelism, political progressivism, and aestheticism in proclaiming Pennsylvania's native son the equal to the world's great painters, sculptors, and writers, while it christened the Lincoln America's new and decidedly more deserving "statue of liberty." It was Hodges's contention that by creating this single work, Barnard had assumed leadership of the nation's first legitimate school of art. "Stirred by a passion for democracy and a profound reverence for Lincoln as its prophet," the sculptor outgrew the ephemeral classicism that had previously enslaved his efforts. In reference to the statues of Borglum and Saint-Gaudens, Hodges was glad to note that no table, chair, or bench disturbed the solitude of Barnard's version. The feet

were like roots "spreading into the common soil;" not a single line had been omitted from the face, and the hands, bony and gnarled, conveyed a sense of tremendous power, of strength held in reserve. Here was symbolized an ideal balance of courage and religious submissiveness that should govern all human and national relationships. Thus, if the leaders of the American Republic seriously intended to honor their moral obligation to "stand and serve" humanity, here was to be found their most valuable lesson.

It was one thing to talk of the statue as a symbol of democracy, but quite another to explain what expectations a viewer was required to bring to such an exceptional statue. Hodges hoped to cover much of this ground in his choice of a new critical language, for conventional discourse limited itself to describing a material object, its pose, styling, and composition. Barnard's Lincoln, he argued, was not a statue at all. Quite to the contrary, it was a genius artist's revelation of a great soul, the transmission "of a sacred legacy through one soul to millions of souls."[40]

Evidence of the power of this transmission was to be found in the spontaneous testimony of witnesses attending the foundry exhibit. A most valued reference was Harrison W. Gourley, an original Lincoln appointee who still held his original post with the United States Customs service. Another was Theodore Roosevelt, who never failed to utter a memorable phrase when visiting an artist's studio. Gourley, whose boyhood experiences much resembled those of the Barnard family legend, had been lifted by Lincoln "higher than any other man in (Springfield) could lift him." While Gourley was at work in a telegraph office years later, Lincoln placed one great hand on his forehead, the very same hand he now observed at the foundry. Roosevelt could claim no personal benedictions, but nonetheless spoke with equal conviction: "'I always have wished I might have seen him—and now I do.'" If these men of vastly differing life experiences could have been similarly affected, Hodges intoned, it was only because Barnard's genius was capable of bringing Lincoln's soul before them.

When Barnard transcribed the remarks of visitors to the 25 November foundry exhibit, he naturally presumed Roosevelt's contribution would have the greatest impact. The first of several amended utterances reads:

> At last we have the Lincoln of the Lincoln-Douglas debates. How long we have been waiting for this Lincoln! I feared that with the passing of years it would never come; but here it is—the living Lincoln. Lincoln was never done with a beard, it hid

his character. But now after long waiting here he is, the true Lincoln. This statue is unique; I know of no other so full of life. The greatest sculptor of our age has revealed the greatest soul of our age. One is worthy of the other. (I commend Barnard with all my heart). He has given us Lincoln, the Lincoln we all know and love.[41]

Barnard's increasing tendency to compare the statue with its model—a common laborer—and associate it with the anarchosyndicalist mystique of the working class, his resentment at having to follow the "orders" and timetable set by wealthy patrons, and his purported resort to a "dream" state of consciousness during the statue's genesis, more than hint at the artist's radical nature. Yet Hodges's article and, more emphatically, Roosevelt's hyperbolic approbation, safely positioned Barnard's work and ultimate achievement within the bounds of progressive democracy and Christian redemption. Despite Charles Taft's eagerness to take credit for seeing the commission through, he was suspicious of Roosevelt's motivations for praising his statue. Nonetheless, his all-important recommendation rendered valuable service in reassuring everyone who might see the statue that Barnard had not strayed too far toward Bakuninism or Bolshevism. It was Roosevelt, after all, who three years earlier had characterized European modernists as the "lunatic fringe" of the New York Armory Show when he drew connections between abstraction and anarchism.[42] What better compliment could he now have paid the Tafts than to rank their artist not only ahead of Borglum but also "the greatest sculptor of our age"?

Part Three
Lincoln on Display

5

The Union Theological Seminary

Efforts to secure a temporary public exhibition of Barnard's statue in Manhattan were spearheaded by Mrs. Prescott A. Hoard, the former Minnie Margaret O'Laughlin, a sculptor, designer, and currently, supervisor of the New York City Public Lecture Bureau of the Board of Education. With the assistance of Atty. Charles E. Le Barbier, Hoard circulated a petition that emphasized the nonpolitical nature of their project.

> It is intended that this appeal, made to the public, through the public, shall do away with any political operation . . . since the story of Lincoln is given to the younger generation by writing, painting and sculpture . . . It is urged that Barnard's statue, expressing so wonderfully and truthfully Lincoln, a man of the people, be placed on view. It is not only the work of a genius, but the great spirit of Lincoln speaking through sculpture to the public, the people he loved.[1]

Laws forbidding temporary sculpture exhibitions on city property prompted Hoard and her volunteers to inspect likely locations at armories, at Madison Square Garden, along upper Riverside Drive, at Columbia Heights, and in Fort Washington Park. Barnard insisted his "Lincoln the Man" be erected close to a city street in full public view. After new appeals, Robert W. De Forest, chairman of the New York City Art Commission, and Cabot Ward, Commissioner of Public Parks of the City of New York, refused to bend the rules. Since armories were controlled by the military, Edwin Seligman urged Atty. Harry Taft to solicit Gov. Charles S. Whitman, but again to no avail. At last, the daughter of Robert

Ogden, who at his death presided over the Union Theological Seminary's board of trustees, succeeded in procuring the temporary use of seminary grounds, which adjoined Columbia University in upper Manhattan. Acknowledging Mrs. George W. Crary's kindness, Barnard observed, "it is very dear to think Lincoln will be shown first on the site planned originally through the efforts of Mr. Ogden."[2]

The Roman Bronze Works erected the statue in the seminary courtyard on 8 December, two days before the opening of an expected weeklong exhibit. However, the impending marriage of Walbridge Taft and William Taft's current speaking tour forced a delay of the Cincinnati unveiling date, thereby allowing an extension of the New York exhibition to 26 February 1917. During the ten weeks, some 9,000 people viewed the statue, with attendance reaching its peak on 18 February when 1,348 visitors were recorded. Even on Sundays, when the exhibition was not advertised, an average of eight hundred persons were counted, making it obvious to one observer the statue was drawing many away from Sunday services. To the seminary's administrative officer, the figures indicated that "either the people of the city and their tastes are developing along artistic lines, or else this must be a work of particular excellence."[3]

Framed by the entrance gate, a profile view of the figure, with a wooden platform before it, rose above a plaster base that imitated a rough-hewn boulder. The surrounding architecture was Tudor revival, a customary style for educational institutions, and from several positions the viewer glimpsed the figure beneath the prominence of Memorial Tower, which resembled the bastions of London's Houses of Parlia-

97

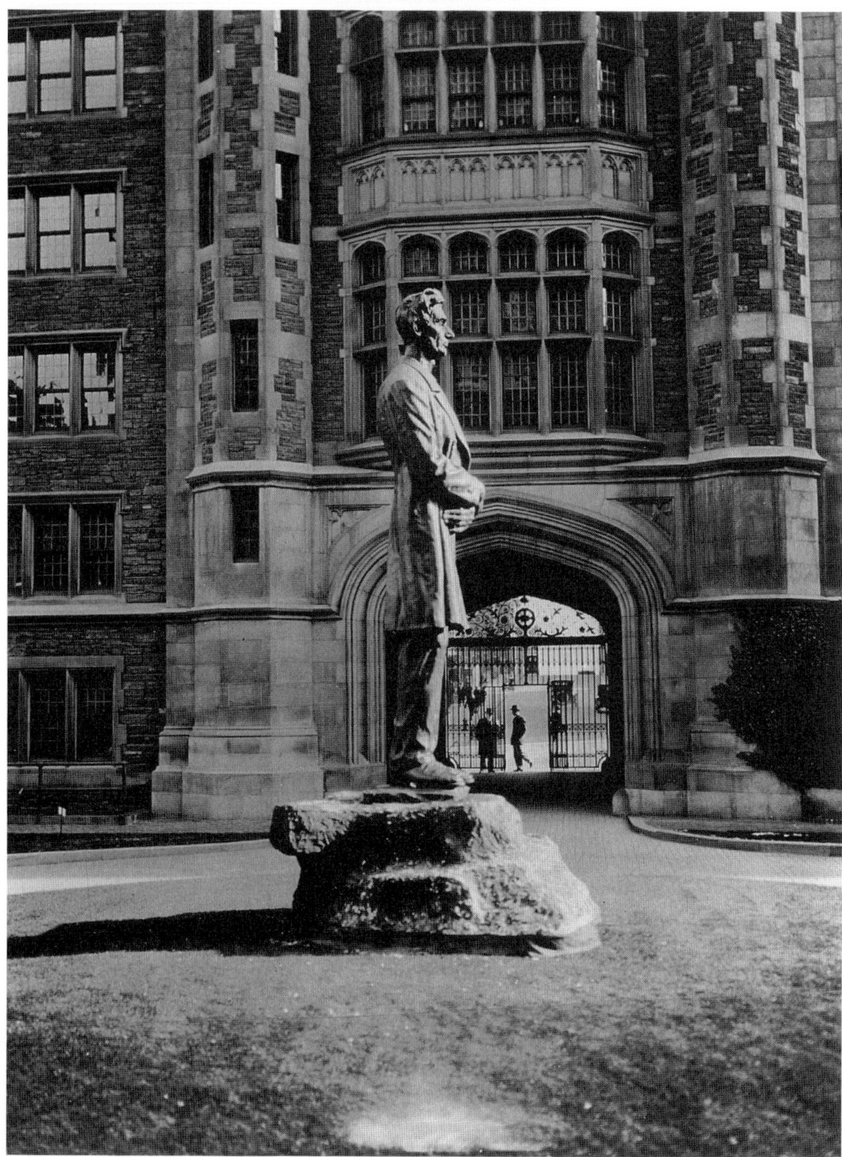

Barnard's Abraham Lincoln *(1st cast) at the Union Theological Seminary, New York City, 1916–17. Photo courtesy of the National Museum of American Art.*

ment. Although by Barnard's usual standards the overwhelming presence of English Gothic architecture left something to be desired, the court was nevertheless a "place of peace and quiet . . . where those who enter could abide with the spirit of Lincoln." He could also take satisfaction in the fact that this apparently tranquil bastion of Presbyterian teaching had recently been swept by theological controversy, just as the neighboring university had become the nation's educational storm center. In justification of Ogden's progressivism, a doctrinal struggle had been decided in favor of liberal reform.[4]

The opening on 12 December was preceded by a press preview on Sunday afternoon, 10 December. Snowy weather lingered through Monday, causing

the statue to be first seen as a looming umbrage under a white cap. Charles and Anna Taft briefly examined it on Monday then returned for a more leisurely inspection under cloudless skies the following day. Viewing it from varying angles, they appreciated its "wonderful power" and happily surmised that its presence before their home "will add to our pleasure and confirm our opinion you [Barnard] have made a new departure in portrait sculpture." Despite the inclement weather of opening day, the elderly Gourley dared to remove his hat. Roosevelt again arrived in the company of Chapman, whose interest had been intensified by the Hodges editorial. Others included Clyde H. Burroughs, who currently directed the Detroit Institute of Arts; Percy MacKaye; Percy Grant, rector of the Fifth Avenue Church of the Ascension; Charles Evans, pastor of New York's First Presbyterian Church; and John D. Rockefeller Jr, who underscored his appreciation by requesting a photograph of the bronze. Among professional artists known to have attended was illustrator Charles Dana Gibson, sculptors F. Edwin Elwell, Charles C. Rumsey, Ralph Goddard, and the Barnards' Dublin neighbor, Abbott Thayer. Personal invitations were sent to *New York Times* publisher Adolph Ochs, to the *New York Herald*'s George E. Pollock, to the *New York American*'s William Randolph Hearst, to the staff of the *New York Post* and *New York Sun,* and to periodical editors Lawrence and Lyman Abbott, Albert Shaw, George H. Putnam, Mary Fanton Roberts, and Frank Crane. Seligman and William Carpenter were sure to have been among the throng of Columbia University personnel, faculty, and students, that stopped by the courtyard.[5]

Ladened with the terms "soul" and "genius," mawkish tributes weighed emotional reactions. A woman wrote that "tears sprang to my eyes—whilst my heart leaped in gratitude to know there was one in our midst who could portray to posterity the soul of our martyred Lincoln." Aesthetician Ralcy H. Bell, who left Barnard a recent publication, most likely *The Philosophy of Painting,* confessed he was so "struck by [Barnard's] noble mastery, your spiritual insight, and your poetic powers," he promised to devote a future study to Barnard's genius. Thayer proclaimed the statue to be an "exquisite art miracle like a Beethoven andante . . . the very note it strikes in Being rather than Seeming." Others explored the way the statue related to its temporary surroundings. Designer Clarence Whybrow was heartened to see it "standing in [its] rugged impressiveness of mind and matter, and, in a calm, strong manner defying the elements, while [Lincoln's] face was just in the quiet repose of the white mantel covering given [it] by Mother Earth." Rumsey remarked on its resemblance to a Gothic tower. The fateful timing of the exhibition was also fully appreciated. Having produced his own fanciful interpretation of Abraham Lincoln for East Orange, New Jersey, in 1912, Elwell saw in Barnard's statue dramatic confirmation of the artistic freedom that could only flourish under an American democracy. Gibson's quoted observation noted that "it seems foreordained by history that at this supreme moment you should bring forth your great statue of Lincoln the Democrat."[6]

Sympathetic editors attempted to head off anticipated public ridicule. The *New York Sun*'s writer, no doubt Henry McBride, the distinguished advocate of Realism and modernist abstraction, boldly suggested

deformity, inelegance, even deliberate caricature could be defended as uniquely American components of sublimity and sacredness. When applied to Lincoln, such factors instructively indicated how little the great American's soul was circumscribed by external appearance. The term "caricature" could be justly applied, he advised, since effective caricature, more than a conventional likeness, was ernest to the point of "exaltation." By contrast, competing examples by Saint-Gaudens and Borglum leaned far too heavily upon story-telling motives. Nevertheless, the editorialist warned, there would be no saving the statue from a misguided public outcry. An instructive example of what was probably in store for it was Mark Twain's unfortunate dismissal of the morose boatman in Puvis de Chavannes's now canonical painting, *The Poor Fisherman*—that he was a seasick man searching for lobelia.[7]

In early January, the *New York Tribune* included the Lincoln in a survey of new American sculpture that celebrated the healthy diversity of the contemporary scene. Dwelling upon one of Leigh Hodges's main points, *New York American*'s Ralph Goddard nominated the statue for placement in New York harbor, where it would reign as a new national symbol. He indignantly scored the resulting irony when a comical Uncle Sam was permitted to represent a nation whose citizens were preparing to sacrifice their lives for democracy, and he deprecated the efforts of Leonard Volk and Daniel French to fashion presidential portraits that too much emphasized the office instead of the man.[8]

In the face of such tributes, the *New York Times*'s inattention was especially curious. Publisher Ochs had long been committed to defending controversial public statuary, including Barnard's Harrisburg groups and his New York Public Library statuary. But it was now with obvious disinterest that his newspaper made passing note of the exhibition. Barnard's problem with this powerful molder of public opinion stemmed in part from his continuing naïveté in regard to public relations. Protected by his own literary acumen, Borglum could afford to step on editors' toes in his vigorous self-promotions and, as we have seen, French learned early that the lasting reputations of a sculptor and statue had less to do with merit than with the manner in which publicity and photographs were released; he knew it to be especially foolhearty to permit one newspaper to receive privileged access to information. That Barnard had permitted a Philadelphia newspaper to "scoop" other hometown journals in reporting the foundry exhibit, made him vulnerable to editorial recrimination.[9]

Even more compromising was the photograph that

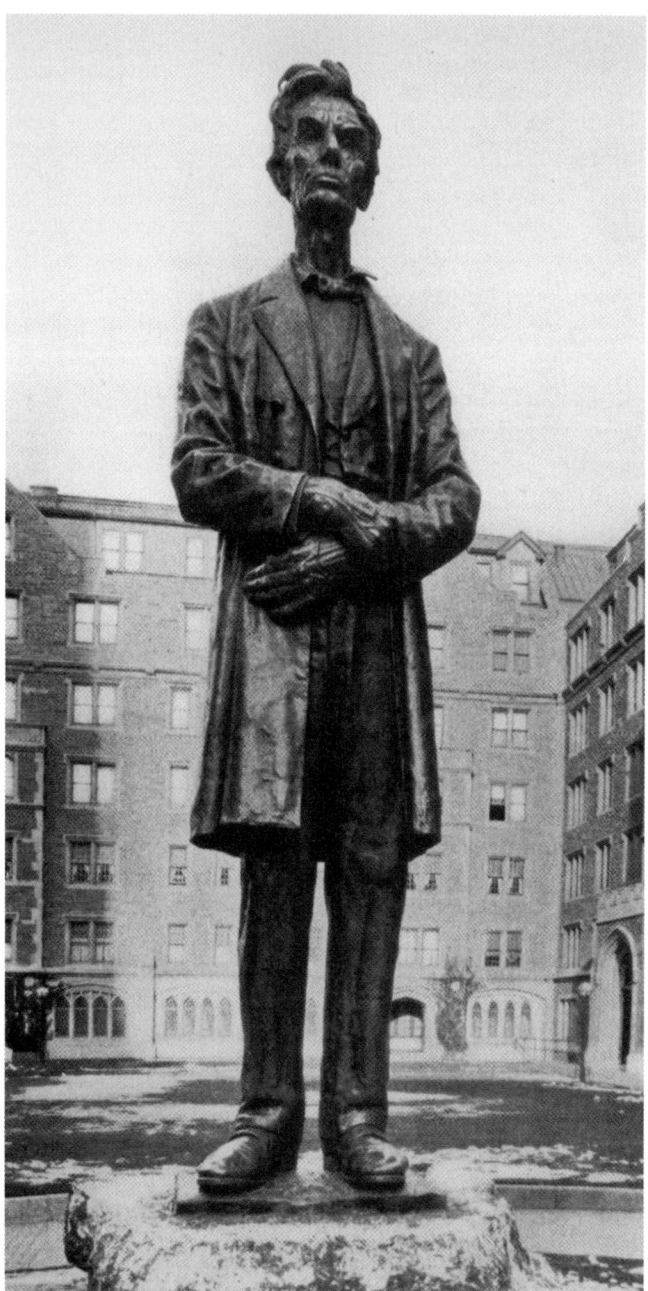

Barnard's Lincoln *(1st cast) at the Union Theological Seminary. From the* Literary Digest *(January 6, 1917).*

first circulated in the New York press. In early January, the *Literary Digest* reproduced a full-length view of the statue beside a Barnard interview. A copyright citation identified the artist as the owner and obvious supplier of an image that markedly distorted the head and upper body by stretching the neck, tilting the chin sharply upward, and squashing the face. It was easy for thousands of subscribers who had not seen the statue to assume that the illustration precisely duplicated what the human eye would have seen from the same position. An editor of a distant newspaper, the *Milwaukee Sentinel,* reacted by con-

ducting a public trial in which the photograph and the testimonies of individuals who had known Lincoln served as primary evidence. Predictably, the decision went against the defendant: the image was "fearfully and wonderfully unlike Lincoln as [the witnesses] knew him."[10]

Barnard had allowed at least two individuals to photograph the statue at the seminary, so long as they agreed to append the copyright notice to any prints that were published, but later he vehemently denied having done so. Reacting to the artist's complaint, the *Literary Digest* relented; ignoring the question of origin, they assumed responsibility for choosing the photograph in place of others, and admitted the photographer failed to gain a proper focus owing to the statue's cramped placement in the courtyard. A corrected image supplied by Barnard represented the statue in relatively even focus from a higher angle and with a soft play of light touching its frontal plane. One of many unpleasant experiences, this incident taught Barnard another critical lesson about monumental statuary: a figure twice as high as life could not be photographed distortion free with conventional equipment from a distance less than one hundred feet.[11]

Despite the *Literary Digest*'s retraction and republication, the psychological damage had been done, and Barnard's enemies were in possession of a powerful weapon that no editorial correction or apology could erase from the public mind: the lingering afterimage of the giraffelike neck and head. Most readers understood a photograph to be inherently "real" and, when positioned beside the verbal descriptions of living witnesses, an incontrovertible document.

Barnard had much to learn about extemporaneous interviews, as well. The day following the opening, J. M. Allison, Hulbert Taft's most trusted editorialist, entered an extensive Barnard monologue in the *Times-Star.* A euphoric Barnard examined the prophetic dimensions of the work, reviewing his mother's memories of Lincoln, and reflected upon Douglas Volk's ritualistic bestowal of the casts. Recounting a theme pressed by Hodges, the sculptor confided that before being assigned to the project, he was an academic artist who followed the styles of successful contemporaries, appropriating the "tricks of techniques" of old masterworks. With the Lincoln at hand, he became an instrument of God's power and lost all control over its design. "It was created utterly without vanity itself," and hence, as Hodges stunningly revealed, the statue "was beyond mere sculpture." Therefore, even though the project had demanded the full extent of his creative and imaginative power, he could also with absolute assurance deny authorship. It was "not for me to say my works are good or bad . . . there are things made by the human hands which speak of mysteries unrevealed," he concluded, "those are the things in which the hand has been guided by an inspiration which may not be defined." He noted his consternation when Edward S. Clark, with mock seriousness, told Charles Taft he intended to keep the Lincoln in New York. "Clark's words sounded like bargaining in something Holy—like changing destiny for a price."[12]

The intermingled themes of mystical Platonism, divine madness, and the creative instrumentation of the *alter deus* that comprised the *Times-Star* interview, were bound to have an impact on a predominantly rural Midwestern Protestant readership. By now familiar with the loftly platitudes of "soul language," as it was routinely applied to creative genius, the Tafts probably anticipated the nature of Barnard's interview. But many less enlightened readers who resided in backwoods locations similar to those lived in by "Lincoln the Man," were less prepared for such lofty affirmations. When, in recognition of a native son's achievement, the *Bellefonte* [Pennsylvania] *Democratic Watchman* reprinted the Cincinnati article in a February 1917 edition, one of Barnard's old acquaintences took offense. In a familiar defense, Barnard claimed to have been misquoted:

> I never took the stand that God had so much to do and I so little in the Lincoln making. I did state I worked much in a sub-conscious manner and also in a way I could not define and analyze. But I would never state or think God was so much and directly responsible for my sculpture that you must have divined. Great indeed above the work of mortals would a statue be if His responsibility were so direct. God helps those who help themselves in art as in other things. I was grieved the article ever went into print as it did first in Cincinnati written by one of their best writers. What can people think when they read such apparent statements by me and then see an ordinary statue of Bronze?

The sweeping renunciation of all he and his supporters had claimed, particularly an insistence the work was not an ordinary statue, was further undermined by Barnard's conclusion: he begged his correspondent not to allow newspapers to print his denial, since "it would only make trouble in Cincinnati."[13]

It was a noticeably more subdued Barnard who next favored the *New York Sun* with an interview that was republished soon after by the *Literary Digest.*

Rhapsodically blending non sequiturs, fragmented syntax, and conflicting metaphors—a model example of Lacanian psychotic discourse—the essay targeted the "scientific" studies of Borglum and Bartlett. It commenced with an assessment of how the Volk mask reconciled art and nature. An exact imprint of what had been divinely created, the physical presence of the mask argued against those misguided artists who wished to disguise ugly lines, thereby thwarting God's will and the vital spirit of democracy. It defied comparisons with the Olympian Zeus, with the Roman emperors, Napoleon, and with the conventionalized Christ, for these iconographic formulas presented iron-willed beings who lived apart from their worshippers. But the mask should not be copied, as Bissell had ardently instructed, for it was a great artist's duty to recover the illusive secrets that underlay its appearance. Through long hours of study Barnard discerned that the head's powerful chin supported an inverted pyramid of widening steps that led to the full roundness of the brain; the entire cranium was like a temple in which each infinitesimal part was essential to the whole.[14] Lines "lead away from self center . . . and forever onward." Beneath the left eye were two mountains, and between them a stream which then proceeded to innundate a circular hill. This was a trail of tears which flowed in times of both joy and sorrow; it traced a path of light downward through a dark valley, then opened into light as it formed a smile at the corner of the lips. To each side of face belonged distinct sexual functions: the left, which Borglum dismissed as being immature and unimpressive, was the female side, the locus of Lincoln's mothering instinct, while the right segment embodied equally pronounced masculine attributes that were made manifest in Lincoln's tremendous physical strength and will. But overall, Barnard insisted, the face determined that the entire stance of the body should convey a sense of passivity and humility, for "he is clothed with cloth worn, the history of labor." The creases and wrinkles thus retraced the records of labor; they were exultant American symbols that answered to their Old World equivalent as it was found in the wings of the Victory of Samothrace.[15]

Whatever publicity advantages the seminary exhibition yielded, it stood in the way of expeditious payouts from the Lincoln account and thus Barnard faced a new round of financial difficulties. On 6 January 1917, a desperate note informed Charles Taft that Barnard's mortgage holder intended to foreclose on his property if taxes were not paid immediately. His plea for an advance of fifteen thousand dollars was coupled with an offer to transfer the mortgage to Taft if he thought his request out of line, but "it would be a great disaster for me to loose my property." Once again Taft yielded, but only in the amount of five thousand dollars, leaving a fifteen-thousand-dollar balance due.[16]

The specter of an artist being forcibly barred from home and studio was a particularly distressing one for wealthy patrons, and when paying bills, Barnard realized it was not unwise to leave mortgage and property taxes to the last. Yet a large real estate transaction gave more substance to Barnard's latest predicament. On 5 January 1917, newspapers announced the sale to an unidentified purchaser of the Billings and Schaefer estates, and of the Hays property, which together comprised all the undeveloped land in Manhattan lying north of Barnard's studio and the Cloisters. The mysterious buyer was a man well known to the sculptor, and one who had much admired his Lincoln statue: John D. Rockefeller Jr. Not only did the sale promise to increase property values, it signaled the start of a tortuous legal struggle between Barnard, Rockefeller, and the Metropolitan Museum of Art over the disposition of Barnard's museum and medieval art collection.[17]

As the seminary exhibition went into its third month, world events took their dramatic turn, leading to increased social ferment and political reaction. Like many Francophiles, a group well represented in America by École des Beaux-Arts-trained artists, Barnard found himself caught between conflicting goals. He espoused the cause of Labor, but rejected organized Labor's neutralist stance. He had no love for monarchical England, even less for Russian czars, but France had been a second home, and he believed its republican views to be an indispensable condition of its cultural superiority. Germany's attack on France was a blow struck against art. As we have noted, he had had his differences with the French government, but by January 1917 old loyalties were solidly reaffirmed. By then, some three hundred fifty French artists had been killed in the conflict. It was also in January that news accounts first described the German conscription of Belgian laborers. Edna Barnard later observed that Wilson's restraint had intensified the savagery of the conflict, since pacifism in the face of aggression "helped no one and no thing." Barnard's sympathies for the French intensified further, when in the spring of 1917, he was briefly reunited with Isadora Duncan. He had last seen her in Paris a year earlier when, almost within range of enemy shells, she danced La Marseillais before weeping throngs in la Place du Trocadero. Now returned to New York following a triumphant tour of the front,

the heroine shared with Barnard, and with the photographer Arnold Genthe, Mary F. Roberts, and Percy MacKaye, new ideas for establishing an American school of dance, another of many schemes destined to be undermined by her tempestuous nature. Yet nothing could erase the memories of Paris and, in commemoration of the Trocadero performances, a grateful French government announced through Barnard that it was commissioning him to sculpt a marble statue of the dancer.[18]

Barnard's rekindled concern for France intensified his esteem for Roosevelt, as well. The colonel's personal offer of military service and strong advocacy of immediate intervention on the side of France, a declaration spurned by the Tafts as another grandstanding maneuver, were extremely heartening. Even if Roosevelt had not offered to raise a division, he remained in Barnard's estimate the legendary hero of San Juan Hill, a man whose "action in rushing to the assistance of Cuba in the interest of suffering humanity" ranked with the American attack on the Barbary Pirates in an earlier time. Naturally, the attention Roosevelt gave Barnard's sculpture in no way lessened this admiration. Thus Barnard needed little prodding when he decided whether or not to volunteer for service in Roosevelt's division. He applied for membership in the Arts of Concealment detachment, noting he had experimented with camouflaging techniques under Abbott Thayer, "the discoverer" of modern protective coloring strategies.[19]

Between mid-March and 25 May 1917, when Roosevelt's request to lead a division was formerly rejected by the Wilson administration, Barnard helped to coordinate recruitment and freely offered advice on policy. He forwarded a demonstrative assessment of Wilson's foreign policy that he assumed Roosevelt was sure to approve. "Of course, I have been Soul Stifled since Belgium lay dying for Liberty, and we, the father of the Republics—offering a cup of water to her parched, bleeding lips. But not a word of reproach or step toward the Brute of Steel, the Dragon of Steel, that trampled with a thousand piercing bayonets over her prostrate body." Alluding to a recent ceremony during which Wilson illuminated the *Statue of Liberty* in New York Harbor, Barnard expressed fear that continued American neutrality meant that the "Great Statue of Liberty, in our heart's door, would serve as a fortress for Prussian Aggression." There was nothing left for him to do but obediently place himself at the Colonel's command: "What can you do with me? I am at your and my country's service when the call comes . . . what can you make of me?"[20]

This rhetorical combination of brutalizing imagery

and personal submissiveness precisely described the contrasting visual modalities of the Lincoln statue, a powerful and potentially active figure in the momentary attitude of obedience and servitude. As such, both Barnard and his statue prepared to mother their nation through humble service and through the healing of wounds. Leigh Hodges imagined Barnard's Lincoln asking God, "What next is there for me to do?" Similarly, here was a master-creator at the summit of his career, offering his services—in effect, his own body—to a national hero for whatever purpose he deemed appropriate for saving France. The expression "What can you make of me?," curiously reminiscent of Isadora Duncan's invitation to her artists, metaphorically signaled an exchange of both sexual and professional roles: Barnard would become the inchoate clay and wax, while Roosevelt, with masculine resolve, would proceed to mold him into a statue of his own design.

Exultant over his assumed transformation, Barnard sent effusive messages to sympathetic friends. Shortly after America's entry into the war, he corresponded with Émile Hovelaque, a member of the Marshall Foch commission which was then meeting with American officials in New York.

The first Prussian heel that trod France gashed its hot iron nails deep into the soul of this Republic. For more than two years they have been festering here, today the balm is applied, wings are taking the place of wounds, winged arms, winged boats, winged action, to repay France our debt of the past, and pay Democracy our debt of the present . . . I am raising a corps to go to France and fight with Roosevelt at once.[21]

Lending force to Barnard's oath, was news of the February Revolution in Petrograd, Russia, and the abdication of the Romanoff regime. Once allied ranks had been purged of the autocrat Czar Nicholas II, prowar advocates could more easily argue that the conflict was entirely between democrats and Prussian dictators. American socialists and radicals more generally threw their support to the Petrograd Soviet of Workers' and Soldiers' Deputies, who demanded an international workers' revolution against governments.[22] Moderates and conservatives could only hope a provisional government would continue to resist the invaders and keep order at home. Barnard's progressive outlook convinced him Russia required a constitutional democracy in order to survive, but some rambling notations he made in the spring and summer of 1917 attest that he, like the radical vanguard, vicariously thrilled to the images of land-starved peasants rising en masse against iron-fisted tyrants and machines of war.

As plans for the dedication of the Cincinnati Lincoln went forward, propagandists ordered replica Barnard Lincolns for foreign cities. In late March two statues were being readied for Paris and Petrograd. The latter project would place a bronze on the high pedestal in Znamenskaia Square, which until recently supported the equestrian statue of Czar Alexander III. The replica intended for an unnamed location in Paris, to be financed by Charles Taft, was endorsed by a mixed consortium of editors, academics, and statesmen. The Paris City Council formally accepted its gift Lincoln on 27 March, several days before Barnard disclosed plans for his proposed Isadora Duncan memorial.[23]

The French presentation committee belatedly explained its position in a terse release several months later: "The committee believes that France is today fighting for the democracy of the world, she is fighting our battle. In appreciation of the gallant spirit of the French people, America presents this statue of Abraham Lincoln, who was more than any man the truest representative of Western Democracy." Hoping to sell the war to resisting socialists, suffragettes, independent elements of Labor, and racial minorities on both sides of the Atlantic, the committee was in accord with the sentiments expressed in a communication sent to Roosevelt by Illinois Rep. Medell McCormick: "we need something so specific that it will in spirit arouse masses of people who by Blood or for some other reasons, understand the hopes of those now subject nations, which desire and are fitted for self government."[24] That specific thing, so difficult to select, obviously should not remind the masses of the ruling class, nor should it be in any way associated with the rootless anarchists who wished to destroy institutional authority once and for all. Therefore, Barnard's "Lincoln the Man," if amended to represent "Lincoln the Democrat," would uniquely combine elements of order and disorder, rugged masculine power and feminine compliance, august, thoughtful leadership and dutiful servitude that would most widely appeal to both the working classes and emerging political leaders. Whether this balance had been sufficiently struck was open to question.

Outside of Albert Shaw, who agreed to coordinate committee activities, Charles Taft, and MacKaye, the French statue presentation committee consisted of few old Barnard supporters. Columbia University faculty were well represented, not by Seligman or the Carpenters, but by journalism professor Talcott Williams and the sociologist Franklin H. Giddings, the latter a surprising inclusion since he was a confirmed Anglo-Saxonist. The best known academicians were Charles W. Eliot, president emeritus of Harvard University, and Felix Adler, who after a career spent teaching Asian literature—like Charles Taft he studied at both Heidelberg and Columbia—had assumed directorship of the internationally supported American Ethical Union. Former Supreme Court Justice Charles Evans Hughes, the Republican presidential candidate who narrowly lost to Wilson in 1912, stood as the committee's highest ranking statesman. Two more names would have made the roster complete: William Howard Taft and Theodore Roosevelt. Barnard expected to obtain the latter's "valuable name and endorsement" above all others, since Roosevelt had warmly praised the statue and would have been joining old political allies on the committee. Roosevelt, however, curtly refused while offering the sculptor his view that "this does not seem to be an opportune time to present a statue of Lincoln to France. France needs bread, and not a stone, and it needs men with rifles in their hands even more than it needs bread. I think our action should be shaped along the lines thus indicated."[25]

There were obviously other than purely practical reasons for this rejection, the most obvious being Roosevelt's general mistrust of the Latin race. Like his confidant, Lord James Bryce, former British Ambassador to the United States, Roosevelt considered the French people to be hopelessly sentimental, overly emotional, undisciplined, and too susceptible to Caesarism.[26] One senses his proposed expedition was aimed as much at saving the French from themselves, as it was at routing the Prussians. He was even more fearful of the Slavs, and thus had even less reason for wanting a Lincoln statue in Petrograd, where its disheveled appearance might have contributed to the social chaos. The hint of irritation in the stiffly worded message also quite obviously reveals Roosevelt's growing impatience with Barnard and his emotional flights of fancy.

William Howard Taft's commendation of the statue at Cincinnati led the sculptor to believe Charles's brother would also readily support the French committee. But pointing to the pressures of work and claiming to already have sufficient representation through his brother, Taft resisted. Since he readily agreed to endorse other committees, one charged with restoring destroyed French monuments, the more likely reasons for the refusal was his felt loyalty to the Lincoln Memorial Commission, and his desire to distance himself from Roosevelt, who he could assume would join the group. Further-

more, over the past several months, William Taft, like Roosevelt, had become ever more fearful of the increasing arrogance of Labor and of the pan-Slavists. At home in Cincinnati he could justly admire Barnard's success in portraying the "habit and garb of [Lincoln's] origin and his life among the plain people," but it was quite another thing to imagine such a statue before unruly throngs of revolutionaries.

The Roman Bronze Works began preparing the Russian replica at once. Obviously the insurgent spirit of revolution, not to mention the standards of high artistic integrity, would not be well served by an industrially reproduced clone. Thus, Barnard proceeded to mystify the way the duplicate statue would be produced. On 22 March he described the second statue as an "exact duplicate" of the Cincinnati statue, having been "struck off from the same wax model" used for the original, and was therefore "just as original as the other." The question of "originality" aside, the statue could not have been made from the same wax model. Barnard's description of the *cire perdue* method stressed that each new cast required a new wax form before the molten bronze was poured into the mold.[27] He was reluctant to admit that the old plaster mold was being used to form a new wax impression, because it was the fixed and unalterable contours of these old plaster husks, and not the living hands of the artist, that would be actively shaping the wax.

Such fine technical distinctions were lost on the American Committee for the Encouragement of Democratic Government in Russia as it desperately searched for a symbol that might help it stave off total anarchy. The driving force behind the committee was Charles R. Flint, who organized its first mass meeting at the Metropolitan Opera House on 25 March. With the backing of Carnegie Endowment for Peace officials Elihu Root, Joseph Choate, and Nicholas Murray Butler, men we shall meet again in future chapters, as well as of Alton B. Parker, who agreed to chair, and having also coaxed an exceedingly disgruntled Theodore Roosevelt to issue a supportive encomium, Flint consulted with the Petrograd Council of Workmen's and Soldiers' Deputies on devising some symbolic gesture.[28] By the time a second mass meeting was held at Carnegie Hall a month later, Flint and his conferees had decided a replica of Barnard's Lincoln should go to the beseiged city. The latter meeting occasioned a violent shouting match between pacifists, who packed the galleries, and pro-war factions seated below. The dissidents' primary target was New York Mayor John T. Mitchel, who in a final moment of exasperation, indiscriminately characterized the prowar group as patriots and the pacifists as traitors. Once calm was restored, a projected image of Barnard's Cincinnati Lincoln was displayed alongside portraits of Russian revolutionaries.

Meanwhile, Barnard revised his notes on the Lincoln statue. The most significant manuscripts are undated, but one is tempted to see in them evidence the artist was drifting to a more radical outlook as the year progressed. This is indicated by a more frequent reference to the mystique of labor and an increased use of feminizing metaphors, figurations that contrasted sharply with the militaristic braggadocio that epitomized Roosevelt's pronouncements. The best example is the prose poem entitled "The Hand." Penciled in emphatically large and broken script, the text contrasts the hand of Labor with that of Autocracy. Labor's hand is loved by the earth as a mother loves her son. The fingers of the other hand, which in the throes of death reach out for a war machine, are "unscared" and "waxen." Ruthless war lords had used the tanklike apparatus to pulverize the very people they had enslaved to make it, those who "riveted it out of the milk of woman's breast" and the blood of man. In return for the "caress of labor's mighty hand," the earth would yield sufficient food for the "body and soul" of humanity. But "the waxen fingers of dying autocracy" for the last time grasped for the machine throttle that would crush labor's hand, just as in history, autocrats had conscripted armies of laborers to fight against their enemies. From social history, Barnard suddenly shifts to the subject of the deified Lincoln. Not only did the Emancipator's hand dignify labor in the world, it was also the instrument that "opened the doors of heaven to the path of labor." Lincoln stood "as God willed man to stand as men wish God to stand, fearless in fellowship for Brotherly Love."[29]

The musings on hands that grapple over the future of mankind provide a specific interpretation that brings the crossing hands of the statue into conflict with one another. By this reading, only the left one, the hand that responds to Lincoln's underlying feminine nature, properly belonged to him, the God of Labor and of the Earth. The grasping hand, by contrast, a figuration of the dying corpus of dictatorship, vainly seeks to overpower its life-giving neighbor in a final paroxism of blind rage.

Barnard's close contact with a new generation of liberal journalists helped inspire these and similar considerations. The invectives he aimed at the twin devil of monarchy and capitalism bear the unmistakeable imprint of the writings of Frank Crane, a syndicated columnist with whom Barnard was on

especially close terms in March and April 1917, and who was active on the French and Russian Barnard Lincoln committees. A Westerner, and a former Methodist minister who espoused the social gospel, Crane exchanged his spiritual calling for journalism at the turn of the century. Thereafter, his syndicated sermonettes reached a daily readership of an estimated fifty million people. Books encapsulating Crane's timely thoughts also enjoyed impressive sales. At the outbreak of the World War, he counciled against American involvement, urging the establishment of a world court similar to that proposed by William Taft. Yet the author's ardent socialism identi-

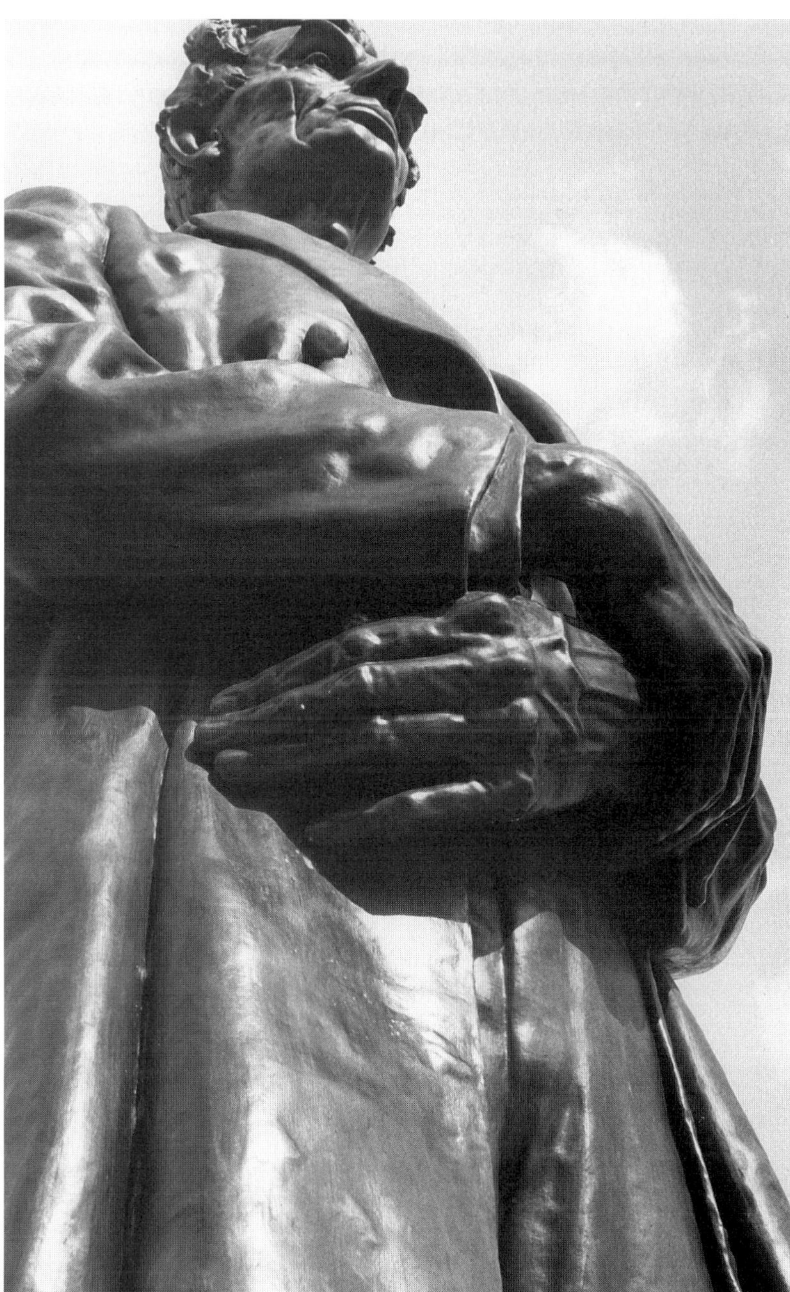

Detail of 1st cast.

fied Christ not as a judge but as a laboring democrat—at one point even as "a tramp working man looking for a job"—who was born to serve humanity. Repudiating the enthroned monarchical God who reigned in history until the Revolutionary age, Crane equated work, or the willingness to work, with godliness. A chapter entitled "A Vision of Hands," in Crane's *The Looking Glass* (1917), identifies hand labor as the sine qua non of man's moral obligation to serve others.[30]

The concept of a Paris Lincoln survived until at least November 1917, while the Petrograd project is last publicly mentioned in an article Crane wrote for the *New York Globe and Commercial Advertiser* in April 1917.[31] Against the backdrop of war and revolution, Crane envisioned for his readers the "gaunt figure of [Barnard's] rail splitter" quietly standing in the place formerly occupied by a warring Romanoff. Once it was atop this imposing pedestal, the journalist imagined Lincoln's "mute lips will say, what is as true of the world as of America: 'A House divided against itself cannot stand.' I believe civilization cannot endure permanently half democratic and half autocratic." Here, then, was a Lincoln that would mark the fulfillment of millenial prophecy.

The second phase of the Russian Revolution, when Lenin and the Soviets ousted the provisional government, put an abrupt end to the proposed Petrograd Lincoln. With the French project destined to be abandoned in the fall, only one other international project remained active. Before discussing this campaign more fully, it will be necessary to briefly return to the Cincinnati Lincoln.

In February of 1917 the Cincinnati park commission began redesigning the park fronting the Taft home. The principal consideration was how the statue would relate to both the commercial and private zones between which it would stand. The Tafts were anxious that it be clearly seen from a considerable distance along Fourth Street, as well as from the portico of their mansion, therefore some last-minute adjustments were required. A public fountain was moved and the statue edged rearward in order to free it from a bank of trees.[32] From the center of a *rondpoint,* it was to face in a westerly direction, fixing its gaze along the approaching street; on fair afternoons the rays of the lowering sun would fully illuminate it, causing the statue's shadow to angle backward in the general direction of the Taft portico. From the north, it would loom high over apartment buildings and, at a comfortable distance, the bandstand. The granite pedestal arrived in Cincinnati on 21 February with the statue following it on 7 March, in plenty

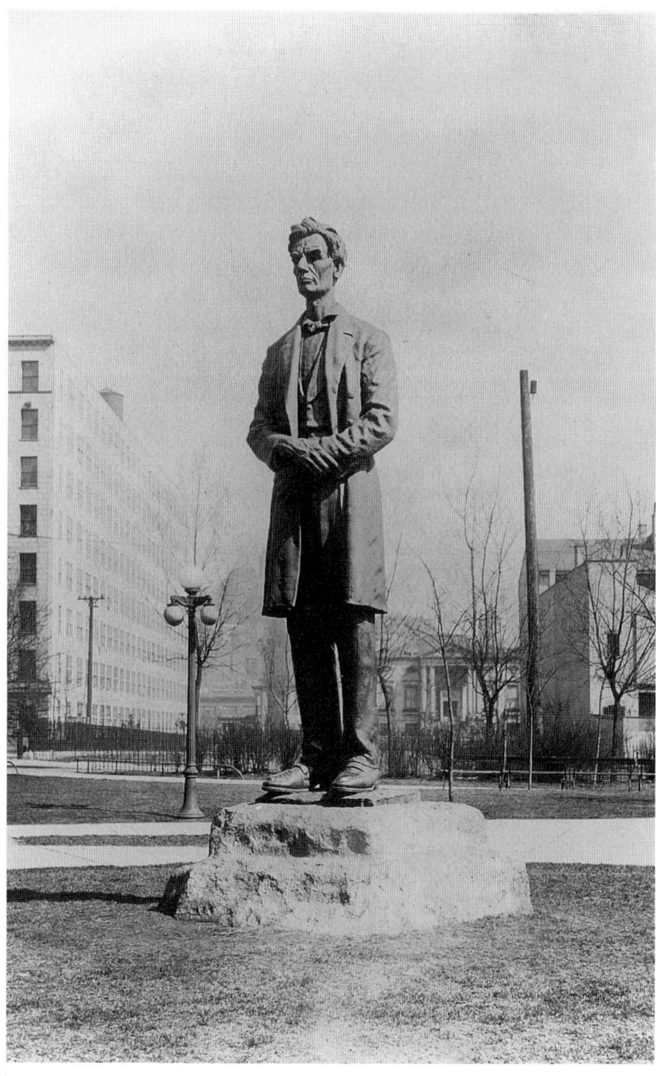

Barnard's Lincoln *(1st cast) in Lytle Park, Cincinnati, ca., 1917. Photo courtesy of the National Museum of American Art.*

of time for the dedication. The Tafts withheld final payment to Barnard until 10 July 1917, after landscaping was completed and installation costs were paid.

Meanwhile Barnard went over the guest list with Allison and Taft. He asked that Crane and Lyman Whitney Allen, a Lincoln scholar who had written a poem on Barnard's statue, be invited. There was never a question as to who would deliver the dedicatory address, but the artist hoped to also involve Roosevelt in the exercises. Fearing Taft's rebuke, Barnard revealed to Allison a plan for making the exercises a political landmark. Assuring him he would not raise such a sensitive issue with Charles Taft himself, Barnard inquired whether they should "take advantage at the dedication of the Lincoln statue to bring together at this supreme moment of the world's history and our own responsibilities and invite Ex. Prest.[*sic*] Roosevelt to be at one with Ex. Prest. Taft gathered around for and to the dedication of our statue of Abraham Lincoln."[33] Naïve though it was, Barnard's suggestion revealed a blind hope still held by many rank and file Republicans that the progressives and conservatives would make amends and thus return the party to its former potency. Just how the image of "Lincoln the Democrat" might fit this equation was a question not easily answered. Barnard's suggestion presumed that both William Taft and Roosevelt believed "magnificently in our point of view, in interpreting the Lincoln," yet he could not be so certain of Taft's attitude. While Roosevelt could be expected to say "splendid things of the statue," and had frequently visited his studio, Taft had seen it only once as a small model four years previously, at a time when he was preoccupied with the Lincoln Memorial, and he did not express an interest in seeing it again.

When following the dedication, Charles Taft wrote Barnard of his and Anna's satisfaction over the final disposition of the Cincinnati project, he entered the postscript, "I do not think our friend, Harry Probasco, has even peeped since the statue was installed."[34] It was true that the former chairman of the Alms Memorial Lincoln committee, ever respectful of wealth and political power, decided against attacking the statue in the local press. This did not mean, however, that Probasco was ready to forgive and forget.

In the intervening years, the Borglum-Probasco correspondence inevitably centered around the slow pace of Barnard's work. In March 1914 the *Times-Star* reacted sharply to a Borglum speech prophesying the eventual failure of the project. Although a spirited reply was drafted, Probasco could not summon the courage to release it to the press. Borglum sent updated reports on the statue's appearance, describing it at one point as a "twisted hunk of bronze," and pressed Probasco to take a public stand. The seminary exhibit brought forth a new series of invectives, and prompted Borglum to describe an incident at a dinner party when a prominent member of the National Sculpture Society compared the statue to a gorilla, then proceeded to imitate the statue's "vulgarity and grossness." Incredulously, Borglum summarized for Probasco the *Sun-Literary Digest* interview in the following terms: "Barnard said he read up on Lincoln, then went to the country and found this most decrepid specimen of manhood to fit his conception, and then had followed him literally. What do you think of that?" Borglum wished no one to think him timid. While anticipating forthcoming appearances at Lincoln birthday celebrations, he indirectly rebuked Probasco's discretion when he asserted he would not be "meally mouthed" over Barnard's statue or its patron. He was fully prepared to expose as false the argument that Taft had out of sympathy been inveigled into commissioning the Lincoln. "If you feel hesitant," he cautioned Probasco, "just wait until the gargoyle is restraining his evident sickness of stomach, as he gulps out over your public square . . . then you will have become very clear in your mind as to what is right to do in this case."[35]

Stirred by Borglum's denunciations, Probasco answered in kind. He assured Borglum of his lasting enmity toward Barnard and the Tafts, whom he characterized as "that old outfit." Before he saw photographs of the model, he predicted Barnard's concept would present "Lincoln as a wet nurse rocking a cradle." After its arrival, Probasco reported everyone in Cincinnati thought it a failure and with horror contemplated the fact "our hero (was) being carried into history in this mongrel shape." With dedication day at hand, he began speaking his mind on the issue during local appearances, but vowed not to author a press release unless Borglum endorsed it, since the Tafts "are our wealthiest people and they have a newspaper of high standing and wide circulation so that I might fare poorly with such odds against me if not supported."[36] On this note of temerity the Borglum-Probasco cabal disbanded.

6

John Stewart's Peace War

IN JANUARY 1917 JOHN STEWART WAS PURSUING TWO RE-lated goals; one, to induce William Howard Taft to lead a newly reorganized Anglo-American peace committee, and the other, to revive a project for erecting a Lincoln statue in London to represent that committee's friendship offering to England. The Union Theological Seminary exhibition suggested a single solution that Stewart brought before Charles Taft. After learning the cast would cost no more than $10,500, Taft immediately directed Barnard to furnish Stewart with photographs and publicity. In February, Stewart met in London with Lord Weardale, chairman of the British reception committee, urging him to accept the Taft Lincoln in place of a previously selected cast of Saint-Gaudens's standing Lincoln under terms negotiated before the War. Soon after, Weardale notified patron and sculptor of his committee's preliminary acceptance, while London's Office of Works, the overseer of the city's public property, agreed to locate the substitute at the same location near the Houses of Parliament and Westminster Abbey that had already been reserved.[1]

Charles was gratified the Taft name would be associated with a gift that promised to improve Anglo-American relations at an extremely portentious moment and, despite his own well-publicized disaffection with the British, Barnard considered the chosen destination "the most superb site in all of England . . . the Gothic background and our Lincoln will marry well together; he is much more like a Gothic Cathedral than a Greek Temple." Charging the sculptor to produce the best possible replica, Charles concurred with Stewart's prediction that the promised London unveiling would be "quite an international episode."[2]

International episodes were routine fare for the fifty-two-year-old John A. Stewart (1865–1928). Late into a career spent as a seminarian, publisher, manufacturer, promoter, and organizer of diverse enterprises, including the Institute for Pictorial Education, and the National Art Film Association, Stewart entered the field of law and politics, taking a law degree from the University of Toronto in 1915, while continuing to manage the politically moderate Republican League of Clubs of the State of New York. In February 1909 he cofounded with Ohio Senator Joseph W. Butler the American Committee for the Celebration of the One Hundredth Anniversary of Peace Among English Speaking Peoples, 1914–1915, hereafter referred to as the American Centenary of Peace Committee, or the ACPC. He chaired the association's executive committee until 1917 when it was reorganized first as the Sulgrave Institution of Great Britain and the United States, and then as the George Washington-Sulgrave Institution, which he continued to direct until his death. An English branch of the American committee was formed in London in 1911 under the presidency of Albert H. G. Grey, the Third Earl of Grey, who was commander in chief and governor general of the province of Canada, and under the chairmanship of Lord Shaw of Dumfermline. Charter members included Baron Philip James Stanhope Weardale, Parliamentarian Arthur Shirley Benn, and prominent British pacifist Harry S. Perris. Australian and Canadian committees were soon established, bringing the combined international membership to over ten thousand at the outbreak of World War I.[3]

The international centenary of peace association was founded upon tenants of Anglo-Saxonism, a sentiment that had guided the policies of England and America through the crisis years spanning the turn of the century.[4] Following the Russo-Japanese War, it lessened as an overt force in international affairs, but like other pan-racial movements opposing it, Anglo-Saxonism found a no less politically effective sanctuary in peace organizations that flourished through 1914. Its mythology maintained that English-speaking peoples and their Teutonic forebearers were in every respect superior to other national populations. This by no means insured a common front. Emerging from a watershed of evolutionist thinking, a belief in Anglo-Saxon-Teutonic preeminence was used to certify every shade of preformed opinion on international affairs. Moderate conservatives like Stewart applied it to peace-at-any-price relations between England, her possessions, and America; Roosevelt progressives were more apt to emphasize the competitive factor, while arguing for greater, rather than less, American vigilance in her dealings with her mother country. American isolationists preferred to locate the seat of Anglo-Saxonism within a new American Empire in the Western Hemisphere.

Stewart endorsed the proposition that peace initiatives undertaken between peoples of similar race, language, and culture were more likely to endure than those which bound dissimilar populations. Following the signing of the Treaty of Ghent on 24 December 1814, the respect emanating from common racial ties had forestalled armed conflict in every dispute between the two nations. Recent provocations arose in Central and South America; one involved a discriminatory toll schedule for the Panama Canal, and another grew out of President Wilson's refusal to militarily protect British corporations operating in Central and South America. The peace Stewart had in mind left open the possibility of an armed American invasion of Mexico, if such action would strengthen Anglo-American comradeship and further extend the uninterrupted history of successful arbitration between the two nations and constituents of the British Empire. The approaching anniversary of the Ghent signing would offer a perfect opportunity for calling world attention to the Anglo-Saxon mastery of international understanding. Stewart anticipated "there will gather in New York one of the most representative bodies of English speaking men that have ever met together in the history of the English speaking race."[5]

The international committee's principal political agenda commemorated William Taft's efforts to construct binding international arbitration treaties between America, England, and her possessions, even though these were eventually emasculated by the Senate amendments of 1912. Taft's legislation envisioned a judiciable settlement of national claims, including those involving national honor, by a world court. This point especially heartened leading British statesmen like Premier Herbert Asquith, who characterized Taft's measure as "the most signal victory in our time in the international sphere of the power of reason and the sense of brotherhood." The British Centenary of Peace Committee (BCPC) was in fact sanctioned by Parliament's Committee to Promote Arbitration between Great Britain and the United States.[6] Under the circumstances, William Taft could not with conscience withhold the use of his name by the American organization, but he remained skeptical of Stewart's intentions and was understandably fearful of the inflammatory effect the ACPC's preamble was having upon components of Labor, racial minorities, and suffragettes. He also deeply regretted the makeup of the membership and thus declined the post of honorary chairman.

Stewart had no recourse but to assign honorary positions to Woodrow Wilson and his top men, William Jennings Bryan and Thomas R. Marshall. Less easy for Taft to ignore was the fact that from 1910 to 1917 the active chairman was Andrew Carnegie, a disaffected Taft Republican who held the former president personally accountable for not properly selling his arbitration measures to the Senate, and who now unhesitatingly proclaimed Wilson the greatest American president since Lincoln.[7] The presence on the ACPC of Carnegie associates Elihu Root, Columbia University President Nicholas Murray Butler, and Joseph B. Choate, a lawyer-diplomat who like Root once served as American ambassador to England, brought the committee under decidedly anti-Taft leadership. Eventually, the honorary chairmanship fell to Roosevelt, who had less to expect of his fellow members than Taft. But as he mounted his final presidential campaign, Roosevelt anticipated some political advantages and, at the least, expected to exercise watchdog surveillance over ACPC deliberations.

Carnegie promoted his own version of Anglo-Saxon-Teutonist political and philosophical ideology through the seemably inexhaustable financial resources of his endowment. Among its administrative divisions, the Endowment for International Peace, the Division of Intercourse and Education, both established in 1910, the Church Peace Union (1914), and the Hague Palace of Peace (1913), provided machinery for arbitrating disputes among a Teutonic brotherhood. During the ACPC's first years Stewart gained Carnegie's full trust and cooperation, but a quarrel in 1914 cast a shadow over future operations. This was precipitated when without ACPC sanction, Stewart offered President Wilson the committee's service in helping him "improve the Mexican matter," a remark Carnegie and his astonished colleagues took to mean his advocacy of an American invasion. As we shall see, this was not the only indiscretion the executive director dared to commit on behalf of what he deemed the best interests of Anglo-Saxon supremacy.[8]

English affiliates viewed Roosevelt's presidency as a sign the organization had wide American support. Hoping to sustain the illusion, Stewart signed on others who would have been the ACPC's most obstreperous critics. Hence *Review of Reviews* editor Albert Shaw, a Wilson intimate who feared British imperialism, was recruited to direct public relations. Despite the ACPC's varied constituency, suffragettes, Labor, and ethnic Americans, as well as patriotic isolationists, effectively blocked any chance for federal sanction or significant financial support. A German-American association, the American Society of Truth, was founded in 1912 specifically to defeat a $7.5 million appropriations bill authored by ACPC loyalists Sen. Theodore Burton and Rep. Martin Littleton for funding peace operations. After Burton eased the measure through the Senate, it met a quick death in the House Foreign Affairs committee, which scourged it for drawing a distinction between England, a former armed combatant, and other countries, excepting Spain, that had never militarily engaged American forces. In 1914, a second and decidedly more modest plea for fifty thousand dollars also failed after a Western legislator, in a retort to a bill sponsored by Virginia Representative Henry Flood, observed that "every time you have one of these celebrations you revive the animosity which comes out of the conduct of the English people a hundred years ago. Why not celebrate the day they burned the capitol building?"[9]

Similar skirmishes over peace celebration funding were joined in many state legislatures, particularly that of New York, between 1912 and 1914. It hardly helped Stewart's cause that charter member Root was a notorious enemy of immigration, a fact that especially enraged Irish-Americans. Nor did the committee's frequent error of associating the Celtic race with "Anglo-Saxonism" in official announcements soothe the wrathful United Irish-American Societies or the American editors of the *Irish Times*. Stewart readily branded these challengers a loathsome minority "that has never been absorbed into American sentiment and feeling but for three generations has considered itself as members of a hyphenated citizenship and in their action, which is political and social, few identified with the religious and intellectual life of America." In retaliation, dissentors laid plans to celebrate key American victories against the British during the War of 1812.[10]

As it touched upon issues of peace and war between the United States, England, and Canada, the ongoing factional struggle took the form of a board game in which players sought to advance public monuments into adversarial territory. Especially troublesome to Stewart was the construction of a million-dollar federal monument honoring Commodore Oliver Perry at Put-in-Bay, Ohio. An unveiling of a massive column in September 1913 was to climax a three-month centennial celebration of the Battle of Lake Erie, an event that might easily have been converted into a patriotic anti-British demonstration. Carnegie quickly advanced Stewart five thousand dollars to fund a clandestine public relations campaign aimed at defusing this eventuality. Like a field officer who was reporting to his commanding general, Stewart advised Carnegie, "they have been pressing us rather hard with reference to the Perry victory celebrations . . . but only the German and Irish press approve." He vowed to energetically lobby the responsible federal committee and in this particular instance the Stewart-Carnegie alliance was remarkably successful. The laying of the monument's cornerstone on 4 July 1913 officially commemorated one hundred years of Anglo-American peace, not, as common sense would otherwise dictate, a spunky, homegrown American hero's defeat of adventurous foreign brigands. The pro-British theme was reinforced several months later when during a second observance the bones of American and British officers killed in the action were reinterred together in the monument's crypt.[11]

The committees vacillated on the question of what monuments should be ordered, where they should be located, and precisely what political message they should convey. There were a number of "trial-balloon" announcements appearing in the press for projects such as one establishing in America a replica of the Earl of Chatham statue in the House of Lords—a proposal that was eventually carried out in a most ignominious fashion—another entailing the construction of a colossal peace monument in the Rocky Mountains, and yet another for the erection of a Museum of the Peaceful Arts in New York State, both of which fell by wayside.[12] Proposals more persistently centered on images of George Washington, Queen Victoria, and Abraham Lincoln. Sidestepping the inevitable arguments over which historical figure would be most appropriate, the English committee also considered raising in London an allegorical tribute to peace that would avoid portraiture altogether.

Protocol weighed heavily. An English resolve to set aside Washington's ancestral home, Sulgrave Manor, in Northhamptonshire, as a shrine and educational center for visiting Americans, caused little dissension. A majority of the English committee consisted of liberal peers who happily overlooked Washington's considerable role in a rebellion that geography and a failed colonial policy rendered inevitable. Conservative British Unionists associated with the BCPC intensely regretted the Revolution and Washington's place in it, but Sulgrave was of fine Tudor vintage, and one could still find there the original coat of arms that legend insisted had inspired the design of the American flag. One could easily conclude that Washington was an English gentleman whose majestic character emblematized a new nation.[13] Additionally, his sponsorship of Jay's Treaty marked him out as the first of his countrymen to have entered into a binding arbitration agreement with America's parent country.

Earl Grey would also have a statue. "A monument to George Washington in Westminster Abbey," he said, would be a "testimony to our ungrudging and generous recognition of the influence for good exerted on successive generations of the British as well as the American people by the example of his splendid qualities." This benefaction came with strings: the Earl politely but firmly inserted an afterword directed at incoming President Woodrow Wilson who he now expected to put national honor and fairness on the line by settling the Panama Canal toll dispute. This the president accomplished with considerable diplomacy when in mid-1914, as the Canal was being prepared for its grand opening, he persuaded the Senate to rescind an exclusive toll-free amendment for Canal-bound American coastal shipping, a mandate of the Hay-Pauncefote Treaty (1901) that particularly offended British leaders. Roosevelt regarded Wilson's surrender to British interests treasonable, while Anglophiles began recognizing an unusual similarity between the living American president's national rectitude and the statecraft of his fellow Virginian, George Washington. The State of Virginia seemed to be acknowledging this when it elected to present a bronze replica of Jean Houdon's standing figure of Washington in the State Capitol at Richmond either to Westminster Abbey or Westminster Hall.[14] It even-

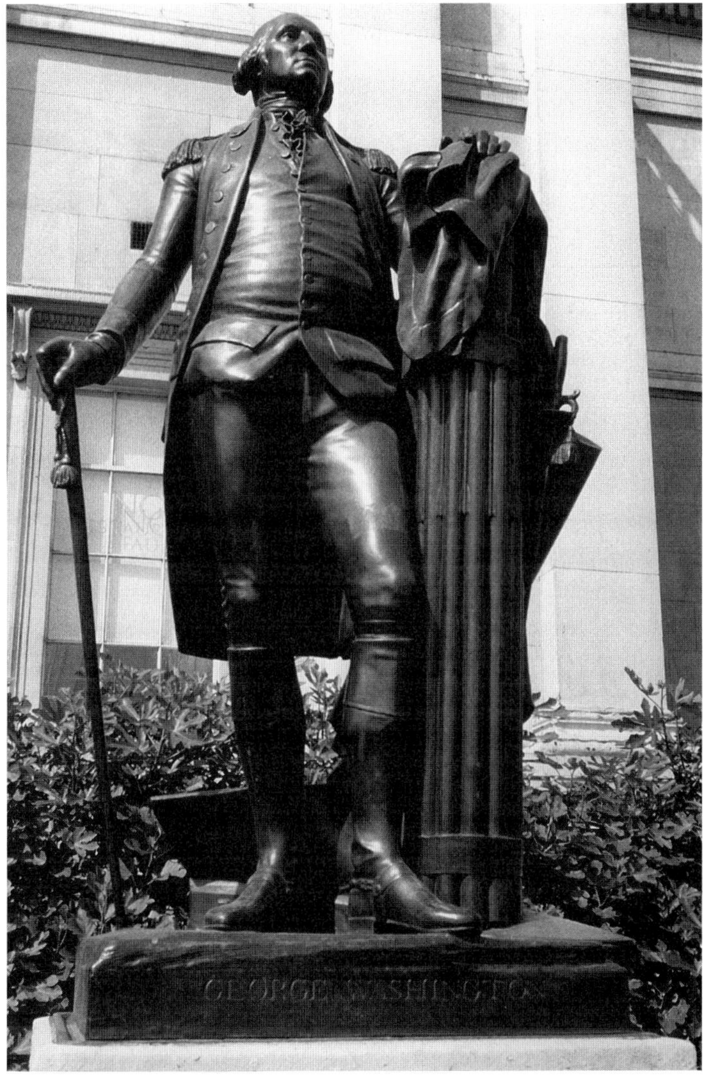

Jean Antoine Houdon, George Washington. *1921. Bronze, figure, 6′2″. Replica of 1791 marble original. Photo: Greg Giacona.*

tually found its way to the front lawn of the National Gallery in Trafalgar Square.

In early 1913, the centenary of peace committees had settled upon a bust of Washington for Westminster Abbey, a statue of Queen Victoria for Washington, D.C., and were considering another nonportrait monument for an unnamed location in London. With demands for female suffrage and Irish Home Rule placed directly before them, committee members quite logically assumed a statue of Queen Victoria would have an ameliorating effect upon all facets of political thought. In her image would be encountered at once a fine example of an Anglo-Saxon-Celt, a woman, and mother, and a crowned head of state who had never taken up arms against the United States.[15]

A statue of Lincoln was a different matter. Even

though Lincoln's paternal ancestors could without difficulty be traced to Samuel Lincoln of Norwich, and some descendants later prospered in Virginia, the later history of the Abraham Lincoln genealogy became mired in itineracy, poverty, and possible illegitimacy. To these stigmas was added the fact a large portion of the English population sided with the Southern plantation owner against the Union cause, since, it reasoned, this profitable trading partner should have been allowed to secede from the Union in much the same manner that America had seceded from the English Empire. Despite Lincoln's resolution of the Trent Affair, an ideal example of the selflessness required for successsful arbitration, as well as his assassination, anti-Lincoln feelings survived into the new century. Even Harry Perris, the most liberal member of the BCPC, remained unconvinced the Civil War was necessary, although he would grant Lincoln the benefit of his doubt.[16]

Braving the threat of protest demonstrations, an English delegation arrived in New York the first of May 1913 for a joint session with their American partners. Suffragettes promised to be particularly active when they discovered that two of the representatives openly opposed women's rights. By association, the Carnegie Mission and the New York hall that bore the benefactor's name, became the opposition's foremost symbols of a male-dominated Anglo-Saxonist capitalist autocracy. From a different perspective, wary observers discerned in the hastily organized and continuously revised schemes for monuments an underlying absurdity of the Anglo-American peace-at-any-price mentality itself.[17]

The most vitriolic critic of the monument exchange was the ACPC's own honorary chairman. After hosting a luncheon at his Oyster Bay estate, Roosevelt shared with Arthur Hamilton Lee his dismay over the proceedings.

> Good Lord Weardale and the other members, both British and American, were filled with a plan in the first place to get a monument to George Washington at Westminster Abbey, where I would regard it as preposterous to put him; and in the next place, to erect a statue to Queen Victoria in Central Park, thereby furnishing a steady occupation for the police force in protecting it from celtic enthusiasts whose life ambition would be to blow it up. Really your proposal about John Paul Jones in front of the Admiralty office, and Ross and Cockburn in Washington, preferably one in front of the White House and the other of the Capital, would, I have not a doubt, be accepted with rapture by that delegation.(i.e., their fickleness).[18]

As he saw it, the committee's naïveté was not the only factor that would undermine an effective distribution of monuments. In the period after he left office, and particularly after his defeat in the 1912 election, Roosevelt could find precious few individuals in England's or America's past or present who were worthy of representation. There were no figureheads, only "college-president-politician types," and "American lawyer-politician" types. He found therefore no appreciable difference between Taft, Bryan, and Wilson, on one hand; the Liberal Prime Minister Herbert Asquith and his cabinet, on the other; or between these individuals together and the most dismal American leaders of the past: Jefferson and Buchanan. Lincoln was the single exception, for as we have seen, Roosevelt was determined to draft him into the living ranks of twentieth-century progressivism.[19]

But there were other far less cynical progressives on Stewart's ACPC who took the broadly proposed statue exchange quite seriously. Oscar S. Straus, Roosevelt's one-time Secretary of Commerce and Labor and, in 1914, the Progressive Party's New York gubernatorial candidate, viewed Wilson's part in the repeal of Panama Canal toll exemptions for American ships as fresh evidence of the power of diplomacy to further the cause of peace. Speaking before the New York Republican Club in March 1914, Straus saddened his Bull Moose colleagues when he thoughtfully compared the present instance of American (and pointedly, Wilsonian) magnanimity with an earlier arbitrated case which England lost to the United States: the "Alabama" indemnity claim that grew out of Civil War naval action. In 1872, an international court ruled that because the ship in question was built and armed by England, that country was liable for the $15.5 million in property loss the vessel inflicted against the Union navy while in Confederate service. But Straus had a more specific reason for wanting to revisit history since he had reason to believe a residue of this claim money was yet being held by the Treasury Department. Decrying the fact that, unlike Canada, the United States government had as yet made no financial pledge to the forthcoming Anglo-American celebrations, he urged that some of the "Alabama" money be freed for financing these events, and for making possible the exchange of permanent monuments that would commemorate the long peace that had existed between the two nations.[20]

Responsibility for ACPC decisions on monuments rested with Andrew B. Humphrey. One of Humphrey's first acts was to appoint John Gutzon Borglum and Frederick Ruckstull art advisors, an assignment that brightened Borglum's hope for winning commissions for some of the peace monuments. The men testified at a joint Congressional hearing on the ill-fated Burton-Littleton bill as to the artistic importance of the peace celebrations. When during the 1913 American conference British centenary committee delegates toured Washington, New York, and Chicago, Borglum joined them on the final leg of their journey. He obviously had little influence in arranging the itinerary, however, since it included Lincoln Park and a pause before Saint-Gaudens's statue. With the memory of this august image fresh in their minds, the entourage, led by Lord Weardale, Benn, and Perris, retired to the University of Chicago for a symposium on British-American relations that was highlighted by Sir Arthur Lawley's rousing tribute, "The Anglo-Saxon Impulse."[21]

The delegates waited until their return to Washington before making known their high opinions of Saint-Gaudens's statue. Even Borglum was surprised by their sudden interest in it, and sent a sharply worded note to Stewart associate William B. Howland that read: "I see the committee is to place a Lincoln. Lest you forget, let me remind you that Lincoln is really one of my children." Press releases simultaneously issued from New York and London on 23 May 1913 confirmed that the BCPC representatives admired the Saint-Gaudens Lincoln but insisted they had proceeded no further in their deliberations than to agree that a heroic Lincoln statue sculpted by a foremost American artist would eventually be chosen for London. Meeting with Stewart at the Lawyer's Club on that day, an American subcommittee decided upon the Saint-Gaudens, although this was not immediately made known to the public or the committee's general membership.[22] It was announced that the Queen Victoria monument for Washington D.C. would be carried forward by a womens' committee led by Mrs. Joseph Choate, and that a third unspecified monument would be delivered to Ottawa as part of a three-way international exchange.

Perris, the single English conferee at the Lawyer's Club, conveyed the American offer to his committee, which then accepted it on 10 June 1913. But still there was no immediate public confirmation of this agreement, and even Borglum and other insiders were kept in the dark. It was not until January 1914, during one of his then frequent London trips, that Stewart officially released the crucial information. When reporting the announcement, the London *Times* misidentified the chosen statue as Saint-Gaudens's "George Washington," an error that may not have been wholly unintended, since many Londoners feared Lincoln's image might altogether replace the promised cast of Houdon's *Washington*. The London *Observer* clamored for updated information, while venturing the judgment that the placement of Washington's portrait at Westminister Abbey would be the single most important event in influencing Anglo-American solidarity. Stewart and London Commissioner of Works Lord Beauchamp conferred on acceptable locations, while in the House of Commons, Benn requested Beauchamp to reserve the southeast corner of the Canning enclosure for the bronze. Americans were informed of the resolution on 16 April. The *New York Times* reported that the ACPC subexecutive committee had "approved a contract" for supplying a Saint-Gaudens duplicate "subject to the agreement of the finance committee." The persistent Augusta Saint-Gaudens, whose campaigning on behalf of her late husband's statue for the Lincoln Memorial was to later provoke Bacon and French, volunteered to oversee the casting of the replica, the estimated cost being set at no more than forty-five thousand dollars. At the same time, it was announced that two other statues had been approved: a Queen Victoria for Washington, D.C., which was budgeted for twenty-five thousand dollars, and a memorial to the American historian Francis Parkman for Ottawa, Canada, at no more than thirty-five thousand dollars. British government clearance was gained for the London duplicate bronze on 2 May 1914 and, on 8 June, with a rhetorical flourish of "hearty thanks to His Majesty's Government," the host committee responded in kind.[23]

Thus, Saint-Gaudens's commanding study of "Lincoln the Man" was to be situated at the very heart of the English-speaking world. From the southwest corner of Parliament Square it would face at a battalion of bronze statesmen neatly attired in historic costumes. There stood Mario Rossi's *Benjamin Disraeli* (1883), Matthew Noble's *Sir Robert Peel* (1877) and *Lord Derby* (1874), and Thomas Woolner's *Lord Palmerston* (1876). Beyond, and to the right of this distinguished company, Hamo Thornycroft's *Oliver Cromwell* (1899) rose impressively against the very walls of Parliament. The oldest statue within sight was Richard Westmacott's portly, toga-clad, *George Canning* (1823), for whom the western edge of the Square was then named. This figure was several paces north, or to the left side, of the proposed Lincoln site. Of all those represented, Canning (1770–1825) had the most to do with ordering the future history of the Western Hemisphere, since it was this sagacious foreign secretary who bequeathed Britian's recogni-

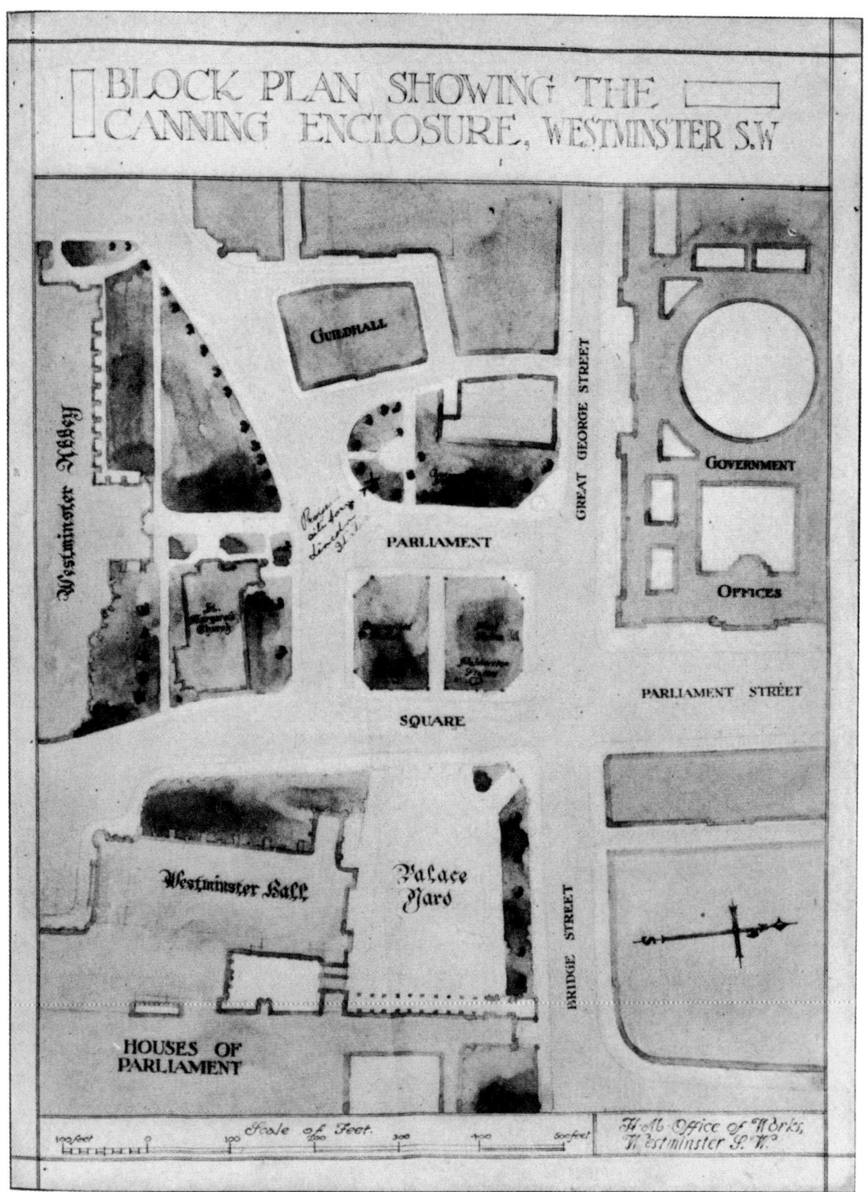

*Block plan of the Canning Enclosure, Westminister, with
inscription and arrow marking the proposed site of statue.
From U. S. Commission of Fine Arts, Eighth Report,
January 1, 1918–July 1, 1919 (Washington, D.C.:
G.P.O., 1920), p. 89.*

tion of independence upon rebelling Spanish possessions in South America.[24] The sensitive international
situation that currently threatened the peace of this
region, and endangered the bonds of friendship existing between the partner nations no doubt helped
induce Benn and Stewart to recommend the enclosure above other locations. Certainly, no statue could
find its place in a more congenial setting than at the
threshold of Parliament and "under the shadow of
the Abbey."

The crucial decision having been made, the English
hosts proceeded to raise money for their part in the
celebrations and the statue exchange. On 5 February
1914, the centenary committee sponsored appearances by the archbishop of Canterbury and Prime
Minister Asquith who spoke of emotional ties that
cut across class and national lines. The archbishop
exemplified the force of racial identity by calling
forth a mental image of the typical Anglo-Saxon
American who with bowed head stood before the
statues in the Abbey, saying, "'Those men are my
forebearers, my chieftains as really as they are
yours.'"[25]

The last published confirmation that the Saint-

Gaudens Lincoln presentation remained on track appeared in the London *Times* on 12 July 1914. Even though the outbreak of war forced the BCPC and ACPC to cancel the scheduled celebrations, Stewart remained hopeful a statue exchange might yet go forward. He therefore ordered a reorganization of the ACPC, and through Nicholas Murray Butler, secured funding from the Carnegie Endowment for International Peace for the purpose of liquidating an outstanding debt of six thousand dollars. The executive committee voted in the spring of 1915 to perpetuate itself for the purpose of placing, war or no war, the Lincoln and Parkman statues at their assigned locations, although it had nothing to say about the Queen Victoria project. Almost a year later, Stewart created within the one-hundred-and-fifty-member executive committee a new ACPC subexecutive committee of fifteen members. Beside Isaac Seligman, who became its treasurer, this council included Joseph Choate, Charles S. Davison, Louis S. Seaman, William C. Demorest, George F. Kunz, Austin G. Fox, Robert C. Morris, Alton Parker, Job E. Hedges, George W. Burleigh, T. Kennard Thomson, and Humphrey Howland. Stewart retained executive power as ex-officio. One would not expect the ailing Andrew Carnegie to be a component of this new directorship, but more conspicuously absent from its roster were Carnegie operatives Nicholas Murray Butler and Root, and Choate was soon to withdraw.[26]

What measures Stewart took to raise the funds for the Saint-Gaudens cast in 1913 and 1914, and during the subsequent tenure of the committee of fifteen, remained a highly contested question. He later maintained he had asked donations from each of the 168 executive members and the 13,000 general membership of the ACPC with no results. Yet he was unable or unwilling to provide a copy of the appeal to inquisitors.[27] The improbability that such a wide canvass would not have yielded some returns weighed heavily in the subsequent investigations into the early stages of the statue campaign.

Aside from the question of Stewart's inaction or malfeasance in regard to the Saint-Gaudens replica, there was no denying the fact that during the two-and-one-half-year hiatus separating the announced statue agreement from the executive director's decision to advance the Barnard substitution, the English had begun to take a decidedly different historical view of Lincoln. Lincoln, the weary civilian commander in chief, not General Washington, became the subject of close study by those weighing America's destined role in the European conflict. Caught in the crossfire between factions, President Wilson was now

inevitably led to compare himself to the Civil War president who, amid raging zealots, dispassionately examined the full consequences of military action. As had Carnegie in his ruminations, Albert Shaw had already drawn this comparison in editorials describing Wilson's "watchful waiting" response to the Mexican crisis.[28] Similarly, some among Britain's upper class began to put aside old prejudices, finally recognizing in Lincoln's "patience, his modesty, his serene optimism" qualities that could now well serve their cause.

An index of this amended view was the Lincoln biography first published in March 1916 by Godfrey Rathbone Benson, or Lord Charnwood. Popularly received on both sides of the Atlantic, it was the first volume to have been written by an Englishman on the life of the Emancipator. This together with the fact that the author was a baron and of a literary family, had gained respect as a political strategist, and that his book appeared at one of history's most fretful moments, aroused special interest. English readers found it unexpectedly affecting. Considering the biography a "model of what the historian's work should be," John Drinkwater adapted it to a play in which Irish actor William J. Rea appeared in the leading role. Unlike Tarbell, Lord Charnwood did not intend to uncover new facts, only to review a familiar biography and a segment of American political history in balanced, temperate English. He claimed to have an advantage over American authors in his ability to bring a "delicacy and sureness of moral perception" to his considerations; his impartiality would rescue Lincoln's life from myopic regional analysis and cloying religious metaphor. Lord Charnwood could not deny that Lincoln's impoverished youth on the frontier imbued in him a respect for the common man, but the sagacity and compassion that would later serve him were more developed in defiance of these social and environmental conditions. To be able, even as a civilian, to win a war was one thing, but for Lincoln to possess the ability to separate out the moral and legal premises that were bound up in the conflict required unique insights. What made the difference in Lincoln's education, Charnwood insists with obvious satisfaction, was his self-directed study of a necessarily limited, but crucial range of literature: the Holy Bible, Shakespeare, *Aesop's Fables, Pilgrim's Progress,* Defoe's *Robinson Crusoe,* and, to a lesser extent, the poetry of Burns. These models instilled within his consciousness a "sort of poetry of its own," which in the end confirmed for Lincoln the plain, logical patterns "of what life should be."[29]

Like many Americans of their day, the Tafts were

drawn to Charnwood's preliminary observation that "[The reverence for Lincoln] is shared to-day by many who remember with no less affection how their own fathers fought against him." Now inviting reconciliation, he offered his nation's apology for its mistreatment of Lincoln, agreeing that Lord Salisbury, Lord Robert Cecil, and Gladstone behaved more as Prussian autocrats than as Britain's moral leaders, when they deprecated the American Union as a business rival. Charnwood well understood Northern fears that England and France might ally against the Union on the side of the Confederates, but he also hastened to absolve the English government of impropriety, reminding American readers that John Bright, Richard Cobden, and Lancashire workingmen, despite the American blockade of cotton exports from Southern states, had stood firm with Lincoln.[30]

It is doubtful that any member of the joint English and American committees had not read and been impressed by Charnwood's book. The Tafts and other Barnard Lincoln apologists wished to believe the Baron had something of Barnard's characterization in mind when he pointed to Lincoln's rude beginnings, and to his refusal thereafter to "introduce tidiness or method into his office" or his personal appearance. In Drinkwater's play, Rea spoke the King's English, but wore a crumpled top hat and a jacket whose pockets brimmed with documents. Lawrence Abbott noted parallels between Charnwood's verbal portrait and a statue in which "uncouthness was transformed into the finest kind of beauty." Having read the biography in the summer of 1917, Charles Taft also recognized confirming resemblances. All agreed that the burden of the Barnard Lincoln's reception in London rested almost entirely upon the fit and nature of its clothing.

In his congratulations to Barnard, caricaturist-illustrator Grant Wright summarily castigated the aristocratic presumptions of the opposition.

> Just think of these grand representatives of Democracy, [Thomas B.] Reed, dead, [Robert] Choate, dead, Robert Lincoln, the man who was ashamed of his father . . . think of them telling the mass of Americans what Lincoln should WEAR to be presentable to the court and what was meant by Democracy—jarring—none of them earned a dollar by the sweat of their brow and long after your great statue is erected Robert Lincoln will be whizzed home from his office in the Pullman Palace Car Co. in his $10,000 benzine buggy with all the windows drawn so he will not be able to see the great mass of the common people, with whom

his father loved to be classed—[Robert Lincoln] exclusive, select, haughty and arrogant aristocrat.

Charles Taft similarly chided those who insisted upon a man "of the tailor-made variety [because] Americans were known in England by their padded shoulders." Albert Shaw, like Wright and the critic McBride, treasured historic cartoons of Lincoln for their capacity to vividly summarize his character, and for that reason, thought Barnard well justified in his portrayal.[31] Could it have been that England's ruling classes were prepared to amend their views not only toward Lincoln's political identity, but also toward the whole question of sartorial refinement? Perris indicated as much.

Barnard transcribed Perris's obviously well-rehearsed panegyric as the Englishman stood before the statue in the company of the ACPC.

> Every English-speaking man, woman and child is today fighting for democracy. Millions are dying for democracy. All English-speaking people are one in this fight—American and English, brothers again under the flag of democracy. Abraham Lincoln, of all men, typifies the ideal we fight for. In the great statue of Abraham Lincoln, as revealed by Barnard, we have a statue that will give the people of England a great lesson in Democracy. This statue is destined to do more for humanity I believe than any other statue existing. I am deeply moved to think of the day when this statue of Abraham Lincoln will be placed in the streets where all London and England will see it. It will register one of the historic days of the world's history. England will rejoice to have another of these statues of Abraham Lincoln in Paris to stand there also as a monument to democracy. It seems to me predestined and fore-ordained that such a statue would be created at this supreme moment of its need in the world.[32]

Yet Charnwood expressed a decidedly different reaction when he finally had an opportunity to see photographs of Barnard's statue. The baron was generally familiar with the public monuments of both countries, frequently traveled through America, and maintained a close friendship with Canadian-born sculptor-anatomist, R. Tait McKenzie, as well as with Charles Moore, chairman of the Commission of Fine Arts. Thoroughly admiring of the Lincolns of Saint-Gaudens and Daniel French, Charnwood took issue with McKenzie for defending Barnard's interpretation. Recounting their dispute for Moore, Charnwood said McKenzie ventured the opinion that Barnard's depiction was "'democratic' or something to that effect and the Saint Gaudens's statue was not. I flatter myself that I converted him by pointing out that St. Gaudens' statue was really like a working man in the clothes which a working man would wear as President or to be sculpted, while Barnard's was not in the least like a working man but much more like a minor poet who had gone under." Obviously, photographs severely tested the author's usually moderate, balanced judgement on humanity. This revulsion equaled in intensity Charnwood's later reaction to Wilson, when during the president's triumphal postwar state visit to England, he archly announced that the term "Anglo-Saxon" no longer rightly applied to the people of the United States.[33]

But until 24 September 1917, when a report on the American controversy over the statue appeared in the London *Times,* few English citizens knew a Lincoln statue was soon to arrive in London courtesy of the Americans. Furthermore, until vengeful *Times* proprietor Lord Northcliffe published a blotchy, unfocused halftone reproduction in the following issue, Perris and Lord Weardale were the only members of the BCPC who had seen the image, the latter via sketches or photographs forwarded by Stewart, the former having actually seen the work in New York. Recalling his initial contact with Stewart, Weardale admitted he was aware a new statue was being offered in place of the Saint-Gaudens, because, as he understood it, the original plan had been aborted. On 11 February 1917, Stewart cabled Weardale the information that the replacement was generally considered a much finer work of art than the Saint-Gaudens, a judgment he ascribed to an unidentified London *Times* art editor who attended the Union Theological Seminary exhibition.[34]

Now charged by his own committee with having withheld from it sketches or illustrations of the Barnard replacement, Weardale denied having seen such materials before the BCPC acceptance vote. It was sufficient for him to know that the work was much admired in America and that a Taft, no matter which Taft, was its presentor, for "our committee could not but welcome a gift made to us by so prominent and responsible a personality as Taft." Confiding that when he finally saw its reproductions he found the statue to be homely, the BCPC chairman speculated that it was for this very reason "[it] appealed to a wider American sentiment." Faced with new anti-Barnard reports in the British and American press and left without a means for rescinding their vote, disgruntled BCPC members cabled Stewart not to forward the statue until after the War was concluded.[35]

Sir Alfred Mond, Lord Beauchamp's successor as First Commissioner of Works, was even more in the dark. His understanding was that in 1914 Lord Beauchamp approved the Canning enclosure for a Saint-Gaudens replica that had been offered by Charles Taft, whom he recognized as the owner of a fine art collection. But, in as much as the Office of Works claimed to have had no power to decide on the aesthetic nature of gifts, the commissioner begged to remain neutral. Weardale also wished to leave the decision to the Americans, but advanced the possibility that two Lincolns by the respective sculptors might stand together in London in a kind of competitive visual dialogue. Perris signaled from New York his willingness to follow Weardale's suggestion.[36] Despite his strong endorsement at the foundry, Perris now waived his right to argue aesthetics; he, too, held it to be sufficient that Roosevelt and William Taft were among Barnard's enthusiasts. It was not a question of superiority and inferiority, rather the simple fact that those who advanced the Saint-Gaudens cast had not been successful in their efforts to fund the work.

To fend off critics who naturally expected the new London-bound statue to be an exact duplication of the Cincinnati bronze, Stewart stressed that it was to be an "original variant" of the first. This implied that a judgment of the first should not be automatically transferred to the second, which might be more satisfying. His ploy also reminded all interested parties that the Saint-Gaudens figure could not escape being a mechanical reproduction since the artist was no longer living. Hoping to push this point to advantage, Barnard again underlined the unique nature of his cast, drawing upon a metaphorical parallel between his onetime encounter with the wax, and the transcendent results this encounter made possible. "Souls that willed for Universal good," he wrote, "have formed the mould into which mould has flowed the red blood of their life." It was important for his clients to realize that every new statue he produced from the wax bore "its own living touch of the artist."[37] Since there were no obvious differences between the two bronzes, the phrase "living touch" bore a decidedly more symbolic than literal connotation.

Rising British concerns and incalcuable complications arising from the war convinced the Barnard team that time was the most critical factor of all. With justice, Stewart's detractors speculated his latest efforts were guided by the single conviction that when "[the statue] is once over there the matter is settled." At first hoping for a July 1917 unveiling in

London, Stewart, Barnard, and Taft urged the Roman Bronze Works forward. Taft remitted five thousand dollars on 13 March and five weeks later a wax model derived from the original plaster piece molds was ready for the artist's inspection. Until the end of April, Barnard was free to retouch or radically change the wax surfaces had he chosen to do so. The wax form was then made ready for a core mold and firing, but Taft's final remittance was withheld until 31 October and another five months were to pass before bronze was actually poured.[38]

Production of the proposed French statue fell hopelessly behind schedule before work was indefinitely suspended. The foundry received the initial contract on 27 June but was forced to wait until 1 November 1917 for the initial payment.[39] Upon its receipt, a third wax model, made from the original piece moulds, was created. This remained in storage for several years while Riccardo Bertelli, director of lost wax operations for the Roman Bronze Works, vainly begged Barnard to complete payments.

Through the fall of 1917, as the tide of criticism directed at the English cast rose to fever pitch, Stewart and Harry Perris held strategy sessions in New York. With increasing obduracy, Stewart insisted a fall unveiling in London was still within the realm of possibility, even if formal dedication ceremonies might have to be delayed until after the armistice. Content to see the Lincoln as a virile image, Stewart urged the pro-Barnard forces to boldly attack their critics in like manner. On the other hand, taken with what his like-minded friends discerned were the statue's passive, reliant characteristics, Perris counseled Barnard to remain silent and not attempt to defend himself. He sweetened this directive by urging that "when a return blow is given to the dastardly attacks that have been made on you and your work—it must be a hard one."[40] Generally, Perris's advice prevailed. But for a final private viewing at the foundry on 19 October that would generate more appreciations, and a brief summary defense issued by the artist in mid-November, there would be relatively few attempts to argue down the philistines. Instead, the team vowed thereafter to take their case to heads of state.

Stewart now had to consider the eminent tightening of export controls by the Federal War Trade Board. Created by a blanket presidential order on 18 September 1917, the board proceeded to compile and publish licensing regulations restricting the exportation of critical produce and industrial materials through 1 November.[41] A marble Lincoln could have been freely exported, but bronze was high on the conservation list. Initially, bronze objects containing less than the United States standard of ten percent copper alloy would have been exempt, but the completed document ruled out even this exception. President Wilson, of course, had the discretion to ease restrictions on any export item he thought would give practical or propaganda assistance to the war effort. There was thus a possibility he might order a license for a bronze statue that seemed destined to raise the morale of an ally, contribute to that country's social stability, and reassure its citizenry about American intentions.

With this discretionary option in mind, members of the House of Representatives passed a nonbinding resolution on 6 October 1917 requesting President Wilson to prevent the statue's shipment. Sponsored by Massachusetts Rep. John J. Rogers, the vote climaxed a five-day hearing that extensively examined testimony, photographs, editorials, and the letters of Robert Lincoln. Rogers believed the resolution was made necessary because Abraham Lincoln was an international figure, a fact made apparent when British Prime Minister Lloyd George, demanding total victory on the European front, quoted a Lincoln resolve on the Civil War. Pennsylvania Rep. J. Hampton Moore's generous approbation of his state's native-born artist earned Rogers's unbridled scorn. In an exchange, Rogers ridiculed a Barnard statement of purpose claiming he "wanted to show the man's soul through his face and hands and feet." Turning to photographs, Rogers instructed his colleagues that if they would inspect "the misshapen, ugly, comic-cartoonist feet, I do not think that you will find that there is much soul there—spelled 's-o-u-l'; although at least two very conspicuous soles (Laughter)." Rather than impugn the patriotic motivations of the sponsers, the avenger asked only that the President "speak that single word" that would prevent the statue's shipment.[42]

Lincoln statues were not Wilson's top concern at the moment, but he was agonizing over human issues that were not unrelated to the Rogers Resolution. The president was defending a selective service law that failed to distinguish between slackers and conscientious objectors, although he officially assured the nation he did not favor conscripting the unwilling. Did the statue he was being asked to judge convey willingness, then, or reluctance? He could not doubt its rude countenance, whether the result of ineptitude, deliberate caricature, or heartfelt emotion, aligned it with what he took to be Lincoln's preference for working-class values. Hence his quandary over Barnard's statue, like the many seemingly unsolvable civil and military problems that confronted him in late 1917 was another cross for him to bear. Until the end of July, Stewart had been confident of Wilson's support. In June he persuaded the president to serve as honorary chairman of the presentation committee. Making no reference to the fact the Barnard was being substituted for another previously-sanctioned work, Stewart convinced Wilson to break a personal rule that forbade his endorsement of private gifts. As he reviewed the Rogers Resolution and other negative reports in early October, the president's attitude had changed. But when a new Barnard defense came to his attention, he confided to his assistant secretary of state, a man strongly critical of the statue, that "I have come to think that perhaps our alarm was not justified."[43]

With the shipping license now his primary concern, Stewart cabled Sir Alfred Mond a lengthy petition on 15 November reassuring the British government that the statue was ready for shipment, provided it could induce the issuance of a shipping licence. Omitting reference to published criticism, the cable emphasized the high political and professional regard for the work.[44] A roster of sponsors was divided into three sections: those who approved the cable, those who had at some time or another praised the work, and, beneath the name of honorary chairman Woodrow Wilson, there appeared an additional list of 250 names, subdivided by states of residence, who comprised the committee of presentation. With the first group were the names of William Taft, Roosevelt, Shaw, Tarbell, MacKaye, Henry McBride, MacMonnies, Goddard, and Thayer.

No longer entirely sure of Wilson's position, Stewart requested William Taft to bring up the matter of the shipping license during a previously scheduled meeting between himself and Wilson on another subject. Stewart considered as well requesting the intervention of American ambassador to England Walter H. Page, who he correctly believed approved of the statue. Page and Taft were attempting to obtain Wilson's approval for a series of Anglo-American diplomatic visits, colloquies Wilson not only opposed but considered conspiratorial to his anti-British views. Thus the Taft-Wilson conference would not be an ideal time for discussing the fate of a statue. Nevertheless, Taft advised Wilson that "it would be wise to give the order."[45]

To the same end, but on his own initiative, Albert Shaw wrote Wilson a long appreciation, since, as he observed, the statue's placement involved a certain sanction on [Wilson's] part." After a period of estrangement, due in part to presidential resolves favoring British interests, Shaw and Wilson were back on good terms. The former was editing a volume of the president's collected papers and the latter was preparing a strong war message to Congress that would please the editor.[46] Shaw obviously saw no reason for restraint or brevity in expressing his opinions.

I have studied [the statue] carefully at the foundry and have a most definite and mature opinion about it. It is a suburb monument, a great piece of creative art. It is amazingly impressive. In my opinion it is the greatest piece of portrait statuary that we have ever produced in America. I am perhaps not competent to speak about works of art considered purely as art. I am, however, competent to speak about Lincoln, because I have been a student of Lincoln's mind but also personality. Whatever else Barnard's Lincoln is most amazing in its accurate recreation for us of the actual Abraham Lincoln. It is by no means a grotesque thing, but it has immense dignity. Anatomically, it is unquestioningly like Lincoln. It is not true that the hands and feet are exaggerated.[47]

In attempting to cover all the points Wilson would likely be considering, Shaw's letter seemed more addressed to Barnard's enemies than to the one man who had the power to advance the statue. Implicating Robert Lincoln as the leader of the anti-Barnard conspiracy, he implied the son did not know his own father as well as did Shaw and others who valued the statue. Shaw criticized out of hand the anatomical structure of the Saint-Gaudens Lincoln, praised Barnard's choice of the beardless candidate—singling out the head as the finest portrait of Lincoln in existence—and repeated without example Stewart's claim that the new work was an original variant, though he admitted the divergence between statues was slight. Shaw summarized with a routine accusation: the critics of the Barnard were men "who have not had the frankness to say to the public that they have not seen the statue and that they have given their names in opposition merely through the earnest solicitation of certain individuals."[48]

Several days before Shaw's lengthy epistle arrived, Wilson received another critique from the painter John Singer Sargent. While posing for a portrait commissioned by the National Gallery of Ireland, Wilson accepted the painter's offer to report on the statue. After meeting with the artist at the foundry, Sargent assured the president that Barnard had agreed to correct the overly tight fit of the clothes and to change the arm and hand gesture, which so suggested the "look of the victim . . . acting his fate" by bringing the arms down to the sides. Wilson was satisfied that if such changes were made, the statue would "probably be worthy of the very unusual distinction which is to be conferred upon it."[49]

The president shared Sargent's response with William Taft and Taft, in turn, was able to cheer John Stewart with this generally positive report. That Wilson had for the time being reaffirmed his position on the statue presentation committee was also encouraging. But these developments did not mean Wilson was prepared to grant the license, or decisively render a public opinion, for he informed Shaw he was suspending all further judgement on the controversy. He did so with one final observation: "my only fear has been that Mr. Barnard has been intent upon being too absolutely realistic and that the mystical spirit of our great President would not be adequately indicated."[50] No "single word" was to be spoken, and consequently, Barnard's second Lincoln cast remained entombed at the foundry for an additional fifteen months.

Perhaps it was a missed opportunity. Had Wilson considered it further, he might have seen advantages in countersigning the shipment of the "absolutely realistic" figure to Parliament Square, since at the moment, Parliament's chief concern seemed not to be the Germans, but how to prevent the Barnard Lincoln's shipment. From mid-October through mid-December, Weardale and Mond stood their ground against shrill accusations and condemnations. Finally, in hearings in the House of Lords on 12 December, Charnwood forced a showdown. He baited Weardale and the Commissioner of Works with one of Robert Lincoln's chief complaints: that Barnard favored the chosen model in part because he happen to have been born on a farm near Lincoln's birthplace. The London *Times* summarized the disputation thus: "A more insufficient recommendation [Charnwood] could hardly conceive. He thought that in the circumstances the Government would show good judgement and good feeling if before committing themselves to a final decision as to giving a site, they consulted American feeling and the opinion of eminent sculptors in London in regard to the merits of the statue." With an assist from the Earl of Crawford, Weardale protested Charnwood's objections by alluding to the transcribed opinion of Roosevelt and the contents of the Sargent-Wilson communication he had just received from Stewart. The debate ended in apparent stalemate as Viscount Harcourt justified the action of the former Commissioner of Works for the reason that "we are notoriously behind other countries in the art of sculpture, and he would be sorry to see the matter judged by the same criterion of taste as that which was responsible for the erection of the Victoria Memorial." With that sentiment, at least, most of the other Lords in hearing were in full agreement.[51]

Part Four
Profiles of Controversy

7

The Judging of William Howard Taft

WILLIAM HOWARD TAFT'S FIRST ATTEMPTS TO DEFUSE Robert Lincoln's anger had little effect. Recurring illness augmented his reactionary temperment, and now in retirement, Lincoln was free to execute his censorial power more vigorously than ever. The present situation required him to not only reprove Theodore Roosevelt but Taft as well. It was easy to account for Roosevelt's widely quoted commendation of the statue, since, as Lincoln observed to his confidant Judd Stewart: "The trouble is that the gun [Roosevelt] fires is a very large one, and when it goes off half-cocked it makes a great deal of noise and is apt to cause a great deal of trouble. But for all this, I should gratefully welcome any form of incantation he should authorize. He, however, is not apt to make his recantation as loudly as his original." Even so, Lincoln was gratified to learn through a mutual acquaintance that Roosevelt objected to the implications of the published statement, claiming that his remarks were directed toward a Lincoln bust, not the statue, which he did not like.[1] Lincoln was left to conclude Roosevelt's failure to correct the record was due to his fear of further angering Taft. But was family loyalty enough to satisfactorily explain Taft's own determination to defend the statue's artistic qualities?

There were other statues for Lincoln to consider. The Art Commission of Illinois invited him to critique Andrew O'Connor's portrait prior to its casting and placement before the state capitol. Illustrating the president-elect bidding a farewell to Springfield's citizens, the beardless figure strides forward with both arms at its sides. A pronounced Adam's apple, thin chest, narrow shoulders, and the stiltlike legs were uncomfortably reminiscent of Barnard's depiction,

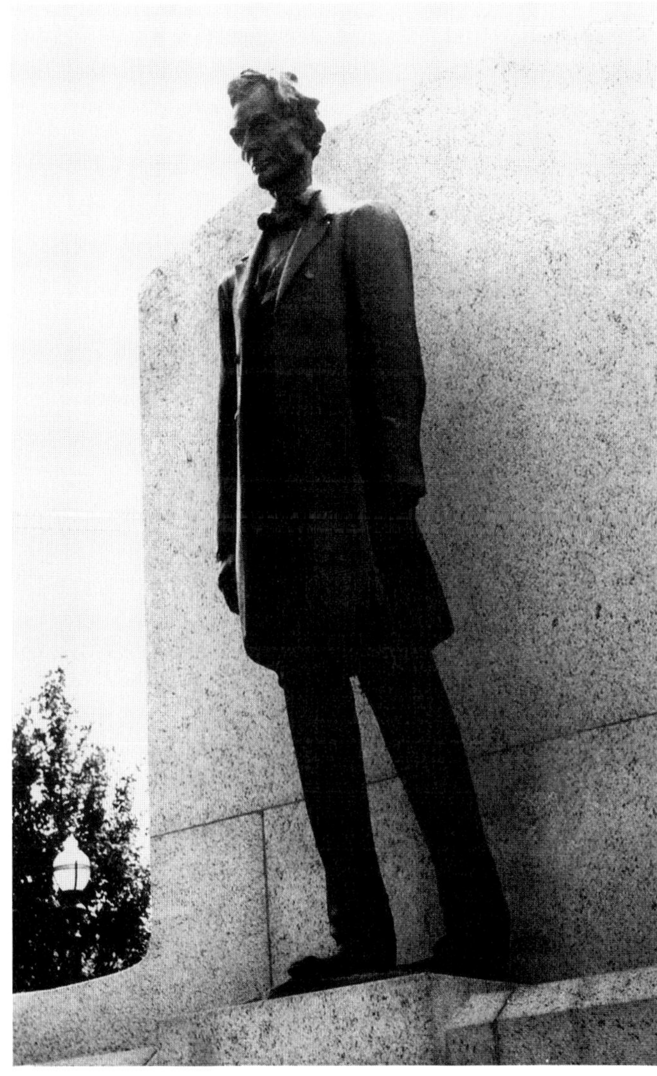

Andrew O'Connor, Abraham Lincoln. *1918. Bronze, 12'. Illinois State Capitol, Springfield.*

123

yet the face reflected no psychological torment, and the pressed outer garments more amply fitted the thin frame beneath them. After an upturned collar had been secured and the waistcoat smoothed over, Lincoln pronounced the figure fit for public display.[2]

There was a difference between Robert Lincoln's begrudging acceptance of a portrait statue, and his underlying attitude toward sculptural representation in general. He admired a family heirloom, an edition of a Leonard Volk *Hermes Bust* that closely followed the features of the life cast, and Robert also frequently commended Saint-Gaudens's and Daniel French's portraits of his father. Nonetheless, he privately confessed he "was not keen on having any statue" of his father in London. Life photographs had the edge over other pictorial media, and in this category, the winning image was the Anthony Berger three-quarter view taken in Brady's Washington studio on 9 February 1864. Statues disappointed him because marble and bronze could never approximate life; the only basis for their acceptance was how well a photographic transcription of a particular statue convincingly restored the modeled or hewn materials to actual flesh, cloth, and hair. Lincoln boasted he had not seen Barnard's "beastly thing and I hope I may never do so. I am quite satisfied that the photographs I have seen do not lie in depicting the various atrocities. Photographs could not show them if they did not exist." And what in this instance was revealed was a figure entirely contrary to his remembrance—never had his father crossed his hands over his stomach in such an agonized manner.[3]

Robert Lincoln's clandestine actions against the statue were aimed at preventing the raising of a statue, not advancing another in its place. His bitter complaint to Taft reflected a belief that if brought under sufficient pressure, the former president would eventually force his brother to yield. Even if this strategy failed, the letter would otherwise be useful in swaying the opinions of influential statesmen. To this end, Lincoln began testing the waters of diplomacy. Harboring warm memories of his tenure as United States minister plenipotentiary to London, he requested his close friend Joseph Choate, a former ambassador to Great Britain, to formally appeal to the British Foreign Office. Choate was only too happy to comply, for after reading Lincoln's letter to Taft and seeing the photographs, he took a strong personal interest in the matter. In early May, Choate reassurred Lincoln that "I have not at all forgotten my promise to write you the needed letter. I have been more taken up since my return from Washington with an effort to stop the sending of a triplicate

of the horrible statue to Russia, the last place where your father ought to be represented by such an effigy." As an honorary vice president of the American Committee for the Encouragement of Democratic Government in Russia, and on good terms with its organizer, Charles Flint, Choate informed Lincoln he had all but convinced Flint to withdraw the Petrograd offer. He further vowed that once his duties on behalf of the Balfour and Joffre reception in New York were fulfilled, he would devote all his energy to turning back the proposals. A week after posting this letter, the eighty-five-year-old lawyer-diplomat died of a heart attack.[4] The official view was that Choate's directorship of the New York peace committee had overtaxed him, but Robert Lincoln and his friends had a more specific diagnosis in mind.

That in his final moments Choate accorded such high priority to defeating the Barnard projects, not only as a favor to Robert Lincoln but also because of personal conviction, did not ease William Taft's personal discomfort when he saw the Choate-Lincoln correspondence in published form. With conviction, Taft wrote Mrs. Choate that a "great man has gone from among us at the height of his powers," for it was obvious Wilson's call to arms had rejuvenated the statesman. Like Taft and other conservatives, Choate had been slow to accept the inevitable, but Belgium had transformed him into a fierce war hawk; thereafter, his speeches compared pacifists and slackers to Civil War Copperheads. Ultimately, he too became convinced Abraham Lincoln was personally leading the nation into the war, and because of this, nothing short of total national effort was required.[5] However, he detected no evidence of this determination in the Taft Lincoln.

Had Choate survived the war years, he would have had a significant influence in the eventual outcome of the controversy. As an active member in Stewart's ACPC and, however briefly, the subsequent Committee of Fifteen, he presumably had full knowledge of the proceedings and could have brought a rapid "open-and-shut" indictment against the executive director. His intimate standing with British politicians would have assisted in breaking through their diplomatic neutrality. Like Robert Lincoln, however, his ultimate objective was to check the passage of the Barnard, not advance the Saint-Gaudens. Despite his participation in the original ACPC negotiations relative to the Saint-Gaudens offer, Choate had little to say in defense of Lincoln statues. He was, after all, a celebrated lecturer on Lincoln and had known him personally. If he preferred the Saint-Gaudens to its substitute, this did not mean it wholly impressed him, since, as he considered it, Choate became convinced no visual artist could overcome the problems visited upon him by Lincoln's appearance.[6] The idea of Lincoln transcended the sculptor's art altogether, while the character of lesser heroes was more suitably captured by it. Among Chicago's portrait statues, for example, Choate more liked Louis Rebisso's Ulysses S. Grant equestrian than Saint-Gaudens's Lincoln.

The circumstances surrounding Choate's last communication to Robert Lincoln gave it an importance second only to the Lincoln-Taft letter. Multiple copies of both texts were widely distributed among such supporters as Judd Stewart and Frederick Ruckstull, the irrepressible editor of the *Art World*. In the spring of 1917 Lincoln forwarded this material along with photographs to Cecil Spring Rice, Great Britain's ambassador to the United States, requesting they be sent through channels to the British Foreign Office. Once arrived, they would normally be passed to American Ambassador Walter Page. But while Spring-Rice was sympathetic to Lincoln's campaign, Page was not. Furthermore, Lincoln did not fully appreciate Spring-Rice's weakened position with Prime Minister Balfour's newly established conservative regieme. When at year's end Robert Lincoln impatiently awaited what he expected to be an official British repudiation of the hated statue, Spring Rice was dismissed from the foreign service. Looking beyond this personnel change, Lincoln correctly surmised John Stewart had also intervened in some manner.[7]

While gathering critical support on the home front, Lincoln elected to send Barnard Lincoln photographs to the Springfield bankers, lawyers, and judges who best knew his father in his professional life. Robert scorned the pro-Barnard commentary of Harrison Gourley, a mere bureaucrat who frequently saw him but seldom heard Abraham Lincoln speak. Infinitely more reliable in his view was the critical refutation of his Yale-trained attorney friend, Clinton L. Conkling. Likewise, St. Louis Appeals Court Judge George D. Reynolds, whose contact with Abraham Lincoln was confined to the years between 1856 and 1861, swore that the illustrative material failed to present a "faithful reproduction" of the man. Reynolds separately forwarded his judgment to William Taft, along with others by St. Louis attorneys Charles P. Johnson and Wells H. Blodgett, also privileged members of Springfield's living witness fraternity.[8]

Drawing from a standard checklist of complaints, Reynolds called Taft's attention to the lugubrious expression, the disheveled clothing, the arm positioning, the long neck, prominent Adam's apple, and the unusually large feet and hands. He recalled a "fighting man, fighting a fight he expected to win" and one who was careful to dress in immaculate linen. It seemed to him that Barnard had fallen into historical error by assuming that the Lincoln of the late 1850s continued to act and look like a laborer, when, in fact, because of his later professional associations, he had already grown "away from the days and ways of manual labor." Similarly, the woebegone expression projected a sorrow yet to come, not the gregarious, genial disposition of the candidate. Having spent much of his professional career defending the Pullman company against the interests of labor, Robert Lincoln obviously found these remarks heartening and no doubt agreed with Reynolds's characterization of the Petrograd offer, a subject Robert was unable to address in his initial letter to Taft. Reynolds viewed the placement of Barnard Lincolns in Cincinnati, Paris, and London enough of an insult to each of the host cities, but like Choate, thought the possibility of a Russian statue far worse, since, to judge from available news photographs, even the proletariat and Bolsheviki "are not so hideously uncouth and ungainly [as the statue]." Quoting scripture, the judge implored Taft to change his mind. Even if committed, he observed, "you are a 'son of man and can repent' [As cited in] 23 Numbers, V:19; although the same book Genesis VI: 6, says that even Deity repented. I guess you have had occasion to change your mind occasionally. I know I have in my nine years on the appellate bench. I ask a rehearing on your judgment approving this enormity." Judd Stewart, another like Robert Lincoln who had rendered Taft political support in his struggle against Roosevelt, now rose to taunt him. An industrialist who claimed ownership of the largest collection of Lincolniana in existance, Stewart called Taft's attention to the same historical inconsistencies that angered Reynolds. Barnard's "immature country lout" might have adequately represented an adolescent, but photographic and descriptive evidence proved that during the Lincoln-Douglas debates, the candidate was fully formed and imbued with the poise of a great man.[9]

A prominent member of the Barnard statue presentation committee chose to send Taft, rather than Stewart, notice of his resignation.[10] William H. P. Faunce, currently the president of Brown University and a popular lecturer on international religious and social issues, professed like Taft to be an amateur in art matters. But he was certain the goal in presenting statues to another country was to provide the host nation with an "interpretation of the highest product of American life." Unlike the others, he allowed that the "weird statue, which in the name of realism presents Abraham Lincoln without dignity or intellect or purpose," might indeed be raised in Russia without fear of unhappy consequences, but certainly not in England where human dignity and intellect were treasured qualities. Few Englishmen knew what an ideal American male looked like, Faunce argued, thus such an image would provoke grave misunderstandings between the two countries.

Taft was also confronted by Yale classmate Edward Lind Morse (1857–1923), a painter who counted himself a thoroughbred professional. The son of artist-inventor Samuel F. B. Morse, he summered at the Stockbridge, Massachusetts, art colony, near the summer retreat of the late Joseph Choate. Following his graduation and ten years of academic study in Germany and France, Morse was unable to emerge from the shadow of his illustrious parent. Perhaps his single most significant achievement was the biography he completed of his father in 1914, a study that dealt frankly with the inventor's racism, bigotry, his uncompromising antagonism both for the emancipation proclamation and its "weak and vacillating" author.[11] Personally disavowing these opinions, Edward nevertheless boldly exhonorated his father as one of the most illustrious men of his age.

In early October 1917, Morse warned Taft "it would be a crime against art and an insult to the great emancipator to let [Barnard's Lincoln] represent him in the British metropolis."[12] He forwarded a *New York Tribune* editorial he thought expressed the feelings of "practically every artist in the United States." While with ironic intent Samuel Morse might have exalted Barnard's rendition, his son was obviously dismayed by the statue's "unmanly" aspects. His favorite, however, was not the Saint-Gaudens but Daniel French's standing Lincoln, which he happened to have seen as a clay model in the artist's studio ten years previously. In contrast to this commanding study of a great personality buried in thought, Barnard's statue was a mere caricature.

Taft delivered Morse a standard response. On aesthetic questions he was an amateur and therefore had only his feelings and the testimony of other laymen to guide him. On this basis, the Barnard had a powerful effect "upon the lay mind as a whole" and Taft added the aesthetic perception that "it grows on one the more one looks at it." As he was about to remind Judge Reynolds and others, the excessive criticism was unjust because it was being generated by accusers who had not actually seen the statue. By so arguing, Taft no doubt had the common law writ of habeas corpus in mind. But he was also most definite about the nature of contracts, affirming that "so far as my

brother is concerned, he made the offer and it was accepted, and, even if he be otherwise minded, as he is not, he could not in honor withdraw." Unimpressed by Morse's standing in the National Academy of Design, Taft confided to his wife: "Ed Morse . . . is a failure protesting against Barnard's statue of Lincoln. He wrote like a Pope as if what he said settled it. I answered differing from him and then asked him if he had seen the statue. I don't believe he has. He was very sore."[13]

Morse demanded further satisfaction, calling attention to a discrepancy between Taft's legal-political views and his aesthetic outlook. In reference to the insurgent strategy advocating public recourse to initiatives, referendums, as well as to the popular recall of justices, and judicial decisions, he agreed with Taft that the "lay mind is not as well able to cope with the problems of the law and of statecraft as the expert." But Taft, after all, had created the Commission of Fine Arts obstensively to render a similar professional judgment of art projects for federal districts. Even though professional artworks were meant to appeal to the nonprofessional viewer, Morse interjected the indefensible claim, "I think you will find that no statue or other work of art has obtained lasting fame, unless it has been endorsed by professional artists." In the present case, a public artwork has been almost universally condemned by laymen and professionals as well as by the memorialized subject's living relative. Admittedly, he had only seen photographs, not the work itself, but neither had he seen Verrocchio's *Colleoni* in Venice, or Saint-Gaudens's standing *Abraham Lincoln,* yet he could venture that the verdict "of posterity will be that the last two are masterpieces and the former a caricature."[14] Taft chose not to answer this second more closely argued rejoinder.

Morse's determination to place the issues of public art on an equal plane with political and judicial issues was no doubt inspired by Charles Moore, who was summering at Stockbridge. Though his affiliation with the continued to be that of a lay member, Moore was to remain the cornerstone of that organization's first years. In 1915, after five years as secretary, Moore advanced to CFA chairman, a post he held until 1937. He was otherwise active in the affairs of the New-York-based American Federation of Arts, he lectured and authored articles on public monuments, and he was Daniel Burnham's chief biographer. What for the moment made him especially useful to the Barnard opposition was his long and reasonably friendly association with William Taft.

In mid-September 1917, Moore sounded Taft out

on the question of jurisdiction. The CFA had been asked to render an opinion on the Barnard-Saint-Gaudens affair and since Taft was "one of the founders and strong supporters of this body," Moore thought it reasonable to ask his personal opinion. Taft flatly denied the commission had any authority in the case, since it was not an official matter, but for the record he would present his personal view. If considered within their proper contexts, both statues had validity. The rough surfaces and informal appearance of the one suited it for placement in a park close to the public, while the classical refinement of the other was a perfect complement to a memorial shrine. Taft found Moore's criticisms unjust; the Barnard was not grotesque—in fact it was probably "truer to life than any of them." But then he backed away, for he assured his correspondent that French's conception "suits me best." He concluded by retreating into the defensive posture of the layman. "Of course I am not an artist, and I only give you the impression that the Barnard statue has made upon me, a wayfaring man, but a fool."[15]

As it happened, Moore's inquiry came as the procedural misunderstanding between Taft and the Senate liaison member of the Lincoln Memorial Commission had abruptly halted French's work on the colossus.[16] As noted above, French awaited a signal from the LMC before ordering and cutting marble sections, but Taft was unaware a formal meeting was required before this next step could be taken. There was no causal relation between this miscommunication and Taft's regard for the Barnard statue, yet because French stood to be blamed for the delay, he, Moore, and chief architect Henry Bacon nevertheless suspected there was a connection, that the LMC chairman had allowed personal feelings to derail his official, dispassionate, responsibilities. That Taft went on record preferring French's portrait over the Barnard, even if only by degree, helped somewhat to allay these fears.

Yet Moore wished to impress upon Taft the fact that the dispute had everything to do with the successful completion of the Daniel French Lincoln. French was taking a personal interest in the outcome of the London statue offer, and, with encouragement from sculptors Paul Bartlett and CFA member Herbert Adams, had informed Barnard of his objections. Now drawing upon the authority of the written word, Moore reviewed the virtues of Saint-Gaudens's portrait, a visualization he compared with the Lincoln tribute of James Russell Lowell. "The American people have idealized the author of the Gettysburg address and the Second Inaugural . . . It was this fact that Richard Watson Gilder taught Saint-Gaudens and it is this idea that Mr. French has embodied in his statue." With his patience wearing thin, Taft indicated the exaggerated nature of Moore's and French's condemnations proved they were "not judicial and not careful." However, he resisted the temptation to add the considerably more pointed remark that was to conclude his answer to Judge Reynolds several months later: "the language that has been hurled [at the Barnard] is so utterly excessive in its abusive character that it must have been prompted by something other than a mere consideration of the statue as a memorial to Lincoln."[17]

The implication that a vengeful political attack on Taft lay beneath what should have remained an honest disagreement among friends over aesthetic priorities was widely held among Barnard's supporters. Frank Chapman could only believe that the venom "so borders on malicious persecution that it carries its own contradiction." After reading strident press critiques as well as a note personally sent him by Robert Lincoln, Isaac Markens sought Taft's reassurance. "There must be something back of all this . . . these sensitive people . . . are always ready to endorse the most absurd idealistic productions when they look pretty. To me the the appealing quality of Lincoln is the simplicity and ugliness, as set forth by Barnard." Accused of having usurped executive privilege, John Stewart wilted under a barrage of indelicately phrased charges.[18]

The verbal onslaught reflected a prominent strain of contemporary art criticism. Strong uncompromising rhetoric had become a popular weapon in the academician's arsenal during the period extending from the "Armory Show" to the conclusion of World War I. Kenyon Cox, Edwin Blashfield, Carroll Beckwith, John Alexander, and Guy Pene du Bois, among other artists and critics, commonly drew upon such terms as "queer," "pervert," "feeble-minded," "insane," "rubbish," "monstrous," and "lunatic fringe" to express moral indignation over antisocial tendencies of postimpressionism and its Modernist progeny. Milton Brown has observed that the war years spawned a language of "frenzied incoherence" and "critical absurdity" that was intended to defend eternal classical values.[19] Even though what went under the rubric of "realist" art was less suspect than the seemingly anarchistic work of Matisse, Cézanne, the cubists, and the futurists, realism earned its share of vituperative discourse, for the reason that it seemed to grow out of a similar self-indulgence and social decrepitude. Still, as Taft, the lay critic, perceived, both realism and classicism were grounded in equally valid social contexts, even though one happened to respond to the real experiences of the underclass, the other to the high idealism of social leaders. He could only conclude the injudicious language was prompted by a fear among fellow patricians that he, the most widely respected spokesman for conservative ideals, had been mysteriously striken by the disease of Bolshevism.

Thus, it was with a sense of urgency that Moore dug for further confirmation of his views on the statues. Anxious to obtain an informed judgment that would not be based solely on photographic evidence and that even the Tafts would respect, he took his case to Joseph H. Gest. Well known to the Tafts, especially Charles, Gest (1859–1935) had long ruled as Cincinnati's most influential art administrator.[20] From 1888 to 1902 he was the assistant director, then, from the latter year until 1929, director of the Cincinnati Museum of Art as well as of the Academy of Art. He was also a mainstay of Rookwood Pottery, advancing to company president in 1914 while continuing to chair its board of directors. He also headed the advisory board of the National Gallery of Art and locally led the Cincinnati Municipal Art League and the Museum association, which played active roles in secondary school art education.

Gest's detailed summation corresponded with William Taft's more hastily expressed views.[21] Couching his assessment in moderate, conciliatory, language, he admitted to Moore the statue "was to me at first a shock," but he then described a slow warming as the power it emitted gradually took hold. Finally, after repeated viewings, he could "feel it throbbing there." There was, Gest lectured, more than one option open for artists of public statues: "realism" allowed for the play of the artist's imagination in expressing his personal emotion, while the combined aesthetic category of tradition and style pointed in a different direction. Even though these had always been irreconcilable approaches, they were equally valid so long as universal standards of artistic sincerity and craftsmanship were involved and so long as one studied the actual statue and not photographs. So too, a private citizen was free to commission statues belonging to these contrasting modes. He admired the Saint-Gaudens not as a statement of "the Man," but as an embodiment of "The President" and, for this reason, had personally placed a photograph of it in a school attended by African-American children. Barnard's realism was appropriate for the prepresidential Lincoln, or "Lincoln the Man," since the early years were so utterly barren and uncultured. But for an overemphasis of certain "realistic details," Barnard had admirably succeeded in capturing the stark essence of a social condition that few Americans had

experienced for themselves or were likely to find attractive. History warranted Barnard's interpretation because Lincoln was so thoroughly immersed in the thoughts and feelings of his time. For this reason, Gest could understand Robert Lincoln's reaction, but there was no reason why a choice had to be made, why the public's exposure to art's many forms should be limited. Gest's conclusion was less conciliatory. Deferring the final question of quality to the "test of time," he entered in the margin a final, more decisive, prediction: "We may well remember that the vitality of this Barnard statue with its homely and common humanity may in the time of social upheaval following this great war convey something of this rugged strength of the highest American character that a more reserved and dignified statue of Lincoln would not."

A clearly disappointed Moore forwarded the Gest and William Taft summations to an incredulous Daniel French. The sculptor was amazed that the veritable bastion of political conservatism could accept at once a sterling example of classicism and a poorly-rendered manifestation of realist portraiture. Equally upsetting was the way Gest "talked all around the issue," refusing to confront the plain fact that Barnard was incompetent. "It is not whether Barnard has made the attempt to portray the man of the people—which would be good—but whether he succeeded in that or anything else worth while." To make his position entirely clear, French directed an unequivocal declaration to Barnard: "It seems necessary now that I should tell you that your statue does not seem to me to represent Lincoln either in person or character and I have to confess that I should regret to see it erected in a foreign city as a portrait of our great President."[22] Stiffly formal though the statement was, Daniel French rarely expressed his opinion of other statues so frankly. But that a man of Taft's intelligence found value in such an obviously irredeemable creation was sufficient to cause him to distrust his own judgment.

This was a common reaction among many of the politicians and civic leaders with whom Taft frequently associated. Wartime service brought him close to lawyers, financiers, and academics who questioned his position in the affair. In 1918, while remaining the League to Enforce Peace's deeply committed president, Taft was an active chairman of the National American Red Cross and cochairman of President Wilson's National War Labor Board, an assignment that forced his return from New Haven to Washington. Several key administrators in this work were themselves active in the American Federation of Arts, one of several organizations that would tirelessly campaign against the Barnard statue.[23] The Federation's presiding officer was corporate lawyer Robert W. De Forest, a Yale graduate whose civic involvements ranged from the presidency of the Metropolitan Museum of Art, to the administration of city philanthropic services, and to the vice presidency of the National American Red Cross. De Forest also headed New York City's Municipal Art Commission, and hence was personally familiar with the early history of the Barnard Lincoln. Elihu Root, Taft's former political mentor, was a charter member of the federation and continued to sit on its board of directors, as he did on the governing bodies of numerous other clubs and institutions, including, as we have mentioned, the Metropolitan Museum of Art. We have already evaluated the rebellion in the ranks of Stewart's ACPC executive committee that led to the resignations of Root, Nicholas Murray Butler, and Joseph Choate, this following the contested Carnegie Endowment "buy-out." Now with a determination equal to that of Robert Lincoln and Choate, Root prepared to advance the federation's attack on the statue. They remained steady correspondents, but Taft and Root with increasing frequency found themselves on the opposite sides of party issues, a situation that obviously did not help moderate the latter's assessment of the statue situation.[24]

Consistent with other conservative art organizations that flourished in the wake of the City Beautiful movement, The American Federation of Arts pledged to foster social reform through a sponsorship of "intelligent" art and architectural design. As was made manifest in the pages of its journal, the *American Magazine of Art,* the organization was determined to cleanse contemporary art of modernistic and realistic impurities by controlling the content and style of public art and by restricting the permissible range of museum exhibitions and collection purchases. The works of William Merrit Chase, James McNeill Whistler, and John Singer Sargent were spotlighted against a backdrop of American impressionism, tonalism, and academic figurative work. During the war years, the periodical gave greater attention to public monuments, emphasizing the inspirational effect that properly designed war memorials could have on citizens living in far-flung communities. As chairman of the federation's General Committee on War Memorials, Moore illustrated talks and articles with a chronological survey of monuments, ranging from the *Winged Victory of Samothrace* to the heroic commemoratives of Jules Dalou and Saint-Gaudens.[25] By creating such models, he argued, artists had given pictorial form to the ideals, feelings of honor, and to the patriotism of their respective societies. A similar theme dominated federation-sponsored presentations by, among others, Lorado Taft, Herbert and Adeline Adams, and Hermon MacNeil.

Despite its populist educational preamble, the federation defined democracy in the narrowist of terms. The people its artists hoped to reach were divided between successes and the "failures, the left-behinds, the incompetents, [who had] to be carried on the shoulders of the intelligent." "Are 'the people,'" Maria Oakey Dewing asked, "hungry, unwashed ragged and imprisoned? Are 'the people' stupid and ignorant? No! a thousand times no! These are no more 'the people' than the very small class who are spoiled with luxury and thoughtless with inexperience." Consequently, the social makeup of the audience, not the test of time, determined the value of art. Even if ragged, unwashed denizens like those Lorado Taft observed on the benches surrounding the Taft Lincoln were to some degree uplifted by the work, the federation otherwise judged them to be incapable and unworthy of an authentic aesthetic experience. The social exclusivity that permeated the federation's deliberations was underlined by MacNeil, whose oeuvre also included a Lincoln statue, when he spoke of the progress of contemporary sculpture at the AFA's 1917 annual convention: "And above all else [the artist's] work must radiate some charm or strength of human character that touches the passer by." The radiated art spirit, he continued, could not be legislated, but was to be discovered in "the hearts of those who make up our better class of citizenship."[26]

AFA Secretary Leila Mechlin, who was also the editor of the *American Magazine of Art,* stoically received news that Barnard's London-bound statue had been cast in early October 1917. She had just completed an editorial for the periodical's November issue that would constitute the federation's opening shot in the publicity war and hopefully lead to Charles Taft's withdrawal of the commission. Mechlin had little interest in the aesthetic side of the question and even conceded Barnard had ability and that his statue was "in its way a work of art." What brought her to the conclusion that "the whole world has gone mad" was the fact William Taft chose to ignore Robert Lincoln's protest.[27] While pressing this point, she quoted the entire text of the letter and secondarily credited the adverse opinions of the living witnesses. To the latter compilation she appended the nonsensical observation that because Barnard could not have remembered Lincoln, it was not surprising he was unable to interpret his appearance and spirit.

Critiques in the December 1917 and January 1918 issues of *American Magazine of Art* were authored by George L. Raymond, a living Lincoln witness who also had written a pyschological study of art, and by Maria Dewing, wife of the painter Thomas W. Dewing. Raymond's fundamental complaint was that the statue was intended to represent Lincoln rather than some other individual, for otherwise its realism held interest, even importance. But with the identity fully indicated, the gestures, physical carriage, and anatomical abnormalities competed with the actual subject's physical being, as well as with the associative ideals of democracy and emancipation. According to Raymond's physiological lexicon, Barnard's portrait envisioned a radical who would have warred with England over the Mason and Sidell affair, and who would have imprudently freed the slaves before Northern opinion was prepared to accept the measure. Barnard was apparently influenced by the satirical caricatures that were distributed to discredit Lincoln during his first campaign. Mrs. Dewing unfavorably compared the "nerveless, ill-formed, weak [and] resignedly laid together" hands of the statue with the vigorous natural hands made visible by the Volk casts.[28]

Although it agreed in principle that the creative act could not be legislated, the federation, in consultation with the CFA, now pushed for federal intervention in all cases involving the presentation of gift statues of a public nature to foreign countries. Cass Gilbert, Root, Moore, and others sought to establish a cooperative link between the federation, which unlike the National Academy of Design claimed a national constituency, and the CFA, and the State Department. The proposal faced enormous difficulties by attempting to federalize private initiative, an issue that when applied to the Barnard work, divided the federation's own membership. However, following a joint session with an ad hoc committee representing the National Academy of Design, the federation passed resolutions it vainly hoped to see made into law. During its annual conference in May 1918, the organization resolved that Barnard's substitute statue should not be sent to London, and urged the enactment of legislation that would prevent private parties from "making gifts of the public representative character to foreign countries . . . without the approval of the proper authorities of the United States Government."[29]

At first independently, then as collaborators, Moore, acting on behalf of the CFA, and Root, in accordance with the AFA resolutions he had largely authored, drew up identical bills that were entered in the Senate and House in September 1918. As amended by the Committees on the Library in both Houses, they authorized the secretary of the treasury to refuse export licenses for any work of art purporting to be a gift made by an individual or an organization to a foreign nation or muncipality [whether or not deemed to be of a "public representative character"] unless by the consent of the secretary of state. The omission of the "public character" clause in the amended version considerably broadened the intent of the original language. But the amendment also struck out a provision pointedly directing the secretary of state to proceed only upon the advise of the CFA, and another—aimed directly at stopping the shipment of the Barnard statue—that insisted the legislation take effect immediately upon passage.[30] Even though the measure did not specifically direct the secretary of state to seek professional advice, Moore and Root trusted it sufficiently inferred the secretary would be guided by CFA consultation.

We shall presently discuss what became known as the Root Bill while examining the harried international negotiations that preceded the placement of the statues in England. Our present focus is on William Taft's relationship with those who wished to expand the CFA's power over the private realm and specifically empower it to retire the Taft Lincoln. Such a move was a sure test of the limits of Taft conservatism and he was undoubtedly relieved that neither bill cleared the Senate or House. However, before the House version failed in committee, the measure was attached to a report by Moore and CFA executive officer Col. C. S. Ridley that recited the history of the statue controversy and urged that the CFA be permitted to fulfill without hindrance its proper function as a federal art censor. Moore directed his remarks as much to Taft as he did to the House, when he explained the proposed legislation would direct,

> that the agency which Congress has seen fit to set up to advise the Government in matters of art shall act in these cases. There is, afterall, a good deal of common sense about questions of art; and there is also a good deal that is technical. It is one thing for a man to know what pleases him; it is quite another thing to know what will please cultivated men and woman not only to-day but decades and centuries hence. There are standards in art, standards in taste, which have been developed through the centuries. If we are to make gifts of American works of art to other countries, let us see to it that they get the very best we have to offer.

He further affirmed that only one Lincoln statue was worthy of export. "Indeed, the present generation of

Americans have had their ideas of Lincoln's personality formed largely by [the Saint-Gaudens] statue, which has been copied for museums and photographed until it is one of the best known works of art in this country."[31]

Anticipating the bill's defeat, Root and Nicholas Murray Butler decided to work within the precincts of the Carnegie Foundation to advance the Saint-Gaudens cast. They were joined in this new endeavor by senior diplomat Henry White (1850–1927). In early 1918, White was balancing assignments as an American Red Cross administrator, and as a delegate with the Wilson mission to the League of Nations conference in Paris, but he could not ignore Robert Lincoln's call for assistance. Before advancing to the ambassadorships of Italy and France, White had loyally served as Robert Lincoln's first secretary in the London legation and personally shared the Lincolns' bereavement following the death in 1890 of their son, Abraham Lincoln II, the same young man who three years previously had unveiled Saint-Gaudens's standing statue of Lincoln in Chicago. The "hardest blow" of White's own career, however, was dealt by President Taft, who, after assuring Roosevelt, Lodge, Root, and other White supporters that he would retain him as the French ambassador, summarily dismissed him in 1909.[32] White preferred to believe an innocent misunderstanding prompted this unkindness, not significant policy differences. Nonetheless, the firing not only drove another wedge between Taft and Roosevelt but it also reflected on Taft's judgment and character in the minds of those who now passionately opposed the exportation of the Barnard statue, most especially in the mind of White himself.

Learning of the new Saint-Gaudens initiative from White in December 1917, just as he realized his personal diplomatic efforts had failed to bring positive results, Robert Lincoln was gradually reconciled to the placement of Saint-Gaudens replicas in London and Paris as the most efficient way for checking the Barnard offers. The only other acceptable alternative would be the placing of a replica of Daniel French's Nebraska statue. Lincoln rejected Judd Stewart's suggestion that an entirely new statue by an American be chosen upon the advice of the National Academy of Design, a move he reasoned would play into the hands of the Barnardites by causing further controversy. Meanwhile, before his call to Paris, White was detailed by Root and Butler to draw up contracts for casting two bronze replicas of the Saint-Gaudens statue, and in late February 1918, Chicago's Lincoln Park commissioners consented to allow the casts to be made.[33] But this development by no means signaled victory, only the beginning of the final moments in an international chess match that was being played out with public statuary.

William Taft was correct when he predicted to Stewart that the excessive criticism would eventually subside. His injured colleagues were to gradually forgive his momentary madness and Taft, proceeding as if nothing had happened, went out of his way to show appreciation for their understanding. Long before the controversy was finally resolved, Taft was appointed honorary chairman of the American Federation of Arts' Committee on War Memorials. The reconciliation accompanied a blossoming personal friendship between Taft and Lord Charnwood. He saluted the British author's critical prowess in his introduction to William Draper Lewis's posthumous *Life of Theodore Roosevelt* (1919), and it was clearly Charnwood's rhetorical forebearance that set the tone for Taft's generous euology. Setting aside his own resentments, Charnwood warmly returned the compliment. Significantly, the men first met in the fall of 1918 while in the company of Charles Moore and an assembly of CFA members before the unfinished shell of the Lincoln Memorial. Charnwood had just completed a western tour that included an address at the unveiling of the O'Connor Lincoln statue in Springfield.[34]

Taft's appointment to the Supreme Court in 1921 also helped repair his friendship with Robert Lincoln. But it was the dedication of the Lincoln Memorial in 1922 that more than any other event ensured the hatchet would remain buried. Seated beside Taft and President Harding before French's massive figure, the son of the immortalized hero forgot his prejudice against sculpted portraits. In the four years remaining to him, Robert often asked to be driven around the memorial and the statue Taft had helped make possible.[35]

8

The Press

IT WAS NOT UNTIL THE FALL OF 1917 THAT THE CONTRO-versy fully blossomed in the American press. Despite the *Literary Digest*'s damaging publication of the distorted photograph, the *Milwaukee Sentinel*'s subsequent ill humor, the foreboding silence of the *New York Times,* and Barnard's lack of candor, the statue's yet semiprivate status seemed to veil it from harsher public judgement.[1] Moreover, until the bronze departed Manhattan, nothing was known of plans for exporting replicas.

Over four months elapsed until the battle was rejoined in the monthly journal, *Art World.* Following another lull, the *New York Times,* in an August editorial endorsing the complaints of the *Art World*'s editor, reopened the case, and by the end of September, the print war had begun in earnest. In New York, the *Tribune, Evening Post, Globe, Sun,* the *Herald, World,* and *American* joined the *Times* and a bevy of Philadelphia dailies, the *North American,* the *Ledger,* and *Evening Telegraph,* in praise or condemnation. The *Times* and the *Tribune* emerged as the most popular forums for the disputation and were editorially the most critical of the proposed gift statues. Between August 1917 and 8 June 1918, when *New York Times* circulation stood at 250,000 readers, letters, features, editorials, and illustrations related to the question appeared in thirty-nine issues, eleven in October and thirteen the following month. In our day, *Times* coverage of the infamous Richard Serra *Tilted Arc* litigation, which ranged over a period three times as long, generated approximately the same number of entries.[2]

Critics Henry McBride, of the *Sun,* and Frank Crane, of the *Globe,* shouldered the minority view.

While the *Evening Post* did not unequivocally defend the sculptor's Lincoln, it scolded its competitors for treating a private, and what seemed to it a relatively inconsequential matter, with such consternation. The *Washington Post* remained noncommittal until late in the controversy, this in marked contrast to the highly partisan views assumed by the London *Times*'s Washington bureau. Unswayed by the presence of two Saint-Gaudens Lincolns in its city, the *Chicago Tribune* also took little interest, but in a single editorial gave Barnard qualified support.[3] Editorial competition did not center entirely on whether one liked or disliked the statue; even anti-Barnard writers sought to outdo one another in excavating the depths of the sculptor's depravity, in characterizing his utter failure as a public artist, in dwelling upon the Tafts' hopeless gullibility, and in ruminating on John Stewart's malicious intent.

The principal contenders among editors of monthly art journals were the *Art World*'s Frederick W. Ruckstull, a strident foe, and Mary Fanton Roberts, whose *Touchstone* was an equally vigorous defender. James B. Townsend, editor of the weekly *American Art News,* like the *New York Times* editors, deferred to Ruckstull's disclosures as a means for keeping the controversy in high gear between the monthly appearances of the *Art World.* In our last chapter, we noted that *American Magazine of Art* editor Leila Mechlin was also an energetic prosecutor. The *Art World* was published from October 1916 until March 1918; *The Touchstone* also first appeared in 1916, but outlasted its adversary by three years. Both were the progeny of a single parent, Gustave Stickley's *The Craftsman,* a once potent voice for the prin-

132

ciples of John Ruskin and William Morris that ceased a fifteen-year run in December 1916. A veteran news reporter and magazine editor, Roberts was *The Craftsman*'s last managing editor; she retained for the new enterprise Stickley's Kelmscott Press format—heavy stock paper, illuminated spots for initial letters, Caslon typography—and continued regular house and garden features. Beyond this, *The Touchstone* was a repository of waning fin-de-siècle aestheticism. Surveys of pictorial, performance, and literary art explored what Isadora Duncan termed the "great wave movement" of Nature, the all-governing force of creation. Soulful tributes to Rodin, Yvette Guilbert, Sarah Bernhardt, Duncan, and Vachel Lindsay, illustrated with soft-focused photographs by Gertrude Käsebier and Arnold Genthe, conveyed the langor of Art Nouveau, notwithstanding the timely updates on humanitarian ministrations behind Europe's battlelines that appeared in many issues.[4]

After its financial collapse in January 1917, *The Craftsman* merged with the *Art World;* thereafter, the successor dutifully retained a house and garden section similar to that of *The Touchstone*. Otherwise, slick paper, conventional type, a folio format, sharply-focused halftones, and a continuing reverence for the Old Masters, submerged the *Art World* in a contrasting scholarly ambiance. Its reactionary defense of the American Renaissance paralleled the editorial perspective of the *American Magazine of Art*. However, the *Art World*'s board of advisors, the Art Society of America, tended to identify more closely with the affiliated American Institute and National Academy of Arts and Letters, an older, more thoroughly literary, and therefore, in certain minds, a more authoritative interprofessional organization, than was the American Federation of Arts. The president of the Art Society of America, Robert Underwood Johnson, was also secretary of the institute, while other society members, the dramatist Augustus Thomas, Daniel French, George de Forest Brush, the illustrator Timothy Cole, the designer Louis C. Tiffany, the symphony conductor Walter Damrosch, and Stickley, each held dual memberships. Ruckstull pledged to defend a "beautiful, sane and decent art" against the degeneracy of realism and modernism, but vowed the journal's editorial language would be decidedly "more sharply cut" than the "sweet Addisonian style, mixed sometimes with hypocracy, born of moral fear" into which conservative critics unfailingly retreated when approaching hard aesthetic issues.[5]

Born in Alsace of what he emphatically insisted were not German, but French, Huguenot parents,

Ruckstull had gained notoriety not so much as the sculptor of pedestrian historical tableaux, including most notably the melodramatic *Lincoln: April 15, 1865,* but as an organizer and bellicose pamphleteer. Barnard knew him as the unyielding administrator of outdoor public sculpture projects for the National Sculpture Society at the turn of the century. Despite his shrill rantings against all he decided was anticlassical, the editor maintained close ties with Charles De Kay, the critic whose insightful submissions to the *New York Times* and *Century Magazine* twenty years earlier had given readers a fresh alternative to the doctrinaire academicism of Kenyon Cox, the primary spokesman for the National Academy of Design. A characteristic analysis is found in De Kay's 1898 appraisal of Rodin's *Monument to Balzac,* a statue viciously maligned by insensitive philistines, who were more prone to talk than to look, to think, and search out the great thought expressed in the work.[6] Now consenting to join the Art Society of America and, as its associate editor, guide the *Art World*'s crusade, De Kay had obviously tired of plumbing the depths of artistic genius. A far more urgent mission was to salvage America from the social and cultural suicide that awaited its innocent acceptance of radical art forms.

The assault began in the *Art World*'s June 1917 issue before the editorial staff knew of the various plans for sending replica statues abroad or of Robert Lincoln's concurrent mission to intercept them. Belatedly reacting to the Union Theological Seminary exhibition, Ruckstull reprinted the *Milwaukee Sentinel*'s reaction to the distorted photograph. Over the next nine months, seven numbers of the magazine ran extensive editorial criticisms and letters of protest, and arranged in gallery fashion photographs of Abraham Lincoln, of the Barnard statue, of other statues, of paintings made from life, and of the Volk life mask, which Ruckstull considered the sine qua non for Lincoln portraitists. Borrowed cartoons, one supplied by Robert Lincoln from a London periodical, others from *Life* magazine, brought a British levity to several editorials.[7] Uncertain of the effect untouched photographs might have upon his subscribers, Ruckstull routinely subjected plates to arbitrary changes of focus, enhanced detailing, and enforced tonal modulations. Redrawn eyelids, pupils, brows, and lips appearing in an imprint of Brady's Cooper Union portrait, subtly transform Lincoln's relaxed expression into a mask of swaggering confidence. Gardner's 1861 seated portrait of Lincoln was subjected to extensive revisions; its general tone was lowered and value contrasts reduced; details of a chair

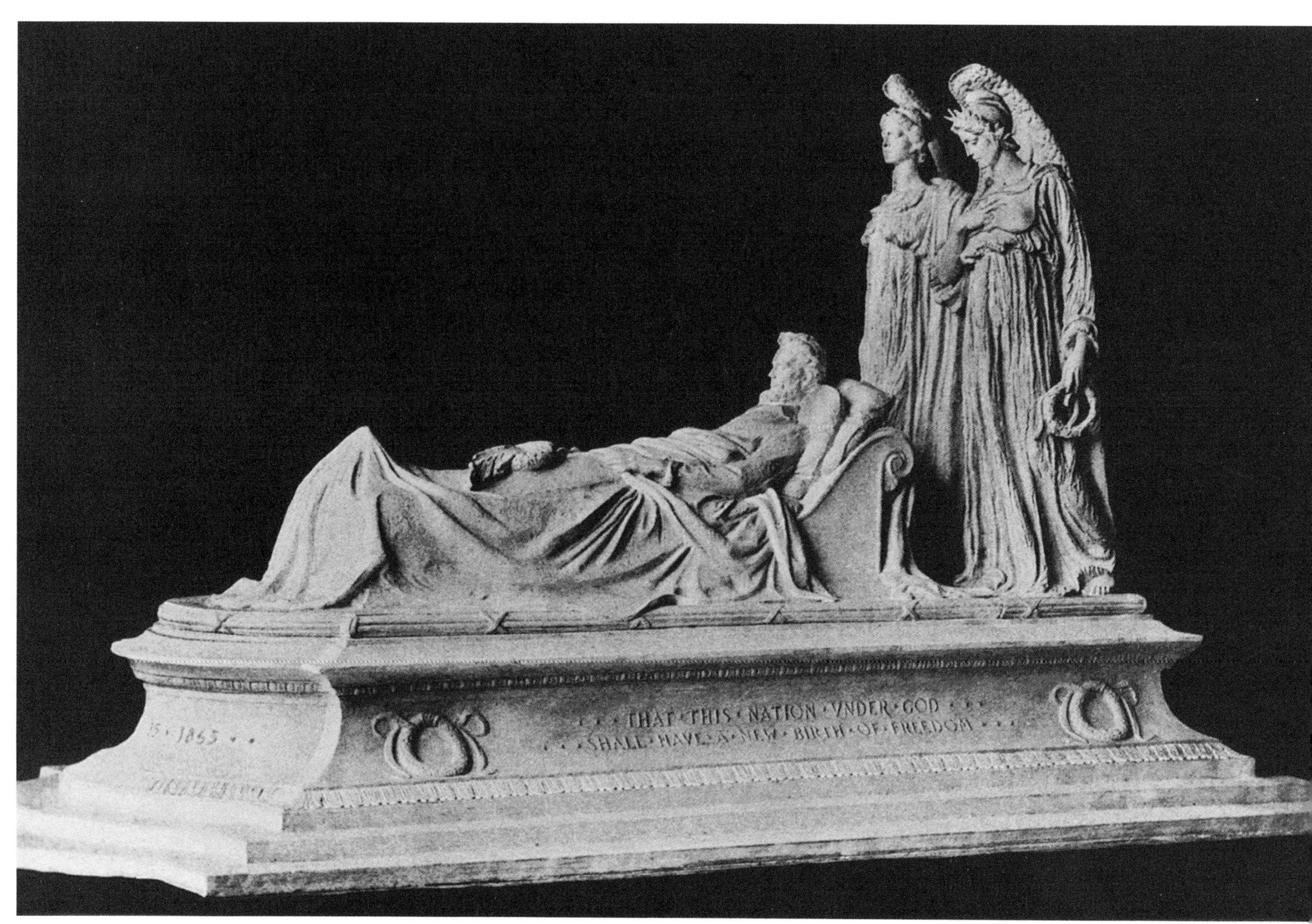

Frederick W. Ruckstuhl and Anthony de Francisci, Lin-coln: April 15, 1865. From the Art World *(May 1917).*

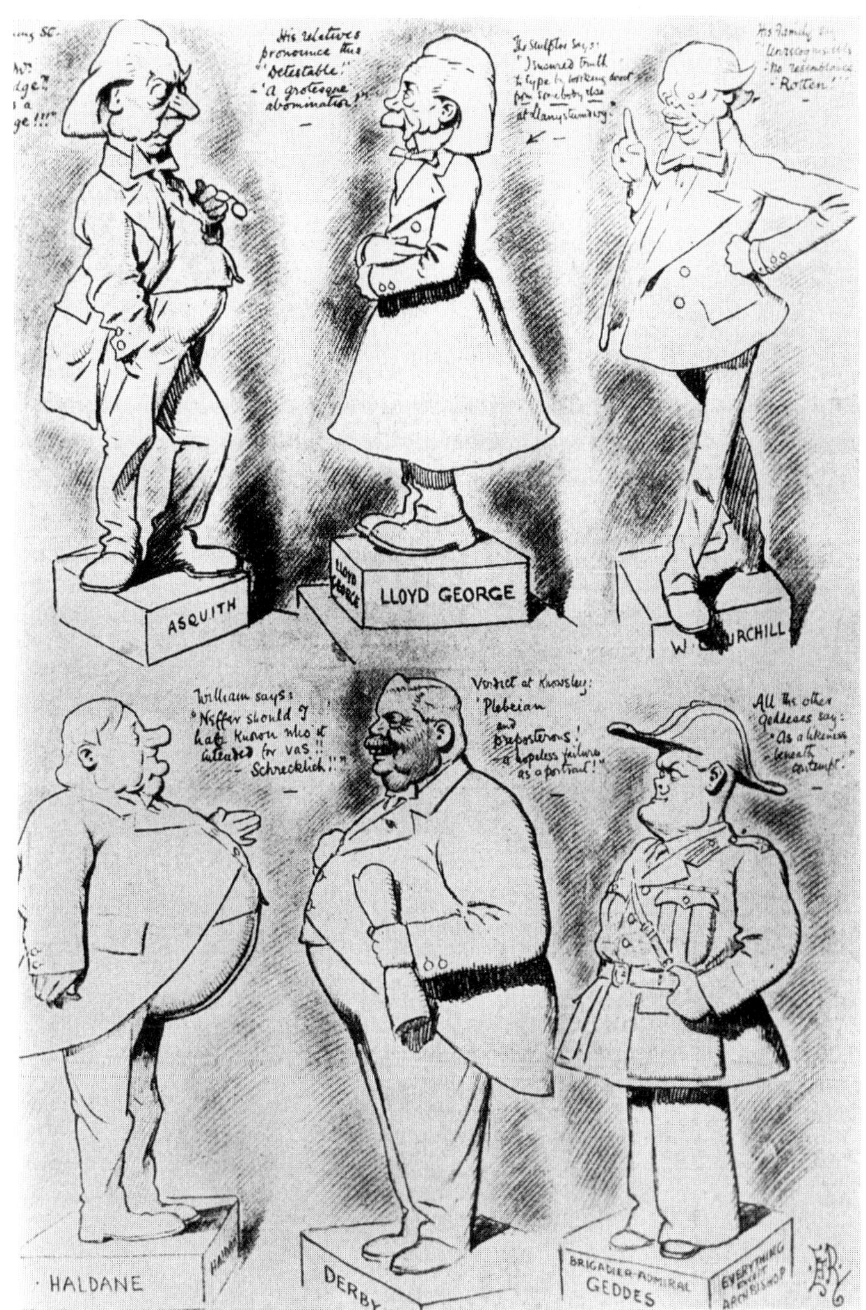

"Why Not Be Getting a Few British Statues Ready?"
From the [London] Bystander, *10 October 1917 as re-*
printed in the Art World *(December 1917).*

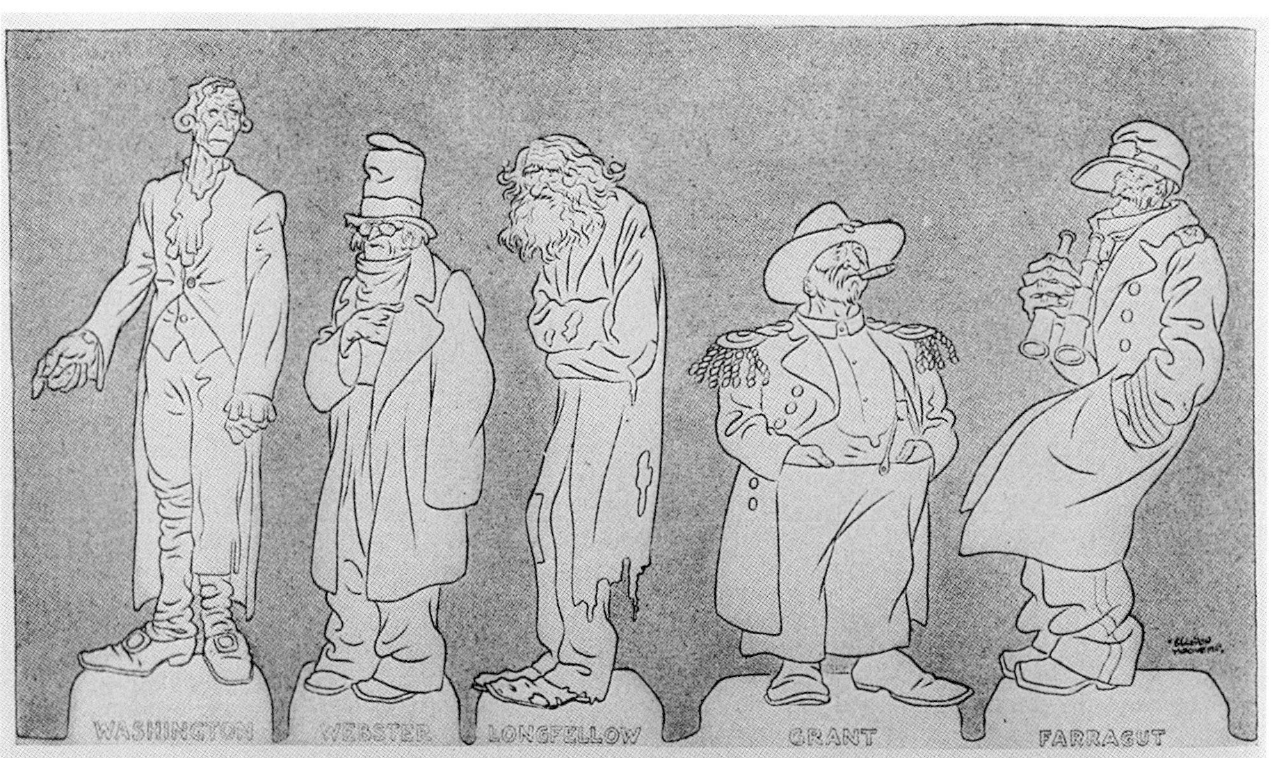

"*If More of Our Public Statues Were Modelled in the Manner of Barnard's Lincoln.*" From Life Magazine, 18 October 1917, as reprinted in the Art World (December 1917).

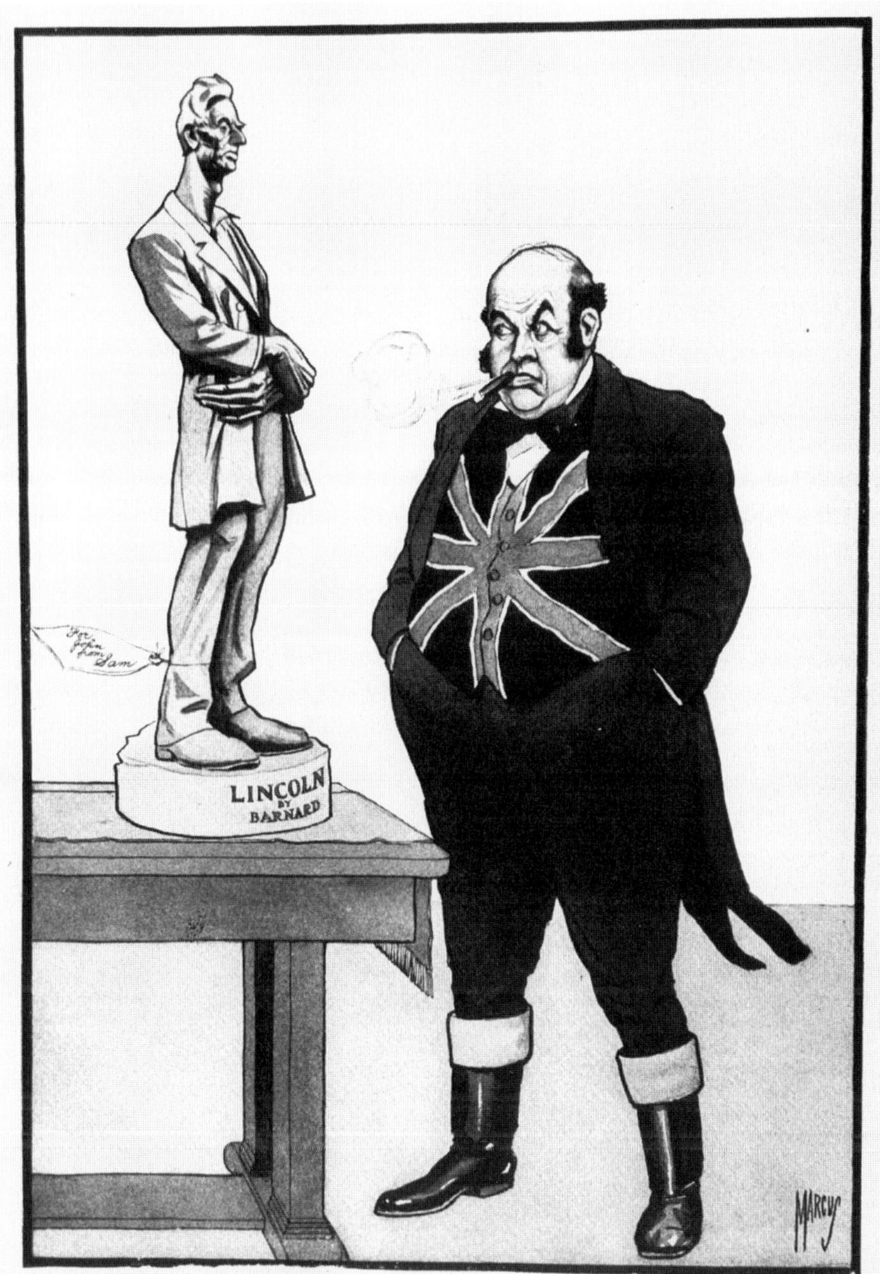

"The Gift." From Life Magazine, 29 November 1917, as reprinted in the Art World (December 1917).

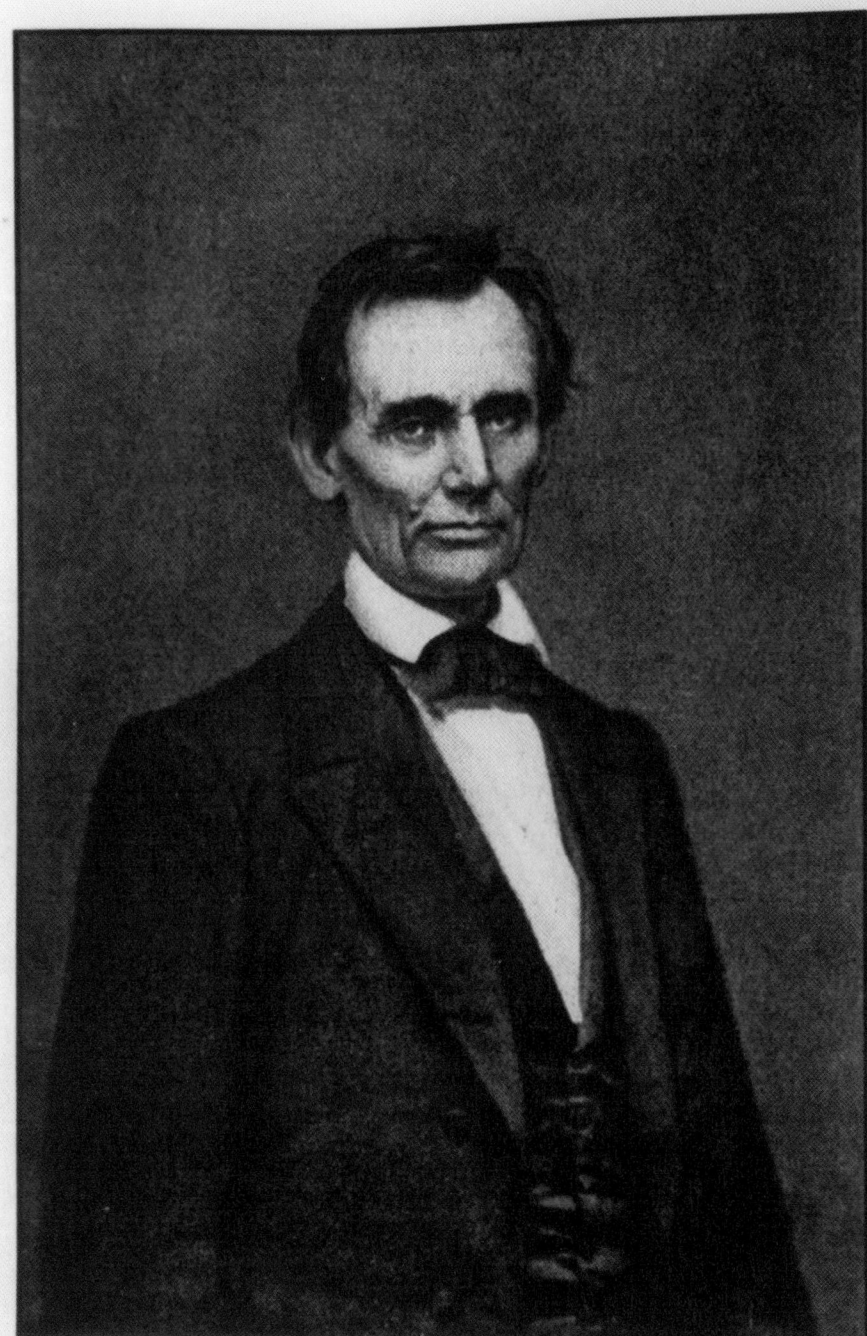

flesh in the face. This is utterly untrue to the life
masks, Figs. 6 and 7, which already accentuated his
leanness, because all human flesh shrinks under
pressure when cast in plaster. And that he was

Mathew Brady, Abraham Lincoln. *1860. Photograph,
as reprinted in the* Art World *(June 1917).*

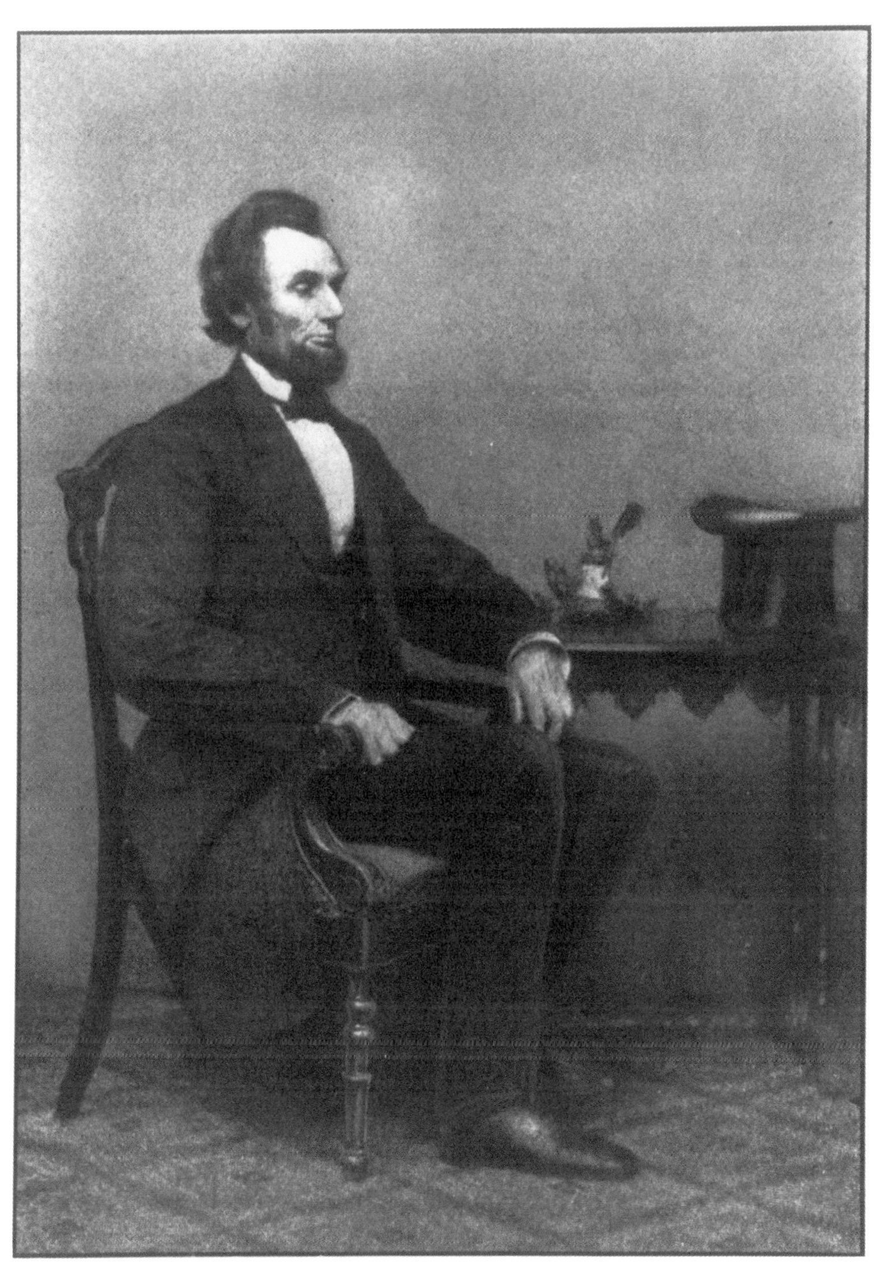

Alexander Gardner, Abraham Lincoln. *Ca. 1861. Photograph, as reprinted in the* Art World *(June 1917).*

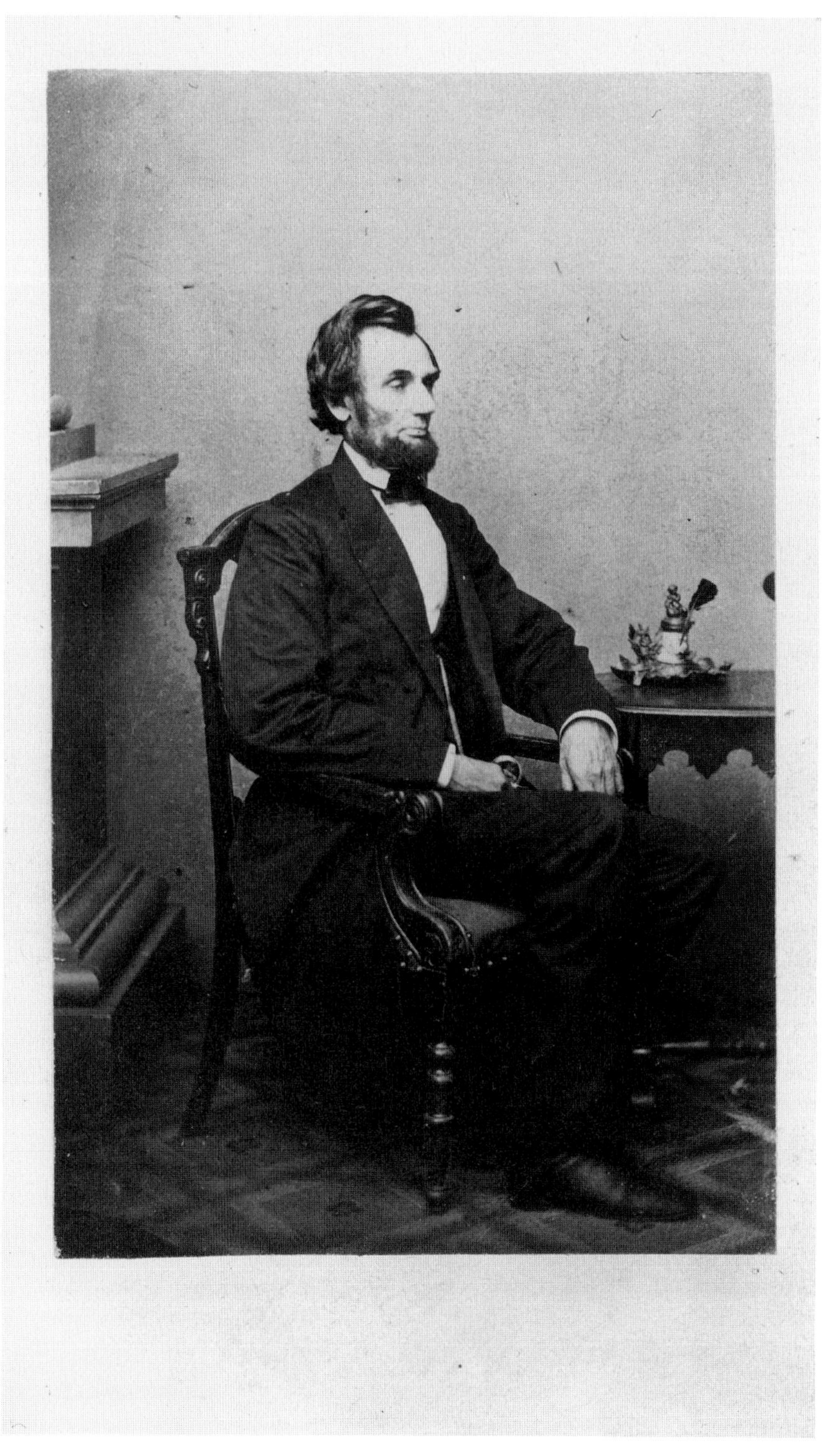

Alexander Gardner, Abraham Lincoln. Ca. 1861. Photograph, albumen silver print, 3⅜″ × 2⅛″. National Portrait Gallery, Smithsonian Institution.

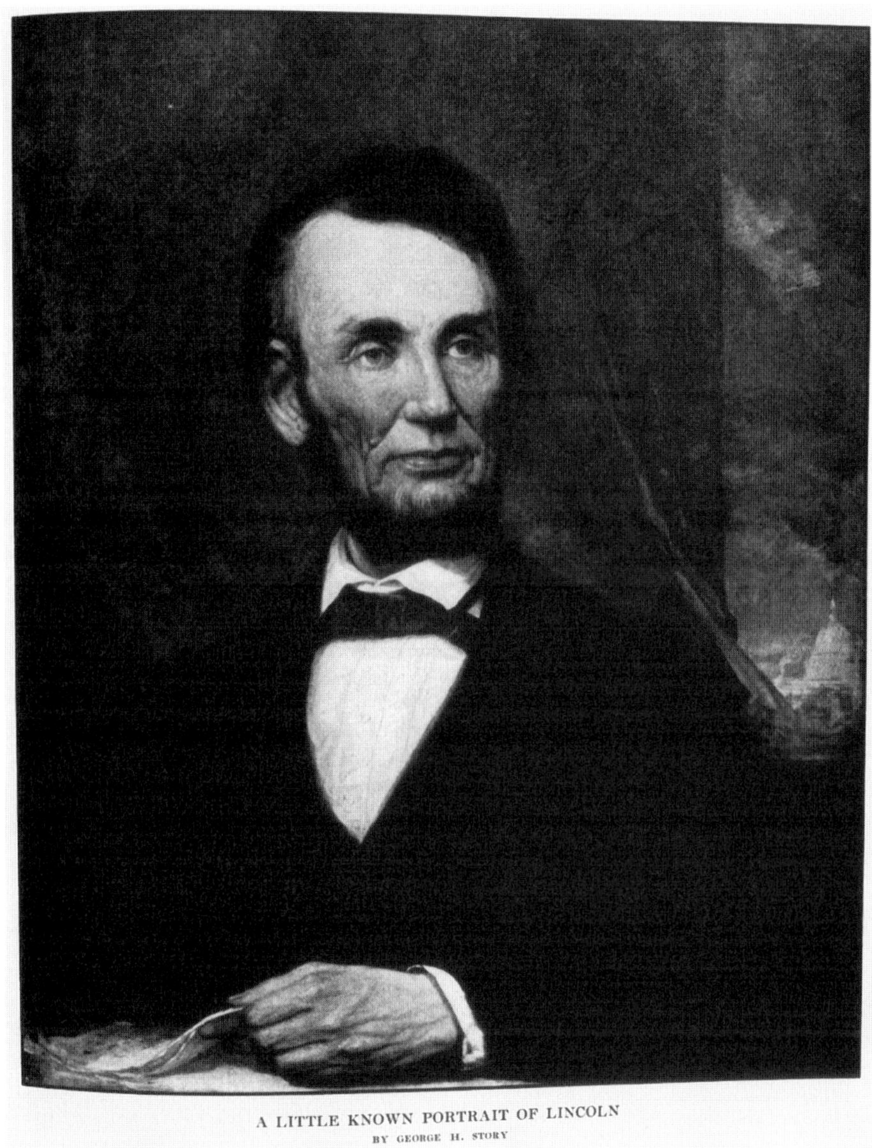

George H. Story, Abraham Lincoln. 1861–66. Oil on canvas. Illinois State Historical Library, as reproduced in the Art World, *(August 1917).*

and wrinkled pant legs that in the original dissolve into shadow, have been reinforced by a light outline and gray wash; an architectural molding has disappeared without a trace.

While altered photographs were intended to settle disputes over physiognomy, or natural truth; photomechanical reproductions of painted and sculpted portraits pressed home the argument that Lincoln courted fashion and dressed accordingly. Ruckstull proudly displayed the elegant, dashing, images found in oils by George H. Story and W. T. Travers. Travers's full-length depicts a singularly graceful and charming figure in evening wear whose imperial stance resembles that of George Washington in Gil-

bert Stuart's Lansdowne portrait. Even though the painter entirely transformed Lincoln, Ruckstull's technicians found further opportunities for reinforcing the contours of the figure and the jacket lapels; but the principal alteration is found in the thin light boundary line that cuts through the murky grey tone enveloping the figure's right side. Reproduced in two issues, Saint-Gaudens's standing Lincoln statue is enveloped in medium-soft illumination and burnished with a fine granular patina.

Because of the frequent shift between photographic "fact" and improvisation, Ruckstull and De Kay lost sight of the essential differences between media. In an examination of what poses Lincoln habitually as-

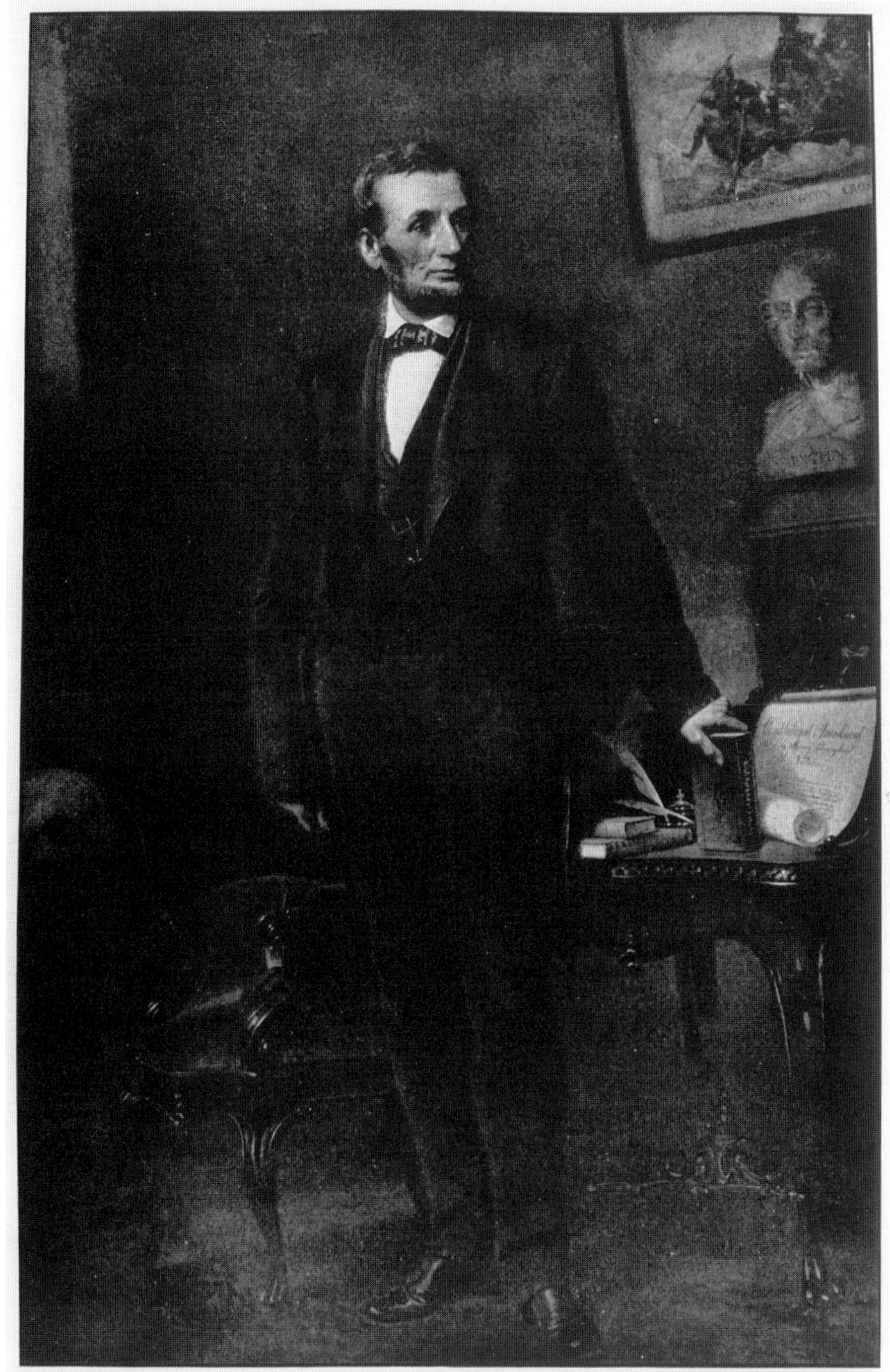

This standing portrait of Lincoln, showing him in full evening dress and painted from life in 1864-5, by W. R. Travers, is reproduced here to show that, when Lincoln deliberately sat for his likeness either to a photographer or a painter, he insisted upon being dressed in the fashion of his day. We trust that this portrait—added to the photographic evidence we gave in our June issue—will be regarded as proof positive that Lincoln really loved elegance of dress and that he was not in the least a downward-leveling and hobo-worshiping slouch.
Read carefully the letter of Ward H. Lamon on page 9.

W. R. Travers, Abraham Lincoln. *Oil on canvas. As reproduced in the* Art World, *(October 1917).*

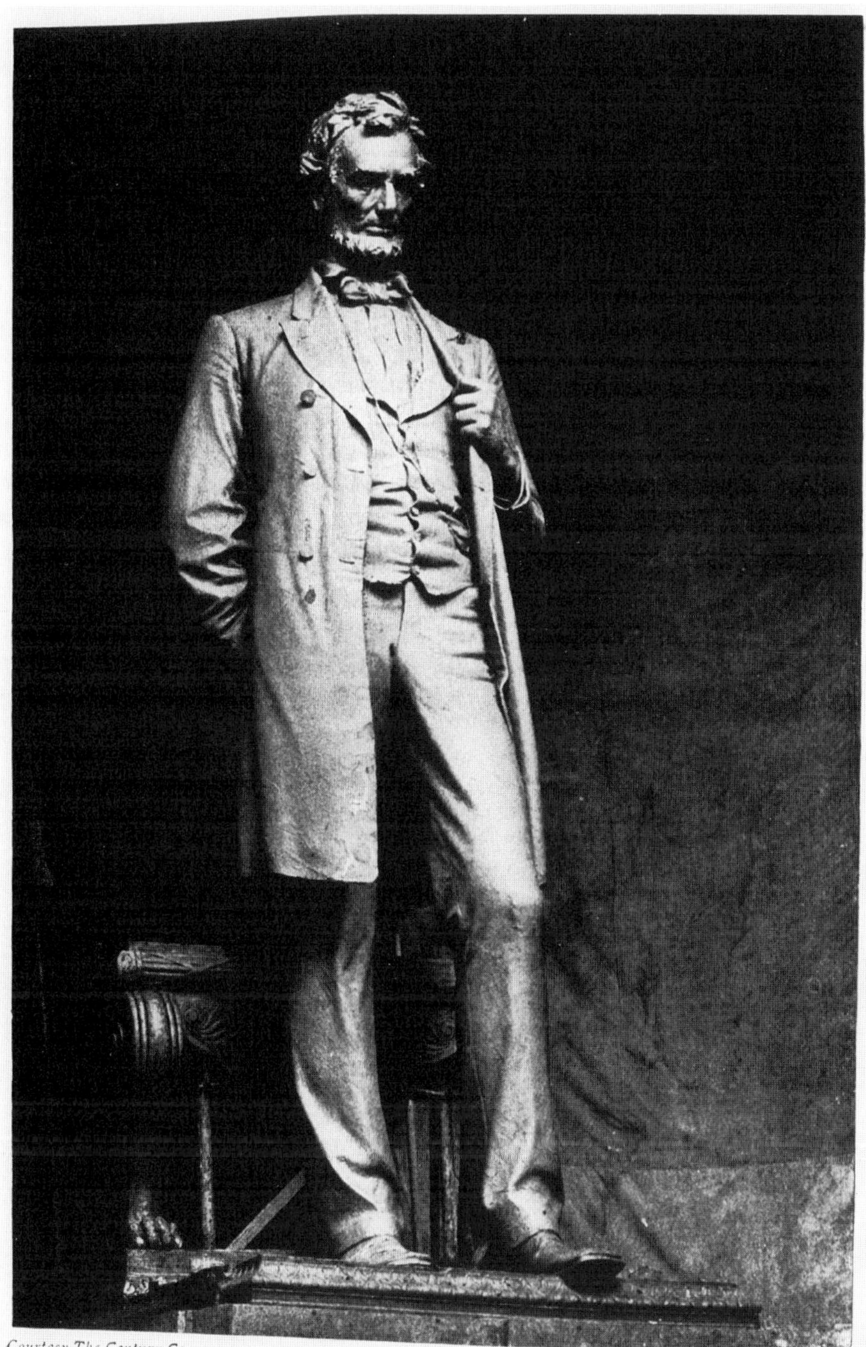

SAINT-GAUDENS'S GREAT STATUE OF LINCOLN IN CHICAGO

If a replica of any existing Lincoln statue is sent abroad, as a gift from the American people to the people of England and France, as an adequate characterization of Lincoln, also to symbolize our democracy, our taste in art and our state of culture, it should be a replica of the above statue—unquestionably the noblest statue so far erected of our great President; among the half-dozen greatest portrait statues created in the nineteenth century. Here we have no lacrimose, whipped weakling, but a serene fighter who conquered in nearly everything he ever undertook.

Augustus Saint-Gaudens, Abraham Lincoln. *1887. Bronze. As reproduced in the* Art World *(June 1917).*

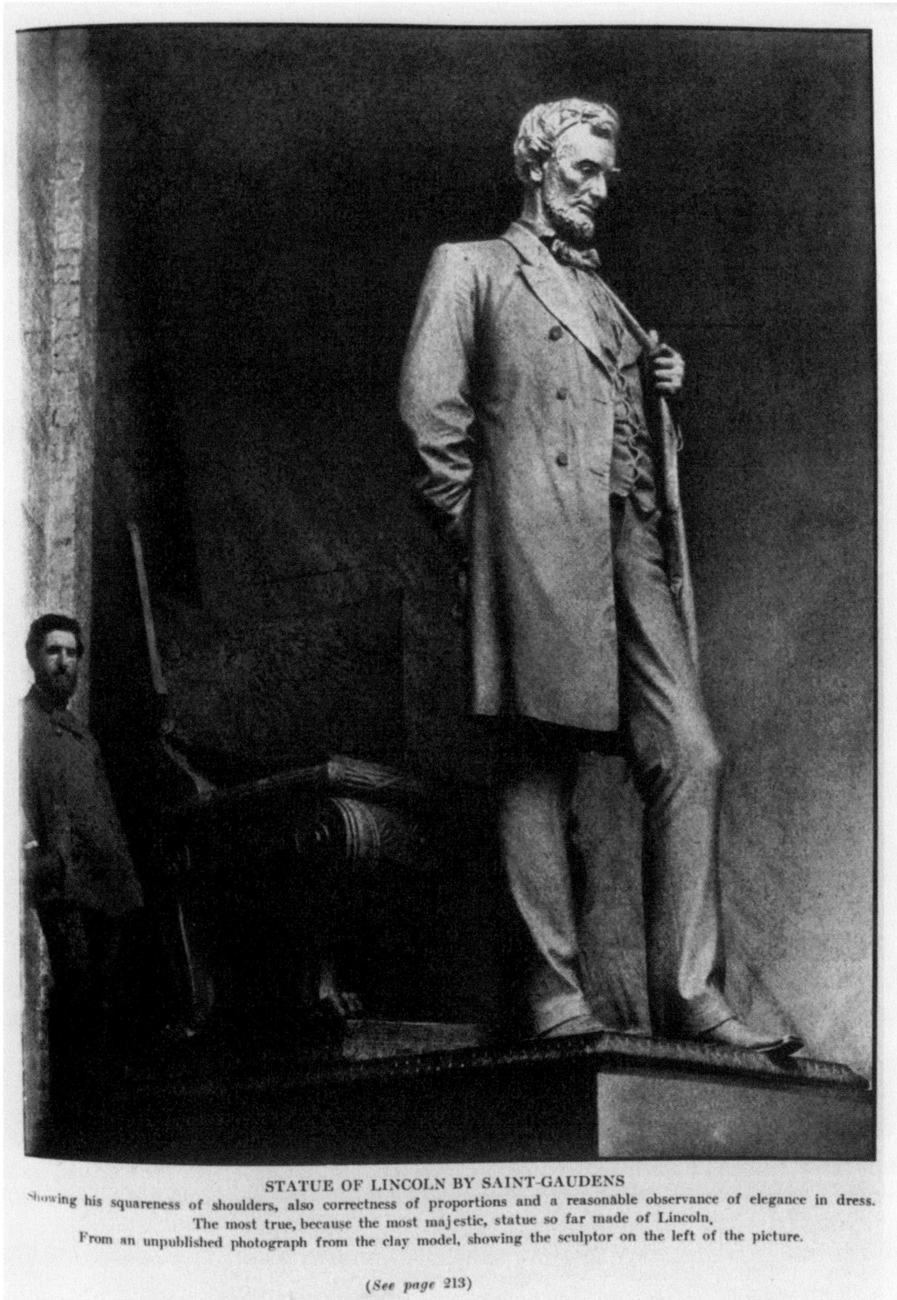

STATUE OF LINCOLN BY SAINT-GAUDENS
Showing his squareness of shoulders, also correctness of proportions and a reasonable observance of elegance in dress.
The most true, because the most majestic, statue so far made of Lincoln.
From an unpublished photograph from the clay model, showing the sculptor on the left of the picture.

(See page 213)

Augustus Saint-Gaudens, Abraham Lincoln. *As reproduced in the* Art World, *(November 1917).*

sumed, the *Literary Digest* had earlier reproduced a photograph of a lost William Morris Hunt painting that presented Lincoln with hands clasped before him. However, *Digest* editors were unaware that the photograph was of a painting and not of the living subject himself. So it was that Ruckstull, without questioning the error, published the same image—albeit after his cosmeticians had done their work—as a live photograph and positioned it beside a photographic cut of Barnard's statue. Ruckstull's objective was to add fuel to his condemnation; even so, the confusion alerted anti-Barnard archivists who now found it necessary to defend photographic authority over artistic invention. Judd Stewart, Truman Bartlett, and Frederick Meserve begged *Art World* patrons to understand that a painting might display a man in any conceivable or inconceivable pose, but no existing photographs showed Lincoln's arms positioned in the manner manifested by the Barnard statue.[8]

Among Ruchstull's chosen illustrations, all but the

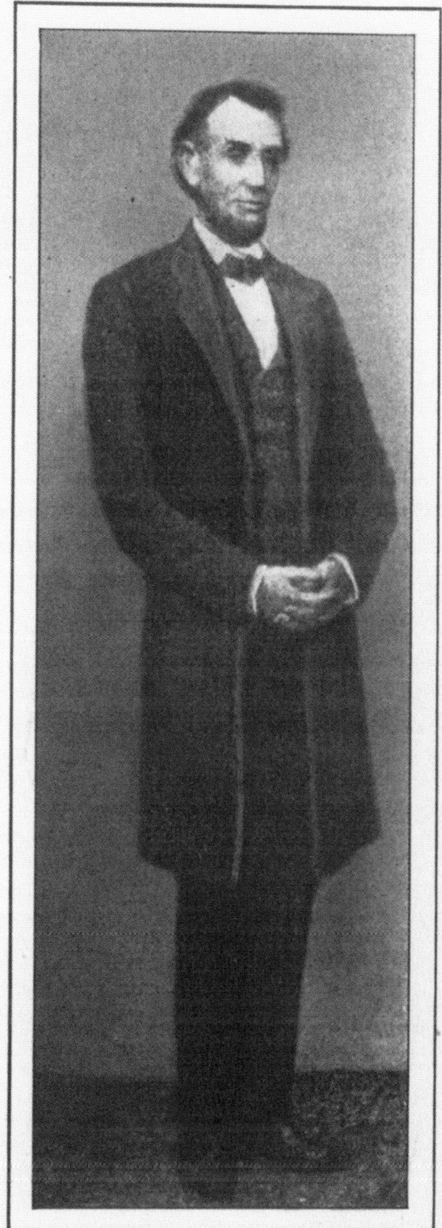

FIG. 8.—FROM A PHOTOGRAPH OF LINCOLN

Showing the squareness of his shoulders, also the elegance of his proportions and that he had a certain amount of grace, also showing that his hands and feet were not large for his size.

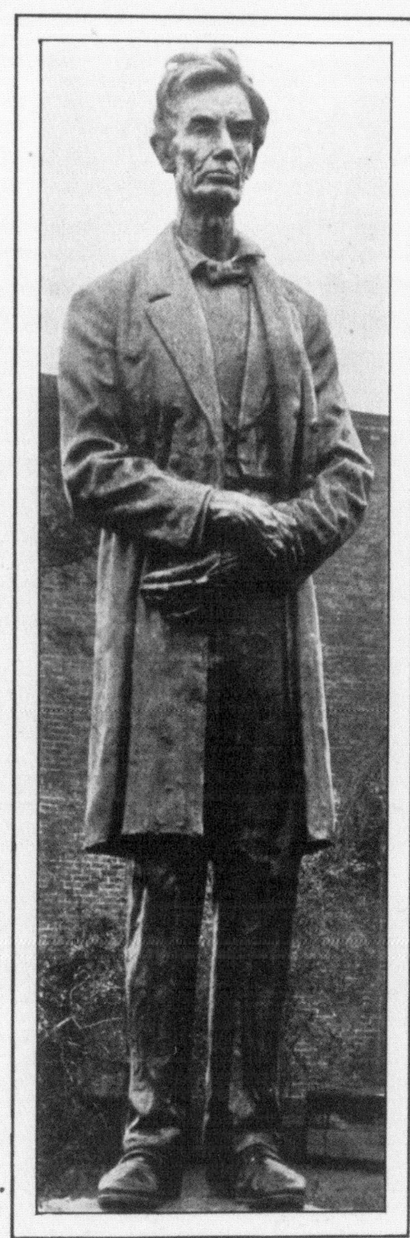

FIG. 9—THREE-QUARTER VIEW OF MR. BARNARD'S STATUE

Showing stooped shoulders, very long neck, enormous hands, gigantic feet and a lugubrious face, untrue to Lincoln.

monument for Boston and mak
size, and worked on this proble
sparing neither time, energy i
not have a "swelled head" like l
trembling respect for public op
artist friends for helpful critic
his model in bronze, and ther

ense beauty. This can be done
e character of any national hero,
e time the sculptor's own artistic
s a number of our sculptors has
ll furnish the public with a mirror

William Morris Hunt, Abraham Lincoln. *and Barnard's* Lincoln. *As reproduced in the* Art World, *(June 1917).*

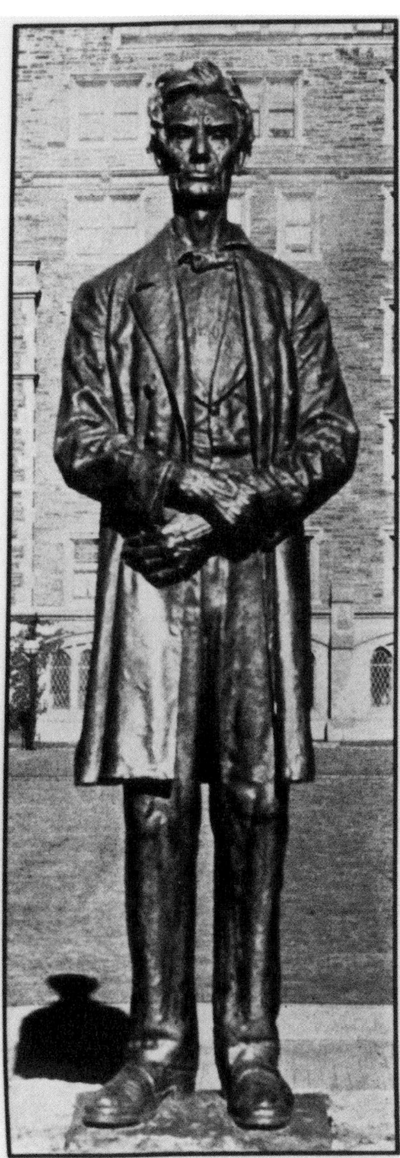

Fig. 10—Front View of Barnard's Statue

Accentuating the size of his hands, etc.; also showing a deliberately introduced element of slouchiness by putting the collar of the coat under a point of the shirt collar and other suggestions of slouchiness untrue to Lincoln.

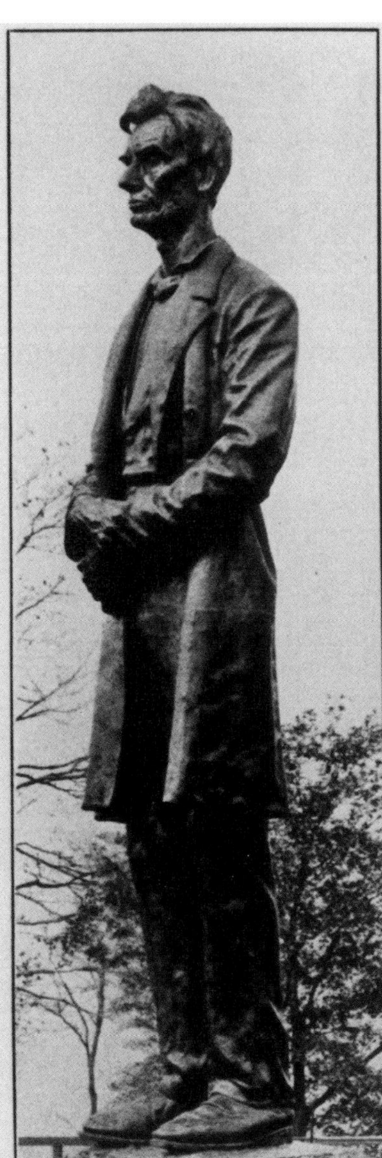

Fig. 11—Another View of the Statue

Showing Lincoln pressing his hands over his stomach as if he had the colic.

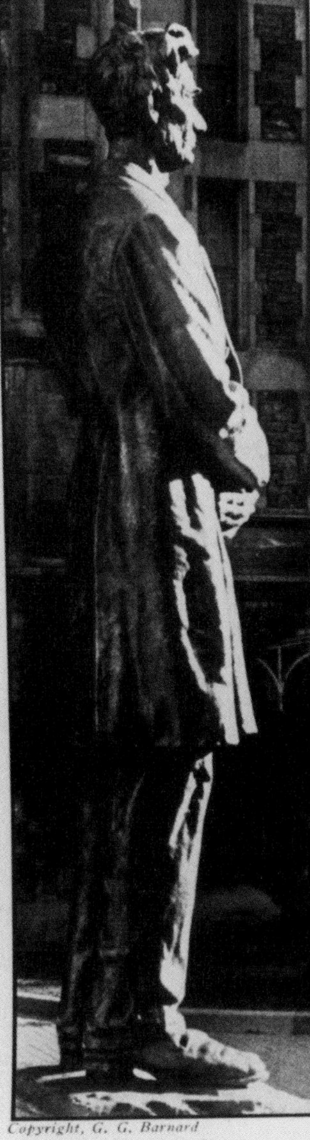

Fig. 12—Another View of the Statue

Showing the clumsy and lumpy feet utterly untrue to Lincoln.

Barnard's Lincoln. *As reproduced in the* Art World *(June 1917).*

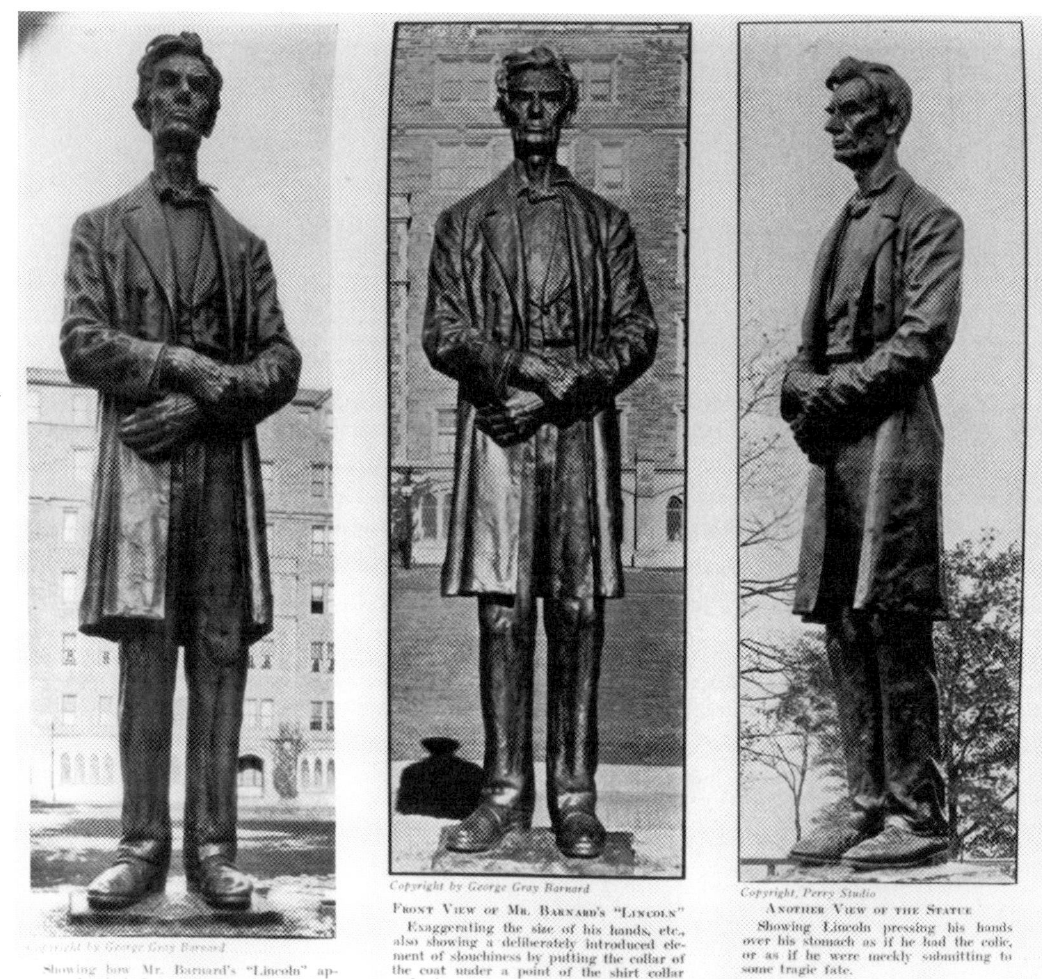

Barnard's Lincoln. *As reproduced in the* Art World *(January 1918).*

images of Barnard's statue were meant to contribute to a format of acceptance. In several issues the outlaw statue is pictured in multiple "line-ups" on a single page that resemble spliced film segments. It is seen in full focus and brightly illuminated, the irregularities of surface and angularity of form being made clearly evident. Nor did Ruckstull fail to include the notorious bandit photograph. Two views of a beardless bust Roberts reported was the preliminary for the head of the standing bronze were also compared with historic photographs of Lincoln which readers were assurred had not been altered.

As pictured in photographs taken by William van der Weyde, this bust sparked a main point of order between the warring editors. Barnard had convinced Mary Roberts the photographed bust, one that was similar to, if not identical with, the twenty-inch high plaster in the Kankakee County Historical Society Museum, was made from the same key molds that were produced for the bronze statue heads. It was, in fact, the model for a quite different work, the large marble head, also with the Museum collection, to which I referred in chapter 4 [see p. 58]. Preferring to believe otherwise—she attributed the unfavorable criticism of the Cincinnati statue to the harsh outdoor lighting that permeated many photographs that reproduce it—Roberts thus advanced the more refined Van der Weyde studio portraits of the smaller bust as improved views of the same head.[9]

Enlargements of the Van der Weyde prints were placed before passersby in the windows of Roberts's New York office, and she freely granted Ruckstull and others permission to publish them. But Ruckstull would not be fooled. The statue head and the bust in the photographs were not the same. Furthermore, Ruckstull contended, even if the decoy was noticeably less lugubrious than the head of the completed statue, it had faults of another sort: it exemplified "neurotic patheticism," and conveyed the image of "a spiritual malcontent about to be hanged or see the

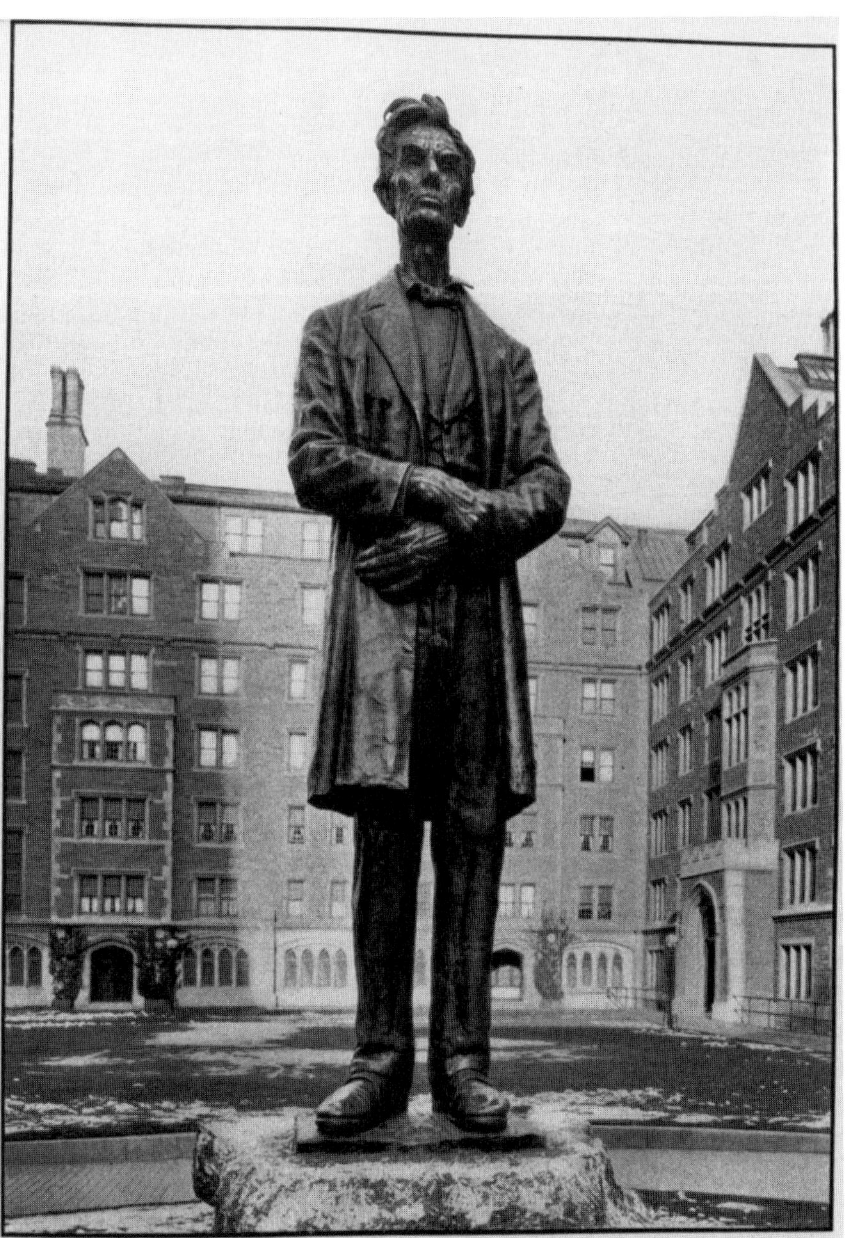

Barnard's Lincoln. *As reproduced in the* Art World *(No-vember 1917).*

William Van der Weyde, Barnard's Bust of Lincoln. *Ca. 1917. Photographs. As reproduced in the* Art World, *(January 1918).*

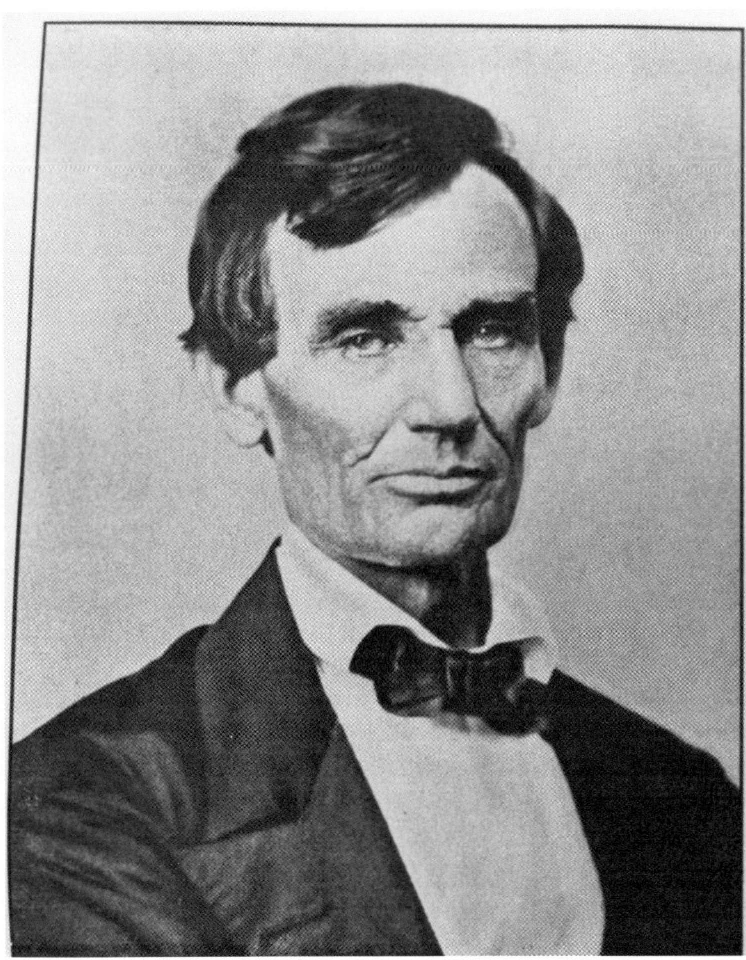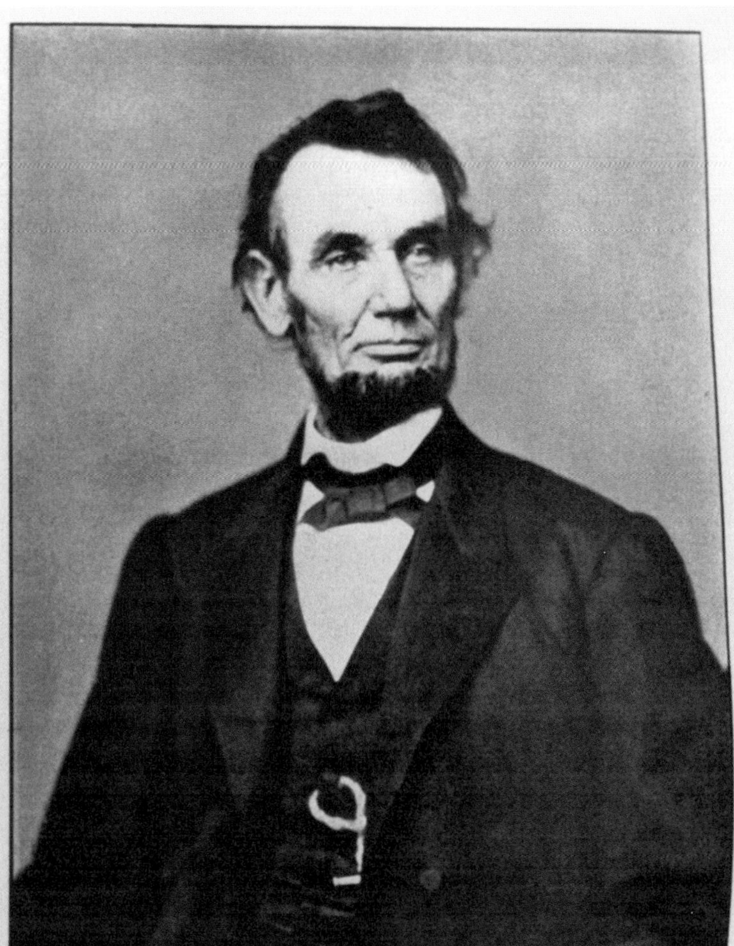

Preston Butler (left) and Matthew Brady; Abraham Lincoln. *1860 and 1874. Photographs (as reproduced in* Art World; *January 1918).*

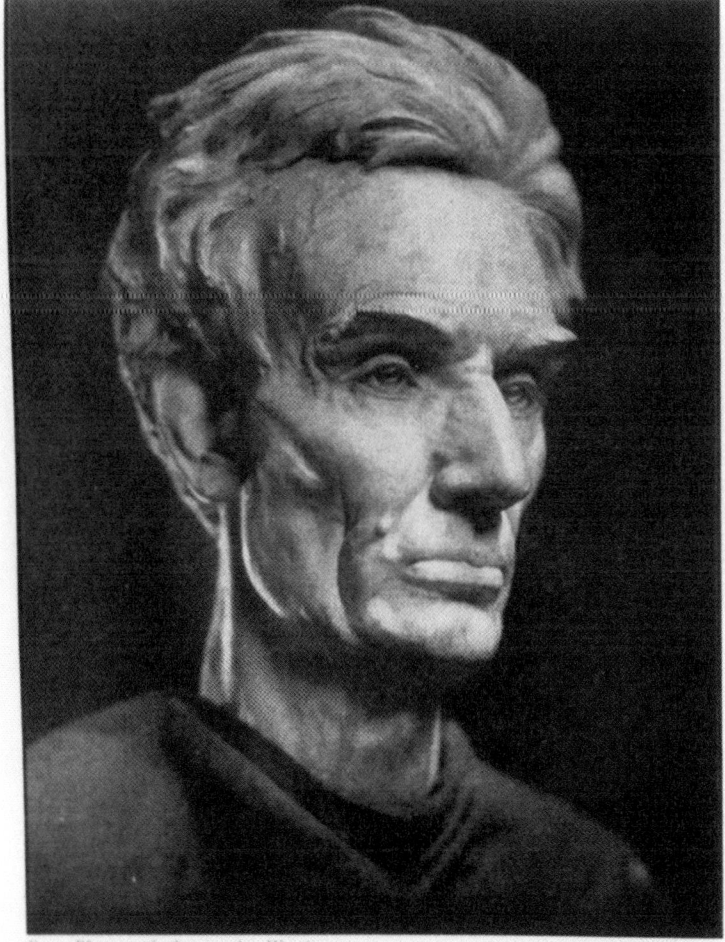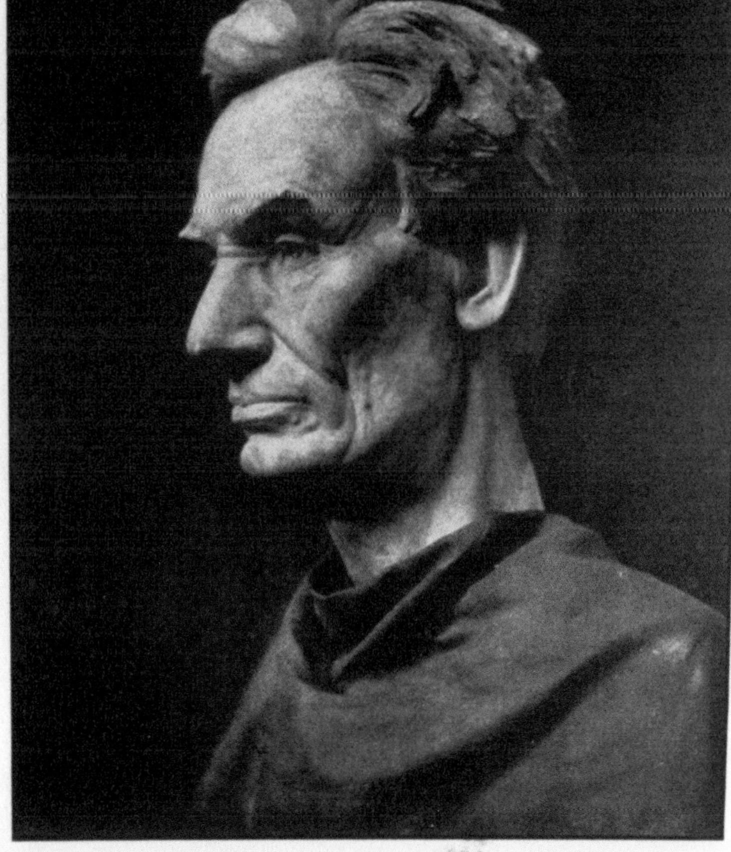

On foregoing pages excellent photographs—all unretouched—show how Lincoln looked at the beginning and near the end of his public career. Here are photographs of a bust by Mr. Barnard which certain magazines have printed as the head on the replicas proposed for London and Paris. This is not the head of the "Lincoln" erected in Cincinnati; it is even worse: showing Lincoln as an aged, sullen, defeated, frightened man, or as he might have looked had he been condemned to the gallows. An attempt to realize the false-pathetic fallacy created by certain writers. Had he looked like this in 1860 he would never have become President because he could never have roused the confidence of the people. Note exaggeration of the depressions in the cheeks; also the wrinkles on the side of the nose, no suggestion of which is found in any photograph or in the life-mask.

world explode."[10] The horizontal corrugations beside the nose reminded him of the snout of a snarling animal, or variously, of a moral criminal, or a "hobo-slave, not a virile working man of the world."

Dogmatic captions forced upon *Art World*'s patrons indisputable truths. Beneath a Brady halftone appeared the notice: "One the grandest heads ever modeled by the Creator." A view of the Saint-Gaudens is addressed as: "Saint-Gaudens's great statue of Lincoln in Chicago. If a replica of any existing Lincoln statue sent abroad, as a gift from the American people to the people of England and France, as an adequate characterization of Lincoln, also to symbolize our democracy, our taste in art and our state of culture, it should be a replica of the above statue." Immediately upon turning the page, one encountered the distorted image of *une belle horreur* which is captioned, "Looks Like Something The Cat Brought In On A Wet Night!" Beneath a frontal view taken during the seminary exhibit, also inscribed with a Barnard copyright, appears a printed list of deformities: "stooped shoulders," an "abnormally long neck; the shirt collar sticking up like a rabbit's ear; the distorted clothing;" "impossible" trousers; and "gigantic clod-hopper feet . . ." Ruckstull trusted that the copyright designation would fend off claims he was unfairly basing his case on bootleg photographs. Thus, he exercised his censorial role by first exposing his audience to what was forbidden, threatening, and pornographic; then rescued it by interjecting the written authority of editorial truth. Desperately hoping to prolong this didactic ritual even beyond the endurance of the most vehement Barnard critics, Ruckstull with idiomatic bluster dared the ACPC to come out of its lair when it failed to respond to his latest insults.[11]

Brandishing the epithets "hobo-democrat," "slouch," "radicalism in rags," and "woeful, wallowing Willie," Ruckstull lashed out at the *Touchstone*'s emphasis upon Lincoln's social depravation to justify the statue. The outgrowth of an "anti-virile" mentality, the inclination to sentimentalize heroes and gods in such a manner undermined civic ideals while also failing to respect the undeniable force of social Darwinism. The real Lincoln descended from hardy Virginian stock that only momentarily experienced hard times in Kentucky. Barnard's "mongrel, white-trash, gnarled and deformed rail-splitter from the backwoods of Kentucky" was thus an imagined aberration. But biological analysis also complemented derisive social references; here was both a social degenerate and a victim of hookworm, dyspepsia, colic, or indigestion. The deformities and grip-

ping gesture invited scientifically-phrased diagnoses; claiming Barnard had cast "a disease in bronze," a physician suggested the model Thomas must have suffered from acromegaly, a recently identified disorder of the hypophysis that caused an individual to develop overly large hands and feet. George Raymond's physiognomical observations regarding the simian-like, "brow-thrown-back-and-chin-forward" configuration, that were initially printed in the *American Magazine of Art,* were reprinted in the *Art World*'s January number.[12] Not incidental to this analysis was an earlier publication of a cartoon showing a brush-wielding simeon Ruckstull and De Kay likened to a "Modernist" artist.

The statue's "deformation of the form," Ruckstull's designation for any work that deviated from classical rectitude and formal coherency, was tantamount to social degeneracy and placed Barnard squarely in the company of Rodin, the cubists, vorticists, and futurists. Without bothering to discriminate among the approaches of this wide-ranging assembly, he branded them all "neurotic, anarchistic Bolsheviki artists" against whom the European war, with American assistance, was being fought. In answer to a MacMonnies's condemnation of censorship that accompanied his approbation of Barnard, Ruckstull countered that all similar appeals for artistic freedom were nothing more than veiled demands for degeneracy. In reference to the Congressional Selective Draft Law, a measure that set firm borders around the limits of freedom in civilized society, the avenging editor lectured that no artist was empowered to place on a "public pedestal" anything he wished. If left uncorrected, he warned, Barnard's vision of "hobo democracy" might well stand as America's only alternative to the militaristic machine art of European autocracies, this because his Lincoln contradicted evolutionary laws that naturally propelled succeeding generations toward the "common-sense" objective of Beauty.[13]

MacMonnies also unhesitatingly placed Barnard with the avant-garde, but one of a more wide-ranging variety. Like the Michelangelos, Rembrandts, Monets, Darwins, Whistlers, Marconis, and Edisons of the past, he faced academic repression, most aptly defined by Kenyon Cox in a recent *New York Times* editorial, that would reduce science and culture to uniform standards. Ruckstull, on the other hand, judged Michelangelo to be a blatant imitator of the Greeks, though he could not resist flavoring this observation with an allusion to the sculptor's reputed "fondling" of the *Torso Belverdere*. A favorite historical example of a futurist or a Barnardite was

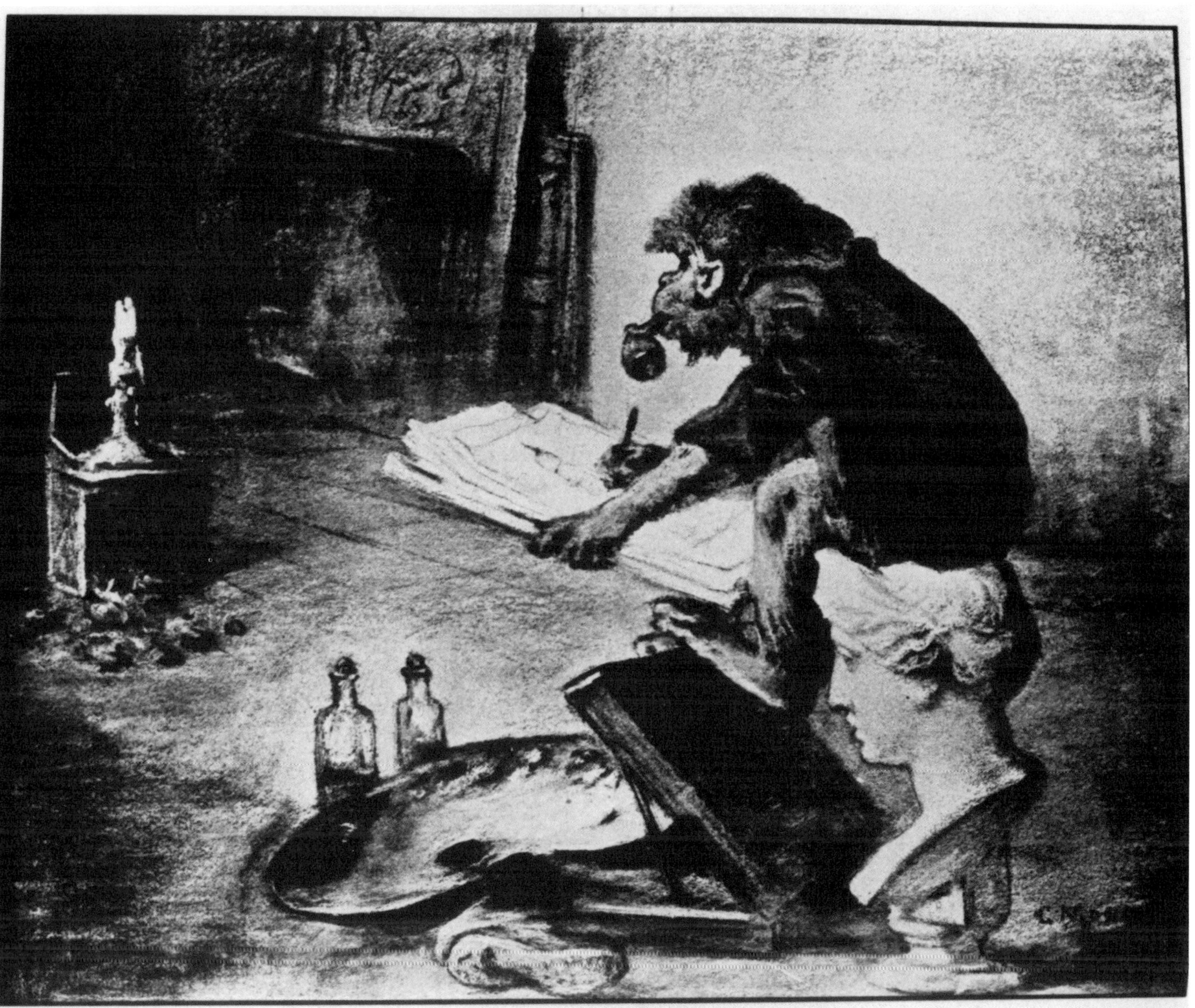

"THE MODERNIST"
Down with the Ideal and up with the Real!
C. Monginot, "The Modernist." From L'Art Français.
As reprinted in the Art World *(August 1917).*

the Florentine Mannerist sculptor Baccio Bandinelli, whose *Hercules and Cacus* set off a storm in the sixteenth century. The egotistical Bandinelli was an especially apt example, since in his zeal to surpass the living Michelangelo and the Greeks, he, like Barnard, refused all advice from artists and the public. During the resulting riots, the patron Alessandro de Medici, a politically powerful man no less blameless than Charles Taft, was forced to order arrests to restore order. Public outrage properly destroyed Bandanelli's

reputation just as the outcry of Parisians against the *Monument to Balzac* had more recently sidetracked Rodin's professional career. By contrast, Ruckstull envisioned a modest Saint-Gaudens, whose "trembling respect for public opinion" induced him to destroy or alter such works as the standing Lincoln, while resisting the selfish impulse to be novel or original. In short, the public sculptor was society's tool and was therefore required to furnish "the public a mirror in which it can contemplate itself with pride and satisfaction."[14] There could be no compromise: "a public monument," he declared, "is a public avenue for the expression by the public of public thought and feelings."

Having gained the trust of Robert Lincoln, Ruckstull was determined to make his journal the official communication center for the critics. The complete text of Lincoln's protest to Taft as well as his other exchanges with Conkling and Choate were printed in the October issue. Sen. Henry Cabot Lodge wrote of his refusal to join John Stewart's committee of presentation. Judd Stewart updated readers on the perfidy of John Stewart, who recently wrote him to say that it was, after all, the British centenary committee, and not the Americans, that was insisting upon receiving the Barnard statue. Editor Henry Watterson revealed he was leading an anti-Barnard campaign in the pages of the *Louisville (Kentucky), Courier-Journal*. Letters also explored a point of contention that divided the anti-Barnardites: whether it was historic photographs or personal recollections that were more reliable for judging the quality of commemorative statues. Long communications authored by Judd Stewart and Meserve gave full credence to the former, while Henry B. Rankin, author of *Personal Recollections of Abraham Lincoln* (1916), condemned the media of painting, sculpture, and photography for not being able to preserve Lincoln's animated countenance.[15]

All too soon, the conflict between the journal's elevated form and debased content became apparent to its unhappy backers; Ruckstull's choice of epithets, language Barnard compared with that of street toughs, clearly contradicted the assiduous attention given to layout and production. Art Society of America members soon realized they risked tarnishing their reputations by continuing their association with Ruckstull. George de Forest Brush, who would privately denounce Barnard's statue with language that closely resembled Ruckstull's, was for the moment more disturbed by the editor's obvious lack of control. Announcing his resignation from the advisory board, Brush summarized the views of many of his American Institute colleagues when he wrote, "When I gave my name on the Art World Committee I thought we at last had a magazine that knew art and would tell big and true things. But it is the same old story. I find people only fighting for their own personal gain . . ." Though as usual he resisted making a public statement, Daniel French voiced similar regrets. He joined Ruckstull's committee in February 1917 without a clear understanding of editorial policy, and, under polite protest, permitted his name to remain on the masthead. For this he was duly rewarded when the *Art World* featured his *Death Staying the Hand of the Sculptor* as one of America's greatest memorials. However, the magazine's August issue proved the ferocity of Ruckstull's language went beyond the bounds of legitimate criticism. French informed the editor that even though he disliked Barnard's conception, he yet honored his adversary's earnest intentions and respected the opinions of individuals like Ida Tarbell. In communications to other Institute colleagues, however, French, like Brush, was far less moderate in his references to Barnard.[16]

Composing her first response to Ruckstull in August 1917, more then a month before the October issue of the *Touchstone* appeared, Roberts was assisted by Tarbell, MacMonnies, and Barnard. Two articles bore the thrust of her complaint against the *Art World*'s arrogance and antagonism. Her "Lincoln, Soul and Body of Democracy—As Shown in the Barnard Statue" set forth a standard comparison between the sadness of Lincoln's life, as evidenced in harsh lines, ragged attire, and crossed arms, and a transcending morality that was the fruit of this labor.[17] But even though these coarse attributes were appropriate signs of Lincoln's careworn life, no fixed aspect of physical appearance could adequately measure the great soul within.

The second article, "The People's Lincoln," excerpts the commentary of Roberts, MacMonnies, and Tarbell, and freely quotes from the Leigh Hodges editorial. MacMonnies asserted the purpose of all great art was to present a personal vision and create a mood. Like Roberts, he underscored the necessary connection between the spirituality of manual labor and a melancholy existence. He, too, dismissed the importance of whether the chosen clothing was or was not historically appropriate. But here MacMonnies wavered, for he had to admit "a man should appear draped in things characteristic of himself and his times" and, as it happened, Barnard's clothing was appropriate, while the clothes worn by Saint-Gaudens's Lincoln were decidedly not "eighteen sixty-five." Tarbell's submission to this article was aimed directly at Ruckstull's interpretation of her comments in a new edition of *The Life of Abraham Lincoln*. In its preface, she declares Barnard's statue to be "the profoundest thing done of the man by any one in any medium" because of its power to summarize Lincoln's spiritual resolution.[18]

Roberts trusted that these intonations of the "pathetic fallacy" would give sufficient answer to the lords of the *Art World* who only groveled in the dust of trivia. "It would seem to us," she concluded, "that perhaps Lincoln's feet trod close enough to God for us to cease to carp about the size of them." She also sought to put to rest Ruckstull's contention there was a distinction between a public and private work of art; what was to be deemed "public perception" began with the private individual, then extended laterally and vertically through the strata of class. A similar principle applied to the question as to which, if any, administrative body should decide upon the appropriateness of gift statues being offered to foreign countries. Roberts's adversaries considered leading professional lay societies the most trustworthy judges; French, Moore, and company looked steadfastly to the federal authority invested in the CFA, while Roberts was perfectly satisfied to give unofficial sponsoring groups like the ACPC sovereign power in deciding such matters.[19]

Outside of her long personal friendship with the sculptor and his wife, there were some very specific reasons why Tarbell should have felt a special kinship to Barnard's statue. Having been raised in Titusville, Pennsylvania, close by Barnard's birthplace, she retained a fierce loyalty to the region's working classes, in whose interests she wrote the stunning exposé of The Standard Oil Company. She was familiar with the cultural environment of Charles Taft's Cincinnati, since her first published article in the *Chautauquan* (1886) surveyed the arts and industries of the city. Tarbell's impoverished apprenticeship in the Latin Quarter coincided with Barnard's last student years in Paris, and she shared his appreciation for the salient characteristics of the French mind and of French culture, particularly when seen in relief against comparable manifestations of Anglo-Saxon society. Similarly, the occasionally coarse treatment she received as a female biographer of Lincoln—she claimed to have been accused of treason for daring to illustrate household details that symbolized Lincoln's early impoverishment; items, she reasoned, lovers of Lincoln and true democrats most wished to dwell with—Tarbell could well sympathize with Barnard in his present predicament.[20]

Tarbell's "Those Who Love Lincoln: A Word For Barnard's Statue," which appeared in the December 1917 *Touchstone,* was as much an apology for her own social precepts as it was an appreciation of her friend's statue. Pointing to the deluded efforts of those who would raise godlike idols in the place of admired leaders, Tarbell ridiculed ongoing attempts to falsify the plain facts of Lincoln's life. There was irony in the fact that the efforts to extricate the man from his rude beginnings were coinciding with the implementation of a national draft, a measure that was bringing an entire generation of socially disenfranchised men into the main stream of American life. Now, more than ever, the truth about Lincoln's origins deserved public examination, even as proponents of social stratification stiffened their stance. Tarbell was inevitably led to compare the leaders of the anti-Barnard campaign to the Copperheads and to the vile Stanton, who not only attacked Lincoln's principles but also his nonconforming appearance and, by implication, his social origins. Similarly, Lincoln's courage seemed comparable to Barnard's daring efforts to reveal "the part [Lincoln's] hardships had in the making of the man."[21] Before Barnard's roughly modeled image, Tarbell discerned the symbolic victim of a primarily Eastern protectionism, the injured manhood of American democracy. Hence, there was no mystery why she found the statue's ennobling spiritual presence overpowering.

Ultimately, Roberts's journalistic fervor served her cause no better than did Ruckstull's unchecked animosity. Instead of resting with MacMonnies's initial definition of art, that it addressed the emotions and was not accountable to material facts, she attempted to engage Ruckstull on his own ground by printing quotations gathered by Barnard that verified Lincoln's uncouthness. The most valued of these sources were drawn from individuals who were leading the attack: Choate, Rankin, and Lincoln biographer George H. Putnam. Moreover, William Herndon's reference to Lincoln's awkward, flat-footed stride was printed beside an account of how the offended Robert Lincoln attempted to sabotage Herndon's not sufficiently complimentary biography. Material fact then had a most important role in the *Touchstone* defense, after all.[22]

Quoted commendations proved to be troublesome. Most originated from Barnard's personal files and had not been specifically cleared for publication in the *Touchstone.* Those of MacMonnies and Thayer remained firm, but other quotes became grist in the mills of the critics. Charles Dana Gibson's enthusiastic "noble presentation of a noble human being," a comment he made in reference to the seminary exhibit, was considerably diluted by an updated submission: "It strikes me one does not need to say much. George Gray [sic] Barnard's Lincoln can defend itself." Sargent's evasive "I have no words with which to tell you how much I like [Barnard's] work," became the source of considerable levity. A Daniel French letter to Barnard not intended for publication was excerpted to read: "You know that I admire profoundly your art and your personality. I have taken umbrage at the way Mr. Ruckstuhl has attacked you and have written to tell him so." Roosevelt's salutation was to be the defenders' trump card:

> At last we have the Lincoln of the Lincoln-Douglas Debates. How long we have been waiting for this Lincoln! I feared with the passing years it would never come; but here it is, the living Lincoln, the Great Democrat. This statue is unique; I know of no other so full of life. The greatest statue of our age has revealed the greatest soul of our age. One is worthy of the other. I congratulate Barnard with all my heart. He has given us Lincoln, the Lincoln we all know and love.[23]

This embellishment differed only slightly, but significantly, from his original commendation, quoted at the end of chapter 4.

The citation was one of several altered versions of a single utterance Barnard transcribed during the foundry preview in 1916. Contrary to Robert Lincoln's information, Barnard insisted Roosevelt was addressing the statue, not the giant Lincoln head, or any of the busts. Sensitive to the delicate balance existing between context and meaning, Barnard thought nothing of rearranging the structure of original quotations, so as to alter or otherwise strengthen inferences. While the original declamation was subjected to a number of cuttings and pastings, the crucial passage in the *Touchstone* entry is "the greatest statue of the age has revealed the greatest soul of our age," a phrase that replaced the "greatest sculptor of our age has revealed the greatest soul of our age" of the original. Believing the second modified quotation was to be included in advanced publicity being forwarded by the ACPC to England, and not in a current magazine article, Roosevelt returned the revision to Barnard on 19 September saying that it "agreed in substance" with the first but wisely avoided both superlatives and comparisons. Yet the Colonel was unhappy to find it in print and complained to Roberts. Even so, the desired correction was inexplicably delayed until the journal's March 1918 issue.[24]

As editorial copy for the October *Touchstone* was being readied, the *New York Times* was firing its first salvo, an editorial deprecating the "long-suffering peasant" that was to stand beside a statue of Oliver Cromwell in London. Roberts mistook the reference to Thornycroft's standing statue for an equestrian, but nonetheless saw clear evidence of a Teutonic conspiracy in the making. She could envision no English statue that more resembled the dull, dispirited, *Siegessaule* in Berlin than her recollected image of the Cromwell. It seemed equally obvious to her that Ruckstull, a man whose original surname and presumed birthplace were German, should in league with publisher Ochs, prefer an autocratic prototype over a democratic rendition of "Our Commoner." Notwithstanding Perris's rule of silence, Roberts urged activists of the ACPC to respond in kind. But it was not until the *New York Times* called attention to the English committee's quandary a month later that ACPC secretary Andrew Humphrey decided to break his silence.[25]

Lashing out at Ruckstull in a *Times* letter printed on 27 September, Humphrey asserted the folded-hand position of Barnard's Lincoln was one of the "most natural" of Lincoln's mannerisms, particularly when he was in a contemplative mood.[26] Advancing a preview of material destined for the forthcoming *Touchstone,* he included the favorable Sargent and Roosevelt quotations, but the latter entry was drawn from the unedited, and to Roosevelt, most objectionable "greatest sculptor of our age" transcription, which Barnard, had he so wished, could have amended in time for the letter's publication. But Humphrey's most grievous tactical error came when, in the spirit of Roberts's reference to race, he challenged the right of "an adopted American" to misrepresent a native-born artist to the public.

As Meyer Berger points out, nothing was printed in *Times* that did not first cross the desk of its publisher and his trusted editor, Charles R. Miller, and Humphrey's slur would have been no exception. Although New York newspapers flourished as never before during the war years, their editors and publishers were obliged to walk the tightrope of public opinion more gingerly than ever. From a conservative's viewpoint, Ochs believed the war was an ideological, rather than a social, struggle and happily threw off the veneer of neutrality when Wilson declared war. Better than most professionals of German ancestry, he realized his international views would be thoroughly scrutinized; any sign of softness or leniency in his support of America's war effort could have grave consequences. Therefore, he would not be a party to sending any American statue to Europe that suggested vulnerability or defeat. On 28 September, an unsigned *Times* editorial rebuked Humphrey and assailed the Barnard statue as unsuitable for placement in London. The writer, quite possibly Miller himself, admitted his paper had often expressed admiration for Barnard's previous work, but now such merit "escaped the eye." Sarcastically alluding to the Sargent and Roosevelt quotations, the writer rejoined, "it is unique," and "we, too, have no words in which to tell Barnard how much we like his work." If the statue were to take its place before

Parliament, the editor predicted the English people would likely take matters into their own hands. By no means did this aggressive tone signify confidence, for at the end of October, Miller privately informed Robert Lincoln that "we have lost the fight as to London."[27]

In the 28 September issue of the *Times,* Ruckstull attempted to set the record straight on the details of his birth and, to prove he had not instigated the campaign against his fellow sculptor, released the texts of Robert Lincoln's correspondence to and from William Taft and Choate ahead of their scheduled appearance in the October *Art World.* He assured readers he had more reason than Humphrey to despise the Prussians, since Humphrey's forebearers had not "been ground down under," as had Ruckstull's. Augustus Thomas wrote a week later to reaffirm the steadfastness of his wounded comrade's patriotism, while also countering Humphrey's assessment of Lincoln's appearance.[28] Thomas knew there were serious sociopolitical implications at stake, hence he took pains to demonstrate through precise measurements that Lincoln's feet were not out of proportion to the size of his body as the pro-Barnardites believed. This went a long way toward proving Lincoln was not a radical. Had he been, Thomas maintained, the problem facing public sculptors, like that which he daily faced as a dramatist, was still to make "immortality safe for democracy;" that is, in Ruckstullian terms, one was obligated to make "democracy" most attractive and not, as Humphrey would have it, "most natural."

If the opposition was hoping for further personal exchanges, they were to be disappointed. Charles Taft would not comment directly, although, he authorized the publication of a key editorial in the *Cincinnati Times-Star.* Privately, he expressed gratification that the *Art World* had helped to make the Taft Lincoln the best known statue in existence. Instead, the defense posted only two other entries in the *Times.* The first consisted of Barnard's "only answer" to his raging critics.[29] Sarcastically prefaced by an editor as "not unworthy of [Barnard's] genius" and "his long solitary thought," this reply recited without further explanation Isaiah 53:

> For he shall grow up before him as a tender plant, and as a root out of a dry ground; he hath no form or comeliness; and when we shall see him, there is no beauty that we should desire him. He is despised and rejected of man; a man of sorrows, and acquainted with grief; and we hid as it were our faces from him; he was despised, and we esteemed him not.

The *Times* thought it a bizarre defense, but one that at least substantiated critical opinion. On the other hand, John Stewart, provoked by suspicious questioning, authored a statement reiterating he had authorized the statue substitution only because of the total failure of the original funding campaign, one that even Robert Lincoln had ignored.[30] Thereafter, the ACPC committee of fifteen accepted Charles Taft's "offer." As we shall see, Stewart's faulty memory of the makeup of this committee, and hazy recollection of the timing of the crucial decision—whether it was before or after Joseph Choate's death—heartened investigators. Fully conscious of his vulnerable position, and quite possibly with Charles Taft's consent, Stewart sought conciliation: the statue presentation committee would fully sanction the second placement of a Saint-Gaudens replica if donors could be found, but such a replica would not be assigned to the Canning enclosure.

Even with the ACPC relatively silent and the embargo apparently holding until the end of the war, New York and Philadelphia editors had no difficulty maintaining a high interest in the controversy through the early months of 1918. The letters-to-the-editor columns continued to burgeon with the outraged commentary of living witnesses and distinguished professionals. The English artist Joseph Pennell, who thought the Saint-Gaudens replica would make an especially salubrious addition to the dreary statue collection in Parliament Square, delivered Barnard a stinging renunciation. The most ironic submission was the *Times* letter of Edwin Stanton's son, Robert. In memory of the "dignified" man who once held him in his arms, Stanton demanded that Barnard's ugly statue be melted down for bullets. An author of a letter published in the *Tribune* demanded that the statue be decapitated.[31]

Newspapers and magazines sampled both popular and "electorate" opinion. *The Philadephia Evening Telegraph* and the *Independent* conducted straw polls that registered overwhelming opposition to the Barnard, although the results of the latter query were inconclusive as to which other Lincoln statue should be sent instead. On the other hand, a more republican form of advocacy was evidenced in published petitions sponsored by professional groups. On 26 October, thirty-three prominent artists, architects, writers, and men of affairs describing themselves as "representative Americans," declared their opposition and called upon various societies, clubs and, ultimately the CFA, to render a final decision. The Council of the National Academy of Design voted 12 November to censure both the proposed Paris and

London statues, although Council chairman Herbert Adams resisted attempts to bring a vote before the full academy membership. The NAD later called for another temporary outdoor exhibition of the bronze statue in order to facilitate a public referendum on its suitability. Following the wishes of Chancellor John Wesley Hill, trustees of the New York based Lincoln Memorial University reinforced their denunciation with a pledge to distribute approved Lincoln statues around the globe, thereby making the world "safe" for democracy. A negative vote of The New York Chapter of the American Institute of Architects was published on 20 February 1918 and that of the American Federation of Arts on 8 June.[32]

These weighty remonstrations did not go entirely unchallenged. Henry McBride belittled the judgment of the NAD council, pronouncing its eight members "unimportant" artists who by passing the resolve "put another smudge on the organization's history." This action immediately reminded the critic of Cardinal Richelieu's censorship of Corneille's *Le Cid,* which everyone else, including the fearful French Royal Academy itself, considered great literature. Like MacMonnies, McBride was quite familiar with the phenomenon of academic censorship. Since the furor that surrounded the New York Armory Show four years earlier, he had made it a point to defend obstensibly heretical challenges to accepted standards.[33]

McBride studied art in New York under John Ward Simpson, an avowed enemy of both the National and Royal Academies, and specifically of John Singer Sargent, and he had taught art and traveled widely. In 1913 he replaced James Huneker and Samuel Swift as the *Sun*'s chief art editorialist, ably continuing the liberal critical tradition marked out for the paper by Charles Fitzgerald and James Gregg. After he agreed to serve on John Stewart's statue presentation committee, McBride repeatedly needled Barnard's adversaries in his Sunday column, "Notes and Activities in the Art World." Expanding upon Jo Davidson's lament that he and other sculptors were seldom so visibly before the public eye as was the sculptor of the Lincoln, McBride acknowledged that thanks to his enemies, Barnard "has cornered the market for reclaim." McBride posed the rhetorical question as to why America was the only country in which reactionary voices like Ruckstull's belonged to a single chorus, while progressive opinion remained divided and disorganized. He answered with the retort: "it is a political matter (I will whisper it in your ear)." While composing these columns, McBride was codirecting with Bryson Burroughs the Thomas Eakins

retrospective exhibition that opened at the Metropolitan Museum of Art on 5 November. He thus found it possible to identify the raw, uncompromising, descriptive power revealed in Eakins's *The Gross Clinic* with the coarse, ungainly features of the Lincoln statue, and to justify both works as brilliant challenges to social authority and academic convention.[34]

The poll conducted by the *Philadelphia Evening Telegraph* returned 96,112 in favor of the Saint-Gaudens replica and 2,016 for the Barnard. A more modest tally conducted by the *Independent* produced a mixed result. Readers were asked to choose between photographic reproductions of six Lincoln statues: the Barnard, the Saint-Gaudens standing figure, Borglum's Newark statue, Ball's *Emancipation Group,* Daniel French's standing portrait, and Bissell's Edinburgh memorial. Even though the artist of the Edinburgh statue was misidentified as a "J. Patrick," and the work would have been far less familiar to readers than the others, the Bissell Lincoln ran second to the triumphant Saint-Gaudens, 3,356 to 9,820. Because the low-angled profile view of Saint-Gaudens's statue was notably unflattering, one must assume the large plurality accorded it was largely based on the public's familiarity with the work. More curious was the narrow gap that existed between Barnard's 1,207, French's 1,467, and Borglum's 2,841. Even though, as expected, the Barnard was least favored, respondents obviously saw no clear distinctions between a statue many professionals considered the spiritual heir of the Saint-Gaudens and one that was widely branded an atrocious caricature. In fact, the *New York Times* leaned more toward Borglum's portraits, than those of Saint-Gaudens or French. Its judgment centered on the close similarity between the Newark Lincoln and an admired historic photograph of the seated president, now attributed to Alexander Gardner. The photo appeared in two issues, the second time in a composite featuring the Borglum, the Saint-Gaudens, and the Barnard. It was hardly accidental that the angled view of the Borglum, which as usual was being overrun by children, is remarkably congruent with the photograph positioned directly beneath it. A week earlier, a *Times* editorial boosted Borglum's marble bust, declaring that its "blunt, generalized contours" and "rich hollows and soft, broad bosses" would best suit the "London of round corners, grey stone, of misty air" (see p. 29).[35]

Wearied by the personal diatribe that filled the press in the fall of 1917, some editors moved to broader issues. They were assisted by the timely issuance in English of Judith Cladel's *Auguste Rodin, l'oeuvre et l'homme* (1908), wherein conceptual distinctions

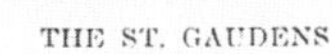

THE ST. GAUDENS
LINCOLN

The statesman and leader is emphasized in the statue below of President Lincoln. It stands in Lincoln Park, Chicago

Press Illustrating

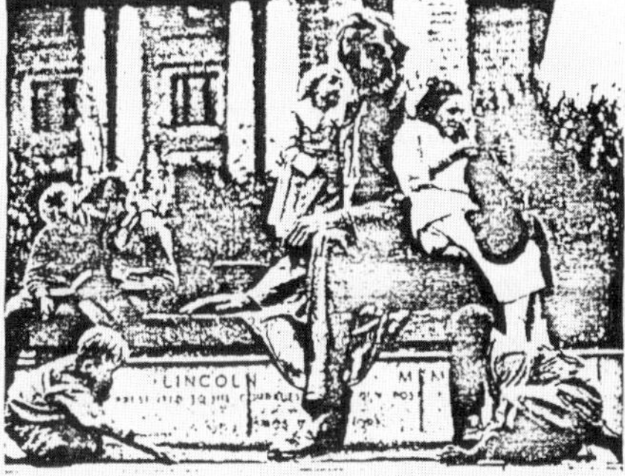

Central News

THE CHILDREN'S CHOICE

Lincoln's love of people, his kindliness, and his sadness, too, are brought out in this statue by Gutzon Borglum. Newark children like to make it one of their favorite playgrounds

LINCOLN IN
WASHINGTON

Daniel Chester French's statue of Lincoln (below) has just been completed for the national Lincoln building at Washington

Press Illustrating

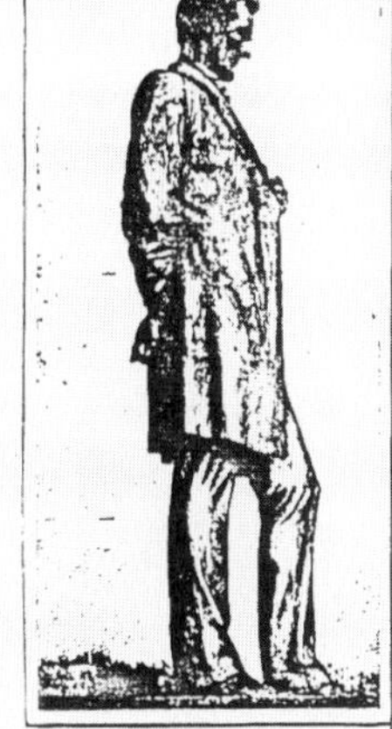

"LINCOLN FREEING THE
SLAVE"

But the statue below has more often been known as "Shine, Sir!" It stands in Boston. The sculptor is Thomas Ball

Press Illustrating

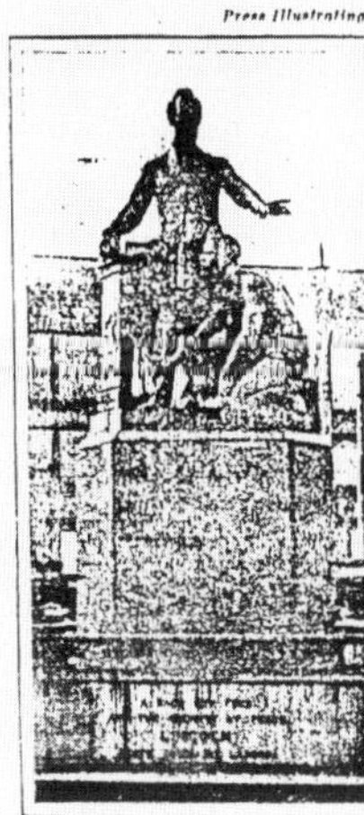

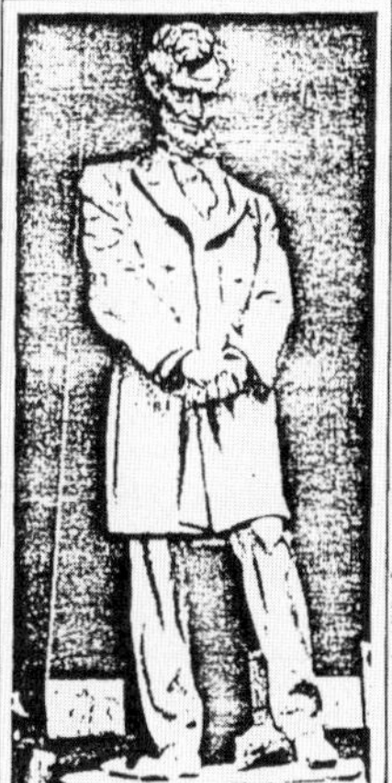

AN EDINBURGH
MEMORIAL

This is the chief British memorial to Lincoln now. It was made by J. Patrick in memory of Scottish-American soldiers

Press Illustrating

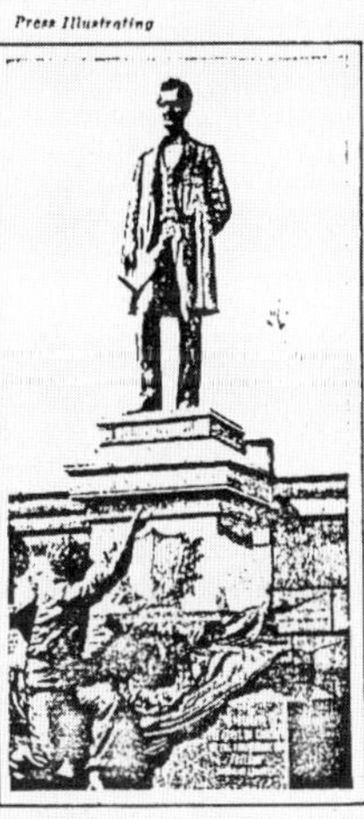

Central News

THE BARNARD STATUE

The proposal to place a replica of this statue in Parliament Square, London, has aroused a storm of controversy as to which Lincoln statue best represents our conception of him. On another page we discuss the six chief examples of Lincoln statues, all photographed here. "When doctors disagree the public is the referee"—tell us which is your choice

The Independent *(November 3, 1917).*

Barnard's Lincoln as a Noted Painter Sees It

Kenyon Cox Points Out the Statue's Faults in Comparison with True Lincoln of Mr. Story's Photograph – Saint Gaudens's Figure Best

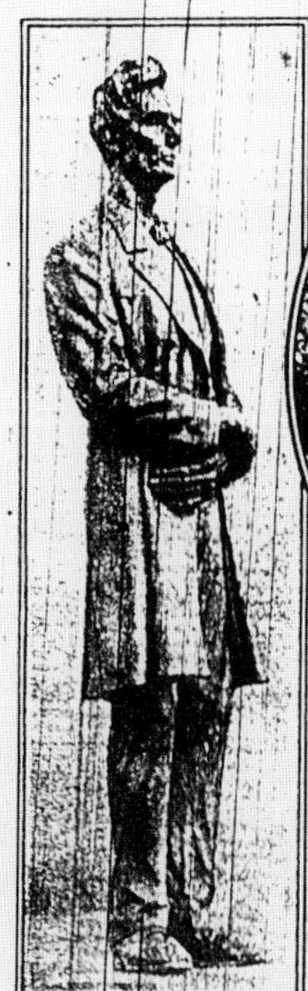

© Pirie Prints.
Barnard Statue, Replica of Which Will Stand in London.

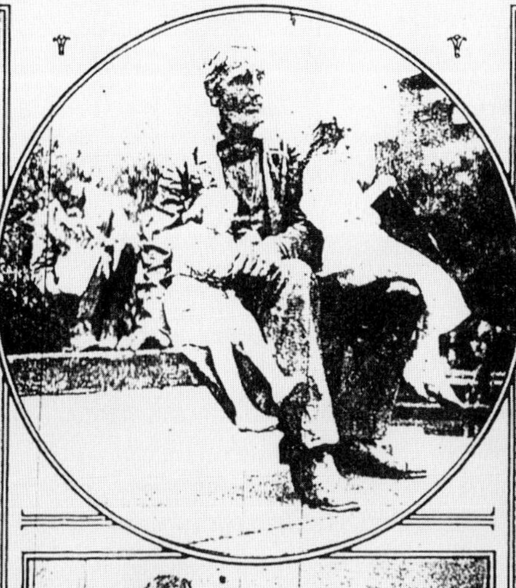

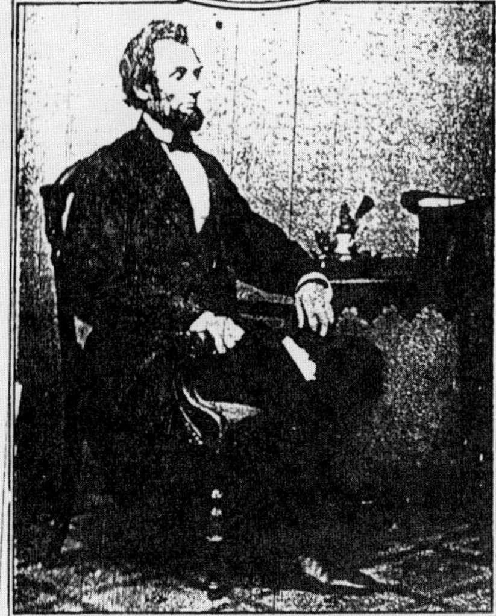

(Above.) Borglum Statue, with Children Playing Over It, at Newark, N. J.
(Below.) Photograph Taken at Brady's Studio, Washington, Feb. 23, 1861, Under Supervision of George H. Story, Painter of Lincoln Portrait That Hangs in the National Gallery.

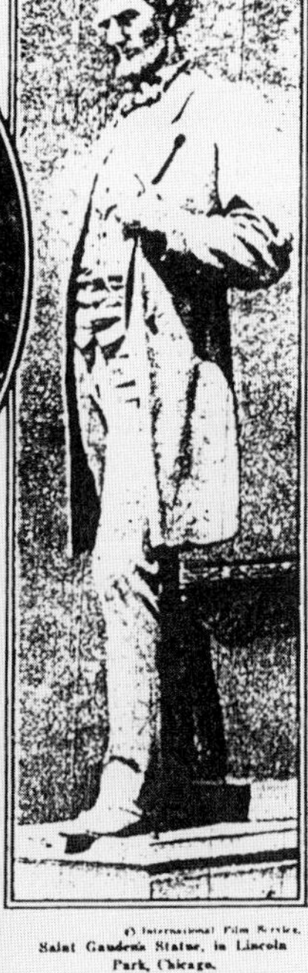

© International Film Service.
Saint Gaudens's Statue, in Lincoln Park, Chicago.

KENYON COX, the painter, is of the opinion that by comparison with the accompanying photograph of Lincoln, taken Feb. 23, 1861, the Saint Gaudens statue is a better likeness of the great President than either the much-discussed statue by George Grey Barnard or that by Gutzon Borglum in Newark. In the light of the photograph, the Barnard statue appears to Mr. Cox as "something like a caricature."

But even if the Barnard statue were shown to be a literal physical portrait of Abraham Lincoln, the painter and art critic would still question the advisability, and criticise the value of such a presentation of the man. And this, it should be added, is a criticism which is expressed almost in the same sentence with Mr. Cox's recognition of Barnard's ability and achievement. As he says, "Mr. Barnard is a man of talent who has done what he tried to do." But what he tried to do, Mr. Cox points out, offers neither a literal likeness of Lincoln—as seen, for example, in the photograph taken just before his inauguration—nor a visualization of what the man really was. Neither as portrait nor symbol, in short, does the Barnard statue represent the real Lincoln, as he is seen in his photographs and held in the hearts of the people of America. At the same time Mr. Cox considers the fitness of such a presentation as Barnard's, in sculpture, open to grave question.

"It is easy to see what Barnard was trying to do, and why," Mr. Cox said. "He was carrying out in his sculpture his ideal of Lincoln. Of course, no artist can make a portrait of the 'real Lincoln.' Lincoln is dead; and in any case all that the artist can do is to carry out his ideal. Barnard's was, as he himself has said, the democratic ideal. He wished to represent Lincoln, the man of the people. And to do that he accented all that was rough and grotesque in his figure and bearing. Barnard has, indeed, done for Lincoln something of what Rembrandt did in his figures of Christ. In representing the Man of Sorrows, the Christ of the people, he made a figure that was often ugly and grotesque. Barnard's ideal is entirely comprehensible.

"But where I join issue is with Mac-Monnies's statement that the fact that Barnard has carried out his ideal is a sufficient answer to criticism. I do not think it is. I think the question is whether Barnard's ideal is our ideal, and whether a statue of Lincoln that is to represent this country abroad should not more truly speak our thought than Barnard's expression of his ideal does. Also there is the question whether Barnard's ideal is a sculpturesque ideal—should it be done in sculpture?

"I think," Mr. Cox added, quickly, "that Barnard is a very able sculptor. I admire his ability. But I do not think that what he has tried to do is the right thing to do in this case. In trying to accent the 'popular' idea of Lincoln he has made something like a caricature of what Lincoln was."

Mr. Cox went on to speak of the question of physical likeness.

"One of the things I have heard said," he remarked, "is that Barnard chose as model for the figure a man who had been a railsplitter for forty years. I do not know whether that true or not. But I do know that if Lincoln had been a railsplitter for forty years, we should never have heard of him! Such a thing as that is not a literal presentation. It is an exaggerated ideal. As a matter of fact, Lincoln became a professional man early in his life. He was not a railsplit-

(Continued on Page 14)

New York Times, *28 October 1917, sec. 7, p. 7.*

between public and private art were demonstrated in familiar historical examples. The *Tribune* set forth what Edward Morse and other academicians believed was the solution to the misunderstanding by defining the adjectives "monumental" and "artistic." The first denoted a work that aspired to a universal, poetic truth; the latter term specified that which was innovative and original in a created work. One was best appreciated in a public setting, the other in a more secluded and private domain. The editorialist would not admit that a dignified classicism necessarily ruled out creative genius, but, with Rodin's *Balzac* in mind, insisted an artist who would serve the public should be encouraged to be safe rather than sorry when undertaking the portrait of a great man. The editor found it ironic that Barnard and his friends had once criticized Rodin while they now based their defense on principles they freely attributed to the French master.[36] Kenyon Cox reasoned that a successful public statue had to be both an inspiring symbol as well as a likeness of an individual. Even though he allowed MacMonnies's comparison between Barnard's Lincoln and Rembrandt's roughly sketched portraits of Christ, and admitted Barnard was a man of talent, Cox emphasized that Rembrandt was not painting a work aimed at advertising abroad the national aspirations of his countrymen. Whether he liked it or not, this was precisely Barnard's obligation.

No hierarchical divisions existed in the minds of those editors who either wished the Barnard statue to be forwarded to Westminister, or who considered the instigators of the controversy themselves guilty of impropriety. With tongue-in-cheek circumspection, the *New York Evening Post* reasoned that despite the fears of the objectors, all would turn out for the best. New York would be spared another sculptural menace and, once erected in London, the uncouth statue would soon be camouflaged by the surrounding atmosphere, if the bronze were not first destroyed in an air raid. Twenty-five years hence, the editor predicted, few would be able to distinguish the difference between the Barnard, the Saint-Gaudens,

or the Borglum. Whether it was a work of genius like the *Balzac,* or a hopeless failure, the statue was recognizably a portrait of Lincoln and, the writer jested, in matters of portraiture, great men always looked out for themselves. Recalling that American Ambassador James Bryce denounced Clark Mill's jaunty equestrian of Andrew Jackson when comparing it to the statuary of his native land, and observing, as well, that the same Americans who were taking strong exception to the Barnard were oblivious to the horrid works that were defacing their own country, an *Evening Post* commentator lightheartedly proposed the two nations enter a treaty.[37] This would permit only American-made monuments to be set up in England, and only those made by British sculptors to be erected in America, thus insuring both nations against offensive statues.

The *Chicago Tribune* facetiously observed that it was a dangerous practice for an artist like Barnard to attempt to express in concrete form an abstract idea, since the public was not prepared to accept artistic innovation in a neutral environment outside the studio or gallery. Sardonically eyeing the magnitude of the protest in the East, the journalist evoked Goethe's precepts directing the observer to first give himself up to a "sympathetic appreciation before judging" a work of art. Otherwise, it was fair to warn the reader that "while you are judging Barnard's statue, Barnard's statue is judging you." Percy MacKaye fully agreed with this maxim. He recalled that Americans first disparaged Whitman's writing in the same manner they were now criticising Barnard's statue. But circumstances brought Whitman to the attention of an enlighted British audience, which without hesitation honored the American's native genius and democratic precepts.[38] So it was with Barnard's portrayal of Lincoln, the Democrat, which was being subjected to harsh rebuke by home critics, even after it was accepted in England in the place of other works. Thus, Cowper's "tenth Muse who now governs the periodical press" had done her best with statues and statesmen.

Part Five
Resolutions

9

On to Westminster

WHEN THE *ART WORLD* BEGAN ITS ASSAULT, BARnard urged Charles Taft to institute legal action against the magazine; the wary patron suggested instead that such an initiative could best be undertaken by his "artistic friends."[1] But what artists might he have counted upon? MacMonnies, Frank Elwell, Abbott Thayer, Charles Rumsey, Maurice Fromkes, and Ralph Goddard had remained faithful. So had one other sympathetic École comrade, who despite substantial differences between them, stood ready to offer Barnard moral, if not legal, support.

Lorado Taft—his American ancestors were unrelated to those of the Cincinnati Tafts—believed the contemporary sculptor's desire to win individual distinction should be tempered by certain social responsibilities. He or she also had to consider the welfare of professional colleagues, and was obligated to educate the public. Since, as he said, "we are all heirs of the ages," and, "all is ours to have and hold if only we desire it," Taft was convinced there could be no higher national priority than that of informing the American people about the evolutionary progression of art from its earliest beginnings to the present day. With this goal in mind, he directed a Chicago sculpture cooperative known as "The Midway Studios," and wrote several popular surveys, *The History of American Sculpture* (1903) and *Modern Tendencies in Sculpture* (1921), the latter an international compilation of figurative work that was based on a lecture series Taft presented at the Chicago Art Institute. He published generous appreciations of Barnard in both texts and, convinced that his New York colleague would make a fine addition to the western art movement, attempted to coax him back to Chicago. Fail-

ing in this, Taft tried to at least make a club man out of Barnard, prompting him to enlist in the American Institute of Arts and Letters.[2] Now, during Barnard's torment over the Lincoln, Taft sought to rouse him with a flattering personal appraisal of the statue, which he composed after visiting Cincinnati in the summer of 1917.

As we approached the little square where the figure is so effectively placed on its low pedestal we suddenly became conscious of its presence. The size and mass of it and its placement pleased me at once and I was startled when my companion said "Well, he's 'Down and Out' all right!" It must be admitted that from a distance and at certain angles the humble knees and reluctant hands give the statue a tramp-like look. The ragged connoisseurs who adorned the benches encircling the square might find a touch of kinship in Barnard's "Lincoln." We drew nearer and my companion's tone became more respectful.

"I guess it's Lincoln's brother, who staid [sic] on the farm and split rails all his life. He is like Lincoln, but so crude." We walked around the figure—and around again. We found a place among the unwashed and sat upon a green bench to study and to talk about this great overpowering work. We were coming under the spell of a mighty achievement. It was not my Lincoln, nor his Lincoln, but we felt that we were looking at a perfectly legitimate and even triumphant expression of George Barnard's ideal of Lincoln—an intensely subjective rendering of a national theme by a sculptor of unusual ability. Details of dress and methods of modeling are entirely irrelevant. This passionate interpretation of Lincoln by a sculptor

163

whose skill has always been my reverent homage is to be esteemed like Rodin's "Burghers of Calais" for its own artistic worth, not as a photograph. It does not claim to be a precise statement. It is the emotion of a poet caught and eternalized by admirably trained hands. One view of that tragic head seemed to be the greatest rendering of the Lincoln theme that I had yet looked upon. Was it the hypnotism of the moment? I must see it again.

Like the claims made by other defenders, Lorado's legitimizes poetic truth over a photographic replication, as he insists upon a progressive and culminative viewing experience for uncovering the expressive potential of the statue. Taft well realized this was not a new kind of critical defense, for it could be found in varied form throughout Western literature. Whenever ancients like Callistratus, Tacitus, Philostratus, Ovid, or Renaissance authors such as George Sandys, or modern-day poets, Rodin admirer Rainer Maria Rilke for example, addressed the romantic idea of the statue that had come to life, it was always in contrast to the statue that was, like the "photographic replication," simply a dead, material record of what no longer existed.[3]

Taft's narrative on the Barnard Lincoln constituted another of many endorsements he extended to his fellow sculptors, even when their chosen styles radically differed from his own. However, he apparently made no move to publish this statement, and hesitated until the press controversy over the Lincoln had peaked before forwarding it to Barnard. For his part, Barnard was no doubt offended by the essay's frankly expressed introduction and possibly sensed a tone of condescension in Taft's remarks since, in his first book, the author acknowledged without reservation that Saint-Gaudens's Lincoln "was considered" the greatest single masterwork of American sculpture.[4] For whatever reason, the embattled Barnard resisted adding this otherwise reassuring communication to his press portfolio.

Barnard preferred to vent his frustration in letters and memoranda. In the draft of a letter to Ruckstull written in July 1917, in which he persistently misspelled his antagonist's surname—we recall the editor retained the Germanic spelling of his surname until the beginning of 1918—Barnard, like Tarbell and Roberts in the forthcoming issues of *Touchstone,* compared him to the Copperheads, and the bronze statue to the unflinching man who felt their wrath.[5] He denied having copyrighted the damning photographs, and charged De Kay with having broken a verbal promise not to publish any images he had not first

approved. Noting Ruckstull reprinted the *Milwaukee Sentinel*'s rebuke, but not the *Digest*'s later retraction, he now demanded a correction and personal apology be printed in the *Art World*'s forthcoming issue. The complaint ends on a suspiciously high note, with Barnard expressing hope Ruckstull's *Lincoln: April 15, 1865* would finally "meet its reward" by being commissioned for a public building. "Thus," Barnard reproved his adversary, "your magazine would do good work in the upbuild of American sculpture and brotherhood in art."

This communication is reasonably moderate in comparison with a dozen pages of penciled notes, possibly intended for a published broadside, which evidence Barnard's effusion of blind rage.[6] In this writing, words progressively expand in size, crowding the borders of pages violently scored by hyphens, underlines, and punctuation; lines tilt precariously and the syntax is repetitive and disorganized. Choosing invectives quite foreign to the soothing remonstrations of Isaiah, and the pacificism urged upon him by Perris, Barnard savors Ruckstull's and De Kay's decrepitude.

De Kay and Rucksthoul, one foreign born, seek to cover the Lincoln statue with [the] mud of their hearts desire, we acknowledge they throw very dirty mud, and any reader readily sees it comes from the depths of their hearts, it is so true an expression of venom and spite [which are] the tools of [the] expression of [anguish?], free from the U-boat tricks that uses lines as these—In these days of the fight for life and death [to, for] Democracy it is a crime one or two men should backed by money assert to the American Republic what they say is good art [and] what they say is bad art (to decide the faith of our growth) they show their own cooperative work asking the public to carry it out.

In a phrase, the editors' affront amounted to "Kaiserism for the big I."

Once the initial complaint is discharged, Barnard launches into a familiar disputation, laced with poetic imagery, that links young Lincoln's unrefined dress with his working-class background. Made by loving mothers in Western homesteads, comfortable clothing was the workingman's standard attire, be he a miner, mill worker, or farmer. In microcosm, the broadcloth's turbulent surfaces resembled a map crossed by the farm roads Lincoln traveled in his youth, or the unfinished logs that sheltered his childhood days. Lincoln's dress was the uniform of all workingmen; it recorded "God's finger prints upon

Page of letter from George G. Barnard to Frederick Ruckstuhl. Ca. July, 1917. George G. Barnard Papers, Archives, Philadelphia Museum of Art.

the life he touches." Scuffed by daily use, the oversized country-made shoes were the American equivalents to the sandals of Apollo. Ruckstull and De Kay would have Lincoln born in the White House parlor, rather than a log cabin. Indeed, Barnard speculates, the Civil War was ultimately fought against the false values symbolized by the mansion's carpeted halls. Yet the artist professed to understand his detractors' disparagement; Ruckstull was of Alsace and, for his entire life, De Kay had been the prisoner of a teaming eastern metropolis. Just as God "loves the worn clothes of labor," the writer ruefully remarked, so He was even tolerant of the likes of dictator publishers who deprecated his statue by describing it as the "Hobo president."[7]

As is borne out by his correspondence to associ-ates, Ruckstull was familiar with a version of this text. In letters to Howard Russell Butler he vowed to "scotch this [Barnard] movement or else Labor will use it to advantage." In December 1918, Ruckstull touched on his favorite topic of conversation: Barnard's rumored insanity.[8] He feigned pity for the "half-witted of the race who will persist in going off at a tangent and flying into a state of neurosis and demi–insanity and will swear that a totem-pole is finer than the Apollo Belvedere." He knew such delusions were the symptoms of mental instability, a manifestation that would be made more serious if certain "intellectuals should swallow [Barnard's] pontifical buncomb."

Decidedly more melodramatic than the responses to Ruckstull was a draft of a proposed Barnard communication to Daniel French. While the two were sparring over French's association with the *Art World*'s advisory committee, as well over the *Touchstone*'s out-of-context quoting of a Daniel French letter to Barnard, the latter issued a pathetic rejoinder: "Little did I dream that while I was planning to give my life to my country you and Ruckstuhl and others . . . a plan was being made among sculptors to cast ignomy on my life's work, and bring disgrace before the world upon my name and my family."[9] He did not discount the importance of verisimilitude in the evaluation of his portrait: "You are right [the Lincolns] differ. Yours is not the Lincoln I meet every where in every description of Lincoln, from his boyhood to his martrydom. In your standing Lincoln you have dealt in [the] superficial and [in] surface arrangements, your treatment of the Lincoln figure and clothes is exactly like your other portrait statues by you. While Lincoln's figure was as unlike one Emerson and others in sculpture as the oak is unlike the cotton-wood." While French's bust of Emerson (1883) in no way resembled his later head of Lincoln, Barnard saw their generic similarity in the artist's intent to deal only with pleasing affectations, not with substance. This proved French had not read the sixty or more biographies that Barnard asserted had informed him about Lincoln's complex character. In a histrionic conclusion, he returned to the conspiracy theory, declaring that "I regret with all my blood and soul I am not at the battlefront, but grateful I am here now to protect my life's work and my family's honor from the knife trusts at my back."

Meanwhile, as discussed in chapter 7, a fretful and disorganized anti-Barnard cartel had resorted to quiet diplomacy and private investigation in an effort to sustain Robert Lincoln's early initiatives. The press had completed its work with mixed results; what clearly was needed were not additional public protests or editorial pontifications, but a "personal" and "confidential" meeting of minds between the most resourceful partners of the opposition. A veil of secrecy attested to the importance of the cabal's deliberations, while it also protected it from public accountability. Lost to us are the informal conversations and satirical mimes that entertained the habitués of Manhattan's professional clubs, most particularly those of the Century Association, a central gathering place for Sen. Elihu Root—the club's incoming president—William Ellsworth, Howard Russell Butler, Nicholas Murray Butler, Robert Lincoln, Ruckstull, and other conspirators.[10] There were few Centurians who did not feel personally obligated to carry forward the unfinished work of their fallen comrades, Choate, Gilder, and Saint-Gaudens.

With the resources of the Carnegie Endowment for International Peace at his disposal, as well as the enthusiastic backing of endowment president Root, Nicholas Murray Butler, who then directed the Peace Endowment, assumed command of the operations. Butler laid a proposal before the executives of the Endowment's Division of Intercourse and Education on 11 January 1918, several weeks before he notified the British of his intent, and a full year of delicate negotiations before Lord Weardale and Mond found it possible to accept his offer. Butler readily gained the consent of his executive board to offer "on behalf of the endowment to the city of London the Saint-Gaudens's statue of Abraham Lincoln, provided a suitable and satisfactory method can be found to have the statue placed upon the site assigned for the Lincoln statue at Westminster." As we have seen, Henry White, with Robert Lincoln's blessing, intended to forward to Paris a second replica which Root and Butler also seemed ready to fund through the endowment. But nothing more is heard of the Paris statue after the German army began its push to the Marne River in late March 1918. Butler's team discussed other possible amendments to the original offer: White and Lincoln raised the possibility of selecting a cast of Saint-Gaudens's yet-unveiled seated Lincoln— now located in Chicago's Grant Park—a statue that perhaps counted in their minds as being more of an "original" than the frequently-reproduced standing portrait.[11] Whatever Butler would ultimately decide, funding would be the least of his problems.

The man's chief concerns were tied to his social philosophy, the rigors of diplomacy, and the gentle art of disguise. When preparing press releases at the end of 1918, Butler and his Peace Endowment assistant Henry S. Haskell, preferred that the public record show that the replica was being offered to England by a volunteer American committee "on behalf of their fellow citizens," that body consisting of Butler, Root, White, and the financier J. P. Morgan. Certainly, such an organization could easily have raised the required funds on its own; indeed, John Gutzon Borglum justifiably argued that "a half-dozen New Yorkers could have [raised the money] in an hour." Nevertheless, the financing was to be arranged by, and "on behalf of the [Carnegie] Endowment," and most, if not all, of Butler's correspondence relating to the project was written on Peace Endowment letterheads. So insistent was he that the endowment be the sole de facto sponsor, he politely ignored Robert Lincoln's request to contribute to all incidental costs not covered by the casting contract. To this end, Lincoln directed Butler to draw disbursements from a twenty-five thousand dollar guaranty fund established with his account at J. P. Morgan's banking house. However, what Butler took to be an extended courtesy was more accurately a demand; while the disappointed Lincoln had not expected the project "to be an entire filial act of my own, I had hoped and expected that I should have some practical part in it."[12] Hence, the unilateral, secretive character of the Butler-Carnegie undertaking began to resemble the John Stewart-ACPC-Sulgrave Institute promotion of the Taft Lincoln against which it was competing.

What may have induced Butler to so strongly favor the endowment's role in the statue war? Was Nicholas Butler, as John Stewart charged in letters to Charles Taft, seeking to lead a Carnegie takeover of the Sulgrave Institute by becoming its chancellor? And, if so, would the eventual location of the Saint-Gaudens Lincoln on the hallowed ground of the Canning Enclosure symbolize the success of this *coup?* Butler quite obviously viewed the situation differently. When in 1916 he dispensed endowment funds to settle all ACPC debts, he believed he was effecting a "buy out" of the committee on the endowment's behalf.[13] He was naturally distressed when Stewart resurrected the organization, first under the umbrella of the Committee of Fifteen, and later, under the joint control of the Anglo-American Society and the American Sulgrave Institution. Beyond questions of aesthetics and suitability, the Barnard Lincoln substitution constituted in the minds of Butler and Root an illegitimate abridgement of an endowment perogrative.

Yet Butler's wish to utilize endowment's resources rather than private capital grew out of deep personal convictions. An expounder of political ethics and international law, he could find no better guardian of civic ideals than the private institution.[14] In the arena of national and international relations, the institution stood between the anarchy of unfettered individualism and the autocratic tendencies that were built into federalism. But it also followed that as it bequeathed public beneficences through education and works, corporations like the Carnegie could afford to act anonymously, especially when their donations impinged upon the delicate fabric of international alliances in times of unprecedented world crisis. From this standpoint, Butler perceived the endowment's active assistance to be a model of a modest benevolence few governments or individuals were capable of achieving. For example, from his perspective inside the endowment administration, Butler could better appreciate Lord Weardale's embarrassment in the present circumstances than could Charles Taft, a private donor who was typically driven by vanity and personal ambition.

Weardale, chairman of what was now designated as the Anglo-American Society, had little enthusiasm for the "modern ultra realistic school" with which he associated Barnard's statue, and was convinced, erroneously, as it turned out, the bronze was too tall for the Canning site. Even so, he and Mond were more afraid of offending the Taft family, an American sculptor who, despite adverse criticism, was yet "admired in certain artistic circles," and the three presidents whose names were affixed to the Stewart petition, than they were of being implicated in John Stewart's shameless gamble. The German offensive added to Weardale's predicament, for it would extend by months an agonizing controversy into which he and Mond were being increasingly drawn. Weardale would have agreed with Ruckstull's prediction that the "Americans will grow to hate the British because of their indifference, at first in secret, but then it will break out." The commissioner of works was in an even more difficult position than Weardale, for right-wing elements were charging that Mond, a leading Jewish politician and corporate director, was a war profiteer and enemy collaborator. Thus with increasing impatience, the two men demanded that the American government, guided by the advice of experts, mercifully relieve them "of a particularly disagreeable and invidious responsibility."[15] Weardale, at least, was determined not to commit the Westminster site to either statue until after the armistice.

Butler's realization in mid-March 1918 that the project was deadlocked was substantiated by Ambassador Page. After interviewing Mond and Foreign Secretary Balfour at Butler's request, Page relayed the information that even though British officials preferred to receive only one Lincoln and generally hoped it would be the Saint-Gaudens, they were loathe to admit this preference. Otherwise, the ambassador could offer Butler no hope and, given his personal views, little sympathy, since Page deemed both the Anglo-American Society and the Butler-Endowment statue offerings to be strictly "none of our government's business." Indeed, some disgruntled AAS members were urging that both the Barnard and Saint-Gaudens orders be replaced with one that would produce an entirely new commission for "an original symbolic statue."[16]

The legal encumbrance left Butler and Root with few satisfactory options. They still hoped the Root bill restricting export of art works would pass both Houses in 1918, thereby settling all uncertainties. As has been noted, the measure was soundly defeated, an outcome that could have hardly surprised its seasoned sponsor. Root and Butler realized they would have to rely upon others who could work outside the domain of the endowment and in close association with official art organizations. There was no lack of eager and capable investigators and strategists, but like Robert Lincoln, most of these were also vain and stridently independent individuals who with one false move could derail the common effort. For example, the chastened Ruckstull still clung to the hope that he might once more publicly thrash John Stewart and Barnard, thereby forcing Charles Taft's withdrawal. Furthermore, without personal knowledge of the endowment's action, the editor was preparing to lead a conscription campaign for funding a Saint-Gaudens replica. Striving once again to gain the center of attention, the irrepressible John Gutzon Borglum also planned to solicit money for what he now sanctimoniously described as the "excellent" Saint-Gaudens, to thus defeat a "plan to usurp the nation's prerogative for private exploitation."[17] Luxuriating in his off-hours disguise as undercover investigator, Judd Stewart remained through 1918 a most energetic plotter and perhaps Robert Lincoln's most trusted confidant. Jealously guarding his expanding archive of incriminating documents, he also sought to direct the crusade. But it was to be Howard R. Butler, the vice president of the National Academy of Design, who Nicholas Butler realized would be the most capable and trustworthy investigator.

Son of prominent New York attorney William Allen Butler—he was unrelated to Nicholas Butler—Howard Russell Butler (1856–1934) had interests that ranged from law, to astrology, scientific photography, landscape architecture, and painting. Degrees from Columbia and Princeton prepared him for a career in patent law. But in the later 1880s, Butler opted to study painting under Frederic Church, Carroll Beckwith, and, in Paris, with Dagnan Bouveret, Roll, and Gervex. Returning from Paris in 1888, he joined the New York art community as a painter and site architect—he assisted Andrew Carnegie in the design, construction and supervision of the magnate's New York properties—and also as a fundraiser, contract supervisor, and officer for the Fine Arts Society and the National Academy Association. In 1916, he was elected president of the latter organization and vice president of the National Academy of Design. In December 1917, after publicly expressing indignation over suspected illegalities in John Stewart's preemptive advancement of the Barnard statue, the NAD Council assigned Butler the task of preparing a history of the ACPC statue initiative. His first objective was to counter Stewart's early advisory to Mond, which maintained that the ACPC generally considered the Barnard to be a "superior substitute" to the Saint-Gaudens. To this end Butler randomly

polled the ACPC membership, discovering that out of more than seventy replies, fifty-one either denounced the Barnard, preferred the Saint-Gaudens, or both; that only one individual unequivocally liked the Barnard, one apparently confused member stood with a Saint-Gaudens that had folded hands, one equally admired both statues, while twenty-one others expressed no preference. Seventeen of the latter respondents indicated they had not been consulted. Butler forwarded the results to Mond and, at the beginning of the new year, published them in the *New York Times*.[18]

By no means was Butler's mission then complete, for he was soon deluged with advice for new initiates from Ruckstull, Lincoln, Judd Stewart, James B. Townsend, editor of the *American Art News,* and Nicholas Butler. Two options aimed at undermining John Stewart's position were now on the table. One was to force the ACPC executive director to release documents detailing ACPC action related to the statue substitution, and the other to test the legitimacy of the names listed on Stewart's cablegram of 15 November 1917 to Mond. Following a considerable delay and an angry exchange between him and former ACPC executive Austin G. Fox, Stewart reluctantly forwarded some archival material. But he was unwilling or unable to make available copies of the reputed solicitation for the Saint-Gaudens replica or a record of an actual ACPC subcommittee vote which activated the substitution. Howard Butler's assignment to verify the names on the cablegram had to proceed under tight security, for the cable was a document that English officials, for fear of added embarrassment, did not wish to fall into the hands of John Stewart's and Taft's accusers. In mid-January 1918, Judd Stewart finally obtained a complete copy of the cablegram from Robert Lincoln. But he was reluctant to release the full text, again out of respect for Lincoln, Weardale, and Mond, and thus urged Howard Butler to individually question those whose names appeared on the cable. Assured of the document's existence, Nicholas Butler and Root requested Howard Butler to carry forward his research and, if he found the results sufficiently compromising, to utilize it in enacting NAD resolves.[19]

Howard Butler's second canvass, that of the names that authorized sending the cable, those who the cable credited as having enthusiastically praised Barnard's Lincoln, and several individuals listed on the statue presentation committee, was completed by April 1918. Butler was highly selective in his contacts; upon Lincoln's and Judd Stewart's advice, he stayed clear of almost all signers who authorized the cablegram, for these—Elwell, Goddard, MacMonnies,

McBride, MacKaye, Tarbell, Thayer, William Taft, George Harvey, Shaw, and Andrew Humphrey— were considered unshakable. Roosevelt was also exempted, although his attitude was more difficult to ascertain. Thus, the brunt of Butler's investigation was directed at a dozen names in the second group, the "enthusiastic" praisers. Despite his intimidating manner of inquiry, four of these stood by Barnard. For example, the painter Maurice Fromkes held fast even after being subjected to a Butler cross-examination. The inquisitor was astonished that Fromkes approved of John Stewart's forced substitution. Conceding that Barnard was attempting to be experimental, Butler lectured his fellow painter that "it seems to us this is no time for experimentation." Frank Chapman, Lawrence Abbott, and F. W. Stokes also withstood similar interrogation, although Abbott wavered enough to admit that, in light of the criticism, the Barnard statue should probably not be classified as a "national" offering.[20] These holdouts brought to six the total pro-Barnard submissions uncovered by Butler's two inspections of over eighty names.

Approximately ten others firmly repudiated Barnard's statue, complaining they had not been consulted. Although his name was listed among the supporters, Robert Clowry stated that illness prevented him from responding to the solicitation.[21] Charles W. Eliot, Charles Evans Hughes, Frederick Coudert, Robert Bacon, Melville E. Stone, and Charles Dana Gibson indignantly condemned John Stewart and Barnard. From the statue presentation list, Secretary of the Treasury William G. McAdoo, Secretary of Commerce William C. Redfield, and Secretary of the Interior Franklin K. Lane each verified they had not authorized use of their names. Most surprising was Butler's assertion that Woodrow Wilson's name was not authorized, since as we have seen, the president had accepted John Stewart's invitation to serve as honorary chairman of the statue presentation committee in June 1917.

However, it was clear that John Stewart had been overly careless in assembling his petition. Quickly learning of Butler's canvas of the cablegram names, he attempted one final face-saving measure. On 1 March 1918 he dispatched a form letter that boldly affirmed "no person's name appears as a member of the Lincoln presentation committee who did not authorized such use of his name in a letter now on file in this office." Otherwise, he would not accommodate the accusers, who he identified as "two men whose motives are almost entirely personal," by issuing a public reply. He passionately decried the slanderous defilement of his artist. "No campaign was ever conducted in this country against any worthy object with so much venom, misrepresentation (disregard of fact) and so much akin to persecution as that campaign which has been conducted in the name of art against poor Barnard and his statue." While he reaffirmed the names of the statue presentation committee, Stewart pointedly did not give similar reassurance that he retained records substantiating the names given as "enthusiastic praisers" of Barnard's statue. Two weeks after Stewart mailed this announcement and, significantly, just days before Germany began its drive on the Marne, he signaled Barnard to prepare the statue for immediate shipment.[22]

Howard Butler compiled the results of his investigations and a history of ACPC and BCPC actions—this obtained by Nicholas Butler from Weardale and Mond—into a fifteen-page council report, to which was appended his extensive correspondence. Its conclusion was unequivocal: the substitution "was brought about by a small clique" led by John Stewart and representing Charles Taft, Barnard, their friends, and "a few spirits in Modern realistic art and whomever they could get to put their names (perhaps unthinkingly) to this lamentable scheme."[23] Their intrigue, the council continued, consisted of nothing less than an insult directed toward "America's greatest sculptor," and it was unwilling "to see one of his noblest works thus elbowed out of its legitimate place to make room for Barnard's questionable production." Furthermore, the Council faulted a method of operation that permitted one man to overstep his authority with such overwhelmingly disastrous results.

Hence, the document assumed the character of a legal brief upon which the NAD, the Fine Arts Federation of New York, the American Federation of Arts, the National Security League, and, most importantly, the CFA, proceeded to base a series of resolutions. As noted earlier, the Council relayed the report to the full membership which, bowing to the wishes of its president, Herbert Adams, declined to put its approval to a vote. Instead, on 1 April the NAD instructed a committee comprised of Howard Butler, Kenyon Cox, and Arnold W. Brunner to lay the report before the CFA, requesting it to present the matter to either the president or the secretary of state for final disposition.[24] Nicholas Butler contemplated an endowment publication of the report, but backed down after no doubt realizing that such a document would only call attention to the organization's critical role in the affair.

Having more than justified the NAD's faith in his investigative abilities, Howard Butler confidently prepared to assist kindred organizations. But not all was smooth sailing. Outside of the NAD, his most significant presentation occurred at Detroit in late May of 1918, on the occasion of the annual convention of the American Federation of Arts. Despite the commanding presence of President George W. De Forest, two members of the committee on resolutions moved to table some of the more severe language aimed at Barnard. Alfred V. Churchill, formerly of Columbia Teachers College and now a member of the Smith College art faculty, objected to the inclusion of Barnard's name and the proposed statement that his statue "has never received the general approval of the American people or the committee named." Recounting the incident for Root, Howard Butler expressed outrage that Henry W. Kent, the newly-appointed secretary of the Metropolitan Museum of Art's Board of Trustees—a man well known and respected by De Forest and Root— dared to support Churchill's protest. Butler was also questioned by resolutions committee chairman George Booth about the relative scarcity of information on the pro-Barnard petitioners. Gently reproving Butler, Booth advised, "let's not give just one side of the question in case it gets before the country; if there were endorsements—these should be considered."[25] Having confronted these obstacles, Butler presented a synopsis of his report to the full AFA membership and, as we have seen in chapter 8, it proceeded to approve two resolutions. The results of the AFA conference were widely reported, but still the statue impasse remained in place.

During the months the Carnegie offer lay on the table, Barnard received unexpected critical support from radical British artists and writers. Northcliffe's initial editorial in the London *Times* produced several letters of protest, one from William Roberts who had attended Barnard's seminary exhibit. More significant was Roger Fry's submission to the *Burlington Magazine,* the erudite art journal he helped establish in 1913. Intending to run his appreciation earlier, Fry delayed publication until the June 1918 issue so that "adequate" photographs could be reproduced.[26] Having apparently obtained the images from the *New York Sun,* Fry reprinted three glossy halftones of the full-standing figure, two taken from angular positions outside Barnard's studio, the other, a more distant frontal view picturing the statue in bright sun against the seminary buildings. Contained within Fry's "A Monthly Chronicle" series, the notice commended the work in a typically understated Bloomsbury tone. Fry contended that since the work in question was a portrait statue it could not rightly qualify as a "pure work of art," neither did it display

the admirable freedom of handling one encountered in Rodin's *Burghers of Calais,* the one bronze in all of London with which the Barnard could otherwise be compared. Nor was it the highest example of modern "synthetic form," an obvious reference to the abstracting work of Eric Gill and Henri Gaudier-Brzeska. But even as a secondary work, the critic maintained, Barnard's statue was far superior to the city's "inimitable collection of bronze dummies," and upon second thought, he even allowed it was a "masterly and profound interpretation of individual character in forms that at least have the unity that appertains to individuality." Next to it, Saint-Gaudens's Lincoln was little more than "trumpery prettiness."

Jacob Epstein registered his endorsement with considerably less equivocation. Since leaving New York's Jewish ghetto, Epstein, along with Gill and Gaudier-Brzeska, assumed a foremost position among England's modernist sculptors, a ranking that spared him neither the aversion of Bloomsbury nor the censure of such archconservatives as the Rev. Bernard Vaughan, who was to take Epstein to task for the deformities of his *Risen Christ.* In such works he strove to express a personal intimacy which was far distant from Barnard's characterization, but his early admiration for the American's independence and intensity at the Art Students League remained undiminished.[27]

In answer to a Sir Claude Phillips's complaint that appeared in the 6 October 1917 *London Daily Telegraph,* Epstein vigorously countered that London's citizens should await the arrival of the statue "with eager expectancy due to an unknown work by a great master." Inferring that ulterior motives had prompted Sir Phillips's attack, Epstein asserted that "like all men of genius, of independent mind, [Barnard] would have ready waiting for him the usual pack, who at first opportunity, would fasten upon him." Like other English critics who in advance of the *Burlington* article condemned the Barnard, Phillips had only the blurred photograph that first appeared in the London *Times* as his single visual reference. But neither could Epstein claim to have seen the statue or other less compromising photographs. The point for him was to know that his old instructor was imbued with Michelangelo's heroic passion—a fact singly demonstrated in *The Two Natures of Man*—and that he, like Epstein himself, had been mishandled by ignorant art critics. However, as Epstein brought the *Risen Christ* to completion over the next several years, it is apparent his interest in Barnard's Lincoln extended considerably beyond a heartfelt sympathy for a maligned artist or shared outrage over pompous cultural autocracies. The statue marked a dramatic change in Epstein's oeuvre of figurative works which quite possibly stemmed from the formal devices he discovered in the Barnard. Before 1914, as Richard Buckle confirms, Epstein considered the human form to be an icon of beauty; thereafter, as "an instrument which could not only inflict but suffer pain."[28] A notable example of this transformation from classicism to social realism, the *Risen Christ* was begun as a portrait study of Barnard Van Dieren in 1917. In 1919, before a yearlong interruption of work, the sculptor added the closely-bound mummylike torso, and overlarge hands with the "accusing finger." There are suggestive parallels between the Barnard and Epstein figures in their stiff immobility and in their archaic distortions, but the most telling detail is found in the Christ's enormous, heavily-veined left hand, which closely resembles Barnard's "hands of labor."

When early in 1920 Rev. Vaughan reacted to the Epstein at an exhibition at the Leicester Galleries, the sculptor's most vigorous defender was George Bernard Shaw. By that time, the noted author had with similar conviction, but with less public attention, unleashed his wit on Barnard's attackers. Urged on by Robert Lincoln, Judd Stewart sent Shaw photographs, copies of newspapers, and a summation of his personal opinion of Barnard's statue. But the Americans badly misjudged the pundit's singular distaste for pretence and lordly manners. Judd Stewart's righteous epistle, which arrived in advance of the photographs and documents, was sufficient to convince Shaw that Barnard had "somehow hit off the right conception for a statue of Lincoln for London," while "the Saint-Gaudens suit of clothes, on which so much stress is layed on your side, would remind everybody here of Sir Charles Wyndham at his gayest on the stage."[29] If the Americans wished their gift Lincoln to resemble the typical British statesman, Shaw rejoined, Stewart should know that he was notoriously ill-dressed. Even so, insofar as his countrymen were concerned, the most appropriate interpretation of Lincoln, the one that Barnard provided, emphasized his saintliness, not his political proficiency. "No doubt," Shaw offered, "some foolish remarks will be made about [Barnard's Lincoln] . . . but the connoisseurs will have to stop and look, to hum and haw, to admit that there is an idea there, to point out that there is a lot of real execution in that head, to ask who did it, and on being told it is by an American, to exclaim 'Nonsense! No American could possibly do work of that class.'" When

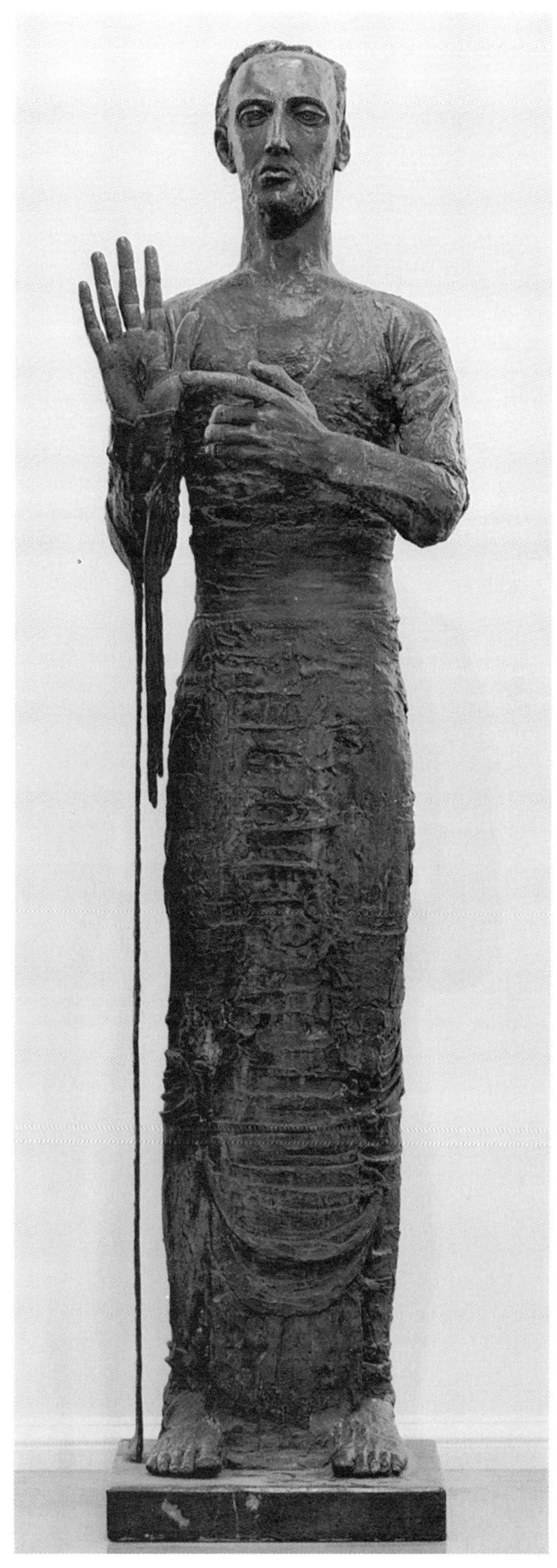

Jacob Epstein, Risen Christ. *1917–20. Bronze, 7'4".
Scottish National Museum of Modern Art, Edinburgh.*

in August 1918 the Allies successfully checked the German advance, and it became apparent the armistice was only weeks away, the American and British Saint-Gaudens operatives anxiously anticipated the day when the United States War Powers Act embargo would be terminated and began concentrating their efforts on securing an accord between the State Department and the CFA. Even if the Root bill was to fail, at least the two governmental agencies could arrive at an understanding that would sufficiently indicate official opinion on the statue matter.

Therefore, in late September, Secretary Balfour forwarded a communication from Mond to Assistant Secretary of State Phillips reaffirming his wish that the statue decision be made by the American government in consultation with a body of experts. At the same time, Charles Moore reminded Phillips the CFA stood ready to offer its opinion. Nicholas Butler then forwarded the Howard Butler report, along with the AFA's two resolutions, to Moore. On 9 October, Colonel C. S. Ridley advised Phillips the CFA had approved the Saint-Gaudens. In early November, several days before the Armistice took effect, Nicholas Butler again pressed Mond. Declaring that his committee was prepared to immediately effect the casting and a shipping of the replica, he enclosed the Butler documents for distribution to British officials. Finally, on 29 November, Weardale transmitted the long-awaited cable to Nicholas Butler. The British government had "definitely" accepted the American's generous proposal and the "issue is now happily ended."[30] Yet the door had not entirely been closed on the Barnard, for in light of his and Mond's scruples, Weardale hoped the rejected statue would yet find its place in another English location. Thus, the British government had been forced into the final decision, after all.

Impatient Americans awaited the issuance of an official statement from London. This did not come immediately. While hosting a joint Sulgrave Institute-Anglo-American Society luncheon in Piccadilly on 20 November, Weardale gently prepared his audience. After suggesting that a statue of President Wilson should be commissioned for London to stand beside the ones of Lincoln and Washington, he mentioned without further comment that Nicholas Butler was recommending the Saint-Gaudens cast for London. The formal announcement came a month later.[31] It confirmed that Barnard's statue would be offered to some other prominent British city and it rejoiced that as a result of the controversy, two Lincoln statues, rather than one, would be placed. Howard Butler broke the news at a meeting of the NAD on 18 December.

It was now time to raise the necessary funds. At an executive committee meeting on 16 December, the Carnegie Endowment's Division of Intercourse and Education earmarked twenty thousand dollars for the cast, its base, transportation, and for labor. But this figure underestimated the amounts for the pedestal and labor, thus the committee was called back to increased its appropriation to thirty-five thousand dollars. An unused balance of six thousand dollars was eventually returned to the endowment treasury. Another full year was to pass before the cast was produced by the Gorham Manufacturing Company of Providence, Rhode Island, under the supervision of Mrs. Saint-Gaudens. Butler had reason to be pleased, since the total cost of the replica was one-third less the amount John Stewart was originally quoted in 1913. Obviously, the sculptor's widow was in a generous mood, as was the Cunard steamship line, which, after reviewing the controversy, waived its transportation fee.[32]

Weardale's decision was announced a week before the American president made a whirlwind visit to England, a tour designed to promote his Fourteen Points for the Covenant of the League of Nations as well as to celebrate the armistice. Immediately after Wilson's departure from London, Perris and John Stewart, acting jointly for the Anglo-American Society and the Sulgrave Institution, and with the consent of Charles Taft, opened a search for a new location, soliciting the town governments of Norwich—the ancestral seat of the American Lincolns—Liverpool, and Manchester. In an effort to counter the stigma of rejection, Perris offered prospective hosts the misinformation that before the War two statues had been offered, only one of which was to be sited in London. He otherwise suggested that the selected host community place the statue in a grassy circle, similar to Cincinnati's Lytle Park, and low to the ground, "not stuck at the top of a high pedestal." Thanks to the Charles Tafts, the work would be presented without cost, but the recipient was expected to bear the expense of erection and maintenance.[33]

Perris's communication to Manchester crossed in the mail with an application from that city's Lord Mayor.[34] John Makeague, the host of Wilson's recent appearance in Manchester, insisted the historic ties and commercial interests existing between the British industrial center and America well qualified it for the honor, as did the fact that, excluding London, Manchester was England's leading art center. Even though Makeague had as yet received no photographs, he left little doubt his city council would enthusiastically approve the statue's acceptance.

Manchester's cultural and business leaders considered the statue's diversion from Westminster to their city to be one of the work's chief assets. They did not regret the socioeconomic divisions that had historically placed the northern industrial region of Lancashire into competition with London and the South, or the fact that in Southern eyes, Manchester was a foreign, and specifically American, enclave. If this indicated the city was driven by commercial greed alone, its defenders only needed to point to the period of the American Civil War when local mill workers, at the expense of their livelihood, participated in the boycott of Confederate cotton, while simultaneously, Londoners sought to aid and comfort the Rebels. Now that American forces had sustained England in the European War, Manchester could claim for herself the added moral vindication of having reinforced strong commercial ties with the United States, a point stressed by Wilson when he spoke at Free Trade Hall.[35] Moreover, the same city that attracted self-motivated industrialists was also home to distinguished social reformers like John Bright and Richard Cobden.

Another factor in the age-old rivalry was Manchester's surprisingly strong artistic life. Art exhibitions, handsome buildings, a wealth of private art collections, and the promulgation of the moral precepts of Ruskin, Morris, the Pre-Raphealites, and of the Arts and Crafts movement, masked the more brutal aspects of the city's industrial existence. Even before its incorporation in the early nineteenth century, Manchester emerged as an important center for public statuary, as it sustained the careers of such prolific sculptors as Matthew Nobel, William Theed, Onslow Ford, Alfred Gilbert, Sir Francis Chantrey, and the Pre-Raphaelite Thomas Woolner. Alfred Waterhouse's Manchester Town Hall, begun in 1868, contained a sculpture hall that was soon filled with standing portraits and busts of national and local heroes. The thoroughfare of Piccadilly, and the confines of the Cathedral and Town Hall, thus offered the citizen, as Palgrave commented, "a city full of diverting commentaries on the taste of the patronizing man of business."[36] But among its Victorian relics, nothing could have adequately prepared its residents for its newest public statue.

In January, Manchester's city council referred Perris's offer to a Lincoln Special Statue Committee consisting of the Mayor as chairman, the deputy chairman of the town art committee, the Parks and Cemetery Committee, and a Town Hall committee. With the matter of acceptance a foregone conclusion, the LSSC focused upon a probable site, recommending the downtown area of Piccadilly, approximate to Noble's statue of Wellington and the old Infirmary,

as its preference. On 29 January Perris informed the Lord Mayor that Manchester had been chosen over two contending cities, but requested that his committee be allowed to negotiate the site and participate in planning the dedication ceremonies. The full city council approved the offer in early February, and, in separate letters, Perris and Stewart informed Barnard they had "bowed to" Charles Taft's wishes that the statue go to Manchester, although Norwich and Liverpool had also applied.[37] Stewart engaged the Mercantile Marine Company to ship the statue and a six-ton granite boulder base from New York on 23 February.

Manchester's council awaited the pleasure of the donors, hoping they would accept a permanent site on Piccadilly. But on 5 May, when Stewart and Perris arrived for the official presentation and a tour of the city, Stewart's inspection of the crowded commercial district with its towering memorials clearly disappointed him. He held out for a location at the edge of Platt Fields, a large recreation park located two miles from city center where the low-set statue could be viewed against a flat, prairielike expanse. Among limitations was one involving a zoning ordinance that forbid the erection of a permanent building—the building clause did not exclude public statuary—within park perimeters. The other drawback, as Stewart envisioned it, was the fact that an eighteenth-century structure, "Old Hall," stood within a hundred feet of the desired setting. Yet, encouraged by the information that Old Hall was soon to be demolished—its conversion into a city art gallery eventually spared it—the Sulgrave director won Platt Fields for temporary placement. He left open the possibility Piccadilly might one day be an acceptable permanent location, especially if proposed architectural renovations were carried out. However, once it was erected there, the figure would remain in Platt Fields for over sixty-five years (see p. 8).[38]

In his luncheon address, Perris covered all political bases. The statue presentation symbolized a resurgence of Anglo-American understanding, it reaffirmed Manchester's historic involvement with the American Union, and, at the present hour, it highlighted Wilson's efforts to establish the League of Nations. The *Manchester Guardian* devoted its 6 May issue to articles and editorials aimed at preparing the public for its first sight of the statue. "There will be a great row about it, as there has been in America, where it has sifted out the sighted from the blind art-critics more successfully than any masterpiece in recent years."[39] The reader was cautioned to remember that such accepted heirlooms as Alfred Gilbert's statue of J. P. Joule had initially been ridiculed for its less than elegant attire. Comparing Barnard's preparatory research into Lincoln's character to the manner in which Rodin and Jacob Epstein approached their subjects, a *Guardian* journalist implored residents to understand the statue's homely details were not to be taken as descriptive facts alone, but as instructive reminders that the mundane accidents of life were ultimately unimportant. What counted was spiritual essence, the "moving grandeur of the essential man" and, except for the Gilbert, a Chantrey, and a Woolner, Manchester had few comparable monuments. Drawn along more practical lines was the appended consideration that the statue would gain the attention of worldly art connoisseurs and that it could be expected to bring to the city throngs of patriotic American tourists.

Having so frankly addressed those aspects of the work that would most likely cause public concern, one might well have expected the *Guardian* to have provided an illustration of the statue in question. Instead, its publication of a left-profile view of the "wonderful head [of the statue]" was in fact a Van der Weyde photograph of the cloth-draped "decoy" bust, over which the *Touchstone* and *Art World* had wrangled the previous fall. By way of proving how closely this image resembled its subject, the paper introduced beneath it two historic photographs, one a Hesler, showing the right profile of Lincoln's beardless face, the other, a straight-on view of the bearded president.

The dedication took place before a crowd of two thousand at the Fields on the sunlit, breezy afternoon of 15 September 1919. Understandably, few of the adversaries who had fought over the statue participated. Weardale, Mond, Perris, the Charles Tafts, Barnard, and John Stewart were made obvious by their absences. Lord Charnwood pointedly boycotted the proceedings. The highest ranking British official was Manchester's new Lord Mayor and Alderman William Kay. Averting the possibility of international repercussions, a reluctant American Ambassador John W. Davis accepted his invitation at the last minute.[40] Judge Alton Parker shouldered the responsibility of representing the Anglo-American Society, the Sulgrave Institution, as well as the Tafts. As British and American flags spanked above the white-shrouded figure, Parker spoke fervently of a new era of world peace and Anglo-American accord. Pulling the cord immediately thereafter, Kay praised "this wonderful and beautiful statue of so fine a man."

A sequence of photographs show the mayor, with rope in hand, standing beside Davis, Parker, the Dean

of Manchester, and Rev. J. E. Robert.[41] Directly behind the mayor stands the Lady Mayoress in white attire, who seems intent on shielding herself from the onlookers. In stark contrast to this shy figure is a robust woman to her right, the Countess of Sandwich, whose father, the New Yorker William Sturgess, had been a close friend of Abraham Lincoln. An unsmiling Lord Mayor, bedecked with a ceremonial necklace, looks downward at the fallen shroud; Davis grimaces as he peers into the statue's face; with respectful smiles, Parker and the clerics affect good humor. In the near foreground, a gentleman with top hat in hand makes haste for an exit. But it is finally the remarkable image of the Countess that is central to this transitory view of the unveiling's aftermath. Steadying herself between a chair and her cane, she, like Davis, scrutinizes the bronze head with extraordinary intensity, her gaze betraying a look of pained incredulity and aggression. Having become interested in the fate of the Barnard statue through his correspondence with Judd Stewart, George Bernard Shaw quite possibly took note of similar news photographs and, if so, would have been highly amused and edified by the contrasting demeanors of the celebrants. Quite obviously the Countess, the Mayor, and Davis, if not Parker, had been been forced to "stop and look" even though the idea behind what they beheld seems for the moment to have assaulted their sensibilities.

These photographs provide more critical information about how the Lincoln was received in Manchester specifically and in England generally than do the two days of speeches that accompanied the unveiling. Intent on advancing a postwar rhetoric that United States Congressional action against the League of Nations had already largely repudiated, the oratory could only disappoint its listeners. So, too, many of those present could not help but identify the "homely plainness of the figure" with what now seemed America's tragic loss of nerve. Yet a *Manchester Guardian's* reporter valiantly attempted to justify the statue, not on the grounds of America's European diplomacy, but on the promised strengths of its personal vision. Even if not immediately apparent, one could apprehend a certain nobility about the head and shoulders. The layman also had to understand something of the problems of scale and perspective.

The sculptor on this scale must also separate unerringly the facts that count from the rest, for this task is one of simplifying, not elaborating. And, above all, if his figure is so clearly larger than life, he must contrive to suggest that it is inhabited by a spirit larger than that of ordinary humanity, and that his man is worthy to be a companion of gods and heroes. In spite of its deliberate ungainliness, the new statue does suggest this greatness of spirit. Note the strength and serenity of the look, the line of the lip, the set of the chin, the modelling of the cheek, the expressiveness of the hands."

Above all else, here stood the man, not the office-holder, while "President" Lincoln better belonged in London. Here, "in the great rugged head of this new statue it has something fitted to touch the spirit of the children of future generations like the Great Stone Face of another American's imagining."[42]

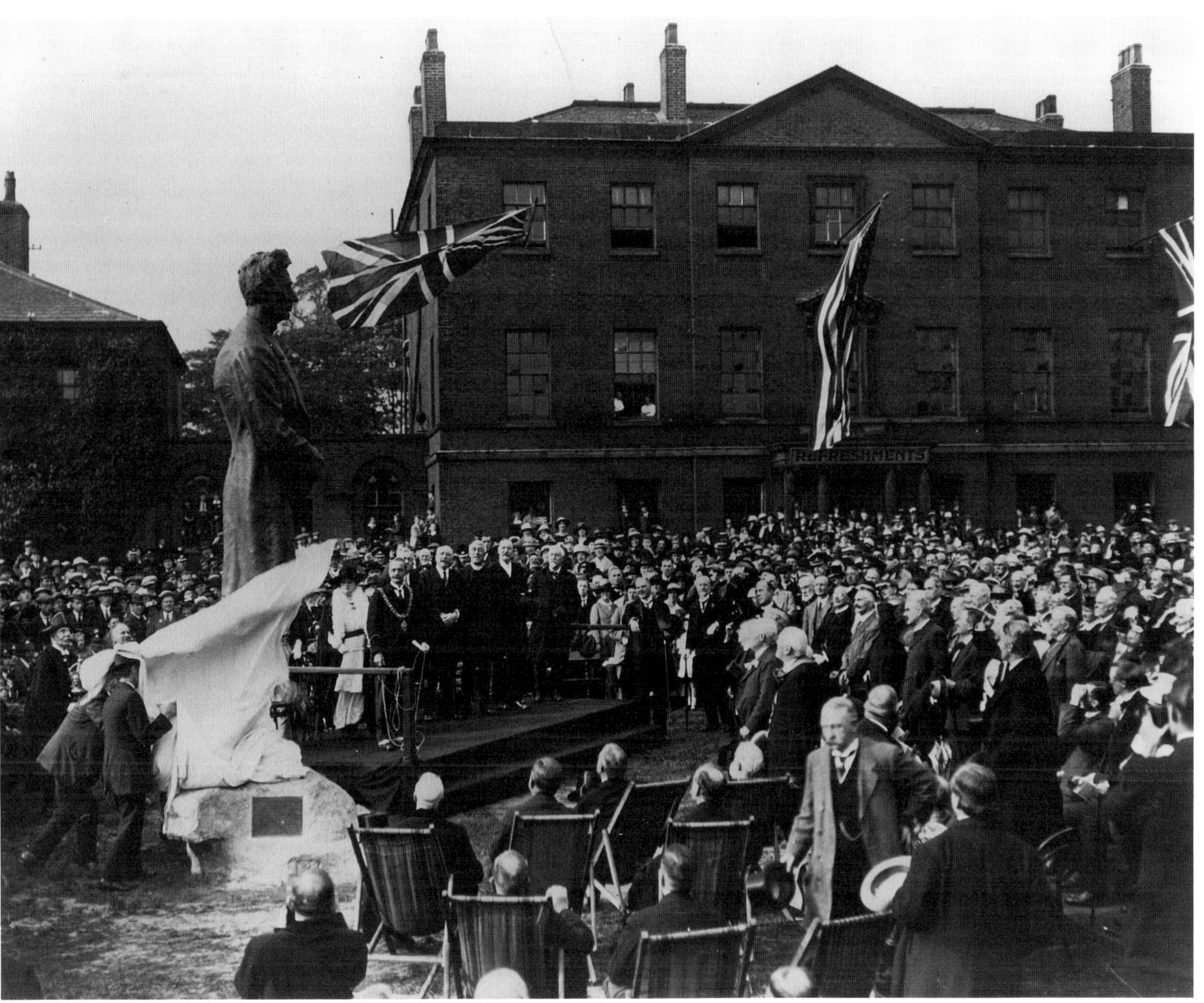

Unveiling of Barnard's Lincoln, *2nd cast, at Manchester, England. Photo courtesy of the National Museum of American Art.*

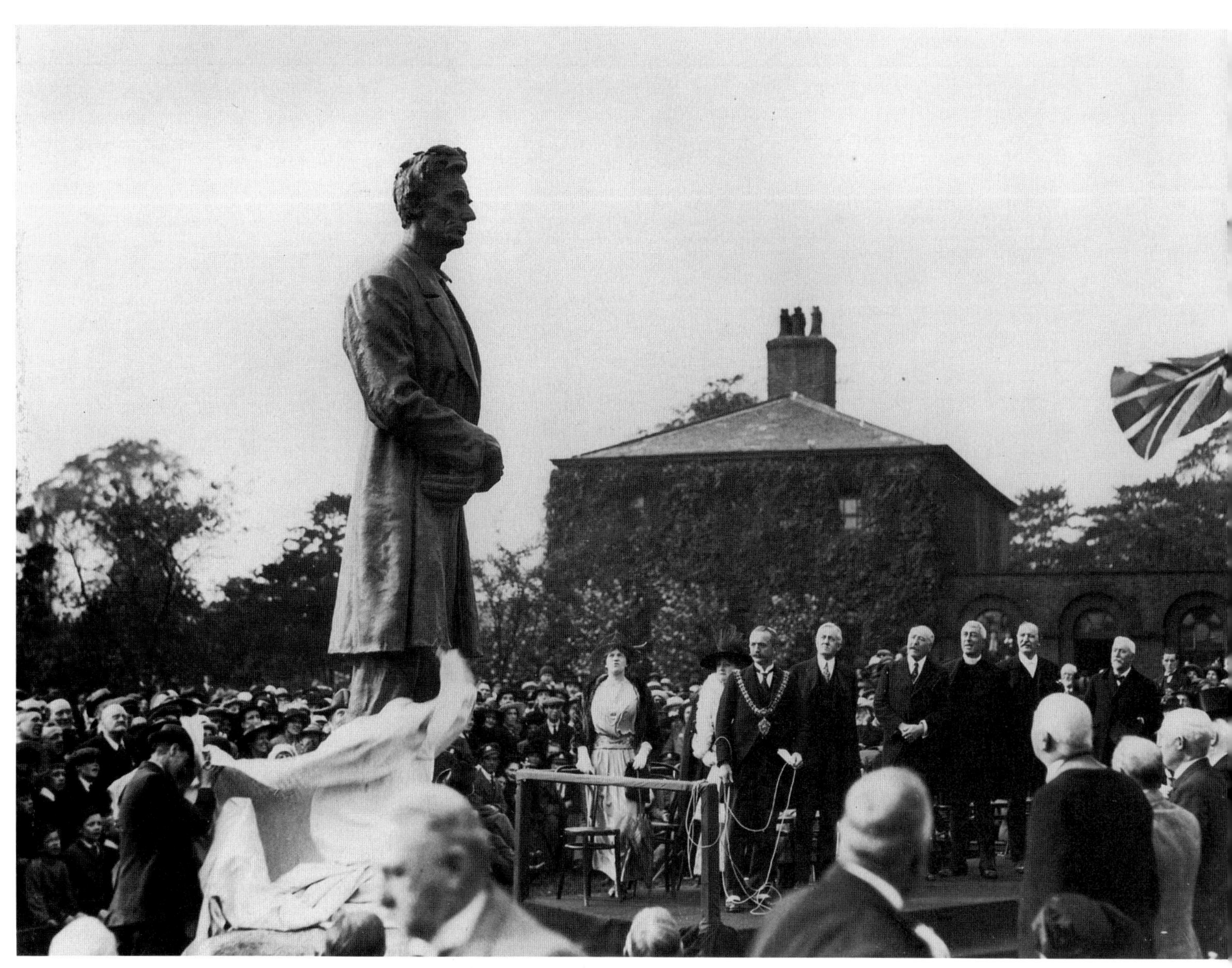

Unveiling of Lincoln, *2nd cast. Courtesy of the Cincinnati Historical Society.*

10

Louisville and the Bernheim Lincoln

T HE SAINT-GAUDENS REPLICA WAS DEDICATED ON A rainy 28 July 1920. Introduced by Lord Bryce as America's most esteemed secretary of state since Daniel Webster, Elihu Root presented the statue to Great Britain "on behalf of the people of the United States" inside Westminster's Central Hall. Following Prime Minister Lloyd George's response, a distinguished company followed a contingent of American Civil War veterans out into the murky thoroughfare toward the Canning Enclosure where the Duke of Connaught performed the unveiling.[1]

For those observers who best knew the Chicago original, the appearance of the new cast in its foreign setting must have been unsettling: here no spacious exedra gave emphasis to Lincoln's lonely meditation. Instead, an eleven-foot granite block elevated the figure five feet above its Chicago counterpart, thereby partially obscuring the Chair of State. Thus the intimacy of the downcast gaze was neutralized; this Lincoln looked not into the faces of living admirers, but stared vacantly into an expanse of pavement and vehicles, although some commentators preferred to believe he fixed his eyes on that "ancient and holy shrine" that rose directly opposite.[2]

In contrast to the meager coverage they accorded the Manchester unveiling, Northcliffe's London *Times* and Ochs's *New York Times* featured this ceremony in multiple articles, the former publishing a lengthy Charnwood appreciation and a Cass Gilbert reminiscence describing the moment Saint-Gaudens conceived the idea for this, his greatest work, while riding an eastbound train. The Anglo-American Oil Company Limited used the occasion to announce it was donating ten thousand pounds to a Westminster

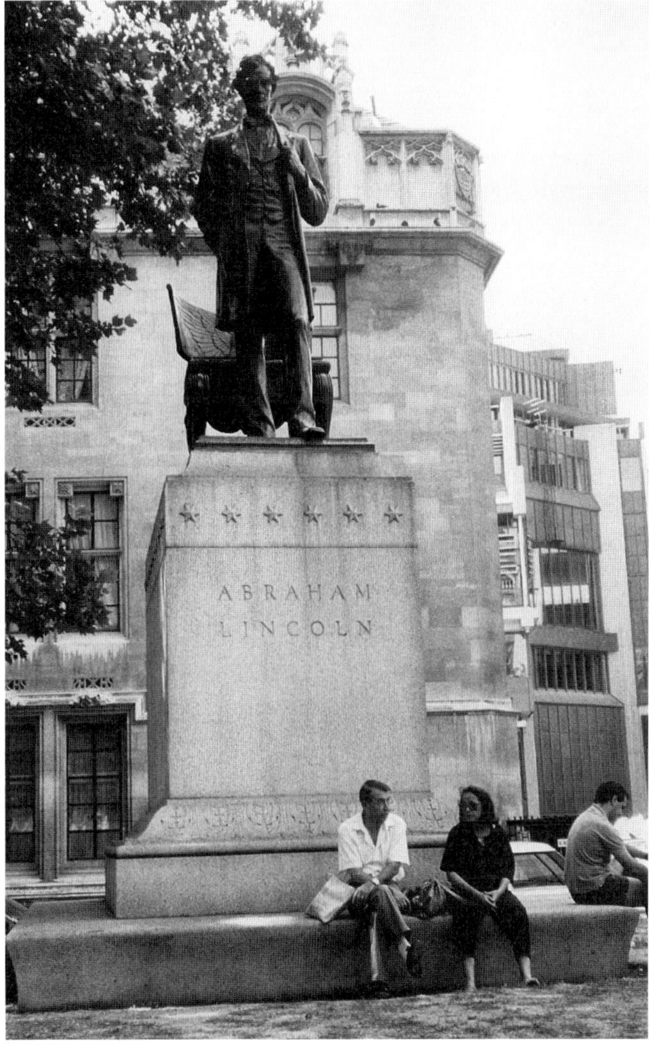

Augustus Saint-Gaudens, Abraham Lincoln, *cast of 1887 original. 1921. Bronze, 12'. London, England. Photo: Greg Giacona.*

Abbey restoration fund that the London *Times* was vigorously promoting. The *New York Times* printed its initial report on page one, returned to the story on 15 August with an editorial praising Lloyd George, then transcribed Root's speech a week later. The dispatches underscored the event's racial significance; its enactment acknowledged Lincoln's rugged countenance was now "more widely known than (that) of any other statesman of the Anglo-Saxon Race." Adolph Ochs's writers advanced a decidedly liberal reading of Bryce's and George's comments: the Prime Minister's affirmation that Lincoln had "lost" his nationality did not mean he had instantly become an Englishman, but rather that had taken his rightful place beside the common people of all races and nationalities. This distinction was not lost on those who compared the Manchester and London unveilings from afar. For example, thousands of American Jews, who with Ochs admired Lincoln no less than did Lloyd George, recalled a long sequence of injustices their people had suffered at the hands of the Saxons, not the least of which was the infamous Lincolnshire massacre. Neither could they dismiss the fact that many dispirited English Jews had joined the tide of immigration that flowed from Eastern and Western Europe to America's Midwest.[3]

Isaac Markens, the Barnard Lincoln defender whose communications to Robert Lincoln and William Taft were discussed above, once had occasion to research the legends that affirmed Abraham Lincoln's close ties with American Jewry. A familiar story involved General Grant's Order Number Eleven. Reacting to incidents of smuggling across Union lines, a flagrancy perpetuated by both gentile and Jewish noncombatants, Grant expelled only the latter from the Department of Tennessee under a twenty-four-hour deadline. After Cincinnati Rabbi Isaac M. Wise and a delegation of Paducah, Kentucky, Jews met with Lincoln, the President immediately countermanded the order, indignantly professing he saw no distinction between the races. Markens also reviewed the valued assistance Lincoln and the incipient Republican party had received from such Jewish politicians as Abraham Jonas, an organizer of the Lincoln-Douglas debates, and went on to document Lincoln's personal friendship and casual dealings with other American Jews, particularly Rabbi Wise. Even though he initially sided with the Copperheads, the assassination turned Wise about. It was then he set forth his variously-quoted observation that "'Abraham Lincoln believed himself to be bone of our bone and flesh of our flesh. He supposed himself to be of Hebrew parentage; he said so in my presence, and

indeed he possessed the common features of the Hebrew race both in countenance and features.'"[4] This contention Robert Lincoln curtly dismissed.

Neither did Markens or Jewish intellectuals give credence to Wise's attestation, but few would contest the Rabbi's persistent claim that among gentiles, "Old Honest Abe" was by far the most Hebraic in character. In the pages of his influential *The American Israelite,* which he published from Cincinnati, Wise wrote: "Attired in the garb of simplicity and good humor, [Lincoln's] modest worth lay concealed under a rough and uncouth exterior" and that he possessed the extraordinary skill of hiding his individuality behind the noble deeds planned in his great intellect . . . [Lincoln] was forgiving in his nature, gentle as a child, and above the low machinations of his foes."[5] Wise's assertion that "his image shall live forever" was less a prediction than a directive aimed at the consciences of American Jews.

Thus, upon the witness of Paducah's Jewry and Rabbi Wise, many Jews of America's heartland accepted the "rough" and "uncouth" Lincoln as one of their own. The legacy persisted in border states where begrudging gentiles remained silent. For example, in Louisville, Kentucky, Lincoln's centennial-of-birth was most notably observed by the city's Temple Adath Isreal. Rabbi Hyman G. Enelow, borrowing the language of Christian socialists, affirmed that the martyred president

> was a child of the soil, he loved the soil, kept in touch with the soil, derived his strength from it, like the giant in the ancient Greek myth, and his life was dedicated to the perpetuation of those ideals which from the beginning of our Republic have hallowed this American soil, and without which it would be deflowered of all its honor and glory.[6]

While wintering at Palm Beach, Florida, during the winter of 1920, a retired Jewish businessman of Louisville once more turned his thoughts to Lincoln. On behalf of himself and his wife Amanda, Isaac W. Bernheim, founder and president of the Bernheim Distilling Company, prepared to donate a Barnard Lincoln to his home city. He trusted this benefaction, like his other selfless acts, would repay Louisville for insuring his prosperity over the past thirty years. He also wanted to leave behind something that would remind citizens "that America is the land of opportunity for all of its children, no matter where born and what their station in life."[7]

Born into a merchant family in Schmieheim, the Grand Duchy of Baden, in 1848, Bernheim's youth was overshadowed by poverty and the anti-Semitic restrictions imposed upon the largely Jewish settlement by the Duchy's *Obrigkeit* statutes. Sustained by the ancestral network that supported his many fellow migrants, Bernheim made his way to America in 1867. Because of disappointing business prospects, he paused only briefly in New York. The following season he toiled as a merchant peddler in the Shenandoah Valley, then moved on to Paducah, Kentucky, where an uncle assigned him to bookkeeping duties. Eventually, Bernheim joined a wholesale liquor firm, became active in Paducah's thriving Jewish community, and married into the prominent Uri family. In partnership with his brother Bernard, who immigrated to Paducah in 1870, Isaac took control of the firm, inaugurated its manufacture of the popular "I. W. Harper" bourbon whiskey blend, and expanded sales through mail advertising. In 1888, the Bernheims transferred their operations to Louisville, and in 1897, opened the Bernheim Distilling Company, which was soon to become the nation's largest producer of Kentucky whiskey. Isaac retired as company president in 1915, five years before the enactment of National Prohibition, but retained control of the plant, its assets, and brand rights until the lifting of Prohibition in 1933. In that year the distillery was sold to the Schenley Distillers Company. While seeking his place in Louisville's secular life, Bernheim became active in the reformist Temple Adath Israel. Inspired by the fellowship and teachings of Adath Israel Rabbi Adolph Moses and the aforementioned Rabbi Wise, the architect of America's Jewish reform movement, he commenced legislating for a liberalization of American Jewish practices and culture. Like Wise, Bernheim castigated old fixtures of tribal religion: Messiah worship, the observance of Saturday rather than Sunday sabbaths, the sanctification of the cantor, the mandated use of Yiddish or German instead of English, the prohibition of Christian participation and, above all else, the Zionist movement, a manifestation of racial separatism that was even more troubling to him than was Anglo-Saxonism. His ideal American Palestine eventually took physical form in the large natural preserve the Bernheim Foundation established south of Louisville.[8] Bernheim Forest was to be a miniaturized Schwartzwald wherein the untouched glory of natural creation would be augmented by the instructive beauty of man's art. Nestled amid ancient trees and free-flowing brooks would be an art museum and noble statues of state and national heroes. All would be welcomed to the sanctuary, but Bernheim would not tolerate on its grounds any discussion of religion and politics, trafficking or trading, or any form of racial or social segregation.

Like Rabbi Wise, Bernheim grimly perceived the American Jew's preoccupation with economic success had too often overruled his solemn duty to improve the culture of his chosen place of residence. The donation of practical services like hospitals and schools was an unwritten requirement. But reformers valued as much that singular fusion of faith and culture "which Isreal's noblest sons have exhibited in all ages and which alone can serve to beautify, consecrate and perpetuate human civilization." The example of Europe and of certain American cities like Cincinnati convinced Bernheim that the donations of public statuary, art museums, and natural preserves were the most appropriate ways in which a successful businessman might broaden a city's cultural, recreational, and moral horizons. He would not be driven to this by the urge for self-aggrandizement, cloying sentimentality, or guilt, because patronage, and the public beneficence it engendered, was bound by the same laws of commerce that governed the business world itself. During celebrations marking his eightieth birthday, Bernheim announced, "Every man who has met with material success must look upon himself as an investment of the community, and that it is his duty to declare such dividends in service, and in other things of value in return for the protection which he has received, and which enabled him to reach success."[9]

Had it been Cincinnati, this affirmation would have been unnecessary, and Bernheim politely pointed to the hardships local businessmen experienced during the Civil War and in subsequent financial panics to excuse what he saw as Louisville's decided neglect of its public duty. Yet, for whatever reasons, the fact remained that the city's first families had been unusually slow to honor the principles of noblesse oblige. To be sure, there were handsome parks, a splendid cemetery, and a nationally-famous racetrack. At the turn of the century, the Louisville Literary Club and Woman's Club did what they could to promote fledgling literary and artistic efforts. The Dupont family had donated a manual training school. But there were no public fountains to honor and refresh the working classes; no art academies, craft industries, or art and design museums to guide native talent; no grand-opera houses, or established orchestras. The opening of a combined public library, art gallery, and museum in 1872 promised to be Western America's answer to the British Museum. However, like many private institutions of its kind, the promised cultural emporium buckled under the weight of poor management, personal bickering, and corrupt promotional schemes.[10] Obviously, the directors of the Louisville and Nashville Railroad, and the Bank of Kentucky, and the legion of wealthy financiers and jurists they sustained, as well as the chiefs of the gambling industry, were accustomed to pouring their dividends back into their own pockets and into the purses of influential politicians, rather than into service or things of public value.

Nor did Louisville's old guard fully appreciate the intellectual diversity and cultural vitality the German element promised to bring to their community's calcified social strata. The annual Saengerfest was a shining example of such revitalizing energy, but, as George Leighton observes, the Germans generally kept to themselves, and even the wealthiest among them "were not received" by socially prominent gentiles. In 1896 Bernheim was elected an "honorary" member of the Commercial Club, an extraordinary honor for a Jew, and for a number of years he shouldered the thankless task of directing Louisville's municipal Gas and Electric Company, but he entertained no illusions about the place his race and origins destined him to occupy within the social hierarchy, especially after the outbreak of the European War, and the resulting upsurge of nativist resentment against German-Jewish residents.[11]

Louisville was not entirely bereft of public statuary. Albert P. Henry's graceless marble bust of Lincoln was presented to the city by a memorial funding committee in 1867. This association was directed by James Speed, Lincoln's attorney general and the brother of the his boyhood confidant, Joshua Speed. Also in 1867, the second of three replicas of Joel Hart's standing figure of Henry Clay, a work which cost local providers ten thousand dollars, was unveiled in the Jefferson County Courthouse. Eight

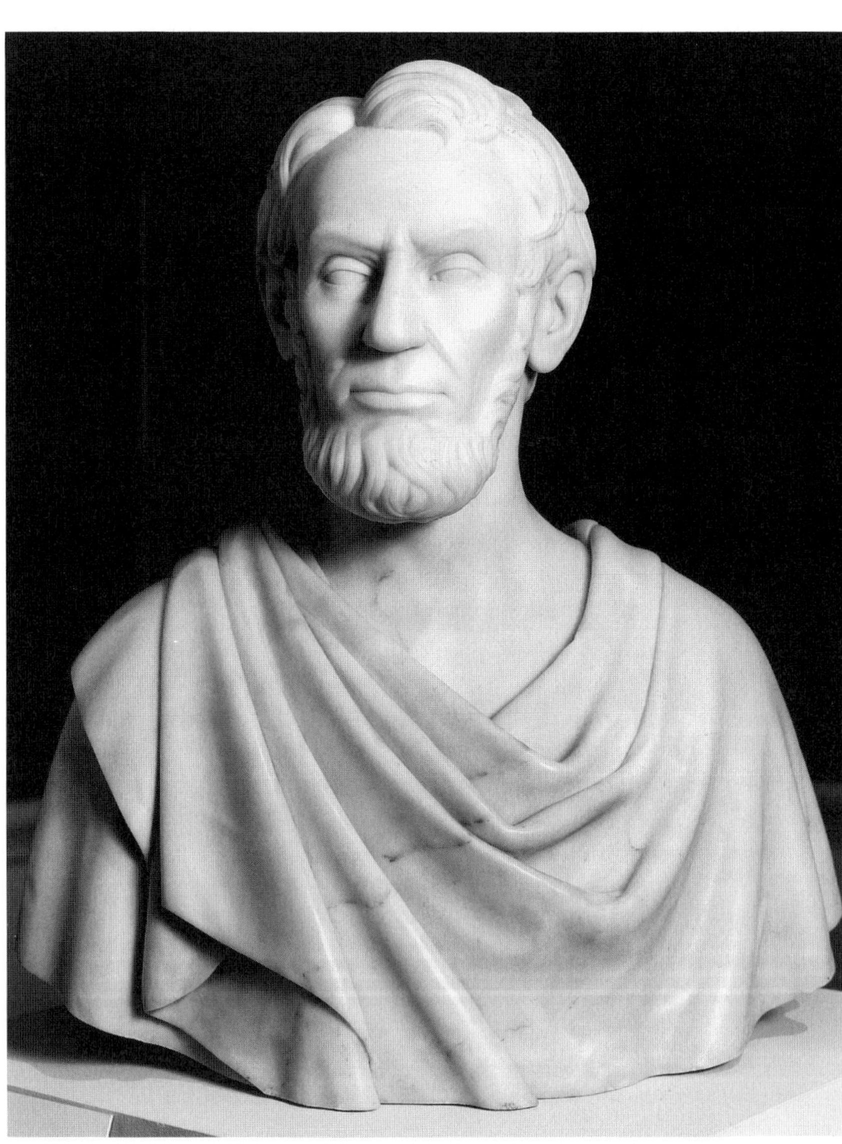

Albert P. Henry, Abraham Lincoln. *1865. Marble, 24".* *(PL 43.1). Deposited by the Citizens of Louisville. Courtesy of the J. B. Speed Memorial Art Museum, Louisville, Kentucky. Photo: Kenneth Hayden.*

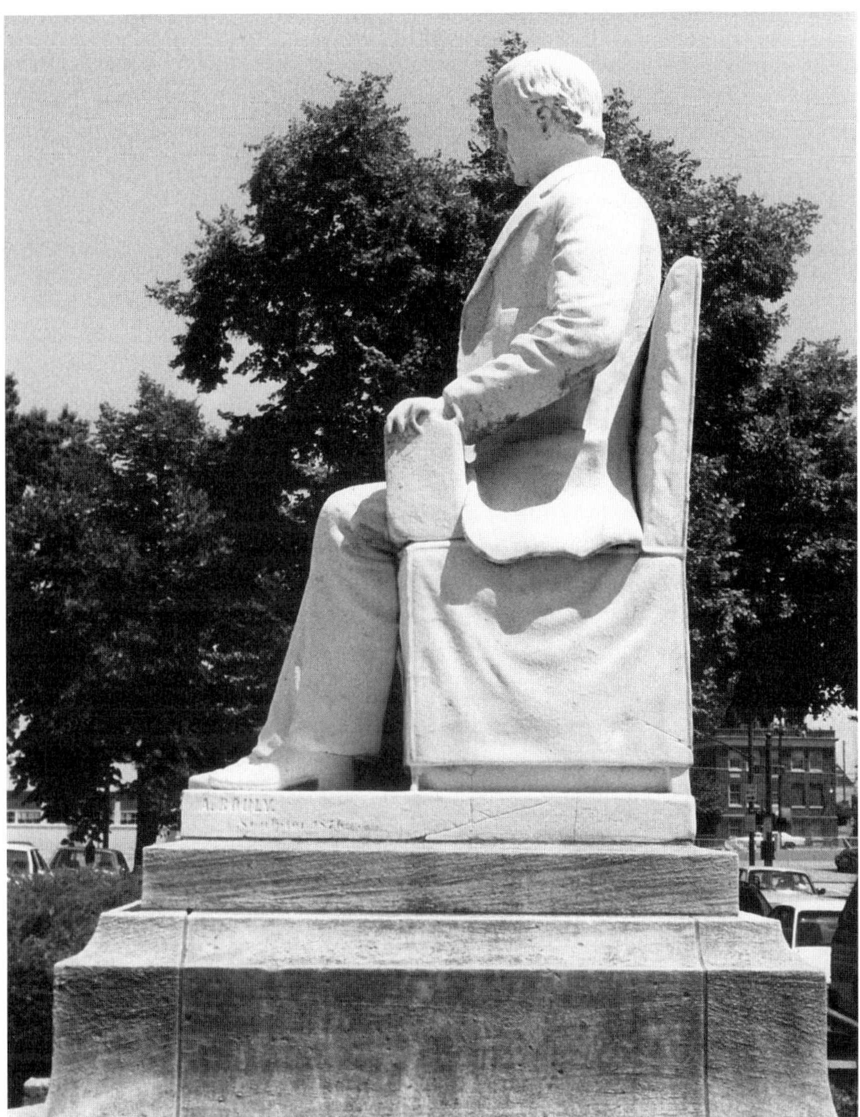

Louis Bouly, George D. Prentice. *1875. Marble, figure,
5′. Free Public Library, Louisville, Kentucky.*

years later, Walter N. Haldeman and Henry Watterson, respectively the owner and managing editor of the *Louisville Courier-Journal,* commissioned a heroic seated portrait of pioneering journalist and onetime Lincoln auxiliary, George D. Prentice.[12] These works comprised a meager and undistinguished repository for a community of Louisville's standing, still, with Henry's bust leading the way, Bernheim could find little to criticize in the choice of subjects, or in the progressive spirit that motivated these few patrons.

But as Louisville entered a new era of monument-building, Bernheim witnessed a disturbing trend. With its completion in 1895, a monument dedicated to the city's Confederate dead became the community's most imposing nonarchitectural structure. Its construction has a complicated history involving a not uncommon dispute over the choice of designs.

As completed, a fifty-foot stone shaft, at the summit of which stands a Confederate sentry alertly eyeing the northern horizon, rises above the southern limits of Louisville's main thoroughfare. Consistent with others of its type, Louisville's monument was financed by local women whose stated mission was to honor patriotism's ultimate sacrifice, not to open old wounds. At the laying of the cornerstone, Rabbi Moses observed that men should fight and die for duty as they see it, whether on the side of a Lee or a Lincoln.[13] Confederate flags were discretely concealed until the ceremonies concluded, yet no rhetorical gloss or concealment could disguise the shaft's true purpose.

This rallying symbol of sectional values acquired an especially acrid connotation in Louisville. Lincoln's personal ties to the community were well

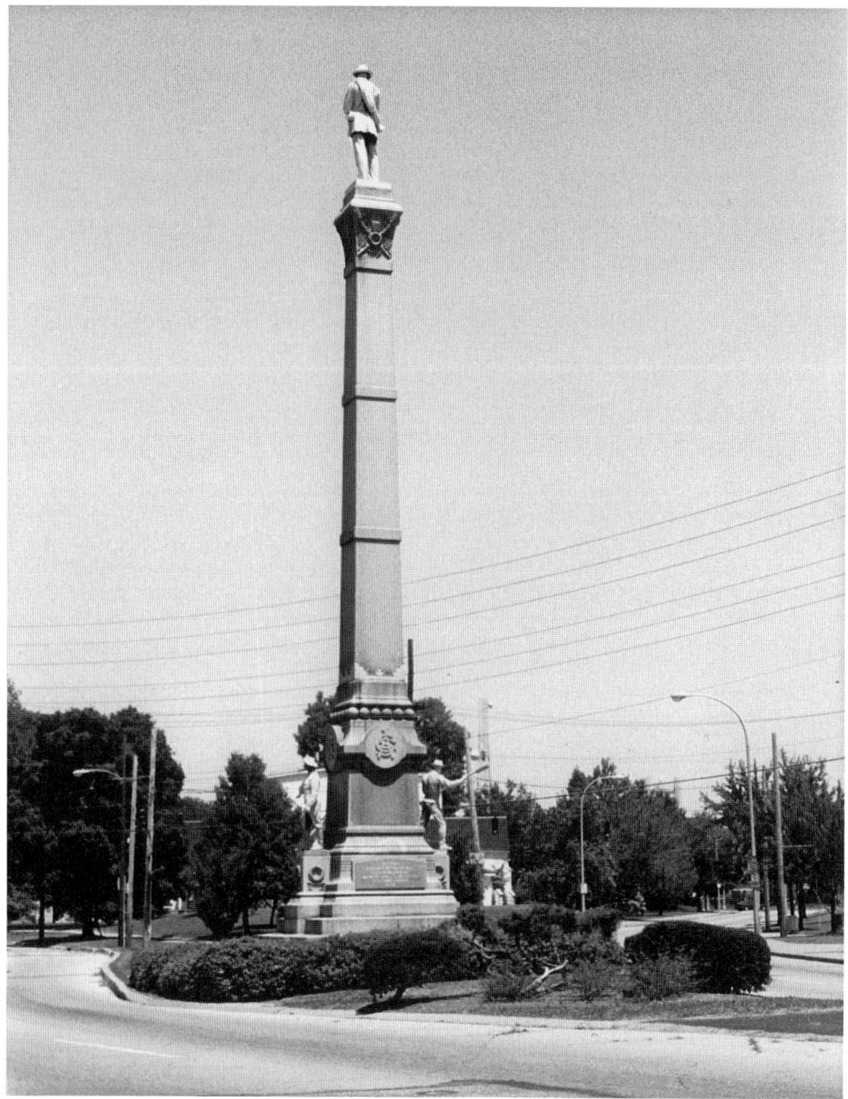

*Ferdinand von Miller (figures) and Michael Mouldoon
(construction),* Monument to the Confederate Dead.
1895. Bronze and granite. 30' Louisville, Kentucky.

known: his recoupment at Joshua Speed's homestead after a broken engagement, his pardoning of the Lousiville-born Confederate Gen. John G. Castleman, as well as his assassination, presented affecting examples of both Lincoln's fragility, as well as his propensity to "mother" even those who defied him. However, such tender evocations could not sway hardened anti-Unionists.

The chief North-South trading center of an officially neutral border state, Louisville lived out the Civil War under federal occupation. Unionist opinion, both pro-slave and abolitionist versions, remained deeply rooted after the Secessionist press was forced into exile. The surrounding countryside remained hostile and unrepentant, and Louisville voters solidly backed Lincoln opponents in both presidential elections. The fact that Cave Hill Cemetery contained the graves of five thousand Union soldiers to a mere two hundred Confederates, did little to dampen the opposition's desire for atonement. Thus, in 1887 the Executive Committee of the Kentucky Woman's Confederate Monument Association, with the moral support of the Confederate veterans who formed the core of Louisville's professional and legal community, hastened to fulfill their obligation.[14]

Bernheim could have expected little more. Only one town south of the Mason-Dixon line, Vanceburg, in Eastern Kentucky, could claim the distinction of having raised a monument to Union dead. Thus, no sooner had the proprietors opened the doors of their distillery, than they began contemplating their sponsorship of monuments that would erase the stain of sectional resentment. Even though Isaac considered a heroic statue of Lincoln from the very

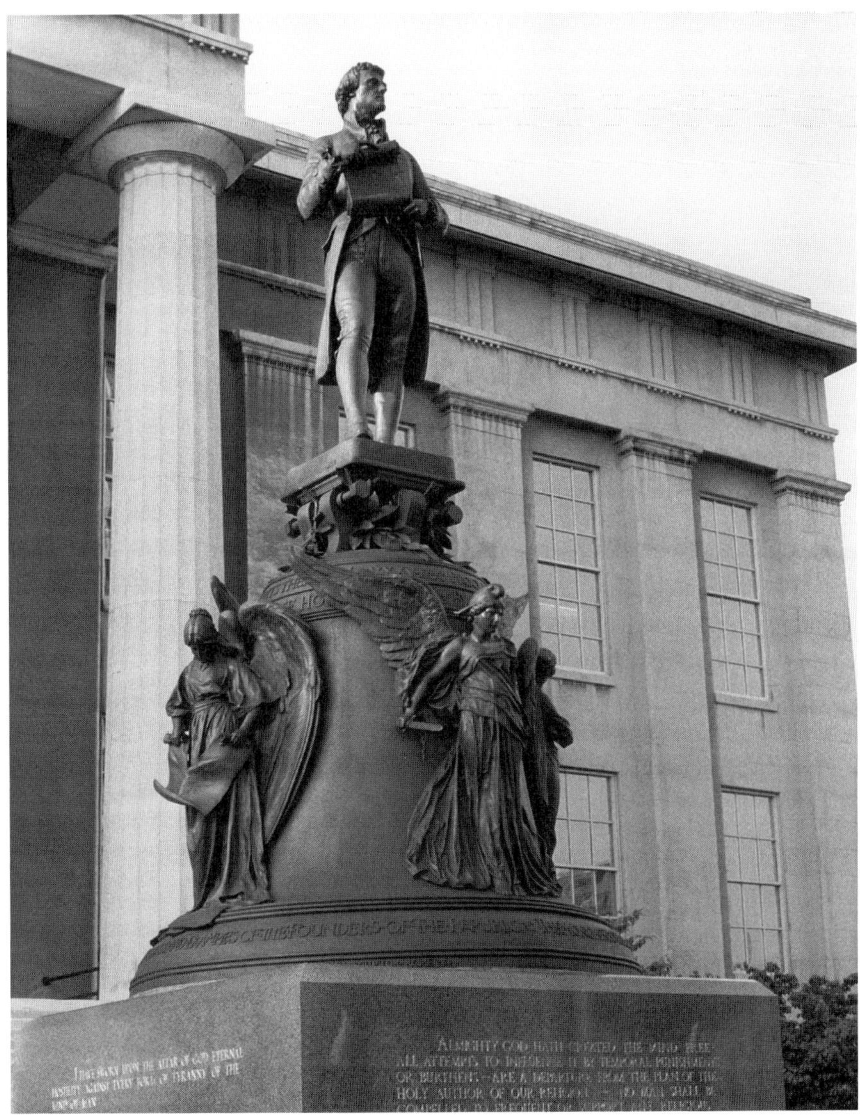

Moses Ezekiel, Thomas Jefferson Memorial. *1899.*
Bronze and granite, main figure, 8'. Louisville, Kentucky.

beginning, he momentarily turned his attention to Thomas Jefferson, the governor who originally granted Louisville its charter, and the one diplomat beside Henry Clay who would have most appealed to Southern Unionists. It was Jefferson, he maintained, who "had done more than any one person to make this country free, and who made our success and happiness possible by inspiring Americans with the truth and justice of that immortal declaration." The Bernheims engaged expatriot American sculptor Sir Moses Ezekiel to fashion a heroic bronze group for placement before the Jefferson County Courthouse. Attended by allegorical figures, a youthful "Sage of Monticello" is shown presenting the charter to an imagined assembly of the Continental Congress.[15]

The decision for Jefferson was entirely appropriate, but in view of Bernheim's earlier inspiration, it also reflected a degree of caution. No heroic Lincoln statues were to immediately appear in Louisville, and almost ten years passed before any were established in the state of his birth. The first of Adolph Weinman's commissions, a seated figure for Hodgenville, was not completed until 1909, and his standing Lincoln for the state capital at Frankfort, was erected two years later (see pgs. 48 and 49). The first was financed by the Kentucky state legislature, while the Frankfort bronze was a personal donation to the state by Louisville's James Breckenridge Speed, nephew of James and Joshua Speed. Kentuckians generally approved Speed's initiative, but another Louisville-bred citizen immediately acted to counter it. Confederate Veteran General William B. Haldeman called upon his comrades, the remnants of Kentucky's famed Orphan Brigade, to build a colossal obelisk at Fairview, Kentucky, to the memory of that other eminent Kentucky-born president, Jefferson Davis. Inching its way skyward over a period of some fifteen years, a 350-foot concrete shaft was finally dedicated in 1924. Meanwhile, the Bernheims returned to Ezekiel with an order for a Lincoln bust which they donated to the Louisville Free Public Library in 1914.[16]

Regarding this bust in the library's upper hall several years later, a Louisville artist thought it fair to say that "we Kentuckians worship at the shrine of Abraham Lincoln." To be sure, the Haldeman faction did not agree with such windy evocations, but the term "worship" accurately describes the ministry's expanding embrace of Lincoln. One local researcher argued that attendance records kept by the Pigeon Creek Baptist Church, located near Lincoln City, proved Lincoln was nurtured in the Hard-Shell faith. Temple Adath Isreal's Rabbi, Hyman Enelow, whose Louisville tenure extended from 1901 to 1912, committed his congregation to a thorough reexamination of Lincoln's faith and patriotism. Furthermore, after a twenty-seven year absence, Ida Tarbell was planning a return to Louisville to prepare her sequel, *In the Footsteps of the Lincolns* (1924), in which she sought to correct Thomas Lincoln's ignominious "white trash" reputation by conclusively verifying Nancy Hank's legitimacy.[17]

But another individual had done even more to reform Western Kentucky's prejudices: the flamboyant journalist and politician Henry Watterson. Associated with Gen. Haldeman in the operation of the *Courier-Journal,* Watterson served as the managing editor since the paper's inception in 1868. Like Haldeman, he was a former Confederate soldier and an exiled Southern editorialist, but unlike his partner remained highly critical of Jefferson Davis and disparaging of the South's postwar glorification of the lost cause. He pledged to make Louisville the territorial cornerstone of sectional healing and racial equality, and gained a reputation as the South's most vigorous Lincoln apologist. He planned a biography and frequently spoke on Lincoln before national audiences. Watterson obliged both Robert Lincoln's and James Speed's requests to be the principal orator at the Hodgenville and Frankfort unveilings. Like the Bernheims, the Speeds, and Tarbell, Watterson respected the unique commemorative power that could be transmitted by public statuary. His modest art collection, later bequeathed to the Free Public Library, contained several bronze portraits of Lincoln, one a small version of Weinman's standing figure.[18] As noted above, Watterson joined with Walter Haldeman, fa-

ther of William and original owner of the *Courier-Journal,* to commission the Prentice statue.

By 1920 Bernheim saw no reason for further delay; the European War had passed and with it the resurgent tide of anti-German feeling. Retirement and the enactment of Prohibition had effectively ended his professional association with Louisville, and he contemplated departing his suburban home in Anchorage for the West. But what artist was he to choose for the task? Ezekiel, who had died in Rome in 1917, had left no heroic Lincolns. Why not another Saint-Gaudens replica, or an original by Weinman, the artist who had more than proven his ability to please the public, or by Niehaus, the sculptor he in fact would favor with several important commissions in the late 1920s?[19]

There can be no mistake that when Isaac Bernheim first queried Barnard in February 1920, just after the national observance of Lincoln's birthday, he was intent on presenting Louisville with a statue that beyond its subject would challenge comfortable ideologies. Beside the recent controversy, Bernheim perhaps knew something of the Cincinnati Lincoln's more distant history, the fact, for example, that Rabbi Louis Grossmann, the close friend and successor of Isaac Wise at Cincinnati's K. K. B'nai Israel, was one of the members of the Alms Memorial Lincoln Committee who supported Charles Taft's fateful decision. Stewart's failed Westminster gambit and the sadly ignored Manchester dedication presented a history of exclusion the patron could understand in personal terms. And he could well predict how the proper Louisvillian, one who seriously regarded the social register's rules of etiquette and appropriate dress, would at first react to the battered, disheveled visage. Though social assimilation was a guiding principle, another Bernheim maxim was upheld in his choice of a statue: the individual should not trust the crowd, should not be afraid to be lonely.[20]

Bernheim preferred it to be placed before the Male High School in time for Lincoln's birthday a year hence, but seemed uncertain as to whether the statue should be an exact replica or an altogether new variation on the Cincinnati type. After Barnard favored him with impressive accounts concerning a new Lincoln statue order for Asia, and the momentarily revived Paris project, the men laid plans for Barnard's visit to Louisville and proceeded to draw up a contract. Dated 28 April 1920, this document specifies that the patron would pay Barnard a total of twenty-five thousand dollars, half the amount due immediately as down payment, the remainder after the casting at the Roman Bronze Works before delivery. In an attempt to relegate shipping costs to the artist, Bernheim asked that the final payment be delayed until the unveiling, but was not disposed to argue this point or contest a later delivery date, this being set for May 1921. The contract left undetermined the question as to whether the product would be an original or a replica, only that the *ciré perdue* process would be employed. But Barnard had made his intentions clear in early March when he informed his new patron that he had obtained Charles Taft's permission to "make a duplicate of the Lincoln for Louisville." After Bernheim promptly advanced a down payment, the sculptor entered into an eleven thousand dollar contract with the Roman Bronze and later signed a fourteen hundred dollar note of indebtedness to the Milford Pink-Victoria Granite Company of Stony Creek, Connecticut, for supplying a ten-ton boulder base.[21] Bernheim's expenses thus totaled less than one-half the amount—sixty thousand dollars—he paid for Ezekiel's Jefferson monument, while Barnard's profits came to half the contract payment.

Carefully measuring his options before making a public announcement, Bernheim was encouraged by recent events. If he had decided to move on his plan several years earlier, Watterson, who revealed his objections to Barnard's statue in the *Art World,* might have thrown the entire editorial weight of his newspaper against the gift statue, this despite the editor's long friendship with Bernheim, and the fact that the distiller had been one of the *Courier-Journal*'s most faithful advertisers. Even if answered by such competitors as the *Louisville Post* or *Herald,* a violent Watterson tirade could have had disastrous effects. No less worrisome was Gen. Haldeman, who held the position of managing editor of the *Courier-Journal*'s companion evening newspaper, the *Louisville Times.* But this double threat eased considerably when both newspapers passed from a controlling consortium comprised of Haldeman heirs William, Bruce, Isabel Haldeman, and Watterson into the hands of the progressive Democratic Judge Robert W. Bingham, and when, as a result, the outmaneuvered Watterson resigned in April 1919.[22] Nevertheless, even if Bingham's political orientation was unswerving, Bernheim had no way to predict how the new owner or his editors might react to the new statue. Therefore, as added insurance, the patron brought the coals to Newcastle by gaining Watterson's consent to deliver the dedicatory address.

Beyond these practical considerations, Bernheim did not question the larger and somewhat contradictory implications of his presentation. He valued Lincoln for freeing the African American, but even more

for preserving the Union, because without that accomplishment the United States would not have emerged as a world power. Standing against the overt racism manifested by Louisville's Democratic machine, Bernheim credited himself and other Republicans for "taking the former slave, giving him an education, and fitting him out as a desirable citizen." Indeed, Louisville prided itself on its relatively progressive policy of providing separate but presumably equal facilities for both the black and white races. Even so, the Male High School, before which he first intended the statue to stand, was an all-white institution, and the alternate locations his site committee selected along the way, Central Park and the Louisville Free Public Library, were likewise off limits to African Americans. While Louisville's White Republicans, Jewish and gentile, depended upon the Black vote, George Wright has argued that the party did relatively little to improve the living conditions, work opportunities, and recreational facilities of their Black constituents, nor did they support Black political candidates, or move to honor patronage demands. Under the Republican regime of Mayor Huston Quin in the early 1920s, polite racism was converted into a "political slavery" as severe as Baden's *Obrigkeit,* for the Black found himself "owned by the Republicans and hated by the Democrats." Consequently, young Black radicals affiliated with Louisville's NAACP seceded from Republican regulars in 1921 to form the "Lincoln Independent Party" in a valiant but vain attempt to correct the misnomer "The Party of Lincoln."[23]

Rather than issue identical press releases, Bernheim assigned his friend Frank N. Hartwell to make a surprise announcement at a special meeting of the Louisville's Board of Education at the Pendennis Club on 18 May.[24] Hosting the dinner meeting in the Bernheims's absence, Hartwell noted the patrons were also making available an endowment to be used in unspecified ways to foster an appreciation of Lincoln, quite possibly an annual essay award similar to that he bequeathed as part of the Jefferson monument donation. He then read from a letter of intent addressed by Mr. and Mrs. Bernheim to the Board of Education.

While still a boy I came to America seeking the opportunity of freedom. During all the years I have enjoyed this blessing there has ever stood out before me the luminous and inspiring career of the lowly rail splitter, who became President and a prophet. It is this feeling which actuates me to ask the privilege of presenting to the Board of Education and thru you gentlemen to the citizens of Louisville, a statue in bronze of Abraham Lincoln by George Gray(sic) Barnard, in the hope that it may serve not only as an inspiration to the generations that are, and that are to come, but also as a reminder that America is the land of opportunity for all of its children, no matter where born and what their station in life.

Without further consultation, the board passed resolutions accepting title to the gift on behalf of the city and acceded to the Bernheims' wishes that the statue be placed before the Male High School. It also prepared to use the Bernheim windfall as a means for bolstering its own municipal image. Seeking to head off the threatened retirement of popular board member Alex G. Barret, as well as what it feared would be the resulting defection of others, the board asked Barret to reconsider a decision not to seek reelection, noting it had been informed the Bernheim gift "is made thru us in recognition of the public services rendered by the members of the Board of Education," and, to a large extent, by Barret himself. Having thus circumvented the mayor's office and played to the competitive self-interests of a city bureaucracy, Bernheim left newspaper editors with few options but to politely accept a fait accompli. Even in Watterson's absence, however, the *Courier-Journal* received the Berheim announcement with restraint, making certain its subscribers were fully apprised of the criticism that had recently been heaped upon the other Barnard statues.[25]

Accompanied by his eleven-year-old daughter Barbara, Barnard spent the first week of June 1920 with the Bernheims at Anchorage. Other than being a press opportunity, the visit was designed to give the artist a chance to veto Bernheim's site proposal if he so desired. Press interviews make it clear the sculptor had fully recovered from the London debacle and the trauma of his mother's death the previous year. The unexpected Bernheim order was heartening enough, even more so was Barnard's momentarily warm relationship with John D. Rockefeller Jr. and the anticipated start of his giant peace memorial. In reference to Rockefeller's projected goodwill mission to China the following year, Barnard had much to tell local reporters about a possible new Lincoln order for that country, as well as about a tenth-century Chinese monastery he expected to soon add to his Cloisters collection. With this new information came also the familiar biographical reminiscences that prophetically linked the Barnard family with Lincoln. Of the recent critical storm, Barnard commented, "I tried to put

the soul of the man even into the wearing apparel. For two years I studied Lincoln's face as no human being had ever done before. I put the same wrinkles as found in it into the trousers and the coat."[26] He added that Kentucky author James Lane Allen had once attempted to interest him in sculpting a state monument and that now he intended to make good on that suggestion.

The breezy enthusiasms and arrogant declamations won the ready attention of Louisville's literati, if not its artists. The most irrepressible visionary among regional poets, dramatists, and essayists was Lucien V. Rule, who would author several Barnard appreciations in the coming years, including the one cited at the beginning of chapter 3. Long before he inaugurated the search for his Kentucky model in 1913, Barnard had also formed close ties with Madison Cawein, a nature poet whose impoverishment and early death became a cause célèbre for Louisville's struggling regionalists, as well as with dramatist-lyricist Cale Young Rice, and his wife, the authoress Alice Hegan Rice. The tie between Barnard and the Rices was reinforced by their mutual friendships with Ida Tarbell, whom Cale and Alice first befriended in 1903—Tarbell's renewed Lincoln pilgrimage in October 1922 was to be spent in the company of the Rices.[27]

Having died of a stroke in December 1914, Cawein was unable to witness the statue controversy, but his bitter indictment of the Eastern "lords" of American literature leaves little doubt as to how he would have assessed the academic tirade that was launched against the Lincolns. The Harvard-educated Rice was more urbane than Cawein and Rule, but he too was irresistibly drawn to Barnard's spiritual passion, creative power, and uncanny ability to "talk, arrestingly and on a high plane," despite a lack of formal education. Looking back to evenings spent discussing art, poetry, and religion, the first during Barnard's June visit, Rice recalled a man who "looked, talked, acted and was the genius so completely, if not wisely, that nothing else mattered to him."[28] It was therefore natural that Bernheim would want to include Rice among those he entrusted to help ease the statue to its eventual berth.

Like others of his wider literary circle, especially Percy MacKaye and Tarbell, Rice tended to separate the individual from his work. While accepting Bernheim's request for his services, he could not with conscience overlook some basic flaws he detected in the photographs; it seemed to him that Barnard had exaggerated certain realistic features because of his determination to avoid sentiment. It also struck him that the intended low placement of the figure on an undressed boulder was inappropriate. Nevertheless, he thought it a "splendid piece," most especially its careworn face and exploding locks.[29]

When Barnard departed Louisville for visits with his father in Madison and old friends in Kankakee, the question of a location was far less certain than before his arrival. Leaving open other options, Barnard ruled out the possible alternative of the Louisville Normal School. It having been determined that the cluttered South Brook Street lawn of the Male High School would not provide sufficient room, Bernheim chose a site committee comprised of Hartwell, Rice, Charles F. Huhlein, and architect Arthur Loomis to make further suggestions. After Bernheim consulted with Barnard in New York at the end of 1920, the committee recommended a level clearing close by the main entrance of Central Park as the most favorable setting. This suggestion was overruled by the women of the Outdoor Art League because a single tree representing a rare breed of sassafras would have to be sacrificed. Foreseeing complications in regard to the low-lying ground of Central Park, consulting landscape architect J. R. Dawson argued for the Free Public Library lawn. He was eventually upheld, but with the stipulation that the statue face west from the library's west lawn. Library trustees received title to the statue from the board of education on 11 April 1922.[30] Thus, in enviroments that had shifted from a school yard, to a shady dell, thence to a library, the identity of the promised statue had likewise imaginatively reverted from that of stern preceptor, to a spellbound nature poet, and, finally, to one more consistent with the monastic scholar.

Designed in 1904 by the New York architectural firm of W. G. Tachau and Lewis F. Pilcher, the Louisville Free Public Library building was funded by a $250,000 Carnegie Corporation grant procured through the efforts of the Louisville Scottish Society. In contrast to an oppressive Neo-Gothicism Pilcher and Tachau commonly employed for their numerous armories, asylums, and prisons, the winning Louisville design followed the simple elegance of Louis Seize vernacular.[31] Except for the columned entrance, the highly ornamented delivery room, and the echo of Mannerism found in the display of lions' heads and grotesque masks, the design is one of studied understatement. Large unadorned rectangular window cases apportion smoothly-dressed limestone walls, and the ornamental friezes that divide the first floor from the basement level. Perhaps the most affecting views are encountered before either of the fa-

cade's end bays, where square sections emerge from angled corners, their topmost boundaries crisply ruled by cornices. The crowning feature in each wall is an empty tabernacle window, dressed in Tuscan Doric ornament, that rises to a height of twenty-five feet. Pan's leering mask appears above the apex of the arched openings. Beside the library building itself, one preexisting structure was to have a significant impact on the statue's environmental setting: the soaring Gothic steeple of the now-demolished Warren Memorial Presbyterian Church rose from a street corner just north of the library's west wing.

Barnard's difficulties with the Bernheim Lincoln began well before his Louisville visit. Orders for piece molds were delayed by the death of his personal molder, Attilio J. Contini. Later, Barnard faced a work stoppage ordered by a plaster molders union. In late spring 1921, after Barnard had at last delivered piece molds to the foundry, and wax impressions had been prepared for casting, fire gutted the Roman Bronze Works' casting department. In the confused aftermath of this disaster, the key plaster model from which the piece molds were formed was believed to have been among the estimated one hundred other original plasters that were destroyed. It was, in fact, safely stored in the artist's studio all the while, thus, Barnard only needed to order new piece molds and arrange for another application of wax.[32]

Nevertheless, this complication, together with the artist's illness at the end of 1921, pushed the dedication day well beyond 4 July 1922, the date Bernheim chose as a backup to the original Lincoln's birthday unveiling. Because the cast was not completed until early August, the earliest practical date for the dedication now fell on the singularly inauspicious date of 26 October 1922. After conferring with his son, Lee, who inspected the cast at the foundry at the end of August, Bernheim forwarded his final payment.[33]

Through the long delay, Bernheim remained understanding of his artist's tribulations. In answer to the sculptor's soul-stirring account of the fire, he soothingly counseled, "every storm is followed by a period of fair weather." In December 1921, following six months of silence from Barnard's studio, Bernheim gently prodded, "No news is good news?" He had, in fact, been unusually forgiving of Barnard's repeated misspelling of his name during the first weeks of their correspondence, a carelessness he might easily have taken to be a racial slur. For his part, Barnard assumed an increasingly imperial tone. When announcing the cast had been completed, he wrote Bernheim, "At last after doing the Lincoln statue (the first was destroyed by fire) the second is finished and is ready for you. I have taken great joy in finishing this statue in the wax, and feel it is my living thumb. Not an atom of the hands and head but is their own surfaces, to be repeated." To this gallantry the patron could only respond that he was pleased the bronze was finished and "that it received anew the deft touch of your thumb, producing a work of art that will measure up to your high standards." It seems obvious Barnard had little interest in attending the unveiling. He planned to be "on the road" when the 4 July date was still pending. A week before the actual unveiling, he wired Bernheim he had once again fallen ill, while newspaper accounts instead attributed the absence to Edna Barnard's illness. Meanwhile, urgent inquiries to Barnard from the site committee's architect regarding the positioning of the base went unanswered.[34]

It was not until a Barnard family sojourn at Dublin ended in early October that the positioning of the foundation was finally set. All but three feet of the massive stone was to be submerged before the library's west wall on line with the empty nitch. Concern over the high water table of the site prompted Loomis to set the boulder upon a subterranean concrete platform, a wise precaution as Louisville's flood of 1937 was to demonstrate. But what could Barnard have thought of the architectural backdrop? He may have appreciated its French styling, yet compared with the cloisters he had daringly rescued from European waste heaps, the library's design was shamefully academic, its classical tabernacle the crowning cliché of an arrogant materialism that had poisoned the Western mind throughout the post-Renaissance era. However, at Bernheim's urging, Barnard was willing

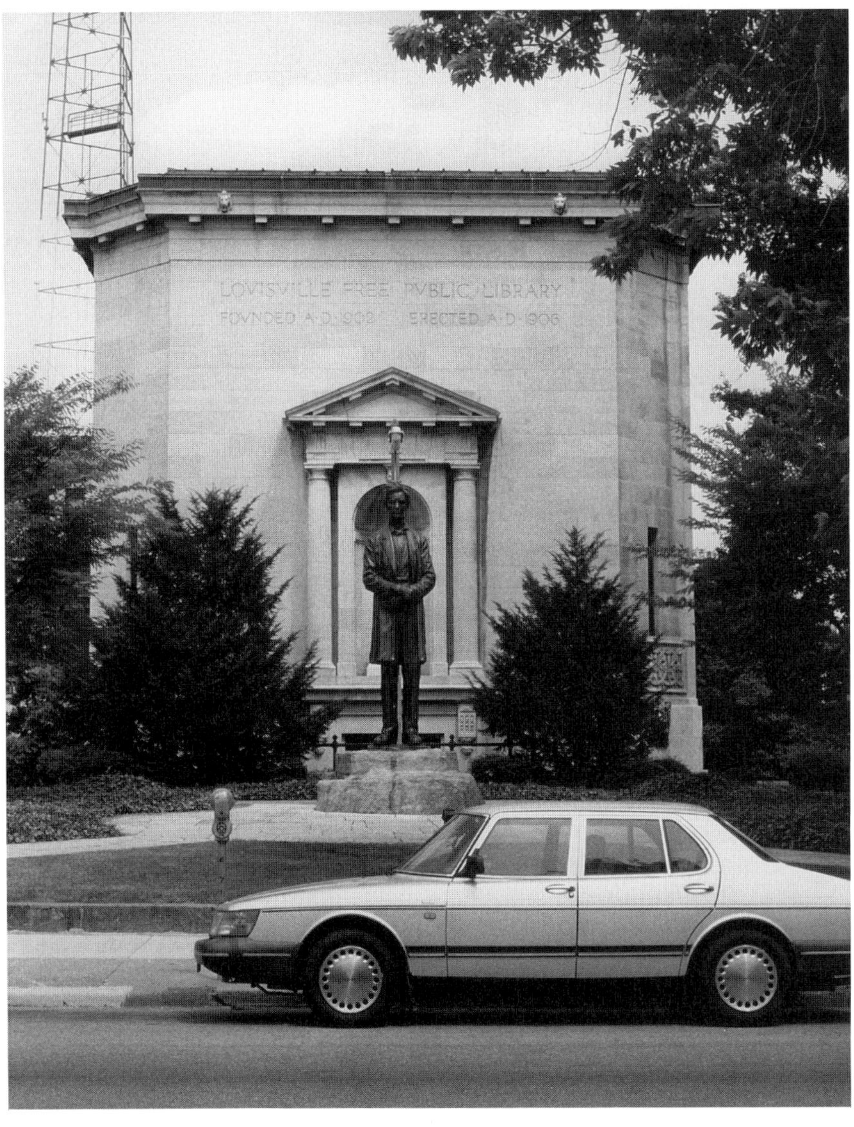

George Grey Barnard, Abraham Lincoln, *3rd cast. 1922. Louisville, Kentucky.*

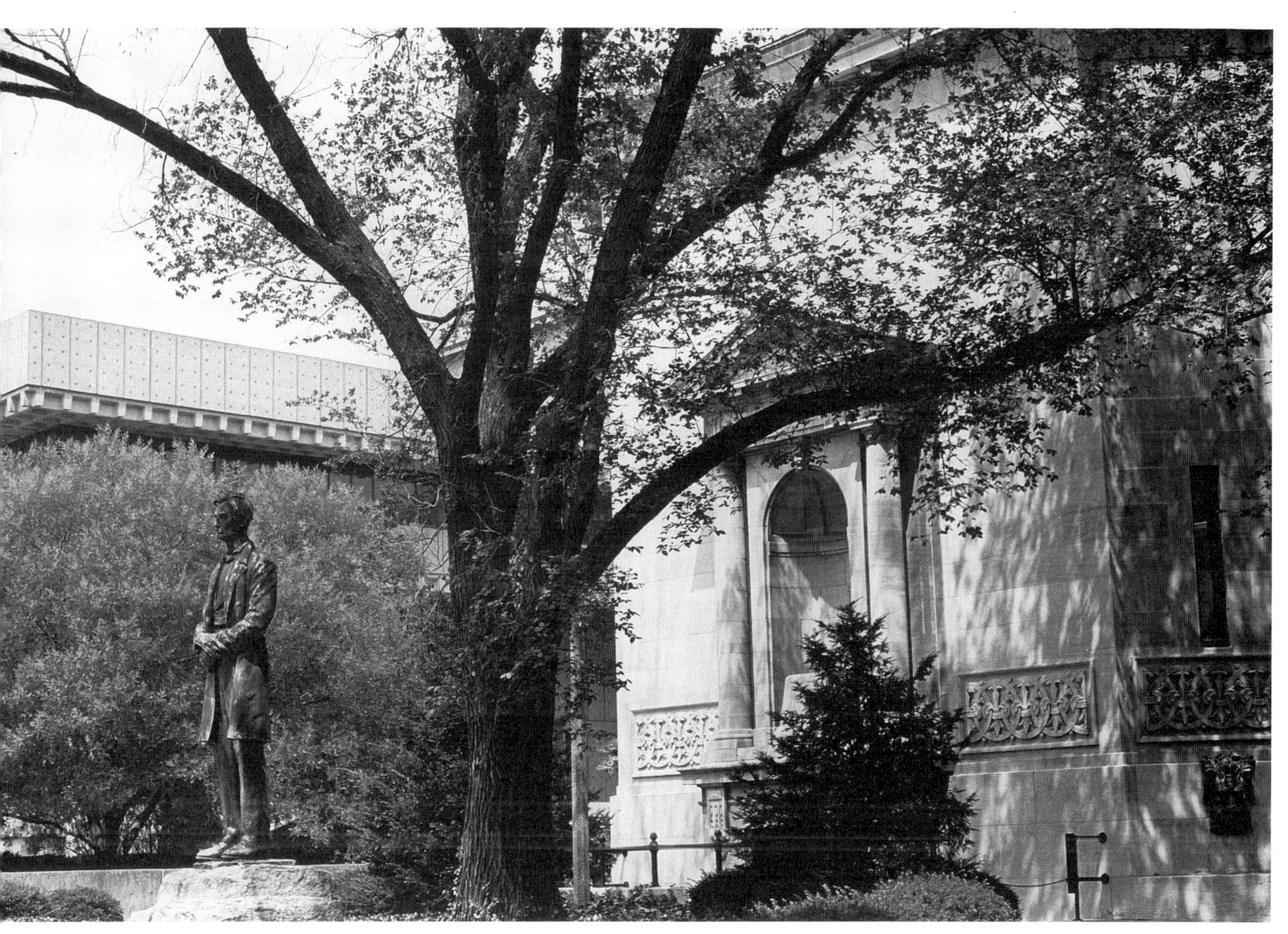

Barnard's Lincoln, *3rd cast.*

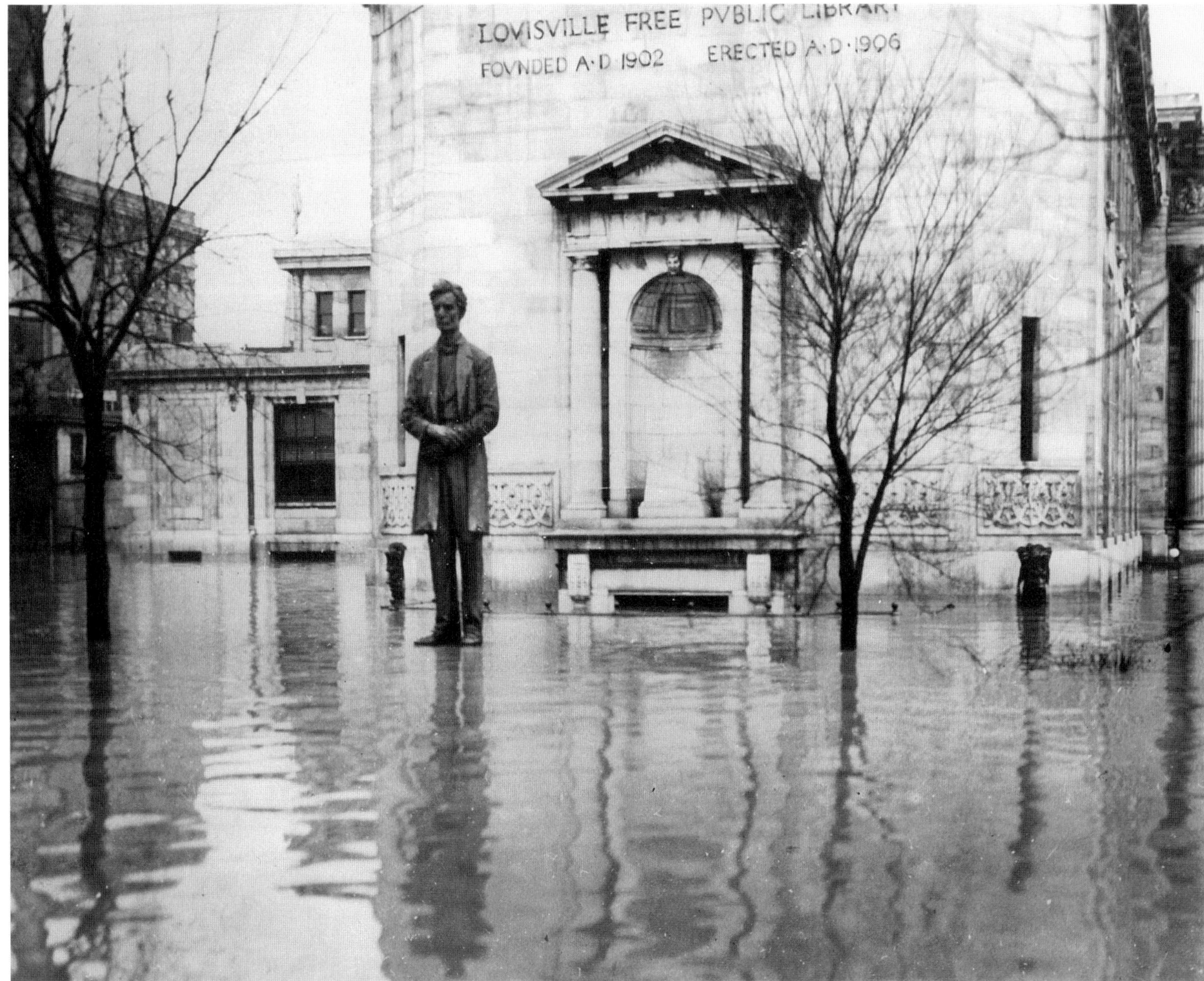

Barnard's Lincoln, *3rd cast, during 1937 flood, Louisville, Kentucky. Courtesy of the Louisville* Courier-Journal.

to acquiesce, so long as the statue would be situated "where the traffic passes near the sidewalk . . . it would then be a part of the City's life, and do the work [Bernheim] wished it to do."[35] In essence, he wanted it as far from the library wall as possible.

But among obvious advantages was the fact that when viewed from the south, the statue's profile appeared beneath the looming church steeple and from this position one hardly knew the library existed. The frontal view also presented a dynamic relationship between statue and architecture the artist may not have anticipated. So snugly does the statue appear to fill the niche, it is difficult to believe the two elements were not designed together. From any position off-axis, however, visual logic suggests the bronze has been displaced from the tabernacle, that somehow the statue has broken free and advanced outward from the wall.

Alongside this visual tension exists another: the familiar critical disparity Barnard found existing between Gothic and Classical form. Stylistically, a union of the figure and architecture is rendered impossible, for it would necessitate the bringing of human disorder and vulnerability into the realm of abstract perfection. Yet, as Barnard surely realized, a similar contradiction had many years ago given added force to Donatello's Florentine statues, especially those like the *Saint George* and *Saint Louis* when

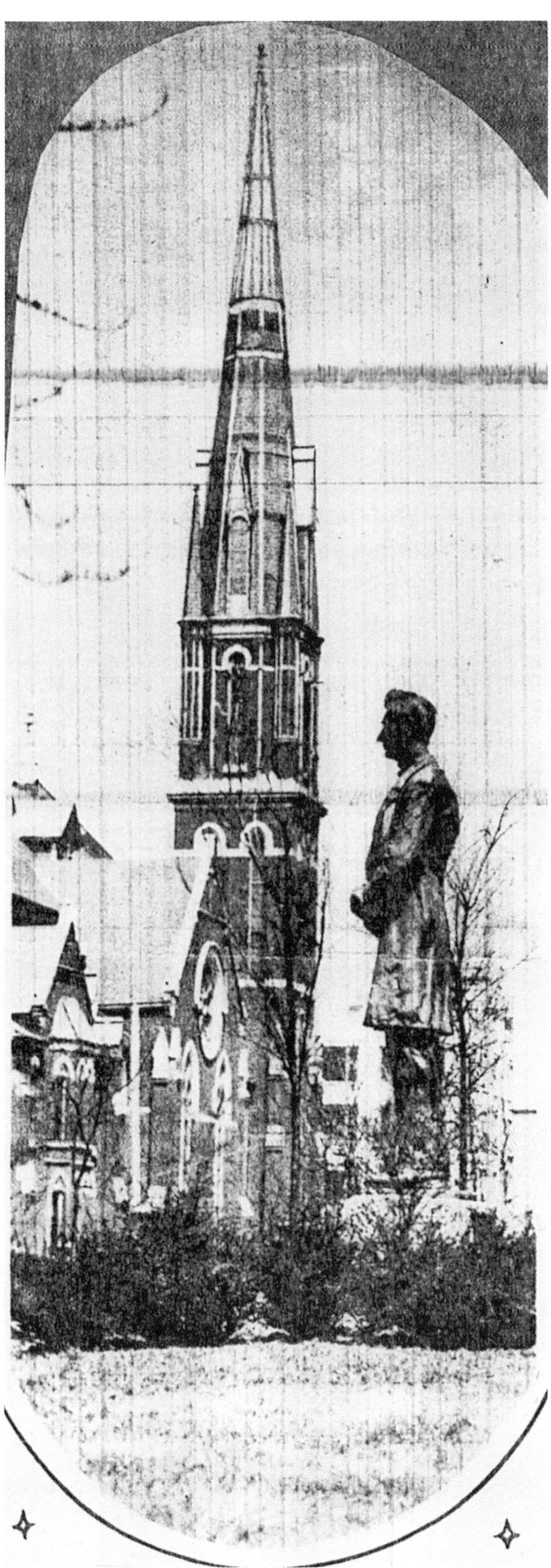

Barnard's Lincoln, *3rd cast. From Louisville* Courier-Journal, *6 May 1928.*

seen enframed by the shallow classical niches originally designed for them. Thus at Louisville, a similar ambiguity emphasizes all the more the tragic dimensions of Barnard's conception.

Once the new cast was revealed, the issue of originality regained its importance. While previously a committee might pardon the distribution of identical statues to separate foreign countries, the present situation involved two fiercely competitive American cities that were within commuting distance. The Louisville press invariably employed the term "replica" to describe the gift statue, while Barnard, who used the term "duplicate" in his earlier letter to Bernheim, now spoke of entirely new forms and surfaces. Directly after the unveiling, the *Courier-Journal* and the *Louisville Times* thoroughly probed the issue, quoting at length Barnard's letter to Bernheim, as well as a similar one written to Hartwell that read: "I have labored with renewed love upon your Lincoln, reasserting the truths as I see them in the remodeling of all the details (or surfaces), in ways that your bronze should have all life touches to any that has left my hand and heart. Less than this I could not do." A skeptical *Times* reporter published a Barnard telegram which read, "The truth cannot be modified. No work leaves my hand for bronze that is not developed, and re-developed in the surfaces of the wax figure before the casting in bronze. I justify each statue with the artist's living and loving touch."[36] An obvious distinction between casts is found in the signing and dating of the plinths: Barnard's name and the date 1922 are handwritten beside the right heel into the upper surface of the plate of the Louisville statue, while the artist's full name and "Sculp" are hand printed into the reverse side of the Cincinnati plinth. No other differences are distinguishable.

With the possible exception of Bernheim, Barnard's communications convinced the site committee that Louisville was not to receive a handed-down Cincinnati Lincoln. The fire at the foundry was proof enough for some that the statue was an entirely original one. Even after a comparison of photographs failed to reveal differences, the desire to believe differences existed proved more powerful than visual evidence. Grasping at straws, Loomis contended he perceived changes about the head and lower part of the body, but when pressed, was unable to be specific. Loomis was in a better position than the others to know if it was an exact replica, since he used the same plumb line verifications, rectified to a quarter of an inch, that Cincinnati architect A. O. Elsner had employed for centering the first bronze.[37]

The *Louisville Times* prepared for an exposé that would both discredit the Barnard statue and boost

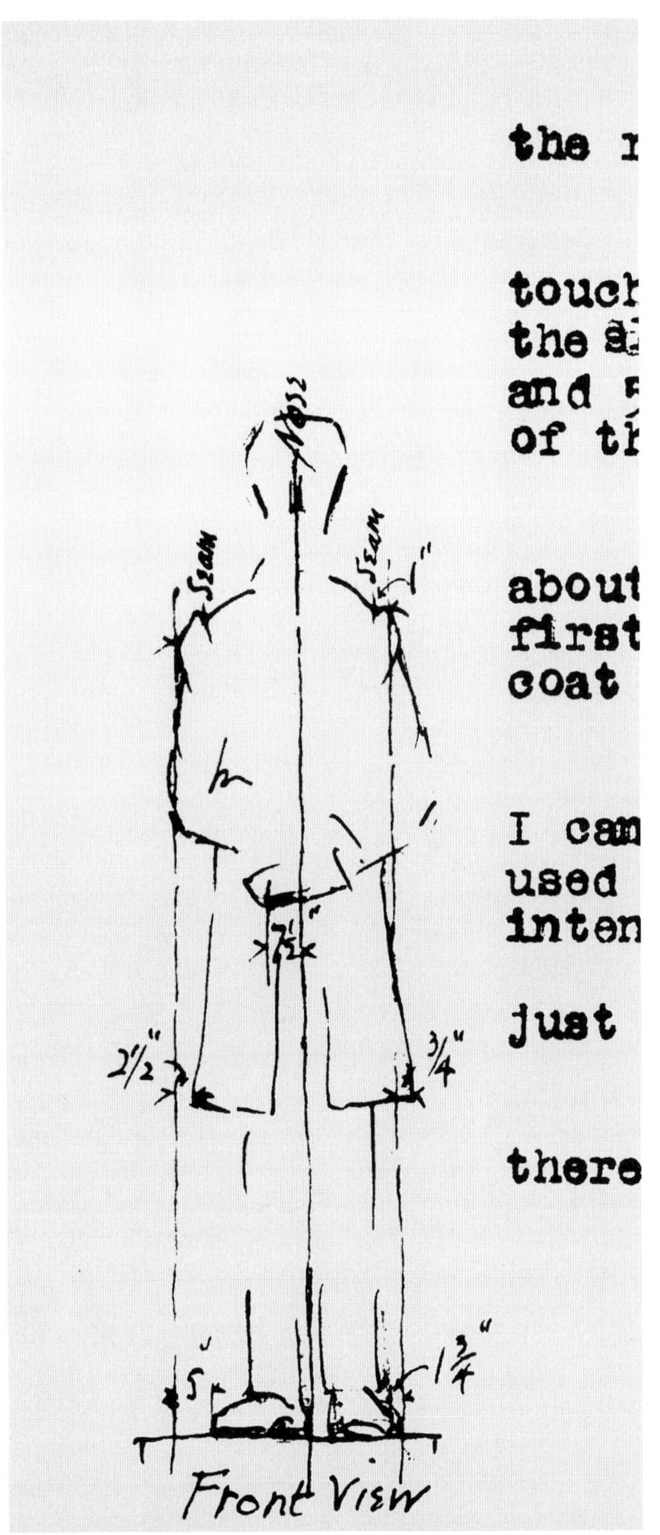

A. O. Elsner, plumb analysis of Barnard's Lincoln, *1st cast. 1922. Courtesy of the Philadelphia Museum of Art Archives.*

notice gave fair warning that if, as rumored, the Barnard statue were identical to the "blatantly physical" Lincoln north of the Ohio, then the newspaper would pronounce it a failure, for that figure lacked "mysterious genius" and soul. Immediately following the ceremonies, however, a *Times* commentator exonerated Louisville's newest statue, since he was now convinced "it has the same strength and daring and yet there is an element of restraint in it which recollections of the Cincinnati and Manchester statues [do] not include." Even its positioning on the stepped base was pleasing, and its ungainly demeanor singularly appropriate. Whether or not this sudden turnabout reflected divided opinions among its staffers, the *Times* thereafter decided to make light of the matter; its parting comment was in the form of a cartoon that illustrated an imagined quarrel between Barnard's bronze, and the library's other heroic public statue—the George Prentiss—that, in effect, hoisted Barnard with his own petard.[38] Columnist Charles Dobbs, a seeming friend of the Barnard, experiments with a newly designed cigarette that accommodates a pronounced Adam's apple like that exhibited by the statue. Images in the lower register depict, first, an imagined self-portrait of Barnard in the guise of his statue, the statue itself, to which is attached the mock-heroic line, "All the days of my appointed time will I wait till my change comes," and, finally, the inevitable confrontation between statues. The latter engagement is accompanied by the observation, "In the original (Cincinnati) Lincoln his hands are merely crossed [while] in the Louisville statue he is pushing back his sleeves," making ready to "knock that baby stare" from his face.

Henry Watterson might well have endorsed the cartoonist's sentiments, although with less evidence of humor. Before his death in December 1921, he had already completed the main body of the address he was to deliver at the unveiling, a typically combative admonishment of nonbelievers.

> One thinks of the world in which Abraham Lincoln lived might have dealt more gently with such a man. He was himself so gentle—so upright in nature and so broad of mind—so simple and unaffected in bearing. But let no Southern man point a finger at me because I canonize Abraham Lincoln, for he was the one friend we had in a country where friends were most in need. He was the one man in power who wanted to preserve us intact.[39]

the lagging Jefferson Davis memorial. The issue that covered the Lincoln unveiling also contained an editorial that upbraided Kentuckians for not supporting Gen. Haldeman's monument campaign. A separate

But if forced to judge the statue on the same basis he judged the man, would he not have been tempted to strike a blow himself? Quite obviously, Watterson

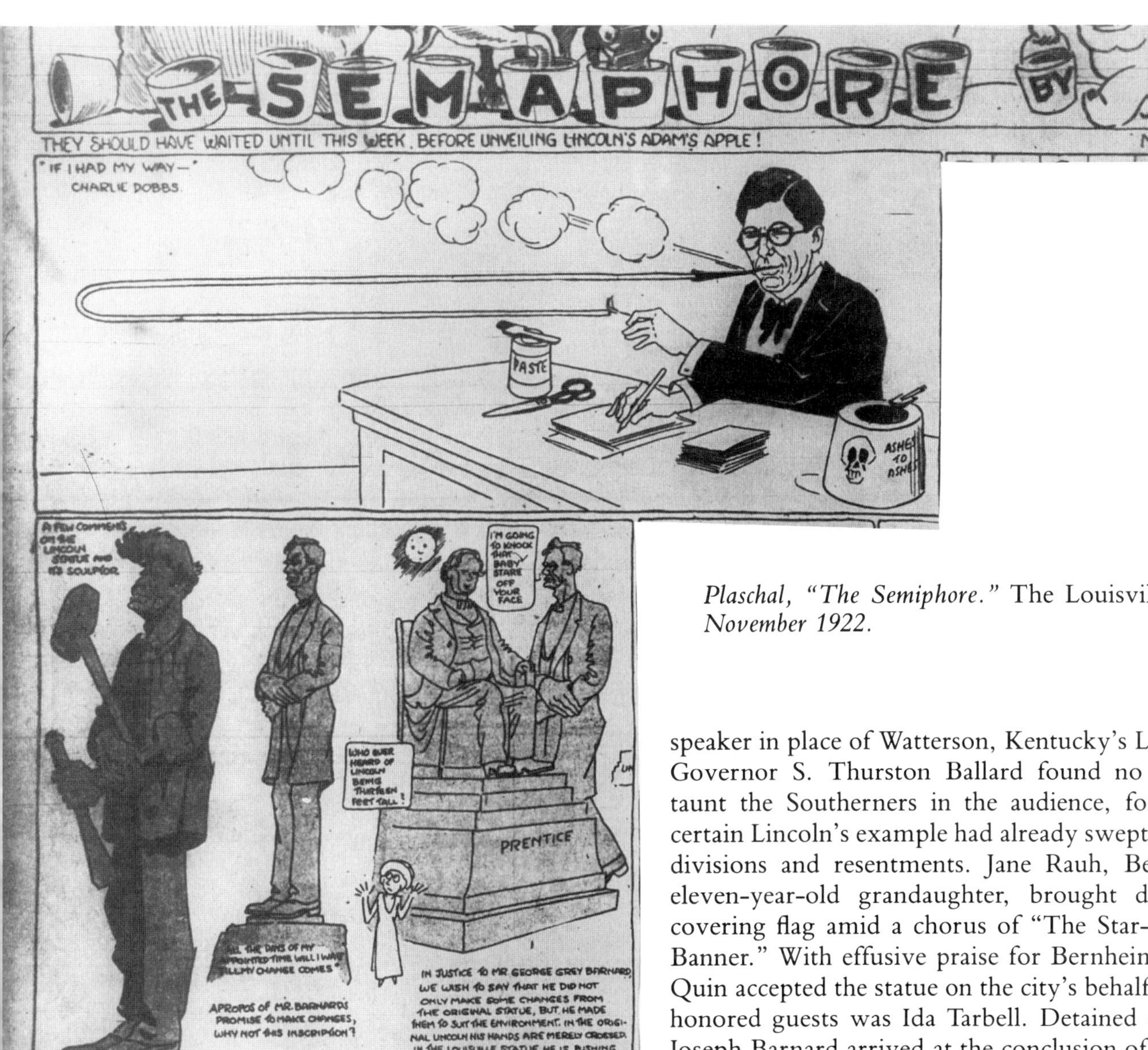

Plaschal, "The Semiphore." The Louisville Times, 4 November 1922.

had no intention of betraying a friend or demeaning a noteworthy occasion.

At high noon on 26 October 1922, the deeply moved Bernheim found gathered about him and his flag-draped statue an assembly comprised of gentile and Jew, of Southerner and Northerner, and of every shade of secular society, which eagerly extended to him its profound appreciation and goodwill.[40] Bernheim's nephew, Memphis Rabbi William H. Finesbriner, delivered an invocation that underscored the hope that an "intrinsic brotherhood" would find its way into hearts of all Americans. Serving as keynote speaker in place of Watterson, Kentucky's Lieutenant Governor S. Thurston Ballard found no cause to taunt the Southerners in the audience, for he was certain Lincoln's example had already swept aside old divisions and resentments. Jane Rauh, Bernheim's eleven-year-old grandaughter, brought down the covering flag amid a chorus of "The Star-Spangled Banner." With effusive praise for Bernheim, Mayor Quin accepted the statue on the city's behalf. Among honored guests was Ida Tarbell. Detained en route, Joseph Barnard arrived at the conclusion of the ceremonies. Jounalists eagerly quoted the comments of less sophisticated participants in order to indicate the statue's elemental appeal. The *Louisville Herald* sought out "a man with three weeks stubble on his chin [who] said, 'Well, that don't look like any of his pictures on the stamps or money or on the Lincoln penny that I've seen; how do you explain that?'" Another exclaimed, "Why, he looks just like a common Kentucky fellow—no style nor nothin. He might be one of us." A child found a remarkable resemblance between the statue and her favorite uncle because it "looks all rumpled up."[41] For these and others, an unfamiliar stylelessness blurred the boundaries separating art and life, the past and present, greatness from the unpretentious existence of their own lives.

A concurrent revelation further brought artifice and the living condition together as one. In February 1922, as Barnard was preparing piece molds for the wax, a Louisville journalist discovered Lincoln model

Charles Thomas living on South Preston Street. Although he had provisional employment with the county, and had served at Camp Knox during the war, Thomas was currently among the state's estimated ten thousand unemployed males. The *Louisville Times* published photographs that were intended to reveal the close similarities between the man and the statue, while an editor stressed the similarities between the early lives of modern Thomas and Abraham Lincoln. This and later reports made clear the fact his posing was the only notable event in the unfortunate man's life. An unskilled laborer trying to survive in a depressed economy, Thomas had little else than his memory of Barnard's studio, a French purse the artist had given him, and a steady trust that "the Lord will provide," to sustain him. He professed no impatience over his current inactivity, but rather was as "happy as a Junebug just because I am living.

It ain't no use worrying about having nothing to do, as that will not do any good." Around the time of the statue's dedication, he secured a permanent construction job with the Louisville Gas and Electric Company, perhaps through Bernheim's assistance. The *Courier-Journal* celebrated the event by printing a photograph of the now presumably happy laborer, pick in hand and ankle-deep in soil, digging into the roots of a tree.[42] But once again, it was his service to art that gave a semblance of worthiness to Thomas's life and labor.

The irony of the situation, which amounted to a kind of inglorious inversion of the Pygmalion myth, could not have been lost on Bernheim, the aging members of Adath Israel, or the many Louisvillian gentiles who were at last prepared to receive this figurative symbol of social, racial, and sectional reconciliation into the public space of their city.

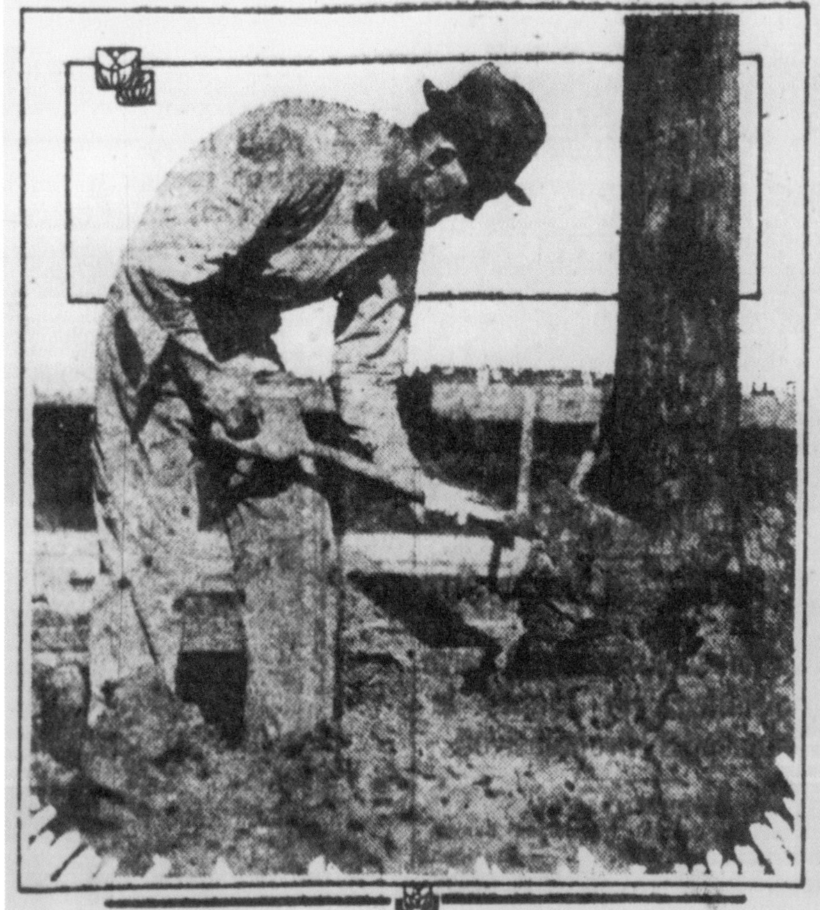

Charles Thomas at Work for the City. From the Louisville Courier-Journal, *16 November 1922.*

Part Six
Renewals

11
The Test of Time

THE "TEST OF TIME" THE BARNARDITES SUMMONED in defense of their statue consisted of something more than the gradual public acceptance that sometimes grows out of familiarity. Time was also in league with environmental factors that threatened to physically destroy the works. Therefore, lingering concerns over the aesthetic or interpretative worthiness of the statues fell to the wayside; they now belonged to a large family of similarly endangered public monuments that had to be rescued before it was too late. In the 1980s preservationists argued that because a large majority of public statues erected throughout the history of this country—some fifty thousand—continued to survive, they deserved protection as well as proper restoration and maintenance. Said one: "Their importance is that they exist."[1]

Clearly, the accumulated effects of weathering, atmospheric contamination, and the overlayering of avian excrement became determining factors in the long-term public perception of the Lincolns. In the absence of such momentous disruptions as vandalism, or removal, resident populations tended to accept as "normal" the gradual day-to-day visual changes. At Barnard's passing in 1938, verdigris was to a varying degree replacing the original chocolate-colored patinas. Before the 1940s, few spectators doubted that light green was the proper color of all outdoors bronze statuary, regardless of original appearances, for such accorded with "the mellow beauty of graceful aging," and ultimately added value to the works. Even in the 1940s and beyond, when bright green streaks resembling spilled paint began overrunning the softer tones, the disfigurements brought a new emphasis to the pathos Barnard had originally sought to express. Revised interpretations were also made appropriate. Insofar as Louisville's Jewish community was concerned, the disfigured personage might easily have passed for Ahasuerus, the despised "Wandering Jew" of Biblical legend. In a more self-referential way, the uncontrolled interaction of chemicals, weather, and time could have been seen as the physical counterpart to the slander and revilement, "the mud," Ruckstull and others had heaped upon an artist's great life work. But watchful preservationists knew the changes were not felicitous.[2]

Of the three, Cincinnati's Lincoln is the most logically positioned. Indeed, a local journalist has suggested it occupies the exact ground where Lincoln walked during a recess in a trial proceedings. This need not be argued, for the bronze's striking prominence at the forward edge of the compact village green, and its perspectival alignment with the Taft portico, seem "just right" to the casual viewer. The statue's placement also marks the center of a patronal sphere of influence. The park was a public space, indeed, one often occupied by the "unwashed," as Lorado Taft described them. But the Taft elders, their descendents, and friends worked diligently to retain for it the same reserved, contemplative air that one encounters inside the Taft home itself. Likewise, no local resident would mistake the fact that Cincinnati's Lincoln was in fact the "Taft Lincoln." The local Optimist Club chose to conduct annual wreath-laying ceremonies at the statue to honor the benevolence of fellow member Charles Taft as well as to commemorate the moment another Optimist, ex-Mayor George Puchta, officially accepted the statue for the city from William Howard Taft.[3]

When Charles Taft died, the Lytle Park neighborhood presented a mixture of industrial, civic, residential, educational, and religious buildings. The Baum-Taft mansion, soon to become the city-owned Taft Museum, was flanked by two factories, the Pugh Building and American Book Company, and a Neo-Renaissance high-rise, the Phelps Apartments, which had been completed in 1926 on East Fourth Street, directly opposite the statue and park entrance. What preservationists decided most lent the neighborhood its unique character, beside the Taft mansion itself, were the three- and four-story vintage brick structures that housed residences, as well as civic, and cultural clubs. Conforming with these older structures was the Neo-Colonial Anna Louise Inn, founded by Anna and Charles Taft in the name of their daughter, as a hostel for working girls. Three clubs were the exclusive domain of women—the Women's City Club, the Cincinnati Catholic Women's Association, and the Cincinnati Business Women's Club—while the remainder comprised the Cincinnati Art Club, the University Club, and the Literary Club, an 1820 structure on East Fourth that had been donated to the association by a faithful member, again Charles Taft. After 1950 separate property holdings owned by Taft daughters Jane Taft Ingalls and Louise Taft Semple were incorporated within the expanded perimeters of the park. Just outside the shaded preserve, in full view of the Lincoln's "inexpressibly sad, care worn" gaze, was full evidence of a modern city's raw, uncaring vitality. The Lytle Park women were quick to weigh the moral implications of this dramatic contrast; Women's City Club president Mrs. Clarence L. Doty defiantly proclaimed:

> Lytle Park gives quality and character to the city of Cincinnati. The Taft Museum stands majestically at one end facing a vista of park and flowers culminating in the beautiful Lincoln statue, with related buildings housing civic and cultural groups . . . all contributing to an individuality of the neighborhood unit in which the whole city for years has taken pleasure and pride. There is no other such spot in the city with these virtues.[4]

The forces of commercial enterprise were to make two assaults upon this womblike compound and its lonely icon, the first of which was easily rebuffed after a public outcry. Hastily reacting to Charles's demise in 1929, and no doubt anticipating Anna's own death the following year, Cincinnati's City Planning Commission proposed in 1930 to rezone the neighborhood from residential to business. In the 1940s a more serious reckoning arose when the federal government chose Cincinnati to be a link on its Interregional System of Highways. This eventually entailed the construction of three north–south expressways, one of which, the Northeast Expressway (I–75, Cincinnati to Columbus), was to be routed through the park. The only alternative to the rejection of the plan, or the outright destruction of the park, was contained in a city master plan, completed in 1948, that proposed that the expressway should be directed through a tunnel that would run beneath the park and its statue.[5]

Civic leaders at first upheld the desirability of the highway project. With a large portion of its cost to be borne by the federal government, it promised to ease inner-city congestion, while insuring tourists improved access to the downtown. A less-advertised consequence of the new system's operation would be the eventual displacement of some of Cincinnati's minority population. However, it was determined in 1958 that two East Fourth Street clubs, the Women's City Club, and the Catholic Women's Club, as well as several adjoining historic buildings, had been slated for demolition, and that no plans existed for replacing these structures once the tunnel was completed. Strongly assisted by long-time councilman and former mayor Charles Phelps Taft II, son of William Howard Taft, the club women laid siege to the offices of the city manager and expressway engineer. Taft warned that the demolition would "eliminate the very type of scarce downtown residential area that the city should be laboring to keep." The park was a place of "permanent [and] continuing beauty," one that perpetuated an atmosphere of "chaste elegance and decorous pride." Giving added force to the argument was a timely article, published in the *Reader's Digest,* that extolled the extent to which significant historic and architectural monuments throughout the country were being replaced by shopping centers, superhighways, skyscrapers, and "sub-utopias." Among the alarming statistics cited was an estimate that within a period of less than twenty years, twenty-five percent of America's "finest" sites had already been lost. Reminding readers that it was a woman, one Ann Pamela Cunningham, who through her own initiative had affected the eventual preservation of Mount Vernon, author Blake Clark seemed to have Lytle Park and its statue specifically in mind when he insisted that "we need authentic, tangible reminders of our national virtues and heroes to make us feel a part of the best of our heritage. Properly presented, they breathe life into past experience."[6]

Finally resigned to the destruction of the original buildings, the Taft coalition prevailed in its insistence that they be replaced with a large new apartment complex styled so as to generally conform with the original simple brick structures. Before this compromise was negotiated, however, long years of disputation between civic, city, state, and federal agents lay ahead. In 1968, a year after actual construction on the tunnel commenced, the statue was removed to the Guilford School. In August 1971, shortly before its scheduled resiting, Eleftherious Karkadoulias, a new resident of Cincinnati, freely offered the park commissioners his services in restoring the bronze.[7]

Born in Markopolo, Greece, in 1936, Karkadoulias learned the ancient art of bronze casting at Marathon, then established a family-owned foundry in the vicinity of Athens. Having immigrated to America in 1967, he moved to Cincinnati in 1969 expressly to direct a sixty-five-thousand-dollar refurbishing project for the *Tyler Davidson Fountain,* which reached completion in October 1971. Directly thereafter, Karkadoulias founded the Karkadoulias Bronze Art Studio in Walnut Hills for the purpose of both restoring many of the area's existing bronzes and/or creating original bronze statuary on commission.[8]

Readily accepting his offer, the park commissioners deferred to the Architectural Review Board a decision as to whether a verdigris or brown patina should be chosen. Karkadoulias then disassembled the six separate bronze sections of the statue at his studio in preparation for the cleaning and repair of the inside and outside of the bronze shell. He applied an unidentified protective coating which the restorer insisted was far superior to the usual wax application in resisting pollution and oxidation. In an effort to calm critics who have questioned Karkadoulias's inscrutability and his reliance upon unorthodox procedures, he maintained that his secret solution was entirely comprised of natural materials.[9]

Certainly, Karkadoulias's ideal bronze restorer differed dramatically from the cautious conservator, the mere "janitor," as he described him, who in collaboration with municipal authorities often works in careful, measured steps. While speaking of his treatment of the Lincoln, Karkadoulias claimed an importance second only to Barnard himself. "The man who created the statue is no longer here, you cannot bring him back and have him keep watch over his own work. Some one has to do it for him. I feel honored to take a great piece of art and restore it to its original state. I think the artists would thank me." The board of park commissioners, which operated without a restoration budget, was not in a position to question the ethics involved, especially after Karkadoulias modestly described his motivation as "a small way

for me to thank the people of Cincinnati for the love they have shown me."[10]

The statue was returned to its approximate original location in a restored and enlarged Lytle Park in 1972. Helping to lend a comforting sense of historical continuity to its return, Sen. Robert Taft Jr., son of Ohio senator Robert Alphonso Taft (1889–1953), and grandson of William Howard Taft—he was born in Cincinnati six days prior to the first Lincoln unveiling—presided over the rededication on 11 November 1972. His address condensed passages in Marquis Adolphe de Chambrun's *Impressions of Lincoln and the Civil War,* a sketch composed in 1865 that detailed Lincoln's forebearance and selflessness in dealing with the defeated Rebels.[11]

Again, the statue was being undraped during wartime, albeit this time a stalemate in Vietnam that was approaching its inglorious end. Again, the ambiguous character of the Barnard Lincoln suggested differing responses to military action and the rubric "national honor." Again, the presentor was a Taft, a well-known party regular whose conservative political agenda in domestic and foreign affairs was coming under increasing fire. After taking degrees at Yale and Harvard (LLB, 1942) and serving in the Second World War, Taft entered the Ohio House of Representatives in 1954. His congressional career consisted of terms in the House between 1963 and 1971 and the Senate, 1971–77.[12]

The Ohio congressman was for the most part a Nixon Republican, especially in regard to the Vietnam War. But his highly publicized amnesty call for draft resisters in 1971 marked a liberalizing trend in his political outlook that would lead to his break with the embattled president in 1974. Taft's bill would have freed five hundred imprisoned draft resisters and pardoned another seventy thousand individuals who had fled the country to escape the draft, so long as they volunteered for noncombat federal service. Even though Taft reasoned some were misguided victims, and others, conscientious objectors, he, like Chambrun's Lincoln, had now decided the time for reconciliation was at hand. This Lincoln-like embrace of misdirected draft dodgers and politically motivated "doves," however, gained him little sympathy from those directing the antiwar movement.[13]

By no means did the reasonably happy outcome of the Cincinnati tunnel project resolve for all time the question of what specific public environment would be most appropriate for the Lincoln statue. The 1948 Metropolitan Plan expected the future park to be the home of museums and historic displays. Here would be the perfect location for crowded gatherings and amusements, not the contemplation and reflection that Charles Taft II and the preservationists most valued. It was in the spirit of this scheme to attract people to the city center that the Greater Cincinnati Chamber of Commerce, through its Downtown Council, chose Lytle Park for its summer afternoon "Parties in the Park" series in the early 1980s, perhaps without realizing the irony such beer-and-music spectacles would present to the disinterested lens of a camera (see p. 7).[14]

Especially in a city that has taken not only old statues but a wide range of modernist sculpture in stride, one finds today an almost unexpected enthusiasm for Barnard's Lincoln. After surveying newly exhibited abstractions by Louise Nevelson, George Rickey, and Donald Judd, journalist Owen Findsen pronounced the Barnard "the best thing in bronze in the city." John Clubbe's appreciation in a recent guidebook boldly affirms Joseph Gest's prediction when he replied to the disappointed Charles Moore three-quarters of a century before:

> Lincoln stands before us, not on the formal plinth usual for statues of presidents (think of those in Piatt Park for Garfield and Harrison), but on a granite boulder, rough hewn, low to the ground. The granite suggests [Lincoln's] rock-like strength in times of crisis. In placing Lincoln so that we look less up to him than at him, Barnard makes a statement about the president's accessibility, even about his vulnerability. With the passing of time, we may admire more readily the unflinching integrity of his vision of Lincoln, more meditative, less heroic than Daniel Chester French's memorial statue in Washington. No other representation of Lincoln I know renders his rough-hewn honesty, his troubled grandeur of soul, so uncompromisingly. He stands before us, gaunt, unsmiling, weary, hair tousled, unbearded, tie askew, vest ill-fitting, big handed, big footed, the reflective eyes fixed on eternity. Barnard did indeed, as Taft hoped, produce 'a great work of art.'"[15]

Clubbe composed his panegyric several years after Cincinnati had emerged from her latest round of public art controversies. The newest public sculpture celebrity was not a statue, wherein history was personalized, but a pedestrian theme park entitled *Cincinnati Gateway*. Designed in 1988 by Minneapolis artist Andrew Leicester for a decayed riverfront industrial zone, *Gateway* features a whimsical synthesis of motifs that typify the city's mercantile and social history. Leicester's insertion of winged pigs into the crowns of simulated steamboat smokestacks was both parodic as well as a thoughtful reference to Cin-

cinnati's extensive hog-butchering tradition and to the ironic social, moral, and psychological implications this tradition evoked. As Leicester fully anticipated, the inevitable public outcry centered on the "flying pig" element. Just as critics had once scorned Barnard for daring to defame Lincoln and his place in history, so latter-day Cincinnatians protested Leicester's attempt to embarrass the "Queen City" and her place in America's history. But rather than closing himself off in a studio, Leicester prepared the way for his project's acceptance by actively seeking public participation during all stages of its development, and by thoroughly researching the city's history before arriving at his designs. Although the contestants aligned themselves with roughly the same broad conflicting issues of "art-for-art-sake" and "social responsibility" that prevailed during the Barnard struggle, the *Cincinnati Gateway* dispute did not occasion the same venomous personal war. After a brief flurry of outcries in the press, and the posting of several public polls which indicated the populace was evenly divided on the issue, the *Gateway* question evolved into a series of comic performances and humorous dialogues between the "Pro-Pig," anti-art-censorship faction, and their "priggish" detractors.[16]

No comforting sense of closure and sentiment occasioned the renewal of Manchester's Lincoln, for this project was undertaken as part of that city's desperate struggle for economic survival. Roughly the same size as Cincinnati, central Manchester was to face a disastrous loss of population and mounting unemployment in the post-World War II era due to a sharp decline of its manufacturing base and textile production, and due to the eventual closing of its seaport canal in 1986. At the same time, a steady immigration from Commonwealth countries, the West Indies, and the Indian subcontinent dramatically changed the ethnic character of the inner city. As early as 1945, city planners made ready to pedestrianize and landscape the downtown area, and moved to construct low-income housing for displaced workers, but actual full-scale construction of the inner-city project did not begin until 1980, well after the effects of the economic downturn revealed the seriousness of the situation. In the beginning, the Lincoln statue had no part in the planning. Instead, it was to be a private corporation that belatedly recognized the statue's potential value to the revitalization program, as well as to its own continued prosperity.

In the 1980s, MEPC reigned as England's second largest real estate investment company and was preparing to venture into the risky American shopping center market. Directed until 1993 by Sir Christopher Benson, a chief executive the London *Times* described as an "iron fist inside a velvet stone," the firm maintained its northwest British headquarters on Manchester's Queen Street, close by Albert Square and the Town Hall. MEPC's local holdings included an unnamed square bounded by Queen and Brazennose streets and several fronting high-rises that it was in the process of renovating. In about 1980, the firm donated the square to the city, which, in accordance with its renewal plan, earmarked it for pedestrianization and landscaping. The square's single amenity was a modest fountain that commemorated the royal wedding of Prince Charles and Lady Diana Spencer.[17]

Having discovered in 1984 that the Lincoln statue at Platt Fields was classified by the city planning office as a temporary listed structure, MEPC's regional office proposed that it and the city cosponsor its relocation to the square, and that the enclosure be named "Lincoln Square." In forwarding this recommendation, regional manager C. John Ellison expressed his belief that the original sponsors and patrons had preferred a central location. In any event, the new square needed a feature that would give it a "greater sense of identity" and thus promise to further benefit of both partners. To sweeten the prospects, Ellison pledged that his firm would bear the expenses of transport and of refurbishing the bronze. Even though his research surely must have impressed upon him the importance that the Tafts, Barnard, and Stewart placed on utilizing a low rustic boulder for the base, Ellison insisted that his company would also provide a tall marble pedestal. Composed of pink British granite, the plinth would match the color chosen for the new brick pavement. There was a note of urgency in the appeal, for MEPC fully expected work to be completed before the end of 1984, or, in several months time.[18]

The city could not refuse. First to respond was Paul Saultert, chief executive of the Manchester Chamber of Commerce and Industry, who agreed that the concept would give special focus to the City Centre Campaign, and would be perfectly timed to coincide with a chamber-sponsored competition, to which MEPC was also a contributor, for devising new roles for empty factories and other "redundant" buildings in the area. In reference to the nearby Gothic city hall and the towering architectural ensemble housing the Prince Albert Memorial outside it, Saulter reasoned that the replanted statue would harmonize with the city's predominantly Victorian heritage. Most of all, MEPC's recommendation would give special emphasis to the strong business ties the chamber continued to maintain with the United States.[19]

Another year passed before the city council moved on final plans for the unveiling, which it then projected for February 1986. Its first choice for unveiler was Alistair Cooke, the erudite Anglo-American television personality who, having been born near Manchester, understood as well as any individual the significance of the historic ties that bound Lincoln and Lancashire textile workers. The council also hoped to persuade Charles Price, American ambassador to Great Britain, to perform the dedication. Security was a major concern from the beginning. The smoothly polished seven-foot plinth was to be equipped with a rounded cornice, not to add a stylish accent to the base but to deter individuals from gaining access to the statue. Before the unveiling the figure was to be covered with sack and chain so as to keep it "secret," and a security guard was to be posted to prevent any last-minute incursions by vandals.[20]

Since the council and MEPC were determined to inscribe lengthy texts on the surfaces of the pedestal, another important matter concerned what texts were to be chosen and how presented. After conferring with MEPC officials in early 1986, city council members had determined that the principal text should excerpt Lincoln's 1863 salutation to the cotton workers that opens with "To the working men of Manchester." This would be imprinted on the forward surface, while separate notations on the sides would refer to the principals and date of the rededication, to the circumstances of the original Taft donation, and to Lincoln's identity.[21] It became clear that what was to be unveiled was more a pedestal than a statue, for the densely printed base, like a leaf from an illuminated manuscript, was to carry the predominant weight of signification.

Obviously intent on making the rededication an instrument for countering ongoing ethnic mistrust of governmental authority, particularly at a moment when the Republic of South Africa was in crisis, the city council made special efforts to invite ethnic minorities to the ceremony, especially members of the "Afro-Caribbean community." After Cooke sent his regrets and Ambassador Price who, unlike his counterpart in 1919, failed to make good on an earlier acceptance, the council secured the services of the African-American Arthur Mitchell, director of the Dance Theatre of Harlem. Mitchell performed the unveiling on 13 November 1986, as the calypso strains of the Mancunian Steel Band of the minority suburb of Hulme reverberated, and a costumed con-

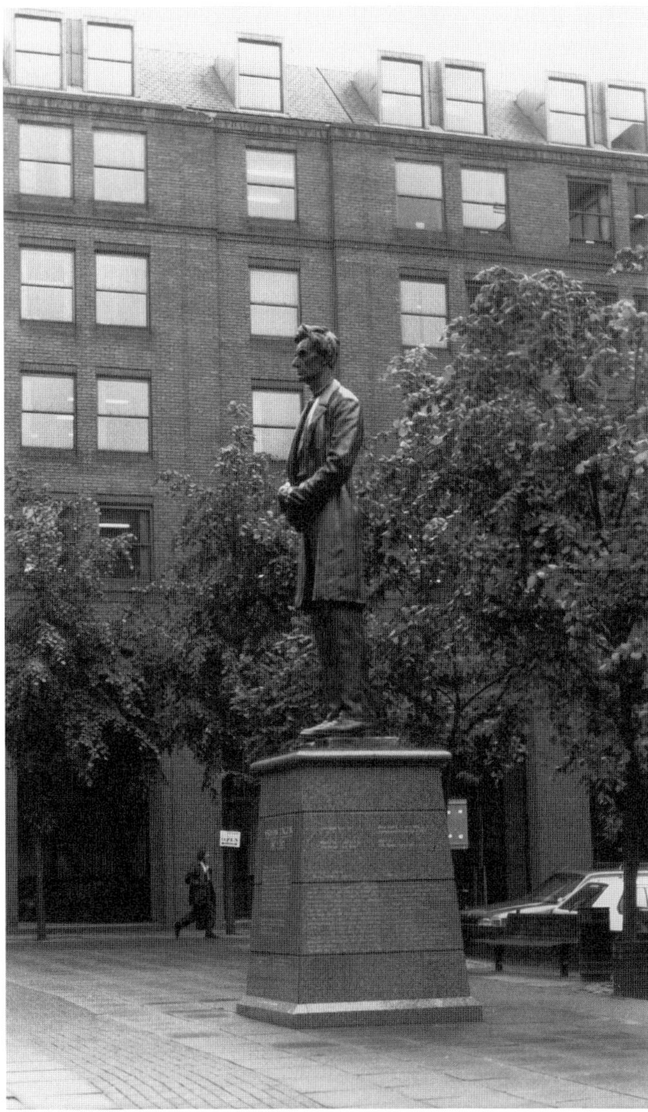

George Grey Barnard, Abraham Lincoln, *2nd cast. Seen in Lincoln Square, Manchester, England, ca. 1989. Courtesy of the Manchester Central Library, Local Studies Unit.*

Barnard's Lincoln, *2nd cast. Courtesy of the Manchester Central Library, Local Studies Unit.*

tingent of the 24th Michigan Regiment of the Union Army performed maneuvers.[22]

What beyond the statue and base was revealed at that moment was the unusual lengths corporate officials would go during Prime Minister Margaret Thatcher's administration to safeguard "political correctness." For, as Mitchell drew aside the covering, it was discovered that Lincoln's printed appreciation was addressed not to the "working men" but the "working people" of Manchester. Similar gender transformations were to be encountered elsewhere and, even more astonishing was the fact that theater was spelled "thearte" in a passage referring to the

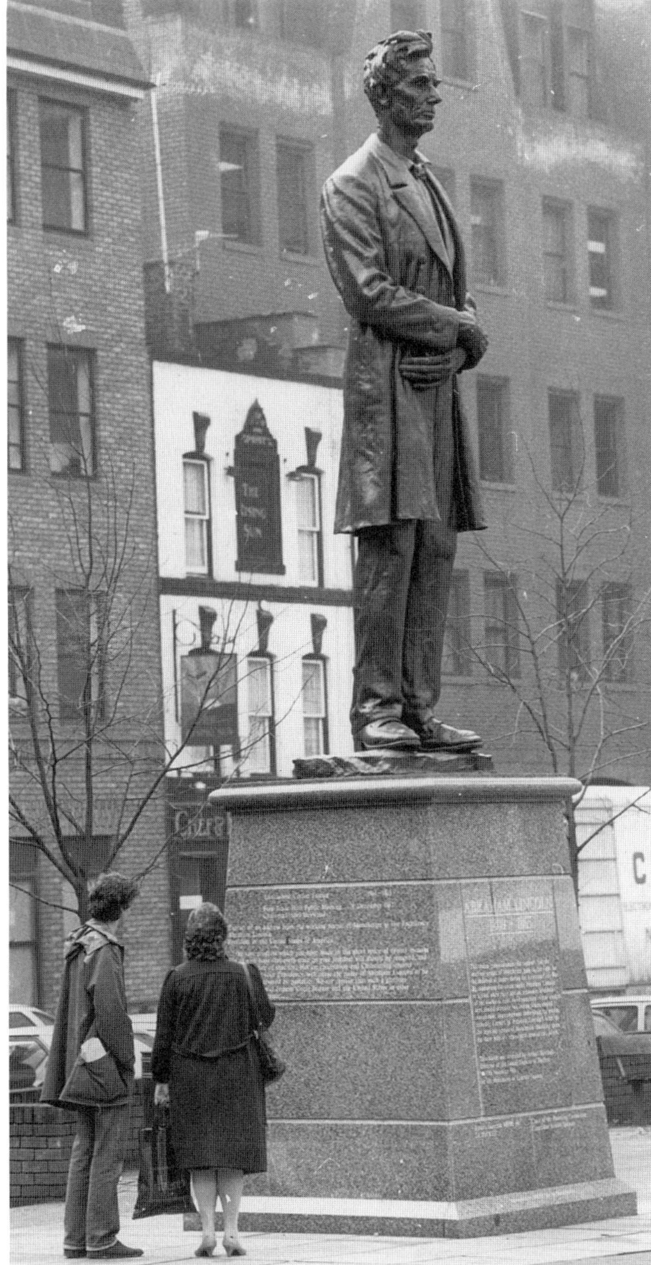

assassination. Former Lord Mayors Fred Balcome and Dame Kathleen Ollerenshaw reacted immediately to the present administration's shameful connivance, Balcome charging that the rewording was a "disgrace to a stateman of such standing who was assassinated for his views." With equal astonishment, Dame Ollerenshaw observed, "These people are rewriting history. History is history. You cannot violate history and change, for example, what Winston Churchill said. I've never heard such bloody nonsense."[23] Evidently, the extraordinary security measures were in part aimed at delaying just this kind of reaction.

In defense, an unnamed MEPC spokesman characterized the text as an abridged version of Lincoln's words, and, as a matter of protocol, Arnold Spencer, chairman of the city council planning committee, assumed responsibility. But neither he nor any city or corporate executive was willing to confess to having personally ordered the revised wording or to having allowed the grievous spelling error to stand uncorrected. The *Manchester Evening News* editorialized blissfully over the implications of this perfidy, noting it was not surprised that such a thing could happen, given the fact that Manchester's city "parents" regard tradition as a "dirty word." Similar in spirit to this revision of history was the fact that, because of the pervading political climate, the office of Lord Mayor had reverted to "comrade chair," that the Queen's portrait had been removed from its former prominent position at city hall, and that a picture of Nelson Mandela, the imprisoned National African Congress leader, not Saint Nicholas, adorned Manchester's official 1986 Christmas greeting card.[24]

In the years that have followed the statue's transfer, Manchester's planning office and cultural service director have been wrestling with another overlooked detail related to the project. The original base, with its bronze dedication plate intact, remains a temporary listed structure at the original Platt Fields location. Those unacquainted with recent events might well be excused for thinking that the Tafts had presented a Connecticut boulder to Manchester, intending it, rather than some stray statue, to be a symbol of Lincoln's steadfastness. After considering the cost of its removal, as well as alternate plans for making the boulder the center of a rock garden, or covering it with another stone, or making it the base of another statue, city planning officer William Showcraft recommended to the keeper of conservation that he simply hide it under a planting of creepers.[25]

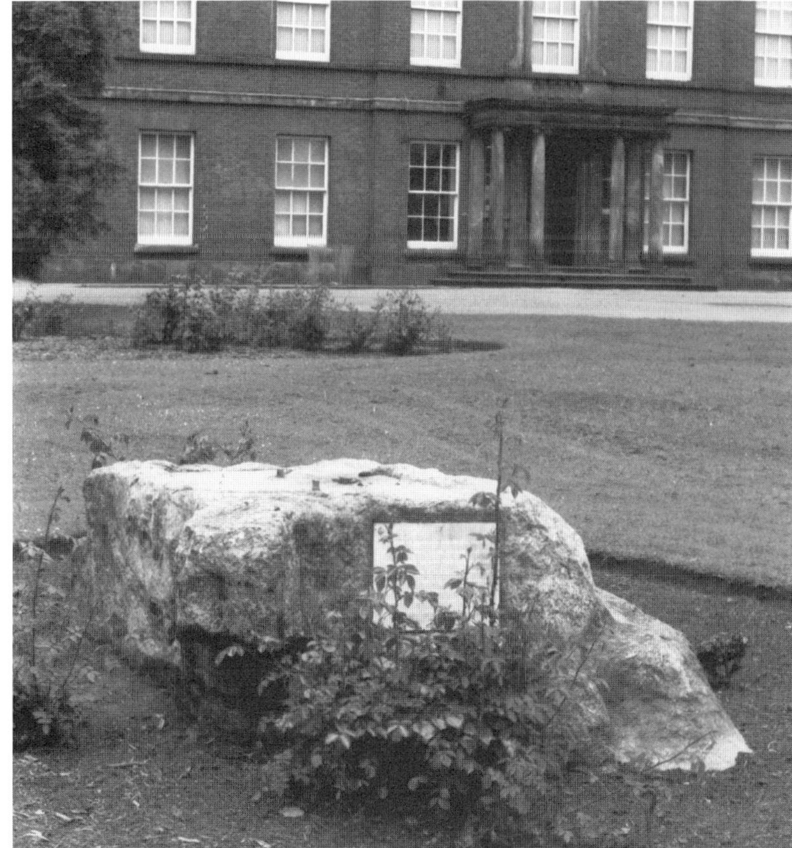

Base of Barnard's Lincoln, *2nd cast. Manchester, England. Photo, 1995.*

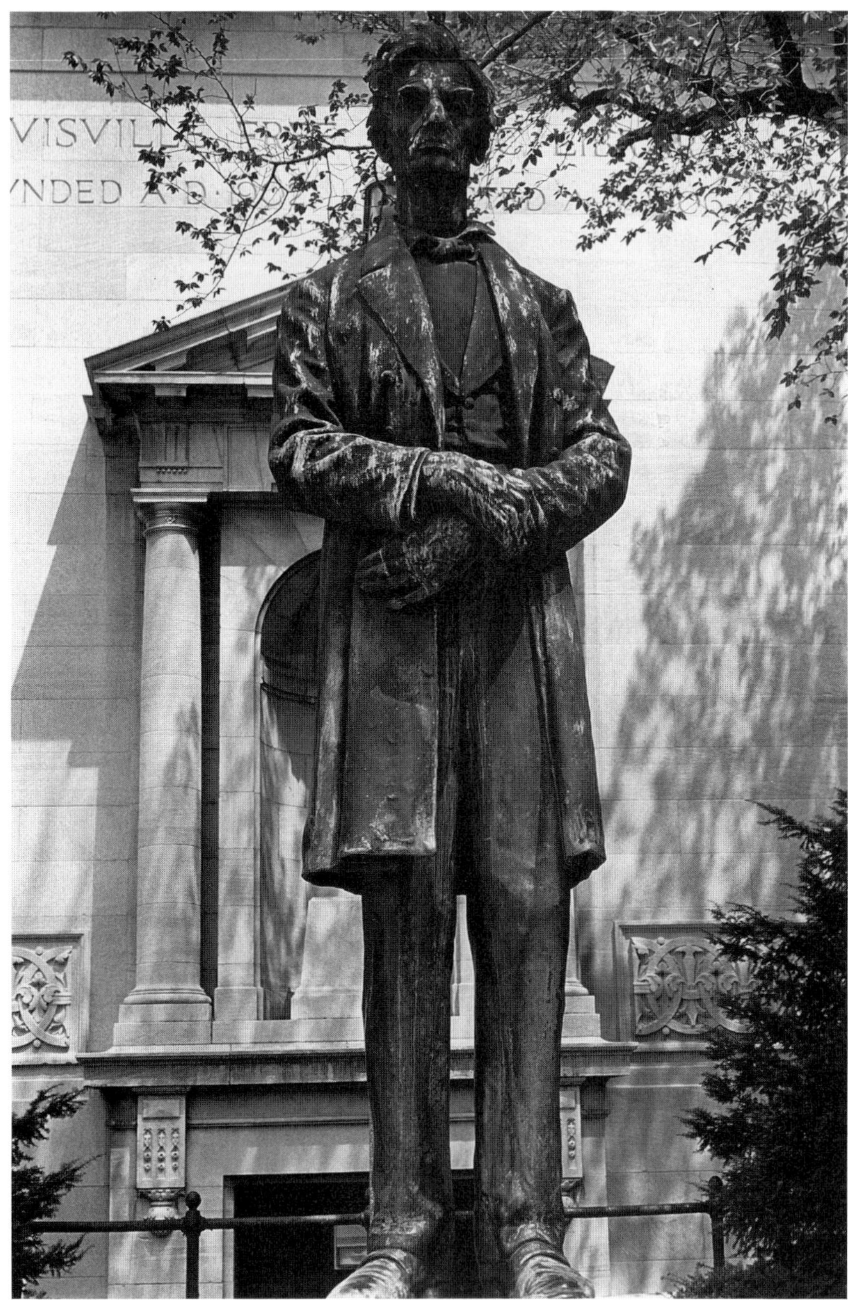

Barnard's Lincoln, 3rd cast. Louisville, Kentucky. Photo, 1988.

Located in a city now well known for its statues and daringly innovative architectural monuments, as well as the world's largest floating fountain, the two-million dollar donation of media heirs Mary and Barry Bingham Jr., the Bernheim Lincoln was recently ranked one of Louisville's "more visible and significant" public works. However, through 1990, it also was classified as the most endangered of the city's some forty public statues and memorials. Mayor Jerry Abramson and his board of alderman saw a parallel existing between the steady erosion of their city's downtown civic structure and the corrosion of public statues. For example, as they considered ways to reverse the Free Public Library's lagging performance in the areas of service and collection de-velopment, they began to consider what to do about the Bernheim Lincoln, as well. A Mayor's Advisory Committee on Public Amenities was formed, and in 1990, Abramson allocated twenty-five thousand dollars for a condition survey and subsequent restoration of public works of art. The following year, the figure for restoration alone jumped to thirty-five thousand dollars with the stipulation that all expended funds be matched by private donations. Acting on the advice to begin with the Lincoln, the city in 1991 entered a fifteen-thousand-dollar contract with a Westport, Connecticut firm. The cultural planning office, which gathered information on the most probable appearance of the statue's original patina, completed the project in mid-October 1991. A routine

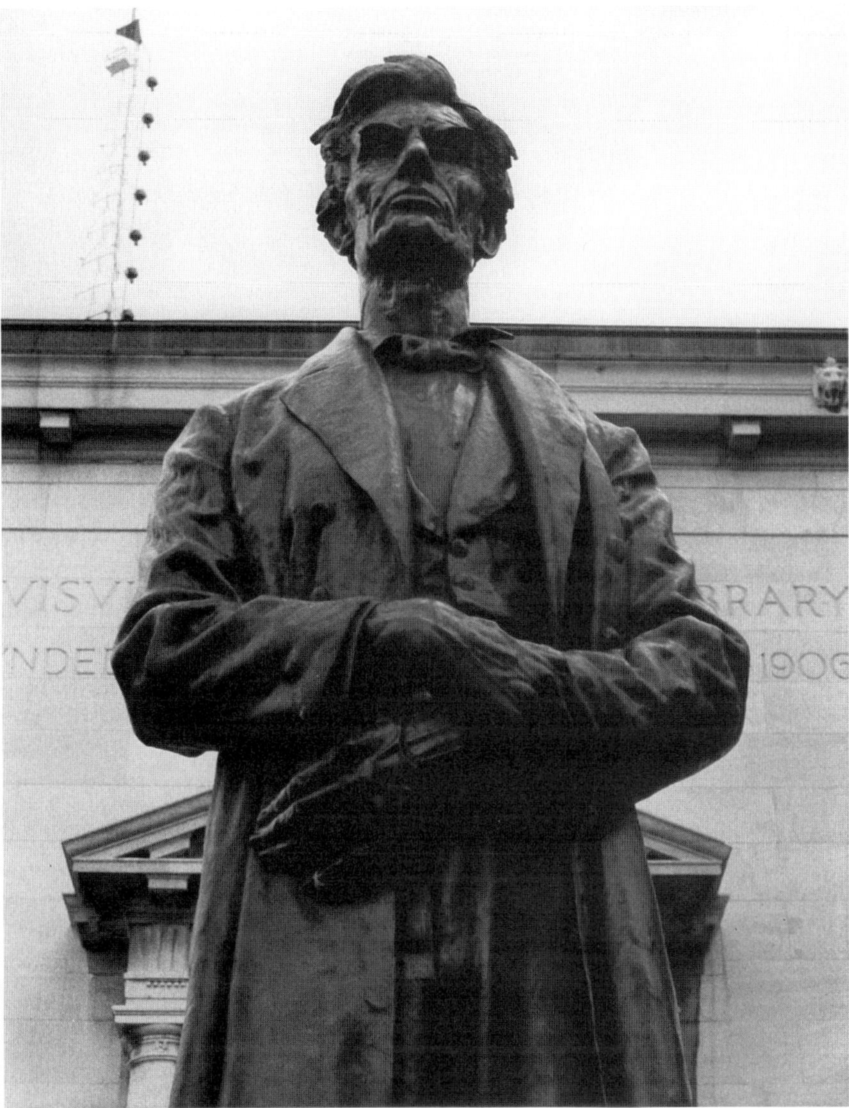

Barnard's Lincoln, *3rd cast. Photo, 1995 (after cleaning).*

process involving low-pressure blasting with walnut-shell fragments, followed by waxing, brought the surface to an almost full black tone, which under sunlight reflects greenish highlights.[26] The statue remained in place during the treatment, and, perhaps because no resiting was required, officials dispensed with a ceremonious unveiling.

Indeed, no amount of personal commitment or money has been able to restore this Lincoln or the others to the ceremonial character that even the most errant of bronze statues once occupied. Bernheim's desire to make his statue the visual focus of an educational program failed to materialize. No wreaths are laid at its feet, no parades pass by, no speeches are presented in its precinct. As Louisville city cultural planner Karolle Swanson commented: "Unfortunately, there is not alot of concern for statues today, they no longer have a place in civic life."[27]

Epilogue

BARNARD ONCE ESTIMATED THAT THE LINCOLN statues earned him a $260,000 profit. Nevertheless, the Bernheim Lincoln was to be Barnard's last heroic bronze; henceforth, debilitating illness was to restrict his activity to the modeling of clay forms he hoped technicians would transfer, under his direction, into flawless, smoothly dressed marble. This marble finishing would also require enormous financial outlays from sympathetic donors, who were in extremely short supply. It is true that in the 1920s there was a national trend away from the routine fine-art casting of large bronzes to statuary made in a variety of other materials; not until the 1970s was the former popularity of bronze statuary close to being restored. Even so, Barnard's final embrace of a glossy, hard-edge, neoclassical relief in place of the expressive potential of bronze says something about the emotional price he paid for his encounter with the "living wax" of the Lincoln. The pathetic human creatures that populated Barnard's *Rainbow Arch,* a one-hundred-foot-high apotheosis to the dead and surviving victims of World War I that occupied the artist throughout the 1930s, closely resembled the armor-plated performers of his Harrisburg, Pennsylvania, tableaux that were completed in a much earlier day. It is to be recalled that in chapter 3, when Barnard was discussing the spiritual power that had guided his work on the Lincoln, he disparagingly categorized all his work made before this statue as "academic." In 1935, when his third and final retrospective exhibition was held at New York's Grand Central Galleries, the official view was that his career had developed out of the classical tradition, then swerved sharply to an "essential realism" represented by the Lincoln statues, and finally had soared into the heights of religious mysticism, from which the artist would probably not return. What characterized this mysticism more than the actual works themselves was his compulsive urge to converse about what he had made or hoped to make; his need to deliver the endless sermon, to summon the the perfect poetic metaphor. An *Art News* critic observed, however, that "in spite of this [latter] preoccupation with the destiny of man, Barnard is likely to be remembered by posterity principally for his representation of Lincoln, the Emancipator."[1]

In chapter 5, I alluded to the settlement reached in 1925 between Barnard, John D. Rockefeller Jr., and the Metropolitan Museum of Art, which brought the first Cloisters (the building and its collection) under the museum's control. It was also in 1925 that Barnard began assembling a new collection of medieval antiques, hoping to sell it to the Museum, and he remained hopeful that with Rockefeller's assistance his dream of establishing a giant national peace memorial on Washington Heights, the northern fringe of Manhattan, might yet be realized. Yet, Rockefeller's desire to distance himself and the museum from Barnard's influence became increasingly apparent in the late 1920's. The final break occurred in 1930, when the patron offered his northern Manhattan acreage to the City of New York for what eventually became Fort Tryon Park, and when Rockefeller declared his intention to move the Cloisters collection out of the old Barnard monastery into a new Cloisters—completed in 1936—which he was to finance and donate to the museum. Not only did this decision put a sudden end to the war memorial and place an eventual death sentence on Barnard's old brick structure, it also meant that the sculptor would have to vacate a studio he had continued to use on the former Billings estate at Rockefeller's pleasure. When the first section of the new Cloisters building was completed, Barnard began installing his second medieval collection in the monastery, and preparing it for its reopening as "L'Abbaye," or "The Monastery." This was to occur in October 1937.[2]

During the mid-1930s, when Barnard began giving his full attention to the *Rainbow Arch,* Edna Barnard and daughter Vivia, as well as a second daughter, Mrs. Barbara MacGregor, lived in Waterford, Connecticut. Son Monroe, who was twice married in the early 1930s, continued to reside with, or near, his father in New York City. George Grey Barnard died at New York's Harkness Pavillion on 24 April 1938 after suffering two heart attacks. Services were conducted at the Abbey just two weeks prior to the official opening of the new Cloisters Museum. Burial was in the Harrisburg, Pennsylvania, Cemetery, close by the Capitol Building and its groups. As details of the sculptor's will were released to daily papers, it became evident that the *Rainbow Arch,* which stood as a monument to the suffering of others, would inflict considerable suffering upon Barnard's survivors. It was disclosed that before his death Barnard had heavily borrowed against the remaining portion of the estate in order to further his collecting, and to meet expenses for the *Arch.* Furthermore, the will stipulated that executors Monroe Barnard and Counsellor Richard Steel were to draw upon what assets remained in order to see the *Rainbow Arch* through to completion. Even though the sculptor attempted to line up civic subscribers, such as the Gold Star Mothers of America, no source, most especially the estate itself, was capable of meeting the estimated five hundred thousand dollars for the supply and cutting of marble, or for funding other considerable real estate and installation expenses. In December 1938 the *Rainbow Arch* model was being dismantled.[3]

In early 1945 the Philadelphia Museum of Art acquired through public auction a major part of Barnard's second collection of medieval antiquities and twenty years later gained possession of the largest single collection of Barnard's personal papers for its library archives. Several years before his death, Barnard decided to donate plaster studio models, including nude studies, to Kankakee Illinois Central School. It was not without controversy that these plasters were received and finally displayed. After having been placed in storage in the late 1940s and '50s, the pieces were moved to the Historical and Arts Building. In 1992 the Kankakee County Historical Society constructed a new wing to house the plasters as well as several marble works. In 1996 Anthony Barnard, grandson of the sculptor, consigned three marble Lincoln heads to Kankakee's Barnard wing on an indefinite loan.

Notes

Introduction

1. J. Seward Johnson sculpted a Lincoln statue for Gettysburg, Pennsylvania, in 1990. See *New York Times,* 23 November 1990.

2. James E. Young, "The Counter-Monument: Memory Against Itself in Germany Today," in W. J. T. Mitchell, ed., *Art and the Public Sphere* (Chicago: University of Chicago Press, 1992), 49–78. Walter Lippmann, *A Preface to Politics* (New York: Mitchell Kinnerley, 1914), 317.

3. F. Luristan Bullard, *Lincoln in Marble and Bronze* (New Brunswick, N.J.: Rutgers University Press, 1952); Donald C. Durman, *He Belongs to the Ages* (Ann Arbor: University of Michigan Press, 1951); Lincoln National Life Foundation, *Heroic Lincoln Statues in Bronze* (Fort Wayne, Ind., 1957); Harriet F. Senie, *Contemporary Public Sculpture: Tradition, Transformation and Controversy* (New York: Oxford University Press, 1992); and Erika Doss, *Spirit Poles and Flying Pigs: Public Art in American Communities* (Washington, D.C.: Smithsonian Institution Press, 1995).

4. Rosalind Krauss, "Sculpture in the Expanded Field," in Hal Foster, ed., *The Anti-Aesthetic* (Port Townsend, Wash.: Bay Press, 1983), 35. Marvin Trachtenberg, *The Statue of Liberty* (London: Penguin, 1976), 15.

5. See, for example, Richard P. Wunder, *Hiram Powers, Vermont Sculptor, 1805–1873,* 2 vols. (Newark: University of Delaware Press, 1991); Betsy Fahlman, *Spirit of the South: The Sculpture of Alexander Galt, 1827–1863* (Williamsburg, Va.: Joseph and Margaret Muscarelle Museum of Art, 1992); John H. Dryfhout, *The Work of Augustus Saint-Gaudens* (Hanover, N.H.: University Press of New England, 1982); Lewis I. Sharp, *John Quincy Adams Ward: Dean of American Sculpture* (Newark: University of Delaware Press, 1985); Millard F. Rogers, Jr., *Randolph Rogers, American Sculptor in Rome* (Amherst: University of Massachusetts Press, 1971); David H. Wallace, *John Rogers, the People's Sculptor* (Middletown, Conn.: Wesleyan University Press, 1967); James M. Dennis, *Karl Bitter: Architectural Sculptor, 1867–1915* (Madison: University of Wisconsin Press, 1967); Hudson River Museum, *The Sculpture of Isidore Konti* (New York: Hudson River Museum, 1975); Michael Richman, *Daniel Chester French: An American Sculptor* (New York: Metropolitan Museum of Art, 1976). Truman H. Bartlett, *The Art Life of William Rimmer* (1890; reprint, New York: Kennedy Graphics, Inc., 1970); Henry James, *William Wetmore Story and His Friends,* 2 vols. (Boston: Houghton, Mifflin, 1903); and Lorado Taft, *The History of American Sculpture* (New York: MacMillan, 1903). Wayne Craven, *Sculpture in America* (1968; rev. ed., Newark: University of Delaware Press, 1984). Daniel Robbins, "Statues to Sculpture: From the Nineties to the Thirties," in Whitney Museum of American Art, *200 Years of American Sculpture* (New York: David H. Godine and Whitney Museum of American Art, 1976), 114–59; George Gurney, *Sculpture and the Federal Triangle* (Washington, D.C.: Smithsonian Institution Press, 1985); Timothy J. Garvey, *Public Sculptor: Lorado Taft and the Beautification of Chicago* (Champaign: University of Illinois Press, 1988); and Michele H. Bogart, *Public Sculpture and the Civic Ideal in New York City, 1890–1930* (Chicago: University of Chicago Press, 1989). Vivien Fryd, *Art and Empire* (New Haven: Yale University Press, 1992).

6. Charles Seymour Jr., *Michelangelo's David: A Search for Identity* (New York: W. W. Norton, 1967); Marvin Trachtenberg, *The Statue of Liberty* (London: Penguin, 1976); Albert E. Elsen, *Rodin's Thinker and the Dilemmas of Modern Public Sculpture* (New Haven: Yale University Press, 1985) and idem, *The Gates of Hell by Auguste Rodin* (Stanford: Stanford University Press, 1985). Harold E. Dickson, "George Grey Barnard's Controversial Lincoln," *Art Journal* 27, no. 1 (fall 1967): 8–15; 19; 23.

7. See Rosalie Goldstein, ed., *Controversial Public Art From Rodin to di Suvero* (Milwaukee, Wisc.: Milwaukee Art Museum, 1984). In an attempt to deal with the eleven projects that have been recently approved for or are presently underway on the National Mall, Congress in 1986 merged the Federal Commission of Fine Arts with the National Planning Commission and the office of the Secretary of the Department of Interior. These new monuments include the World War II Memorial, Korean War Veterans Memorial, Franklin Delano Roosevelt Memorial Park, Vietnam Women's Memorial, Women in Military Service for America Memorial, Black Revolutionary War Patriots Memorial, African Americans Who Served with the Union Army Memorial, Memorial to Japanese American Patriots, National Peace Garden, George Mason Memorial, and Thomas Paine Memorial. Competing designers engaged one another in court during the planning stages of the Korean War memorial. See Michael Hedges, "National Mall: How Many Monuments are too Many in Washington, D.C., Park?," Scripps Howard News Service, 26 May 1996; *New York Times,* 5 July 1987; 15 and 19 December 1990; 19 January 1991; 15 June 1992.

Chapter 1: The Tafts and Their Lincolns

1. Cincinnati *Times-Star,* 31 March 1917; Cincinnati *Enquirer,* 31 March 1917. The program was reprinted with additions in *Barnard's Statue of Lincoln* (Cincinnati, Ohio: Stewart and Kidd, 1917).

2. The standing bronze figure of Garfield was sculpted in 1885 by Charles H. Niehaus. Erected in Piatt Park, it was financed by public subscription. Louis Rebisso's bronze equestrian

of Harrison, completed 1896, is also in Piatt Park. The *Tyler Davidson Fountain* was commissioned by Henry Probasco in memory of his Cincinnati business partner. Cast under the direction of Ferdinand von Miller at the Royal Bronze Foundry, Munich, the fountain was designed by August von Kreling. It was unveiled in October 1871.

3. Marvin Trachtenberg, *Statue of Liberty* (New York: Penguin, 1976), 15. James T. McCleary, "A Bill for Funding a Monument to Commodore John Barry," in U.S. Congress, *House of Representatives,* 59th Cong., 1st Sess., 1906, HR 355, p. 1802. Alphonso Taft to Delia Torrey, 1 February 1857, William Howard Taft Papers, Library of Congress, Washington, D.C., hereafter TP. The Tafts attended Emerson's lecture series on "Beauty" at the Cincinnati Unitarian Church in January of 1857. Alphonso Taft to William Howard Taft, 1 August 1869 and 28 April 1883, TP.

4. The open competition procedure for selecting sculptors was especially subject to abuse. In his version of the Harrison statue affair (in Joseph Gutmann and Stanley F. Chyet, eds., *Moses Jacob Ezekiel: Memoires from the Baths of Diocletian,* [Detroit, Mich.: Wayne State University, 1975], 375, 376), Ezekiel revealed that the Ohio governor had granted prominent Cincinnati lawyer and Civil War veteran Maj. Frank J. Jones a free hand in choosing whomever he wished to sculpt the Harrison statue. Even though he was determined to throw the commission to his long-time friend Louis Rebisso, Jones nevertheless convened a large committee of civic leaders for a national judging of models. After secret balloting determined a vast majority wanted Ezekiel, Jones disbanded the committee and reappointed another in its place that consisted primarily of himself and his former Civil War commander Gen. Andrew Hickenlooper. Ezekiel was not surprised when this new jury unanimously approved Rebisso's model in 1892. After a friend of Ezekiel sought redress in the courts, a judge exonerated Jones on the basis of his carte blanche status. A similar hoax was at the same moment being perpetrated on the national level in connection with the competitive judging for the Gen. William T. Sherman monument for the Washington, D.C. mall. See "Art Judges Disgusted," *New York Times,* 31 May 1896, 11.

5. Daniel J. Ryan, "Lincoln and Ohio," *Ohio Archealogical and Historical Society Publications,* 32, no. 1 (January 1923): 14–15; 17–21; 134–45.

6. Ibid., 69–101. Loyd D. Easton, *Hegel's First American Followers* (Athens: Ohio University Press, 1966), 128–50.

7. Ishbell Ross, *An American Family: The Tafts 1678–1964* (Cleveland, Ohio: World Publishing Co., 1964). Lewis A. Leonard, *Life of Alphonso Taft* (New York: Hawkes Publishing Co.[1920]), 133–41. Ross, 22–25 and Easton, *passim.* Louisa Taft to Delia Torrey, 2 January 1861, TP. AT to Daniel Potter, 2 January 1861; to Aaron Perry, 3 January 1861; to William Cutter, 12 May 1862 and 6 August 1862; to Ben F. Wade, 19 May 1862; Louise Taft to Delia Torrey, 9 March 1862 and 5 October 1862; William Cutter to Alphonso Taft, 18 May 1862, TP.

8. Alphonso Taft to Delia Torrey, June 1862. Louisa Taft to Anna D. Torrey, 18 April 1865, TP.

9. Thomas Ball, *My Threescore Years and Ten* (Boston: Robert Brothers, 1892), 252–53, 281–85; *Washington Evening Post,* 15 April 1876.

10. *Barnard's Statue of Lincoln,* 62.

11. Edna Monroe, "Between the Lines," ms., 171–77, George Grey Barnard Papers, The Cloisters Museum, New York. *Cincinnati Post,* 29 March 1917.

12. Ibid.

13. *Cincinnati Post,* 31 March 1917. Ibid. *Barnard's Statue of Lincoln,* 15–17. Edwin Markham, "Its a Statue for All America," *Cincinnati Times-Star,* 17 November 1917, 1. Ibid.

14. Ms., "Abraham Lincoln" file, George Grey Barnard Papers, Philadelphia Museum of Art and microfilm, Archives of American Art, Washington, D.C. *Barnard's Statue of Lincoln,* 34–35, 57–58.

15. David H. Burton, *The Learned Presidency* (Rutherford, N.J.: Fairleigh Dickinson Press, 1988), 91–98.

16. Ken Hechler, *Insurgency: Personalities and Politics of the Taft Era* (New York: Russell and Russell, 1964). For William Howard Taft's personal perspective on the issue, see William Taft, (hereafter WHT) to Charles P. Taft, 10 September 1910, TP.

17. F. Lauriston Bullard, *Lincoln in Marble and Bronze* (New Brunswick, N.J.: Rutgers University Press, 1952).

18. *New York Times,* 13 February 1909 and 30 May 1911. Roosevelt's views in this regard were most fully defined in the Osawatomie, Kansas address of 31 August 1910. See Theodore Roosevelt, *The Letters of Theodore Roosevelt,* Etting E. Morison, ed., (Cambridge: Harvard University Press, 1954), 7: 108, 113, 122, 123, 797.

19. John S. Goff, *Robert Todd Lincoln: A Man In His Own Right* (Norman: University of Oklahoma Press, 1969). *New York Times,* 29 April 1912; 30 March 1912; and 8 May 1912. Judd Stewart, "Abraham Lincoln on Present-Day Problems and Abraham Lincoln As Presented by Theodore Roosevelt" (Columbus, Ohio: by the author, 1912).

20. *New York Times,* 10 November 1911. Ibid.

21. See Paolo E. Coletta, *The Presidency of William Howard Taft* (Lawrence: University Press of Kansas, 1973) wherein no mention is made of the Commission of Fine Arts or the Lincoln Memorial commission. Of Taft's cultural perspective the author notes (p. 2), "He liked music and enjoyed playing cards but had no interest in art." Edward F. Conckling, *The Lincoln Memorial* (Washington, D.C.: Government Printing Office, 1927), 83–84.

22. Conckling, *The Lincoln Memorial,* 83–84.

23. Ibid. Charles Moore, *Daniel Burnham: Architect Planner of Cities,* 2 vols. (Boston: Houghton Mifflin, 1921), 2: 16–22, 137–233, and John W. Reps, *Monumental Washington* (Princeton: Princeton University Press, 1967), 84–96; 104–7; 136. Moore, II, 137. Ibid., 147, 157, 168. Secretary of the Senate Park Commission and long-time CFA member, Moore described Burnham's approach to planning thusly: "[While he designed] the fleeting, the transitory, the ephemeral, the self-assertive, the struggle for originality, all seemed to drop out of mind, leaving a desire to discover and use in the work of a new nation those forms which have satisfied age after age."

24. Charles McKim to George Wetmore, 29 March 1902, Charles Moore Papers, Library of Congress. McKim gave Wetmore sketches of the proposed statue. He calculated Saint-Gaudens's fee at $250,000. Daniel Burnham to WHT, 19 May 1910, TP.

25. When serving as secretary of war, Taft also held jurisdiction over federal buildings and grounds. Thus, with the Senate representative to the Committees on the Library, he represented the president at meetings of the Senate Park Commission. In 1904 Taft commissioned Burnham to supply city plans for Manila and Baguio, the Philippines.

26. U.S., Congress, Senate. *Commission of Fine Arts,* 62d Cong., 3d Sess., 1912, S. Doc. 690, 9, 10, 20. Of the approximate fifteen statue and monument committees Taft chaired during his tenure as secretary of war, negotiations surrounding ongoing projects for the Ulysses S. Grant and Philip H. Sheridan monuments proved to be especially difficult to administer.

27. French accepted the appointment in January 1915. Daniel Chester French to WHT, 11 January 1915, Daniel Chester French Papers, Library of Congress, hereafter FP. U.S., Congress. Senate, *Lincoln Memorial Commission Report,* 62d Cong., 3d Sess., 1912, S. Doc. 965, 13. Ibid., plate 6. Henry Bacon to Franklin W. Hooper, 15 February and 23 May 1913, FP. See also French to WHT, 25 February 1914, TP. Michael Richman, *Daniel Chester French: An American Sculptor* (New York: Metropolitan Museum of Art, 1976), 121–29. Bacon to Hooper, 23 May 1913, FP.

28. Daniel Burnham to Frank Millet, 12 April 1912, FP. Charles P. Taft (hereafter CPT) to WHT, 16 December 1910 and WHT to CPT, 19 December 1910, TP. WHT to Bacon, 18 February 1914, TP. Born in Palermo in 1886, Cartaino di Sciarrino Pietro made busts of John Burroughs, Charles Sargent, and Elihu Root. He also began work on a bust of Mrs. William Taft. He died in 1918. Bacon to WHT, 25 February 1914, TP. Richman, 173; Bacon to Hooper, 23 May 1913, FP. Of Mrs. Saint-Gaudens's intervention, Bacon commented, "Saint-Gaudens would turn in his grave." Myron T. Herrick to WHT, 8 October 1913, TP.

29. "Suggestion for Letter," encl. in Herrick to WAT, ibid.

30. Francis F. Byers, "Why a Greek Colonnade to Lincoln? Ask American Architects," *New York Herald,* 26 May 1912; "Lincoln as a Greek God," *Independent,* 8 February 1912, 321–2; "How Lincoln Would Have Laughed," *Independent,* 6 February 1913, 280. For the official AIA response to Borglum's charges, see C. Grant LaFarge, editorial, *Independent,* 27 March 1913, 693–94. John Gutzon Borglum to Sen. George P. Wetmore, 23 February 1912, as printed in the *New York Sun,* 15 January 1912. Ibid. At this time CFA members included three architects, Burnham, Thomas Hastings, and Cass Gilbert; the landscape architect Frederick L. Olmsted Jr.; painter Francis D. Millet; and sculptor Daniel French. Charles Moore served as a lay member. On 5 July 1912, Taft named another architect, Pierce Anderson, to fill Burnham's position.

31. Richman, *Daniel Chester French,* 3–32.

32. French to Raymond A. Beardslee, 23 December 1914, FP. French to William W. Harts, 1 May 1916, FP.

33. Moore, *Daniel Burnham* 2: 133. Archie Butt, *The Intimate Letters of Archie Butt* (Garden City, N.Y.: Doubleday, Doran and Co., 1930) 1: 212.

34. "Lincoln Memorial File," FP. Working models for the statue and pedestal were completed by 12 April 1916. French to William Harts, 12 April 1916, FP. Richman, 178, 179. French ordered Lincoln presidential photographs in quantity. French to Ario B. Cammerer, 22 March 1916; to the Rice Photographic Studio, 30 June 1916, FP., and Richman, 178.

35. Richman, 179. French to Harts, 1 May 1916 and 16 June 1916; French to WHT, 23 May 1916; French to Joseph Blackburn, 30 June 1916, FP. French to Bacon, 16 October 1916 and 2 May 1917; French to Harts, 1 June 1917 and 20 July 1917, FP.

36. French to Charles Moore, 8 August 1917, FP. WHT to Woodrow Wilson, 19 November 1913; WHT to Robert Lincoln, 9 November 1913 and 19 October 1913, TP. U.S., *Cong. Rec.* 64th Cong., 1st Sess., 1916, 103, Pt. 3, 2592–603. Cannon urged that a deficiency appropriation of $594,000 be passed over and above the $2,000,000 ceiling Congress previously established for Memorial construction costs. Lamenting his "tenderfoot days" when he took the minority position on the LMC, Cannon now sought to make amends for his error. The purpose of the deficiency measure was to finance new construction of the steps, landscaping, electrical wiring, bronze ceilings, an eliptical mound, and Jules Guerin's murals.

37. WHT to Helen H. Taft, 23 March 1917, TP. Robert Lincoln to WHT, 22 March 1917, TP. In 1892, a thirty-five thousand dollar commission for a commemorative equestrian statue of Gen. Philip H. Sheridan for Washington, D.C., to be jointly administered and funded by the Society of the Army of the Cumberland and the War Department, was awarded to John Quincy Adams Ward, patriarch of the National Sculpture Society. After delays pushed the project six years beyond the original 1898 deadline and prompted the society to pass a resolution that would rescind its contract, Ward continued to work on a definitive model through 1905. Hoping to clarify the federal government's procedural obligation, Secretary of War Taft solicited the views of Mrs. Sheridan, her son, and officers who had served under the general, concerning Ward's most recent model. Their negative comments induced Taft to personally ask Ward to resign the commission. He agreed, but not before filing a law suit against the Society of the Army of the Cumberland. In an action many assumed to have been personally directed by President Roosevelt, Taft, without procedural authority and even before a model had been ordered, awarded the contract to Gutzon Borglum on 31 July 1907. Ward's revised statue was finally accepted by the State of New York for placement in Albany, the general's hometown. See WHT to HHT, 27 March 1917, TP and Lewis I. Sharp, *John Quincy Adams Ward: Dean of American Sculpture* (Newark: University of Delaware Press, 1985), 84–87.

38. WHT to RL, 3 April 1917, TP.

39. *Cincinnati Commercial-Tribune,* 1 April 1917.

Chapter 2: The Charles Tafts in Art

1. The sittings are discussed in CPT to WHT, 8 December 1902; 20 December 1902; 26 December 1902, TP. Unless otherwise indicated all Taft correspondence is with TP.

2. Leonard, *Life of Alphonso Taft,* 195–209. Alphonso Taft to Peter Taft, 16 October 1872.

3. Louise Taft to Delia Torrey, 23 March 1874.

4. Theodore H. Price, "A 100,000-Acre Business," *World's Work,* January 1913, 271–5. Works Project Administration, *Texas, A Guide to the Lone Star State* (New York: Hastings House, 1940), 655–56.

5. For an assessment of the sociopolitical environment of the city during this period, see Zane L. Miller, *Boss Cox's Cincinnati: Urban Politics in the Progressive Era* (New York: Oxford University Press, 1968). The Tafts contributed to the Cincinnati Urban Bethel, an ecumenical settlement house, which according to Miller, sought to "mediate separateness" through "scientific and progressive philanthropy."

6. Richard C. Cote, "The Baum-Taft House: An Architectural History," in Edward J. Sullivan, ed., *The Taft Museum: The History of the Collections and the Baum-Taft House* (New York: Hudson Hills Press, 1995), 41–59; Joseph D. Ketner, "The Robert S. Duncanson Murals at the Taft Museum," *The Taft Museum,* 60–71; Henry A. Ford and Kate B. Ford, *History of Cincinnati, Ohio* (Cleveland, Ohio: L. A. Williams and Company, 1881), 235–45; Charles List, *Cincinnati in 1841: Its Early Annals and Future Prospects* (Cincinnati, Ohio: by the author, 1841), 133–42. See also Robert C. Vitz, *The Queen and the Arts* Cultural Life in Nineteenth-Century Cincinnati (Kent, Ohio: Kent State University Press, 1989), 22–33. Abby S. Schwartz, "Nicholas Longworth: Art Patron of Cincinnati," *Queen City Heritage* 46 (spring 1988): 17–32; Denny Young, "The Longworths: Three Generations of Art Patronage in Cincinnati," in Kenneth R. Trapp, ed., *Celebrate Cincinnati Art* (Cincinnati, Ohio: Cincinnati Art Museum, 1982), 29–47.

7. Schwartz, "Nicholas Longworth," 20–32.

8. *Cincinnati Enquirer,* 5, 6, and 7 October 1871. For a biographical account of Probasco, see *New York Times,* 30 October 1902. The story of the building of the fountain is summarized in *Cincinnati Landmarks: A Bicentennial Exhibition* (Cincinnati, Ohio, CAM. 1976), 41–45. *Cincinnati Enquirer,* 7 October 1871.

9. Roger B. Stein, "Artifact as Ideology," in Metropolitan Museum of Art, *In Pursuit of Beauty: Americans and the Aesthetic Movement* (New York: Rizzoli, 1986), 23–45.

10. Louise Taft was a central figure in early fund-raisers of the WAMA. Carol Macht, "Introduction," in *The Ladies, God Bless 'Em* (Cincinnati Art Museum, Ohio: 1976), 8. The Tafts also proved generous benefactors of the Cincinnati Symphony Association (Vitz, *The Queen and the Arts,* 126–30). Endowed by Longworth's son, Joseph, the Academy grew out of the Cincinnati School of Art and Design established at the University of Cincinnati. See "Western Art Movement," *Century Illustrated Monthly Magazine,* August 1886, 578–80. *The Ladies, God Bless 'Em,* 17. Conway lectured on the South Kensington Museum and

School on 14 October 1880. Ruth K. Meyer, "An Introduction to the Art Collection of Charles Phelps and Anna Sinton Taft," in Sullivan, *The Taft Museum,* 21; idem, "The Taft Collection: The First Ten Years of Its Development," *Queen City Heritage* 46 (spring 1988): 7–8.

11. "Western Art Movement," 579. Ibid., 12. Rookwood exhibits won a gold medal at the Universal Exposition, Paris, 1889 and the Grand Prix for the American Department of Varied Industries, Universal Exposition, Paris, 1900. Kirsten H. Keen, "Rookwood Pottery at the Turn of the Century: Continuity and Change," in *Celebrate Cincinnati Art,* 71–87; and Herbert Peck, *The Book of Rookwood Pottery* (New York: Crown, 1968), 66–68. With Taylor as president and treasurer, Rookwood was incorporated in 1890. Peck, 58. Charles Taft served on the building committee for the second Hotel Sinton, the interior of which was trimmed with Rookwood-designed panels. *Cincinnati Landmarks,* 48–50.

13. Aline Saarinen, *The Proud Possessors* (New York: Vintage Books, 1968), 56–94; 103–17. Ibid., 112.

14. Meyer, "An Introduction to the Art Collection," 22–30. See, for example, CPT to WHT, 8 December 1902; 18 April 1903; 25 February 1904 and 19 March 1904. William lamented that Cincinnati's manufacturers were "lazy about smoke." WHT to CPT, 2 May 1905.

15. Edward J. Sullivan, "Introduction to the Collection of European and American Paintings in the Taft Museum," and Catalogue, in idem, *The Taft Museum* (New York: Hudson Hills Press, 1995) 123–30; 131–311; Meyer, "An Introduction"; Cf. Katherine Hanna, *The Taft Museum Catalogue* (Cincinnati, Ohio: by the author [ca. 1956]); *New York Times,* 8 August 1909; Maurice W. Brockwell, *A Catalogue of Paintings in the Collection of Mr. and Mrs. Charles P. Taft at Cincinnati, Ohio* (New York, 1920).

16. Visiting the collection in 1909, Joseph Duveen declared it the finest in America. Joseph Duveen to CPT, 15 February 1909, Charles Taft Papers, Archives, The Taft Museum; see also William Bode, "Old Art in the United States," *New York Times,* 31 December 1911, sec. 5.1, "Exhibition in New York of Paintings From the Collection of Mr. and Mrs. Charles P. Taft," *Burlington Magazine* 16 (February 1910): 363, 366, 368; *New York Times,* 6 and 21 November 1909; Elizabeth L. Cary, "Some Masters of Portraiture," *Putnam's Magazine,* February 1910, 528; Arthur Hoeber, "Some Pictures from the Collection of Mr. and Mrs. Charles P. Taft," *International Studio* 39, no. 155 (January 1910): lxxi–lxxiv. *New York Times,* 8 August 1909.

17. "Exhibition in New York of Paintings," 368.

18. Brockwell, 72 81. Ibid., 81. Ibid., xv. Frantz Funck-Brentano considered the Taft Millet to be the best example of that painter's work. CPT to WHT, 13 February 1905.

19. CPT to WHT, 26 December 1902; cf., CPT to WHT, 11 February 1903, and 8 December 1902. Whitlaw Reid to Helen H. Taft, Howard Taft, 20 September 1910.

20. *Cincinnati Enquirer,* 1 January 1909; CPT to WHT, 2 January 1909; WHT to CPT, 5 January 1909. *New York Times,* 9 January 1909. CPT to WHT, 29 March 1909.

21. WHT to Mrs. William Howard Taft, 24 September 1910. Archie Butt to Clara Butt, 24 August 1909 in Butt, *The Intimate Letters,* 1: 192. Butt offers that Taft "echoed his [own] thoughts" about Frick using his influence with Secretary of State Philander Knox to "buy" his way into society in the same manner he acquired pictures from dealers.

22. *New York Times,* 6 and 21 August 1909. President Taft signed the tariff bill on 6 August, two days before Charles's purchase was announced. The effect of the tariff on art collecting is discussed at length in "$250,000 for Two Pictures," *New York Times,* 31 December 1911, sec. 3 and 4, 1.

23. CPT to WHT, 15 March 1904. It is tempting to believe Taft was referring to George Grey Barnard's *Solitude (Adam and Eve),* one of several small variations on the *Urn of Life* (ca. 1895–98, and 1918, Carnegie Museum of Art) that Barnard produced after 1900 and that came into the Taft collection at an unknown date (*The Taft Museum* #1931.373). But Diana Strazdes, in "American Paintings and Sculpture," (in Edward Sullivan, ed., *The Taft Museum Catalog,* 310–11) assigns the marble to a date of ca. 1906, and estimates that it passed directly from the artist to Charles Taft in ca. 1917. Barnard's *Urn of Life,* which remained unfinished, was intended to contain the ashes of Anton Seidl, conductor of the New York Metropolitan Opera and former assistant to composer Richard Wagner.

24. Henry Probasco to Mrs. A. Howard Hinckle, 16 March 1909, Archives, Cincinnati Historical Society. *Cincinnati Commercial Tribune,* 2 and 3 June 1909. Henry Probasco to John Gutzon Borglum, 1 September 1909. Unless otherwise indicated, all Gutzon Borglum correspondence cited in this chapter is from the John Gutzon Borglum Papers, Library of Congress, Washington, D.C., hereafter GBP.

25. Charles T. Greve, *Centennial History of Cincinnati and Representative Citizens* (Chicago: Biographical Publishing Co., 1904), 2: 190–92; *Cincinnati Commercial Tribune,* 1 July 1922. WHT to CPT, 10 November 1906. During Taft's presidential campaign, Probasco offered to help restore the candidate's standing with Black voters in the wake of the Brownsville, Texas, massacre in exchange for his appointment to state district attorney. Having already promised the post to Henry Williams, Taft curtly refused Probasco. HP to WHT, 10 August 1908; 29 August 1908; 14 September 1908; WHT to HP [1908] and 28 April 1909.

26. Warren G. Partridge, *The Life of Frederick H. Alms* (Cincinnati, Ohio: Jennings and Graham, 1904).

27. *Cincinnati Enquirer,* 11 February and 24 December 1902.

28. A. Mervyn Davies, *Solon H. Borglum: A Man Who Stands Alone* (Chester, Conn.: Pequot Press, 1974), 134–37. John Gutzon Borglum to Henry Probasco, 29 July 1909. GB to HP, 7 September 1909 and GB to Elihu Root, 12 October 1909.

29. HP to GB, 2 August 1909. GB to HP, 7 September 1909.

30. Lathrop Pack to GB, 11 September 1909; GB to Lathrop Pack, 9 September 1909.

31. Like Roosevelt, Root highly commended Borglum's bust of Lincoln. Elihu Root to CPT, 16 October 1909 and Auguste Rodin to HP, 16 October 1909; Frank Hitchcock to HP, 9 December 1909, GBP. Woodrow Wilson to HP, 20 December 1909, as quoted in Howard Shaff and Aubray K. Shaff, *Six Wars at a Time* (Darien, Conn.: Permelia Publications, 1985), 121, 122. Hulbert Taft to GBP, 28 September 1909, GB; and HP to GB, 10 January 1909. A sympathetic feature on Borglum's career by Paul K. M. Thomas was reprinted in the *Cincinnati Times-Star,* 2 January 1909.

32. Robert H. Davis to George R. Chester, 15 January 1910, GBP. HP to GB, 25 March 1910. HP to GB, 16 May 1910. GB to HP, 24 March 1910.

33. GB to HP, 19 March 1910.

34. GB to HP, 24 March 1910. GB to HP, 3 May 1910. See chapter 1, n. 36.

35. GB to HP, 3 May 1910. *New York Times,* 12 August 1909. GB to [Richard Tyler], 4 May 1910. Journalists friendly to Borglum were alerted to his plight by Probasco. Robert H. Davis, fiction editor for *Muncey's Magazine* and George R. Chester, a freelance humorist who authored the "Get Rich Quick Wallingford" sketches for *McClure's* magazine in 1908, exchanged mirthful notes while scheming to plant a "corking good press agent story" about Barnard in a Cincinnati newspaper. Chester assured Davis that "any scandal you dig up about Barnborn [sic] and transmit it to Probasco will be thankfully received." They presumed Charles Taft was attempting to collect an alleged twenty-five thousand dollars he had loaned Barnard. See George R. Chester to Richard H. Davis, 11 April 1910, GBP; GB to HP, 3 June 1910. *Cincinnati Post,* 8 December 1910. *New York Evening Journal,* 21 December 1910. *Cincinnati Times-Star,* 17 December 1910.

36. Harold Dickson, "George Grey Barnard's Controversial Lincoln," *Art Journal* 27 (fall 1967): 8.

37. The events and interviews are summarized in *Cincinnati Times-Star,* 17 December 1910; *Cincinnati Enquirer,* 18 December 1910; and *New York Times,* 17 and 19 December 1910. CPT to WHT, 9 December 1910.

38. WHT to CPT, 18 December 1910.

39. *New York Times,* 20 December 1910. GB to WHT, 21 December 1910 and GB to CPT, 21 December 1910, GBP.

40. GB to HP, 16 January 1911. GB to HP, 27 December 1910. HP to GB, 29 December 1910.

Chapter 3: The Genius of George Grey Barnard

1. Lucien Rule, *Forerunners of Lincoln in the Ohio Valley* (Louisville, Ky.: Brandt and Fowles, 1927), 1–33.

2. Rule, 1–49; *Memories of the Ohio Valley* (Madison, Wisc.: Federal Publishing Co., 1905), 1: 202–3. Obituaries for Martha and Joseph appear respectively in *Madison Daily Herald,* 1, 2, and 3 December 1919, and 26 April 1926.

3. J. M. Allison, "God-Sent Inspiration Says Sculptor," *Cincinnati Times-Star,* 11 December 1916, 1. The Joseph Barnard mss. in the George Grey Barnard Papers, Archives of American Art, Smithsonian Institution, Washington, D.C., hereafter, GGB, AAA. Rule, 39; Joseph Barnard, "Climbing," ms., n.d., AAA. Joseph Barnard, untitled ms., n.d., AAA.

4. Rule, *Forerunners,* 39.

5. Martha Barnard to George G. Barnard [ca. 1896], George Grey Barnard Papers, Archives, Philadelphia Museum of Art, hereafter GGBP.

6. Ruth Morris, "Project for a Biography of George Grey Barnard," ms., 1941, 3, 6., GGB, AAA. Morris contends Barnard was jealous of his wife, and insisted that she give up her musical career. The artist's son, Monroe G. Barnard, is quoted as saying his father was often "off the deep end." Throughout the remainder of his life, Barnard regularly corresponded with old Kankakee comrades Harry Troup and "Kit" N. G. Halsey, with whom he nostalgically shared recollections of hunting alley cats, swimming, fishing, and exploring nearby "Indian Cave." Such memories left the writer "homesick beyond words." GGB to Harry Troup, 18 July 1919, George Grey Barnard Papers, Kankakee County Historical Society, Kankakee, Illinois. Evan G. Barnard, *A Rider on the Cherokee Strip* (Boston: Houghton Mifflin, 1936), 10. William A. Coffin, "A New American Sculptor," *Century Illustrated Monthly Magazine,* April 1897, 877–82. *Muscatine* [Iowa] *Journal,* 27 November 1899.

7. Charles Caffin, *American Masters of Sculpture* (New York: Doubleday, Page and Co., 1913), 23–25. "Western Art Movement," *Century Magazine,* 587–88. Allison, "God-Sent Inspiration."

8. William J. Clark, Jr., *Great American Sculptures* (Philadphia: Gebbie and Barrie, 1878), 34. Caffin, *American Masters,* 23.

9. *Chicago Evening Post,* 24 April 1897.

10. *Muscatine Journal,* 27 November 1899. Sara Kimbrough, *Drawn From Life: The Story of Four American Artists Whose Friendship and Work Began in Paris During the 1880's* (Oxford: University of Mississippi Press, 1976), 139.

11. Harold Dickson, "Barnard and Norway," *Art Bulletin* 44, no. 1 (March 1962): 55.

12. *New York Daily Tribune,* 13 July 1902; E. T. M. [Ned Moron], *A Man Who Lived For Men* (privately printed, 1896), passim; Bruce Webber, "Robert Frederick Blum and the Clark Family," ms., n.d., National Museum of American Art, Smithsonian Institution, Washington, D.C. For an overview of fin de siècle homoeroticism in art see Bram Dijkstra, *Idols of Perversity* (New York: Oxford University Press, 1986).

13. Viktor Rydberg, *Roman Days,* trans. Alfred Corning Clark (New York: G. P. Putnam's Sons, 1879). Dickson, "Barnard and Norway," 55–57. In about 1887, Barnard took spacious new quarters on Rue Boissonade that connected with a downstairs studio. In his final year in Paris he resided in a garden apartment at 84 Boulevard Garibaldi that also connected with a studio.

14. Maurice Z. Shroder, *Icarus, The Image of the Artist in French Romanticism* (Cambridge, Mass: Harvard University Press, 1961), 8. Of *Sartor Resartus,* Barnard commented, "What a state I was in when I read it!" Regina Armstrong, "The Sculptor of Pan," *Critic,* November 1898, 354. Shroder, 87–89.

15. Dickson, "Barnard and Norway," 56; Alfred Corning Clark, *Lorentz Severin Skougaard* (New York: G.P. Putnam's Sons, 1885), 128 et passim.

16. The motif illustrates early man's struggles with the Serpent of Migaard, whose coils encircled the earth. Clark was familiar with a version of the narrative appearing in Victor Rydberg, *Teutonic Mythology* (London: Norroena Society, 1906) 3: 731, first published as *Undersokningan i germansk mytologi,* between 1886 and 1889.

17. Harold Dickson, "Log of a Masterpiece," *Art Journal* 20, no. 3 (spring 1961): 139–43.

18. S. J. Woolf, "The Stormy Petrel of the Ocean of Art," *New York Times Magazine,* 7 December 1930, 18.

19. At the time of his death, Clark owned five paintings by Bilinska. See "Inventory" (Contents of Alfred Corning Clark residence, #7 West 22nd Street, N.Y.C.), ms., 1896, New York State Historical Association, Cooperstown. Société des Artistes Français, *Salon de 1890,* #219. A pupil of Tony Robert Fleury and Bouguereau, Bilinska specialized in portraits and landscapes. She won a gold medal at the Universal Expositions in Paris, 1889 and in Berlin, 1891.

20. Coffin, "A New American Sculptor," 897. Among more "manly" Victories and combative figures by contemporary artists that probably influenced Barnard's conception are Albert Lanson's *L'age de fer,* Emile Boisseau's *Le Genie du Mal,* and Laurent Margueste's *Perse et Gorgone,* as well as his *Le Centaur Nessus.* Photographs of these works are in GGB, AAA. James M. Saslow, *Ganymede in the Renaissance, Homosexuality in Art and Society* (New Haven: Yale University Press, 1986), 105. Dickson notes Barnard's obvious debt to Michelangelo's Medici tomb figures and also argues Barnard's rendition of Pan derives from the Elizabeth Barrett Browning poem *Musical Instrument* (1860) wherein the god is pictured in a watery setting. However, the author does not allude to the specific sexual undercurrents of the work, nor to the suggestive nature of the Clark-Barnard relationship (Harold E. Dickson, "The Other Orphan," *American Art Journal,* 1, no. 2 [fall 1969]: 110–15). Rydberg, *Roman Days,* 188–208; reference is to the "San Ildefonso Group." Three editions of Symond's *Life of Benvenuto Cellini* appeared in New York and London in 1888; five more releases occurred in 1895. Symond's *Renaissance in Italy* was issued in five volumes in 1887 and 1888, and his illustrated *Life of Michelangelo Buonarroti* was published in 1892. Norman Bryson identifies sexual desire as a means by which artists have overcome their "belatedness" to art and artists of the past. Norman Bryson, *Tradition and Desire* (Cambridge: Cambridge University Press, 1984), 132.

21. Henry D. Allison, *Dublin Days, Old and New* (New York: Exposition Press [1952]), 110.

22. Dickson, "Log of a Masterpiece," 142. George G. Barnard, ms., 20 November 1930, GGBP.

23. Truman Bartlett, "Auguste Rodin, Sculptor," *American Architect and Building News* 25 (1 June 1889): 263. Laura C. Dennis, "A Great American Sculptor," *Review of Reviews,* January 1899, 138.

24. Edna's constancy is made startlingly evident in a letter addressed to her husband eight months following his death. "And, so, my beloved, thank you for this beautiful year and for the years to come—for keeping yourself (in this harried world) so fine and decent and holding fast to the ideals—our ideals that we

both cherish." Edna Monroe to George G. Barnard, 25 December 1938, Barnard Papers, The Cloisters Museum, N.Y.C. Despite this and many similar loving declarations of spiritual accord found in Edna's late letters to George (BP), the two lived separately the final ten years of their marriage—a period in which the sculptor's artistic obsessions intensified and his physical and mental health continued to deteriorate. Percy MacKaye, *Epoch* (New York: Boni and Liveright, 1928), 1: 157–61, 222–25, 252.

25. MacKaye, 1: 157–59; 2: 226 et passim.

26. Ibid., 1: 161, and Edwin O. Grover, *Annals of an Era; Percy MacKaye and the MacKaye Family, 1826–1932* (Hanover: Dartmouth College, 1932), passim.

27. Arvia MacKaye Ege, *The Power of the Impossible: The Life Story of Percy and Marion MacKaye* (Falmouth, Maine: Kennebec River Press, 1992), 151–53. For other contacts between the Barnards and MacKayes, see pp. 109, 134, 166, 192, 276, and 405. The MacKayes were also close friends with their Cornish neighbors Augustus and Augusta Saint-Gaudens. Arvia MacKaye Ege, Percy's daughter and biographer, listed both Saint-Gaudens and Barnard as "particular friends" of the MacKayes, though one was "at the end, the other at the beginning of [Percy's] career." The fact that both were professional sculptors set them apart from the typically literary and theatrical circle in which the MacKayes traveled, but this exception was far overbalanced by their "common concern for a renaissance of art" (149).

28. George G. Barnard to Percy MacKaye, 16 October 1906, as quoted in Grover, 13.

29. Successfully cast on 22 August and measuring 11 feet, 4 inches long by 5 feet, 3 inches wide, *The Great God Pan* was to that moment the largest work to have been sandcast as a single piece by an American foundry. Head-molder Jean Leroy and several assistants labored for eight months to adjust some seventeen hundred individual sand units into the mold. As celebrants looked on and Henry-Bonnard foreman Eugene Veillard waved an American flag, 6,450 pounds of liquid bronze were released into the mold. With heady patriotism, the *Scientific American* crowed: "This casting is by all odds the most difficult piece of work ever attempted in this country, and it is very doubtful if there is a bronze foundry in Europe which could care to risk the casting of such an artistic piece of work in one piece" ("A Phenomenal Piece of Bronze Casting," *Scientific American*, 10 September 1898, 165). See also Charles De Kay, "Barnard's Pan for Central Park," *Art Interchange*, clipping, GGBP, AAA; "Casting of George Grey Barnard's Colossal Figure of Pan," *Monumental News*, 1 October 1898, 568, 569; Regina Armstrong, "The Sculptor of Pan," 354–56. The statue had been offered by the Clark estate to the city two years previously as a fountain motif for Central Park, with expenses for casting and installation to be paid by the estate. However, squeamish city officials blocked this plan and *Pan* was eventually placed (in 1907) in a fountain on the campus of Columbia University. See Harold E. Dickson, "The Other Orphan," *American Journal*, 1 (fall 1969): 108–18. Dickson, "Log of a Masterpiece," 143. The *Two Natures* was accepted by the Metropolitan Museum on 2 December 1896, but not displayed until a new wing was opened ten years later. In 1902 Barnard had completed work on *Maidenhood, The Wooden Clock,* a second version of *Brotherly Love, The Urn of Life, The Hewer,* and *Transportation,* the Henry B. Plant Memorial Fountain for a Tampa hotel. This fountain design derived from the Electric Tower sculpture he produced the previous year for the Buffalo Pan-American Exposition. A bronze duplicate of *The Hewer* was exhibited at the St. Louis World's Fair in 1904 before being presented by its donors to the city of Cairo, Illinois, in honor of Capt. William P. Halliday. See text and illustrations for "Americans of To-morrow—George Grey Barnard, Sculptor," *Harper's Weekly*, 23 August 1902, 1133–34, 1155. The marble version of *The Hewer* was eventually purchased by John D. Rockefeller Sr. for his estate at Tarrytown, New York. For background information on *The Hewer*, see Dickson, "Barnard's Sculptures for the

Pennsylvania Capitol," *Art Quarterly* 22, no. 3 (summer 1959): 128. In 1900 and 1901 Barnard gave weekly critiques to Art Students League evening school students. Epstein remembered a typical session as follows: "He would look at the study and give you a penetrating glance (he had a cast in his eye), and then start his talk, in which he would usually lose himself for the rest of the evening. The students would gather round him, and as he was a man of great earnestness, he was very impressive. Barnard was ascetic in his habits, and deplored the possibility his students drank or were at all Bohemian . . ." Jacob Epstein, *Epstein, An Autobiography* (London: Vista Books, 1963), 10.

30. Anthony E. Grimaldi, "Indiana Soldiers' and Sailors' Monument and Its Dedication: A Study of a Nineteenth Century American Monument and Its Allied Arts of Pageantry" Ph.D. diss. Ohio University, 1982. *Chicago Evening Post,* 24 April 1897. On 25 July 1894, Barnard was offered a contract to sculpt "Religion" and "Michelangelo" for the Reading Room with a completion deadline set for October 1895. After he refused the contract, the commission was given to Theodore Bauer and Paul Bartlett. Lewis I. Sharp, *John Quincy Adams Ward, Dean of American Sculpture,* 249–50. Michele H. Bogart, *Public Sculpture and the Civic Ideal in New York City, 1890–1930,* 177–81. In March 1915 Barnard announced he was suing the firm that cut the marble for his "History" and "The Arts" groups, which occupied the library's north and south pediments, respectively, because of incompetence. The subcontractor, the Donnelly and Ricci Company, immediately filed a countersuit charging that Barnard's plaster molds, which guided their work, were defective to begin with. A *New York Times* editorial upheld Barnard's view. See "$50,000 Damage Suit Over Library Art."

31. As seen through the eyes of the fictional painter Eugene Witla, "there was a world of sculptors, for instance, in which some thirty or forty sculptors had part—but they knew each other slightly, criticized each other severely and retired for the most part into a background of relatives and friends." Theodore Dreiser, *The Genius* (New York: John Lane Co., 1915), 107.

32. Bogart, *Public Sculpture and the Civic Ideal,* 48–52. Barnard applied through Ruckstull for work on the *Dewey Arch.* GGB to Frederick Ruckstull, 22 June 1899, GGBP. Barnard was listed as a member of the NSS in 1895. See Bogart, 331, n. 8.

33. Frederick Ruckstull to GGB, 19 October 1898, GGBP.

34. *New York Times,* 29 January 1898; 11 June 1898; 9 July 1898; 31 July 1898 and *New York Daily Tribune,* 24 May 1898 and 6 June 1898. *Indianapolis News,* 4 October 1898. Rodin's appraisal of Barnard's Paris work is in a summary of quoted citations in GGBP, AAA.

35. John Gutzon Borglum, "Auguste Rodin," *The Artist* 32, January 1902, 194. Daniel Rosenfeld, "Rodin's Carved Sculpture," in Albert E. Elsen, ed., *Rodin Rediscovered* (Washington, D.C.: National Gallery of Art, 1981), 81–201.

36. Isadora Duncan, *My Life* (New York: Boni and Liveright, 1927), 100, 216–18. Duncan's premier performance at the Metropolitan Opera House was attended by MacKaye, William V. Moody, and Barnard, who all sat "spellbound" as if confronted by "some vision out of Beethoven's mind" (Ege, *The Power of the Impossible,* 192). Barnard's rectitude was amply demonstrated during a MacKaye visit with the Barnards in Dublin in July 1907. On this occasion George arranged for Percy to spend the night with him in a separate cabin to prevent him from seeing Edna Barnard in her night gown (Ege, 154).

37. Mary Trombley, "George Grey Barnard—His Statues for the Pennsylvania Capitol," *World's Work,* February 1909, 11256–67; "Barnard's Mighty Sculptures for the Pennsylvania Capitol," *Current Literature,* August 1910, 207–9; Harold Dickson, "Barnard's Sculptures for the Pennsylvania Capitol," 126–47. "Americans of To-morrow—George Grey Barnard, Sculptor," 1155.

38. Dickson, "Barnard's Sculptures for the Pennsylvania Capitol," 126–30.

39. M. S. Young, "George Grey Barnard and the Cloisters,"

Apollo 104 (November 1977): 332–39; J. L. Schrader, "George Grey Barnard: The Cloisters and the Abbaye," *Metropolitan Museum of Art Bulletin* 37, no. 1 (May 1979): 2–53; Harold Dickson, "Origin of The Cloisters," *Art Quarterly* 28, no. 4 (fall 1965): 252–75; William H. Forsyth, "Five Crucial People in the Building of the Cloisters," in Elizabeth C. Parker and Mary B. Shepard, eds., *The Cloisters: Studies in Honor of the Fiftieth Anniversary* (New York: Metropolitan Museum of Art, 1992), 51–62.

40. Schrader, 6. Roger Fry to Sir Purdon Clarke, 16 August 1906 in Denys Sutton, ed., *Letters of Roger Fry* (New York: Random House, 1972), 1: 267–68.

41. Sutton, 22–30; RF to PC, 16 August 1906 (281). Fry also wrote Edward Robinson, the museum's curator of sculpture, about the Burgos patio Barnard hoped to sell. RF to ER, 3 January 1907 (279).

42. *New York Times,* 25 November 1910, and "George Grey Barnard on the Vicissitudes of a Sculptor," *New York Times,* 27 November 1910.

43. This view, expressed by Reverend Henry Bellows, was generally supported by Joseph Choate and the other "men of affairs" who helped found the Metropolitan Museum of Art in 1870. See Calvin Tomkins, *Merchants and Masterpieces* (New York: E. P. Dutton, 1970), 17. GGB to Adolph Ochs, 7 December 1916, GGBP. "George Grey Barnard on the Vicissitudes of a Sculptor."

44. *New York Times,* 16 and 27 March; 3 and 10 April 1910. *Le Siècle,* 3 June 1910.

45. Dickson, "Barnard's Sculptures for the Pennsylvania Capitol," 128. Gov. Edwin J. Stuart to WHT, 13 January 1910, TP. Chandler Hale to Fred W. Carpenter, 17 January 1910, TP.

46. Adrian Buck to Gutzon Borglum, 16 June 1910, GBP. A reporter criticized Barnard for attempting to "marry modern realism with classical conventionalism" and predicted the "austerity and lack of warmth" of the figural groups would make them unpopular. *New York Times,* 1 May 1910. John Gutzon Borglum to HP, 24 June 1910, GBP.

47. Dickson, "Barnard's Sculptures for the Pennsylvania Capitol," 142. Percy MacKaye, "To George Grey Barnard," in Howard Flower and Walter John Coates, *Vases of Verse* (Hartland, Vt.: Solitarian Press, 1931), 38.

Chapter 4: The Modeling of Lincoln

1. Atty. Henry W. Taft, of Strong and Caldwalader, New York, to GGB, 22 May 1911, PMAA. (Unless otherwise indicated mss. references are to the George Grey Barnard Papers, PMAA). Frederick G. Bourne to GGB, 10 August 1917.

2. FGB to GGB, 16 May 1911. Ibid.

3. HWT to GGB, 22 May 1911.

4. Charles D. Hilles to Walbridge Taft, 16 February 1912, TP. Walbridge forwarded a Barnard query about photographs to the White House. Richard Watson Gilder, "Lincoln the Leader," *Century Illustrated Monthly Magazine,* February 1909, 479–507. The *Seated Lincoln,* or *Abraham Lincoln: The Head of State,* for which Saint-Gaudens received one hundred thousand dollars from Chicago magnate John Crerar, was begun in 1897. A studio fire destroyed the first model, but during the artist's final illness his assistant, Henry Hering, completed a second figure, based closely on the original, that measures 9 feet 1 inches. Even though it was not installed in its elaborate architectural setting in Chicago's Grant Park until 1924, both the plasters and the bronze version of the figure were widely exhibited from 1908 to 1915. During the latter year, it was on view at the Panama-Pacific International Exposition, San Francisco. See John H. Dryfhout, *The Work of Augustus Saint-Gaudens* (Hanover: University Press of New England, 1982), 278–79. Newspaper clipping, 4 December 1912. GGBP, PMAA. Newspaper clipping, n.d., GGBP, PMAA.

5. Truman H. Bartlett, "The Physiognomy of Lincoln," *McClure's* Magazine, August 1907, 391–407. Ibid., 407.

6. E. W. Thompson, "Letter to the Editor," *Boston Evening Transcript,* clipping, n.d., GGBP, PMAA. Ibid.

7. William G. Frost to GGB, 13 February 1913. Frost forwarded a copy of the *Berea Quarterly* 16 (June 1913).

8. CPT to GGB, 23 November 1911. The view that Thomas was unusually ambitious and embued with a "restless pioneer spirit," was advanced in Ida Tarbell, *The Early Life of Abraham Lincoln* (New York: S. S. McClure, 1896), 36, 51. CPT to WHT, 30 October 1911, TP.

9. Harold E. Dickson, "George Grey Barnard's Controversial Lincoln," 10. GGB to L. A. Ault, President of the Cincinnati Board of Park Commissioners, 7 April 1912. GGB to Walbridge S. Taft, 29 March 1912. WST to GGB, 27 April 1912; Summary cash statement, CPT to GGB, 10 July 1917.

10. GGB to L. A. Ault, 7 April 1912. Ibid. M. C. Longenecker, Secretary of Cincinnati Board of Park Commissioners, to GGB, 10 May 1912.

11. WST to GGB, 22 July 1912. The full-sized version of *The Prodigal Son* is owned by the J. B. Speed Art Museum, Louisville, Kentucky. Barnard was first invited to submit an entry by Gutzon Borglum, the temporary chairman of the sculpture committee of the organizing Association of American Painters and Sculptors, and the vice president of the Association. Borglum was soon replaced by John Mowbray-Clark who worked out arrangements for the *Prodigal Son*'s shipment. JGB to GGB, 28 December 1912. Four of Barnard's *Urn of Life* variations were also exhibited at the Armory Show.

12. In reference to the *National Indian Memorial* see GGB to WST, 19 March 19, 1913; Daniel Chester French to GGB, 3 and 12 March 1913; Robert Ogden, Vice President of the Indian Association, to GGB, 29 January; 6, 7, 8 and 24 February 1913; GGB to George Von L. Meyer, Secretary of the Navy, 14 and 26 February 1913; GVLM to GGB, 3 March 1913. French was solicited by a Federal commission to supply sketches with the understanding the competition would proceed only if they were found unsatisfactory. After Ogden recommended Barnard to the commission, consideration was given to a collaborative effort between the contenders, an option French quickly rejected. President Taft and his cabinet attended groundbreaking ceremonies. The project was not completed. Barnard's European excursion is discussed in GGB to WST, 19 March 1913. Although the St. Michel cloister was part of his initial purchase in 1907, the French government moved to block its shipment. Left with no options, Barnard presented the remaining fragments to France. *New York Times,* 30 April; 11, 17, 31 May; and 15 June 1913. Shrader (61), summarizes details of Barnard's barnstorming exploits during the Clark excursion. Barnard's expected return was noted in Vivia Monroe to WST, 5 May 1913.

13. Alice Nevitt Millett, "George Grey Barnard" (M.A. thesis, University of Louisville, 1944), 32.

14. Taine (1828–93) was perhaps best known for his *Les origines de la France contemporaine* (6 vols. 1876–94). His twenty-year term as professor of aesthetics and history at the École ended in 1884, Barnard's first year at the school. Rainer Maria Rilke, *Auguste Rodin,* trans. Robert Firmage (Santa Barbara, Calif.: Peregrine Smith, 1979), 66. The volume was first published in Berlin in 1903. Also see Albert E. Elsen, *Rodin* (London: Secker and Warburg, 1974), 93. Rodin embarked on his research journey in 1891. Truman H. Bartlett, "An Old Likeness of Lincoln," *Harper's Weekly,* 10 February 1912, 9–10. John Gutzon Borglum, untitled ms., GBP and John Gutzon Borglum, "The Beauty of Lincoln," *Everybody's Magazine,* February 1910, 217–20.

15. Supra, n. 16.

16. Charles A. Thomas to GGB, 15 June 1913, with the inscription, "Come see me," dated 18 June 1913. Thomas weighed 180 pounds. See also *Louisville Courier-Journal,* 21 July 1980. GGB to [John H.] Grigsby, n.d.

17. Millett, "George Grey Barnard," 32; Dickson, "Barnard's Controversial Lincoln," 10.

18. Charles A. Thomas to GGB, 6 September 1914. Ibid. and CAT to GGB, 22 and 24 August, 1913. Thomas will be further discussed in chapter 10. Dickson, 10.

19. Victor Hugo, *The Hunchback of Notre Dame* (New York: The Book League of America, 1940), 112.

20. I draw upon Jean-François Lyotard's analysis as presented in David Carroll, *Paraesthetics* (New York: Methuen, 1987), 38, 39. In his *Delusions and Dreams in Jensen's "Gradiva,"* a narrative about an obsessive archeaologist who believes a figure on an ancient relief has come to life, and most especially in the essay, "The Moses of Michelangelo" (1914), Freud fully explores the psychoanalytical implications of the "living" statue fantasy. For this and a broad survey of other literary considerations on the theme of the animated statue, see Kenneth Gross, *The Dream of the Living Statue* (Ithaca: Cornell University Press, 1992), 37, 38, 184–97 et passim.

21. See, for example, Pierre Puvis de Chavannes, *Le Pauvre Pêcheur,* oil, 1881 in the National Museum of the Luxembourg, Paris, and Arnold Bochlin, *Odysseus und Kalipso,* oil and tempera, 1882–83 in the Museum of Art, Basel, Switzerland. Frank Harris, *Contemporary Portraits* (London, 1915); 1, as quoted in Albert E. Elsen, *Rodin* (New York: Museum of Modern Art, [1963]), 96 and CC.25.

22. Dickson,"George Grey Barnard's Controversial Lincoln," 10. CAT to GGB, 6 September 1914. CAT to GGB, 24 August 1913. *Louisville Courier-Journal,* 10 October 1952.

23. Dickson, 10. WST to GGB, 1 January 1914. Thomas expected to begin posing the second week of July. CAT to GGB, 19 June 1914.

24. Alex O. Jones to CPT, 22 July 1914. Barnard also complained directly to Anna Taft, GGB to APT, 30 June 1914.

25. CPT to AOJ, 29 July 1914.

26. Dickson, "Barnard's Controversial Lincoln," 11.

27. Jean Jules Jusserand, French Ambassador to the United States, to GGB, 16 April 1912. The French government's reception of the head was delayed until 1921. In that year a newly-executed marble bust was deposited in the American Room of the Luxemburg Gallery, Paris. Just prior to its shipment, Barnard presided at an unveiling of this new head which was conducted by the Rubenstein Club at the Waldorf-Astoria. See *New York Times,* 8 May 1921 and 5 June 1921, sec. 3, 15.

28. Dickson, 12; GGB to TR, 12 September 1917. Barnard later contemplated erecting four bronze casts of the bust along the Lincoln Highway. In 1963 the sculptor's son Monroe Barnard offered a plaster of the colossal head to Texas Governor John Connelly to serve as a memorial in Dallas to assassinated president John F. Kennedy. Before its destruction at an unknown date, the plaster was stored in Poughkeepsie, New York. The ladder is the central metaphor in Joseph Barnard's undated sermon entitled "Climbing" (AAA). This deals with interconnections between the ascent of the Christian soul and man's instinctive desire to triumph over adversity.

29. In *Le Temps,* as quoted by Trachtenberg, 44.

30. George Bissell to GGB, 7 April 1915.

31. CPT to GGB, 17 June 1915. APT to GGB, 29 July 1915.

32. L. Ward Bannister to George L. Burr, 29 December 1915.

33. For Chapman's response, see FMC to GGB, 25 November 1915 and CPT to FMC, 23 November 1915. See also Charles Taft's ingratiating acknowledgment to William Carpenter, CPT to WC, 30 November 1915.

34. CPT to GGB, 11 December 1915. Quoted from CPT to FMC, 23 November 1915.

35. Trial contract, 4 February 1916. GGB to CPT and AST, 6 May 1916; CPT to GGB, 14 and 27 November 1916.

36. A. L. Shannon, Barnard's secretary, to CPT, 4 October 1916. Ibid. At this point, Dublin was a bustlng art colony. See Barbara B. Buff, "Dublin, New Hampshire," *The Magazine Antiques* 121 (April 1982): 946.

37. GGB to CPT and AST, 4 October 1916. GGB to CPT and AST, 21 April 1916. Anna [AST to GGB, 24 January 1916] disclosed that she and her husband were "with great interest" reading the Saint-Gaudens biography, adding, "think you would enjoy it."

38. GGB to CPT and AST, 22 October 1916 and telegram, GGB to CPT, 30 October 1916. Telegram, CPT to GGB, 23 November 1916.

39. Hodges was the only journalist invited to the foundry preview. Telegram, CPT to GGB, 27 November 1916. CPT to Leigh Hodges, 2 December 1916.

40. Leigh Hodges, "A New Tradition in American Art."

41. Photocopy, GGBP, PMAA.

42. Milton W. Brown, *The Story of the Armory Show* (Greenwich, Conn.: New York Graphic Society, 1963), 118–19.

Chapter 5: The Union Theological Seminary

1. The former Minnie Margaret O'Laughlin, Mrs. Hoard was born in Iowa, studied at the Art Students League, and at Teachers College, Columbia University. In 1914 she received appointment as a member of L'Union Internationale des Beaux-Arts et des Lettres. She was best known for her marble, *Eve,* (1914) which was acquired by the Metropolitan Museum of Art. She also specialized in wallpaper design and was an historian of glassmaking. Her sculpture received an award at the Panama-Pacific International Exposition, San Francisco, 1915. See *New York Times,* 31 October 1944 and Metropolitan Museum of Art, *American Sculpture: A Catalog of the Collection of the Metropolitan Museum of Art* (New York: New York Graphic Society, 1965), 138.

2. Margaret Hoard to Ida Tarbell, 17 November 1916. GGBP, PMAA. (Unless otherwise indicated, correspondence is with the GGBP, PMAA). Telegram, GGB to CPT, 21 November 1916. MH to Cabot Ward, 22 November 1916; CW to MH, 27 November 1916; GGB to CW, 18 November 1916. GGB to Mrs. and Mrs. CPT, 16 November 1916. GGB to Dr. and Mrs. George W. Crary, 6 December 1916. She was the former Julia Treadwell Ogden.

3. Clinton Price to GGB, 26 February 1917.

4. The buildings were completed in 1910 by the Boston firm of Allen and Collins. GGB to Clinton Price, 4 December 1916. *The Outlook,* December 1910, 802 and 26 May 1915, 153. *Literary Digest,* 14 June 1913, 1337.

5. CPT to GGB, 14 December 1916. *Barnard's Statue of Lincoln,* 29, and Harrison Gourley to GGB, 20 November 1916. Frank Chapman to TR, 3 December 1916. John D. Rockefeller Jr. to GGB, 6 January 1917. Invitations to the opening are found in GGB to William Randolph Hearst, 7 December 1916; GGB to George E. Pollock, 7 December 1916; GGB to Adolph Ochs, 7 December 1916; GGB to William M. Carpenter, 7 December 1916.

6. Mrs. Ernest C. Brown to GGB, 21 December 1916. See Ralcy H. Bell, *The Philosophy of Painting* (New York: G. P. Putnam's Sons, 1916). In his analysis, Bell (1861–1930) focused upon rhythmic patterns shared by all fine arts media that precipitated pure feeling. The chief by-product of pure feeling was moral enlightenment, and an unselfish love for all creation, animate and inanimate. Bell's alliterative pairing of the words "soul" and "soil" was a semiotic code for aesthetic exaltation. "Soul" connoted the aesthetic emotion in duration, while "soil" grounded this consciousness in the subject of human labor. The genius artist was required to be of the soil, if not literally a farmer, then at least one who has known the suffering, self-abnegation, and defeat common to the life of a laborer, and he was obliged to

treat themes that conformed with the notion of labor. Like the artist, the beholder was obliged to assume a humble attitude, removing from his mind all thoughts of the material world. It was essential that he place himself before the aesthetic object, the essential transmitter, and not rely upon photographic reproductions or, worse, verbal description. If these procedures were followed, the viewer could expect to find his moral and aesthetic consciousness growing within him like a plant. Abbott Thayer to GGB, n.d. Clarence Whybrow to GGB, 12 December 1916. C. C. Rumsey to GGB, 9 March 1917. F. Edwin Elwell is quoted in "summary of support," typed ms. Charles Dana Gibson to GGB, April 1917.

7. *New York Sun,* 17 December 1916.

8. *New York Tribune,* 7 January 1917; *New York American,* 17 February 1917.

9. *New York Times,* 11 December 1916.

10. Barnard's 'Lincoln,'" *Literary Digest,* 6 January 1917, 18. "Doing Lincoln Justice," *Literary Digest,* 10 February 1917, 338–39.

11. GGB to Mr. Latimer, Union Theological Seminary, 20 December 1916. "Allow William Hearfield to take photos he desires, for publication use only and are to be copyrighted in the name of George Grey Barnard." William D. Goodwin [to GGB, 23 December 1916] requested permission to take photographs that "shall be marked copyright by George Grey Baranard." In GGB to Theodore Roosevelt, n.d., Barnard refers to "malacious photos stated copyrighted by me, I have never had a Lincoln photograph copyrighted." "Doing Lincoln Justice," 339. GGB to Elmer Foote, 23 April 1918.

12. J. M. Allison, "God-Sent Inspiration Says Sculptor," *Cincinnati Times-Star,* 11 December 1916.

13. GGB to Mr. Humes, n.d.

14. Reprinted in "Barnard's 'Lincoln','" 18–19. A summary of Lacanian studies on the "*écrits* of the mad," particularly the resulting feminization of such language, is found in John Rajchman, *Micheal Foucault; The Freedom of Philosophy* (New York: Columbia University Press, 1985), 20–22. The role Jacques Lacan assigns to the phallus in centering such language offers a fruitful application to Barnard's writing and the statue. See, for example, Madelon Sprengnether, *The Spectral Mother: Freud, Feminism and Psychoanalysis* (Ithaca: Cornell University Press, 1990), 195–99.

15. "Barnard's 'Lincoln,'" 19.

16. GGB to CPT, 9 November 1916. GGB to CPT, 6 January 1917. GGB to CPT, 9 January 1917.

17. *New York Times, New York Tribune* and *New York Sun,* 5 January 1917. Rockefeller was angered when the *Sun* (6 January 1917) disclosed he was the buyer. Shortly after the Armistice, Barnard commenced trying to interest Rockefeller and the City of New York in a plan whereby The Cloisters would be incorporated into a giant theme park known as the National Peace Memorial, a metropolis of inspirational statuary and reassembled architectural monuments that would encompass the entire northern end of Manhattan. At its center would be Barnard's collossal *War Memorial Arch,* later known as the *Rainbow Arch,* which after 1933 was to exist in a full scale plaster version only. In the early 1920s the sculptor began searching for a new home for his museum, particularly after having been engaged to advise the City of Los Angeles on its elaborate Palos Verdes beautification project. Before the Palos Verdes plan failed in 1922, The Cloisters, for which the artist was asking one million dollars, would have formed the central motif of a fourteen-mile long coastal park. The abandonment of this scheme occurred at the same moment Rockefeller, for whom Barnard was concurrently sculpting his *Adam and Eve,* began contemplating the purchase of The Cloisters and Barnard's collection on behalf of the Metropolitan Museum of Art. After three years of haggling, Barnard accepted the patron's $650,000 offer. As a result of this transaction, Barnard hoped to retain some curatorial authority over his former property. while also proceeding with his ambitious memorial project

and forming an entirely new collection of medieval art and antiquities. Even though the Metropolitan Museum continued to house its medieval collection in the old Barnard monastery, its administrators distanced themselves from Barnard and his new collection. When Rockefeller donated his north Manhattan property to the city for use as a park, (eventually Fort Tryon Park), and began planning the construction of a new Cloisters museum at its center that would replace the old brick monastery, Barnard's much publicized plans for "God's Thumb," as he called Manhattan's northern tip, were nullified. See especially J. L. Shrader, "George Grey Barnard and the Abbaye," *Metropolitan Museum of Art Bulletin* 37 (summer 1979): 1–52.

18. An interview with Belgian poet Emil Cammaerts· was published by the *Sun* on 24 December 1916 beneath headlines that read "Germany Striking at Belgium's Soul." An eyewitness account of the conscription at Wavre appeared in the *New York Herald,* 7 January 1917. Edna Barnard, "Between the Lines," typed ms., 177, Barnard Papers, The Cloisters Museum library. Fredricka Blair, *Isadora* (New York: McGraw-Hill, 1986), 256. Arnold Genthe, *As I Remember* (New York: Reynal and Hitchcock, 1936), 184–86. Duncan chastised her wealthy backer, Paris Singer, when at a dinner in her honor that was also attended by Barnard, Genthe, MacKaye, and Roberts, he announced the purchase of an option on Madison Square Garden in order that it might become the site of Duncan's new School of the Dance. MacKaye and Barnard approved of the plan, the latter envisioning it as an American art center where painters, sculptors, and performing artists could study without financial worry. *New York Times,* 1 April 1917. The announcement of the statue commission came by way of Minister of War Paul Painleve.

19. Thayer began his research in 1896 and, in 1898, with assistance from George de Forest Brush, presented his ideas to Secretary of the Navy Theodore Roosevelt. After settlement in Dublin, New Hampshire, in 1901, Thayer continued to examine the relationship of protective coloring in birds and animals to a system of camouflage for military equipment. Even though supported by such specialists as Frank Chapman, Thayer's theories brought him into increased conflict with predominant scientific opinion, which he deemed hopelessly "unpoetic." One of his foremost critics was Roosevelt, himself, who authored articles aimed at unmasking Thayer's charlatanism. See Ross Anderson, *Abbott Handerson Thayer* (Syracuse, N.Y.: Everson Museum, 1982), 113–25. Barnard's "studies" with Thayer seem to have consisted more of enraptured conversations than a systematic analysis of natural coloring principles. After several such sessions, Thayer wrote the sculptor: "subliminally I knew that you and I should so flame up in enthusiastic talk as to weaken my health, but so necessary part, my old hardened artery head—I am full of this business and loaded and primed ready to show it to Joffre." AT to GGB, 10 November 1914. Another communication reads: "you are so fatally inspiring a being, that after our phone talk, my sore old brain boiled and boiled—perpetually, uncontrollably, one long fiftieth review of all my job for 3 or 4 days and nights, and set back my ship and solider color-nerve a lot." AT to GGB, 5 September 1916.

20. GGB to TR, 20 March 1917.

21. GGB to Emile Hovelacque, 25 April 1917, Theodore Roosevelt Papers, Library of Congress, [hereafter TRP].

22. Philip S. Foner, *The Bolshivik Revolution: Its Impact on American Radicals, Liberals and Labor* (New York: International Publishers, 1967), pp 15, 16.

23. It was around the base of the yet intact statue of Tzar Alexander that the first student worker rallies were organized against the regime. See W. Bruce Lincoln, *Passage Through Armageddon* (New York: Simon and Schuster, 1986), 224–26. The *Cincinnati Times-Star* (28 March 1917) misindentified the statue as Etienne-Maurice Falconet's equestrian, *Peter the Great,* 1766–82, which not only withstood the first revolution, but the second, as well. *Le Temps,* 28 March 1917. Premier Alexandre Ribot

accepted the statue "which is being offered by the United States in sympathetic regard to her sister democracy." As reported in the *Cincinnati Times-Star* (28 March 1917), Adrian Mithouard, president of the Paris municipal council, wrote Primier Ribot, "We see in this [gift] a new and precious pledge of traditional friendship, and I beg you to transmit to the organizing committee our acceptance and our cordial thanks."

24. *New York Sun,* 12 August 1917. Medell McCormick to TR, 25 April 1917, TRP.

25. Members also included Wall Street banker Henry P. Davison, Barnard's banker John Munroe, former French ambassadors Myron Herrick and Robert Bacon, Columnist Frank Crane, Associated Press general manager Melville E. Stone, and George H. Putnam, a Civil War veteran, Lincoln biographer, and publisher. TR to GGB, 21 March, 1917.

26. Stuart Anderson, *Race and Rapprochement: Anglo-Saxonism and Anglo-American Relations, 1895–1904* (Cranbury, N.J.: Associated University Presses, 1981), 65.

27. George Grey Barnard, "The Cire Perdue Process," in *Barnard's Statue of Lincoln,* 65, 66.

28. *New York Times,* 24 April 1917. The society gained much of its financial support from Jewish philanthropist Jacob H. Schiff who was presently vacationing at White Sulphur Springs. Also appearing on the rostrum in support of the War was moderate pacifist Rabbi Stephen S. Wise. "Root Predicts Fall of Central Rulers," *New York Times,* 26 March 1917, 4, and Charles R. Flint, *Memories of an Active Life* (New York: G. P. Putnam's Sons, 1923), 231–34.

29. George Grey Barnard, "The Hand," ms., n.d.

30. Frank Crane, *The Looking Glass* (New York: John Lane Co., 1917), 185–87. See also his *God and Democracy* (Chicago: Forbes and Company, 1912).

31. Frank Crane, "Lincoln at Petrograd," *Globe and Commercial Advertizer,* 26 April 1917.

32. Bryant Anderson to GGB, 1 February 1917. GGB to CPT, 22 February 1917.

33. GGB to J. N. Allison, 22 February 1917.

34. CPT to GGB, 18 May 1917.

35. GB to HP, 25 February, 1914; HP to GB, 3 March, 1914. GB to HP, 9 March 1914. GB to HP, 18 December 1916. GB to HP, 15 January 1917. GB to HP, 24 January 1917. GB to HP, 31 January 1917, GBP.

36. HP to GB, 12 March 1914; HP to GB, 4 February 1915. HP to GB, 4 February 1915.

Chapter 6. John Stewart's Peace War

1. CPT to GGB, 27 January 1917. GGBP, PMAA. Unless otherwise indicated, all correspondence is in GGBP, PMAA. GGB to John A. Stewart, 31 January 1917. JAS to CPT, 22 February 1917. GGB to CPT, 12 March 1917. The dates of official action on the statue are summarized in Lord Weardale, Chairman of the British Centenary of Peace Committee, to Sir Alfred Mond, His Majesty's Commissioner of Works, 22 February 1918, as contained in "Lincoln Statue Controversy," Howard Russell Butler Papers, Archives of American Art, Smithsonian Institution, Washington, D. C. CPT to GGB, 14 March 1917. In his Philadelphia *North American* feature [25 November 1916], Leigh Hodges retold the story of Barnard's first crossing of England while on his way to Paris and why he felt it necessary to travel as fast as possible. This was because he did not want to sleep in a country ruled by a monarch.

2. GGB to CPT, 12 March 1917. CPT to GGB, 14 March 1917.

3. *Who Was Who in America, 1897–1942* (Chicago: A. N. Marquis Co., 1943), 1 : 1185. *New York Times,* 2 November 1928. JAS to Andrew Carnegie, 7 May 1914, Andrew Carnegie Papers, Library of Congress [hereafter ACP]. JAS to William Howard Taft, 17 March 1917, TP.

4. Stuart Anderson, *Race and Rapproachement.* Stewart introduced his overall program in "Worldwide Celebration of the Centenary of Peace," *New York Times,* 31 December 1911, sec. 5, 9, passim.

5. JAS to AC, 5 March 1913, ACP.

6. [Harry] S. Perris, *Pax Brittanica* (New York: MacMillan, 1913), 287. London *Times,* 14 December 1911.

7. In 1914 Wilson and Vice President Marshall were listed along with William Howard Taft as unclassified members at the top of the committee masthead. Bryan was included among numerous honorary vice chairmen. Other members in 1914 and 1915 were John D. Crimmins, Edward F. Dunne, Eugene M. Foss, Edwin Ginn, William C. Osborn, Thomas N. Page, Daniel Smiley, and Oscar S. Straus, vice chairmen; Charles W. Fairbanks, Richard Bartholdt, Theodore Burton, Martin H. Glynn, Emmett O'Neal, Herman Ridder, Jacob H. Schiff, Oswald West, and J. Horace McFarland, executive committee; Cornelius Vanderbilt, chairman, and William C. Demorest, Bernard N. Baker, William A. Clark, Crimmons, Charles S. Davison, Charles M. Dow, James B. Forgan, Jacob Langeloth, J. Pierpont Morgan, Francis B. Reeves, Ridder, William Salomon, and Francis L. Stetson, vice chairmen of the finance committee. Alton B. Parker chaired the committee on legislation. Joseph F. Wall, *Andrew Carnegie* (New York: Oxford University Press, 1970), 995–1005.

8. Carnegie Endowment for Internation Peace, *A Manual of the Public Benefactions of Andrew Carnegie* (Washington, 1919). Both Root and Butler would occupy important positions within the Carnegie administrative hierarchy. Root was appointed chairman of the Carnegie Institute of Washington in 1913 and, between 1915 and 1925, served as president of the Carnegie Endowment for International Peace. At Butler's urging, Carnegie established the Endowment for International Peace. From 1910 to 1945 Butler directed the Carnegie Division of Intercourse and Education and in 1925 succeeded Root as president of the Peace Endowment, while also continuing to serve as a trustee. Choate was vice president and active trustee of the Peace Endowment. JAS to Woodrow Wilson, 28 April 1914, Woodrow Wilson Papers, Library of Congress [hereafter WWP]. JAS to AC, 4 and 7 May 1914, ACP. AC to Joseph H. Tumulty, 7 May 1914, ACP. Stewart's excessive use of executive privilege is discussed in Alton B. Parker to John Gutzon Borglum, 9 March 1915, GBP. Stewart became increasingly wary of the Carnegie faction and later quashed its attempt to advance Nicholas Murray Butler to the position of first chancellor of the Sulgrave Institution, vowing as he did, to break all ties with the Carnegie Foundation. In an effort to interest William Howard Taft in the chancellor's position, Stewart identified Carnegie officials Butler and Root as the primary enemies of Taft's League to Enforce Peace [JAS to CPT, 11 and 15 March 1918, TP.].

9. JAS to AC, 14 December 1911, ACP. JAS to AC, 21 December 1911, ACP. Letterhead [American Committee, British-American Centenary of Peace Committee]. JAS to AC, 16 December 1911, ACP. U. S. House, *To Approve of the Celebration of the One Hundreth Anniversary of the Treaty of Ghent,* 62nd Cong., 2d Sess., 1912, 2421. The House bill was introduced on 24 February 1912 by New York Rep. Martin W. Littleton. A proviso of the bill called for an equal matching of the appropriated funds by the British Centenary of Peace Committee. U.S. Senate, *To Approve the Celebration of the One Hundreth Anniversary of the Treaty of Ghent,* 62d Cong., 3d Sess., 1912, 4256. JAS to AC, 14 May 1912, with clipping, ACP. *New York Times,* 2 May 1912. U. S. House, Committee on Foreign Affairs, *Hearings, Centenary of Peace and Amity between the United States and Other Nations,* 63rd Cong., 2d Sess., 1914, 11325.

10. The Saxe bill, introduced into the New York State Legislature in 1912, requested five hundred thousand dollars as the state's share in the cost of the celebrations. See *New York Times,*

28 February; 2 March; 2 and 13 May 1912. JAS to AC, 14 May 1912, ACP. See also London *Times*, 2 July 1914. Proposed memorials were to commemorate the American Revolutionary General Nicholas Herkimer, Gen. John Sullivan, and War of 1812 naval commanders Thomas Macdonough and Oliver Perry. Stewart expected the Mcdonough celebrations on Lake Champlain, and those scheduled for Detroit, to be particularly insulting to the Canadians [JAS to AC, 16 February 1912, ACP.].

11. JAS to AC, 23 November 1913 and 5 September 1912, ACP. JAS to AC, 5 September 1912, ACP. *New York Times*, 5 July 1913. *New York Times*, 12 September 1913.

12. *New York Times*, 26 and 30 January 1914. "British-American Peace," London *Times*, 19 December 1912, 7, 8. At the request of American women residing in London, Royal Academician Francis D. Wood completed a seven-foot marble portrait of the First William Pitt, Earl of Chatham, in 1915, which the *London Times* [26 January 1914] described as a copy of Patrick MacDowell's (1799–1870) portrait of the subject in the House of Lords. Led by the Duchess of Marlborough, the women offered the statue to the United States as an expression of their continuing love for the land of their birth, or of their adoption. Amid considerable confusion, the statue arrived unannounced at Hoboken, New Jersey, in December 1919, whereupon it was consigned to the reponsibility of the State Department. In 1920, the State Department persuaded the National Museum of the Smithsonian Institution to accept the work and pay for its transport. It was first displayed in the foyer of the National Museum (presently the National Museum of Natural History), then in 1972, it was transferred to the National Portrait Gallery of the Smithsonian Institution. It is presently in storage. See "Pitt Statue," ms., National Portrait Gallery archives.

13. Perris, *Pax*, 252. "British American Peace."

14. Beyond their common goal of breaking down legislative resistance, Wilson and his British advisors wanted to create the illusion that no foreign pressure had been brought to bear, that by rescinding the American toll exemption Congress was simply acting on its own to right a wrong. Wilson signed the measure on 15 June 1914. Articles on the toll question appear almost daily in the *New York Times* through April 1914; see especially "Mexican Crisis Aids Toll Repeal," *New York Times*, 16 April 1914. The quiet diplomacy of the British to bring about the repeal is best revealed in the correspondence of British Ambassador Sir Cecil Arthur Spring-Rice written in late winter and spring of 1914. See Woodrow Wilson, *The Papers of Woodrow Wilson*, Arthur S. Link, ed. (Princeton: Princeton University Press, 1966–1979), 29: 217, 231, 232 et passim. For Roosevelt's reaction see *New York Times*, 25 June 1914. JAS, letter to Centenary Committee members [1914], ACP. John Blackwood, *London's Immortals* (London: Savoy Press, 1989), 230–31.

15. *New York Times*, 16 April 1914.

16. Perris, *Pax*, 273.

17. "Trying to Spoil Peace Celebration," *New York Times*, 1 May 1913, 3. From her London cell, British suffragette Mrs. Flora Drummand sent a warning to her American sisters of the Centenary Committee's arrival. Her smuggled letter referred to alleged instances of torture committed on women who were incarcerated in British prisons. Since Carnegie Hall had been the chosen site for celebrations supporting pending American-British-French arbitration treaties in December 1911, and since the opposition considered Lord Weardale and his British delegation to be Carnegie puppets, laborites and suffragettes readily identified the "Carnegie Mission" with the ongoing Capitalist suppression of the working classes, of racial minorities, and of women. Despite the adverse publicity thrown at the visitors and their American hosts, nothing like the violent demonstrations that greeted the 1911 Carnegie Hall celebration reoccurred during the joint Anglo-American peace conferences of 1913.

18. TR to Arthur Hamilton Lee, 7 July 1913, as quoted in *Letters of Theodore Roosevelt*, 7: 738.

19. TR to Frederick Scott Oliver, 22 July 1915 and to Arthur Lee, 17 June 1915, quoted in *Letters* 7: 935–36, 949.

20. "Wants Us to Keep Our Canal Pledges," *New York Times*, 8 March 1914, 12. A Jewish philanthropist, politician, author, international diplomat—he also served under Taft as United States Ambassador to Turkey—Straus naturally had little to say in defense of the "Anglo-Saxon feeling." His position on the toll contradicted the Progressive Party platform on the issue.

21. TR to Charles G. Washburn, 23 January 1915, Morison, 7: 941 and Burton, *The Learned Presidency*, 40. GB to JAS, 25 February 1913 and JAS to GB, 4 April 1912, GBP. Frederick Ruckstull to Howard Russell Butler, 5 February 1918 in Howard Russell Papers, AAA. JAS to GB, 16 April 1912, GBP. *Chicago Tribune*, 15 May 1913. *Chicago Tribune*, 17 May 1913.

22. GB to WBH, 3 June 1913, GBP. London *Times*, 23 May 1913. Weardale, "Lincoln Statue Controversy." Present at the conference were Stewart, Joseph Choate, William B. Howland, Alton Parker, Charles Hilles, William C. Demorest, George T. Wilson, and Andrew Humphrey.

23. Weardale, "Lincoln Statue Controversy." In a letter to Borglum (H. S. Perris to GB, 3 September 1913, GBP), Perris did not refer to the Saint-Gaudens replica, *London Times*, 30 January; 14 February; 15 February; and 10 March 1914. "Peace Committee Cables to Queen," *New York Times*, 16 April 1914, 4. Weardale, "Lincoln Statue Controversy."

24. Blackwood, *Lincoln Immortals*, 184, 190, 192, 194, 208, 178–79.

25. London *Times*, 5 February and 12 July 1914.

26. Isaac Seligman to JAS, 3 February 1916; IS to Nicholas Murray Butler, 6 February 1916, Howard Russell Butler Papers [hereafter HRBP]. JAS to H. S. Perris, 6 May 1916, HRBP. JAS to IS et al., 7 February 1916, HRBP. JAS to IS, 3 July, 1916, HRBP. JAS to Joseph B. Choate, 7 February 1916, HRBP.

27. Howard R. Butler, "The Proposed Gift to Great Britain of a Statue of Lincoln," *American Magazine of Art* 9, no. 9 (July 1918): 375.

28. Woodrow Wilson, *On Being Human* (New York: Harper and Brothers, 1916), 42, 47–48. Albert Shaw, "Progress of the World," [American] *Review of Reviews*, April 1914, 391. R. W. Macan's poem, "Lincoln: Wilson," appeared in the London *Times*, 7 April 1917, 7.

29. Lord Charnwood, *Abraham Lincoln* (New York: Henry Holt and Company, 1917). John Drinkwater, *Abraham Lincoln* (Boston: Houghton Mifflin, 1918), viii. Charnwood, 10, 11, 103, 105.

30. Charnwood, 1: 258, 260, 263.

31. American reviews are summarized in "Charnwood," *Book Review Digest* 12, no. 12 (February, 1917): 106, 107. Lawrence Abbott, president of the Outlook Company, to GGB, 10 November 1917, and to JAS, 11 March 1918, HRBP. CPT to GGB, 19 September 1917. Grant Wright to GGB (ca. August, 1917). Wright authored *The Art of Caricature* (New York: Baker Taylor Co., 1904). CPT to GGB, 13 June 1917. Albert Shaw, *Abraham Lincoln; His Path to the Presidency (A Cartoon History)*, (New York: Review of Reviews, 1929), ix, 5, 131. The cover bore a embossed reproduction of the head of Barnard's bronze statue. The author refers to Elihu B. Washburne's 1847 description of the shabbily-dressed Lincoln (130–31). Shaw earlier published *Lincoln in Contemporary Caricature* (New York: Review of Reviews Company, 1901).

32. "Mr. Perris . . . spoken before the statue and the American committee," typescript, n.d. Perris probably made the comments during the 19 October private viewing at the foundry. He also saw the statue in situ at Cincinnati while visiting that city several days earlier (H. S. Perris to GGB, 17 October 1917).

33. R. Tait McKenzie (1867–1938) was born in Canada, graduated from McGill University with a medical degree, and, from 1904 until his death, was professor of physical education at the University of Pennsylvania in Philadelphia. After 1911, when his

Youthful Franklin was unveiled in Philadelphia, he specialized in producing bronzes of youthful male athletes. He was especially well known in England, where he volunteered for medical service during the First World War. Widely exhibited, McKenzie's first major retrospective opened at the Fine Arts Society in London in 1920. In connection with his military service, he practiced plastic surgery, a procedure he made the subject of a textbook. See Andrew J. Kozar, *R. Tait McKenzie, The Sculptor of Athletes* (Knoxville: University of Tennessee Press, 1975). Lord Charnwood to Charles Moore, 1 May 1920, Charles Moore Papers, Library of Congress. Charnwood reasoned McKenzie's favorable response stemmed from the fact that "artists seem apt to be carried away by the perception of some small detail of technical merit or of some unfulfilled good intention in works of art which are unquestionably in their whole effect failures." (Charnwood to CM, 23 February 1920, Moore Papers.) Edward Bell to Lawrence L. Winslow, 31 December 1918, in *Papers,* 53: 574. Charnwood commented to Moore (1 May 1920), "How terribly your Mr. Wilson has fulfilled his gloomy forebodings as to the result of his journey . . ."

34. "Lincoln's Statue for London," London *Times,* 24 September 1917, 7. Having achieved notable success directing the (London) *Daily Mirror,* Lord Northcliffe (Alfred Charles William Harmsworth, 1865–1922), took on the proprietorship of the financially troubled *Times* in 1908. This liberal statesman was to lead the British war mission to the United States and, after the War, assisted in affecting an Irish settlement, but he proved to be no friend of the Barnard statue. JAS to WW, 27 June 1917, WWP.

35. "The Lincoln Statue," London *Times,* 26 September 1917, 8. Weardale erred in supposing that the Cincinnati statue had been erected by a public commission. With this misconception in mind, he wondered why Robert Lincoln had not openly opposed its unveiling there. "Two Statues of Lincoln; Statement by the Peace Committee: The Official View," London *Times,* 25 September 1917, 7. "A Statue of Lincoln for Westminster," London *Times,* 14 September 1917, 9.

36. "Action of the Office of Works," London *Times,* 25 September 1917, 7. "The Lincoln Statue." *New York Times,* 21 October 1917.

37. JAS to Jacob Gould Shurman, 12 September 1917, HRBP. GGB, undated ms. If the intended recipients wished to press the issue of originality, Barnard could legitimately point to foundry records that confirm a new head was cast and, on 4 March 1918, attached to the bronze torso of the figure destined for England (Roman Bronze Works, billing statements, 1917–18, GGBP.)

38. Judd Stewart to Howard Russell Butler, 26 January 1918, HRBP. Roman Bronze Works, billing statements.

39. Roman Bronze Works, billing statements.

40. JAS to WHT, 30 October 1917, TP. HSP to GGB, 19 November 1917.

41. United States, War Trade Board, *Rules and Regulations of the War Trade Board* (Washington: G.P.S., 1917), 36.

41. U.S., Congress, House, *Resolved that the President be requested to use his good offices to prevent the shipment from the United States to England of the George Grey Barnard statue of Abraham Lincoln which it is proposed to set up in London as gift to the people of England,* 65th Cong., 1st Sess., 1917, 7605–919. Rogers deplored the crossed-arm gesture, which to him suggested the figure was "awaiting an ambulence," the prominent Adam's apple, the "shapeless canal boots," the "shabby, ill-fitting clothes," the "simion-like slovenly appearance" (7865–66). Ibid., 7866.

43. WW to JAS, 28 June 1917, WWP. WW to William Phillips, Assistant Secretary of State, 26 October 1917, WWP.

44. Telegram, JAS to Alfred Mond, 15 November 1917, WWP, HRBP, and TP.

45. The former editor of *World's Work* and publishing partner of Frank N. Doubleday, Page had a keen interest in art and literature. Though a Democrat, his conservatism aligned him more with Taft Republicans than with the rank-and-file of his own party. After Wilson appointed him ambassador to the Court of St. James in 1917, the president became highly critical of Page's pro-British sympathies. Stewart's comment suggests Barnard and Page—who are known to have corresponded—exchanged ideas on how to move the statue to London. When preparing a biography of Page, Burton J. Hendrick, (*The Life and Letters of Walter H. Page,* 2 vols. [Garden City, N.Y.: Doubleday, Page and Co., 1925]), with obvious impatience, attempted to obtain this correspondence from Barnard. After putting Hendrick off for four years, Barnard declared the papers had been lost. (GGB to Burton J. Hendrick, 8 April 1925). JAS to WHT, 30 October 1917 and WHT to JAS, 15 December 1917, TP. Stewart asked Taft to personally meet London officials in order to clear the way for the shipment.

46. Albert Shaw to WW, 8 November 1917, WWP. AS to WW, 8 December 1917, WWP.

47. AS to WW, 8 November, 1917, WWP.

48. Ibid.

49. "The Sargent Portrait of the President, Exhibited 10 December–10 January in the Corcoran Gallery of Art," *American Magazine of Art* 9, no. 4 (February, 1918): 162; *New York Times,* 13 January 1918, sec. 2, 4; 19 May 1918, sec.7, 14. The portrait was funded by the Hugh Lane estate, which was coadministered by the International Red Cross and the National Gallery of Ireland. See also Sanley Olsen, *J. S. Sargent, His Portraits* (London: MacMillan, 1986), 257. Although he had little interest in critical theory, Sargent (1856–1925) had become Britian's unofficial art censor, especially because of his parentage, in matters concerning American art. Unchallenged as England's foremost portraitist, he faithfully served the Royal Academy as a member of its hanging committee and as a governor at the British School at Rome. Though he disliked administration, he finally agreed in 1921 to chair the faculty at the School in Rome. See Evan Charteris, *John Sargent* (New York: Benjamin Blom, Inc., 1972), 222, 250. John S. Sargent to WW, 6 November 1917, WWP. If the suggested changes to the hands and clothing were carried out, Sargent added, "the statue would be quite worthy of any destination." WW to JSS, 8 November 1917, WWP.

50. WHT to JAS, 15 December 1917. WW to AS, 12 November 1917, WWP.

51. "Parliament," London *Times,* 12 December 1917, 12. To Moore (1 May 1920, Moore Papers) Charnwood confided, "I am afraid I think most of our War memorials that I have seen very poor—nor have we much in the way of recent public buildings to compare with yours."

Chapter 7: The Judging of William Howard Taft

1. RL to Judd Stewart, 8 January 1918, Robert Lincoln Papers, Henry E. Huntington Library, San Marino, California, hereafter, RLH. RL to Frederick Ruckstull, 22 February 1918, RLH.

2. Durman, *He Belongs to the Ages,* 178. Lorado Taft (in *Modern Tendencies in Sculpture,* 134) predicted the O'Connor would provoke criticism because of its slender build, but argued the head was beyond reproach and that some considered it superior to the Saint-Gaudens standing Lincoln. John S. Goff, *Robert Todd Lincoln: A Man in His Own Right* (Norman: University of Oklahoma Press, 1969), 251.

3. RL to Frederick Ruckstull, editor of the *Art World,* 28 November 1917, RLH. RL to Judd Stewart, 23 November 1917, RLH. Goff, 249. RL to Isaac Markens, 14 September 1917, GGBP. RL to Truman H. Bartlett, 27 October 1917, as quoted in Goff, 249.

4. Flint, *Memories,* 126, 127. Joseph H. Choate to RL, 7 May 1917, as quoted in the *Art World* no. 3 (October 1917): 8. Among memorial services for Choate was one conducted in London at

Saint Margaret's Church which abutted the proposed site for Barnard's Lincoln.

5. Excerpts from the letter were first published by Ruckstull in the *New York Times,* 28 September 1917. Mr. and Mrs. William Howard Taft to Mrs. Joseph H. Choate, 15 May 1917, TP. Choate's assessment is included in remarks made before a meeting of the Associated Press on 24 April 1917, as quoted in Theron G. Strong, *Joseph H. Choate* (New York: Dodd, Mead and Co., 1917), 107.

6. While serving as Ambassador to England (1899–1905), Choate became the first American of his generation to address British audiences on Abraham Lincoln. See especially his "Lincoln's Life Work," which was delivered before a meeting of the Philosophical Institution of Edinburgh in 1900, *New York Times,* 14 November 1900, 6. Edward S. Martin, *The Life of Joseph Hodges Choate* (London: Constable and Company, 1920), 1: 217–18. JHC to Mrs. Choate, 22 March 1892, as quoted in Martin, 1: 436. Choate was the principal orator at the unveiling of Saint-Gaudens's *Admiral David Farragut Memorial* in New York's Madison Square in May 1887. See "Unveiling the Statue," *New York Times,* 26 May 1887, 8.

7. RL to Judd Stewart, 11 December 1917, RLH. RL to Judd Stewart, 28 December 1917, RLH. RL to Judd Stewart, 3 December 1917, RLH.

8. RL to Isaac Markens, 28 August 1917, GGBP. Clinton L. Conkling to RL, 23 April 1917, as quoted in the *Art World,* op. cit. George D. Reynolds, Judge of the St. Louis Court of Appeals, to RL, 30 January 1918, with encl. (William B. Thompson to George Reynolds) in GDR to WHT, 5 February 1918, TP.

9. GDR to WHT, 5 February 1918 and GDR to WHT, 6 February 1918, TP. Albert N. Marquis, ed., *Who's Who in America* (Chicago: A. N. Marquis and Co., 1916–17) 9:2353. Judd Stewart to WHT, 14 October 1917, TP.

10. William H. P. Faunce, President of Brown University, to WHT, 17 October 1917, TP.

11. *New York Times,* 11 June 1923, 13. Edward Lind Morse, *Samuel F. B. Morse; His Letters and Journals* (New York: Houghton Mifflin, 1915) 2: 424.

12. Edward Morse to WHT, 8 October 1917, TP.

13. WHT to ELM, 9 October 1917, TP. WHT to HHT, 11 October 1917, TP.

14. ELM to WHT, 15 October 1917, TP.

15. Charles Moore, Chairman of the Commission of Fine Arts, to WHT, 17 September 1917, TP. In 1917 the CFA membership consisted of Frederick L. Olmsted Jr., Thomas Hastings, Herbert Adams, J. Alden Weir, Charles A. Platt, and William M. Mitchell. WHT to CM, 21 September 1917, TP.

16. CM to WHT, 5 October 1917; WHT to CM, 8 October 1917; WHT to Sen. Joseph C. S. Blackburn, Special Resident Commissioner, Lincoln Memorial Commission, 8 October 1917; JCSB to WHT, 9 October 1917, TP.

17. CM to WHT, 5 October 1917, TP. WHT to CM, 8 October 1917, TP. WHT to GDR, 25 February 1918, TP.

18. Frank M. Chapman to Howard Russell Butler, 4 April 1918, Howard Russell Butler Papers, Archives of American Art, Smithsonian Institution, Washington, D.C., hereafter HRBP. IM to WHT, 29 August 1917, TP. JAS to WHT, 1 March 1918, TP.

19. Milton W. Brown, *American Painting From the Armory Show to the Depression,* 82.

20. "Joseph Henry Gest," *Art News,* 13 July 1935, 12. *New York Times,* 27 June 1935, 21; WHT to Guion M. Gest, brother of Joseph H. Gest, 20 February 1913, TP; and Robert C. Vitz, *The Queen and the Arts: Cultural Life in Nineteenth-Century Cincinnati* (Kent, Ohio: Kent State Press, 1989), 244, 245, 256.

21. Joseph H. Gest to CM, 6 October 1917, Charles Moore Papers, Library of Congress, hereafter CMP.

22. Daniel Chester French to CM, 3 November 1917, CMP. DCF to GGB, 4 October 1917, GGBP.

23. In 1918 the following were elected to three year terms on the board of directors of the American Federation of the Arts: Mrs. John W. Alexander, Andrew W. Crawford, Charles L. Hutchinson, H. W. Kent, Florence L. Levy, Elihu Root, and Joseph E. Widener. Edwin H. Blashfield, Glenn Brown, Archer Huntington, Henry White, John L. Porter, and Arthur Fairbanks were appointed vice presidents. See the *American Magazine of Art* 9, no. 9 (July 1918): 363. Robert W. De Forest (1848–1931) was for many years general counsel of the Central Railroad of New Jersey. In company with Choate and Root, he considered art patronage a necessary lubricant in the maintenance of a healthy, vigorously commercial, society. His father-in-law was John Taylor Johnson, the first president of the Metropolitan Museum. His own long association with the museum began in 1889, when he was made a trustee. In 1913 De Forest succeeded J. P. Morgan as museum president, a post he held for eighteen years. While he chaired the executive committee of the Free Art League, this organization successfully lobbied the Taft administration for the removal of tariffs on art. See "Robert W. De Forest," *New York Times,* 7 May 1931, 1.

24. Contributing to the friction between them was Taft's dislike for Root's position on the Covenant of the League of Nations and his contention that the guiding principles of the League to Enforce Peace were hopelessly idealistic. When Nicholas Murray Butler and other Republicans boosted Root's presidential nomination in 1916, Taft supported Charles E. Hughes. Once he was in command of the Carnegie Corporation, Root proved notably unsympathetic to grant requests submitted by the League to Enforce Peace. See Richard W. Leopold, *Elihu Root and the Conservative Tradition* (Boston: Little, Brown, and Company, 1954), 184, 185. Root possibly alluded to the Barnard situation when in early-1918 he remarked to Taft "as matters are going, I am buffeted about by a greater number and variety of violent emotions than any man of my age is entitled to have. Among them, thank the Lord, is a tendency to laugh sometimes at things which are really funny, and there are some now at this very present time to which Rabelais himself could not do justice" (Elihu Root to WHT, 25 January 1918, TP).

25. Charles Moore, "Memorials of the Great War," *American Magazine of Art* 10, no. 7 (May, 1919): 233–34.

26. Maria Oakey Dewing, "The People in Art," ibid., 233–34. Lorado Taft to GGB, 17 November 1917, GGBP. The letter, which reports on Taft's personal inspection of the Cincinnati Lincoln, is discussed in chapter 10. Hermon MacNeil completed a five-foot working model for his *Lincoln as Lawyer* at the beginning of 1918. It presents a full-length, beardless, individual, standing before a classical bench upon which a cloak has been loosely thrown. The figure looks confidently ahead, with arms crossed over the chest, and with its right leg advanced. Hermon MacNeil, "Sculpture—A Report of Progress," *American Magazine of Art* 9, no. 9 (July 1918): 414.

27. Leila Mechlin, "The Barnard Lincoln," *American Magazine of Art* 9, no. 1 (November 1917): 32, 33.

28. Raymond's best known publication was *Painting, Sculpture and Architecture: An Essay in Comparative Aesthetics* (New York: Putnam and Sons, 1909). The author's father was a member of the Illinois State Convention that nominated Lincoln for the presidency. He frequently saw Lincoln both before and after he left the state for the White House. *American Magazine of Art* 9, no. 3 (January 1918): 117. George L. Raymond, "The Barnard Lincoln, An Open Letter," ibid., 9, no. 2 (December 1917): 72, 72. Maria Dewing, "The People in Art," 118.

29. Cass Gilbert to Leila Mechlin, 8 October 1917 and to CM, 29 January 1918 and 21 February 1918, CMP. "Resolutions Adopted By the American Federation of Arts in Convention at Detroit, Michigan, 23 and 24 May 1918," *American Magazine of Art* 9, no. 9 (July 1918): 372.

30. U.S. Senate Committee on the Library, *Authorizing the Secretary of the Treasury to Refuse to Permit the Exportation of Any Work of Art,* 65th Cong., 2d Sess., 1918, S 4910, 9919; and House

Committee on the Library, 65th Cong., 2d Sess., 1918, H.R. 12981, 10625. "Resolutions Adopted by the American Federation of Arts."

31. U.S., House of Representatives, Committee on the Library, *Restrictions As to the Exportation of Certain Works of Art,* 65th Cong., 3d Sess., 1919, H. Rept. 1031 to accompany H.R. 12981, 1–3.

32. Allan Nevins, *Henry White: Thirty Years of American Diplomacy* (New York: Harper and Brothers, 1930), 307–448. White's name appears on the slate of newly appointed vice presidents of the American Federation of Arts for 1918.

33. RL to Judd Stewart, 21 February 1918, and to Frederick Ruckstull, 22 February 1918, RLH. RL to Judd Stewart, 28 December 1917, RLH.

34. RL to Judd Stewart, 21 February 1918, RLH. WHT to JAS, 4 March 1918, TP. Robert W. de Forest to WHT, 11 January 1919, and WHT to RWD, 14 January 1919, TP. William Howard Taft, "Introduction," in William Draper Lewis, *The Life of Theodore Roosevelt* (United Publishers of the United States and Canada, 1919), vii. Noting the short interval that had elapsed between Roosevelt's death and the appearance of the book, Taft wrote, "But Dr. Lewis is able to tell the events of Roosevelt's life and give to the world the benefit of personal observation. He will thus explain much, and greatly aid the future historian, who after fifty years, shall write a life like that of Charnwood's 'Life of Lincoln.'" Just then Charnwood was preparing to write his own brief biography of Roosevelt, whom, along with Gladstone, he compared with Lincoln. See Godfrey Rathbone Benson Charnwood, *Theodore Roosevelt* (Boston: The Atlantic Monthly Press, 1923). Taft described Roosevelt as the "most brilliant personality in American public life since Lincoln." Ibid., xxii. Lord Charnwood to WHT, 1 February 1920; [Lady] Dorothea Charnwood to WHT, 21 October 1918; WHT to Lord Charnwood, 15 March 1920, TP. Charnwood appointed Taft president of the English-Speaking Union in 1918. Charles Moore to WHT, 31 October 1918, and WHT to CH, 6 November 1918, TP. The unveiling of O'Conner's statue took place on 6 October 1918. Charnwood's address compared the American Union with present-day Europe. "With the help of Mr. O'Connor's work, and that of other artists, with the help of some of those old friends of Lincoln, a few of whom I have had the privilege of meeting this day, we seem to see the man himself as we read his character in some of those simple sentences of his, 'I am here,' he seems to say, 'I must do the best I can to bear the responsibility of taking the course which I feel I ought to take.'" "Address of Lord Charnwood at the Dedication of the Statue of Abraham Lincoln on the State House Grounds, October 6, 1918," *Journal of the Illinois State Historical Society* 12, no. 4 (January, 1920): 500.

35. Acknowledging Lincoln's felicitations on the appointment, Taft replied that he was especially heartened by the support offered him by his "real friends, among whom, my dear Mr. Lincoln, I am proud to claim you and Mrs. Lincoln." WHT to RL, 19 July 1921, TP.

Chapter 8: The Press

1. A highly complimentary review of the seminary exhibit appeared in the same journal that published John Gutzon Borglum's insurgent views. Milton Bronner, "A Sculptor of Democracy," *Independent,* 26 February 1917, 355.

2. Cf. Barnard Lincoln controversy, *New York Times Index,* July–December 1917, January–June 1918, with Serra's *Tilted Arc* controversy, *New York Times Index,* 1985–89.

3. "The London Lincoln," *New York Evening Post,* 18 October 1917, 8. See, for example, "Lincoln's Statue for London," London *Times,* 22 September 1917, 7. "Barnard's Lincoln," *Chicago Tribune,* 20 October 1917, 8.

4. John C. Freeman, *The Forgotten Rebel* (Watkins Glen,

N.Y.: Century House, 1965), 9–11, and Mary Fanton Roberts, "One Man's Story," *The Craftsman* 30 (May 1916): 188–200. See also Mary Ann Smith, *Gustav Stickley, The Craftsman* (Syracuse, N.Y.: Syracuse University Press, 1983). Denys Amiel, "Rodin—The Treasure-Maker," *Touchstone* 2, no. 4 (January 1918): 331–42.

5. F. Wellington Ruckstuhl, "A Standard of Art Measurement, Part I," *Art World* 1, no. 1 (October 1916): 323, and Robert Underwood Johnson, "A Growing Force in Art and Letters," in ibid., 48. Ruckstuhl had changed the spelling of his surname by January 1918.

6. Ruckstull (in "Lincoln: April 15, 1865," *Art World,* 2, no. 1 [May 1917]: 158), described the composition as follows: "Lincoln is shown lying on his death bed. Back of his bier stands a winged Fame with a serene expression of satisfaction on her face as if having claimed and gained as her own that which America lost—a great soul. Having quickly descended from the skies she has placed across Lincoln's body a palm of glory and a wreath of immortality, while in her right hand, at rest, she holds a trumpet. By her side has arrived, a moment later, sorrowing America, the incarnation of a mourning people, also to place a wreath upon his bier. Fame, having preceded her, places her left hand on the shoulder of America, as if to console her for the loss of her great and long-suffering hero." Charles De Kay, "An Open-Air Impression of Balzac," *New York Times,* 31 July 1898, 4.

7. [Frederick W. Ruckstuhl], "A Mistake in Bronze," *Art World* 2, no. 3 (June 1917): 211. Robert Lincoln to Frederick W. Ruckstuhl, 6 November 1917, RLH. The editor made mention of Lincoln's collaboration. See "[Frederick Ruckstuhl], "The Effect on Caricature of the Lincoln Controversy," *Art World* 3, no. 3 (December 1917): 194.

8. The photo of Hunt's portrait was first reproduced in "Doing Lincoln Justice," *Art Digest,* 10 February 1917, 339. "Letter from Mr. Judd Stewart," *Art World* 3, no. 3 (December 1917): 197. Hunt's full-length posthumous portrait was commissioned by the art dealers Doll & Richards shortly after the assassination. It was destroyed in the Boston Fire of 1872. A badly-damaged print of the photograph is currently with The American Architectural Foundation, The Octagon Museum, Washington, D.C. See Sally Webster, *William Morris Hunt,* (Cambridge: Cambridge University Press, 1991), 66, 67. While the *Art Digest* was attempting to pay Barnard his dues by printing a photographic image that had at least a remote resemblance to his statue, Ruckstull chose to emphasize how much more elegant the print was in comparison to the statue.

9. [Mary Fanton Roberts] "Lincoln As His Friends and Admirers Knew Him During His Lifetime," *Touchstone* 2, no. 2 (November 1917): 194.

10. [Frederick Ruckstull], "How to Give Europe a Worthy Lincoln Monument," *Art World* 3, no. 4 (January 1918): 277.

11. *Art World* 2, no. 5 (August 1917): 421; ibid., 3, no. 2 (November 1917): 102; ibid., 3, no. 1 (October 1917): 11; ibid., 3, no. 3 (December 1917): 194.

12. "Barnard's 'Lincoln' Once More," ibid., 192. Arthur C. Jacobson, associate editor of *Medical Times,* reprinted from the *New York American,* 2 December 1917, in "The Public on the Lincoln Matter," *Art World* 3, no. 4 (January 1918): 279. George L. Raymond, "To the Editor" [originally the *American Magazine of Art*], reprinted in ibid., 279–80.

13. "A Mistake in Bronze," 211. "Barnard's 'Lincoln' Once More," 190. "A Mistake in Bronze," 217–20.

14. [Frederic MacMonnies] "Barnard's Lincoln," *North American Review,* December 1917, 837–39. MacMonnies' appreciation supplemented those of architect Thomas Hastings and critic Richard Fletcher. "Mr. Barnard's 'Lincoln' Once More," 215.

15. "Mr. Barnard's 'Lincoln' Once More—Some Public Comments," *Art World* 3, no. 1 (October 1917): 7. "A Calamity in Bronze," *Art World* 3, no. 3 (November 1917): 100. "A Letter from Mr. Judd Stewart," ibid., 197.

16. "The People's Lincoln," *Touchstone* 2, no. 1 (October

1917): 63. DCF to FWR, April 18, 1917, DCFP. A Timothy Cole's wood engraving that replicated *Death and the Young Sculptor* appeared as the frontispiece in the November issue. Brush's painting *The Indian and the Water-Lily* was similarly featured in the April 1917 number. DCF to FWR, 15 August and 26 September 1917, DCFP. DFC to Edwin Blashfield, 30 August 1917, DCFP.

17. *Touchstone* 2, no. 1 (October 1917): 54.

18. Ibid., 57–63.

19. Ibid., 61.

20. Kathleen Brady, *Ida Tarbell, Portrait of a Muckraker* (New York: SeaView/Putnam, 1984), 52–85. Ida M. Tarbell, "The Arts and Industries of Cincinnati," *Chautauquan*, November 1886, 160–62. Ida M. Tarbell, "The Charm of Paris," *Scribner's*, (April 1900): 387–404. "'Those Who Love Lincoln': A Word for Barnard's Statue by Ida Tarbell," *Touchstone* 2, no. 3 (December, 1917): 225.

21. Ibid., 224–28.

22. [Mary Fanton Roberts], "Lincoln As His Friends and Admirers Knew Him During His Lifetime," 194–96.

23. "The People's Lincoln," 58–63.

24. GGB to TR, 12 September 1917, TRP. Barnard spliced and rearranged paragraphs from separate Roosevelt mailings. These included personally signed form letters relating to the volunteer division which the artist then photocopied to produce what appears to be a single original, GGBP, AAA. TR to GGB, 19 September 1917, TRP. "George Gray [*sic*] Barnard's Lincoln: A Corrected Letter From Theodore Roosevelt," *Touchstone* 2, no. 6 (March, 1918): 605.

25. "Not the Real Lincoln," *New York Times*, 26 August 1917, sec. 2, 2. "The People's Lincoln," 62.

26. "Statue of Lincoln Held As True Art," *New York Times*, 27 September 1917, 13.

27. Gerald W. Johnson, *An Honorable Titan* (New York: Harper and Bros., 1946), 368, 242–43. "Letters," *New York Times*, 28 September 1917, 10. As quoted by Robert Lincoln in RL to FWR, 30 October 1917, RLH.

28. Frederick W. Ruckstuhl, "Defends Criticism of Lincoln Statue," *New York Times*, 28 September 1917, 11. Augustus Thomas, "The Problem of Making Immortality Safe for a Democracy," *New York Times*, 2 October 1917, 12.

29. "Charles P. Taft Silent," *New York Times*, 1 January 1918, 17. Taft (in CPT to GGB, 27 March 1918, GGBP), shares with Barnard the news that the *Art World* was ceasing publication. Although the patron observed that "that class of art publication will never succeed," he was glad of the attention it focused upon the statue. "Mr. Barnard Answers His Critics," *New York Times*, 18 November 1917, 2.

30. "Had No Money For the Saint-Gaudens Lincoln," *New York Times*, 3 January 1918, 8.

31. GGB to Lorado Taft, 20 April 1929, GGBP. Pennell's equally harsh criticism of the Pennsylvania groups so deflated Barnard that he vowed never to return to Harrisburg; he did, however, consent to be entombed near the capital. Robert B. Stanton, "To the Editor," *New York Times*, 14 October 1917, 2. Beatrice S. De Camp, "To the Editor," *New York Tribune*, 18 October 1917, 8.

32. Bullard, *Lincoln in Marble and Bronze*, 230. "Which is Your Lincoln?," *The Independent*, 3 November 1917, 207. "Oppose Barnard's Lincoln," *New York Times*, 26 October 1917, 14. "Condemns Barnard's Statue," *New York Times*, 15 November 1917, 12. "Had No Money for Saint-Gaudens Lincoln." "Barnard's Statue Still Under Fire," *New York Times*, 25 November 1917, sec. 9, 5. "Architects Oppose Statue," *New York Times*, 20 February 1918, 4. "The Question of the Lincoln Statue," *New York Times*, 9 June 1918, sec. 6, 15.

33. Henry McBride, "Notes and Activities in the World of Art," *New York Sun*, 18 November 1917, sec. 5, 12. Brown, *American Painting*, 89, 177.

34. Lincoln Kirstein, "Henry McBride," in M. Knoedler Galleries, *To Honor Henry McBride* (New York: by the Gallery, 1949). n.p. McBride, "Notes and Activities in the World of Art," *New York Sun*, 4 November 1917, sec. 5, 12. McBride, "Notes and Activities in the World of Art," *New York Sun*, 11 November 1917, sec. 5, 12. McBride, "Notes and Comment in the World of Art," *New York Sun*, 4 November 1917, sec. 5, 12.

35. Bullard, *Lincoln in Marble and Bronze*, 230. "Which Is Your Lincoln?" See photo caption, "The True Abraham Lincoln," *New York Times*, 21 October 1917, sec. 5, 1. The photograph was lent to the newspaper by painter George H. Story, curator emeritus of the Metropolitan Museum of Art, who hoped to put to rest allegations that Lincoln was ill-proportioned. The accompanying text states the image was made under Story's supervision in Brady's Washington studio on 23 February 1861. The Story photograph also appeared in much altered form in the June number of *Art World*. "Barnard's Lincoln As a Noted Painter Sees It," *New York Times*, 28 October 1917, sec. 7, 7, 14. "Fight Over Barnard's Lincoln Still Raging," *New York Times*, 21 October 1917, sec. 7, 12.

36. Judith Cladel, *Rodin, The Man and His Art*, trans. S. K. Star (New York: Century Co., 1917), 103. "On Monuments," *New York Tribune*, 4 October 1917, 8. "Barnard's Lincoln As a Noted Painter Sees It."

37. "The London Lincoln," *New York Evening Post*, 10 October 1917, 8.

38. "Barnard's Lincoln," *Chicago Tribune*, 20 October 1917, 8. Percy MacKaye, "Barnard's Lincoln," *New York Evening Post*, 22 October 1917, 10.

Chapter 9: On to Westminster

1. CPT to GGB, 13 June 1917, GGBP.

2. Ida Bartlett Taft, *Lorado Taft, Sculptor and Citizen*, (Greensboro, N.C.: May Taft Smith, 1946), 84. Lorado Taft, *The History of American Sculpture* (New York: Macmillan Co., 1903; rev. ed., 1917) and idem, *Modern Tendencies in Sculpture* (Chicago: University of Chicago Press, [1921]). A photograph of the Saint-Gaudens Lincoln appears as the frontispiece of the first volume while a photograph of Saint-Gaudens himself introduces the second. A reprint of the Scammon lectures delivered at the Art Institute of Chicago in 1917, *Modern Tendencies* featured the work of Saint-Gaudens and Rodin. LT to GGB, 28 October 1935, GGBP. The Midway Studios opened in 1906. Taft was best known for his "Clay Talks," the impromptu studio demonstrations he conducted throughout regional America. His final years were spent legislating for a Chicago-based "Dream Museum," wherein would be displayed plaster replications of the world's outstanding sculptural masterworks. These would be be arranged on the pattern of a cathedral plan, with aisles reserved for a chronological progression of monuments that belonged with a single nation or race, and transcepts forming time intersections across these national groupings.

3. LT to GGB, 17 November 1917, GGBP.

4. *The History of American Sculpture*, 292. For a stimulating discussion of ekphrastic speculation on the animated statue see Kenneth Gross, *The Dream of the Moving Statue* (Ithaca: Cornell University Press, 1992). Gross compares Roland Barthes's ontological analysis of the photograph, as found in his classic study, *Camera Lucida: Reflections on Photography* (1981), to the statue that Gross (15) perceives to be "a once living thing whose life has been interrupted; it is a creature stilled, emptied of life, turned to stone or bronze or plaster; captured, thus possibly needing to escape; dead, thus needing ressurrection or galvinization; frozen, thus needing the warmth if hands . . ."

5. GGB to FR, draft, summer 1917, GGBP

6. GGB to FR, draft, summer 1917, GGBP.

7. Ibid.

8. FR to HRB, 26 November 1917, HRBP. FR to HRB, 23 December 1918, HRBP.

9. GGB to DF, draft, fall 1917, GGBP.

10. At a meeting in early-January 1918, the Century Club voted unanimously to condemn the Barnard. Charles Dana Gibson, who, as we have seen, Barnard quoted as having praised the statue was present for the vote. See Robert Lincoln to Judd Stewart, 17 January 1918, RLPH.

11. E. B. Sayre, "Saint-Gaudens' Statue of Abraham Lincoln in Canning Enclosure, Westminster," ms., 12 December 1938, in Nicholas Murray Butler Papers, Rare Book and Manuscript Library, Columbia University, hereafter NMBP. Nicholas Murray Butler to HRB, 4 March 1918, HRBP. Robert Lincoln to HRB, 19 August 1918, HRBP.

12. Henry Haskell for NMB to HRB, 19 December 1918, HRBP. GB to HRB, 30 December 1917, HRBP. Nicholas Murray Butler, *Across Busy Years* (New York: Charles Scribner's Sons, 1940), 383–84. RL to NMB, 17 December 1920, NMBP.

13. JAS to CPT, 11 March 1918, WHTP. JAS to Austin G. Fox, 29 January 1918, HRBP.

14. Nicholas Murray Butler, "Patriotism," in *A World in Ferment,* (New York: Charles Scribner's Sons, 1917), 69–83.

15. Lord Weardale to NMB, 2 March 1918, HRBP. Lord Weardale to NMB, 24 March 1918, HRBP. FR to HRB, 5 February 1918, HRBP. In a dispute distantly resembling the Dreyfus Affair, Barrister Percival F. Smith charged that Mond, who before the war was chairman of the Mond Nickel Company, gained an excessive profit from the firm, and had formed secret alliances with antiwar Bolshiviks and Germans. The charges were dismissed. See "King's Bench Division. The Charges Against Sir Alfred Mond," London *Times,* 24 October 1918, 2. Lord Weardale to NMB, 24 March 1918, HRBP.

16. Walter H. Page, United States Ambassador to Great Britain, to NMB, 19 March 1918, HRBP. JAS to Austin G. Fox, 6 March 1918, HRBP.

17. FR to HRB, 9 January 1918, HRBP. GB to Judd Stewart, encl., in Judd Stewart to HRB, 26 January 1918, HRBP.

18. F. Newlin Price, *Howard Russell Butler* (Princeton: Princeton Univesity Press, 1936), n.p. Howard Russell Butler, "Gift to Great Britain of a Statue of Lincoln," ms., 6, HRBP, and as summarized in "The Proposed Gift to Great Britain of a Statue of Lincoln," *Magazine of Art* 9 (July 1918): 374. "Gift to Great Britain . . . ," 6–16. "Barnard's Statue is Again Opposed," *New York Times,* 1 January 1918, 17.

19. JAS to Austin G. Fox, 16 March 1918 and AGF to JAS, 22 March 1918, HRBP. Fox warned him that Stewart's continued refusal to forward a record of the resolution Choate allegedly had endorsed "would suggest unpleasant inferences." Judd Stewart to HRB, 30 January 1918, HRBP. NMB to HRB, 5 February 1918, HRBP.

20. "Gift to Great Britain . . ." HRB to Maurice Fromkes, 14 March 1918, HRBP. Lawrence Abbott to JAS, 11 March 1918, HRBP.

21. RL to HRB, 15 March 1918, HRBP.

22. JAS to William Howard Taft, 5 February 1918, WHTP. GGB to CPT, 16 March 1918, GGBP.

23. "Gift to Great Britain . . . ," 16.

24. National Academy of Design, "Resolutions and Reports, 1918," ms., HRBP.

25. HRB to Jones, 30 May 1918, HRBP. HRB to Elihu Root, 25 May 1918, HRBP. As Butler reports it, he and De Forest obliged Churchill and Kent by deleting from the proposed preamble a passage reading: "Whereas the danger may still exist that this substitution being acquiesced in by the British committee and authorities through motives of courtesy may plant in London a representative Lincoln which is false to the American remembrance, the American understanding, and the American ideal of the great American." Howard Russell Butler, "Address," in American Federation of Arts, "Proceedings," ms., May 1918, n.p., HRBP.

26. William Roberts, "To the Editor" and Gordon Edwards, "To the Editor," London *Times,* 25 September 1917, 10. Roger Fry, "A Monthly Chronicle," *Burlington Magazine* 32 (June 1918): 240.

27. Richard Buckle, *Jacob Epstein, Sculptor* (Cleveland: World Publishing Co., 1963) 100. Jacob Epstein, *Let There Be Sculpture* (New York: G. P. Putnam's Sons, 1940), 205–7.

28. Epstein, 207. Buckle, 99.

29. Epstein, 92. George Bernard Shaw to Judd Stewart, 11 January 1918, as quoted in Bullard, *Lincoln in Marble and Bronze,* 231, 232.

30. Col. C. S. Ridley to William Phillips, 9 October 1918, HRBP. CM to HRB, 28 September 1918, HRBP. HRB to CM, 30 September 1918, HRBP. NMB to AM, 6 November 1918, encl., in Henry S. Haskell to HRB, 6 November 1918, HRBP. NMB to HRB, 2 December 1918, HRBP.

31. "Comrads in Blood," London *Times,* 21 November 1918, 3. "Two Lincoln Statues," London *Times,* 21 December 1918, 3.

32. E. B. Sayre, "Saint-Gaudens' Statue of Abraham Lincoln in Canning Enclosure, Westminister," 1, 2.

33. H. S. Perris to the (Manchester) Town Clerk, 1 January 1918, as quoted in City of Manchester, *Proceedings of the Council 1918–1919* (Manchester: Henry Blacklock and Co., 1919) 1: 168, 169.

34. John Makeague, Lord Mayor, Manchester, to the Anglo-American Committee of Fine Arts, London, 31 December 1918, in ibid., 167, 168.

35. Editorial, London *Times,* 31 December 1918, 9.

36. J. L. Hammond and Barbara Hammond, *The Town Laborer, 1760–1832* (London: Longmans, Green and Co., 1918) 1: 45–47. "Introduction" in John H. G. Archer, ed., *Art and Architecture in Victorian Manchester* (Manchester: Univesity of Manchester Press, 1985), 21, 22. Archer, 11, 12. Benedict Read, *Victorian Sculpture* (New Haven: Yale University Press, 1982), 107–13. Read, 112.

37. City of Manchester, *Epitome of Proceedings of Committees, 1918–1919* (City of Manchester, 1919), 116, 117. H. S. Perris to Lord Mayor of Manchester, 31 January 1919, in *Epitome,* 164. JAS to GGB, 11 February 1919; HSP to GGB, 11 February 1919, GGBP.

38. "Choosing a Site," *Manchester Guardian,* 6 May 1919. Approval was delayed until 4 July. *Epitome,* 405.

39. "Anglo-American Friendship," *Manchester Guardian,* 6 May 1919. "The Barnard Lincoln," *Manchester Guardian,* 6 May 1919.

40. "Lincoln Statue Unveiled," London *Times,* 16 September 1919, 5, and "Judge Parker Presents Statue," *New York Times,* 16 September 1919, 12. The Lord Mayor's invitation to the unveiling (Collection of the Manchester Public Libraries) states, "It is hoped that His Excellency The American Ambassador will be present."

41. The photograph reproduced on p. 176 appeared in the Photogravure section (6) of the *New York Times,* 5 October 1919.

42. "The Statue," *Manchester Guardian,* 16 September 1919.

Chapter 10: Louisville and the Bernheim Lincoln

1. "Unveiling Lincoln Statue," London *Times,* 28 July 1920, 12; "Lincoln Statue Unveiled," London *Times,* 29 July 1920, 13; "'Bleeding World' Needs Our Help, Says Lloyd George," *New York Times,* 29 July 1920, 1.

2. "The United States and the Abbey" and "Westminster Abbey," London *Times,* 28 July 1920, 17.

3. Cass Gilbert, "Augustus St. Gaudens," London *Times,* 29 July 1920, 8; Lord Charnwood, "Abraham Lincoln, A Reading

of His Character," London *Times,* 28 July 1920, 11. "The United States and the Abbey." "'Bleeding World' Needs Our Help;" "Revaluing Public Men," *New York Times,* 15 August 1920, sec. 2, 2; "Elihu Root's Address on Abraham Lincoln," *New York Times,* 22 August 1920, sec. 6, 6. "'Bleeding World' Needs Our Help." "Revaluing Public Men." Howard M. Sachar, *A History of the Jews in America* (New York: Alfred A. Knopf, 1992), 5.

4. Isaac Markens, "Lincoln and the Jews," in Abraham J. Karp, ed., *The Jewish Experience in America* (New York: KTAV Publishing House, Inc., 1969), 3: 220–76. Markens's article first appeared in *American Jewish Historical Society* 17 (1909), 228–31; 234; 222. Markens here quotes from the *Cincinnati Commercial,* 20 April 1865. Cf., Wise's statement in the *American Isrealite* 2, no. 43 (21 April 1865): 339, as quoted in James G. Heller, *Isaac Wise* (New York: Union of American Jewish Congregations, 1965), 371.

5. Heller, 371.

6. Felix A. Levy, *Selected Works of Hyman G. Enelow,* (Chicago: privately printed, 1935) 2: 293.

7. "Replica of Statue of Lincoln to be Presented to Louisville," *Louisville Courier-Journal,* 19 May 1920, 2.

8. Isaac Wolfe Bernheim, *Closing Chapters of a Busy Life* (Denver: Welch-Haffner Printing Co., 1929), 1–16. William L. Downard, *Dictionary of the History of the American Brewing and Distilling Industries* (Westport, Conn.: Greenwood Press, 1980), 20. Downard, 21. Bernheim, 36–41. Herman Landau, *Adath Louisville* (Louisville, Ky.: by the author, 1981), 19–20; Sachar, 99; Bernheim, 41, 83–88. Mrs. Adolph Ochs, wife of the publisher, was Isaac Wise's daughter. Bernheim, 80; Frank H. Bunce, "Dreams From a Pack—Isaac Wolfe Bernheim Forest, *Filson Club History Quarterly* 47, no. 4 (October, 1973): 323–28.

9. Levy, *Selected Works,* 1, 12. Bernheim, *Closing Chapters,* 74.

10. Federal Works Agency, *Libraries and Lotteries* (Cynthiana, Ky.: Hobson Book Press, 1944), 32–34. Ibid., 34–78.

11. George R. Leighton, *Five Cities; The Story of Their Youth an Old Age* (New York: Harper and Brothers, 1939), 68. Isaac W. Bernheim, *The Reform Church of the American Isrealites,* pamphlet, Buffalo, New York, 1921, 10–11. The speaker scores the continued usage of such terms as "Jew," "Judaism," "Synagogue," and "Temple" because of their acquired pejorative connotations.

12. "Yesterday at the Academy," *Louisville Journal,* 13 February 1867, 2. James Speed's oration highlighted a gala reception which attracted high-ranking Confederate veterans. Kentucky-born Albert Henry (1836–72), a colonel in the Union Army, apparently had no formal art training. Following his release from Libby Prison, he completed a plaster portrait of Lincoln from life. Local tradition maintains the plaster was a model for the marble bust which he carved in Hiram Power's Florentine studio. See Robert L. Kincaid," Forgotten Bust of Lincoln," *Lincoln Herald* 45, no. 1 (February 1943): 16–19, and "The Lincoln Bust," *Lincoln Herald* 45, no. 2 (June 1943): 27. Samuel Price *Old Masters of the Blue Grass* (Louisville, Ky.: J. P. Morton and Co., 1902), 163; Craven, *Sculpture in America,* 199. The Prentice statue was among the last works of Louis-Alexis-Achille Bouly (1805–76), a resident of Amiens, France. A brief history of the commission appears in "Prentice Paid Tribute Anew," *Louisville Courier-Journal,* 30 June 1914, 4.

13. The Kentucky Woman's Confederate Monument Association originally accepted a design by Louisville-born Enid Yandall that featured a female allegorical figure at the apex of a seventy-five foot obelisk. A consortium of interested male residents succeeded in overturning the association's decision. See "To the Confederate Dead," *Louisville Courier-Journal,* 20 September 1894, 6; "Rejected the Report," *Louisville Courier-Journal,* 2 October 1894, 6; "Mr. Mouldoon Says A Word," *Louisville Courier-Journal,* 5 October 1894, 6 and "The Tribute of Women," *Louisville Courier-Journal,* 31 July 1895, 1. Justus Bier, "A Forgotten Work by Ferdinand von Miller the Younger: A Contribution to the History of the Confederate Monument," *Kentucky Historical Society Register* 54, no. 187 (April 1956): 125–33. Bier corrects common misattributions to the artist as "Von Muller," or "Von Mueller."

14. "Put in Place," *Louisville Courier-Journal,* 26 May 1895, 4. Mrs. Walter N. Haldeman, wife of the newspaper publisher, chaired the executive committee of the Kentucky Woman's Monument Association. Prominent among male supporters was Confederate Gen. Basil W. Duke, an attorney who served as chief political lobbyist for the Louisville and Nashville Railroad and Capt. John H. Leathers, a prominent banker.

15. "Shaft to North in South, "*Louisville Courier-Journal,* 5 June 1921. Erected in 1884, the Vanceburg shaft depicts a Union soldier standing at parade rest. Bernheim, 102–3. "Unveiled," *Louisville Courier-Journal,* 10 November 1901, sec. 4, 1–2. A replica of the Jefferson is at the University of Virginia, Charlottesville. Born in Virginia, Sir Moses Ezekiel (1844–1917) attended the Virginia Military Institute and participated in the Battle of New Market. In the late 1860s he studied sculpture in Cincinnati with Thomas D. Jones and J. Insco Williams, was admitted to Berlin's Royal Academy of Art in 1869, and, after winning a stipend for his ensemble *Israel* four years later, he transferred to Rome. Knighted by the Italian Government, he maintained a studio in the Baths of Diocletion, where he produced a large number of portraits and allegorical works for the American market, particularly its major expositions. Bernheim met the sculptor in Rome in 1896. The Jefferson monument was commissioned in 1897 during one of Ezekiel's infrequent visits to America. See K. H. Wrenshall, "An American Sculptor in Rome," *World's Work,* November 1908, 12256–64, and Craven, *Sculpture in America,* 337–38. Marion Porter, "Quotations of Jefferson to be Dedicated July 4," *Filson Club Historical Quarterly* 17, no. 4 (October 1943): 191–92. Under "Brotherhood" is inscribed the opening line of the Declaration of Independence; beneath "Freedom," who tears the laws of Primogeniture, is written, "I have sworn upon the altar of God eternal hostility against every form of tyranny of the mind of man;" and accompanying "Justice" are the words, "Equal and exact justice to all men, of whatever state or persuasion, religious or political."

16. Bullard, *Lincoln in Marble and Bronze,* 132–33. "Thousands Witness Dedication at Davis Memorial at Fairview," *Louisville Courier-Journal,* 8 June 1924, 1; "Dedicate Memorial to Jefferson Davis," *New York Times,* 7 June 1924, 3. William Haldeman, who died several months after the dedication, was commander in chief of the United Confederate Veterans and president of both the Jefferson Davis Home Association and the Jefferson Davis Memorial Association. Capt. Leathers was treasurer of the Home Association. Bernheim first offered the Ezekial bust to the State of Kentucky for placement under the rotunda of the new capitol before he was aware that Weinman's heroic statue had been earmarked for that location. See Gov. Augustus E. Willson to Isaac and Bernard Bernheim, 30 May 1910, as quoted in Bernheim, *Closing Chapters,* 145. Upon the evidence of standard biographical accounts, this bust or another one it replicated, was produced in 1880. Also see Craven, *Sculpture in America,* 338.

17. Bessie Laub, "The Art Corner," *Louisville Courier-Journal,* 22 July 1917, sec. 4, 2. A painter as well as a journalist, Laub had visited Ezekiel's Roman studio some years earlier. Thomas B. McGregor, "Some New Facts About Abraham Lincoln's Parents," *Kentucky Historical Society Register,* 20, no. 2 (May 1922): 213–18. See, for example, Hyman G. Enelow, "The Religious Element in Lincoln" and "Lincoln, The Patriot," in Levy, 2: 285–99, and Temple Adath Isreal, *Lincoln Centenary Services,* 1909 (Louisville, Ky.). Helen B. Crocker, "Ida Tarbell Follows Lincoln's Footsteps," *Filson Club History Quarterly* 61, no. 2 (April 1987): 217–33.

18. Isaac F. Marcosson, *Marse Henry* (New York: Dodd, Meade and Co., 1951), 82–84, and Joseph F. Wall, *Henry Watterson* (New York: Oxford University Press, 1956), 87–113,

209–22. *Catalog of Art in the Louisville Free Public Library, Painting, Statuary, Etchings, Prints, Photographs and Bronze Tablets* (Louisville, Ky., 1928), 218, 219. Both the Watterson and Bernheim art collections, which remained separately grouped in the library at least until 1944, have now been dispersed. Number 218 is listed as Ames Van Wart's *Youth of Lincoln* (bronze) and 219 as Weinman's *Abraham Lincoln,* a "bronze replica of Statue in the Rotunda in the State Capital."

19. On behalf of the State of Kentucky, Bernheim presented Niehaus's life-sized statues of Henry Clay and Ephraim McDowell to the United States government for placement in the Capitol's Statuary Hall. Replicas of both works flank Weinman's Lincoln at the Frankfort capitol. See House, *Acceptance and Unveiling of the Statues of Henry Clay and Dr. Ephraim McDowell,* 70th Cong., 2d Sess., 1929, H. Doc. 614.

20. C. K., "Isaac W. Bernheim, A Personal Study," in Bernheim, *Closing Chapters,* 120.

21. Isaac W. Bernheim to GGB, 14 February 1920, GGBP (unless otherwise indicated Barnard correspondence is with GGBP). GGB Secretary to IWB, 28 April 1920. GGB Secretary to IWB, 17 February 1920. Contract for executing Bernheim Lincoln, 28 April 1920. IWB to GGB, 20 April 1920. GGB Secretary to IWB, 10 March 1920. Contract for casting Bernheim Lincoln with the Roman Bronze Works, 10 May 1920. Milford Pink-Victoria Granite Company to GGB, 11 September 1922.

22. Susan E. Tifft and Alex S. Jones, *The Patriarch* (New York: Summit Books, 1991), 117–18 and Wall, 323–28. Huston Quin, "Gift of Millions for Kentucky," *Louisville Board of Trade Journal* 21, no. 1 (January 1938): 5. Bernheim, *Closing Chapters,* 112.

23. Bernheim, 112. George C. Wright, *Life Behind a Veil; Blacks in Louisville Kentucky, 1865–1930* (Baton Rouge: Louisiana State University Press, 1985), 248. Wright, 249. Ibid., 247.

24. "Lincoln Statue is Gift to City," *Louisville Post,* 19 May 1920.

25. "Replica of Statue of Lincoln to be Presented to Louisville."

26. "Urges 'God's Thumb' As Memorial Site," *New York Times,* 17 October 1920, sec. 2, 8. "'Masque of Cloisters' in Old World Setting," *New York Times,* 15 May 1920, 15. "Noted Sculptor Finds Kentucky Rich in Material," *Louisville Times,* 1 June 1920.

27. See chapter 3, n. 1 and Lucien V. Rule, "George Grey Barnard's Lincoln and 'Let There Be Light,'" *Louisville Courier-Journal,* 5 January 1930. Cawein was close friends with painter-illustrator Eric Pape, the husband of Edna Barnard's sister, Alice. When Barnard arrived in Louisville to search for a model, Cawein wrote a friend, "He is a brilliant man, and most enthusiastic about art and poetry. I told him to go to the mountains [to find a model]. He is going for he is a man that brooks no delay and is filled with energy." See Otto A. Rothert, *The Story of a Poet: Madison Cawein* (Louisville, Ky.: John P. Morton and Co., 1921), 316.

28. Crocker, "Ida Tarbell Follows Lincoln's Footsteps," 217–33. Rothert, 309. Cale Young Rice, *Bridging the Years* (New York: D. Appleton-Century Company, 1939), 109.

29. "Lincoln Statue Will Please Louisville, Artists Believe," unidentified clipping, ca., 20 May 1920, Local History file, Louisville Free Public Library. Rice, *Bridging the Years,* 108.

30. "Lincoln Statue Probably Will Be in Central Park," *Louisville Herald,* 5 January 1921. "Park Proposed As Statue Site," *Louisville Herald,* 4 May 1921. "Mrs. C. F. Huhlein Heads Outdoor Art League," *Louisville Times,* 7 May 1921. "Artist to Urge Library Lawn As Site for Statue of Lincoln," *Louisville Courier-Journal,* 22 May 1921. "Lincoln Bronze Site is Selected, *Louisville Courier-Journal,* 9 March 1922.

31. Federal Works Agency, 84. Pilcher served as New York State architect for the first two decades of the century. See A. D. T. Hamlin, "The State Architect and His Works," *Architectural Record* 53, no. 292 (January 1923): 27–43.

32. GGB to Roman Bronze Works, 14 May 1920, and GGB Secretary to IWB, 5 December 1921. GGB to RBW, 30 August 1920, and GGB to IWB, 19 January 1921. "Fierce Blaze at Brooklyn Plant," *New York Times,* 12 May 1921, 2. "100 Models Destroyed by Flames," *New York Times,* 14 May 1921, 18.

33. IWB to GGB, 30 August 1922.

34. IWB to GGB, 3 June 1921. "Controversy About Lincoln Statue Not Allayed by Sculptor," *Louisville Courier-Journal,* 28 October 1922. IWB to GGB, 12 August 1922. Secretary GGB to IWB, 17 March 1922. GGB to IWB, draft for telegram, n.d. Arthur Loomis to GGB, 17 August 1922, and AL to GGB, 6 October 1922.

35. AL to GGB, 18 April 1922. GGB Secretary to IWB, 5 December 1921.

36. "Controversy About Lincoln Statue Not Allayed by Sculptor." "'Truth' Remains in Lincoln Work," *Louisville Times,* 27 October 1922, 1, 16.

37. "Controversy About Lincoln Statue Not Allayed by Sculptor." A. O. Elsner to GGB, 6 October 1922.

38. "Jefferson Davis Monument," *Louisville Times,* 26 October 1922, 6. "Lincoln in Bronze," ibid.; "The Lincoln," *Louisville Times,* 28 October 1922, 6. Plaschal,"The Semaphor," *Louisville Times,* 4 November 1922.

39. Jean H. Coady, "Nostalgia," *Louisville Courier-Journal,* 21 July 1980.

40. "Thousands See Flag Drop From Lincoln Statue," *Louisville Times,* 26 October 1922, 1.

41. "Statue Draws Admiration Of Layman and Critic," *Louisville Herald,* 28 October, 1922.

42. "Model for Barnard's Statue of Lincoln Seeks Work Here," *Louisville Times,* 17 February 1922. "Charles Thomas, Model for Barnard's Lincoln," *Louisville Courier-Journal,* 16 November 1922.

Chapter 11: The Test of Time

1. Leslie George Katz, as quoted in Lee Friedlander, *The America Monument* (New York: Eakins Press Foundation, 1976), n.p.

2. "Lincoln Statue is Green, Not With Envy or Grime, But With Artistic Patina," *Cincinnati Enquirer,* 9 February 1944; "Lincoln Revered at Two Statues," *Cincinnati Enquirer,* 13 February 1944. In J. Gene Hibbs to the Editor, *Louisville Courier-Journal,* 7 September 1992, the correspondent complained specifically about the removal of the verdigris from the John Castleman statue. Comparable objections were voiced in regard to the Manchester Lincoln in John Prince, "Old Abe's Deep Tan is a Real Turn-off," *Manchester Evening News,* 9 April 1991, 4, and in Derek Brumhead to the Editor, *Manchester Evening News,* 13 April 1991, 8. Micheal W. Panhorst, "Brief History of Outdoor Sculpture and Monuments in the United States," in National Museum of American Art and National Institute for the Conservation of Cultural Property, Inc., "SOS, Surveyor's Handbook," typescript [Washington, D.C.: ca. 1991], 38, 42.

3. *Cincinnati Enquirer,* 12 February 1933. The annual observances were routinely covered in the *Enquirer* and *Cincinnati Times-Star.*

4. Cincinnati Historical Society, *A Guide to the Queen City and Its Neighbors* [WPA Guide to Cincinnati], 162–68. Jana C. Morford, "Preserving a 'Special Place:' The Lytle Park Neighborhood, 1948–1976," *Queen City Heritage* 44, no. 3 (fall 1986): 13.

5. Morford, 4, 5.

6. Ibid., 6. Charles Phelps Taft II (1897–1983), who headed Cincinnati's Charter Party, was one-time mayor and a sixteen-term city councilman. In 1947 he became the first layman to be selected president of the World Council of Churches. Blake Clark, "Wanton Disregard of Our Heritage," [condensed from

The Diplomat] *Reader's Digest,* January 1959, 120–23. "Lytle Park Example of 'Sacrifice,'" *Cincinnati Post and Times Star,* 2 January 1959, 2

7. Morford, "Preserving," 6–19; Cincinnati Park Commission, Minutes of Meeting, 18 August 1971, Book 31 (1971–74), Cincinnati Park Board.

8. Howard Wilkenson, "Artist Takes Pride in Statue Repairs for Local Parks," *Cincinnati Enquirer,* 13 June 1983, C-1; Biographical Supplement, *Cincinnati Enquirer,* 9 October 1988, 45.

9. Cincinnati Architectural Board of Review, Minutes of Meeting, 25 April 1972; Box 22, Folder 6, Papers of Charles Phelps Taft II, Cincinnati Historical Society. Serving at that moment as a member of the Review Board, Taft moved that Karkadoulias proceed with a brown, rather than green, finish. Wilkenson, E-2.

10. Wilkenson; John M. Kennedy, "Lincoln and Karkadoulias," *Cincinnati Post,* 17 November 1972, 2, 3.

11. "Back Where He Belongs," *Cincinnati Enquirer,* 11 December 1970; ibid., 19 August 1971; "Robert A. Taft Jr. Pulls Rope," *Cincinnati Post,* 17 November 1972.

12. Eleanora W. Schoenebaum, *Political Profiles: The Nixon-Ford Years, Part 5* (New York: Facts on File, Inc., 1979), 631, 632.

13. Bill Kovack, "Amnesty Bill for Foes Of Draft is Introduced in Senate by Taft," *New York Times,* 4 December 1971, 4. A representative response by protestors to Taft's overture is found in Allan Gelbin, "Amnesty or Punishment," *New York Times,* 28 January 1972, 44.

14. *Cincinnati Enquirer,* 18 May and 21 June 1983; *Cincinnati Post,* 18 May 1983.

15. Owen Findsen, "Art Lives . . . Here, There, Everywhere," *Cincinnati Enquirer,* 13 July 1980, 15. John Clubbe, *Cincinnati Observed: Architecture and History* (Columbus: Ohio State University Press, 1992), 135.

16. Erika Doss, *Spirit Poles and Flying Pigs: Public Art and Cultural Democracy in American Communities* (Washington, D.C.: Smithsonian Institution Press, 1995), 197–236. The author uphold's Leicester's *Cincinnati Gateway* as an ideal standard for other public sculptors to follow.

17. "A Quiet Pilot Revs Up MEPC," *Sunday Times* (London), 16 August 1987, sec. A, 49. C. J. Ellison, Manager, MEPC Regional Office, to V. Cressey, Manchester Town Clerk's Department, 5 April 1984, collection of The City of Manchester Planning Department, hereafter MPD.

18. Ellison to Cressey.

19. Paul R. Saulter, Chief Executive, Manchester Chamber of Commerce and Industry to C. J. Ellison, 2 April 1984, MPD.

20. Ken Strath, Chairman, Manchester City Council, to Alistair Cooke, 24 September 1985, MPD. Manchester City Council, "Note of a Meeting to Consider the Arrangements for the Unveiling of the Abraham Lincoln Statue," 16 January 1986, MPD.

21. "Note of a Meeting."

22. "Note of a Meeting." "Abe Waits for Fresh Start," *Manchester Evening News,* clipping, 1986, MPD. Ray King, "In a Word, History is Changed!," *Manchester Evening News,* 13 November 1986, 1.

23. "In a Word, History in Changed!"

24. "Rewriting History," *Manchester Evening News,* 14 November 1986, 6

25. William Showcraft, Manchester City Planning Officer, to P. A. Sykes, Manchester Keeper of Conservation, 2 February 1990, MPD.

26. Sheldon Shafer, "Hot Wax and Walnuts to Brighten City's Lincoln Statue," *Louisville Courier-Journal,* 9 July 1991, sec. B, 1, 6.

27. Interview, Karolle Swanson, 2 August 1993.

Epilogue

1. Michael E. Shapiro, *Bronze Casting and American Sculpture, 1850–1900* (Newark: University of Delaware Press, 1985), 147. The full-scale model for the *Rainbow Arch* was placed on public view in 1933 at a power house off Broadway at 216th street, Manhattan. Plaster relief figures averaging nine feet high were hung against a temporary wood-and-canvas screen. Measuring 105 feet high by 60 feet wide, the ensemble was intended to be positioned against a mosaic of colored marble formed into an arch. In the central space below was a graveyard representing Flanders Field. A printout containing Barnard's description reads in part, "The Rainbow (of Hope—that wars will end). The souls of the nation's boys in human form, as living, and pure as the sculptor could create them. Each has his personal emotion, as he realizes the dawn of immortality." See R. P., "American Sculptor; George Grey Barnard," *Arts and Decoration* 62 no. 1 (November 1934): 33–39. For his Grand Central Gallery exhibition, see L. E., "Barnard Holds a Retrospective at Grand Central, *Art News,* April 20, 1935, 3, 4.

2. J. L. Schrader, "George Grey Barnard; The Cloisters and The Abbaye," 45–52; Ethel W. Everett, "Prefiguring the Nation's War Memorial," *New York Times,* sec. 3, 15.

3. "Barnard, Sculptor, is Dead at 74," *New York Times,* 25 April 1938, 1, 3. A *New York Times* editor (26 April 1938, 20) pointed to an irony in the fact that Barnard died almost on the eve of the new Cloisters opening. "Artists Present at Barnard Rites," *New York Times,* 28 April 1938, 23. "Burial Rites for Barnard," *New York Times,* 29 April 1938, 21. It was disclosed that the artist had distributed $300,000 of the $650,000 Cloister sale proceeds to his family, but that he later borrowed $50,000 of this back from Edna Barnard's share "for my collection." The will also noted that an additional $100,000 loan was taken out "to perfect the collection" and directed that the executors consider selling the collection, his house, and his property south of the Cloisters in order to settle the debt and help pay for the completion of the *Arch.* Only the old brick monastery itself was not to be sold, for it was to be in front of it that the *Rainbow Arch* was to be installed. See "Barnard Willed Estate for Arch," *New York Times,* 4 May 1938, 24. "Rainbow Arch Memorial Dismantled," *New York Times,* 1 December 1938, 17.

Select Bibliography

Books

Allison, Henry Darracott. *Dublin Days, Old and New; New Hampshire Fact and Fancy.* New York: Exposition Press, 1952.

Anderson, Ross. *Abbott Handerson Thayer.* Syracuse, N.Y.: Everson Museum, 1982.

Anderson, Stuart. *Race and Rapproachement: Anglo-Saxonism and Anglo-American Relations,* 1895–1904. Cranbury, N.J.: Associated University Presses, 1981.

Archer, John H. G., ed. *Art and Architecture in Victorian Manchester.* Manchester, England: University of Manchester Press, 1985.

Ball, Thomas. *My Threescore Years and Ten: An Autobiography.* Boston: Robert Brothers, 1892.

Barnard, Evan G. *A Rider on the Cherokee Strip.* Boston: Houghton Mifflin, 1936.

Barnard's Statue of Lincoln. Cincinnati: Stewart and Kidd, 1917.

Bell, Ralcy Husted. *The Philosophy of Painting: A Study of the Development of the Art From Prehistory to Modern Times.* New York: G. P. Putnam's Sons, 1916.

Bernheim, Isaac Wolfe. *Closing Chapters of a Busy Life.* Denver: Welch-Haffner Printing Co., 1929.

Blackwood, John. *London's Immortals.* London: Savoy Press, 1989.

Blair, Fredricka. *Isadora: Portrait of the Artist As a Woman.* New York: McGraw-Hill, 1986.

Bogart, Michele H. *Public Sculpture and the Civic Ideal in New York City, 1890–1920.* Chicago: University of Chicago Press, 1989.

Brady, Kathleen. *Ida Tarbell, Portrait of a Muckraker.* New York: Harper and Bros., 1946.

Brockwell, Maurice W. *Catalogue of Paintings in the Collection of Mr. and Mrs. Charles P. Taft at Cincinnati, Ohio.* New York: privately published, 1920.

Brown, Milton W. *The Story of the Armory Show.* Greenwich, Conn.: New York Graphic Society, 1963.

———. *American Painting From the Armory Show to the Depression.* Princeton: Princeton University Press, 1955.

Buckle, Richard. *Jacob Epstein, Sculptor.* Cleveland: World Publishing Co., 1963.

Bullard, Frederic Luristan. *Lincoln in Marble and Bronze.* New Brunswick: Rutgers University Press, 1952.

Burton, David Henry. *The Learned Presidency: Theodore Roosevelt, William Howard Taft, Woodrow Wilson.* Rutherford, N.J.: Fairleigh Dickinson University Press, c. 1988.

Butler, Nicholas Murray. *Across Busy Years.* New York: Charles Scribner's Sons, 1940.

———. *A World in Ferment.* New York: Charles Scribner's Sons, 1917.

Butt, Archibald Willingham. *Taft and Roosevelt, The Intimate Letters of Archie Butt.* 2 vols. Garden City, N.Y.: Doubleday, Doran and Company, 1930.

Caffin, Charles Henry. *American Masters of Sculpture; Being Brief Appreciations of Some Phases of Sculpture in America.* New York: Doubleday, Page and Co., 1903.

Carnegie Endowment for International Peace. *A Manual of the Public Benefactions of Andrew Carnegie.* Washington, D.C.: by the endowment, 1919.

Charnwood, Godfrey Rathbone Benson. *Abraham Lincoln.* New York: Henry Holt and Co., 1917.

Charteris, Evan. *John Sargent.* New York: Benjamin Blom, Inc., 1972.

Cincinnati Art Museum. *Cincinnati Landmarks: A Bicentennial Exhibition.* Cincinnati, 1976.

Cincinnati Historical Society. *A Guide to the Queen City and Its Neighbors [WPA Guide to Cincinnati].* Cincinnati: by the society, 1940.

City of Manchester. *Epitome of Proceedings of Committees, 1918–1919.* Manchester, England.

Cladel, Judith. *Rodin, The Man and His Art.* Trans. by S. K. Star. New York: Century Co., 1917.

Clark, Alfred Corning. *Lorentz Severin Skougaard.* New York: G. P. Putnam's Sons, 1885.

Clark, William J. *Great American Sculptures.* Philadelphia: Gebbie and Barrie, 1878.

Clubbe, John. *Cincinnati Observed; Architecture and History.* Columbus: Ohio State University Press, 1992.

Conckling, Edward Franklin. *The Lincoln Memorial.* Washington, D.C.: Government Printing Office, 1927.

Crane, Frank. *The Looking Glass.* New York: John Lane Co., 1917.

————. *God and Democracy.* Chicago: Forbes and Co., 1912.

Craven, Wayne. *Sculpture in America.* 1968. Rev. ed., Newark: University of Delaware Press, 1984.

Dijkstra, Bram. *Idols of Perversity; Fantasies of Feminine Evil in Fin-de-Siècle Culture.* New York: Oxford University Press, 1986.

Doss, Erika. *Spirit Poles and Flying Pigs; Public Art and Cultural Democracy in American Communities.* Washington, D.C.: Smithsonian Institution Press, 1995.

Dreiser, Theodore. *The Genius.* New York: John Lane Co., 1915.

Drinkwater, John. *Abraham Lincoln.* Boston: Houghton Mifflin, 1918.

Dryfhout, John H. *The Work of Augustus Saint-Gaudens.* Hanover, New Hampshire: University Press of New England, 1982.

Duncan, Isadora. *My Life.* New York: Boni and Liveright, 1927.

Durman, Donald C. *He Belongs to the Ages; The Statues of Abraham Lincoln.* Ann Arbor: University of Michigan Press, 1951.

Easton, (Loyd David). *Hegel's First American Followers.* Athens: Ohio University Press, 1966.

Ege, Arvia MacKaye. *The Power of the Impossible: The Story of Percy and Marion MacKaye.* Falmouth, Maine: Kennebec River Press, 1992.

Elsen, Albert E. *Rodin's Thinker and the Dilemmas of Modern Public Sculpture.* New Haven: Yale University Press, 1985.

————. *Rodin Rediscovered.* Washington, D.C.: National Gallery of Art, 1981.

————. *Rodin.* London: Secker and Warburg, 1974.

Epstein, Jacob. *Epstein, An Autobiography.* London: Vista Books, 1963.

————. *Let There Be Sculpture.* New York: G. P. Putnam's Sons, 1940.

Flint, Charles (Ranlett). *Memories of an Active Life: Men, and Ships, and Sealing Wax.* New York: G. P. Putnam's Sons, 1923.

Foner, Philip (Sheldon). *The Bolshivik Revolution: Its Impact on American Radicals, Librals, and Labor.* New York: International Publishers, 1967.

Ford, Henry A. and Kate B. *History of Cincinnati, Ohio, With Illustrations and Biographical Sketches.* Cleveland, Ohio: L. A. Williams and Co., 1841.

Friedlander, Lee. *The American Monument.* New York: Eakins Press Foudations, 1976.

Genthe, Arnold. *. . . As I Remember.* New York: Reynal and Hitchcock, 1936.

Goff, John S. *Robert Todd Lincoln; A Man in His Own Right.* Norman: University of Oklahoma Press, 1969.

Goldstein, Rosalie. *Controversial Public Art From Rodin to di Suvero.* Milwaukee, Wisconsin: Milwaukee Art Museum, 1984.

Greve, Charles Theodore. *Centennial History of Cincinnati and Representative Citizens.* 2 vols. Chicago: Biographical Publishing Co., 1904.

Gross, Kenneth. *The Dream of the Living Statue.* Ithaca, N.Y.: Cornell University Press, 1992.

Grover, Edwin O. *Annals of an Era; Percy MacKaye and the MacKaye Family, 1826–1932.* Hanover, N.H.: Dartmouth College, 1932.

Hanna, Katherine. *The Taft Museum Catalogue.* Cincinnati: The Taft Museum, c. 1956.

Hechler, Ken. *Insurgency; Personalities and Politics of the Taft Era.* New York: Russell and Russell, 1964.

Heller, James G. *Isaac Wise.* New York: Union of American Jewish Congregations, 1965.

Hendrick, Burton Jesse. *The Life and Letters of Walter H. Page.* 2 vols. New York: Doubleday, Page and Co., 1922–25.

Johnson, Gerald W. *An Honorable Titan.* New York: Harper and Bros., 1946.

Kimbrough, Sara. *Drawn From Life: The Story of Four American Artists Whose Friendship and Work Began in Paris During the 1880s.* Oxford: University of Mississippi Press, 1976.

Kozar, Andrew J. *R. Tait McKenzie, The Sculptor of Athletes.* Knoxville: University of Tennessee Press, 1975. Rev. ed., 1991.

Landau, Herman. *Adath Louisville.* Louisville: by the author, 1981.

Leighton, George R. *Five Cities: The Story of Their Youth and Old Age.* New York: Harper and Bros., 1939.

Levy, Felix A. *Selected Works of Hyman G. Enelow.* 2 vols. Chicago: privately printed, 1935.

Lincoln, W. Bruce. *Passage Through Armageddon: The Russians in War and Revolution.* New York: Simon and Schuster, 1986.

List, Charles. *Cincinnati in 1841; Its Early Annals and Future Prospects.* Cincinnati: by the author, 1841.

Leonard, Lewis Alexander. *The Life of Alphonso Taft.* New York: Hawkes Publishing Company, 1920.

Leopold, Richard W. *Elihu Root and the Conservative Tradition.* Boston: Little, Brown and Co., 1954.

Lewis, William Draper. *The Life of Theodore Roosevelt.* United Publishers of the United States and Canada, 1919.

Lincoln National Life Foundation. *Heroic Lincoln Statues in Bronze.* Fort Wayne: by the author, 1957.

MacKaye, Percy. *Epoch: The Life of Steele MacKaye, Genius of the Theater, in Relation to His Times and Contemporaries.* 2 vols. New York: Boni and Liveright, 1928.

Marcosson, Isaac F. *Marse Henry.* New York: Dodd, Meade and Co., 1951.

Martin, Edward S. *The Life of Joseph Hodges Choate*. 2 vols. London: Constable and Co., 1920.

Memories of the Ohio Valley. 2 vols. Madison, Wis.: Federal Publishing Co., 1905.

Miller, Zane L. *Boss Cox's Cincinnati: Urban Politics in the Progressive Era*. New York: Oxford University Press, 1968.

Moore, Charles. *Daniel Burnham: Architect Planner of Cities*. 2 vols. Boston: Houghton Mifflin, 1921.

[Moran, Ned]. *A Man Who Lived for Men*. Privately printed, 1896.

Nevins, Allan. *Henry White: Thirty Years of American Diplomacy*. New York: Harper and Bros., 1930.

Olsen, Stanley. *J. S. Sargent, His Portrait*. London: MacMillan Co., 1986.

Partridge, Warren G. *The Life of Frederick H. Alms*. Cincinnati: Jennings and Graham, 1904.

Peck, Herbert. *The Book of Rookwood Pottery*. New York: Crown Publishers, Inc., 1968.

Perris, Harry S. *Pax Brittanica*. New York: MacMillan Co., 1913.

Price, F. Newlin. *Howard Russell Butler*. Princeton, N.J.: Princeton University Press, 1936.

Read, Benedict. *Victorian Sculpture*. New Haven: Yale University Press, 1982.

Reps, John William. *Monumental Washington: The Planning and Development of the Capital*. Princeton, N.J.: Princeton University Press, 1967.

Rice, Cale Young. *Bridging the Years*. New York: D. Appleton-Century Co., 1939.

Richman, Micheal T. *Daniel Chester French: An American Sculptor*. New York: Metropolitan Museum of Art for the National Trust for Historic Preservation, 1976.

Roosevelt, Theodore. *The Letters of Theodore Roosevelt*. Edited by Etting E. Morison. 8 vols. Cambridge: Harvard University Press, 1954.

Ross, Ishbell. *An American Family; The Tafts, 1678–1964*. Cleveland, Ohio: World Publishing Co., 1964.

Rule, Lucien V. *Forerunners of Lincoln in the Ohio Valley*. Louisville, Ky.: Brandt and Fowles, 1927.

Rydberg, Viktor. *Roman Days*. Trans. by Alfred Corning Clark. New York: G. P. Putnam's Sons, 1879.

Saarinen, Aline. *The Proud Possessors*. New York: Vintage Books, 1968.

Saslow, James M. *Ganymede in the Renaissance, Homosexuality in Art and Society*. New Haven: Yale University Press, 1986.

Shaff, Howard and Aubray K. *Six Wars At a Time*. Darien, Conn.: Permelia Publications, 1985.

Shapiro, Micheal E. *Bronze Casting and American Sculpture, 1850–1900*. Newark: University of Delaware Press, 1985.

Sharp, Lewis I. *John Quincy Adams Ward, Dean of American Sculpture: With a Catalogue Raisonne*. Newark: Delaware: University of Delaware Press, 1985.

Shaw, Albert. *Abraham Lincoln; His Path to the Presidency (A Cartoon History)*. New York: Review of Reviews, 1929.

———. *Lincoln in Contemporary Caricature*. New York: Review of Reviews, 1901.

Shroder, Maurice C. Icarus, *The Image of the Artist in French Romanticism*. Cambridge: Harvard University Press, 1961.

Strong, Theron G. *Joseph H. Choate*. New York: Dodd, Meade and Co., 1917.

Sutton, Denys, ed. *Letters of Roger Fry*. 2 vols. New York: Random House, 1972.

Taft, Ida Barlett. *Lorado Taft, Sculptor and Citizen*. Greensboro, N.C.: May Taft Smith, 1946.

Taft, Lorado. *The History of American Sculpture*. New York: MacMillan Co., 1903.

Taft, Lorado. *The History of American Sculpture*. New York: MacMillan Co., 1903; Rev. ed., 1917.

Tarbell, Ida M. *The Early Life of Abraham Lincoln; Containing Many Unpublished Documents and Unpublished Reminiscences of Lincoln's Early Friends*. New York: S. S. McClure, 1896.

———. *In the Footsteps of the Lincolns*. New York: Harper and Bros., 1924.

Tomkins, Calvin. *Merchants and Masterpieces*. New York: E. P. Dutton, 1970.

Trachtenberg, Marvin. *The Statue of Liberty*. London: Penguin, 1976.

Vitz, Robert. *The Queen and the Arts: Cultural Life in Nineteenth-Century Cincinnati*. Kent State, Ohio: Kent State University Press, 1989.

Wall, Joseph F. *Andrew Carnegie*. New York: Oxford University Press, 1970.

———. *Henry Watterson*. New York: Oxford University Press, 1956.

Wilson, Woodrow. *On Being Human*. New York: Harper and Bros., 1916.

———. *Papers*. Edited by Arthur S. Link. 69 vols. Princeton, N.J.: Princeton University Press, 1966–1979.

Works Project Administration. *Texas, a Guide to the Lone Star State*. New York: Hastings House, 1940.

Wright, George C. *Life Behind a Veil: Blacks in Louisville Kentucky, 1865–1930*. Baton Rouge: Louisiana State University Press, 1985.

Wright, Grant. *The Art of Caricature*. New York: Baker Taylor Co., 1904.

Articles and Collected Essays

Allison, J.M. "God-Sent Inspiration Says Sculptor," *Cincinnati Times-Star*, 11 December 1916. "Americans of To-morrow—George Grey Barnard, Sculptor." *Harper's Weekly*, 23 August 1902: 1133–34; 1155.

"Barnard, Sculptor, is Dead at 74," *New York Times,* 25 April 1938, 1, 3.

"Barnard's Lincoln As a Noted Painter Sees It," *New York Times,* Sunday, 28 October 1917, sec. 7.

"Mr. Barnard's 'Lincoln' Once More—Some Public Comments." *Art World* 3, no. 1 (October 1917): 7.

Bartlett, (Truman Howe). "Augustus Rodin, Sculptor." *American Architect and Building News* 25 (1 June 1889): 263.

———. "The Physiognomy of Lincoln." *McClure's Magazine* (August 1907): 391–407.

Borglum, (John Gutzon). "The Beauty of Lincoln." *Everybody's Magazine* (February 1910): 217–20.

Butler, Howard Russell. "The Proposed Gift to Great Britain of a Statue of Lincoln." *American Magazine of Art* 9, no. 9 (July 1918): 375.

Crane, Frank. "Lincoln at Petrograd," [New York] *Globe and Commercial Advertizer* (New York), 26 April 1917.

Crocker, Helen B. "Ida Tarbell Follows Lincoln's Footsteps." *Filson Club Quarterly* 61, no. 2 (April 1987); 217–33.

De Kay, Charles. "An Open-Air Impression of Balzac," *New York Times,* 31 July 1898.

Dickson, Harold E. "George Grey Barnard's Controversity Lincoln." *Art Journal* 27, no. 1 (fall 1967): 8–15, 19, 23.

———. "Barnard and Norway." *Art Bulletin* 44, no. 1 (March 1962): 55–59.

———. "Log of a Masterpiece," *Art Journal* 20, no. 3 (Spring 1961): 139–143.

———. "The Other Orphan." *American Art Journal* 1, no. 2 (fall 1969): 108–18.

———. "Barnard's Sculptures for the Pennsylvania Capitol." *Art Quarterly* 22, no. 3 (summer 1959): 126–47.

———. "Origin of the Cloisters." *Art Quarterly* 28, no. 4 (fall 1965): 252–75.

Editorial, *Times* (London), 31 December 1918.

"Exhibition in New York of Paintings in the Collection of Mr. and Mrs. Charles P. Taft." *Burlington Magazine* 16 (February 1910): 363, 366, 368.

Fry, (Roger Eliot). "A Monthly Chronicle." *The Burlington Magazine* 32 (June 1918): 240.

"George Grey Barnard on the Vicissitudes of a Sculptor," *New York Times,* 27 November 1910.

Gilder, Richard Watson. "Lincoln the Leader." *Century Illustrated Monthly Magazine,* February 1909, 479–507.

Hodges, Leigh. "A New Tradition in American Art." *North American* (Philadelphia), 25 November 1916.

"Judge Parker Presents Statue," *New York Times,* 16 September 1919.

King, Ray. "In a Word, History is Changed!," *Manchester (England) Evening News,* 13 November 1986.

"Lincoln Statue Unveiled," *Times* (London), 16 September 1919.

Macht, Carol. "Introduction," in *The Ladies, God Bless 'Em; The Women's Art Movement in Cincinnati,* 7–13. Cincinnati: Cincinnati Art Museum, 1976.

[MacMonnies, Frederick]. "Barnard's Lincoln," *North American Review,* December 1917, 837–39.

Markens, Isaac. "Lincoln and the Jews." Reprinted from American Jewish Historical Society Publications. In *The Jewish Experience in America.* Edited by Abraham J. Karp, Jr., 220–76. vol. 3. New York: KTAV Publishing House, Inc., 1969.

Meyer, Ruth Krueger. "An Introduction to the Art Collection of Charles Phelps and Anna Sinton Taft." In *The Taft Museum; The History of the Collections and the Baum-Taft House.* Edited by Edward J. Sullivan, 17–39. New York: Hudson Hills Press, 1995.

Moore, Charles. "Daniel Chester French's Statue of Lincoln." *Art and Archaeology* 13 (June 1922): 257.

Morford, Jana C. "Preserving a 'Special Place:' The Lytle Park Neighborhood, 1948–1976." *Queen City Heritage,* 44, no. 3 (fall 1986): 2–22.

"The People's Lincoln," *Touchstone* 2, no. 1 (October 1917): 63.

P. R. "American Sculptor: George Grey Barnard," *Arts and Decoration* 62, no. 1 (November 1934): 33–39.

"The Proposed Gift to Great Britain of a Statue of Lincoln, *The Magazine of Art* 9 (July 1918): 374.

Robbins, Daniel. "Statues to Sculpture: From the Nineties to the Thirties." In Whitney Museum of American Art, *200 Years of American Sculpture,* 112–59. New York: David H. Godine and the museum, 1976.

[Roberts, Mary Fanton]. "Lincoln As His Friends and Admirers Knew Him During His Lifetime." *Touchstone* 2, no. 2 (November 1917): 194.

Ruckstuhl, (Frederick Wellington). "A Standard of Art Measurement," part 1. *The Art World* 1, no. 1 (October 1916): 323.

———. "A Mistake in Bronze." *The Art World* 2, no. 3 (June 1917): 211.

———. "The Effect on Caricature of the Lincoln Controversy." *The Art World* 3, no. 3 (December 1917): 194.

[Ruckstull, Frederick Wellington]. "How to Give Europe a Worthy Lincoln Monument." *The Art World* 3, no. 4 (January 1918): 277.

Rule, Lucien V. "George Grey Barnard's Lincoln and 'Let There be Light'." *Louisville Courier-Journal,* 5 January 1930.

Ryan, Daniel J. "Lincoln and Ohio." *Ohio Archaelogical and Historical Society Publications* 32, no. 1 (January 1923): 1–145.

Schrader, J. L. "George Grey Barnard: The Cloisters and the Abbaye." *Metropolitan Museum of Art Bulletin* 37, no. 1 (May 1979): 2–53.

Schwartz, Abby S. "Nicholas Longworth: Art Patron of Cincinnati." *Queen City Heritage* 46 (spring 1988): 17–32.

"The Statue," *Manchester* (England) *Guardian,* 16 September 1919.

Stein, Roger B. "Artifact as Ideology," in Metropolitan Museum of Art. *In Pursuit of Beauty; Americans and the Aesthetic Movement,* 23–45. New York: Rizzoli, 1986.

"Those Who Love Lincoln: A Word for Barnard's Statue by Ida Tarbell," *Touchstone* 2, no. 3 (December 1917): 225.

"Thousands See Flag Drop From Lincoln Statue," *Louisville Times,* 26 October 1922.

"Urges 'God's Thumb' As Memorial Site," *New York Times,* Sunday, 17 October 1920, sec. 2.

Van Rensselaer, (Mariana Griswold). "Saint Gaudens Lincoln." *Century Monthly Illustrated Magazine,* November 1887, 37–39.

"The Western Art Movement, *Century Monthly Illustrated Magazine,* August 1886, 578–80.

Woolf, (Stuart Joseph). "The Stormy Petrel of the Ocean of Art," *New York Times Magazine,* 7 December 1930.

Young, Denny. "The Longworths: Three Generations of Art Patronage in Cincinnati." In *Celebrate Cincinnati Art: In Honor of the One Hundreth Anniversary of the Cincinnati Art Museum, 1881–1981,* 29–47. Edited by Kenneth R. Trapp. Cincinnati: Cincinnati Art Museum, 1982.

Young (Mahonri Sharp). "George Grey Barnard and the Cloisters." *Apollo* 104 (November 1977): 332–39.

Pamphlets

Bernheim, Isaac Wolfe. "The Reform Church of the American Isrealites." Buffalo, N.Y.: privately printed, 1921.

Stewart, Judd. "Abraham Lincoln on Present-Day Problems and Abraham Lincoln As Presented by Theodore Roosevelt." Columbus, Ohio, by the author, 1912.

Public Documents

U.S. Congress. Senate. *Lincoln Memorial Commission Report.* 62d Cong., 3de sess., 1912. Sen. doc. 965..

U.S. House Committee on Foreign Affairs. *Hearings; Centenary of Peace and Amity between the United States and Other Nations.* 63rd Cong., 2nd sess., 1914.

U.S. Congress. House. *Resolved that the President be requested to use his good offices to prevent the shipment from the United States to England of the George Grey Barnard statue of Abraham Lincoln which it is proposed to set up in London as a gift to the people of England.* 65th Cong., 1st sess., 1917.

U.S. Senate Committee on the Library. *Authorizing the Secretary of the Treasury to Refuse to Permit the Exportation of Any Work of Art.* 65th Cong., 2nd sess., 1918. S 4910, 9919.

Other collections

The Joseph M. Huston Papers, Pennsylvania State Archives, Harrisburg, Pennsylvania.

The George Grey Barnard Papers, Archives, Philadelphia Museum of Art, Philadelphia, Pennsylvania.

The George Grey Barnard Collection, The Kankakee County Historical Society, Kankakee, Illinois.

The George Grey Barnard Papers, Library, The Cloisters Museum, New York City.

The George Grey Barnard Archives, Archives of American Art, Smithsonian Institution, Washington, D.C.

The George Grey Barnard Collection, National Museum of American Art, Smithsonian Institution, Washington, D.C.

The Charles Phelps Taft II Papers, Cincinnati Historical Society, Cincinnati, Ohio.

The George Grey Barnard Abraham Lincoln files, Cincinnati Historical Society, Cincinnati, Ohio.

The George Grey Barnard Abraham Lincoln files, Park Board, Cincinnati, Ohio.

The Howard Russell Butler Papers, Archives of American Art, Smithsonian Institution, Washington, D.C.

The Robert Todd Lincoln Papers, Henry E. Huntington Library, San Marino, California.

The Nicholas Murray Butler Papers, Rare Book and Main Library, Columbia University, New York City.

The George Grey Barnard files, Centre County Historical Society, Bellefonte, Pennsylvania.

Unpublished manuscripts

Millet, Alice Nevitt. "George Grey Barnard." Masters thesis. Department of Fine Arts, Humanities Division, University of Louisville, Louisville, Kentucky, 1944.

Morris, Ruth. "Project for a Biography of George Grey Barnard." George Grey Barnard Papers, Archives of American Art, Smithsonian Institution, Washington, D.C.

Webber, Bruce. "Robert Frederick Blum and the Clark Family." Typescript, n.d. Vertical files, National Museum of American Art, Smithsonian Institution, Washington, D.C.

Williams, Dan. "Biography of George Grey Barnard." Typscript, 1938. George Grey Barnard Papers, Archives, Philadelphia Museum of Art.

Archival Sources

In the Library of Congress, Washington, D.C.

The John Gutzon Borglum Papers.
The Andrew Dale Carnegie Papers.

The Daniel Chester French Papers.
The Charles Moore Papers.
The Theodore Roosevelt Papers.
The William Howard Taft Papers.
The Woodrow Wilson Papers.
The Alton Parker Papers.

Index

233